U0921007

东莞统计年鉴

DONGGUAN STATISTICAL YEARBOOK

2013

（总第23期 NO.23）

东 莞 市 统 计 局
国家统计局东莞调查队 编

Compiled by
Dongguan Municipal Bureau of Statistics
Survey Office of the National Bureau of Statistics in Dongguan

图书在版编目（CIP）数据
东莞统计年鉴. 2013 / 东莞市统计局，国家统计局东莞调查队编.
－－ 北京 ：中国统计出版社，2013. 8
ISBN 978－7－5037－6882－8

Ⅰ. ①东…
Ⅱ. ①东… ②国…
Ⅲ. ①统计资料－东莞市－2013－年鉴
Ⅳ. ①C832. 653－54

中国版本图书馆 CIP 数据核字（2013）第 170464 号

东莞统计年鉴－2013

作　　者/ 东莞市统计局　国家统计局东莞调查队
责任编辑/ 陈越月
装帧设计/ 冯　坚　钟锦漩
出版发行/ 中国统计出版社
地　　址/ 北京市丰台区西三环南路甲 6 号
邮政编码/ 100073
电　　话/ 邮购（010）63376909　书店（010）68783171
网　　址/ http：//csp. stats. gov. cn
印　　刷/ 东莞市本色印刷有限公司
经　　销/ 新华书店
开　　本/ 890mm × 1240mm　1/16
字　　数/ 1300 千字
印　　张/ 36. 38 印张
版　　别/ 2013 年 8 月第 1 版
版　　次/ 2013 年 8 月第 1 次印刷
定　　价/ 350. 00 元

如有印装差错，由本社发行部调换。

编 者 说 明

一、《东莞统计年鉴—2013》（以下简称年鉴）是一部反映东莞国民经济和社会发展情况的资料性年刊，本书收录了东莞 2012 年大量的统计数据和历史主要年份的一些主要统计数据，旨在全面系统地反映东莞在经济和社会方面的发展变化，为社会各界和海内外人士了解和研究东莞提供翔实的资料。

二、全书分三部分。第一部分，概述；第二部分，统计资料，具体分为综合、人口与劳动力、农业、工业、固定资产投资与建筑业、运输邮电、国内贸易、价格指数、对外经济贸易与旅游、财政、金融与保险、人民生活、社会事业、能源、镇街主要指标、村（居）委会主要指标、历年国民经济和社会发展主要指标、东莞与全国、全省、三角洲主要指标比较等 17 部分；第三部分，基本单位情况。

三、本年鉴资料大部分来自政府统计部门和调查队的各种统计报表、抽样调查资料，部分来自中央省属单位和市属各主管部门的统计资料。

四、使用本年鉴时，请注意指标的统计口径，计量单位及计算价格。本年鉴指标计算所采用的价格除注明外均为当年价格。

五、年鉴统计表中的符号说明：“#”表示其中主要项；“空格”表示该项统计指标数据不详或无该项数据。

六、本年鉴在编辑出版过程中，得到省统计局、有关部门和镇街的大力支持，在此表示衷心感谢。限于编辑水平，本书难免有疏漏之处，敬请批评指正。

《东莞统计年鉴－2013》
编委会和编辑出版人员

编　委　会

主　编： 梁佳沂　王志勋　叶力强

副主编： 李向阳　梁昶成　冯　坚　梁　泉　黎建锋　钟锦漩
叶应涛　李红生

委　员（以姓氏笔划为序）：

邓立峰　刘曙光　苏慧英　李妙荷　肖永梅
邹　燕　罗伟文　周志彪　郭玮珉　黄才凤
黄焕娣　黄耀晃　蔡学良　潘　雷

编辑工作人员

编辑部主任： 钟锦漩

编辑部副主任： 李妙荷　李盛武

责任编辑： 陈越月

编辑人员（以姓氏笔划为序）：

王相东　王锦容　叶丽萍　叶煦麟　卢明芬　朱沃权
朱敏铭　刘韦材　刘凤琼　刘达铭　李雪锋　李琳达
李碧芸　张昌彦　张贵平　林彩凤　周晓君　秦曼诗
凌柱均　萧燕毅　蔡建娣　蔡盟芳　谭灿培　廖康文
樊丽娟　黎晓艳

英文翻译： 马晓威　王锦容　朱敏铭　李玉忠　李盛武
陈德斌　唐宁斌

目　　录
CONTENTS

第一部分　概　述
Part One　Outline

2012 年东莞市国民经济和社会发展统计公报 …… (3)
Dongguan Statistical Communique on National Economic and Social Development 2012
政府工作报告 …… (33)
Report on the Work of the Government

第二部分　统计资料
Part Two　Statistics

一、综　合
General Survey

1－1　东莞行政区划（2012 年） …… (47)
Divisions of Administrative Areas in Dongguan (2012)
1－2　历年东莞行政区划 …… (49)
Divisions of Administrative Areas in Dongguan over Years
1－3　主要年份户数、人口与自然资源 …… (50)
Number of Households, Population and Natural Resources in Main Years
1－4　历年土地与自然资源 …… (51)
Land and Natural Resources over Years
1－5　主要年份国民经济主要指标 …… (53)
Main Indicators on National Economy in Main Years
1－6　主要年份国民经济和社会发展主要比例与效益指标 …… (56)
Main Indicators on National Economy and Social Development in Main Years
1－7　国民经济主要指标分月变化情况（2012 年，累计绝对数） …… (59)
Main Indicators on National Economy by Month (2012, *Accumulative Figures in Value Terms*)

1－8　国民经济主要指标分月变化情况（2012 年，比上年同期增长） ……………………………（61）
Main Indicators on National Economy by Month（2012，*Compare with Same Period of Preceding Year* %）
1－9　历年地区生产总值 ………………………………………………………………………………（63）
Gross Domestic Product over Years
1－10　历年地区生产总值指数 ………………………………………………………………………（64）
Indices of Gross Domestic Product over Years
1－11　历年地区生产总值产业构成 ………………………………………………………………（65）
Composition of Gross Domestic Product over Years
1－12　各行业增加值项目（2012 年） ……………………………………………………………（66）
Composition of Value-added by Industry（2012）
1－13　主要年份支出法地区生产总值 ……………………………………………………………（67）
Gross Domestic Product by Expenditure Approach in Main Years
1－14　主要年份资本形成总额及构成 ……………………………………………………………（67）
Gross Capital Formation and Its Composition in Main Years
1－15　主要年份最终消费支出及构成 ……………………………………………………………（67）
Final Consumption Expenditure and Its Composition in Main Years
1－16　全市企业和个体工商户登记注册年末实有数量（2005－2012 年） ………………………（68）
Enterprises and Self-employed Individuals Registered at Year-end（2005－2012）
1－17　个体工商户情况（2012 年） …………………………………………………………………（68）
Statistics on Self-employed Individuals（2012）
1－18　私营工商企业基本情况（2012 年） …………………………………………………………（69）
Basic Statistics on Private Industrial & Commercial Enterprises（2012）
1－19　历年总供售电 …………………………………………………………………………………（70）
Gross Electricity Supply over Years
1－20　历年国民经济主要指标人均水平 ……………………………………………………………（71）
The Per Capita Level of Main National Economic Indicators over Years
主要统计指标解释 ……………………………………………………………………………………（72）
Explanatory Notes on Main Statistical Indicators

二、人口与劳动力
Population and Labor Force

2－1　历年总人口数与人口密度 ……………………………………………………………………（77）
Total Population and Density over Years
2－2　主要年份户籍人口与劳动力指标 ……………………………………………………………（78）
Main Indicators of Household Population and Labor in Main Years

2－3 历年户籍人口自然变动情况 …… (79)
Changes of Household Population over Years
2－4 历年户籍人口迁移变动情况 …… (80)
Changes of Household Migration over Years
2－5 历年外来暂住人口与外来劳动力 …… (81)
Temporary Residents and Labor over Years
2－6 主要年份城镇在岗职工年末人数 …… (83)
Number of Employed Persons in Urban Areas at Year-end in Main Years
2－7 历年分行业城镇在岗职工人数 …… (84)
Numbers of Employers by Sector in Urban Areas over Years
2－8 主要年份国有单位分行业年末城镇在岗职工人数 …… (85)
Number of Employed Persons in Urban State-owned Units at Year-end by Sector in Main Years
2－9 主要年份集体单位分行业年末城镇在岗职工人数 …… (86)
Number of Employed Persons in Urban Collective-owned Units at Year-end by Sector in Main Years
2－10 主要年份其他所有制单位分行业年末城镇在岗职工人数 …… (87)
Number of Employed Persons in Urban Other Ownership Units at Year-end by Sector in Main Years
2－11 工业、建筑业企业年末城镇在岗职工人数（2012 年） …… (88)
Number of Urban Employed Persons in Industrial and Construction Enterprises at Year-end (2012)
2－12 按经济类型分行业城镇在岗职工人数及构成（2012 年） …… (89)
Employed Persons in Urban Areas by Registration Status and Sector (2012)
主要统计指标解释 …… (90)
Explanatory Notes on Main Statistical Indicators

三、农业
Agriculture

3－1 主要年份农业指标 …… (93)
Main Indicators of Agriculture in Main Years
3－2 主要年份农村经济比例和效益指标 …… (95)
Main Indicators of Proportions and Efficiency in Rural Economy in Main Years
3－3 主要年份农村集体（经联社、经济社两级）资产负债及收益分配 …… (96)
Assets, Liabilities and Income Distribution of Rural Collective Economy in Main Years
3－4 历年农产品人均拥有量 …… (97)
Per Capita Possession of Agricultural Products over Years

3－5　主要年份基层组织情况 …………………………………………………………………………………（99）
Basic Statistics on Rural Grassroots Units in Main Years

3－6　历年耕地面积 ………………………………………………………………………………………………（100）
Area of Cultivated Land over Years

3－7　历年耕地面积变动情况 ……………………………………………………………………………………（101）
Changes of Cultivated Land over Years

3－8　历年乡镇从业人员（按性别、产业分） ………………………………………………………………（102）
Township Employees over Years（by Sex and Industry）

3－9　历年乡镇从业人员（按主要行业分） …………………………………………………………………（103）
Township Employees over Years（by Main Sectors）

3－10　历年农林牧渔业总产值及指数 ……………………………………………………………………（104）
Gross Output Value and Indices of Agriculture over Years

3－11　历年农林牧渔业增加值 ……………………………………………………………………………（106）
Added Value of Agriculture over Years

3－12　历年农作物播种面积 ………………………………………………………………………………（107）
Total Sown Area of Farm Crops over Years

3－13　历年农作物产量 ……………………………………………………………………………………（108）
Total Output of Farm Crops over Years

3－14　主要年份农作物播种面积、亩产及总产量 ………………………………………………………（109）
Sown Area, Yield Per Acreage and Total Output of Farm Crops in Main Years

3－15　主要年份农机总动力、水利、化肥、农药及农村用电量 …………………………………………（112）
Basic Statistics on Total Power of Agricultural Machinery, Water Conservancy, Consumption of Chemical Fertilizers and Pesticides, and Electricity Consumed in Rural Areas in Main Years

3－16　历年水果面积及产量 ………………………………………………………………………………（113）
Planted Area and Output of Fruits over Years

3－17　历年林业生产 ………………………………………………………………………………………（114）
Basic Statistics on Forestry Production over Years

3－18　历年畜牧业生产及产品产量 ………………………………………………………………………（115）
Production of Animal Husbandry and Output of Livestock Products over Years

3－19　历年水产品产量及养殖面积 ………………………………………………………………………（116）
Output and Cultured Area of Aquatic Products over Years

3－20　主要农产品产量与最高年份比较（2012 年） ……………………………………………………（117）
Output of Main Agricultural Products in Comparison with Peak Year（2012）

主要统计指标解释 ……………………………………………………………………………………………（118）
Explanatory Notes on Main Statistical Indicators

四、工业
Industry

4－1　主要年份工业主要指标 ………………………………………………………………（121）
Main Indicators of Industry in Main Years

4－2　历年工业企业单位数（按经济成份分） ………………………………………………（122）
Number of Industrial Enterprises over Years（*by Ownership*）

4－3　主要年份工业企业单位数（按不同类型分） …………………………………………（123）
Number of Industrial Enterprises in Main Years（*by Ownership*）

4－4　历年工业增加值 ……………………………………………………………………（124）
Value-added of Industry over Years

4－5　规模以上工业企业单位数（2012 年） ………………………………………………（125）
Number of Industrial Enterprises above Designated Size（2012）

4－6　规模以上工业增加值（2012 年） ……………………………………………………（126）
Value-added of Industrial Enterprises above Designated Size（2012）

4－7　规模以上工业企业主要财务指标（2012 年） ………………………………………（127）
Main Financial Indicators of Industrial Enterprises above Designated Size（2012）

4－8　规模以上工业企业主要指标（2012 年） ……………………………………………（128）
Main Indicators of Industrial Enterprises above Designated Size（2012）

4－9　规模以上工业企业主要经济效益指标（2012 年） …………………………………（132）
Main Indicators on Economic Benefit of Industrial Enterprises above Designated Size（2012）

4－10　规模以上国有及国有控股工业企业主要经济指标（2012 年） ……………………（133）
Main Indicators of State-owned and State-holding Industrial Enterprises above Designated Size（2012）

4－11　规模以上国有及国有控股工业企业主要经济效益指标（2012 年） ………………（135）
Main Indicators on Economic Benefit of State-owned and State-holding Industrial Enterprises above Designated Size（2012）

4－12　规模以上集体工业企业主要经济指标（2012 年） …………………………………（136）
Main Indicators of Collective-owned Industrial Enterprises above Designated Size（2012）

4－13　规模以上集体工业企业主要经济效益指标（2012 年） ……………………………（138）
Main Indicators on Economic Benefit of Collective-owned Industrial Enterprises above Designated Size（2012）

4－14　规模以上外商投资工业企业主要经济指标（2012 年） ……………………………（139）
Main Indicators of Industrial Enterprises above Designated Size with Foreign Funds（2012）

4－15　规模以上外商投资工业企业主要经济效益指标（2012 年） ………………………（141）
Main Indicators on Economic Benefit of Industrial Enterprises above Designated Size with Foreign Funds（2012）

4－16 规模以上港澳台商投资工业企业主要经济指标（2012 年） …………………………… （142）
Main Indicators of Industrial Enterprises above Designated Size with Hong Kong, Macao and Taiwan Funds (2012)
4－17 规模以上港澳台商投资工业企业主要经济效益指标（2012 年） ……………………… （144）
Main Indicators on Economic Benefit of Industrial Enterprises above Designated Size with Hong Kong, Macao and Taiwan Funds (2012)
4－18 规模以上私营工业企业主要经济指标（2012 年） ……………………………………… （145）
Main Indicators of Private Industrial Enterprises above Designated Size (2012)
4－19 规模以上私营工业企业主要经济效益指标（2012 年） ………………………………… （147）
Main Indicators on Economic Benefit of Private Industrial Enterprises above Designated Size (2012)
4－20 大中型工业企业主要经济指标（2012 年） ……………………………………………… （148）
Main Indicators of Large and Medium-sized Industrial Enterprises (2012)
4－21 大中型工业企业主要经济效益指标（2012 年） ………………………………………… （150）
Main Indicators on Economic Benefit of Large and Medium-sized Industrial Enterprises (2012)
4－22 主要年份规模以上工业企业经济效益指标 ……………………………………………… （151）
Main Indicators on Economic Benefit of Industrial Enterprises above Designated Size in Main Years
4－23 主要年份规模以上国有经济工业企业经济效益指标 …………………………………… （151）
Main Indicators on Economic Benefit of State-owned and State-holding Industrial Enterprises above Designated Size in Main Years
4－24 主要年份规模以上集体经济工业企业经济效益指标 …………………………………… （152）
Main Indicators on Economic Benefit of Collective-owned Industrial Enterprises above Designated Size in Main Years
4－25 主要年份大中型工业企业经济效益指标 ………………………………………………… （152）
Main Indicators on Economic Benefit of Large and Medium-sized Industrial Enterprises in Main Years
4－26 主要年份规模以上港澳台商投资工业企业经济效益指标 ……………………………… （153）
Main Indicators on Economic Benefit of Industrial Enterprises above Designated Size with Hong Kong, Macao and Taiwan Funds in Main Years
4－27 主要年份规模以上外商投资工业企业经济效益指标 …………………………………… （153）
Main Indicators on Economic Benefit of Foreign-funded Industrial Enterprises above Designated Size in Main Years
4－28 主要年份规模以上工业产品产量 ………………………………………………………… （154）
Output of Main Industrial Products of Industrial Enterprises above Designated Size in Main Years
4－29 规模以上五大支柱产业及四个特色产业主要经济指标（2012 年） ……………………… （156）
Main Indicators of Five Pillar Industries & Four Characteristic Industries above Designated Size (2012)

4 - 30 规模以上电子信息、电气机械及仪器仪表制造业主要指标（2011 - 2012 年） …………… (157)
Main Indicators of Electronic Information, Machinery and Instrument Manufacturing above Designated Size (2011 - 2012)
4 - 31 规模以上先进制造业企业主要经济指标（2012 年） ……………………………………… (158)
Main Indicators of Advanced Manufacturing Enterprises above Designated Size (2012)
4 - 32 规模以上高技术制造业企业主要经济指标（2012 年） …………………………………… (161)
Main Indicators of High-tech Manufacturing Enterprises above Designated Size (2012)
4 - 33 规模以上 IT 制造业企业主要经济指标（2012 年） ……………………………………… (164)
Main Indicators of IT Manufacturing Enterprises above Designated Size (2012)
主要统计指标解释 …………………………………………………………………………………… (167)
Explanatory Notes on Main Statistical Indicators

五、固定资产投资与建筑业
Investment in Fixed Assets and Construction

5 - 1 主要年份固定资产投资与建筑业主要指标 ……………………………………………………… (173)
Main Indicators of Investment in Fixed Assets and Construction in Main Years
5 - 2 历年固定资产投资 …………………………………………………………………………… (174)
Total Investment in Fixed Assets over Years
5 - 3 按登记类型和行业分的固定资产投资（2012 年） ……………………………………… (175)
Total Investment in Fixed Assets by Registration Status and Sector (2012)
5 - 4 固定资产投资主要指标（2012 年） …………………………………………………… (176)
Main Indicators of Total Investment in Fixed Assets (2012)
5 - 5 固定资产投资分类情况（2012 年） …………………………………………………… (179)
Basic Statistics on Total Investment in Fixed Assets by Type (2012)
5 - 6 房地产开发主要指标 ………………………………………………………………………… (179)
Main Indicators of Real Estate Development
5 - 7 房地产开发企业主要经济指标（2012 年） …………………………………………… (180)
Main Indicators of Real Estate Enterprises (2012)
5 - 8 房地产开发投资情况（2011 - 2012 年） ……………………………………………… (181)
Investment in Real Estate Development (2011 - 2012)
5 - 9 房地产开发企业、房屋建筑面积及价值（2011 - 2012 年） ………………………… (181)
Floor Space and Value of Buildings in Real Estate Development (2011 - 2012)
5 - 10 商品房屋销售情况（2012 年） ……………………………………………………… (182)
Sale of Commercialized Buildings (2012)
5 - 11 建筑施工企业主要指标（2011 - 2012 年） ………………………………………… (182)
Main Indicators of Construction Enterprises (2011 - 2012)

主要统计指标解释 …………………………………………………………………………… (183)
Explanatory Notes on Main Statistical Indicators

六、运输邮电
Transport, Postal and Telecommunication Services

6－1 主要年份运输邮电主要指标 ………………………………………………………………… (187)
Main Indicators of Transport, Postal and Telecommunication Services in Main Years
6－2 历年运输线路长度与公路密度 ……………………………………………………………… (188)
Length of Transportation Routes and Road Density over Years
6－3 主要年份运输线路长度 …………………………………………………………………… (189)
Length of Transport Routes in Main Years
6－4 主要年份运输工具拥有量 ………………………………………………………………… (189)
Possession of Main Means of Transport in Main Years
6－5 历年客货运输量 ………………………………………………………………………… (190)
Passenger and Freight Traffic over Years
6－6 历年主要运输工具年末拥有量 ……………………………………………………………… (193)
Possession of Main Means of Transport at Year-end over Years
6－7 主要年份邮电通信业务基本情况 …………………………………………………………… (194)
Basic Statistics on Postal and Telecommunication Services in Main Years
6－8 历年邮电通信业务主要指标 ……………………………………………………………… (195)
Main Indicators of Postal and Telecommunication Services over Years
6－9 主要年份邮电通信企业财务指标 …………………………………………………………… (196)
Main Financial Indicators of Postal and Telecommunication Enterprises in Main Years
主要统计指标解释 …………………………………………………………………………… (197)
Explanatory Notes on Main Statistical Indicators

七、国内贸易
Domestic Trade

7－1 历年社会消费品零售总额 …………………………………………………………………… (201)
Total Retail Sales of Consumer Goods over Years
7－2 历年批发零售贸易企业与个体户数 …………………………………………………………… (202)
Wholesale and Retail Trades Enterprises and Self-employed Individuals over years
7－3 批发零售业商品销售总额（2012 年） …………………………………………………… (203)
Total Sales of Commodities in Wholesale and Retail Trades (2012)

7－4 限额以上住宿业和餐饮业经营情况（2012 年） …………………………………………… (204)
Business of Hotels and Catering Services above Designated Size (2012)
7－5 限额以上批发和零售企业财务状况（2012 年） …………………………………………… (205)
Main Financial Indicators of Enterprises above Designated Size in Wholesale and Retail Trade (2012)
7－6 限额以上住宿和餐饮企业财务状况（2012 年） …………………………………………… (209)
Main Financial Indicators of Enterprises above Designated Size in Hotels and Catering Services (2012)
7－7 历年住宿餐饮企业与个体户数 …………………………………………………………… (213)
Enterprises and Self-employed Individuals in Hotels and Catering Services over Years
7－8 历年限额以上企业商品购进、销售、库存总额 ………………………………………… (214)
Total Purchases, Sales and Stock of Commercial Enterprises above Designated Size over Years
7－9 市场分类基本情况（2011－2012 年） ………………………………………………… (215)
Basic Statistics on Market Classification (2011－2012)
7－10 历年城乡集市贸易 ………………………………………………………………………… (216)
Statistics on Urban and Rural Trade Fairs over Years
主要统计指标解释 ………………………………………………………………………… (217)
Explanatory Notes on Main Statistical Indicators

八、价格指数
Price Indices

8－1 历年物价总指数（以上年价格为 100） ……………………………………………… (221)
General Price Indices over Years (*Preceding Year* = 100)
8－2 居民消费价格分类指数（2012 年，以上年价格为 100） ………………………………… (222)
Consumer Price Indices by Category (2012, *Preceding Year* = 100)
8－3 居民消费价格分月指数（2012 年，以上年同月价格为 100） ……………………………… (223)
Consumer Price Indices by Month (2012, *Same Month of Preceding Year* = 100)
8－4 居民消费价格分月指数（2012 年，以上月价格为 100） ………………………………… (225)
Consumer Price Indices by Month (2012, *Preceding Month* = 100)
8－5 居民消费价格分月指数（2012 年，以上年 12 月价格为 100） …………………………… (227)
Consumer Price Indices by Month (2012, *December of Preceding Year* = 100)
8－6 商品零售价格分类指数（2012 年，以上年价格为 100） ………………………………… (229)
Retail Price Indices by Category (2012, *Preceding Year* = 100)
8－7 主要年份食品全社会综合平均价格 ……………………………………………………… (230)
Comprehensive Average Prices of Food in Main Years

8－8 工业生产者出厂价格指数（2012 年，以上年价格为 100） …………………………… （231）
Producer Price Index（PPI）for Manufactured Goods（2012，*Preceding Year* = 100）
主要统计指标解释 ………………………………………………………………………… （232）
Explanatory Notes on Main Statistical Indicators

九、对外经济贸易与旅游
Foreign Trade and Tourism

9－1 主要年份对外经济与旅游业主要指标 ……………………………………………… （235）
Main Indicators of Foreign Trade and Economic Cooperation and Tourism in Main Years
9－2 主要年份进出口贸易 ……………………………………………………………… （236）
Total Imports and Exports in Main Years
9－3 历年进出口总额 …………………………………………………………………… （237）
Total Value of Imports and Exports over Years
9－4 分国别（地区）进出口总值（2011－2012 年） ………………………………… （238）
Total Value of Imports and Exports by Countries（*Regions*）（2011－2012）
9－5 主要商品类别出口总值（2008－2012 年） ……………………………………… （239）
Total Export Value by Category of Main Commodities（2008－2012）
9－6 主要商品进口数量与金额（海关口径，2010－2012 年） ………………………… （240）
Main Import Commodities in Volume and Value（*Custom Statistics*）（2010－2012）
9－7 主要商品出口数量与金额（海关口径，2010－2012 年） ………………………… （242）
Main Export Commodities in Volume and Value（*Custom Statistics*）（2010－2012）
9－8 历年新签利用外资协议（合同）宗数 …………………………………………… （244）
Number of Signed Agreements or Contracts of Utilization of Foreign Capital over Years
9－9 历年新签利用外资协议（合同）规定外商投资额 ………………………………… （245）
Amount of Signed Agreements or Contracts of Utilization of Foreign Capital over Years
9－10 历年实际利用外资 ………………………………………………………………… （246）
Foreign Capital Actually Utilized over Years
9－11 主要年份“三资”企业利用外资 ………………………………………………… （247）
Utilization of Foreign Capital of Enterprises with Foreign Investment in Main Years
9－12 主要年份分方式、分国别（地区）实际利用外资 ………………………………… （249）
Foreign Capital Actually Utilized by Type and Countries（*Regions*）*in Main Years*
9－13 外商直接投资分行业情况（2011－2012 年） ……………………………………… （250）
Foreign Direct Investment by Sector（2011－2012）
9－14 主要年份宾馆酒店接待能力和接待人数 ………………………………………… （250）
Capacity and Tourists Received by Hotels in Main Years

9 – 15 历年旅游业情况 …… (251)
Basic Statistics on Tourism over Years
主要统计指标解释 …… (252)
Explanatory Notes on Main Statistical Indicators

十、财政、金融与保险
Finance, Banking and Insurance

10 – 1 主要年份财政收支主要指标 …… (255)
Main Indicators of Government Revenue and Expenditure in Main Years
10 – 2 财政收支主要指标（2006 – 2012 年） …… (256)
Main Indicators of Government Revenue and Expenditure (2006 – 2012)
10 – 3 历年财政收入 …… (257)
Government Revenue over Years
10 – 4 历年财政支出 …… (258)
Government Expenditure over Years
10 – 5 税务登记情况及税种征收情况（2011 – 2012 年） …… (259)
Taxes (2011 – 2012)
10 – 6 历年金融机构各项人民币存贷款余额 …… (261)
Balance of RMB Deposits and Loans over Years
10 – 7 保险行业主要指标（2006 – 2012 年） …… (262)
Main Indicators of Insurance (2006 – 2012)
主要统计指标解释 …… (263)
Explanatory Notes on Main Statistical Indicators

十一、人民生活
People's Living Conditions

11 – 1 主要年份人民生活主要指标 …… (267)
Basic Statistics on People's Living Conditions in Main Years
11 – 2 历年城镇在岗职工工资总额与平均工资 …… (268)
Total and Average Wage of Employed Persons in Urban Areas over Years
11 – 3 城镇在岗职工工资总额及平均工资（2012 年，按经济类型、行业分） …… (269)
Total and Average Wage of Fully Employed Persons in Urban Areas (2012, *by Status of Registration and Sector*)
11 – 4 主要年份各种分组的城镇在岗职工平均工资 …… (270)
Average Wage of Employed Persons in Urban Areas by Item in Main Years

11－5 各种经济类型分行业城镇在岗职工工资总额、平均工资（2011－2012 年） …………… (271)
Total and Average Wage of Employed Persons in Arban Areas by Status of Registration and Sector (2011－2012)
11－6 国有企、事业和机关单位城镇在岗职工工资总额及平均工资（2012 年） ……………… (272)
Total and Average Wage of Employed Persons in Urban State-owned Enterprises, Institutions and Government Agencies (2012)
11－7 工业、建筑业城镇在岗职工工资总额和平均工资（2012 年） ………………………… (273)
Total and Average Wage of Employed Persons in Urban Industrial and Construction Units (2012)
11－8 历年居民收支、农民收入 ……………………………………………………………… (274)
Income and Expenditure of Urban Households and Net Income of Rural Households over Years
11－9 历年城市居民家庭户基本情况 ………………………………………………………… (275)
Basic Conditions of Urban Households over Years
11－10 历年人均总收入分类 …………………………………………………………………… (276)
Per Capita Total Income over Years
11－11 历年人均消费性支出分类 ……………………………………………………………… (277)
Per Capita Living Expenditure over Years
11－12 不同收入等级年人均可支配收入与消费性支出水平 ………………………………… (278)
Per Capita Annual Disposable Income and Consumption Expenditure by Level of Income
11－13 主要年份城市居民家庭基本情况 ……………………………………………………… (279)
Basic Conditions of Urban Households in Main Years
11－14 主要年份城市居民人均消费性支出及构成 …………………………………………… (280)
Consumption Expenditure of Urban Households in Main Years
11－15 历年城市居民家庭平均每百户主要耐用消费品拥有量 ……………………………… (281)
Ownership of Durable Consumer Goods Owned per 100 Urban Households over Years
11－16 按收入等级分的城市居民家庭基本情况（2012 年） ………………………………… (282)
Basic Conditions of Urban Households by Level of Income (2012)
11－17 按收入等级分的城市居民家庭平均每人全年现金收入（2012 年） ………………… (283)
Per Capita Annual Cash Income of Urban Households by Level of Income (2012)
11－18 城市居民家庭平均每人全年消费性支出（2012 年） ………………………………… (284)
Per Capita Annual Consumption Expenditure of Urban Households (2012)
11－19 农村居民人均实际收入与实际支出（2006－2012 年） ……………………………… (285)
Per Capita Actual Income and Expenditure of Rural Households (2006－2012)
11－20 农村居民人均实际收入（2006－2012 年） …………………………………………… (285)
Per Capita Actual Income of Rural Households (2006－2012)
11－21 农村居民人均消费支出（2006－2012 年） …………………………………………… (286)
Per Capita Consumption Expenditure of Rural Households (2006－2012)

11－22 每百户农村居民家庭主要耐用消费品拥有量（2006－2012 年） ……………………… （286）
Ownership of Durable Consumer Goods Owned per 100 Rural Households（2006－2012）
主要统计指标解释 …………………………………………………………………… （287）
Explanatory Notes on Main Statistical Indicators

十二、社会事业
Social Undertakings

12－1 主要年份社会事业主要指标 ………………………………………………………… （291）
Main Indicators of Social Undertakings in Main Years
12－2 科技活动基本情况（2012 年） ……………………………………………………… （292）
Basic Statistics on Scientific and Technological Activities（2012）
12－3 研究与试验发展（*R&D*）基本情况（2009－2012 年） ………………………………… （293）
Basic Statistics on Research and Development（*R&D*）（2009－2012）
12－4 主要年份国有企事业单位科学技术人员 ………………………………………………… （294）
Scientific and Technical Personnel in State-owned Enterprises and Institutions in Main Years
12－5 主要年份三种专利申请量与授权量 ……………………………………………………… （294）
Three Kinds of Patents Application Accepted and Granted in Main Years
12－6 主要年份各类技术合同签订情况 ……………………………………………………… （295）
Basic Statistics on Technical Contracts Signed by Type in Main Years
12－7 主要年份高新科技发展情况 ………………………………………………………… （295）
Basic Statistics on High-tech Development in Main Years
12－8 主要年份科学技术成果项数 ………………………………………………………… （296）
Achievements for Scientific and Technological Research in Main Years
12－9 科技创新平台情况（2010－2012 年） ……………………………………………… （296）
Basic Statistics on Technology Innovation Platform（2010－2012）
12－10 历年国有企事业单位科学技术人员数 ………………………………………………… （297）
Scientific and Technical Personnel in Enterprises and Institutions over Years
12－11 历年三种专利与技术合同签订情况 ………………………………………………… （298）
Basic Statistics on Three Kinds of Patents and Technical Contracts Signed by Type over Years
12－12 历年科学技术成果项数 ………………………………………………………………… （299）
Scientific and Technological Achievements over Years
12－13 主要年份各类学校情况 ………………………………………………………………… （300）
Basic Statistics on Schools by Type in Main Years
12－14 历年各类学校在校学生数 ……………………………………………………………… （302）
Number of Students Enrollment by Type of School over Years

12-15 历年各类学校当年招收学生数 …… (303)
Number of New Students Enrollment by Type of School over Years

12-16 历年各类学校当年毕业生数 …… (304)
Number of Graduates by Type of School over Years

12-17 历年各级各类学校专任教师数 …… (305)
Number of Full-time Teachers by Level and Type of School over Years

12-18 历年各类学校入（升）学率与高考入围人数 …… (306)
Number of Passing College Entrance Examination and Proportion of Students Entering Schools over Years

12-19 历年文化艺术、文物事业机构数 …… (307)
Number of Institutions in Culture and Cultural Relics over Years

12-20 主要年份广播电视事业发展情况 …… (308)
Basic Statistics on Radio and Television Industry in Main Years

12-21 主要年份安全生产事故中火灾事故情况 …… (308)
Basic Statistics on Fire of Production Accidents in Main Years

12-22 主要年份交通事故发生情况 …… (309)
Basic Statistics on Traffic Accidents in Main Years

12-23 各类卫生事业机构及床位、人员数（2012 年） …… (309)
Number of Health Care Institutions, Beds and Employed Personnel by Type of Institution (2012)

12-24 主要年份卫生事业机构各类人员数 …… (310)
Number of Personnel in Health Institutions in Main Years

12-25 医疗机构服务情况（2012 年） …… (310)
Services in Medical Institutions (2012)

12-26 历年卫生事业机构、床位、人员数 …… (311)
Number of Health Care Institutions, Beds and Personnel over Years

12-27 历年体育运动情况 …… (312)
Basic Statistics on Sports over Years

12-28 主要年份体育比赛成绩 …… (313)
Basic Statistics on Sports Achievements in Main Years

12-29 主要年份群众体育活动情况 …… (313)
Basic Statistics on Activities of Mass Sports in Main Years

12-30 主要年份治安案件情况 …… (314)
Basic Statistics on Public Security Cases in Main Years

12-31 主要年份刑事案件情况 …… (315)
Basic Statistics on Criminal Cases in Main Years

12－32 主要年份道路交通违法情况 …………………………………………………… (316)
Basic Statistics on Traffic Offense in Main Years

12－33 主要年份律师、公证、基层司法及普法教育 ………………………………………… (316)
Basic Statistics on Lawyers, Notarization, Grassroots Judicial Work and Law Education in Main Years

12－34 历年计划生育情况 …………………………………………………………… (317)
Basic Statistics on Family Planning over Years

12－35 主要年份优抚和社会救济、福利事业 ………………………………………… (319)
Basic Statistics on Special Care, Social Relief and Welfare in Main Years

12－36 主要年份婚姻登记情况 ……………………………………………………… (320)
Basic Statistics on Marriage Registration in Main Years

12－37 主要年份环境保护基本情况 …………………………………………………… (320)
Basic Statistics on Environmental Protection in Main Years

12－38 主要年份社会保险事业情况 …………………………………………………… (321)
Basic Statistics on Social Insurance in Main Years

12－39 主要年份最低生活保障情况 …………………………………………………… (321)
Basic Statistics on Minimum Income Relief in Main Years

12－40 主要年份市政建设情况 ……………………………………………………… (322)
Basic Statistics on Municipal Construction in Main Years

12－41 主要年份液化石油气及天然气供应情况 ……………………………………… (322)
Basic Statistics on Supply of Liquefied Petroleum Gas and Natural Gas in Main Years

12－42 历年环境保护基本情况 ……………………………………………………… (323)
Basic Statistics on Environmental Protection over Years

主要统计指标解释 …………………………………………………………… (324)
Explanatory Notes on Main Statistical Indicators

十三、能源
Energy

13－1 主要年份能源主要指标 ……………………………………………………… (329)
Main Indicators of Energy in Main Years

13－2 主要年份综合能源平衡表 …………………………………………………… (330)
Overall Energy Balance Sheet in Main Years

13－3 主要年份石油平衡表 ……………………………………………………… (331)
Petroleum Balance Sheet in Main Years

13－4 主要年份煤炭平衡表 …… (332)
Coal Balance Sheet in Main Years
13－5 主要年份全社会用电量 …… (333)
Total Consumption of Electricity in Main Years
13－6 规模以上工业综合能源消费量（2012 年） …… (334)
Overall Energy Consumpiton of Industrial Enterprises above Designated Size (2012)
主要统计指标解释 …… (335)
Explanatory Notes on Main Statistical Indicators

十四、镇街主要指标
Main Indicators of Towns

14－1 镇街生产总值 …… (339)
Gross Domestic Product by Town
14－2 镇街第三产业增加值（2012 年） …… (350)
Value-added of the Tertiary Industry by Town (2012)
14－3 镇街户籍户数与人口数（2012 年） …… (351)
Population of Household by Town (2012)
14－4 镇街户籍人口自然变动情况（2012 年） …… (352)
Population Household by Town (2012)
14－5 镇街人口迁移变动情况（2012 年） …… (353)
Population Migration by Town (2012)
14－6 镇街土地面积和人口密度（2012 年） …… (354)
Land Area and Population Density by Town (2012)
14－7 镇街常住人口（2011－2012 年） …… (355)
Permanent Population by Town (2011－2012)
14－8 镇街外来暂住人口数（2011－2012 年） …… (356)
Migrant Population by Town (2011－2012)
14－9 镇街计划生育情况（2012 年） …… (357)
Basic Statistics on Family Planning by Town (2012)
14－10 镇街农林牧渔业总产值（2012 年） …… (358)
Gross Output Value of Agriculture by Town (2012)
14－11 镇街主要农产品生产及产品产量（2012 年） …… (359)
Production and Output of Main Agricultural Products by Town (2012)
14－12 镇街农机总动力、机耕面积及农村用电量（2012 年） …… (362)
Basic Statistics on Total Power of Agricultural Machinery, Area of Tractor Ploughing and Electricity Consumption in Rural Areas by Town (2012)

14－13 镇街农村集体（经联社、经济社两级合计）经济收益分配（2012 年） …………………… （363）
Income Distribution of Rural Economy by Town (2012)

14－14 镇街规模以上工业企业主要经济指标（2012 年） …………………………………………… （364）
Main Indicators of Industrial Enterprises above Designated Size by Town (2012)

14－15 镇街规模以上工业企业主要经济效益指标（2012 年） …………………………………… （367）
Main Indicators on Economic Benefit of Industrial Enterprises above Designated Size by Town (2012)

14－16 镇街规模以上工业企业 R&D 人员情况（2012 年） ……………………………………………… （368）
R&D Personnel of Industrial Enterprises above Designated Size by Town (2012)

14－17 镇街规模以上工业企业 R&D 人员全时当量情况（2012 年） ………………………………… （369）
R&D Personnel Full-time-equivalent of Industrial Enterprises above Designated Size by Town (2012)

14－18 镇街规模以上工业企业 R&D 经费情况（2012 年） ……………………………………………… （370）
The R&D Funds of Industrial Enterprises above Designated Size by Town (2012)

14－19 镇街规模以上工业企业全部 R&D 项目情况（2012 年） ……………………………………… （372）
Basic Statistics on R&D Projects of Industrial Enterprises above Designated Size by Town (2012)

14－20 镇街规模以上工业企业办科技机构情况（2012 年） ………………………………………… （373）
Basic Statistics on Scientific and Technological Institutions of Industrial Enterprises above Designated Size by Town (2012)

14－21 镇街规模以上工业企业高新技术产品情况（2012 年） ……………………………………… （374）
Basic Statistics on High-tech Products of Industrial Enterprises above Designated Size by Town (2012)

14－22 镇街固定资产投资总额（2012 年） …………………………………………………………… （375）
Total Investment in Fixed Assets by Town (2012)

14－23 镇街邮电局、所通信能力及服务网点（2011－2012 年） …………………………………… （376）
Communication Capacity and Service Establishments of Telecommunication Offices by Town (2011－2012)

14－24 镇街商贸情况（2012 年） ………………………………………………………………………… （377）
Statistics on Commerce by Town (2012)

14－25 镇街注册工商企业及个体户数（2012 年） …………………………………………………… （378）
Registered Industrial & Commercial Enterprises and Self-employed Individuals by Town (2012)

14－26 镇街集市贸易市场数及私营个体户注册资金额（2011－2012 年） ………………………… （379）
Fair Trades and Registered Capital of Private Enterprises & Self-employed Individuals by Town (2011－2012)

14－27 镇街来料加工装配签约宗数、出口值及引进设备价值（2012 年） ………………………… （380）
Contracts of Processing and Assembling of Import Materials, Export Value and Value of Equipments Imported by Town (2012)

14－28 镇街“三资”企业签约、实际利用外资及出口值（新口径）（2012年） …………………（381）
Contracts, Foreign Capital Actually Utilized and Export Value of Enterprises with Foreign Investment by Town (2012)

14－29 镇街进出口总额（2011－2012年，海关口径） ……………………………………………（382）
Total Value of Exports and Imports by Town (2011－2012, *Custom Statistics*)

14－30 镇街实际利用外资（2011－2012年） ……………………………………………………（383）
Foreign Capital Actually Utilized by Town (2011－2012)

14－31 镇街税收总额（2011－2012年） …………………………………………………………（384）
Taxes by Town (2011－2012)

14－32 镇街本级可支配财政收入和财政支出（2011－2012年） ……………………………………（385）
Disposable Government Revenue and Expenditure by Town (2011－2012)

14－33 镇街资产负债总额（2011－2012年） ……………………………………………………（386）
Total Assets and Liabilities by Town (2011－2012)

14－34 镇街各项人民币存贷款余额与城乡居民储蓄存款余额（2011－2012年） ………………（387）
Balance of Deposits and Loans by Town and Savings Deposit of Urban and Rural Household (2011－2012)

14－35 镇街普通中学情况（2012年） ……………………………………………………………（388）
Basic Statistics on Regular Secondary Schools by Town (2012)

14－36 镇街小学情况（2012年） …………………………………………………………………（389）
Basic Statistics on Primary Schools by Town (2012)

14－37 镇街卫生事业机构、床位及人员数（2012年） ……………………………………………（390）
Number of Health care Institutions, Beds and Personnel by Town (2012)

14－38 镇街优抚和社会救济基本情况（2012年） ………………………………………………（391）
Basic Statistics on Special Care and Social Relief by Town (2012)

14－39 镇街专利申请与授权数（2012年） ………………………………………………………（392）
Basic Statistics on Patents Application Accepted and Granted by Town (2012)

14－40 镇街总用电量和总供水量（2011－2012年） ……………………………………………（393）
Gross Electicity Comsumption and Water Supply by Town (2011－2012)

十五、村（居）委会主要指标

Main Indicators of Villagers'（Neighborhood）Committees

15 村（居）委会主要指标（2012年） ……………………………………………………………（397）
Main Indicators of Villagers' (*Neighborhood*) *Committees* (2012)

十六、历年国民经济和社会发展主要指标

Main Indicators of National Economy and Social Development over Years

16 历年国民经济和社会发展主要指标 ··· (415)

Main Indicators of National Economy and Social Development over Years

十七、东莞与全国、全省、三角洲城市主要指标比较

Comparison of Main Indicators between Dongguan and China, Guangdong Province, the Cities of the Pearl River Delta

17－1 主要年份全国国民经济与社会发展指标 ··· (429)

Main Indicators on National Economy and Social Development of China

17－2 主要年份广东省国民经济与社会发展指标 ··· (431)

Main Indicators on National Economy and Social Development of Guangdong Province

17－3 主要经济指标东莞占全国、全省的比重（2012 年） ·· (433)

Proportion of Main Indicators of Dongguan to China and Guangdong Province (2012)

17－4 主要经济指标东莞占全国、全省的比重（2011 年） ·· (434)

Proportion of Main Indicators of Dongguan to China and Guangdong Province (2011)

17－5 主要经济指标人均水平东莞与全国、全省的比较（2012 年） ································· (435)

Comparison of Per Capita Level of Main Economic Indicators between Dongguan and China, Guangdong Province (2012)

17－6 主要经济指标人均水平东莞与全国、全省的比较（2011 年） ································· (435)

Comparison of Per Capita Level of Main Economic Indicators between Dongguan and China, Guangdong Province (2011)

17－7 珠江三角洲国民经济和社会发展主要指标（2012 年） ·· (436)

Main Indicators of National Economy and Social Development of the Pearl River Delta Economic Zone (2012)

17－8 长江三角洲国民经济和社会发展主要指标（2012 年） ·· (440)

Main Indicators on National Economy and Social Development of the Yangtze River Delta Economic Zone (2012)

第三部分　基本单位情况

Part Three　Basic Units

1－1　按行业分的法人单位、产业活动单位数（2012 年）………………………………………（445）

Number of Corporate Units and Industrial Establishments by Sector（2012）

1－2　按注册类型分的法人单位、产业活动单位数（2012 年）………………………………（448）

Number of Corporate Units and Industrial Establishments by Registration Status（2012）

1－3　按地域分的法人单位、产业活动单位数（2012 年）………………………………………（449）

Number of Corporate Units and Industrial Establishments by District（2012）

1－4　营业收入超 5000 万元的内资企业（2012 年）……………………………………………（450）

Domestic-funded Enterprises with Business Revenue over RMB 50 Million（2012）

1－5　营业收入超 5000 万元的外资企业（2012 年）……………………………………………（495）

Foreign-funded Enterprises with Business Revenue over RMB 50 Million（2012）

1－6　星级酒店名单（2012 年）……………………………………………………………………（541）

List of Star-ranking Hotels（2012）

1－7　高新技术企业名录（2012 年）………………………………………………………………（544）

List of High-tech Enterprises（2012）

东莞市生产总值(亿元)

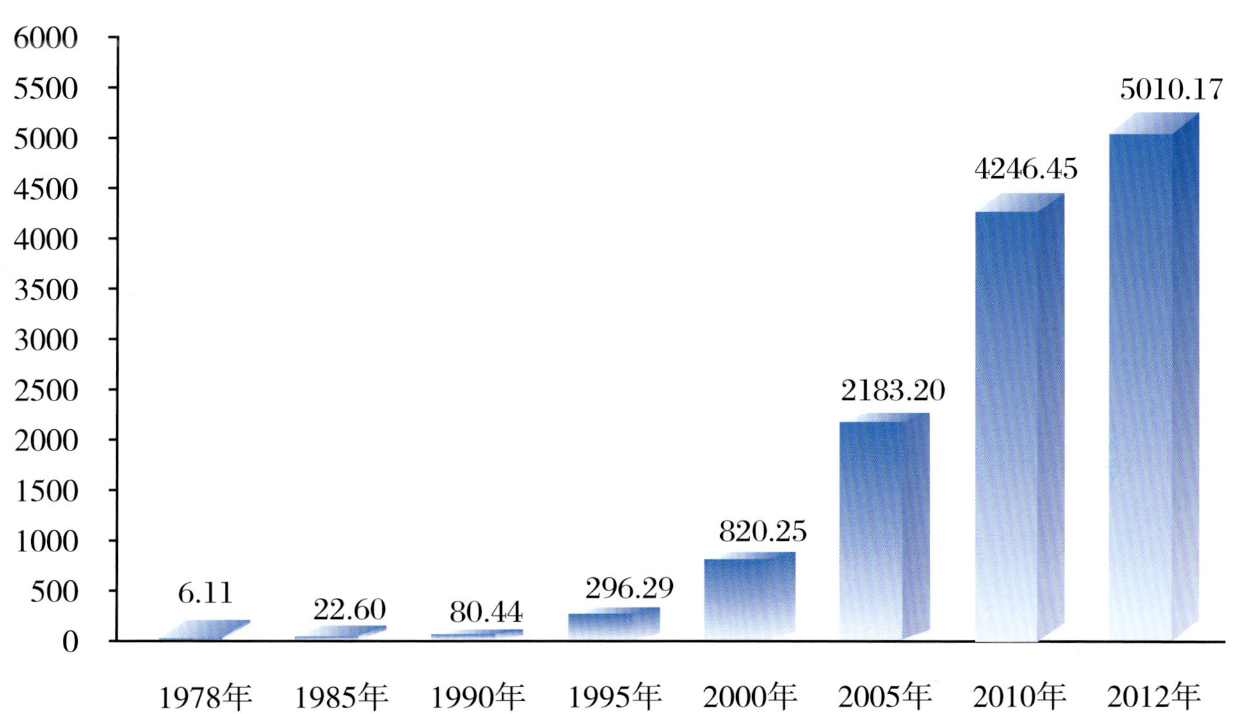

东莞市生产总值构成(%)

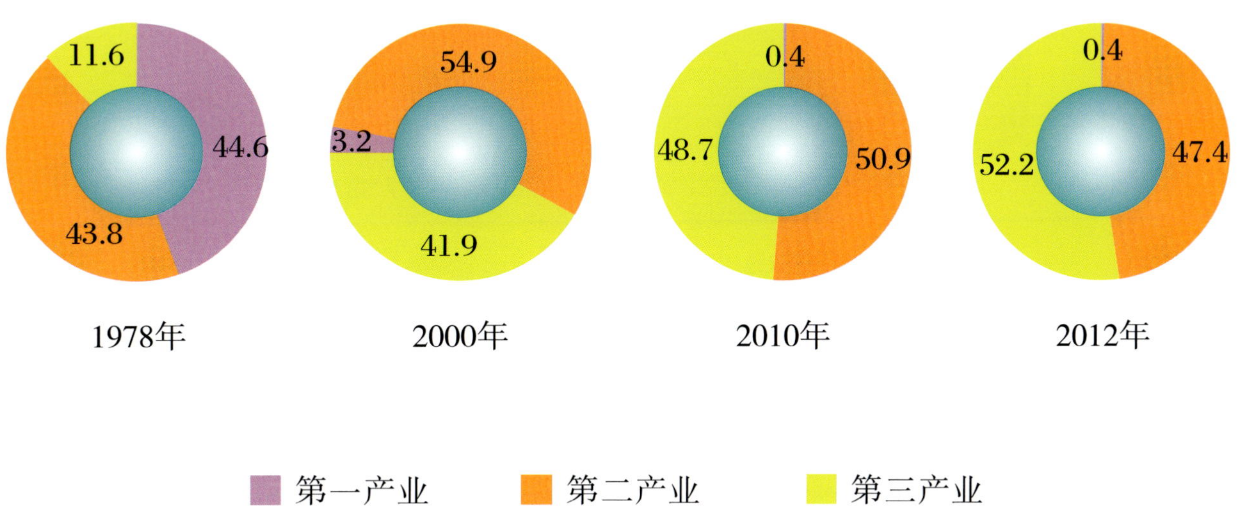

工业增加值（亿元）

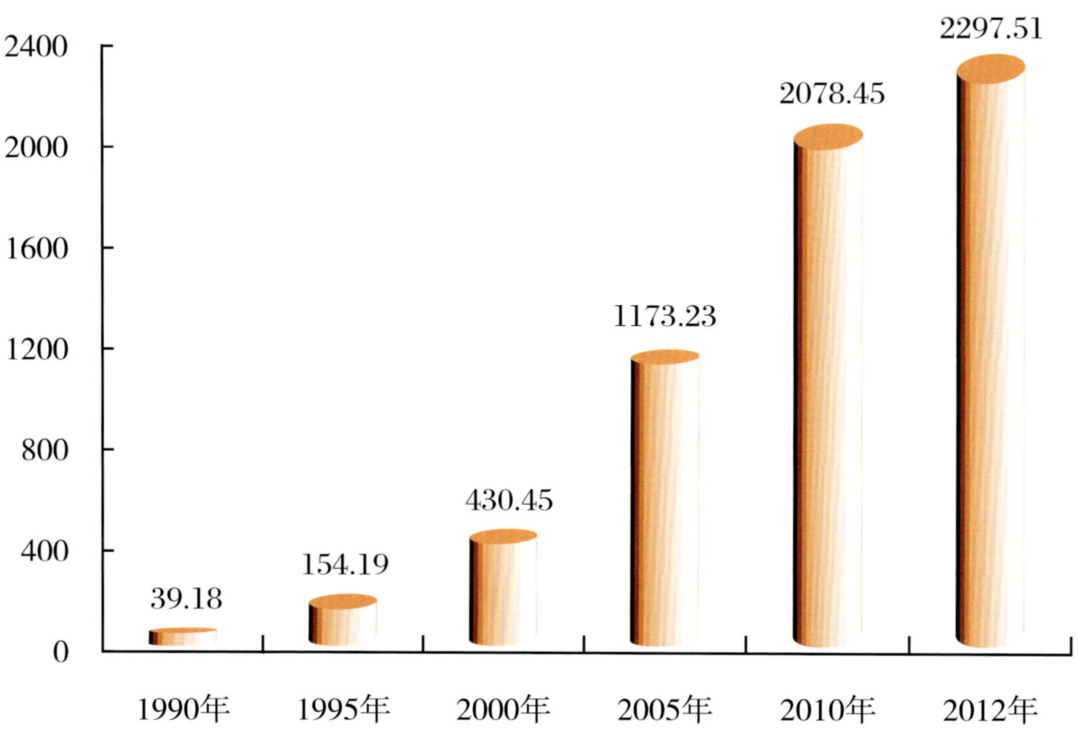

规模以上制造业增加值行业结构(%)

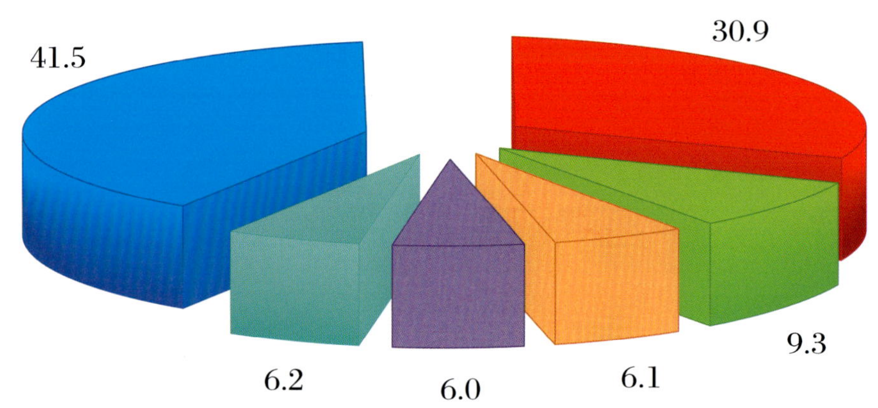

计算机、通信和其他电子设备制造业　电气机械和器材制造业
皮革、毛皮、羽毛及其制品和制鞋业　橡胶和塑料制品业
纺织服装、服饰业　其它制造业

进口总额、出口总额（亿美元）

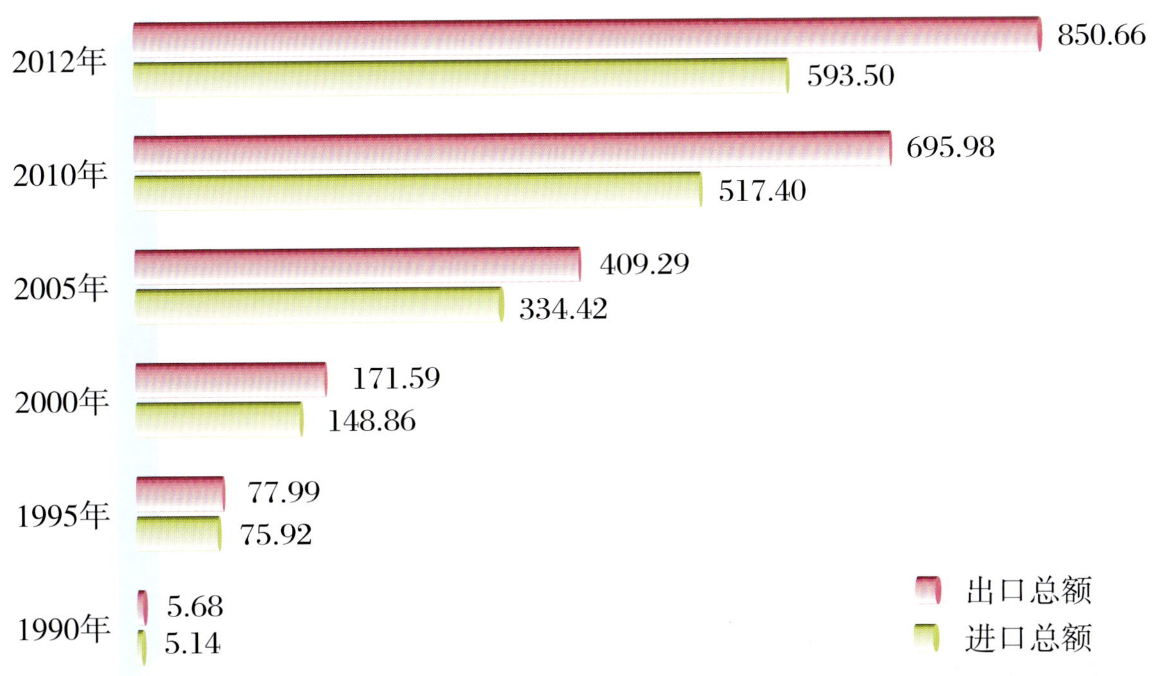

实际利用外资(新口径)（亿美元）

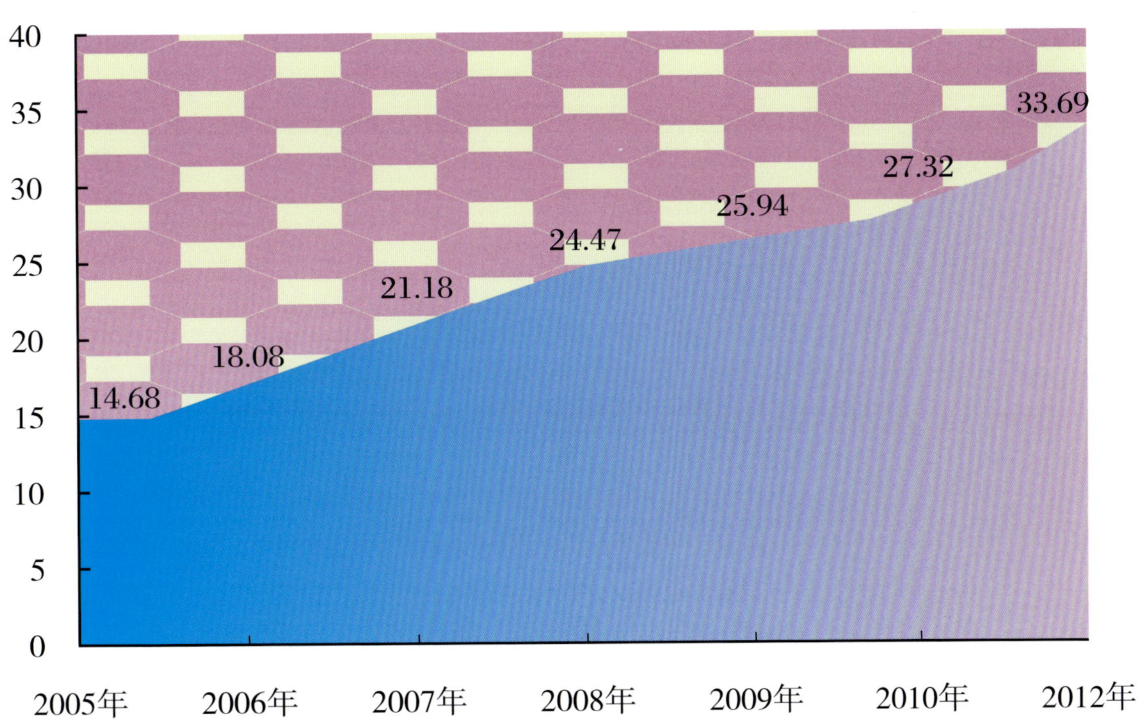

来源于东莞的财政收入（亿元）

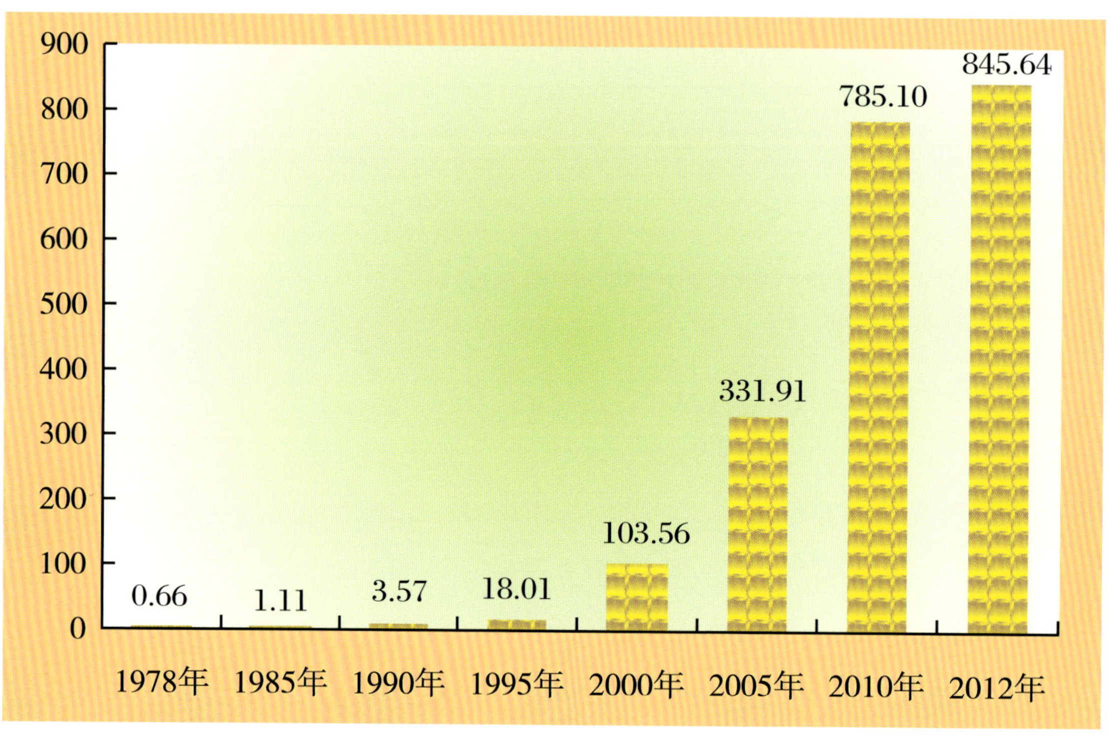

注：1995年及以前年份，来源于东莞的财政收入不含关税。

各项人民币存贷款余额(亿元)

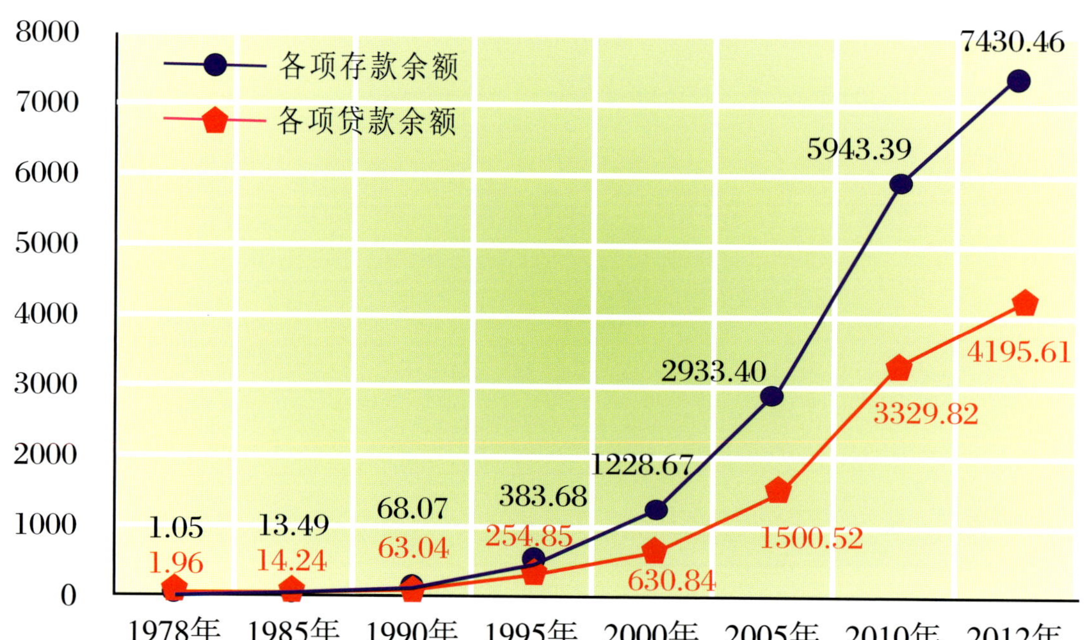

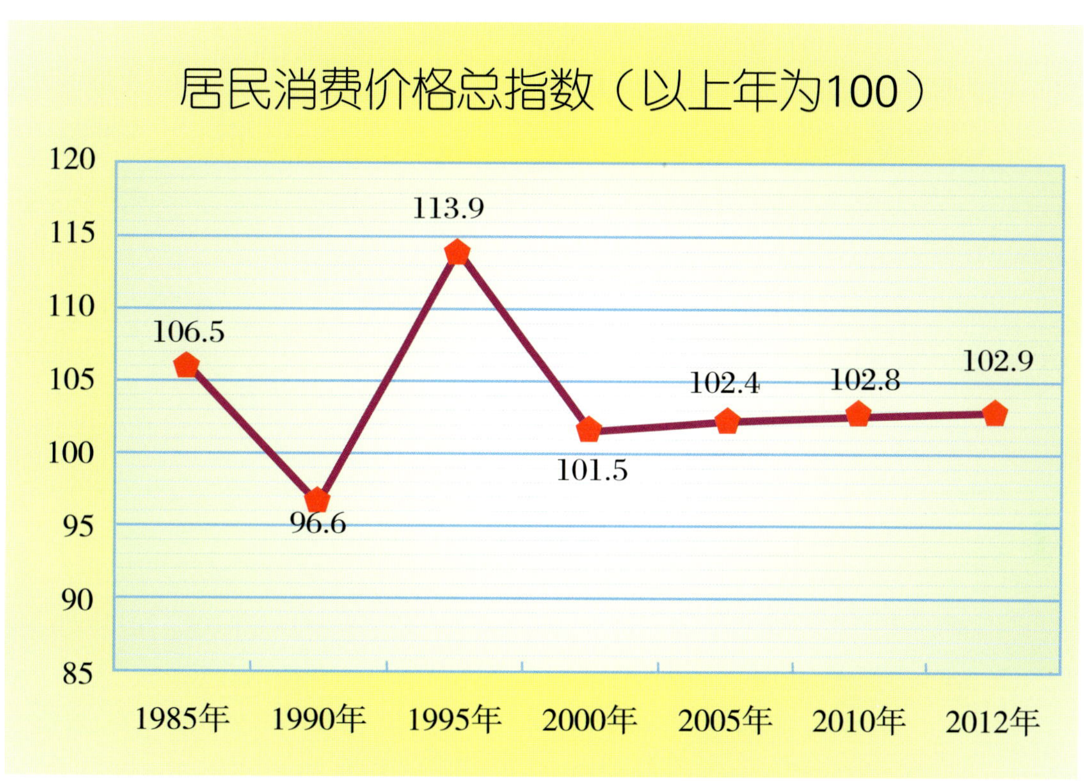
居民消费价格总指数（以上年为100）
120
115
110
105
100
95
90
85
106.5
96.6
113.9
101.5
102.4
102.8
102.9
1985年
1990年
1995年
2000年
2005年
2010年
2012年

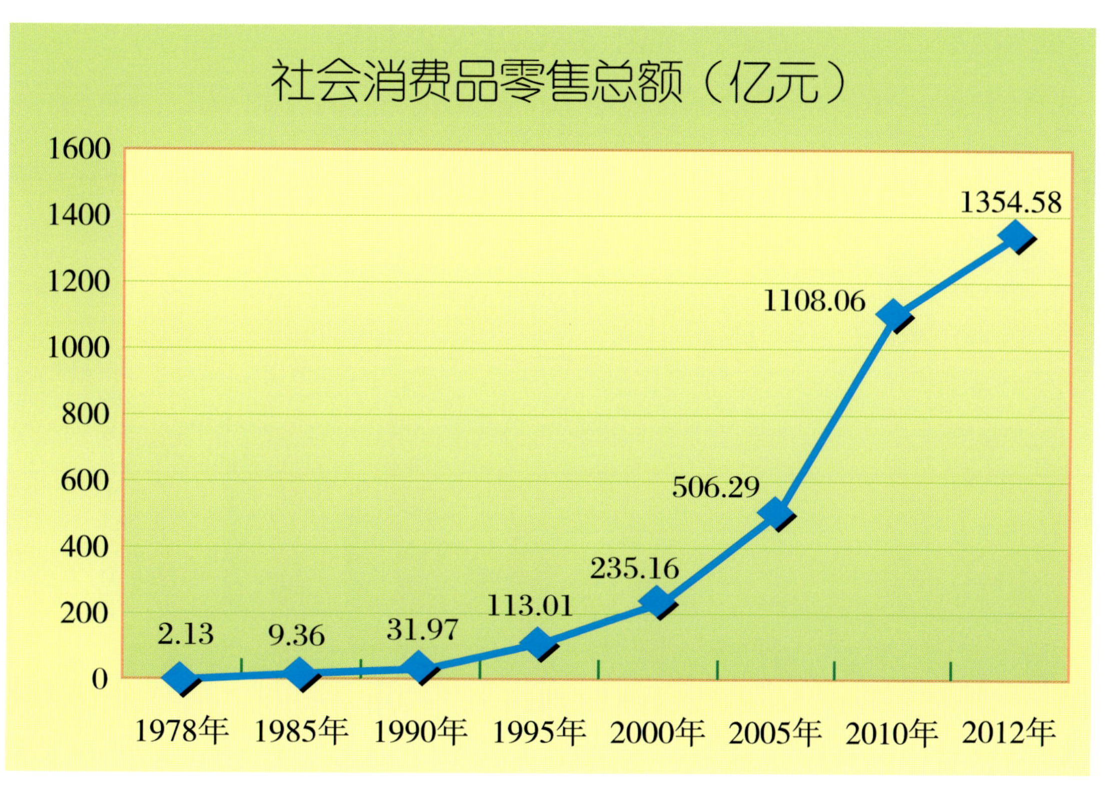
社会消费品零售总额（亿元）
1600
1400
1200
1000
800
600
400
200
0
2.13
9.36
31.97
113.01
235.16
506.29
1108.06
1354.58
1978年
1985年
1990年
1995年
2000年
2005年
2010年
2012年

城乡居民人民币储蓄存款余额(亿元)

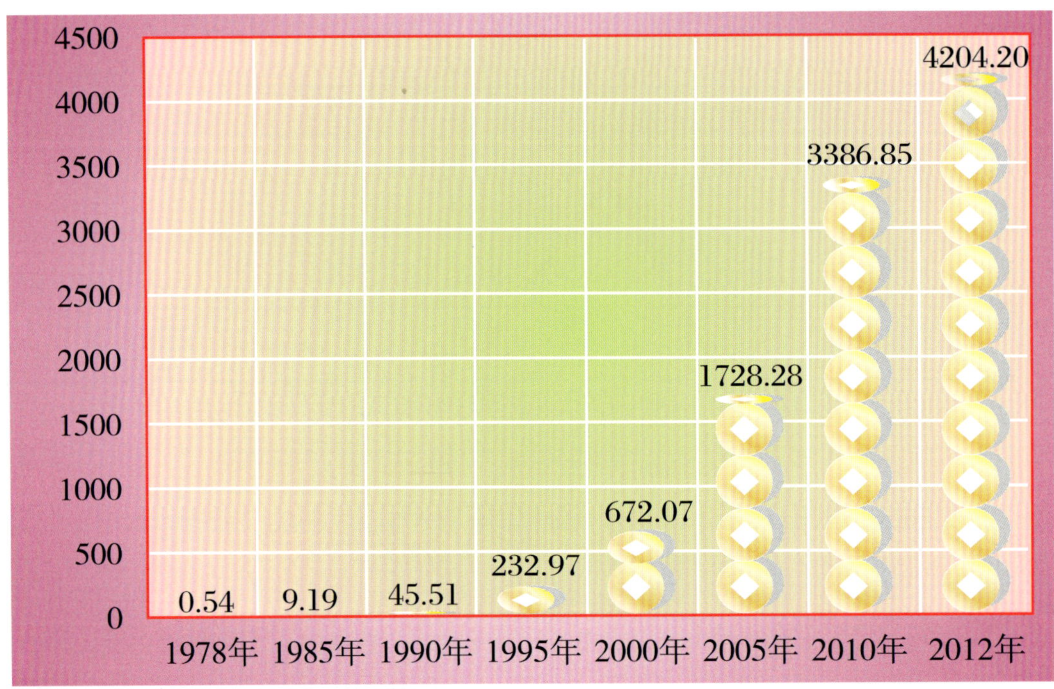

城乡居民人均收入(元)

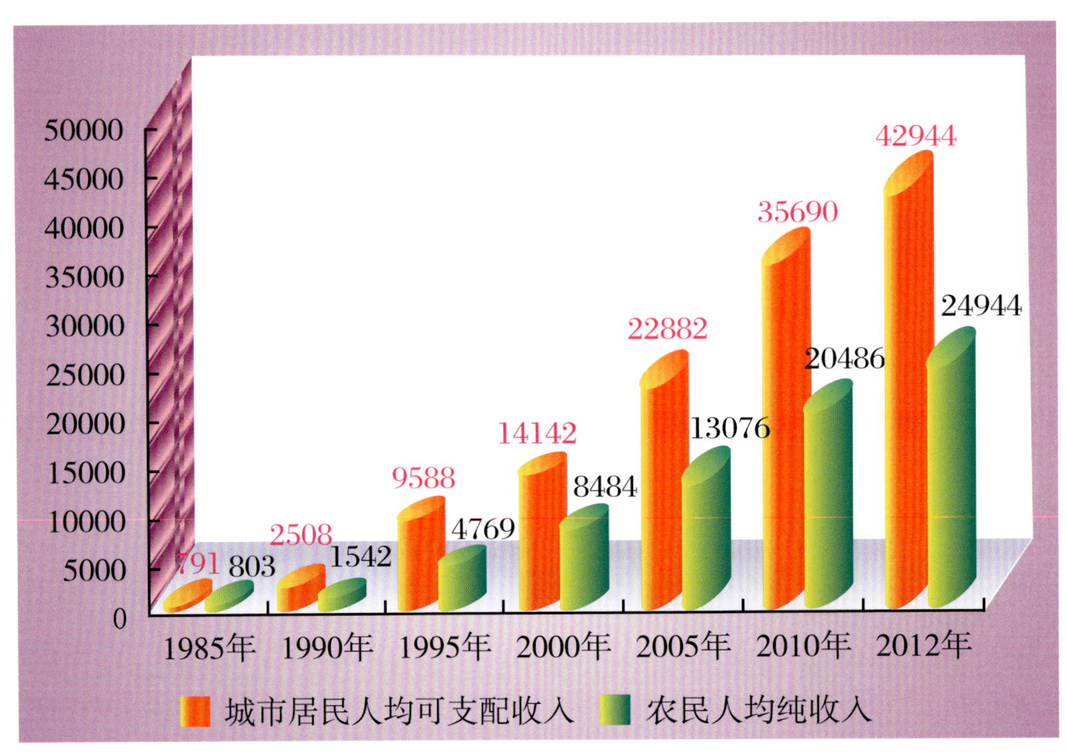

固定资产投资总额(亿元)

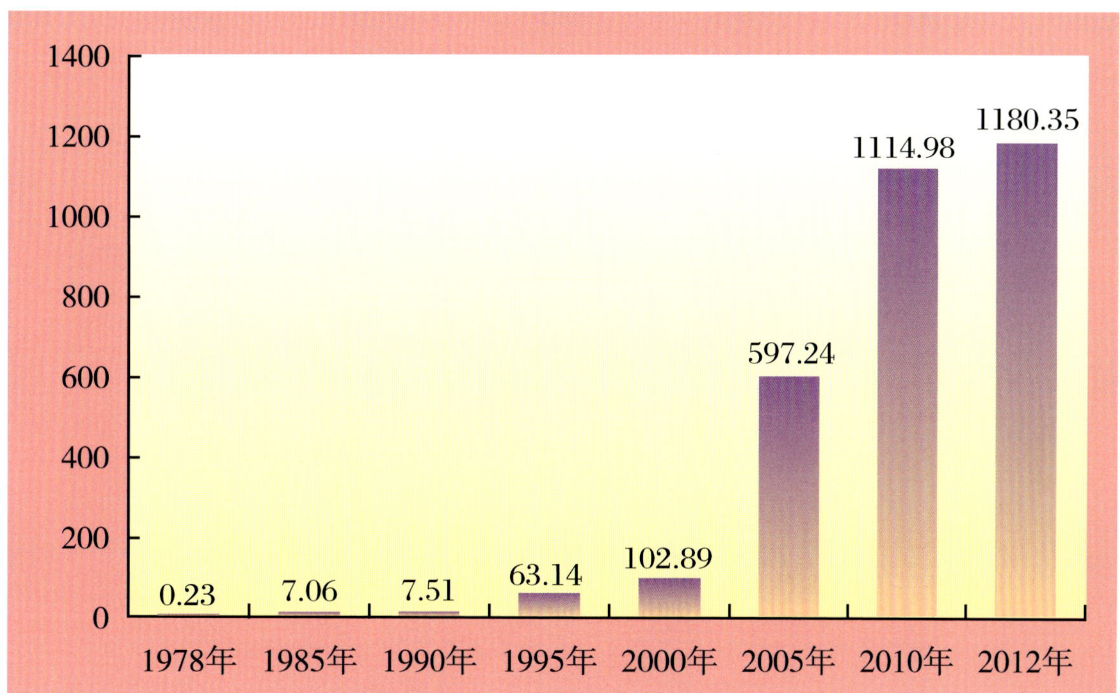

总供电量和总售电量(亿千瓦时)

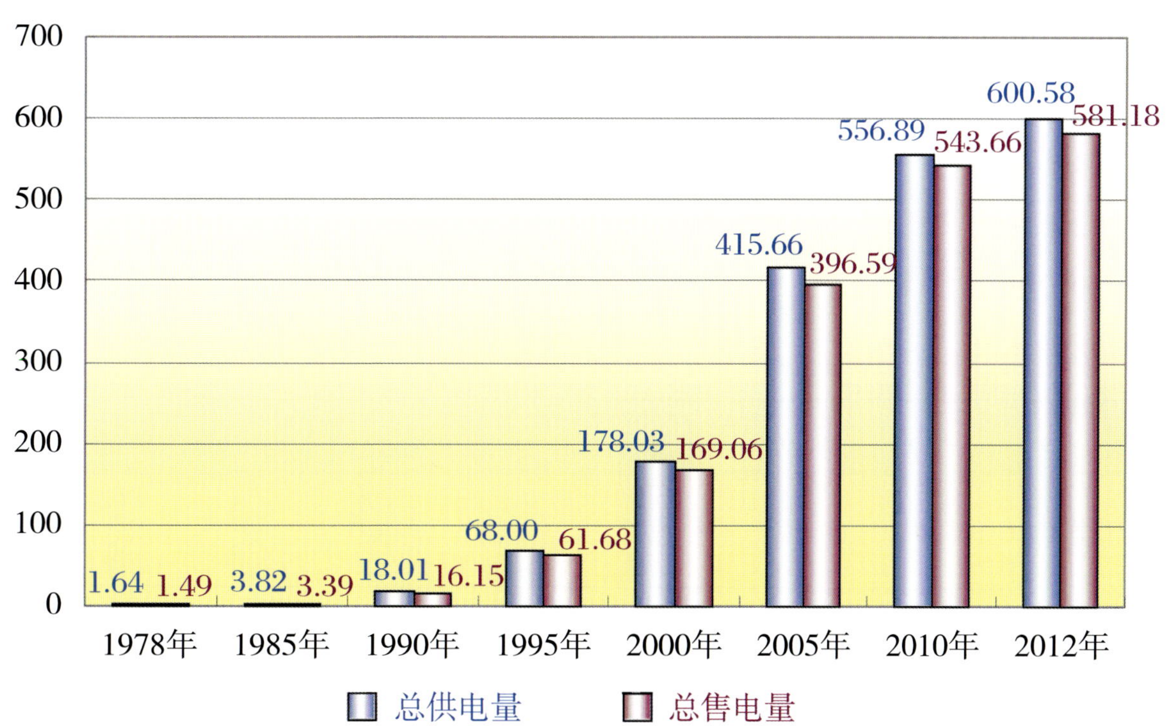

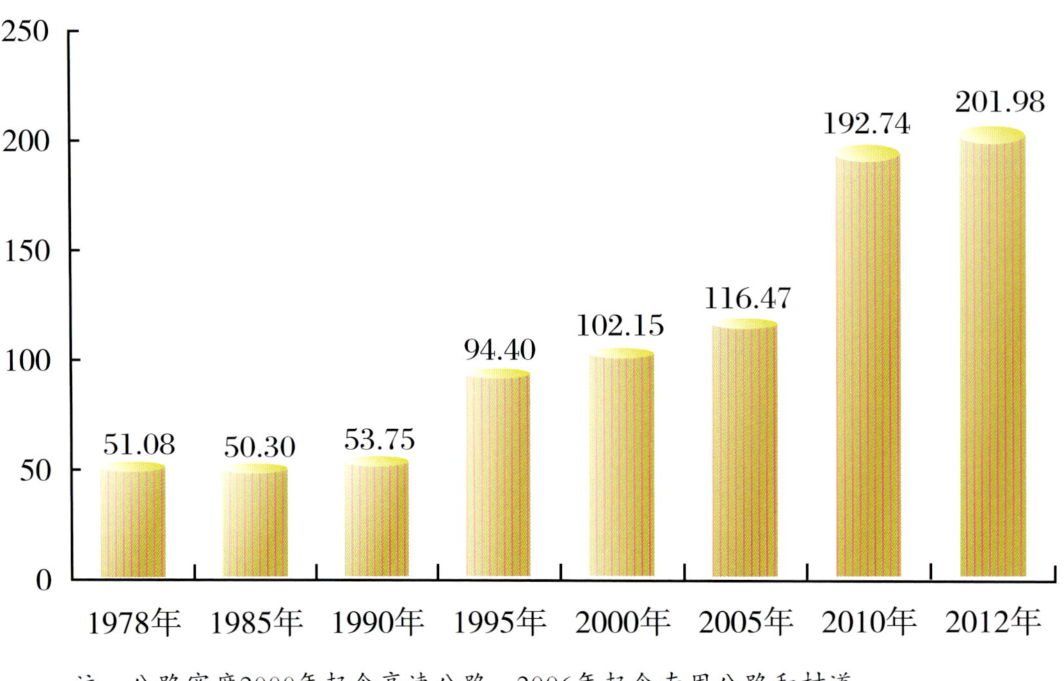

注：公路密度2000年起含高速公路，2006年起含专用公路和村道。

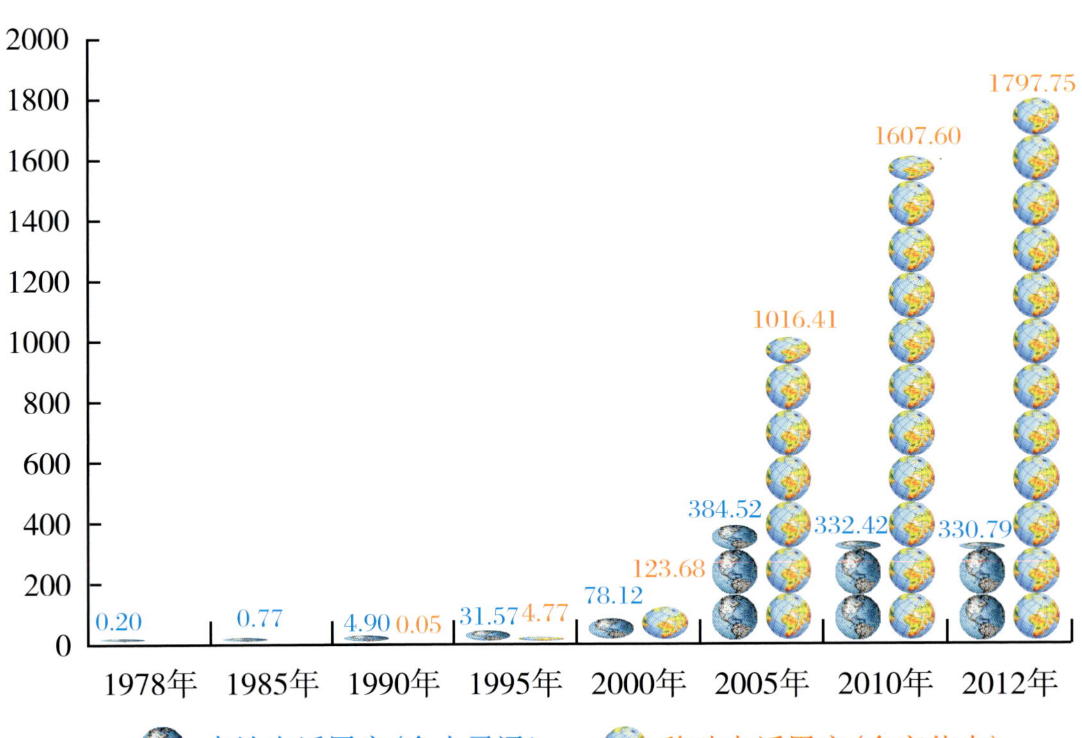

第一部分　概　述

Part One　Outline

2012年东莞市国民经济和社会发展统计公报

2012年，全市人民在市委、市政府的坚强领导下，从容应对复杂严峻的发展形势，以科学发展观为指导，围绕“加快转型升级、建设幸福东莞、实现高水平崛起”的战略目标，组织实施“三重”建设、水乡地区统筹发展、科技金融产业融合发展、农村综合改革、法治化国际化营商环境营造等系列政策措施，经济增长稳步回升，社会和谐稳定，为顺利实施高水平崛起奠定了坚实基础。

一、综　合

初步核算，2012年东莞生产总值（GDP）5010.14亿元，比上年增长6.1%。分产业看，第一产业增加值19.19亿元，增长1.2%；第二产业增加值2351.78亿元，增长5.6%；第三产业增加值2639.17亿元，增长6.7%。三大产业比例为0.4∶46.9∶52.7。人均地区生产总值60556元，增长5.7%。

在现代产业中，规模以上先进制造业增加值739.87亿元，增长8.5%；现代服务业增加值1543.91亿元，增长8.0%。

在第三产业中，交通运输、仓储和邮政业增长15.2%，批发和零售业增长2.7%，住宿和餐饮业增长1.5%，金融业增长14.1%，房地产业增长4.8%，其他服务业增长7.8%。

图一　2006-2012年地区生产总值及增长速度

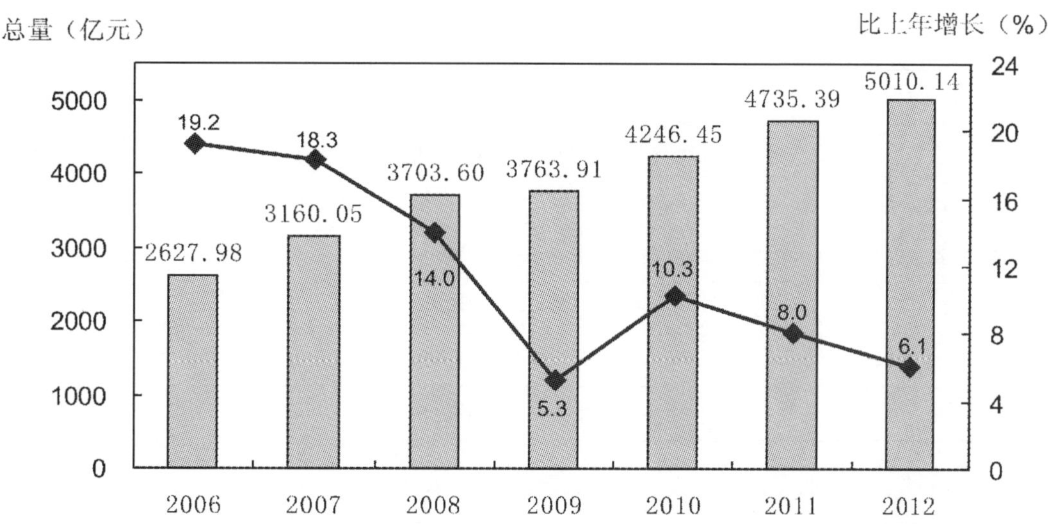

全年居民消费价格总水平上涨2.9%。其中居住类上涨1.5%，娱乐教育文化用品及服务类上涨1.8%，衣着类上涨1.0%，食品类上涨6.1%，医疗保健和个人用品类上涨4.8%，烟酒类上涨1.4%，交通和通信类下降1.2%，家庭设备用品及维修服务类上涨1.4%。此外，全年商品零售价格上涨2.4%。工业生产者出厂价格下降0.2%。

图二 2006-2012年居民消费价格总指数（上年=100）

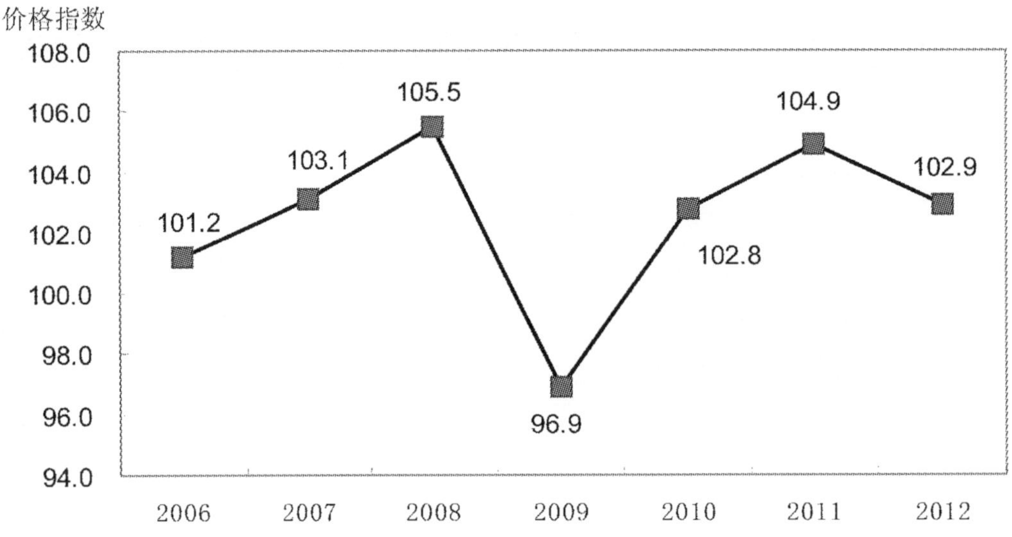

表一　2012 年价格变动情况

类　　别	价格指数（上年＝100）	比上年升降幅度（%）
居民消费价格指数	102.9	2.9
食　品	106.1	6.1
其中：粮食	103.7	3.7
肉禽及其制品	102.6	2.6
油脂	105.0	5.0
蛋	101.1	1.1
菜	124.5	24.5
水产品	108.3	8.3
烟　酒	101.4	1.4
衣　着	101.0	1.0
家庭设备用品及维修服务	101.4	1.4
医疗保健和个人用品	104.8	4.8
交通和通信	98.8	-1.2
娱乐教育文化用品及服务	101.8	1.8
居　住	101.5	1.5
商品零售价格指数	102.4	2.4
工业生产者出厂价格指数	99.8	-0.2

全年来源于东莞的财政收入845.62亿元，增长0.8%。市公共财政预算收入356.32亿元，增长13.8%。市公共财政预算支出385.58亿元，增长9.6%。其中，一般公共服务支出36.20亿元，公共安全支出49.43亿元，教育支出92.80亿元，社会保障和就业支出24.19亿元。全年全市税收总额939.11亿元，增长11.3%。

年末城镇实有登记失业人数1.22万人，全年失业人员安置就业人数1.02万人，城镇登记失业率为2.3%。

经济社会发展中存在的主要问题：资源环境瓶颈约束加剧，自主创新能力不强，转型升级和提质增效任务艰巨，企业生产经营仍面临着不少困难；“三重”项目的推进力度和区域统筹发展力度仍需加大；治安管理、教育公平、医疗改革等公共服务推进步伐有待加快等。

二、农　业

全年全市完成农林牧渔业总产值32.01亿元，（按可比价计算，下同）增长0.6%。其中农业产值16.93亿元，下降2.2%，占农林牧渔业总产值的52.9%；林业产值0.17亿元，同比下降22.7%，占0.5%；牧业产值6.32亿元，增长3.3%，占19.7%；渔业产值7.64亿元，增长5.2%，占23.9%。全年农作物播种面积37.25万亩、水果种植面积17.87万亩。全年粮食产量1.25万吨；水产品产量7.70万吨；蔬菜产量39.11万吨，增长0.6%；生猪出栏28.63万头，增长2.6%；家禽出栏784.70万只，增长7.2%。

全年新增8家农民专业合作社、1家国家级龙头企业、4个名牌产品，目前全市共有农民专业合作社46家（入社农户1000多户）、农业龙头企业19家（省级以上8家，其中国家级3家）、省级农业类名牌产品40个。

三、工业和建筑业

全年全市规模以上工业实现增加值1733.12亿元，增长5.6%。在规模以上工业中，重工业增加值948.73亿元，增长8.3%，占54.7%；轻工业增加值784.39亿元，增长2.4%，占45.3%。

全年全市规模以上五大支柱产业完成增加值1173.41亿元，增长7.8%；四个特色产业完成增加值199.56亿元，增长1.3%。

全年高技术制造业增加值增长13.1%，其中，医药制造业增长16.4%，电子及通信设备制造业增长17.0%，电子计算机及办公设备制造业增长8.0%，医疗设备及仪器仪表制造业下降26.8%。

全年先进制造业增加值增长8.5%，其中，装备制造业增长9.5%，钢铁冶炼及加工业下降8.7%，石油及化学行业下降3.4%。装备制造业中，汽车制造业增长11.7%，船舶制造业、环境污染防治专用设备制造业分别下降12.9%和38.5%；钢铁冶炼及加工业中，炼铁业下降3.7%，钢压延加工下降8.9%；石油及化学行业中，石油加工、炼焦及核燃料加工业下降22.0%，化学原料及化学制品制造业下降2.4%，橡胶制品业下降11.8%。

全年优势传统产业增加值下降0.6%，其中，纺织服装业增长1.5%，食品饮料业增长2.4%，家具制造业下降5.2%，建筑材料下降6.5%，金属制品业增长1.3%，家用电力器具制造业下降9.1%。

规模以上工业综合经济效益指数为129.47，实现利润总额248.90亿元，资产负债率为57.3%。

全年全市建筑业实现增加值78.12亿元，下降1.5%。建筑企业完成总产值142.2亿元，增长9.5%；施工面积705.13万平方米，下降6.7%；竣工面积345.56万平方米，下降14.5%。建筑企业按施工产值计算的全员劳动生产率人均27.4万元，增长20.7%。

表二　2012 年规模以上工业主要产品产量

产品名称	计量单位	产量	增长（%）
啤酒	千升	575383	3.5
果汁和蔬果类饮料类	万吨	228.79	-6.0
服装	万件	108932	-3.8
轻革	万平方米	485.54	-15.4
人造板	万立方米	17.25	8.3
人造板表面装饰板	万平方米	777.55	-45.8
复合木地板	万平方米	66.09	-16.7
家具	万件	4758.80	-18.1
纸浆（原生浆及废纸浆）	万吨	58.36	0.4
机制纸及纸板（外购原纸加工除外）	万吨	1200.74	6.4
塑料制品	万吨	154.30	-4.4
水泥	万吨	249.16	-0.6
瓷质砖	万平方米	1975.81	-11.5
平板玻璃	万重量箱	3286.83	-5.5
卫生陶瓷制品	万件	166.72	-12.5
金属集装箱	万立方米	946.09	13.9
数码照相机	万台	31.37	-36.1
模具	万套	25.39	-22.7
电力电容器	万千乏	455.33	
太阳能热水器	万平方米	11.44	18.4
灯具及照明装置	万套（万台、万个）	22097.87	15.5
电子计算机整机	万台	99.73	28.4
打印机	万台	113.06	6.1
电话单机	万部	3883.18	-5.1
移动通信手持机（手机）	万台	6728.96	27.8
数字激光音、视盘机	万台	1471.54	-27.2
电视接收机顶盒	万台	208.52	19.5
集成电路	万块	6340	105.2
电子元件	亿只	11166	3.3
印制电路板	万平方米	1335.12	-37.4
汽车仪器仪表	万台	49.03	-24.2
光学仪器	万台（万个）	117.48	14.0
眼镜成镜	万副	4692.21	1.4
自来水生产量	万立方米	173413	-2.7

四、固定资产投资

全年固定资产投资 1180.35 亿元，增长 9.4%。按登记注册类型分，国有经济投资 114.10 亿元，下降9.7%，占固定资产投资总额的9.7%；集体经济投资124.13亿元，增长4.0%，占10.5%；民营经济投资669.24亿元，增长2.4%，占56.7%；外商及港澳台商投资294.21亿元，增长33.2%，占24.9%。

图三　2006—2012年固定资产投资总额及其增长速度

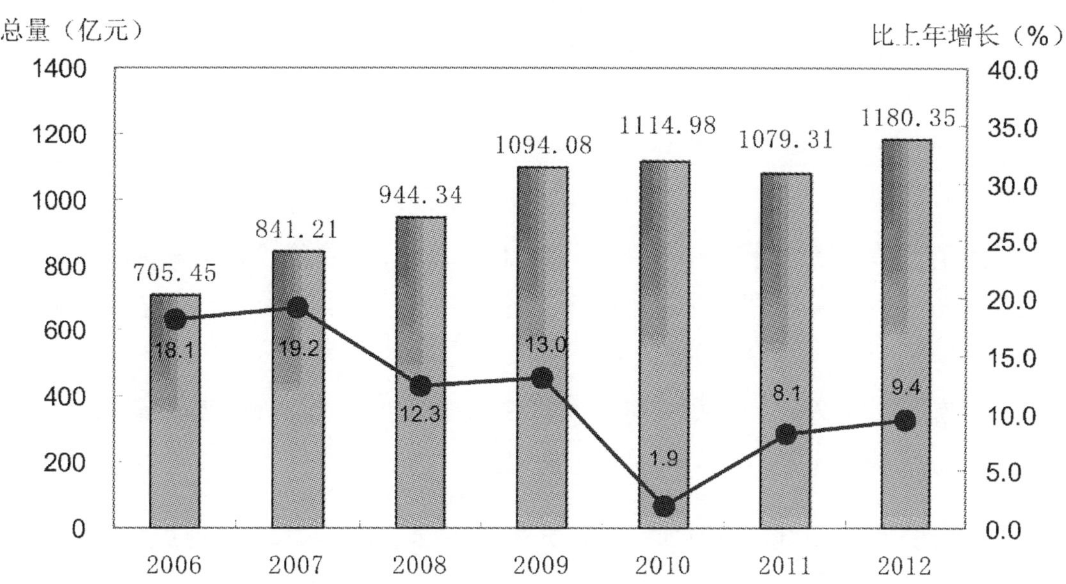

从产业投向看，投资集中在第二、三产业。第二产业投资414.89亿元，其中制造业投资382.60亿元；第三产业投资763.49亿元。全年完成投资5000万元以上项目338个，共完成投资582.56亿元。

表三　2012年分行业固定资产投资额情况

行　　业	投资额（万元）	增长（%）
总　计	11803493	9.4
农、林、牧、渔业	19710	228.8
制造业	3826025	26.6
电力、燃气及水的生产和供应业	320667	-34.3
建筑业	2193	49.4
交通运输、仓储和邮政业	1279006	17.0
信息传输、计算机服务和软件业	218614	9.7
批发和零售业	195376	-26.0
住宿和餐饮业	101943	121.1
金融业	25898	33.5
房地产业	4419691	9.5
租赁和商务服务业	25679	-65.6
科学研究、技术服务和地质勘查业	99097	27.8
水利、环境和公共设施管理业	852023	-16.9
居民服务和其他服务业	8015	-53.2
教育	245393	4.4
卫生、社会保障和社会福利业	55031	-25.3
文化、体育和娱乐业	66813	-4.8
公共管理和社会组织	42319	-0.5

全年完成房地产开发投资377.32亿元，增长1.1%。商品房施工面积2453.93万平方米，增长2.5%；竣工面积362.47万平方米，增长49.6%；销售面积639.12万平方米，增长7.3%，其中商品住宅销售面积583.38万平方米，增长7.9%。全年商品房销售额542.38亿元，增长18.0%，其中商品住宅销售额472.52亿元，增长14.3%。

五、国内贸易

全年全市批发和零售业实现增加值486.88亿元，增长2.7%；住宿和餐饮业实现增加值180.22亿元，增长1.5%。

全年全市社会消费品零售总额1354.58亿元，增长9.3%，扣除物价因素影响，实际增长6.7%。分行业看，批发零售贸易业零售额1234.09亿元，增长9.5%；住宿餐饮业零售额120.49亿元，增长6.7%。

在限额以上批发和零售业中，食品、饮料、烟酒类零售额增长12.8%；服装鞋帽、针、纺织品类增长11.9%；日用品类增长8.2%；汽车类增长10.0%。

图四　2006—2012年社会消费品零售总额及其增长速度

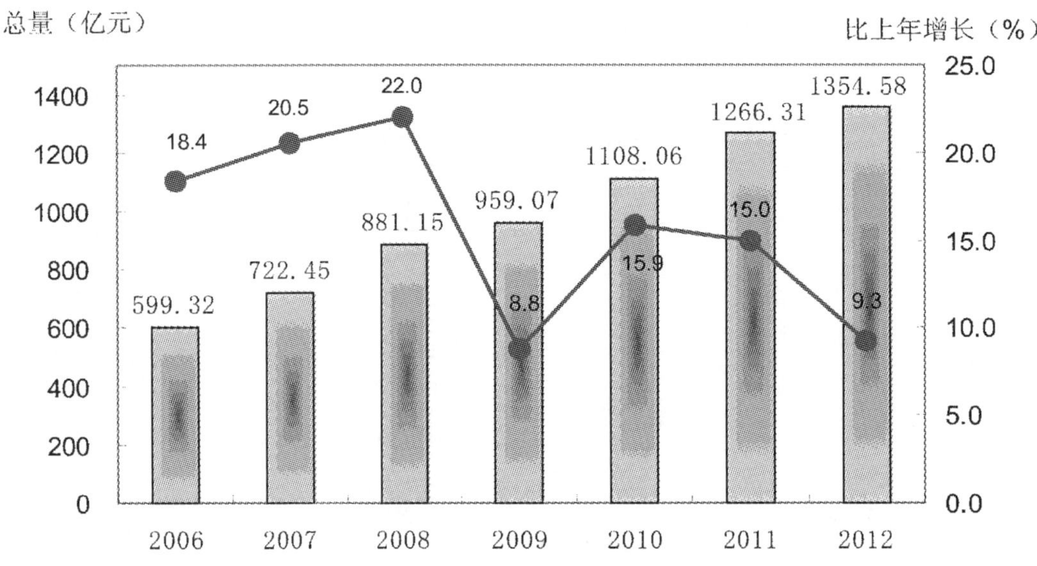

六、对外经济

全年全市进出口总额1444.16亿美元，增长6.8%。其中进口593.50亿美元，增长4.2%；出口850.66亿美元，增长8.6%。

按贸易方式分，一般贸易出口169.23亿美元，增长26.2%；加工贸易出口661.51亿美元，增长4.2%；其他出口19.92亿美元，增长38.4%。

按出口的地区分，对亚洲出口445.11亿美元，增长8.9%；对北美洲出口221.89亿美元，增长11.1%；对欧洲出口138.72亿美元，增长2.1%；对拉丁美洲出口27.48亿美元，增长12.7%；对大洋洲出口10.49亿美元，增长8.7%。

全年机电产品出口 607.69 亿美元，增长 10.3%，占出口总额的 71.4%；高新技术产品出口 297.39 亿美元，增长 8.9%，占 35.0%。

表四　2012 年主要商品出口情况

商　品　名　称	金额（万美元）	增长（%）
机电产品（包括本目录已具体列名的机电产品）	6076866	10.3
高新技术产品	2973879	8.9
自动数据处理设备及其部件	614184	0.3
服装及衣着附件	565121	22.5
静止式变流器	359454	-4.4
自动数据处理设备的零件	375361	8.1
家具及其零件	395838	16.4
鞋类	298888	-2.7
有线电话机（包括无绳电话机）	192299	-0.2
旅行用品及箱包	198731	9.4
电线和电缆	212470	23.2
玩具	186212	8.2
纺织纱线、织物及制品	167082	1.8
录、放像机	77044	-52.4
通断保护电路装置及零件	196629	21.6
电视、收音机及无线电讯设备的零附件	133727	-7.2
手持或车载无线电话机	138665	0.2
数字式相机	70123	-45.6
塑料制品	142073	11.8
游戏机	115326	63.2
电视机（包括整套散件）	92070	-4.2

按新口径统计，全年全市新签外商直接投资项目 690 宗，合同外资金额 38.10 亿美元，增长 8.6%。实际利用外资 33.69 亿美元，增长 10.5%。其中电子及通信设备制造业实际利用外资 6.06 亿美元，下降 7.7%；专用设备制造业实际利用外资 1.62 亿美元，下降 18.8%。

表五　2012 年分行业利用外资情况

行　业　名　称	合同外资金额（万美元）	增长（%）	实际利用外资（万美元）	增长（%）
总　　计	381031	5.9	336938	11.3
农、林、牧、渔业	369	-59.7	297	-24.8
制造业	293911	0.03	251960	-3.0
纺织业	4676	-63.6	8496	-49.0
纺织服装、鞋、帽制造业	7918	-31.0	7667	-32.9
家具制造业	2746	13.6	2088	-47.5
通用设备制造业	4190	-27.9	5015	-43.1

续上表

行业名称	合同外资金额（万美元）	增长（%）	实际利用外资（万美元）	增长（%）
专用设备制造业	33696	144.1	16186	-18.7
电气机械及器材制造业	23932	-36.0	31165	12.3
通信设备、计算机及其他电子设备制造业	75113	-10.2	60606	-7.7
金属制品业	15291	-11.0	12060	9.1
塑料制品业	26460	-10.2	16901	-7.8
文教体育用品制造业	7837	-35.3	7930	4.9
造纸及纸制品业	17908	4.5	24157	54.4
其他制造业	74144	46.8	59689	12.6
信息传输、计算机服务和软件业	19	-90.5	90	-91.4
批发和零售业	45295	60.4	42680	81.1

七、交通、邮电和旅游

全年全市交通运输、仓储和邮政业实现增加值124.87亿元，增长15.2%。

年末全市境内公路通车里程（含乡村道路）4969公里，公路密度201.98公里/百平方公里。年末全市机动车保有量（民用）148.68万辆，增长4.9%。其中汽车保有量120.70万辆，增长13.7%。

全年公路货物运输量8421万吨，货物周转量54.36亿吨公里；水路货物运输量2770万吨，货物周转量242.35亿吨公里。全年公路运输完成客运量7.97亿人次，旅客周转量156.67亿人公里；水路运输完成客运量32.00万人次，旅客周转量2106万人公里。全年港口旅客吞吐量32.30万人次，货物吞吐量9228万吨。

表六　2012年客（货）运量、周转量

指标	单位	数值	增长（%）
客运量	万人	79739	-0.7
# 公路	万人	79707	-0.7
旅客周转量	亿人公里	156.88	7.5
# 公路	亿人公里	156.67	7.5
货运量	万吨	11191	10.1
# 公路	万吨	8421	2.6
货物周转量	亿吨公里	296.71	58.3
# 公路	亿吨公里	54.36	2.3

全年完成邮电业务收入169.96亿元，增长3.1%。邮政发送信函5065万件，特快专递148万件，邮政汇款汇出金额196.36亿元。年末全市固定电话用户（含小灵通）325.11万户，比上年增加5.56万户；移动电话用户1754.10万户，增加76.33万户。全年长途电话通话时长215.19亿分钟，年末互联网用户209.59万户，比上年增加18.88万户；宽带接入用户204.72万户，增加20.29万户。

图五　2006-2012年年末电话用户数

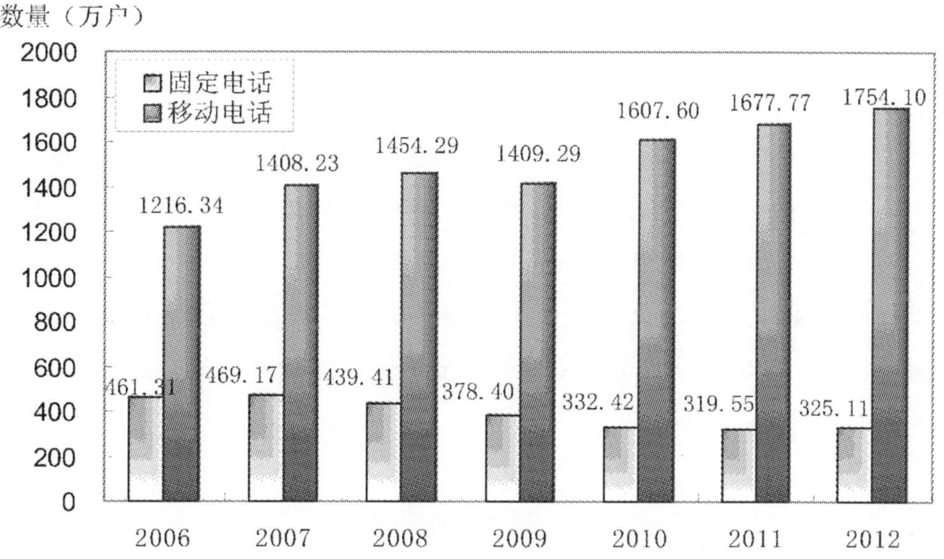

年末全市有星级酒店89家，其中五星级酒店20家。全市有旅行社61家，全年接待国际及港澳台游客414.92万人次，增长16.1%。其中接待外国游客134.81万人次，增长11.0%；接待港澳台游客280.11万人次，增长18.7%。国际旅游外汇收入12.69亿美元，增长39.5%。全年接待国内游客2328.92万人次，增长3.1%。国内旅游总收入306.35亿元，增长22.9%。全年东莞组团外出旅游185.34万人次，增长1.2%。其中，国内旅游167.54万人次，增长0.1%；出境旅游17.80万人次，增长12.6%。

八、金融

全年全市金融业实现增加值213.51亿元，增长14.1%。

图六　2006－2012年城乡居民储蓄存款余额及其增长速度

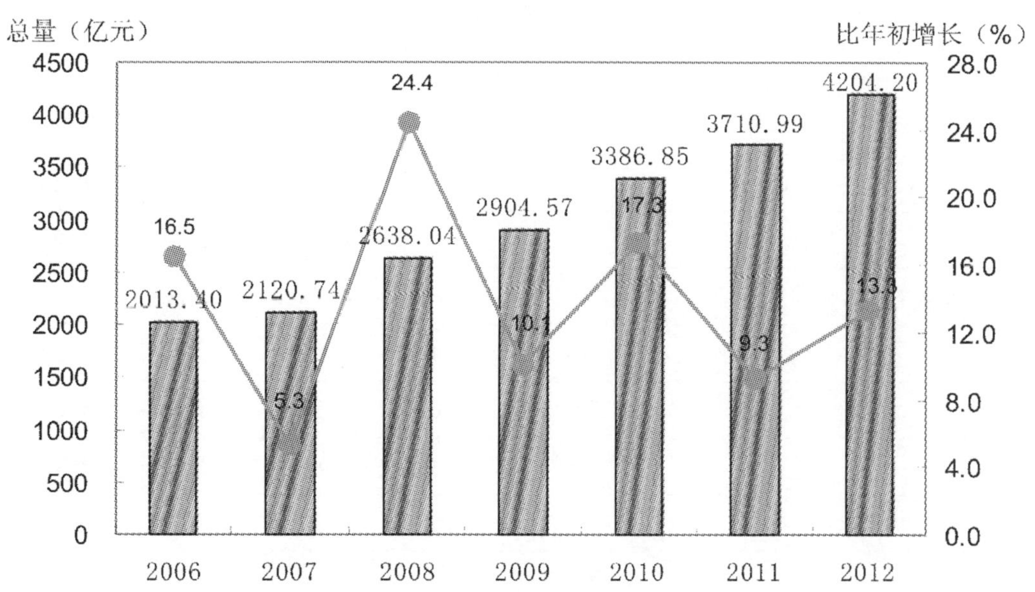

年末全市有各类金融机构97家，其中银行类机构31家，保险类机构41家（不含保险代理机构），证券期货类机构25家。年末全市金融机构各项人民币存款余额7430.46亿元，比年初增长12.4%。其中城乡居民储蓄存款余额4204.20亿元，增长13.3%。各项人民币贷款余额4195.61亿元，增长12.9%。在个人消费贷款余额中，个人住房按揭贷款余额833.28亿元，增长8.5%；个人汽车消费贷款余额9.21亿元，下降43.3%。全市金融机构不良贷款率比年初下降0.08个百分点。

年末全市各类证券公司共开户95.41万户，比上年增加5.93万户。全年股票总成交额6100.59亿元，下降25.7%。年末保证金余额78.37亿元，增长12.3%。

全年全市各类保险保费收入177.66亿元，增长8.6%。其中财产险保费收入61.05亿元，增长10.8%；人寿险保费收入116.61亿元，增长7.4%。全年保险赔款与给付金额32.87亿元，综合赔付率为53.8%。

九、科技和教育

全年新增国家高新技术企业150家，总数达537家。全市专利申请量29199件，增长19.4%，其中发明专利5568件，占专利申请量比例为19.1%；专利授权量20900件，增长8.0%，其中发明专利授权量1381件，增长82.2%。

全年新增3家省级企业工程中心和2家省级企业重点实验室；新增2个国家专利优秀奖，99项科研成果获得市科技奖；新增5个广东省创新科研团队，目前团队总数达14家。

全市有幼儿园791所，比上年增加42所。3－6周岁在园（班）幼儿25.57万人，入园（班）率为97.0%。全市有小学322所，在校学生60.81万人；本市户籍学龄儿童入学率达100%，小学毕业生升学率达100%。全市有初中163所，在校学生19.21万人，初中入学率为100%。全市高中阶段学校有64所，在校学生12.59万人，其中普通高中（含完中）40所，在校学生7.59万人，中职学校24所（含技工学校1所），在校学生5.01万人。全市有普通高等院校6所，在校学生5.24万人。全年普通高等院校共招收本科、专科学生2.05万人，毕业生1.26万人。

表七　教育情况

指　　标	招生（万人）	增长（%）	在校生（万人）	增长（%）	毕业生（万人）	增长（%）
普通本专科	2.05	21.8	5.24	16.2	1.26	33.4
成人本专科	0.60	-5.5	1.88	-8.5	0.63	-9.5
各类中等职业技术教育(不含技工学校)	1.70	2.0	4.73	4.5	1.31	-6.0
普通高中	2.58	0.4	7.59	3.0	2.34	5.9
初中	7.06	1.6	19.21	1.4	5.61	2.4
小学	12.33	7.4	60.81	5.2	8.77	9.0
学前教育	10.71	25.2	25.57	12.3	8.33	21.9
特殊教育	0.006	-29.5	0.04	9.6	0.006	

十、文化、卫生和体育

年末全市有群众艺术馆1个，文化站33个，公共图书馆649个，博物馆31个，艺术表演场所12个，电影放映单位59个，网吧1042间。全市有公共广播节目52套，公共电视节目21套。全年共发行报纸8912.96万份，其中《东莞日报》4481.5万份；各类杂志138.54万册，电影放映29.1万场次，观众537.1万人次。

年末全市有医疗机构2218个，其中门诊、诊所、医务室、卫生站、社区卫生服务机构等基层医疗机构2142个。全市卫生技术人员4.06万人，医疗机构病床2.46万张。全市建成并投入使用的社区卫生服务中心（站）387个。全年诊疗总人数上升18.2%。

全年全市运动员共获得137枚金牌、105枚银牌、99枚铜牌。其中夺得全国赛金牌10枚；广东省赛金牌127枚、银牌95枚、铜牌92枚。全年举办市级综合和单项比赛12次，参加人数0.37万人次。全市有体育彩票发行网点1016个，销售总额10.71亿元，体彩公益金7522万元。

十一、人民生活、社会保障和安全生产

全年城市居民人均可支配收入42944元，农村居民人均纯收入24944元，分别增长8.7%和9.2%。

图七　2006-2012年城市居民人均可支配收入及其增长速度

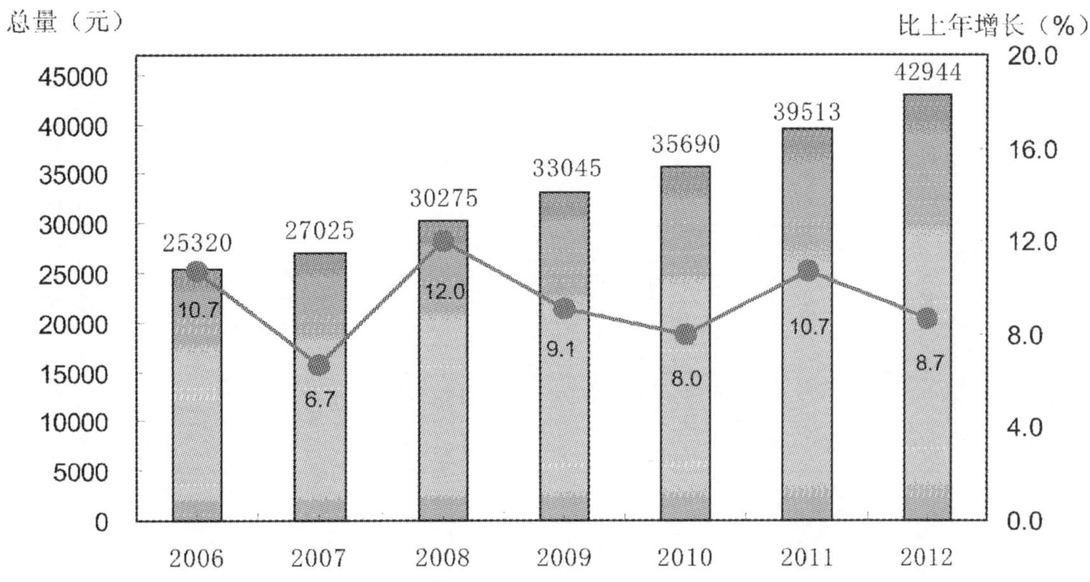

全年城市居民人均消费性支出31369元，增长14.1%，城市居民人均住房建筑面积58.44平方米。全年农民生活消费现金支出16103元，增长14.6%，农村居民人均住房建筑面积50.33平方米。

全市五大险种参保总人次为2553.93万人次，增长3.7%。基本医疗保险616.86万人，失业保险312.78万人，工伤保险494.14万人。全年社会保险基金总收入207.92亿元，保险基金总支出86.7亿元，年末保险基金累计余额591.59亿元。全年累计征缴各项保险（不含机关养老保险）基金187.17亿元，增长19.0%。

图八　2006-2012年农民人均纯收入及其增长速度

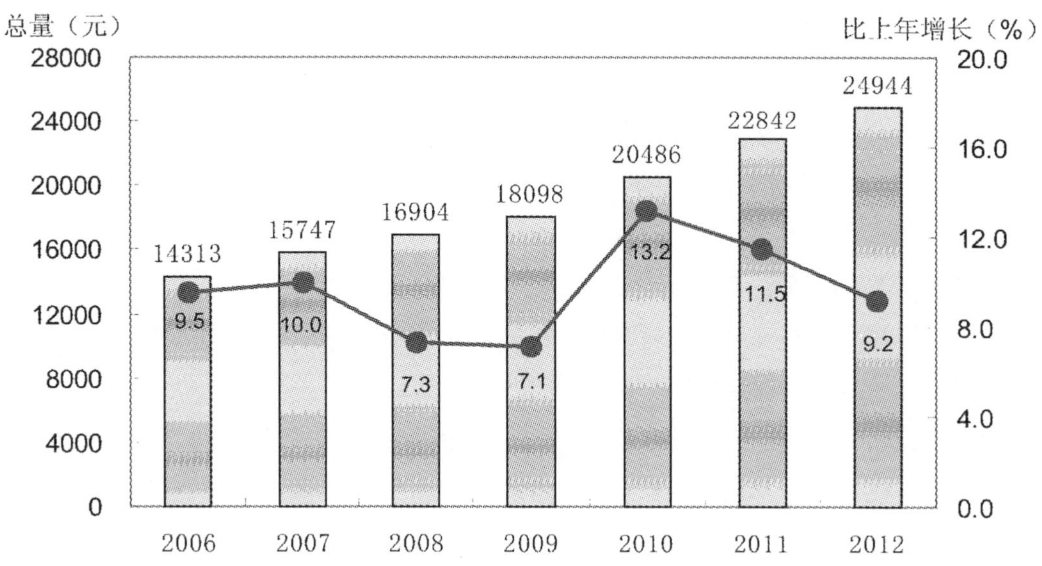

表八　2012 年城市居民收支情况

指　　　　标	金额（元）	增长（%）
城市居民人均可支配收入	42944	8.7
工资性收入	30518	11.9
财产性收入	9099	21.6
转移性收入	3484	-20.3
城市居民人均消费性支出	31369	14.1
食品	11103	16.7
衣着	2121	17.4
居住	2852	34.0
家庭设备用品及服务	2173	14.3
医疗保健	1521	21.6
交通和通信	6108	1.2
教育文化娱乐服务	4348	11.9
其他商品和服务	1143	17.4

年末全市有收养类福利事业单位 34 个，其中社会福利院 1 个，社会福利中心 1 个，敬老院 31 个，敬老院供养老人 709 人。社会福利事业单位收养 2269 人，全年社会救济 2.47 万人。全市居民最低生活保障支出 8906.6 万元，社会救济福利事业费用 2.93 亿元，自然灾害生活救助支出 274.2 万元，慈善基金结余 2.07 亿元。全市纳入“五保户”对象有 1015 人，“五保户”费用支出 1702.9 万元。

全年共发生各类伤亡事故 4341 宗，下降 4.1%；死亡 534 人，受伤 4835 人，分别下降 1.1% 和 3.6%；直接经济损失 5325.39 万元，增长 704.1%。其中，道路交通事故 4299 宗，下降 4.3%；造成死亡 490 人，受伤 4831 人，分别下降 1.0% 和 3.4%。亿元地区生产总值生产安全事故死亡率为 0.106，道路交通事故万车死亡率为 3.31。

十二、人口、资源和环境

年末全市户籍人口187.02万人。全年出生人口2.47万人，出生率为13.3‰；死亡人口9684人，死亡率为5.2‰；人口自然增长率为8.1‰。年末全市常住人口829.23万人，其中城镇常住人口735.28万人。人口城镇化率为88.67%。

全年雨日天数205天，日照时数1708.7小时，平均气温22.6摄氏度，相对湿度78%，降水量1838.6毫米。

年末全市有森林公园18个，林业用地面积90.29万亩，生态公益林32.96万亩，林木积蓄量291.03万立方米，林木总生长量14.61万立方米。

年末全市建成区土地面积888.39平方公里，公共管理与公共服务用地面积59.71平方公里。林业用地面积90.29万亩，森林覆盖率为37.1%，林地绿化率为97.0%；城市建成区绿地率为42.4%，绿化覆盖率为45.0%，人均公园绿地面积16.53平方米；全市已建成公园广场1057个，面积1.21万公顷。

注：1. 本公报数为初步统计数，最后统计数据以《东莞统计年鉴－2013》为准。

2. 地区生产总值、各行业增加值、农业总产值绝对数按当年价格计算，增长速度按可比价格计算。

3. 自2012年起，“地方一般预算收入”和“地方一般预算支出”统一更名为“地方公共财政预算收入”和“地方公共财政预算支出”。

4. 五大支柱产业：电子信息制造业（即通信设备、计算机及其他电子设备制造业）、电气机械及设备制造业（包括电气机械及器材制造业，仪器仪表及文化、办公用机械制造业，通用设备制造业，专用设备制造业以及交通运输设备制造业）、纺织服装鞋帽制造业（包括纺织业，纺织服装、鞋、帽制造业以及皮革、毛皮、羽绒及其制品业）、食品饮料加工制造业（包括食品制造业，饮料制造业，农副产品加工业）、造纸及纸制品业。

四个特色产业：玩具及文体用品制造业（即文教体育用品制造业）、家具制造业、化工制品制造业（包括化学原料及化学制品制造业，橡胶制品业，石油加工、炼焦业及核燃业）、包装印刷业（即印刷业、记录媒介的复制）。

5. 农村居民人均纯收入采用农村住户抽样调查口径。

6. 阅读本公报时，请注意统计指标的时间、口径和计算方法等。

Dongguan Statistical Communique on National Economic and Social Development 2012

In 2012, under the strong leadership of the municipal government, with the guidance of scientific concept of development, giving prominence to the strategic objectives of " changing the way of development, constructing the happy Dongguan, to achieve the high level rise" . By implemented the policies and measures of organized and implemented the construction of major projects, coordinating the development of the water region, converge the development of the science and finance industry, implementing the comprehensive rural reform, building the legal and international environment for business, the economic development recovery steady and the social harmony and stability, providing the steady foundation of implementing high level rise policies successfully.

I Comprehensive

According to preliminary accounting, Dongguan realized a GDP of RMB 501. 01 billion in 2012, up by 6. 1% over the previous year calculating at comparable price . In specific terms, primary industry contributed RMB 1. 92 billion, up by 1. 2% ; secondary industry contributed RMB 235. 18 billion, up by 5. 6% ; and tertiary industry contributed RMB 263. 92 billion, up by 6. 7%. The added value of primary, secondary and tertiary industries respectively accounted for 0. 4% , 46. 9% and 52. 7%. The per capita GDP realized RMB 60. 56 thousand, up by 5. 7%.

In the modern industry, the added value of the modern above-scale manufacturing industry realized RMB 73. 99 billion, up by 8. 5% ; the value of the modern services industry realized RMB 154. 39 billion, up by 8. 0%.

In the tertiary industry, the growth of the transportation, storage and postal services was 15. 2% , the wholesales and retail trade up by 2. 7% , the housing and catering services up by 1. 5% , the finance up by 14. 1% , the real estate up by 4. 8% , the others up by 7. 8%.

The CPI (consumer price index) was up by 2. 9% of Dongguan in 2012, among which residence up by 1. 5% , recreational, education and culture articles up by 1. 8% , clothing up by 1. 0% , food prices up by 6. 1% , healthy care and personal articles up by 4. 8% , tobacco, liquor and articles up by 1. 4% , transportation and communication down by 1. 2% , household facilities, articles and services up by 1. 4%. The retail price was up by 2. 4% and PPI (producer price index) down by 0. 2% over the pervious year in 2012.

Figure 1: Gross Domestic Product and Its Growth, 2006-2012

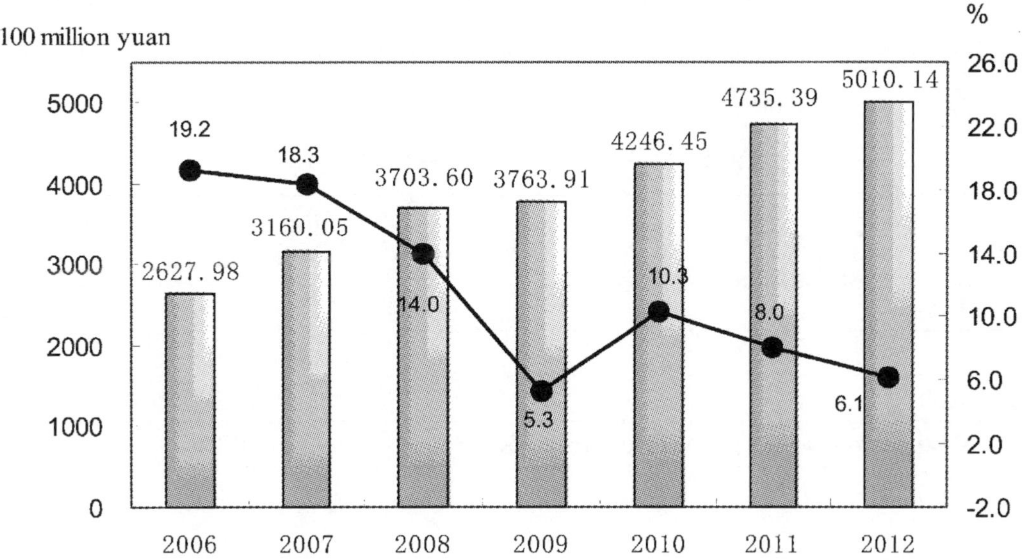

Figure 2: Change in Consumer Prices, 2006-2012

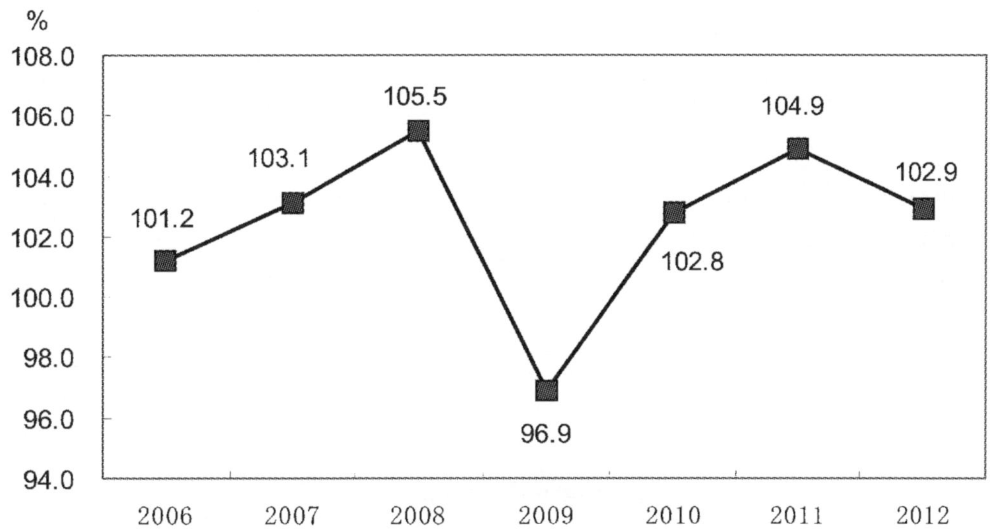

Fiscal revenue rooted in Dongguan was RMB 84. 56 billlion for the year, up by 0. 8% , in which, the General budgeted revenue was RMB 35. 63 billion, up by 13. 8%. General budget expenditures amounted to RMB 38. 56 billion, up by 9. 6% , in which the general public services expenditures totaled RMB 3. 62 billion; the expenditure for public security was amounted to RMB 4. 94 billion; for education was RMB 9. 28 billion; for social security and employment effort was RMB 2. 42 billion. The total tax revenue was RMB 93. 91 billion, up by 11. 3%.

The number of urban registered unemployed amounted to 12. 2 thousand at the end of 2012, the number of job placement for unemployed was 10. 2 thousand persons, The unemployment rate on record in urban areas was 2. 3%.

The main problems of economic and social development: the resource and environment bottleneck more severe, independent innovation capability is still not strong, transformation and upgrading of the industry, and raising quality and efficiency of the production was arduous, and operation of enterprises were still facing many difficulties; the three kind major programs and coordinating regional development need for more efforts; security management, educational equity, health care and other public services should be promoted at a quicker pace.

Table 1: Change of Prices in 2012

Item	Price Index (%)	Increase over 2011 (%)
Consumer Price Index	102. 9	2. 9
Food	106. 1	6. 1
Of Which: Grain	103. 7	3. 7
Meal, Poultry and Processed Products	102. 6	2. 6
Oil or Fat	105. 0	5. 0
Eggs	101. 1	1. 1
Fresh	124. 5	24. 5
Aquatic Products	108. 3	8. 3
Tobacco, Liquor and Articles	101. 4	1. 4
Clothing	101. 0	1. 0
Household Facilities, Articles Services	101. 4	1. 4
Health Care and Personal Articles	104. 8	4. 8
Transportation and Communication	98. 8	-1. 2
Recreation, Education and Culture Articles	101. 8	1. 8
Residence	101. 5	1. 5
Retail Price Index	102. 4	2. 4
Producer Price Index	99. 8	-0. 2

Ⅱ Agriculture

In 2012, the gross output value of agriculture was RMB 3. 2 billion, up by 0. 6% calculating at comparable price. Specifically, the output value of farming was RMB 1. 69 billion, down by 2. 2%, accounting for 52. 9%; the output value of forestry was RMB 17 million, dowm by 22. 7%, accounting for 0. 5%; the output value of animal husbandry RMB 632 million, up by 3. 3%, accounting for 19. 7%; the output of fishery increased 5. 2% to RMB 764 million, accounting for 23. 9%. In 2012, the sown area of grain was 24. 83 million square meters, the fruit planting area was 11. 91 million square meters. The total output of grain was 12. 5 thousand tons; the total output of aquatic products was 77 thousand tons, the total output of vegetables was 391. 1 thousand tons, up by 0. 6%. The number of slaughtered fattened hogs was 286. 3 thousand, up by 2. 6%; and that of poultry was 7. 85 million, up by 7. 2%.

In 2012, there were 8 new farmers's specialized cooperation units, 1 newly approved leading agricultural enterprises at the national level, 4 famous brand products. At the end of 2012, there were 46 farmers's specialized cooperation units, 19 leading agricultural enterprises; 40 provincial level leading products on agricultural industrialization respectively.

Ⅲ Industry and Construction

In 2012, the total added value of the sector industry above the designated size was RMB 173.31 billion, up by 5.6%. Specifically, heavy industry realized an output value of RMB 94.87 billion, up by 8.3%, accounting for 54.7% of the output value of industry above the designated size; that of light industry was RMB 78.44 billion, up by 2.4%, accounting for 45.3%.

The total added value of 5 Pillar Industries in 2012 was RMB 117.34 billion, up by 7.8%. The added value of 4 Characteristic Industries was RMB 19.96 billion, up by 1.3%.

The annual added value of high-tech manufacturing industries increased by 13.1%, of which the pharmaceutical manufacturing industries increased by 16.4%, the electronic and communications equipment manufacturing industries increased by 17.0%, the computer and office equipment manufacturing industries increased by 8.0%, and the medical equipment and instrumentation manufacturing industries declined by 26.8%.

The total added value of the advanced manufacturing industries in 2012 increased by 8.5%. Specifically the equipment manufacturing industries increased by 9.5%, the iron and steel smelting and processing industries decreased by 8.7%, the petroleum and chemical industries decreased by 3.4%. Specifically the automobile manufacturing industries got an increase of 11.7%, the added value of the ship manufacturing industries and special equipment manufacturing industries for environmental pollution control decreased by 12.9% and 38.5%. Among the iron and steel smelting and processing industries' added value, the iron-smelting industries decreased by 3.7%, the steel rolling processing industries decreased by 8.9%. Among the petroleum and chemical industries' added value, the petroleum processing, coking and nuclear fuel processing industries, chemical materials and products manufacturing industries and rubber products manufacturing industries got a decrease of 22.0%, 2.4% and 11.8%.

In 2012, the added value of the traditional superior industries was down by 0.6%, among which, the textile and garment industries up by 1.5%, the food and beverage industries up by 2.4%, the furniture manufacturing industries down by 5.2%, the building materials manufacturing industries down by 6.5%, the metal product industries up by 1.3%, the household appliances manufacturing industries down by 9.1%.

The sector industry above the designated size realized a total profit of RMB 24.89 billion, of which the assets liability ratio was 57.3% and the comprehensive index of economic efficiency levels was 129.47.

Table 2: Output of Major Industrial Products of Industrial Enterprises above the Designated Size and the Growth, 2012

Industry	Unit	Qty	Increase over 2011 (%)
Beer	1000 L	575383	3.5
Fruit and vegetable drinks	10000 Tons	228.79	-6.0
Garment	10000 Pcs	108932	-3.8
Light Leather	10000 Sqm	485.54	-15.4
Wood-based Panel	10000 Sqm	17.25	8.3
Surface Finishing of Wood-based Panel	10000 Sqm	777.55	-45.8
Solid Wood-Flooring	10000 Sqm	66.09	-16.7
Furniture	10000 Pcs	4758.80	-18.1
Pulp	10000 Tons	58.36	0.4
Machine-made Paper & Paperboard	10000 Tons	1200.74	6.4
Plastic Products	10000 Tons	154.30	-4.4
Cement	10000 Tons	249.16	-0.6
Porcelain	10000 Sqm	1975.81	-11.5
Plate Glass	10000 Weight Boxes	3286.83	-5.5
Sanitary Pottery	10000 Pcs	166.72	-12.5
Metal Container	10000 Sqm	946.09	13.9
Digital Camera	10000 Sets	31.37	-36.1
Mould	10000 Sets	25.39	-22.7
Power Capacitors	10000 Kilovars	455.33	
Solar Energy Water Heater	10000 Sqm	11.44	18.4
Lamps and Lighting Equipments	10000 Sets	22097.87	15.5
Computer	10000 Sets	99.73	28.4
Printing Machine	10000 Sets	113.06	6.1
Telephone Set	10000 Sets	3883.18	-5.1
Mobile Phone	10000 Sets	6728.96	27.8
DVD Player	10000 Sets	1471.54	-27.2
Set-top Box	10000 Sets	208.52	19.5
Integrated Circuit	10000 Sets	6340	105.2
Electronic Components	10000 Pcs	11166	3.3
Print Circuit Board	10000 Sqm	1335.12	-37.4
Automobile Instrument	10000 Sets	49.03	-24.2
Optic Instrument	10000 Sets	117.48	14.0
Eyeglass	10000 Sets	4692.21	1.4
Production of Running Water	10000 Cbm	173413	-2.7

The annual added value of construction was RMB 7.81 billion, down by 1.5% over the previous year. The total output value of buildings completed of construction enterprises was RMB 14.22 billion, up by 9.5%; the floor space of buildings under construction was 7.05 million square meters, down by 6.7%; the floor space of buildings completed was 3.46 million square meters, down by 14.5%. Calculated at the output value of buildings completed, the overall labor productivity was RMB 274 thousand per person, up by 20.7%.

IV Investment in Fixed Assets

The total investment in fixed assets reached RMB 118.04 billion in 2012, an increase of 9.4% over 2011. Specifically, state owned economy investment was RMB 11.41 billion, down by 9.7%, collective economic investment RMB 12.41 billion, up by 4.0%, private economic investment RMB 66.92 billion, up by 2.4%, foreign and Hong Kong, Macao and Taiwan investment RMB 29.42 billion, up by 33.2%, accounting for 9.7%, 10.5%, 56.7% and 24.9%.

Figure 3: Investment in Fixed Assets and Its Growth, 2006-2012

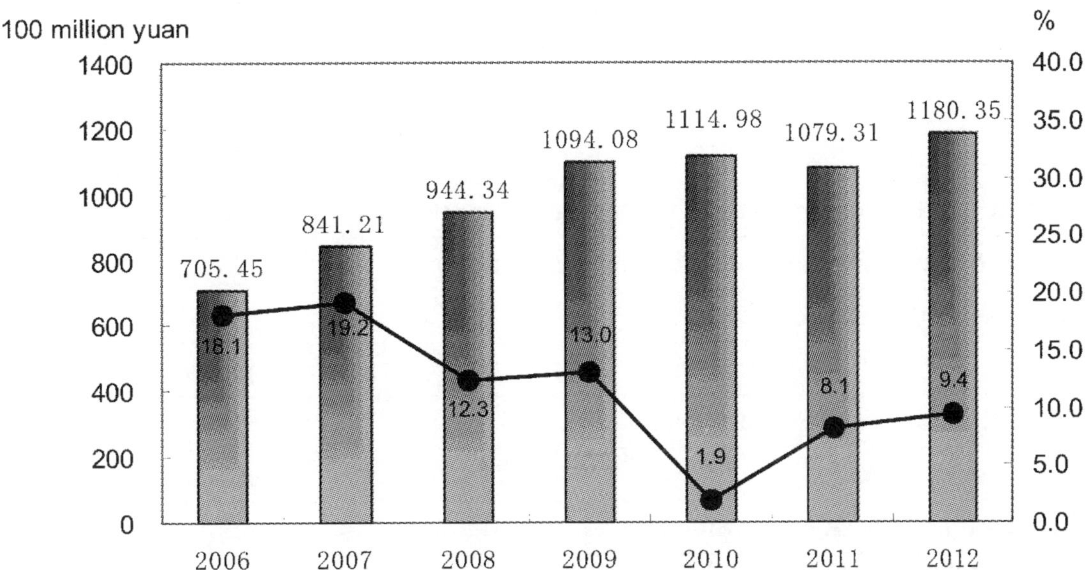

With regard to industries, the investment was concentrated toward the secondary and tertiary industries. Investment in secondary industry was RMB 41.49 billion, including manufacturing industry investment of RMB 38.26 billion; investment in tertiary industry was RMB 76.35 billion. The total completed investment reached 58.26 billion, 338 project units above 50 million of investment completed.

The investment in real estate development staged a increase of 1.1% to RMB 37.73 billion. The construction area of commercialized buildings was 24.54 million square meters, up by 2.5%; the floor space of commercialized buildings completed was 3.62 million square meters, up by 49.6%. The sales area of commercialized buildings was 6.39 million square meters, up by 7.3%.

Specifically, the sales area of commercial residential buildings was 5.83 million square meters, up by 7.9%. The sales volumes of commercialized buildings was RMB 54.24 billion, up by 18.0%. Specifically, the sales volumes of commercial residential buildings was RMB 47.25 billion, up by 14.3%.

Table 3: Investment in Fixed Assets by Sector in 2012

Sector	Investment	Increase over 2011 (%)
Total	11803493	9.4
Farming, Forestry, Animal Husbandry and Fishery	19710	228.8
Manufacture	3826025	26.6
Production and Supply of Electric power, Gas and Water	320667	-34.3
Construction	2193	49.4
Transport, Storage and Postal Services	1279006	17.0
Information Transmission, Computer Services and Software	218614	9.7
Wholesale and Retail Trade	195376	-26.0
Hotel and Catering Services	101943	121.1
Finance	25898	33.5
Real Estate	4419691	9.5
Leasing and Business Services	25679	-65.6
Scientific Research, Technical Services and Geological Prospecting	99097	27.8
Water Conservancy, Environment and Public Facilities Management	852023	-16.9
Resident Services and Other Services	8015	-53.2
Education	245393	4.4
Health Care, Social Security and Social Welfare	55031	-25.3
Culture, Sports and Recreation	66813	-4.8
Public Administration and Social Organization	42319	-0.5

V Domestic Trade

The total value-added of wholesale & retail sales was RMB 48.69 billion in 2012, up by 2.7% over the previous year; that of the lodging and catering industry was RMB 18.02 billion, up by 1.5%.

The total retail sales of social consumer goods reached RMB 135.46 billion, up by 9.3% over the previous year, and up by 6.7% calculating at comparable price. Specifically, the retail value of wholesale and retail trade reach RMB 123.41 billion, up by 9.5%, the retail value of lodging and catering industry reached RMB 12.05 billion, up by 6.7%.

With regard to enterprises above designated size of wholesale and retail trade, of food, beverages, tobacco and liquor was up by 12.8%; clothing, shoes, hats and textiles up by 11.9%; daily necessities up by 8.2%; automobiles up by 10.0%.

Figure 4: The Retail Sales of Consumer Goods and Its Growth, 2006-2012

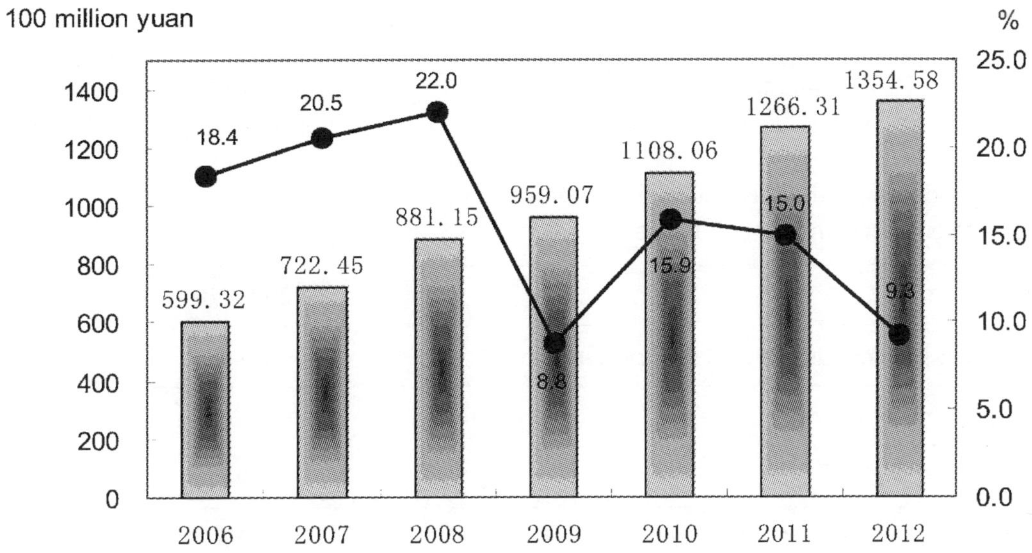

VI Foreign Trade

The total value of imports and exports in 2012 reached $ 144.42 billion, up by 6.8% over the previous year, of which the total value of imports reached $ 59.35 billion, up by 4.2%; the total value of exports reached $ 85.07 billion, up by 8.6%.

Divided by mode of trade, the export value of general trade reached $ 16.92 billion, representing an increase of 26.2%; The export value of processing trade reached $ 66.15 billion, up by 4.2%; other trades for export reached $ 1.99 billion, representing an increase of 38.4%.

Divided by regions of export, the exports to Asia reached $ 44.51 billion, up by 8.9%; the exports to North America reached $ 22.19 billion, up by 11.1%; the exports to EU reached $ 13.87 billion, up by 2.1%; the exports to Latin America reached $ 2.75 billion, up by 12.7%; the exports to Oceania reached $ 1.05 billion, up by 8.7%.

The total export volume of electromechanical products reached $ 60.77 billion, up by 10.3%, accounting for 71.4%. The export of hi-tech products reached $ 29.74 billion, up by 8.9%, accounting for 35.0%.

According to the new statistical caliber, the number of recently signed projects of foreign direct investment was 690, the amount of contracted foreign capital reached $ 3.81 billion, up by 8.6% over the previous year. The amount of foreign capital actually utilized reached $ 3.37 billion, up by 10.5%, of which, the amount of foreign capital actually utilized by manufacture of electronic equipment and communication equipment reached $ 0.61 billion, down by 7.7%; the amount of foreign capital actually utilized by manufacture of special purpose machinery reached $ 0.16 billion, down by 18.8%.

Table 4: Main Export Commodities in Value and the Growth, 2012

Commodities	Value (10000 US dollars)	Increase over 2011 (%)
Electromechanical products (including the electromechanical products that have been listed in the catalogue)	6076866	10.3
Hi-tech products	2973879	8.9
Automatic Data processing machines and components	614184	0.3
Clothes and clothing accessories	565121	22.5
Static converters	359454	-4.4
Parts of automatic Data processing machines	375361	8.1
Furniture and components	395838	16.4
Shoes	298888	-2.7
Cable telephone (including cordless telephone)	192299	-0.2
Traveling articles and cases (value)	198731	9.4
Insulated Wire or Cable	212470	23.2
Toys	186212	8.2
Spinning Yarn, Fabric and Products	167082	1.8
Video Recorder and Video Player	77044	-52.4
Electric Apparatus for Switching or Protecting Electrical Circuits	196629	21.6
Parts of Television, Radio and Wireless Telecommunication Equipment	133727	-7.2
Handle Mobiles and Car Telephones	138665	0.2
Digital cameras	70123	-45.6
Plastic Articles	142073	11.8
Game machines	115326	63.2
Automatic Data processing machines and components	92070	-4.2

Table 5: Total Value of Foreign Capital Actually Utilized and the Growth by Sector in 2012

Sector	contracted foreign capital (10000 US dollars)	Increase over 2011 (%)	Foreign Capital Actually Utilized Value (10000 US dollars)	Increase over 2011 (%)
Total	381031	5.9	336938	11.3
Agriculture, Forestry, Animal Husbandry and Fishing	369	-59.7	297	-24.8
Manufacturing	293911	0.03	251960	-3.0
Textile Industry	4676	-63.6	8496	-49.0
Manufacture of Textiles, garments, shoes and hats	7918	-31.0	7667	-32.9
Manufacture of furniture	2746	13.6	2088	-47.5
Manufacture of General Machinery	4190	-27.9	5015	-43.1
Manufacture of Special Purpose Machinery	33696	144.1	16186	-18.7
Manufacture of Electric Machinery and Equipment	23932	-36.0	31165	12.3
Manufacture of Communication Equipment, Computers and other Electronic Equipment	75113	-10.2	60606	-7.7
Manufacture of Metal Products	15291	-11.0	12060	9.1
Manufacture of Plastics Products	26460	-10.2	16901	-7.8
Manufacture of stationery and sporting Products	7837	-35.3	7930	4.9
Manufacture of papermaking and Paper Products	17908	4.5	24157	54.4
Manufacture of others	74144	46.8	59689	12.6
Information Transmission, Computer Services and Software	19	-90.5	90	-91.4
Wholesale and Retail Trade	45295	60.4	42680	81.1

VII Transportation, Post, Telecommunications and Tourism

The value added of the transportation, storage, post and telecommunications sector reached RMB 12.49 billion in 2012, up by 15.2% over the previous year.

At the end of 2012, the total length of highways in Dongguan (including the highway in the rural area) was 4969 km; the highway density was 201.98 km per 100 km. The possession of motor vehicles (for civil use) reached 1.49 million units, up by 4.9%. Of which, the possession of automobiles was 1. 21 million units, up by 13. 7%.

In 2012, the freight traffic of highways was 84. 21 million tons, the freight ton-kilometers of highways were 5. 44 billion ton-kilometers; the freight traffic of waterways was 27. 7 million tons, the freight ton-kilometers of waterways were 24. 24 billion ton-kilometers. The number of passengers traffic of highways was 0. 8 billion in 2012, the passenger-kilometers of highways was 15. 67 billion passenger- kilometers, the passengers traffic of waterways was 320 thousand persons, the passenger-kilometers of waterways was 21. 06 million passenger- kilometers. The volume of freight handled by ports in Dongguan throughout the year totaled 92. 28 million tons and passengers traffic totaled 0. 32 million persons.

Table 6: Passenger (freight) Traffic and Passenger (freight) flows in 2012

item	unit	volume	Increase over 2011 (%)
Total passenger traffic	million persons	797. 39	-0. 7
Highways	million persons	797. 07	-0. 7
Passenger flows	100 million person-kilometers	156. 88	7. 5
Highways	100 million person-kilometers	156. 67	7. 5
Total freight traffic	million tons	111. 91	10. 1
Highways	million tons	84. 21	2. 6
Freight flows	100 million ton-kilometers	296. 71	58. 3
Highways	100 million ton-kilometers	54. 36	2. 3

The turnover of post and telecommunication services totaled RMB 17 billion, up by 3. 1% over the previous year. In post services, the number of mail delivery reached 50. 65 million, express delivery 1. 48 million, and postal remittance RMB 19. 64 billion. The number of fixed telephone subscribers (including PHS) at year-end of 2012 was 3. 25 million, an increase of 55. 6 thousand subscribers over 2011. The number of mobile phone subscribers reached 17. 54 million, an increase of 763. 3 thousand subscribers. The length of long-distance calls totaled 21. 52 billion minutes in 2012. At the end of 2012, there were 2. 1 million internet subscribers, an increase of 188. 8 thousand, and 2. 05 million broad band subscribers, an increase of 202. 9 thousand.

At the end of 2012, there were 89 star-rated hotels in Dongguan, including 20 five-star hotels. There were 61 travel agencies, receiving 4. 15 million tourists from foreign economic zones and Hong Kong, Macao and Taiwan, up by 16. 1%. Among them, the number of foreign tourists was 1. 35 million, up by 11. 0%, the number of tourists from Hong Kong, Macao and Taiwan was 2. 8 million, up by 18. 7%. The foreign exchange income from international tourism increased 39. 5% to 1. 27 billion US dollars. The number of domestic tourists was 23. 29 million, up by 3. 1% over the previous year, and the total income from domestic tourism staged an increase of 22. 9% to 30. 64 billion. The passengers of travel tours of Dongguan was 1. 85 million in 2012, up by 1. 2%, of which, the tourists traveling domestic areas totaled 1. 68 million, up by 0. 1% , traveling aboard totaled 178 thousand, up by 12. 6%.

Figure 5:Number of Phone Subscribers, 2006-2012

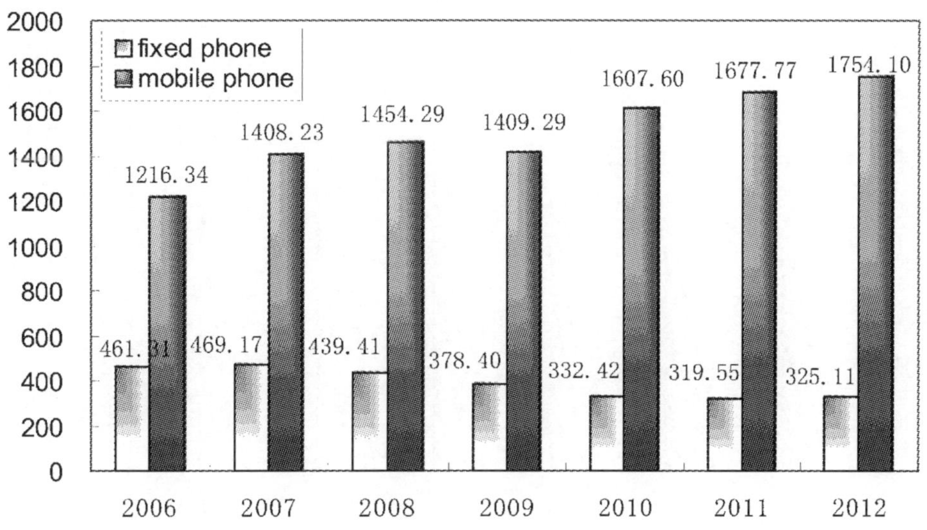

VIII Financial Intermediation

The added value of finance was RMB 21. 35 billion in 2012, up by 14. 1%.

By the end of 2012, Dongguan had 97 financial institutions, including 31 banks, 41 insurance institutiongs (excluding insurance agencies), and 25 securities and futures institutions. The savings deposits of financial institutions totaled RMB 743. 05 billion in all items at the end of 2012, up by 12. 4% since the beginning of the year, in which, the deposits by urban and rural residents totaled RMB 420. 42 billion, up by 13. 3%. Loans in all items of financial institutions reached RMB 419. 56 billion, up by 12. 9%. With respect to the personal individual consumption loans, the balance of personal housing loans reached RMB 83. 33 billion, up by 8. 5% , personal auto loans totaled RMB 0. 92 billion, down by 43. 3%. The NPLs of Dongguan financial institutions reduced 0. 08 index since the beginning of the year.

The total number of all kinds of securities trading accounts was 954. 1 thousand by the end of 2012, an increase of 59. 3 thousand over the previous year. The total turnover of stock trading was down by 25. 7% to RMB 610. 06 billion. The guarantee fund balance totaled RMB 7. 84 billion, up by 12. 3%.

The premium received by the insurance companies in Dongguan totaled RMB 17. 77 billion in 2012, up by 8. 6% over the previous year. Of which, the property insurance premiums was RMB 6. 11 billion, up by 10. 8% ; the life insurance premiums was 11. 66 billion, up by 7. 4%. The claim and payment reached RMB 3. 29 billion, and comprehensive compensation rate reached 53. 8%.

Figure 6: Savings Deposits of Urban and Rural Households and Tts Growth, 2006-2012

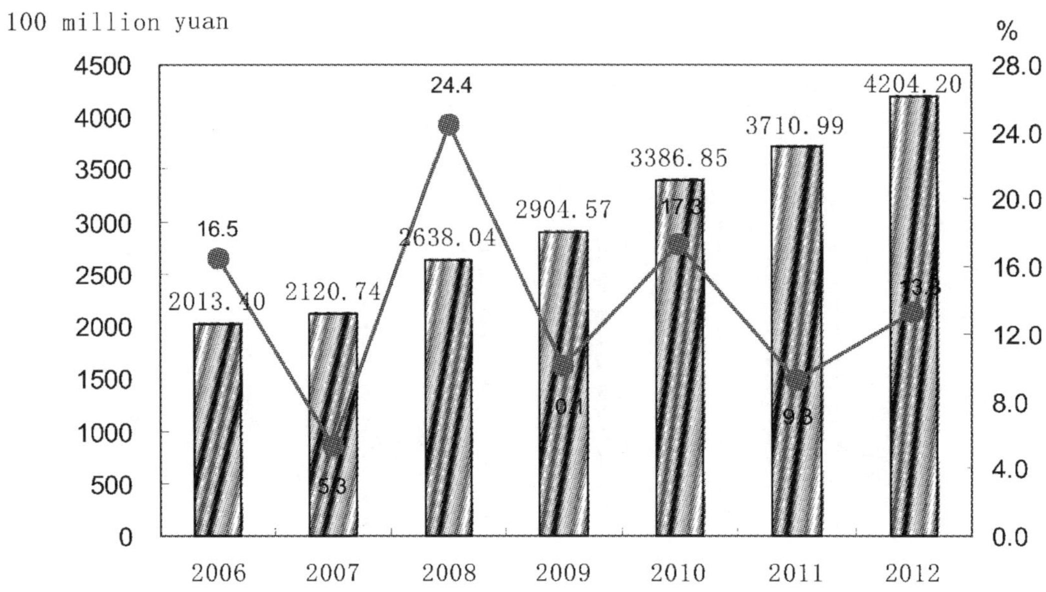

IX Science and Technology

The city saw 150 new national high-tech enterprises with a total of 537 units. The number of patents application accepted reached 29199 units, up 19. 4% over the previous year, of which, 5568 units were patents of invention, accounting for 19. 1%. The number of patents application granted reached 20900 units, up by 8. 0% , of which, 1381 units were patents of invention, up by 82. 2%.

3 new provincial-level enterprise engineering centers and 2 new provincial-level enterprise key laboratories were approved in 2012; 2 new national patents award of excellence were won and 99 scientific research achievements were rewarded the city's scientific and technical prize; 5 new Guangdong innovation research teams were approved in 2012, and the total number of teams increased to 14.

There were 791 kindergartens in Dongguan, 42 more than the previous year. There were 255. 7 thousand three to six year old children enrolled, and the enrollment rate of kindergarten reached 97. 0%. There were 322 primary schools in Dongguan, and 608. 1 thousand students enrolled in primary school; the enrollment ratio of school-age children with residence registration was 100% , and the promotion rate from primary schools to junior secondary schools was 100%. There were 163 junior secondary schools, with 192. 1 thousand enrolled students, and the net enrollment ratio of junior secondary schools was 100%. There were 64 senior secondary schools with 125. 9 thousand students in Dongguan. Specificallg there were 40 senior secondary schools (including six-grade secondary schools) with 75. 9 thousand students and 24 secondary vocational schools (including 1 technical school) with 50. 1 thousand students. There were 6 institutions of regular higher education with 52. 4 thousand students. In 2012, in institutions of higher education, there were totally 20. 5 thousand students new-enrolled and 12. 6 thousand students graduated.

Table 7: Education

Item	new students (10 thousand)	Increase over 2011 (%)	students (10 thousand)	Increase over 2011 (%)	students graduated (10 thousand)	Increase over 2011 (%)
college	2. 05	21. 8	5. 24	16. 2	1. 26	33. 4
adult college	0. 60	-5. 5	1. 88	-8. 5	0. 63	-9. 5
secondary vocational school (except technical school)	1. 70	2. 0	4. 73	4. 5	1. 31	-6. 0
senior secondary school	2. 58	0. 4	7. 59	3. 0	2. 34	5. 9
junior secondary school	7. 06	1. 6	19. 21	1. 4	5. 61	2. 4
primary school	12. 33	7. 4	60. 81	5. 2	8. 77	9. 0
kindergarten	10. 71	25. 2	25. 57	12. 3	8. 33	21. 9

X Culture, Health and Medicine

At the end of 2012, there were 1 mass art center, 33 cultural stations, 649 public libraries, 31 museums, 12 arts performance places, 59 movie screening units and 1042 internet cafes. Dongguan had 52 public radio programs and 21 public television programs. In 2012, 89. 1 million copies of newspapers, 1. 39 million copies of magazines were published. Dongguan Daily had 44. 82 million copies circulation. There were 291 thousand film screenings and 5. 37 million viewers in 2012.

At the end of 2012, Dongguan had 2218 health care institutions, including 2142 grass-roots health care institutions such as outpatient departments, clinics, health stations, infirmaries and community health service centers, with 40. 6 thousand medical technical personals and 24. 6 thousand hospital beds. 387 community health service institutions had been built and put into service. The patients who received treatment throughout the year were increased by 18. 2%.

Dongguan athletes won 137 gold, 105 silver and 99 bronze medals in 2012, including 10 gold medals in national tournaments, 127 gold medals, 95 silver medals and 92 bronze medals in provincial tournaments. Dongguan held 12 municipal integrated and individual competitions, of which, 3. 7 thousand people participated in 2012. Dongguan had 1016 sports lottery networks, with a total sales of RMB 1. 07 billion, and public welfare fund of sports lottery was RMB 75. 22 million.

XI People's Living Conditions, Social Security, Safe production

Annual per capita disposable income of urban residents was RMB 42,944, per capita net income of rural was RMB 24,944, an increase of 8.7% and 9.2% respectively.

Annual per capita consumption expenditure of urban residents was RMB 31,369, an increase of 14.1%. Per capita housing construction area of urban residents was 58.44 square meters. Annual per capita cash consumption expenditure of farmers was RMB 16,103, an increase of 14.6%. Per capita housing construction area of rural residents was 50.33 square meters.

Figure 7: Per Capital Disposable Income of Urban Households and Its Growth, 2006-2012

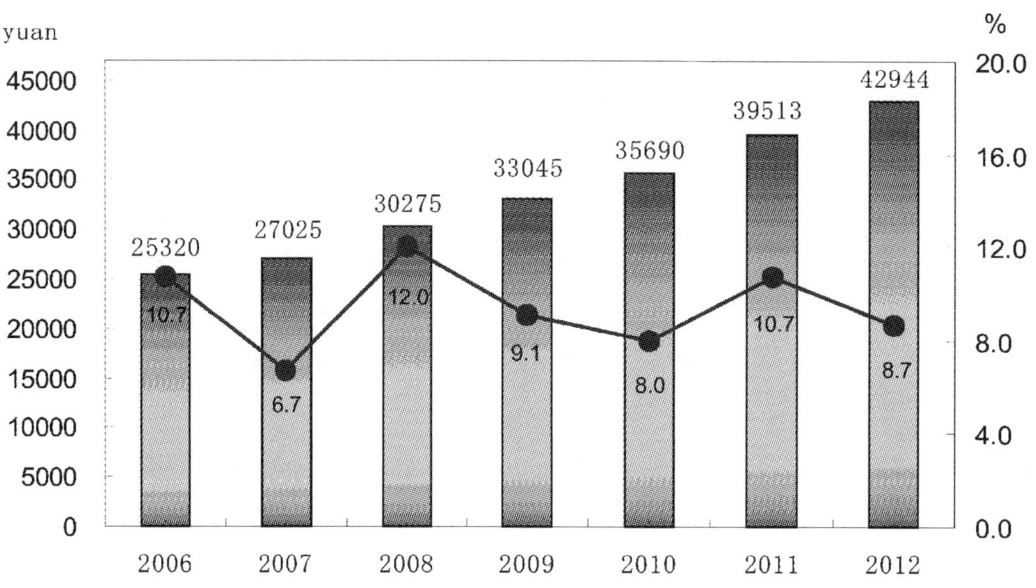

Figure 8: Per Capital Disposable Income of Rural Households and Its Growth, 2006-2012

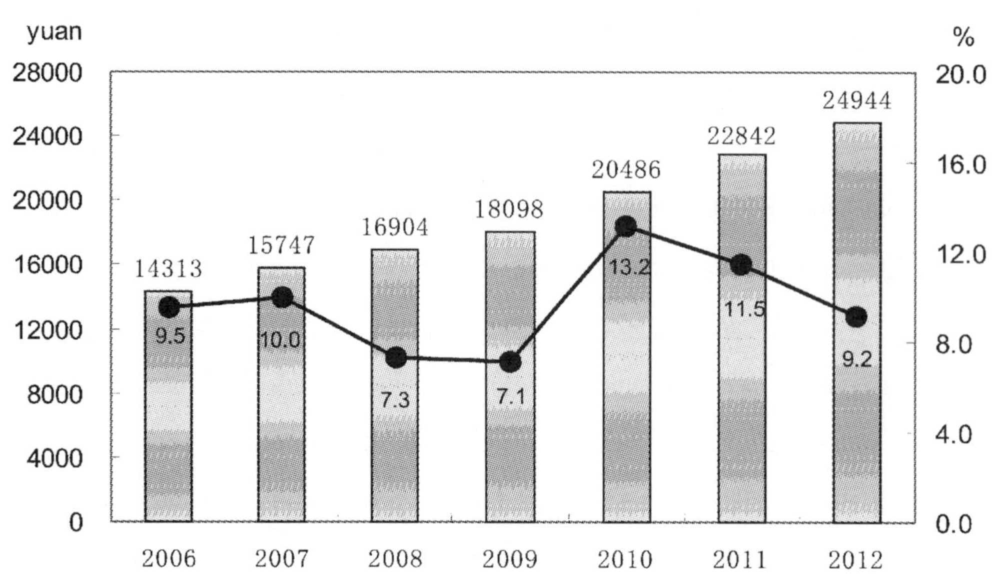

The total number of insured by Five Major Insurances was 25. 54 million, increased by 3. 7%. Of this total, 6. 17 million were insured by basic medical insurance, 3. 13 million were insured by unemployment insurance, and 4. 94 million were insured by injury insurance. The total revenue of social insurance fund was RMB 20. 79 billion. The total expenditure of social insurance fund was RMB 8. 67 billion. At the end of 2012, accumulated balance of insurance fund was RMB 59. 16 billion. Annual cumulative collection of insurance fund (excluding pension insurance of executive authorities) was RMB 18. 72 billion, increased by 19%.

Table 8: Income and Expenditure Of Urban Households 2012

Item	Income or expenditure (RMB)	Increase over 2011 (%)
Per Capita Disposable Income of Urban Residents	42944	8. 7
Income from Wages and Salaries	30518	11. 9
Income from Properties	9099	21. 6
Income from Transfer	3484	-20. 3
Per Capita Consumption Expenditure of Urban Residents	31369	14. 1
Food	11103	16. 7
Clothing	2121	17. 4
Residence	2852	34. 0
Household Facilities, Articles and Services	2173	14. 3
Health Care and Medical Services	1521	21. 6
Transport and Telecommunication	6108	1. 2
Educational, Cultural Recreation Services	4348	11. 9
Miscellaneous Goods and Services	1143	17. 4

In 2012, 24. 7 thousand persons received social assistance. At the end of year, there were 34 adotive welfare units with 2269 persons adopted in Dongguan, including 1 social walfare institute, 1 social welfare center and 31 gerocomiums where maintained 709 old people. The expenditure of urban minimum living allowance was RMB 89. 07 million. Expenditure of social relief totaled RMB 293 million. Expenditure of social relief for natural disaster was RMB 2. 74 million. Balance of Charity Fund was RMB 207 million. 1015 persons were brought into the " Five-Guaranteed households" project, and cost RMB 17. 03 million.

In 2012, 4341 cases of industrial accident occurred in Dongguan, decreased by 4. 1% over the previous year; 534 persons died and 4835 persons were injured, decreased by 1. 1% and 3. 6% respectively; direct economic losses was RMB 53. 25 million, increased by 704. 1%. Of this total, the number of road traffic accidents was 4299, decreased by 4. 3%, which resulted in 490 deaths and 4831 injured, decreased by 1. 0% and 3. 4% respectively. Production-related accident mortality rate per 100 million GDP was 0. 106 and road traffic mortality rate per 10 thousand vehicles was 3. 31.

XII Population, Resources and Environment

At the end of 2012, Dongguan's registered population reached 1. 87 million. There were saw 24. 7 thousand births, a crude birth rate of 13. 3 per thousand, and 9684 deaths, and a crude death rate of 5. 2 per thousand in 2012. The natural growth rate was 8. 1 per thousand. Resident population was 8. 29 million. Of this total, resident population in urban was 7. 35 million. Population urbanization rate reached 88. 67%.

Throughout the year, rainy days numbered 205 days, sunshine hours were 1708. 7 hours, average temperature was 22. 6 degrees Celsius. Relative humidity was 78%. Precipitation of the year was 1838. 6 millimeters.

At the end of 2012, there were 18 forest parks, 601. 9 square kilometers of forest area and 219. 7 square kilometers of ecological public forest, which contained 2. 91 million cubic meters of tree storage and 146. 1 thousand cubic meters of total tree growth in Dongguan.

At the end of 2012, built-up area of land area reached 888. 39 square kilometers in Dongguan. Land area of public administration and services was 59. 71 square kilometers. With forest coverage rate of 37. 1%, with 97% greening rate in woodland and 42. 4% greening rate in urban built-up area, the total greening coverage rate was 45% in Dongguan. 1057 parks and plazas had been built, which covered an area of 121 square kilometers. Per capita green area was 16. 53 square meters.

政府工作报告

REPORT ON THE WORK OF THE GOVERNMENT

——2013年1月8日在东莞市第十五届人民代表大会第三次会议上

东莞市人民政府市长　袁宝成

各位代表：

现在，我代表市人民政府向大会报告2012年政府工作，对2013年工作提出建议，请予审议。并请政协各位委员和其他列席人员提出意见。

2012年工作回顾

刚刚过去的2012年，是东莞承前启后、加快转型的关键一年。一年来，在上级和市委的坚强领导下，全市各级各部门以科学发展观为指导，围绕市第十三次党代会确立的“加快转型升级、建设幸福东莞、实现高水平崛起”的战略目标，按照优化发展、好中求进的方针，从容应对复杂严峻的发展形势，经济增长稳步回升，社会保持和谐稳定，市第十五届人大一次会议确定的年度工作任务基本完成。预计全市实现生产总值5010亿元，同比增长6.1%。人均生产总值6万元，增长4.9%。来源于东莞的财政收入845.6亿元，其中市公共财政预算收入356.3亿元，增长13.8%。进出口总额增长6.8%左右，出口增长8.5%左右。城市居民人均可支配收入42872元，农民人均纯收入24898元，分别增长8.5%和9%。

过去一年，是高水平崛起谋篇开局、凝心聚力的一年。紧紧围绕市委决策部署，提质提效提精神，强力强势抓执行。大力推进“六个东莞”建设，紧盯“三重一大”建设、科技金融产业融合、水乡地区统筹发展、镇村集体经济转型等突破口，出台实施一系列新举措，抓出了工作实效，实现了良好开局。

过去一年，是创新型经济扬帆起步、坚实推进的一年。一批关系城市未来的战略性、创新型产业项目纷纷落户，众多著名高校院所与创新团队竞相进驻，科技孵化和风投创投机构迅速增长，为新一轮产业大发展积蓄了较大后劲。东莞在《福布斯》中文杂志大陆创新能力最强城市的评比中名列第十三位。

过去一年，是城市形象不断提升、工作亮点纷呈的一年。生产总值突破五千亿元大关，工业投资、服务业吸引外资逆势增长，财政收入、利用外资等多项指标位居全省前列。中国加工贸易产品博览会作为我市首次举办的国家级重大展会，为东莞增添了一张亮丽的城市名片。全省加工贸易转型升级现场会、世界莞商大会、中国图书馆年会等重大活动成功举办，“三打两建”、广深高速沿线景观整治等专项行动强力实施，商事登记、行政审批等重大改革锐意推进，全国文明城市、全国双拥模范城市、中国制造业最优投资环境城市、中国十佳宜业城市等荣誉称号的蝉联获取，进一步彰显了东莞创新活力的经济形象、宜居生态的城市形象、安定和谐的社会形象。

一年来，我们主要抓了以下工作：

——突出推进“三重一大”建设，以产业增量扩张促进存量调整。集全市之力开展重大项目招商。制定实施“1+5”政策，实行“一站通”工作机制，开展日韩台招商活动，赴以色列、德国进行经贸考察，到京拜访央企总部，落实土地资源保障，引进了投资超600亿元的粤海装备技术产业园、123亿元的中粮集团粮油食品加工园区、100亿元的华为终端总部等项目。全市共引进重大项目81宗，投资总额达1972亿元，为下一阶段发展注入了新的强大动力。**扎实推进重大平台和重大项目建设。**松山湖启动中以国际科技合作产业园、两岸生物技术产业合作基地的建设，台湾高科技园升格为省级平台。虎门港成功跨入百万标箱港口行列。生态园基础设施建设加快。长安新区用海规划通过国家评审。市属重大项目完成投资278.3亿元，增长18.6%，带动全社会固定资产投资1178亿元，增长9.1%。**切实加快产业转型升级步伐。**推进外经贸“十个100”计划，全年新增来料加工转法人企业536家，外资企业新设研发机构220家，总数达到670家。外资企业产品内销总额增长15.1%，省级以上名牌名标达580个。主营业务超百亿元企业增至3家。促进信息化和工业化融合，省两化融合“4个100”示范工程标杆企业增至37家。大力发展现代服务业，社会消费品零售总额增长9.2%，服务业增加值占生产总值比重超过50%。

——力促科技、金融与产业融合，增强经济创新驱动力。积极实施招科引智战略。组团拜访商务部、科技部、教育部等部委及北大、中科院等高校院所，达成50多项合作意向。与北大共建光电研究院，与华南理工共建协同创新研究院，与中科院共建云计算中心，推进散裂中子源项目建设。全市公共创新平台增至13家。启动松山湖大学创新城规划建设。引进省创新科研团队5个，总数达14家，排名全省第三。科技合作周暨招才引智大会升格为部省共同举办。**完善激励创新政策体系。**制定实施科技金融产业融合“1+4”政策，完善“科技东莞”政策，引导更多社会资金投入科技创新。全市R&D占生产总值的比重提高到1.58%。先进制造业、高技术制造业增加值分别占规模以上工业增加值的42.7%和32.3%。专利申请量、授权量位居全省第三。**发挥金融创新引领作用。**设立20亿元创业投资引导基金，成功引进深创投、中科招商等企业，风投创投等股权投资类企业增至98家。上市企业增至12家。加快金融商务区规划，推进松山湖科技金融产业融合试点。新设和引进金融机构15家，跨境人民币结算突破1000亿元。我市成为粤台金融合作试点城市，台湾玉山银行东莞分行正式开业。

——加大水乡统筹与集体经济转型力度，促进区域协调发展。作出统筹水乡地区发展的重大决策。出台实施方案，全面铺开十镇一港规划编制工作，启动了龙湾滨江片区、水乡大道改造提升工程等12个总投资额307亿元的先期项目。水乡发展已被纳入省幸福导向型产业体系行动计划。**推进镇村集体经济改革发展。**出台了一系列含金量高、操作性强的政策，加大力度破解集体经济发展难题。开展清产核资，建成集体资产交易试点平台，严控一般性支出和超前分配。镇街平均可支配收入8.3亿元；村组两级纯收入增长9.4%，其中欠发达村纯收入增长15%。镇村债务负担有所减轻，收不抵支的村（社区）减少34个。**强化深莞惠等区域合作与对接。**深莞惠规划衔接、产业融合、交通对接等日益加强，石马河联合整治取得阶段性成效。主动加强穗莞战略合作。加快莞韶、莞惠产业转移园建设。认真抓好援疆援藏工作，圆满完成对韶关、云浮的帮扶开发“双到”任务，对口援助广西河池、重庆巫山工作扎实推进。与韩国牙山市结为友好城市。

——**打造法治化国际化营商环境，增创政府服务“加一”和综合成本“减一”优势。力推商事登记和行政审批制度改革。**在大朗进行商事登记制度改革试点，企业注册时间平均缩短60%以上，市场主体同比增长79.3%，成为全省发证最快、同期发证最多的试点地区。去年12月份起在全市铺开该项改革，市本级不再保留任何涉及市场准入的前置审批事项。东莞被国家工商总局确定为全国商事登记改革试点城市。大力深化行政审批制度改革，第一批取消和转移行政审批事项296项，减幅41.3%。**积极帮助企业减负和解决实际问题。**开展市镇领导“访企业、送服务、促转型”大走访。全面取消个体工商户和工商企业治安联防费，减半收取流动人员调配费，为企业年减负3.8亿元。海关、检验检疫等口岸单位主动为企业减免收费近2亿元。进一步规范镇村收费。实施新10亿元融资支持计划。**深入开展“三打两建”行动。**以罕见力度严查大要案、斩断利益链、深挖保护伞，加快建设社会信用体系和市场监管体系。累计查办欺行霸市、制假售假及商业贿赂案件3万多宗，查处保护伞233人，促进形成风清气正的政务环境、公平诚信的市场秩序。**不断创新提升政府服务。**在全国率先推出加工贸易管理服务平台，实现了外经贸、海关、检验检疫和企业“四方联网”。推进依法行政，开展“市民评机关”活动，对服务窗口进行明查暗访，着力解决推诿扯皮、办事拖拉、效率低下等问题，优化了政府服务，提高了行政效率。

——**深入推进城乡环境整治，提升城市建设管理水平。高效完成广深高速、虎门大桥东莞段景观综合整治。**用短短五个月时间，清理广告标牌1333块，清拆违法和临时建筑44.7万平方米，沿线脏乱差的面貌有较大改观。以对城市未来发展高度负责的态度，强力开展在建违法建筑清理专项行动。**加快轨道交通等重大基础建设。**组建东实集团，推进轨道交通融资。地铁R2线工程进展顺利，3个站点完成主体封顶。新火车站等15项重点工程竣工，市民艺术中心等21项重点工程加快推进。新建改造高速路、国省道、镇村联网路147.7公里，建成一批水电气管网和水利防灾减灾工程。加快“三旧”改造步伐。新增和更新公交车、出租车近千辆。**加强环境生态保护。**划定27个重点饮用水源保护区，启动水源保护隔离工程。推进生态景观林带和森林公园建设，植树造林2226公顷，新建绿道324公里。城镇生活垃圾无害化处理率达85.2%。深化运河综合整治，落实节能减排任务，加强环境执法和污染企业监管。

——**加强社会建设与管理创新，着力保障和改善民生。积极创建全省创新社会管理引领区。**成立社会建设研究院。完成社会组织孵化基地建设。出台政府购买服务目录。稳步推进村级体制改革。加强网上信访大厅建设，全省率先实现视频信访系统镇街全覆盖。建立全市统一的劳动关系预警系统。强化综治信访维稳平台建设，做好矛盾隐患排查化解，引导民众理性表达个人意愿与爱国诉求。**切实强化社会安全管理。**推进“四化五警”建设，开展警务前移、出租屋治安管理等试点，推广执法办案格式化，启动智能综合视频监控系统建设，“两抢一盗”立案下降9.6%，老虎机赌博现象基本绝迹。严格落实安全生产“一岗双责”，推进消防安全网格化管理试点，深入开展校车隐患等专项整治行动，强化食品药品监管，全市未发生重特大安全事故。**大力发展以改善民生为重点的社会事业。**市财政全年共投入205亿元用于民生事业。基本完成向社会承诺的十件实事。落实幼儿园财政补助，上调镇街中小学公用经费标准。全市高考录取率、每万户籍人口升重点人数等四项主要高考指标均居全省第一。深入实施提升公共文化服务水平工程，健全文化产业、文化精品扶持政策，一批优秀文艺作品获省级以上重大奖项。成功举办漫博会。出台公立医院改革试点实施方案，全面启用市中医院新院。建设十分钟体育圈，莞籍运动员首获残奥会金牌。发行新社保卡，上调离退休人员基本养老金和居家养老服务补助标准。加强劳动力培训和就业援助。向困难群众发放临时救助金和物价补贴。国防人防、统计审计、人口计生、外事侨务、工青妇幼、民族宗教、档案方志、科普法普、气象、打私等工作扎实推进。

各位代表！一年来，全市上下凝心聚力，提振精神，以强烈的使命感克难前行，以高效的执行力扎实推进，朝着高水平崛起的道路迈出了坚实的步伐。在此，我代表市人民政府，向全市广大干部群众，向人大代表和政协委员，向各民主党派、人民团体、社会各界人士，向各驻莞单位、驻莞部队，以及参与、支持和关心东莞建设发展的港澳台同胞和海外侨胞，致以崇高的敬意和衷心的感谢！

与此同时，我们也清醒地看到，东莞还处于转型攻坚期和矛盾凸显期，资源环境瓶颈约束加剧、产业结构不尽合理、自主创新能力不强、体制机制不够完善等深层次问题仍然存在，需要长期不懈努力破解。从当前来看，也有不少困难和问题值得我们高度重视：**一是经济企稳回升的基础仍需巩固。**尽管全市经济呈现出回暖向好的态势，但由于受国际经济环境影响，生产总值、工业、消费等指标与年度目标任务仍有一定距离。企业生产经营也面临着不少困难。**二是重大项目的带动效应尚未真正显现。**一大批“三重”项目虽已签约启动，但要真正落地动工、建成投产、发挥效益，还需付出艰辛努力。**三是统筹发展的力度有待进一步加大。**集体经济转型困难不小，区域发展不够协调，镇村债务负担仍然较重，水乡地区统筹发展等工作仍需深入推进，对土地资源的整合力度亟待加大。**四是城市规划建设管理的水平有待进一步提升。**城市顶层设计相对缺乏，经营管理需要创新理念，违法建筑等问题不容忽视。**五是惠及民生的工作仍待加大力度。**十件实事涉及的52项具体工作中，有2项未能完成年度目标。群众对物价上涨、公交出行、人才入户等问题反映依然较多，治安管理、教育公平、医疗改革等任务比较艰巨。**六是机关作风建设仍需加强。**一些干部的精神状态与高水平崛起的要求仍有一定的差距，办事效率、服务水平和管理能力有待进一步提高。对这些问题，我们必须以强烈的责任感和紧迫感，积极寻求破解之策。

2013年工作安排

今年是全面贯彻落实十八大精神的开局之年，也是东莞加快推动高水平崛起的奋进之年，机遇与挑战并存。世界经济正在经历新一轮的再平衡过程，低速增长态势仍将延续，总需求不足和产能相对过剩的矛盾有所上升，企业经营成本增加和创新能力不足的问题并存，经济发展和资源环境硬约束的矛盾有所加剧。与此同时，党的十八大胜利召开为今后发展指明了方向，跨国公司和大型央企民企酝酿着新一轮生产布局调整，第三次工业革命雏形初现，国内城镇化、工业化、信息化融合步伐不断加快，新兴产业和重大项目进驻东莞势头强劲，为我市经济稳健回暖与产业加速升级提供了良好契机。今年政府工作的总体要求是：**认真贯彻落实党的十八大、中央经济工作会议、省委十一届二次全会和市委十三届三次全会精神，以习近平总书记视察广东和胡春华书记莅莞调研重要讲话精神为指导，深入实践科学发展观，坚定不移地推动转型升级，脚踏实地推进改革发展，把握好稳中求进的主基调，以提高经济增长质量和效益为中心，以打造创新型经济为主攻方向，着力优环境、上项目、强统筹、抓改革，为加快转型升级、建设幸福东莞、实现高水平崛起不断开创新局面。**

具体来讲，**优环境，**就是要加大力度降低综合成本，提升政府服务，提高城市承载力，推动东莞成为综合营商环境最优越的城市之一。**上项目，**就是要坚定不移地抓产业、盯项目，全力谋求重大项目招商与建设的新突破，加快推进经济结构战略性调整。**强统筹**，就是要按照主体功能定位和产业转型升级的要求，下更大力气推动水乡统筹、土地统筹、招商统筹，以此为突破口优化资源配置，促进协调发展，提升发展层次。**抓改革**，就是要以自我革命的勇气和决心，大刀阔斧地推进行政体制、社会管理等重点领域改革，坚决破除思想观念和体制机制约束，不断增创新的制度红利。

综合考虑各方面因素，今年全市发展的**预期目标是：生产总值增长7%，人均生产总值增长6%，市公共财政预算收入增长10%，固定资产投资总额增长10%，社会消费品零售总额增长10%，出口总额增长7%；服务业增加值占生产总值比重50%，先进制造业、高技术制造业增加值占规模以上工业增加值比重分别达到42.5%和33.8%，发明专利申请量和授权量分别增长15%和60%；城市居民人均可支配收入增长8.5%，农民人均纯收入增长9%，单位生产总值能耗下降4.86%，城镇登记失业率、居民消费价格涨幅分别控制在3%以内和3%左右。**

围绕以上目标要求，我们必须坚持加快转型升级、推进发展方式转变不动摇，矢志不渝地把转型升级作为东莞践行科学发展观的核心任务，继续加大产业结构调整力度，以**"工作落实年"**为主题，切实抓好转型升级各项重大决策的贯彻落实，抓好重大项目的跟踪落实，抓好市委1号文和市政府1号文等政策措施的细化落实。重点做好几方面工作：

一、打造最佳营商环境，进一步提升开放型经济水平

争做综合营商成本最具竞争力的城市。进一步清理和规范涉企收费，全面放开再生资源回收市场，建立统一交易平台，全年为企业减轻行政收费、中介服务收费、中间环节成本35亿元以上。办好一年一度的加博会，发挥台博会、漫博会等平台作用，推广"一达通"、"大麦客"等商业模式，探索规划和申报综合保税区，增加车检场保税物流相关功能，推进省市共建物联网产业基地，大力发展现代流通业，帮助企业降低渠道成本和物流成本。落实领导走访、专人跟进和跨部门服务等机制，开展竞争性高峰电力电量交易试点，帮助企业解决用工、用电、融资等困难以及物业产权等历史遗留问题。巩固"三打两建"成果，加大打击力度，总结石龙镇社会信用体系建设、食品行业市场监管体系建设等试点经验，在全市铺开"两建"工作。

增强城市对优秀人才的吸引力。全面梳理和改革人才入户政策，进一步降低门槛和简化程序。大力引进创新科研团队、领军人才、紧缺人才和高技能人才。妥善解决人才住房问题，出台企业人才子女入学办法，做好家属安置工作，营造有利于吸引和留住人才的软硬环境。推进留学人员创业园、博士后工作站等载体建设。打造大学生入户快速通道。

实施创新驱动发展战略。加快松山湖大学创新城等平台建设，发挥现有平台作用，促进与专业镇和产业集群对接。用好财政引导资金，继续引进风投创投机构，加大金融创新和企业上市培育力度。扶持高端电子、生物技术、新一代互联网、3D打印等战略性新兴产业发展，与省共建云计算应用产业基地。实施高成长型中小企业培育计划，支持中小微企业和民营经济发展。积极创建全国质量强市示范城市。办好科技合作周活动。

大力发展电子商务。出台扶持电子商务发展的政策措施。支持专业镇和专业市场搭建电子商务营销配送网络，带动产业集群整合升级，助推传统产业向价值链高端延伸。深入开展"莞货网上行"等活动。加力引进和培育电子商务企业，对在莞设立总部的电商予以奖励。探索实行"零门槛"的电子商务企业网上注册登记制度，吸引各地电商在莞集聚。

深化加工贸易转型与内外开放合作。用好国家赋予的先行先试政策，鼓励加工贸易企业外包供应链管理，向研发设计、品牌营销、物流配送转型。抓好外贸转型升级示范基地建设，扩大设备及先进技术进口，提高一般贸易占比，促进对外贸易多元平衡发展。推动两岸生物技术产业合作基地建设，用好专项投资基金，铺开基础设施及首期项目。推进粤台金融合作试点。加快台湾高科技园详细性规划编制和招商工作，推进中以国际科技合作产业园建设。落实珠三角规划纲要，加强深莞惠在规划、交通、产业等方面的对接，推进穗莞和莞港澳合作。

二、深入实施“揽月行动”，构建“星月同辉”的产业格局

建立统筹有力的招商机制。认真落实“1+5”招商政策，建立重大项目招商信息共享、布局统筹、选址流转和利益分享机制，将镇街、园区和部门跟踪接洽的重大项目全部纳入统一数据库，避免过度竞争和无序引进。建立项目评估准入、比选和约束机制，制定投资强度、单位产出、产业链配套等项目评价体系，健全企业失信惩戒和享受优惠政策的退出机制，强化对重大项目招商工作的指导。

以高效服务推动粤海等重大项目动工建设。进一步强化与粤海集团的战略合作，尽快完成粤海园区概念性总体规划和产业规划，力争项目于今年动工。加快启动“三纵三横”配套路网一期工程建设。推动华为终端总部项目年内动工。对所有重大项目实行挂钩督导、部门联审、“六个一”包干等制度，提供从立项审批到办证开工“一条龙”服务。

科学从容推进园区开发建设。完善松山湖功能配套，严格筛选项目，提升产出效益，争创国家创新型科技园区。加快生态园征地拆迁和土地平整，完善产业规划和招商指引，积极申报国家城市湿地公园。加快长安新区围填海工程与基础设施建设。深化虎门港与沙田镇统筹发展，突出产业链招商，推进集装箱码头和保税物流中心建设，做大增值服务，做旺港口经济。

争创全国城乡土地生态利用制度综合改革试点城市，为产业发展进一步拓展空间。推进土地统筹整合，优化国土空间开发格局，未来三年力争腾挪拼接出1000亩以上地块50块、面积10万亩，强化重大项目用地保障。探索实行土地规划发展权和开发建设权分离，试行闲置土地置换、项目分期供地、土地绩效评估等制度。落实土地未开发收回政策。加快“三旧”改造步伐。创建全国节约集约用地模范市。对新增用地指标实行分类比例控制和差别化管理。

三、强力统筹水乡地区十镇一港发展，打造全省幸福导向型产业发展示范区

建立健全规划体系和统筹开发机制。高标准编制水乡地区统筹发展总体规划和专项规划，一盘棋考虑城乡建设、生态保护和产业布局。加快完善投融资、利益平衡、项目把关等机制，强化统筹发展的制度保障。推动农村管理体制、土地统筹机制等改革在水乡地区先行先试。

完善一体化的水乡交通体系。市财政安排20亿元，加快水乡大道、疏港大道粤晖大桥、望牛墩横海大桥、石龙红海大桥等先期项目建设，迅速启动中洪路、望万路等干线联网工程。统筹推进基础设施和公共服务设施建设。探索道路建设与统筹开发沿线土地相结合的城建投融资新模式。

打造具有水乡特色的标志性片区。提前启动望洪枢纽站周边15平方公里土地统筹和建设，致力打造东莞城市次中心、水乡核心片区。加快建设总投资超百亿元的龙湾滨江片区，促进商住休闲旅游综合开发。加快推进中堂、望牛墩10.5平方公里的水乡风情区规划，实行整体招商，成片开发。加快建设麻涌4平方公里世界农场项目，打造集都市农业、观光旅游、创意休闲等于一体的新型农场。启动挂影洲中心涌沿线片区更新改造，促进污染治理、环境美化与产业发展有机结合。

逐步构建亲水宜居的优质生活圈。通过生物净化、湿地生态改造等手段，积极推进水环境治理，改善水体质量和生态景观。实施城乡环境综合治理行动，不断改善村容村貌，加强土地管理，集约节约利用土地，提高土地利用效率。推进亲水环境建设，打造具有岭南水乡特色的区域景观。

四、力推重点领域综合改革，增创新的制度红利

东莞改革开放30多年来的成功经验，很关键的一条就是以敢为人先的精神和改革创新的锐气，不断推进体制机制上的众多首创改革，从而适应了市场经济发展的要求，破解了瓶颈制约，赢得了发展先机。我们要拿出前几代东莞人破釜沉舟、筚路蓝缕的勇气，向改革要方法、要动力，冲破束缚发展的思想观念和路径依赖，冲破利益固化的藩篱，攻坚克难，在转型升级上杀出一条新的血路，形成各项改革协同推进的正能量。

以商事登记为突破口深化行政体制改革。按照宽进严管原则，完善商事登记改革配套政策，推行网上年检，强化后续监管，优化后续审批，进一步发挥商事登记改革的综合影响力，推动与商事主体改革相关的其他改革向纵深发展。完成行政审批制度改革，落实配套工作，推行并联审批、网上审批和“一站式”服务。今后未经市政府批准一概不许增设审批事项。适时扩大简政强镇改革范围。探索推进大部门体制改革。

推进农村综合改革和转型发展。全面推进农村综合改革各项任务。市镇财政加大投入，逐步统筹承接村一级的治安、环卫和行政管理开支。推进社区政务服务中心建设。完善和落实欠发达镇村扶持政策。通过税收分成、生态补偿、结对帮扶等途径，让基层分享土地统筹、“三重”建设等带来的实惠。引导基层通过集中统租、稳妥投资等方式，实现集体资产保值增值。

推进省市共建全省创新社会管理引领区。深化警务机制改革，在现有基础上再推动公安市局10%、分局20%的警力下沉。整合全市治安联防队伍。加力整治治安重点场所和黄赌毒现象，严打各类犯罪活动。落实安全生产“一岗双责”，抓好危险化学品、消防、交通安全等专项整治，创新食品药品和农产品安全监管模式，推进应急管理综合一期平台建设，落实领导接访下访、信访包案等制度，打造平安东莞。培育和规范社会组织发展，新建10个市级社区综合服务中心示范点。

抓好医疗、公交、水务等领域的改革。按照公益化方向加快公立医院改革步伐，组建市属公立医院管理中心。启动公交公益化改革，提升服务质量和管理水平，整治公交不准点、冒黑烟及车内治安等群众关注的问题。深化水资源管理体制机制改革，推进镇街水务一体化，实现市镇村三级水务分级管理。

五、切实加强经济调节，夯实可持续发展的制度保障

加强财政资金及财政投资项目的绩效管理。全面强化财政专项资金、财政投资重大基建、重大民生支出和政府融资项目的绩效评价，进一步提高财政资金使用效益。建立绩效评价结果反馈与应用机制，实行评价结果与预算安排相结合。加强审计监督。严肃查处非法骗取财政扶持资金的行为。

进一步规范镇村经济管理。建立农村集体资产交易平台和“三资”管理信息监控平台。加强对大额开支和敏感性开支的监控，严控非生产性支出。强化债权债务管理，推进镇村已到期债务清偿。今后凡镇村借债，必须经上一级政府批准。

完善与国有资产规模相适应的监管机制。全面调查摸底和分类梳理，建立健全科学合理的人事、审计、工资、业绩考核等监管机制，强化国资管理部门对市属国有企业的监督管理。做优做强做活国有企业，推动国有资本更多地投向关系经济命脉的行业和领域。摸清财政投资建设的场馆、医院、学校等国有资产底数，探索构建新型监管模式。

六、提升城市承载力，建设更具生态文明的美丽东莞

优化城市顶层设计。以新一轮总体规划修编为契机，构建疏密有致的城市格局。以轨道交通建设为纽带，加强沿线土地统筹开发，拓展和优化城市空间布局。加快南城国际商务区、中央商圈、生态休闲区和松山湖大道两侧区域的规划建设，提高城市首位度。推进从莞高速东莞段、东江梨川大桥、松山湖大道延长线等建设，完善城市基础网络和配套功能。

加强环境综合治理。推广广深高速景观综合整治经验，切实加强全市公路沿路景观和广告标牌管理。推进四大环保行动计划，加快环保产业基地建设，创建国家生态市。加强东江水保护，深化运河与内河涌整治，加快截污次支管网铺设。加快垃圾处理厂建设，整治垃圾填埋场，推广垃圾分类处理。严格落实节能减排责任，抓好国家级工业能耗在线监测试点工作。逐步淘汰黄标车。大力植树造林，加快森林公园、镇村公园、慢行道等建设，提高绿道使用效益。深入创建宜居社区。

提升城市精细化管理水平。建设“智慧城市”和“数字城管”，在大市区率先推行网格化管理，将绿化环卫、城市照明、户外广告等纳入监管范围。全面清理在建违法建筑，完善长效管理机制。推进“智慧交通”建设，大力整治交通拥堵，加快主要堵塞点的改造和分流。统筹市政地下管线铺设，在新开发区域推广管线集中统一铺设的共同沟建设。加强工程招投标管理，保证市场公平与工程质量。

创新投融资平台建设。发挥好新组建的东莞实业等投融资平台作用，强化建设及监督管理，有效整合多种资源，创新投融资机制，撬动更多社会资本参与城市建设和发展。重点抓好轨道交通融资，探索通过发行市政债券、利用股权信托资金等方式，筹集资金加快建设。

七、在改善民生中加强社会建设，努力让市民过上美好生活

完善保障有力的社保体系。认真办好十件实事。加大就业创业扶持力度，重点解决大学毕业生、困难家庭等群体的就业问题。提高最低生活保障和五保供养标准。扩建市社会福利中心，将居家养老服务扩大至120个社区。发行300万张新社保卡，加大重大疾病和意外伤害医疗保障力度。加强平价商店和价格调节基金运营管理，减少物价上涨对群众的影响。

增强文化整体实力和竞争力。全面推进文化名城建设，继续实施“百千万文化惠民”工程，建好国家公共文化服务体系示范区。加大文化产业和文化精品扶持力度，办好“我们的节日”、读书节等活动，加强非物质遗产和历史文物的保护与开发利用，实施文化人才“三个100”工程。

努力办好群众满意的教育。新建5所公办幼儿园，给予民办学校在校生公用经费和教科书补助。增加新莞人子女积分入学学位。统一全市初中公用经费标准，加强民办学校规范化建设，推进免费中职教育。启用东莞理工学校新校区、技师学院和高技能公共实训中心，开设市外国语学校，扩建市特殊教育学校。加强在莞高校学科建设，提高服务地方发展能力。

全面发展体育卫生人口计生等各项事业。大力发展群众体育和竞技体育，增加社区体育设施，提升篮球、羽毛球等品牌。推进市人民医院分院、儿童医院、台心医院等建设。发挥好社区卫生服务机构的作用，为市民提供优质价廉的医疗服务。探索设立市国医馆，推进中医药进社区。实施优生健康惠民工程和妇女两癌免费筛查。稳步扩大住房公积金制度覆盖面。落实好新疆兵团农三师的对口支援计划，推进支援西藏林芝的项目建设。继续帮扶韶关、云浮、广西河池、重庆巫山等地发展。

八、进一步加强作风建设，塑造高效廉洁的政府形象

落实中央“八项规定”，深入改进工作作风。精简会议和文件，改进会风文风，力戒形式主义、文牍主义。严格控制各类庆典、多重检查、评比及达标创建活动。加强调查研究，推广现场办公。开展明查暗访，落实首问责任、限时办结等制度。加强政府执行力建设，着力治庸治懒治散治奢，整治

“吃拿卡要”等行为，推动机关作风进一步好转。

推进“大数据”战略，加快电子政务建设。运用云技术集成企业登记、信用监管、数据统计等功能，构建全市信息共享和内部监管平台。拓展加工贸易“四方联网”，打造地方电子口岸。优化提升网上办事平台，推动90%的行政审批事项、80%的公共服务事项上网，打造全国一流的网上办事大厅。推进数据开放工程，在财政、环保、招投标等领域开展数据公开试点。

强化内外监督，打造为民务实清廉的政府。落实廉洁从政各项规定和廉政责任制，强化政府内部监督，坚决惩治腐败行为。加快法治政府建设，落实重大行政决策程序和政务公开制度，主动接受人大政协及社会监督，重视和发挥网络媒体监督作用，促进形成清廉高效、务实为民的良好政风。

各位代表！九万里风鹏正举，党的十八大绘就了夺取中国特色社会主义新胜利的宏伟蓝图，中华民族伟大复兴的目标已越来越接近，得改革开放风气之先的东莞没有理由不认真把握这一千载难逢的发展机遇。站在新的起跑线上，我们将牢记使命，勤勉进取，在中共东莞市委的坚强领导下，与全市人民一道，同心同德，攻坚克难，朝着高水平崛起的目标奋勇前进，用实干托起我们的东莞梦和伟大的中国梦！

名词注解：

六个东莞：市委市政府制定了《关于建设“六个东莞”营造法治化国际化营商环境的意见》，提出打造平安东莞、法治东莞、信用东莞、效率东莞、活力东莞、开放东莞。

三重一大：“三重”指重大项目、重大产业集聚区、重大科技专项；“一大”指重大项目招商。

风投创投：即风险投资和创业投资，一种投入到高新技术领域具有巨大潜力和风险的投资方式。

“1+5”招商政策：“1”指《关于加强重大项目招商引资工作的意见》，“5”指东莞市《重大项目招商引资奖励办法》、《招商引资重大项目认定管理办法》、《重大项目招商引资“一站通”工作机制》、《招商引资队伍建设管理办法》、《招商引资产业指导目录》。

“一站通”工作机制：指由市重大项目招商引资工作领导小组统筹负责，形成一条从项目信息收集、招商洽谈、拍板签约到后期服务的快速反应通道。

粤海装备技术产业园：位于谢岗镇，计划投资超600亿元，为东莞建市以来投资规模最大的项目。重点引进汽车装备制造等高端制造业。

中粮集团粮油食品加工园区：位于麻涌镇，总投资123亿元。项目建成投产后，预计年产值达200亿元。

华为终端总部项目：位于松山湖，总投资100亿元，主要发展与手机等所有终端关联的研发、销售和增值业务。

中以国际科技合作产业园：位于松山湖，被国家科技部授予“国际科技创新园”称号，主要承接和引进以色列及欧美等国家和地区的水处理技术。

两岸生物技术产业合作基地：位于松山湖，主要承接两岸在新药中药研发、医疗器械制造、基因产业和健康产业等方面的合作项目。

外经贸“十个100”计划：即培育百家总部形态企业、壮大百家内销龙头企业、扶持百家自主品牌企业、发展百家高新技术企业、打造百家“升转”示范企业、锻造百名外经贸“专才”、拜访百家目标企业总部、落实百家千万美元项目、引进百家新兴产业项目、帮扶百家民企“走出去”。

信息化与工业化融合“4个100”示范工程：指我省2009年起在生产流程、装备制造数字化改造及节能减排、清洁生产信息技术应用等四方面评选标杆企业各100家，促进“两化”融合。

云计算：一种基于互联网的计算方式，可将大量用网络连接的计算资源统一管理和调度，将共享的软硬件资源和信息，按需提供给终端计算机和其他设备。

科技金融产业融合“1+4”政策：“1”指《关于促进科技、金融与产业融合的意见》，“4”指东莞市《产业升级转型及创业投资引导基金管理暂行办法》、《促进股权投资基金业发展的若干意见》、《金融创新奖评选暂行办法》、《金融招商奖励办法》。

R&D：即研究与开发经费支出。

十镇一港：指统筹水乡地区发展涉及范围，包括中堂、望牛墩、麻涌、洪梅、道滘、石龙、万江、石碣、高埗、沙田等10个镇街，以及虎门港。

四方联网：东莞、黄埔海关、广东检验检疫局、省外经贸厅四方共同搭建的加工贸易管理服务平台，在全国第一个做到了企业联网申报、外经贸联网审批、海关联网备案、检验检疫联网共享数据。

四化五警：“四化”即治安管理网格化、治安巡逻常态化、治安监控全面化、治安打击精确化；“五警”即科技兴警、人才强警、动态布警、从严治警、从优待警。

“一达通”商业模式：指整合所有企业进出口环节所需银行、海关、物流、税务、保险、外汇等机构或供应商，实现在线业务申报办理。

“大麦客”商业模式：指我市部分台商企业以“大麦客”统一品牌，打造集内销仓储批发为一体的大卖场经营模式。

3D打印：指通过电脑软件对设计出的产品按三维空间分层切片，由3D打印机对粉末状金属或塑料等原材料进行层叠式粘合，直接构造形成零件或成品，多应用于模具制造、工业设计领域。目前正在向规模化生产、生物器官打印等方向发展。

“六个一”包干制度：即“一个重大项目、一名领导挂帅、一个部门牵头、一笔专门经费、一个责任目标、实行一抓到底”的工作制度。

望洪枢纽站：穗莞深城际轨道、莞惠城际轨道、市域轨道R1线的接驳换乘站，规划设在望牛墩镇和洪梅镇交界处。

四大环保行动计划：包括空气清洁、重点流域整治、重金属污染整治和农村环境保护等四项行动。

智慧城市：指用信息通信技术手段，感测、分析、整合城市运行核心系统的各项关键信息，对民生、公共安全、城市服务等各种需求做出智能响应，实现城市智慧式管理和运行。

数字城管：指用信息化和移动通信技术手段来处理、分析和管理整个城市的所有城管部件和城管事件信息。

智慧交通：综合运用先进的资讯、通信、网络、自动控制等技术，改善交通运输状况，提高运输效率和安全性。

我们的节日：是我市开展的系列文化活动，从镇街精选出一批项目进行创新整合，包括东坑卖身节、桥头荷花节等。

文化人才“三个100”工程：即从全市相关企事业单位、社会团体中选拔100名优秀人才充实文化人才队伍，从文化系统中选拔100名优秀干部到先进地区挂职锻炼，在全国范围内公开招聘100名各艺术门类专业优秀人才。

“大数据”战略：大数据是一种对信息爆炸时代产生的海量数据的描述，是对利用云计算等互联网信息技术，对经济、商业、政府管理等进行数据化、电子化变革的统称。

第二部分　统计资料

Part Two　Statistics

一、综　合

General Survey

1-1 东莞行政区划（2012年）

Divisions of Administrative Areas in Dongguan (2012)

镇街	村（居）委会		
	个数		名称
合计	村委会	350	
	社区居委会	245	
莞城	社区居委会	8	东正 市桥 北隅 西隅 罗沙 博厦 兴塘 创业
石龙	村委会	7	西湖 忠维 林屋 蒲溪 新维 王屋洲 黄家山
	社区居委会	3	中山东 中山西 兴龙
虎门	社区居委会	30	虎门寨 东方 则徐 大宁 树田 白沙 沙角 怀德 博涌 镇口 村头 新联 九门寨 居岐 金洲 南面 北栅 小捷滘 北面 陈村 东风 武山沙 黄村 南栅 龙眼 宴岗 赤岗 路东 新湾 民泰
东城	社区居委会	23	岗贝 花园新村 东泰 温塘 桑园 周屋 余屋 鳌峙塘 峡口 柏洲边 上桥 下桥 樟村 梨川 堑头 主山 石井 同沙 光明 牛山 立新 火炼树 星城
万江	社区居委会	28	万江墟 万江 石美 莫屋 拔蛟窝 黄粘洲 蚬涌 谷涌 小享 滘联 上甲 新村 新谷涌 共联 水蛇涌 大莲塘 牌楼基 严屋 大汾 流涌尾 金泰 曲海 坝头 胜利 官桥滘 简沙洲 新和 新城
南城	社区居委会	18	鸿福 宏远 胜和 元美 亨美 三元里 篁村 新基 周溪 袁屋边 白马 石鼓 蛤地 西平 雅园 水濂 新城 宏图
中堂	村委会	15	潢涌 三涌 湛翠 凤冲 袁家涌 吴家涌 鹤田 中堂 一村 东向 蕉利 槎滘 下芦 马沥 四乡
	社区居委会	5	中心 斗朗 红锋 东泊 江南
望牛墩	村委会	21	李屋 望东 扶涌 赤滘 五涌 下漕 上合 聚龙江 望联 洲湾 洲涡 杜屋 寮厦 芙蓉沙 官桥涌 横沥 福安 石排 官洲 朱平沙 锦涡
	社区居委会	1	望牛墩
麻涌	村委会	13	麻一 麻三 麻四 大步 东太 新基 川槎 鸥涌 华阳 南洲 大盛 漳澎 黎滘
	社区居委会	2	麻涌 麻二
石碣	村委会	14	石碣 唐洪 黄泗围 西南 单屋 梁家村 沙腰 刘屋 水南 四甲 鹤田厦 涌口 横滘 桔洲
	社区居委会	1	城中
高埗	村委会	18	冼沙 卢溪 宝莲 塘厦 草墩 护安围 保安围 三联 横滘头 低涌 朱磡 新联 欧邓 芦村 高埗 凌屋 上江城 下江城
	社区居委会	1	新创
道滘	村委会	13	南城 南丫 闸口 大鱼沙 小河 永庆 北永 昌平 厚德 九曲 大罗沙 大岭丫 蔡白
	社区居委会	1	兴隆
洪梅	村委会	9	洪屋涡 新庄 梅沙 氹涌 黎洲角 夏汇 尧均 乌沙 金鳌沙
	社区居委会	1	洪梅
沙田	村委会	16	中围 和安 大流 泥洲 杨公洲 福禄沙 阇西 民田 先锋 西大坦 穗丰年 大泥 齐沙 稔洲 义沙 西太隆
	社区居委会	2	横流 滨港
厚街	社区居委会	24	竹溪 厚街 珊美 宝屯 三屯 陈屋 赤岭 河田 寮厦 汀山 环冈 大迳 新围 桥头 南五 新塘 涌口 双岗 溪头 沙塘 宝塘 下汴 白濠 湖景
长安	社区居委会	13	长盛 涌头 霄边 咸西 锦厦 新安 乌沙 新民 沙头 上沙 厦岗 厦边 上角

1-1　续表

(2012年)

镇　街	村（居）委会		
	个　数		名　　称
寮　步	村委会	20	西溪　凫山　石龙坑　石步　良边　富竹山　塘唇　向西　霞边　上屯　下岭贝　竹园　上底　药勒　刘屋巷　浮竹山　陈家埔　井巷　小坑　长坑
	社区居委会	10	寮步　塘边　横坑　岭厦　新旧围　缪边　牛杨　泉塘　坑口　良平
大岭山	村委会	21	太公岭　大塘朗　下高田　连平　鸡翅岭　马蹄岗　金桔　大沙　百花洞　大塘　水朗　杨屋　矮岭冚　颜屋　大片美　梅林　元岭　大岭　新塘　旧飞鹅　大环
	社区居委会	3	大岭山　农场　领居
大　朗	村委会	16	高英　洋乌　洋坑塘　松柏朗　黎贝岭　松木山　犀牛陂　水平　宝陂　石厦　杨涌　沙步　新马莲　佛子凹　蔡边　水口
	社区居委会	12	大朗　佛新　巷头 巷尾　大井头　屏山　竹山　求富路　长塘　黄草朗　圣堂　长富
黄　江	社区居委会	7	新市　田美　三新　梅塘　宝山　北岸　长龙
樟木头	社区居委会	10	圩镇　樟罗　百果洞　樟洋　石新　柏地　官仓　裕丰　金河　樟新
清　溪	村委会	20	浮岗　上元　清厦　铁松　铁场　谢坑　青皇　大埔　长山头　三中　九乡　三星　渔樑围　厦坭　大利　土桥　重河　松岗　罗马　荔横
	社区居委会	1	清溪
塘　厦	社区居委会	22	塘厦　三局　林村　石潭埔　四村　振兴围　大坪　莆心湖　平山　诸佛岭　桥陇　龙背岭　石鼓　田心　横塘　蛟乙塘　凤凰岗　莲湖　沙湖　石马　清湖头　塘新
凤　岗	村委会	11	雁田　官井头　油甘埔　凤德岭　塘沥　黄洞　竹塘　竹尾田　三联　五联　天堂围
	社区居委会	1	凤岗
谢　岗	村委会	11	黎村　窑山　南面　大龙　大厚　赵林　稔子园　五星　曹乐　谢岗　谢山
	社区居委会	1	泰园
常　平	村委会	31	岗梓　塘角　苏坑　袁山贝　金美　还珠沥　朗贝　桥沥　卢屋　九江水　朗洲　陈屋贝　司马　霞坑　漱旧　漱新　黄泥塘　元江元　横江厦　沙湖口　白石岗　松柏塘　上坑　木棆　下墟　板石　田尾　白花沥　桥梓　麦元　土塘
	社区居委会	2	常平　新民
桥　头	村委会	11	田头角　李屋　朗厦　岗头　屋厦　禾坑　邓屋　邵岗头　东江　山和　石水口
	社区居委会	6	莲城　田新　桥头　大洲　迳联　岭头
横　沥	村委会	16	石涌　隔坑　半仙山　田头　田坑　横沥　村头　长巷　田饶步　六甲　村尾　水边　新四　山厦　月塘　张坑
	社区居委会	1	恒泉
东　坑	村委会	14	东坑　坑美　角社　塔岗　黄麻岭　初坑　凤大　黄屋　寮边头　长安塘　新门楼　井美　彭屋　丁屋
	社区居委会	2	草塘　骏达
企　石	村委会	19	铁岗　深巷　湖美　博夏　上洞　江边　旧围　清湖　东平　上截　下截　东山　莫屋　杨屋　新南　南坑　铁炉坑　企石　霞朗
	社区居委会	1	宝石
石　排	村委会	18	石排　下沙　福隆　庙边王　沙角　黄家壆　赤坎　向西　水贝　田寮　横山　埔心　谷吓　塘尾　李家坊　田边　中坑　燕窝
	社区居委会	1	太和
茶　山	村委会	16	上元　茶山　下朗　横江　增埗　卢边　寒溪水　南社　塘角　博头　冲美　粟边　孙屋　超朗　京山　刘黄
	社区居委会	2	茶山圩　茶溪
松山湖	社区居委会	1	松山湖
虎门港	社区居委会	1	虎门港

1-2 历年东莞行政区划

Divisions of Administrative Areas in Dongguan over Years

单位：个

年　份	镇　街	村(居)委会		
			村委会	社区居委会
1978	33	526	496	30
1979	33	531	501	30
1980	33	545	515	30
1981	34	554	524	30
1982	34	561	531	30
1983	34	561	531	30
1984	34	542	512	30
1985	33	546	516	30
1986	33	560	530	30
1987	34	580	537	43
1988	33	582	542	40
1989	33	583	544	39
1990	33	583	543	40
1991	33	586	546	40
1992	33	590	549	41
1993	33	590	549	41
1994	33	592	551	41
1995	33	592	551	41
1996	33	593	552	41
1997	33	594	551	43
1998	32	594	551	43
1999	32	593	546	47
2000	32	675	546	129
2001	32	678	546	132
2002	32	678	546	132
2003	32	616	487	129
2004	32	596	440	156
2005	32	596	404	192
2006	32	596	394	202
2007	32	591	386	205
2008	32	591	383	208
2009	32	598	383	215
2010	32	599	383	216
2011	32	594	350	244
2012	32	595	350	245

注：2010年起社区居委会数含松山湖高新区及虎门港。

1-3 主要年份户数、人口与自然资源

Number of Households, Population and Natural Resources in Main Years

项　　目	单 位	1978年	1990年	1995年	2000年	2005年	2010年	2011年	2012年
户　数									
年末户籍总户数	万户	24.82	32.73	36.43	41.40	46.50	53.05	53.90	54.41
#非农业户	万户	4.37	8.91	10.06	11.44	18.90	27.08	27.69	28.09
人口与劳动力									
年末常住人口	万人		175.62	336.45	644.84	656.07	822.48	825.48	829.23
年末户籍人口	万人	111.23	131.85	143.65	152.61	165.65	181.77	184.77	187.02
#非农业人口	万人	18.49	30.87	35.38	39.61	65.84	92.09	94.46	95.96
人口密度(常住人口)	人/平方公里		712	1365	2616	2662	3343	3356	3371
人口密度(户籍人口)	人/平方公里	451	535	583	619	672	739	751	760
土　地									
土地面积	平方公里	2465	2465	2465	2465	2465	2460	2460	2460
年末耕地面积	万亩	118.39	88.26	70.86	66.33	50.29	57.69	57.19	
人均耕地面积	亩	1.06	0.67	0.49	0.43	0.30	0.32	0.31	
建成区面积	平方公里			82.48	147.68	620.31	798.48	854.30	888.39
#城区建成区面积	平方公里				28.13	108.10	91.65	100.80	106.53
气　候									
年降水量	毫米	1748.3	1602.9	1664.8	2019.3	1837.6	2165.9	1298.6	1838.6
年平均气温	摄氏度	21.9	22.8	22.4	23.2	22.7	22.4	22.1	22.6
极端最高气温	摄氏度	35.7	37.8	36.2	37.0	37.4	36.1	36.2	36.7
极端最低气温	摄氏度	2.7	4.3	6.7	5.6	1.8	1.9	3.2	4.1
年日照时数	小时	1958.8	1910.2	1935.7	2059.5	1736.3	1699.7	2120.1	1708.7
森　林									
有林地面积	万亩		83.48	91.48	92.16	89.23	87.30	87.38	87.55
林木蓄积量	万立方米		167.18	123.02	136.11	175.38	255.82	272.98	291.03
森林覆盖率	%		31.4	29.7	30.6	33.1	36.7	36.9	37.1
水资源									
大陆海岸线总长度	公里	61.4	61.4	61.4	115.9	92.1	97.2	97.2	97.2
海水养殖可养面积	万亩	5.0	5.0	5.5	2.6	16.9	2.0	1.1	1.1
淡水养殖可养面积	万亩	30.0	30.0	28.0	14.3	30.7	10.0	10.0	10.0

注：1. 土地面积数据来源于市国土局，不包括海域面积。
2. 人均耕地面积按户籍人口计算。
3. 大陆海岸线从2000年起以咸水为界定。
4. 常住人口2006-2010年数据，根据东莞市第六次全国人口普查数据结果重新修订，下同。

1-4 历年土地与自然资源

Land and Natural Resources over Years

年　份	土地面积(平方公里)	气候				
		年降水量(毫米)	年平均气温(摄氏度)	极端最高气温(摄氏度)	极端最低气温(摄氏度)	年日照时数(小时)
1978	2465	1748.3	21.9	35.7	2.7	1958.8
1979	2465	2007.1	21.9	36.5	2.9	1991.4
1980	2465	1434.7	22.3	37.7	3.3	2157.1
1981	2465	2394.9	22.1	35.6	3.2	1792.2
1982	2465	1454.1	22.1	37.5	3.8	1754.1
1983	2465	1947.1	21.8	35.8	3.3	1909.7
1984	2465	1444.5	21.5	35.9	3.1	1749.2
1985	2465	1678.0	21.8	35.8	4.2	1671.7
1986	2465	1665.2	22.2	35.9	3.0	2098.1
1987	2465	1908.8	22.9	37.0	4.3	1816.6
1988	2465	1735.0	22.0	37.0	7.0	1836.5
1989	2465	1567.2	22.5	37.6	5.2	1926.0
1990	2465	1602.9	22.8	37.8	4.3	1910.2
1991	2465	1219.6	23.0	36.6	1.2	1968.8
1992	2465	1827.1	22.3	37.0	4.5	1854.5
1993	2465	2393.6	22.5	35.6	3.0	1965.7
1994	2465	1809.1	23.0	38.2	5.4	1828.6
1995	2465	1664.8	22.4	36.2	6.7	1935.7
1996	2465	1547.4	22.7	37.1	3.4	2036.0
1997	2465	2074.0	22.8	36.3	6.1	1558.1
1998	2465	1844.5	23.6	36.5	5.6	1699.0
1999	2465	1614.5	23.3	37.8	3.1	2015.8
2000	2465	2019.3	23.2	37.0	5.6	2059.5
2001	2465	2042.6	23.3	36.6	6.6	1978.2
2002	2465	1557.4	23.6	36.7	4.5	2046.9
2003	2465	1416.7	23.0	36.1	3.8	2268.7
2004	2465	1705.8	22.8	38.0	3.5	2192.9
2005	2465	1837.6	22.7	37.4	1.8	1736.3
2006	2465	2412.0	22.7	36.8	4.7	1616.4
2007	2465	1806.9	22.9	35.9	6.7	1876.7
2008	2465	2710.9	22.2	36.8	4.8	1879.3
2009	2465	1881.6	22.8	36.3	5.3	1967.8
2010	2460	2165.9	22.4	36.1	1.9	1699.7
2011	2460	1298.6	22.1	36.2	3.2	2120.1
2012	2460	1838.6	22.6	36.7	4.1	1708.7

注：土地面积数据由市国土资源局提供，不包括海域面积，下同。

1-4 续表

年份	森林			水资源		
	森林面积(万亩)	林木蓄积量(万立方米)	森林覆盖率(%)	大陆海岸线总长度(公里)	海水养殖可养面积(万亩)	淡水养殖可养面积(万亩)
1978				61.4	5.0	30.0
1979	44.4	110.3	14.7	61.4	5.0	30.0
1980				61.4	5.0	30.0
1981				61.4	5.0	30.0
1982				61.4	5.0	30.0
1983				61.4	5.0	30.0
1984	76.6	160.5	21.9	61.4	5.0	30.0
1985	78.3	156.0	28.6	61.4	5.0	30.0
1986	82.4	157.8	30.0	61.4	5.0	30.0
1987	83.9	183.9	34.5	61.4	5.0	30.0
1988	84.3	169.1	34.7	61.4	5.0	30.0
1989	80.9	164.8	31.1	61.4	5.0	30.0
1990	83.5	167.2	31.4	61.4	5.0	30.0
1991	85.0	169.2	31.6	61.4	5.0	29.0
1992	86.3	169.8	31.3	61.4	5.5	29.0
1993	87.3	168.9	31.9	61.4	5.5	28.0
1994	86.1	116.8	28.3	61.4	5.5	28.0
1995	91.5	123.0	29.7	61.4	5.5	28.0
1996	91.9	115.7	29.9	61.4	5.5	28.5
1997	93.5	121.1	29.9	61.4	5.7	28.7
1998	93.4	126.0	30.1	61.4	5.7	28.7
1999	92.2	120.4	30.1	115.9	4.8	28.7
2000	92.2	136.1	30.6	115.9	2.6	14.3
2001	93.3	146.0	31.2	116.0	2.8	12.9
2002	93.8	155.0	31.7	115.9	4.1	11.7
2003	93.3	165.1	32.2	92.1	4.2	10.4
2004	93.3	165.1	32.2	92.1	4.0	10.0
2005	89.2	175.4	33.1	92.1	16.9	30.7
2006	88.9	194.4	35.1	92.1	16.6	30.5
2007	89.1	215.1	35.5	92.1	16.9	30.7
2008	88.6	227.9	36.2	97.2	2.5	15.0
2009	90.1	241.4	36.5	97.2	2.0	10.0
2010	87.3	255.8	36.7	97.2	2.0	10.0
2011	87.4	273.0	36.9	97.2	1.1	10.0
2012	87.6	291.0	37.1	97.2	1.1	10.0

1-5 主要年份国民经济主要指标

Main Indicators on National Economy in Main Years

项　　目	单位	1978年	1990年	1995年	2000年	2005年	2010年	2011年	2012年
国民经济核算									
地区生产总值	亿元	6.11	80.44	296.29	820.25	2183.20	4246.45	4735.39	5010.17
第一产业	亿元	2.72	13.28	21.43	25.91	20.55	16.57	17.88	18.76
第二产业	亿元	2.68	40.53	166.97	450.71	1227.86	2160.82	2366.20	2375.64
#工业	亿元		39.18	154.19	430.45	1173.23	2078.45	2288.41	2297.51
第三产业	亿元	0.71	26.63	107.89	343.64	934.78	2069.07	2351.32	2615.78
农村经济									
农林牧渔业总产值	亿元	4.24	23.64	42.69	54.64	42.05	28.31	30.66	32.01
农村集体经营总收入	亿元		7.18	41.23	77.50	120.57	143.38	148.48	155.05
年末耕地面积	万亩		88.26	70.86	66.33	50.29	57.69	57.19	
工　业									
规模以上工业企业指标									
工业增加值	亿元		23.76	111.02	360.11	979.34	1708.31	1642.45	1978.13
主营业务收入	亿元	2.69	47.27	275.84	988.91	3912.15	7708.17	8454.92	9612.66
年末固定资产原值	亿元	0.78	14.29	60.14	728.85	1856.09	3216.25	3304.96	3746.45
年末固定资产净值	亿元	0.51	11.95	46.26	470.19	1105.26	1783.69	1823.77	2064.06
流动资产合计	亿元	0.26	1.74	21.28	529.82	1873.28	3788.83	4173.21	4590.03
资产总额	亿元		13.51	52.98	1122.60	3345.33	6001.71	6612.71	7206.02
负债总额	亿元				563.04	1858.09	3525.30	3877.06	4189.56
资产负债率	%				50.2	55.5	58.7	58.6	58.1
利税总额	亿元				84.10	183.10	469.59	483.30	518.84
综合效益指数	%				114.0	119.9	130.3	128.3	134.4
能源消费									
地区能源消费总量(等价值)	万吨标准煤					1885.78	2812.65	2896.05	2935.73
地区能源消费总量(当量值)	万吨标准煤					1800.14	2438.84	2512.46	2437.34
电力消耗	亿千瓦时					419.83	562.00	586.07	604.28
单位GDP能耗(等价值)	吨标准煤/万元					0.864	0.619	0.632	0.604
单位GDP能耗(当量值)	吨标准煤/万元					0.825	0.599	0.548	0.501
规模以上工业综合能源消费量(当量值)	万吨标准煤					1203.77	1496.06	1482.56	1385.42

注：1.2005年以前地区生产总值采用全国第一次经济普查资料修订的数据；2005-2008年采用第二次经济普查资料修订的数据；2004年以前使用旧行业分类，2004年起使用新行业分类，下同。

2.规模以上工业企业1997年及以前为独立核算企业口径，1998-2005年为全部国有及年销售收入500万元以上非国有企业口径，2006-2010年为年主营业务收入500万元及以上口径，2011年起为年主营业务收入2000万元及以上口径，下同。

3.2005年以前工业相关数据采用第一次经济普查资料修订的数据，2008年采用第二次经济普查资料修订的数据，下同。

4.单位GDP能耗(等价值)和单位GDP能耗(当量值)2006-2010年按2005年可比价计算；2011年开始按2010年可比价计算。

1-5 续表 1

项　　目	单 位	1978年	1990年	1995年	2000年	2005年	2010年	2011年	2012年
运输邮电									
公路通车里程	公里	1259	1325	2327	2518	2871	4751	4828	4969
#高速公路	公里				89	154	217	251	319
旅客周转量	亿人公里	0.94	32.22	44.62	100.19	118.53	129.07	145.88	156.88
水　运	亿人公里	0.43	0.15	0.19	0.14	0.33	0.20	0.20	0.21
公　路	亿人公里	0.51	32.07	44.43	100.05	118.20	128.87	145.68	156.67
货物周转量	亿吨公里	1.51	18.47	26.46	40.47	42.48	109.03	187.48	296.71
水　运	亿吨公里	1.42	11.25	13.66	15.86	15.23	57.95	134.35	242.35
公　路	亿吨公里	0.09	7.22	12.80	24.60	27.25	51.08	53.13	54.36
港口货物吞吐量	万吨	293	233	201	746	2280	5657	6848	9228
邮政业务收入	亿元						6.32	7.37	7.82
电信业务收入	亿元						149.02	157.49	162.14
局用交换机容量	万门		6.98	52.29	103.13	286.25	365.02	357.00	364.00
年末移动电话交换机总容量	万户			4.80	154.20	1059.10	1657.00	2066.00	2219.30
本地电话用户(含小灵通)	万户	0.20	4.90	31.58	78.12	384.52	332.42	319.55	330.79
移动电话用户(含充值卡)	万户		0.05	4.77	123.68	1016.41	1607.60	1677.77	1797.75
#充值卡	万户				42.71	839.58	1433.56	1432.99	1354.88
互联网用户	万户			0.05	13.78	52.90	153.92	190.72	209.59
供用电									
总供电量	亿千瓦时	1.64	18.01	68.00	178.03	415.66	556.89	579.35	600.58
#网供	亿千瓦时	1.64	11.18	38.48	134.91	342.26	547.33	569.93	591.18
总售电量	亿千瓦时	1.49	16.15	61.68	169.06	396.59	543.66	566.69	581.18
#工业用电	亿千瓦时	1.08	11.93	48.79	134.58	330.31	435.57	445.76	452.29
固定资产投资									
固定资产投资总额	亿元	0.23	7.51	63.14	102.89	597.24	1114.98	1079.31	1180.35
#房地产开发	亿元			8.52	11.25	144.43	298.99	373.31	377.32
房地产开发当年房屋施工面积	万平方米					1160.20	2060.54	2393.57	2453.93
房地产开发当年房屋竣工面积	万平方米					132.90	296.59	242.28	362.47
商品房销售面积	万平方米					321.90	511.25	595.61	639.12
商品房销售额	亿元					119.40	373.77	459.61	542.38
新增固定资产	亿元					173.30	577.86	578.89	623.85
固定资产交付使用率	%					29.0	51.8	53.6	52.9
国内贸易									
批发和零售业商品销售总额	亿元	7.49	43.41	155.69	279.19	824.82	1957.18	2346.18	2522.89
社会消费品零售总额	亿元	2.13	31.97	113.01	235.16	506.29	1108.06	1266.31	1354.58

注：1. 2006年起公路通车里程含专用公路和村道，与往年数据不可比，下同。
2. 1995年全社会固定资产投资总额含沙角C厂投资126374万元。
3. 2009年起，客货运输量中，公路和水路运输量统计改用新调查方法，与往年不可比，下同。
4. 2005年以前国内贸易相关数据采用第一次经济普查资料修订的数据，2005-2008年采用第二次经济普查资料修订的数据，下同。

1-5 续表 2

项目	单位	1978年	1990年	1995年	2000年	2005年	2010年	2011年	2012年
城镇	亿元							1179.00	1263.83
乡村	亿元							87.31	90.74
物价指数(以上年价格为100)									
商品零售物价总指数	%	100.4	94.9	109.7	100.1	103.0	103.2	104.7	102.4
居民消费价格总指数	%		96.6	113.9	101.5	102.4	102.8	104.9	102.9
消费品价格指数	%		94.9	109.7	100.1	103.0	102.8	105.7	103.6
服务项目价格指数	%		111.0	128.9	112.8	100.4	102.6	103.0	101.1
对外经济贸易、旅游									
进出口总额(海关口径)	亿美元		10.82	153.91	320.45	743.72	1213.38	1352.24	1444.16
进口总额	亿美元		5.14	75.92	148.86	334.42	517.40	568.95	593.50
出口总额	亿美元		5.68	77.99	171.59	409.29	695.98	783.29	850.66
#一般贸易	亿美元			2.32	2.09	17.55	95.41	134.11	169.23
来料加工装配	亿美元			43.46	83.43	161.17	195.54	169.35	121.65
进料加工	亿美元			32.02	85.84	230.43	394.62	465.43	539.86
其他	亿美元			0.19	0.22	0.14	10.40	14.39	19.92
新签利用外资协议(合同)数	宗					773	869	1324	690
合同外资金额(新口径)	亿美元					29.80	25.97	35.08	38.10
实际利用外资(新口径)	亿美元					14.68	27.32	30.51	33.69
全年接待旅游人数	万人次		125	89	291	1156	2251	2615	2744
#国际及港澳台旅游者	万人次		27	27	106	169	327	357	415
旅游外汇收入	万美元				7617	28189	67592	90975	126924
财政、金融									
来源于东莞的财政收入	亿元	0.66	3.57	18.01	103.56	331.91	785.10	838.52	845.64
市公共财政预算收入	亿元			11.56	30.47	103.97	277.84	313.06	356.32
市公共财政预算支出	亿元	0.18	2.28	12.42	33.61	117.04	289.83	351.92	385.58
金融机构各项人民币存款余额	亿元	1.05	68.07	383.68	1228.67	2933.40	5943.39	6609.39	7430.46
金融机构各项人民币贷款余额	亿元	1.96	63.04	254.85	630.84	1500.52	3329.82	3716.08	4195.61
人民生活									
全市职工平均工资	元						16108	21739	25658
城镇在岗职工平均工资	元	474	3552	9682	14051	28253	46576	50398	57007
城市居民人均可支配收入	元		2508	9588	14142	22882	35690	39513	42944
城市居民人均消费性支出	元		2038	9220	12529	21768	25733	27495	31369
农民人均纯收入	元	149	1542	4769	8484	13076	20486	22842	24944
城乡居民人民币储蓄存款余额	亿元	0.54	45.51	232.97	672.07	1728.28	3386.85	3710.99	4204.20

注：1. 城镇在岗职工工资总额和人均工资2000年前是城镇职工工资，2000年起是城镇在岗职工工资，不含乡镇及以下办企业职工，下同。
2. 全年接待旅游人数和旅游外汇收入2002年起是旅游局口径，与往年数不可比。
3. 农民人均纯收入采用农村住户抽样调查口径，相应调整了往年数，下同。
4. 1995年及以前年份，来源于东莞的财政收入不含关税，下同。

1-6 主要年份国民经济和社会发展主要比例与效益指标

Main Indicators on National Economy and Social Development in Main Years

项　　目	单 位	1990年	1995年	2000年	2005年	2010年	2011年	2012年
户籍人口								
出生率	‰	17.07	17.59	12.11	10.62	10.90	10.92	13.32
死亡率	‰	4.76	4.84	4.59	4.60	4.68	4.79	5.22
自然增长率	‰	12.31	12.75	7.52	6.02	6.23	6.13	8.10
人口性别比(男/女)	%	97.1	100.4	102.4	103.1	103.1	103.0	103.1
地区生产总值中三次产业比重								
第一产业	%	16.5	7.2	3.2	0.9	0.4	0.4	0.4
第二产业	%	50.4	56.4	54.9	56.2	50.9	49.9	47.4
工　业	%	48.7	52.0	52.5	53.7	48.9	48.3	45.9
建筑业	%	1.7	4.3	2.5	2.5	1.9	1.6	1.6
第三产业	%	33.1	36.4	41.9	42.8	48.7	49.7	52.2
全社会劳动生产率	元/人				59743	70910	75477	79531
(按全社会从业人员、增加值计算)								
第一产业	元/人				14238	24017	29980	31479
第二产业	元/人				50634	51150	49512	49502
第三产业	元/人				86154	122064	163827	181529
农　业								
农林牧渔业总产值结构								
农　业	%	54.9	45.7	39.6	25.5	52.3	52.2	52.9
林　业	%	1.8	2.1	0.7	0.4	1.0	0.7	0.5
牧　业	%	19.2	30.0	41.4	57.7	19.6	20.8	19.8
渔　业	%	13.3	16.1	14.9	14.9	24.0	23.3	23.9
农林牧渔服务业	%				1.5	3.0	3.0	2.9
工　业								
规模以上工业企业效益								
固定资产利税率	%	8.5	10.7	11.5	9.9	26.3	26.5	25.1
资金利税率	%	6.3	7.7	7.5	5.5	7.8	7.3	7.8
产值利税率	%	5.4	10.0	9.2	4.6	6.1	5.7	5.5

注：2003年起新增农林牧渔服务业。

1-6 续表 1

项　　目	单 位	1990年	1995年	2000年	2005年	2010年	2011年	2012年
建筑业								
技术装备率	万元/人		0.37	0.43	0.68	1.02	0.98	1.00
产值利税率	%		3.9	5.4	7.5	8.1	7.4	6.9
劳动生产率(按总产值计算)	元/人	18636	42766	60849	108136	218076	207555	280706
固定资产投资								
固定资产投资相当于地区生产总值比例(投资率)	%	9.3	17.0	12.5	27.4	26.3	22.8	23.6
全社会房屋建筑面积竣工率	%	45.2	34.1	60.7	22.5	20.7	12.8	14.0
财　政								
来源于东莞的财政收入相当于地区生产总值比例	%	4.4	6.1	12.6	15.2	18.5	17.7	16.9
市公共财政预算支出相当于地区生产总值比例	%	2.8	4.2	4.1	5.4	6.5	7.4	7.7
外经外贸								
利用外资结构								
外商直接投资	%	41.2	63.6	66.0	75.2	86.4	94.8	91.7
外商其他投资	%	58.8	36.4	34.0	24.8	13.6	5.2	8.3
实际利用外资额相当于协议规定外商投资额比例(旧口径)	%	80.6	31.9	89.7	78.9	103.0	86.9	89.5
进出口总额比例								
进口总额	%	47.5	49.3	46.5	45.0	42.6	42.1	41.1
出口总额	%	52.5	50.7	53.6	55.0	57.4	57.9	58.9
#一般贸易	%		3.0	1.2	4.3	13.7	17.1	19.9
来料加工装配	%		55.7	48.6	39.4	28.1	21.6	14.3
进料加工	%		41.1	50.0	56.3	56.7	59.4	63.5
其他	%		0.2	0.2		1.5	1.9	2.3
交通运输								
货运量中各种运输方式比例								
公　路	%	58.2	55.7	63.3	71.7	82.0	80.8	75.2
水　运	%	41.8	44.3	36.7	28.3	18.0	19.2	24.8

1-6 续表 2

项　　目	单 位	1990年	1995年	2000年	2005年	2010年	2011年	2012年
金　融								
各项人民币存款相当于生产总值比例	%	84.6	129.5	149.8	134.5	140.0	139.6	148.3
各项人民币贷款相当于生产总值比例	%	78.4	86.0	76.9	68.8	78.4	78.5	83.7
各项人民币存款余额中主要存款比例								
#单位存款	%					40.4	41.4	40.4
财政性存款	%	1.2	2.2	0.3	0.9	0.8	0.5	0.7
储蓄存款	%	66.9	60.7	54.7	58.9	57.0	56.1	56.6
各项人民币贷款余额中主要贷款比例								
#短期贷款	%	90.5	64.6	84.2	48.9	37.1	39.8	41.9
中长期贷款	%	2.1	10.8	7.4	46.7	59.1	55.7	53.3
科技、教育、文化、卫生								
科教文卫事业费占财政支出比例	%	28.7	24.5	25.8	17.8	27.9	34.0	34.0
学龄儿童入学率	%	99.9	100.0	100.0	100.0	100.0	100.0	100.0
小学毕业生升学率	%	95.4	99.2	99.8	99.9	100.0	100.0	100.0
初中毕业生升学率	%	44.1	85.4	90.3	94.1	97.9	98.0	97.8
普通高中毕业生升学率	%	31.2	64.9	70.5	96.5	95.1	94.5	95.9
每一教师负担学生数								
普通高等学校	人		13.7	20.1	15.4	17.6	18.5	19.2
职业技术学校	人	20.6	21.8	19.0	18.2	20.3	20.0	20.5
普通中学	人	20.7	21.1	22.4	19.8	17.7	17.2	16.9
小学	人	24.0	24.2	34.3	27.5	23.3	23.3	24.0
人民生活								
城市居民消费结构								
食品类	%	63.5	39.5	32.3	27.7	33.9	34.6	35.4
衣着类	%	4.7	6.6	3.9	5.9	6.6	6.6	6.8
其　他	%	31.8	53.9	63.8	66.4	59.5	58.8	57.8

1-7 国民经济主要指标分月变化情况（2012年，累计绝对数）

Main Indicators on National Economy by Month (2012, Accumulative Figures in Value Terms)

项　目	单位	1 月	1-2 月	1-3 月	1-4 月	1-5 月	1-6 月
规模以上工业增加值	亿元		250.50	402.26	550.98	646.19	785.04
#国有经济	亿元		15.30	22.42	31.74	43.92	54.77
外资型经济	亿元		190.15	308.09	420.43	485.48	588.07
#民营企业	亿元		49.85	79.28	110.27	128.64	156.69
#五大支柱产业	亿元		173.62	279.29	383.44	436.23	528.12
#四个特色产业	亿元		25.02	43.60	57.96	75.18	91.58
规模以上工业销售产值	亿元		1185.11	1880.94	2615.71	3369.30	4082.48
规模以上工业出口产品产值	亿元		622.54	967.20	1347.74	1761.89	2151.15
规模以上工业产品产销率	%		103.7	100.8	101.7	100.2	100.1
规模以上工业企业主营业务收入	亿元		1150.29	1910.23	2637.50	3380.48	4104.50
规模以上工业企业利润总额	亿元		19.89	38.04	52.68	72.87	94.54
固定资产投资总额	亿元		85.75	174.29	264.68	347.63	443.18
#房地产开发	亿元		44.63	68.37	97.81	129.75	154.31
来源于东莞的财政收入	亿元	95.25	153.56	206.16	281.98	349.20	419.45
市公共财政预算收入	亿元	33.99	63.42	89.45	117.88	144.78	173.23
市公共财政预算支出	亿元	30.40	50.82	77.60	98.09	122.23	151.11
金融机构各项人民币存款余额	亿元	6167.51	6196.02	6657.98	6384.27	6488.36	6913.25
#城乡居民储蓄存款余额	亿元	3540.55	3533.70	3757.38	3602.70	3681.71	3945.78
金融机构各项人民币贷款余额	亿元	3745.62	3758.08	3818.50	3880.92	3935.20	3983.68
进出口总额(海关口径)	亿美元	91.10	186.95	306.85	415.21	539.50	664.48
#出口总额	亿美元	56.64	108.41	177.34	240.71	311.50	385.29
新签项目宗数	宗	63	99	137	186	249	298
合同规定外商投资额	亿美元	4.25	6.93	9.29	12.15	16.02	20.93
实际利用外资	亿美元	2.71	4.62	7.73	10.19	13.48	16.91
社会消费品零售总额	亿元		232.52	336.88	445.92	553.26	669.97
居民消费价格总指数	%	105.0	104.6	104.5	104.4	104.3	104.2
服务项目价格指数	%	104.6	103.7	103.3	103.0	102.7	102.6
总供电量	亿千瓦时	30.46	70.66	118.64	165.85	220.93	277.34
总售电量	亿千瓦时	45.02	74.78	114.58	160.77	207.86	261.43
邮电业务收入	亿元	13.31	26.77	41.78	59.96	71.27	84.59
城市居民人均可支配收入	元			14878			24247
城市居民人均消费性支出	元			8063			15342

注：1. 物价指数以上年同期为100；各项指标1-12月累计不等于年报数。
2. 城市居民收支为季报数据。

1-7　续表

(2012年，累计绝对数)

项　　目	单位	1-7 月	1-8 月	1-9 月	1-10 月	1-11 月	1-12 月
规模以上工业增加值	亿元	935.01	1090.07	1258.58	1409.15	1569.41	1733.12
#国有经济	亿元	66.06	77.52	90.17	100.87	110.89	119.94
外资型经济	亿元	694.72	809.23	934.55	1046.05	1163.58	1283.91
#民营企业	亿元	187.22	218.93	252.01	282.33	316.32	353.07
#五大支柱产业	亿元	628.20	731.71	845.54	946.77	1058.05	1173.41
#四个特色产业	亿元	109.22	127.21	146.07	163.52	181.41	199.56
规模以上工业销售产值	亿元	4852.37	5635.38	6518.45	7293.15	8093.88	8924.31
规模以上工业出口产品产值	亿元	2551.65	2981.56	3395.18	3806.71	4224.24	4652.41
规模以上工业产品产销率	%	100.0	99.6	100.0	99.8	99.8	99.7
规模以上工业企业主营业务收入	亿元	4888.62	5702.15	6536.52	7316.76	8120.62	8938.49
规模以上工业企业利润总额	亿元	116.88	138.86	167.00	193.82	220.23	248.90
固定资产投资总额	亿元	549.05	663.76	822.81	910.87	1006.53	1180.35
#房地产开发	亿元	181.15	204.87	250.72	291.18	319.21	377.32
来源于东莞的财政收入	亿元	509.25	568.94	627.18	717.10	785.16	845.62
市公共财政预算收入	亿元	201.89	229.17	257.84	285.95	319.74	356.32
市公共财政预算支出	亿元	202.78	227.13	265.31	296.82	325.85	385.96
金融机构各项人民币存款余额	亿元	6667.86	6716.70	7015.95	6861.17	6959.90	7430.46
#城乡居民储蓄存款余额	亿元	3791.45	3826.05	3993.72	3880.94	3913.53	4204.20
金融机构各项人民币贷款余额	亿元	4023.25	4078.19	4118.18	4132.45	4140.50	4195.61
进出口总额(海关口径)	亿美元	788.98	920.80	1058.52	1188.22	1312.52	1444.16
#出口总额	亿美元	457.44	536.12	619.06	697.08	766.34	850.66
新签项目宗数	宗	368	425	492	544	610	690
合同规定外商投资额	亿美元	24.24	28.90	31.58	33.13	35.72	38.10
实际利用外资	亿美元	20.61	24.69	28.15	30.38	31.31	33.69
社会消费品零售总额	亿元	781.65	895.47	1008.26	1123.14	1237.69	1354.58
居民消费价格总指数	%	103.9	103.7	103.4	103.1	102.9	102.9
服务项目价格指数	%	102.3	102.2	101.9	101.6	101.3	101.1
总供电量	亿千瓦时	337.94	400.16	455.48	505.72	553.39	600.58
总售电量	亿千瓦时	315.75	373.91	434.95	488.80	539.03	581.18
邮电业务收入	亿元	98.30	112.98	127.21	141.61	156.01	169.96
城市居民人均可支配收入	元			33566			42944
城市居民人均消费性支出	元			23658			31369

1-8 国民经济主要指标分月变化情况（2012年，比上年同期增长）

Main Indicators on National Economy by Month

(2012, Compare with Same Period of Preceding Year %)

项　　目	单位	1 月	1-2 月	1-3 月	1-4 月	1-5 月	1-6 月
规模以上工业增加值	%		-12.5	-1.6	-0.9	0.7	0.9
#国有经济	%		-0.9	6.3	7.6	8.0	8.2
外资型经济	%		-12.4	-0.3	-0.1	1.7	2.1
#民营企业	%		-16.3	-7.4	-5.2	-4.1	-3.9
#五大支柱产业	%		-12.0	-0.6	0.4	2.4	2.5
#四个特色产业	%		-17.0	-0.7	-3.0	-2.8	-1.8
规模以上工业销售产值	%		-11.1	1.1	2.8	3.9	3.5
规模以上工业出口产品产值	%		-9.3	3.5	2.9	5.7	5.6
规模以上工业产品产销率	%		2.4	0.5	2.0	0.6	0.4
规模以上工业企业主营业务收入	%		-17.3	0.9	1.7	3.0	2.6
规模以上工业企业利润总额	%		-62.2	-33.6	-33.2	-29.5	-21.9
固定资产投资总额	%		17.9	10.7	10.2	5.0	3.8
#房地产开发	%		77.2	8.3	5.0	7.6	-0.1
来源于东莞的财政收入	%	-3.8	4.8	0.3	-3.1	-4.1	-1.7
市公共财政预算收入	%	5.4	7.9	10.3	10.5	11.7	10.5
市公共财政预算支出	%	56.9	-18.9	-13.3	-16.9	-14.7	-13.6
金融机构各项人民币存款余额	%	-6.7	-6.3	0.7	-3.4	-1.8	4.6
#城乡居民储蓄存款余额	%	-4.6	-4.8	1.3	-2.9	-0.8	6.3
金融机构各项人民币贷款余额	%	0.8	1.1	2.8	4.4	5.9	7.2
进出口总额(海关口径)	%	-17.8	4.1	5.0	3.2	5.1	6.1
#出口总额	%	-10.6	6.6	7.6	5.9	7.2	7.8
新签项目宗数	%	-24.1	-33.6	-49.1	-55.5	-60.3	-64.8
合同规定外商投资额	%	3.9	14.4	6.5	4.4	2.1	5.3
实际利用外资	%	5.7	5.6	6.0	8.2	10.2	12.8
社会消费品零售总额	%		7.4	11.0	10.7	10.6	10.8
居民消费价格总指数	%	5.0	4.6	4.5	4.4	4.3	4.2
服务项目价格指数	%	4.6	3.7	3.3	3.0	2.7	2.6
总供电量	%	-25.7	0.5	2.0	2.1	3.9	4.0
总售电量	%	-4.3	-10.2	-0.8	0.4	0.8	2.8
邮电业务收入	%	-3.8	2.1	5.3	6.7	6.1	4.8
城市居民人均可支配收入	%			10.2			10.7
城市居民人均消费性支出	%			24.8			20.7

注：存贷款增速为比年初增长，下同。

1-8 续表

(2012年，比上年同期增长)

项　　目	单位	1-7 月	1-8 月	1-9 月	1-10 月	1-11 月	1-12 月
规模以上工业增加值	%	1.6	1.4	3.2	3.2	4.7	5.6
#国有经济	%	8.0	8.0	7.5	7.1	6.7	5.8
外资型经济	%	2.9	2.8	4.9	3.9	4.2	4.5
#民营企业	%	-2.8	-3.2	-1.5	-1.8	0.1	1.8
#五大支柱产业	%	3.1	2.9	5.3	5.1	6.8	7.8
#四个特色产业	%	-1.1	-1.5	-0.8	-1.5	-0.2	1.3
规模以上工业销售产值	%	2.8	3.4	5.2	5.4	4.9	5.3
规模以上工业出口产品产值	%	5.8	5.4	5.6	4.8	5.2	5.5
规模以上工业产品产销率	%	-0.8	0.03	0.1	0.2	0.2	0.1
规模以上工业企业主营业务收入	%	3.3	3.9	3.7	2.7	3.1	3.0
规模以上工业企业利润总额	%	-16.5	-17.0	-14.0	-11.2	-10.2	-7.5
固定资产投资总额	%	8.1	8.7	8.9	9.2	9.2	9.4
#房地产开发	%	-1.4	-7.2	-5.3	-1.7	-1.1	1.1
来源于东莞的财政收入	%	-2.3	-2.1	-3.1	-2.4	-0.4	0.8
市公共财政预算收入	%	11.3	12.9	13.4	13.2	13.6	13.8
市公共财政预算支出	%	4.0	-5.7	2.5	4.0	4.2	8.3
金融机构各项人民币存款余额	%	0.9	1.6	6.2	3.8	5.3	12.4
#城乡居民储蓄存款余额	%	2.2	3.1	7.6	4.6	5.5	13.3
金融机构各项人民币贷款余额	%	8.3	9.7	10.8	11.2	11.4	12.9
进出口总额(海关口径)	%	5.9	5.6	6.2	7.0	6.4	6.8
#出口总额	%	7.4	7.2	8.0	9.1	7.6	8.6
新签项目宗数	%	-61.9	-61.0	-58.7	-56.2	-52.8	-47.9
合同规定外商投资额	%	6.4	6.3	5.1	5.2	5.9	8.6
实际利用外资	%	14.2	14.0	11.8	12.3	11.3	10.5
社会消费品零售总额	%	10.2	10.0	9.6	9.3	9.0	9.3
居民消费价格总指数	%	3.9	3.7	3.4	3.1	2.9	2.9
服务项目价格指数	%	2.3	2.2	1.9	1.6	1.3	1.1
总供电量	%	3.9	3.7	3.6	3.9	3.7	3.7
总售电量	%	3.0	3.1	3.1	3.4	3.4	2.6
邮电业务收入	%	3.6	3.6	3.3	3.5	3.5	3.1
城市居民人均可支配收入	%			9.0			8.7
城市居民人均消费性支出	%			17.7			14.1

1-9 历年地区生产总值

Gross Domestic Product over Years

年　份	地区生产总值（万元）	第一产业	第二产业	第三产业	人均地区生产总值（元）
1978	61122	27235	26781	7106	553
1979	66233	26460	29244	10528	593
1980	72199	26323	33290	12586	643
1981	91131	32772	42980	15379	802
1982	114322	37257	58137	18927	991
1983	130340	39847	68962	21531	1115
1984	159632	45671	78091	35869	1350
1985	226033	61475	116584	47973	1885
1986	300167	81416	135735	83016	2462
1987	392859	98236	177249	117373	3170
1988	554583	118888	282771	152924	4408
1989	609202	126568	279724	202910	4768
1990	804401	132787	405290	266325	6173
1991	959073	134523	503220	321330	5095
1992	1108922	144115	592701	372106	5038
1993	1570491	143953	873114	553424	5850
1994	2170341	174796	1194928	800616	6357
1995	2962892	214306	1669723	1078863	7421
1996	3617502	248645	1994826	1374031	8444
1997	4485981	256388	2432816	1796777	9747
1998	5579964	259437	3056779	2263749	11265
1999	6672386	257863	3670519	2744004	12494
2000	8202530	259087	4507072	3436372	13679
2001	9918905	260968	5405092	4252845	15268
2002	11869374	248791	6488109	5132474	18131
2003	14525186	228165	7981954	6315068	22174
2004	18060258	227087	10160382	7672789	27554
2005	21831961	205546	12278624	9347791	33287
2006	26279791	120089	15065985	11093717	39173
2007	31600489	118991	17546573	13934924	45057
2008	37036004	148251	19016068	17871685	50471
2009	37639142	147877	18230836	19260428	48988
2010	42464527	165719	21608153	20690656	52798
2011	47353949	178776	23662018	23513155	57470
2012	50101727	187556	23756366	26157806	60557

注：1. 地区生产总值绝对值按当年价计算，指数按可比价计算,下同。
2. 人均地区生产总值1990年及以前按户籍人口计算，1991年起按常住人口计算，与以前年份不可比。
3. 人均地区生产总值2006-2010年数据，根据东莞市第六次全国人口普查数据结果重新修订，下同。

1-10 历年地区生产总值指数

Indices of Gross Domestic Product over Years

年份	地区生产总值指数(上年=100)	第一产业	第二产业	第三产业	人均地区生产总值指数(上年=100)	人均地区生产总值指数与地区生产总值指数之比
1979	99.5	86.5	107.0	146.4	98.6	0.991
1980	102.7	90.3	117.3	113.9	102.0	0.993
1981	116.6	115.0	122.1	110.8	115.4	0.989
1982	116.9	105.3	131.0	117.6	115.1	0.985
1983	110.4	104.8	115.7	111.3	108.9	0.987
1984	114.2	109.0	107.0	140.9	112.9	0.988
1985	132.3	118.9	144.5	132.7	130.5	0.986
1986	126.1	111.9	110.3	174.7	124.0	0.983
1987	122.5	111.6	127.7	126.0	120.5	0.984
1988	115.7	90.6	143.7	103.0	114.0	0.985
1989	107.1	99.8	106.2	113.7	105.5	0.985
1990	123.2	104.4	127.6	128.0	120.8	0.980
1991	117.5	103.1	121.5	118.6	108.8	0.926
1992	108.3	100.0	112.6	105.1	92.6	0.855
1993	127.9	79.4	139.2	129.0	104.8	0.820
1994	122.5	107.2	124.7	122.3	96.3	0.786
1995	127.4	110.5	135.1	116.8	108.9	0.855
1996	117.5	109.4	115.5	123.5	109.5	0.932
1997	119.6	104.5	119.8	121.8	111.3	0.931
1998	121.8	100.9	122.1	124.5	113.1	0.929
1999	119.7	102.3	120.6	120.3	111.0	0.928
2000	119.7	99.8	120.7	120.0	106.6	0.891
2001	119.9	103.0	121.6	118.9	110.7	0.923
2002	120.5	97.6	122.6	119.1	119.6	0.992
2003	120.5	90.2	122.3	119.7	120.4	0.999
2004	121.0	90.0	125.6	115.8	120.9	0.999
2005	119.5	102.3	120.0	119.3	119.4	0.999
2006	119.2	58.9	121.9	117.1	116.6	0.978
2007	118.3	89.9	114.8	123.3	113.1	0.957
2008	114.0	110.6	106.1	124.0	109.0	0.956
2009	105.3	102.3	99.7	111.4	100.5	0.955
2010	110.3	101.6	116.7	104.1	105.3	0.955
2011	108.0	100.5	107.0	109.0	105.4	0.976
2012	106.1	100.0	105.8	106.5	105.7	0.996

1-11 历年地区生产总值产业构成

Composition of Gross Domestic Product over Years

单位：%

年 份	地区生产总值	第一产业	第二产业	第三产业
1978	100.0	44.6	43.8	11.6
1979	100.0	40.0	44.2	15.9
1980	100.0	36.5	46.1	17.4
1981	100.0	36.0	47.2	16.9
1982	100.0	32.6	50.9	16.6
1983	100.0	30.6	52.9	16.5
1984	100.0	28.6	48.9	22.5
1985	100.0	27.2	51.6	21.2
1986	100.0	27.1	45.2	27.7
1987	100.0	25.0	45.1	29.9
1988	100.0	21.4	51.0	27.6
1989	100.0	20.8	45.9	33.3
1990	100.0	16.5	50.4	33.1
1991	100.0	14.0	52.5	33.5
1992	100.0	13.0	53.5	33.6
1993	100.0	9.2	55.6	35.2
1994	100.0	8.1	55.1	36.9
1995	100.0	7.2	56.4	36.4
1996	100.0	6.9	55.1	38.0
1997	100.0	5.7	54.2	40.1
1998	100.0	4.7	54.8	40.6
1999	100.0	3.9	55.0	41.1
2000	100.0	3.2	54.9	41.9
2001	100.0	2.6	54.5	42.9
2002	100.0	2.1	54.7	43.2
2003	100.0	1.6	55.0	43.5
2004	100.0	1.3	56.3	42.5
2005	100.0	0.9	56.2	42.8
2006	100.0	0.5	57.3	42.2
2007	100.0	0.4	55.5	44.1
2008	100.0	0.4	51.3	48.3
2009	100.0	0.4	48.4	51.2
2010	100.0	0.4	50.9	48.7
2011	100.0	0.4	49.9	49.7
2012	100.0	0.4	47.4	52.2

1-12 各行业增加值项目（2012年）

Composition of Value-added by Industry (2012)

单位:万元

项　　　目	增加值	劳动者报　酬	生产税净　额	固定资产折　　旧	营业盈余
地区生产总值	50101727	24234022	6323853	9080424	10463428
第一产业	187556	172882		14674	
第二产业	23756366	13262112	2885532	2989523	4619199
工业	22975137	12843167	2735064	2929839	4467067
建筑业	781228	418945	150468	59684	152132
第三产业	26157806	10784355	3438321	6090901	5844229
交通运输、仓储和邮政业	1360939	510005	88635	445279	317020
交通运输和仓储业	1296249	481747	85900	437316	291285
邮政业	64690	28257	2734	7963	25735
信息传输、计算机服务和软件业	1998316	355610	111052	338831	1192822
批发和零售业	5021959	2354644	2127246	220078	319991
住宿和餐饮业	1679436	1372849	80928	204931	20728
金融业	1999080	627469	250144	37766	1083701
#银行业	1717326	536546	166127	33888	980765
房地产业	4653249	392437	512027	3085195	663591
房地产开发经营	1266871	263831	434081	21918	547042
物业管理	274161	94944	18302	135868	25048
房地产中介服务	31196	14357	4172	4258	8409
其他房地产活动	228430	19304	55472	70560	83092
居民自有住房服务	2852591			2852591	
租赁和商务服务业	5189197	2148557	169433	888037	1983169
科学研究、技术服务和地质勘查业	327383	97099	15697	133944	80643
水利、环境和公共设施管理业	111429	53219	4004	32707	21498
居民服务和其他服务业	929517	765807	27987	81868	53854
教育	935165	755165	4809	164283	10908
卫生、社会保障和社会福利业	602006	451981	9484	61250	79290
文化、体育和娱乐业	286654	141154	36117	92370	17013
#娱乐业	180503	85124	29069	74203	-7893
公共管理和社会组织	1063476	758358	758	304359	

1-13 主要年份支出法地区生产总值

Gross Domestic Product by Expenditure Approach in Main Years

项　目	1995年	2000年	2005年	2010年	2011年	2012年
支出法地区生产总值(万元)	2962892	8202530	21831961	42464527	47353949	50101727
最终消费	1502524	4342481	11201390	22984391	26194232	27381203
资本形成总额	1210079	2369818	7148513	12757774	12692672	13614456
货物和服务净出口	250290	1490232	3482058	6722362	8467045	9106068
资本形成率(投资率)(%)	40.8	28.9	32.7	30.0	26.8	27.2
最终消费率(消费率)(%)	50.7	52.9	51.3	54.1	55.3	54.7

1-14 主要年份资本形成总额及构成

Gross Capital Formation and Its Composition in Main Years

项　目		1995年	2000年	2005年	2010年	2011年	2012年
资本形成总额(万元)		1210079	2369818	7148513	12757774	12692672	13614456
固定资产形成总额		884671	1775228	6115306	10513989	11221377	12071618
存货增加		325407	594590	1033207	2243785	1471295	1542838
比重(资本形成总额=100)	固定资产形成总额	73.1	74.9	85.5	82.4	88.4	88.7
	存货增加	26.9	25.1	14.5	17.6	11.6	11.3

1-15 主要年份最终消费支出及构成

Final Consumption Expenditure and Its Composition in Main Years

项　目		1995年	2000年	2005年	2010年	2011年	2012年
最终消费(万元)		1502524	4342481	11201390	22984391	26194232	27381203
居民消费		1262972	3752814	9798031	19852461	22421136	23421319
政府消费		239552	589666	1403359	3131930	3773095	3959884
比重(最终消费=100)	居民消费	84.1	86.4	87.5	86.4	85.6	85.5
	政府消费	15.9	13.6	12.5	13.6	14.4	14.5

1-16 全市企业和个体工商户登记注册年末实有数量（2005-2012年）

Enterprises and Self-employed Individuals Registered at Year-end (2005-2012)

单位：户

项　　目	2005年	2006年	2007年	2008年	2009年	2010年	2011年	2012年
工商登记户数合计	353266	403403	476125	504978	505502	518513	506061	540104
内资企业	13898	12953	13401	13074	12493	12439	12820	13264
#国有	1977	1554	1404	1313	1141	1058	1014	1005
集体	6478	4989	4487	3385	2899	2180	1968	1846
有限责任公司	1606	1468	1493	7017	7886	7649	8271	8767
外商投资企业	7675	7695	7973	9437	9748	10113	11240	11974
#合资	1013	822	718	860	1206	1120	1197	1243
合作	482	379	307	218	197	179	177	167
独资	6177	6492	6946	6956	7678	8280	9492	10243
“三来一补”企业	9552	8206	7417	6552	5748	4906	4047	3231
私营企业	29017	38282	48955	63241	74229	88650	104689	122703
个体工商户	293124	336267	398379	412674	403284	402405	373265	388932

注：本表数据来源于市工商局。

1-17 个体工商户情况（2012年）

Statistics on Self-employed Individuals (2012)

项　　目	户　数（户）	从业人员（人）	资金数额（万元）	其中城镇		
				户　数（户）	从业人员（人）	资金数额（万元）
合　　计	388932	886813	910823	203703	434763	448696
农、林、牧、渔业	226	784	3683	85	288	577
工　业	65746	277252	304290	24507	100825	111192
建筑业	604	1544	2514	346	842	1159
交通运输、仓储和邮政业	1702	4494	6014	963	2437	3177
信息传输、计算机服务和软件业	1573	2506	1370	877	1304	765
批发和零售业	258931	443756	422739	143699	241307	234465
住宿和餐饮业	27512	77641	86526	15213	43905	50421
房地产业	35	70	89	28	56	69
租赁和商务服务业	3293	7330	8699	1980	4385	5035
居民服务和其他服务业	28584	69100	66978	15563	37950	36574
卫生、社会保障和社会福利业	29	63	111	25	53	90
文化、体育和娱乐业	420	1599	6991	271	1058	4725
其他行业	277	674	819	146	353	447

注：本表数据来源于市工商局。

1-18 私营工商企业基本情况（2012年）

Basic Statistics on Private Industrial & Commercial Enterprises (2012)

项目	户数（户）	投资者人数（人）	雇工人数（人）	注册资本（万元）	其中：1. 独资企业			
					户数（户）	投资者人数（人）	雇工人数（人）	注册资本（万元）
合计	122703	231728	722605	15269267	8451	8318	76683	288478
农、林、牧、渔业	595	975	8809	90083	287	281	6418	24183
工业	45159	88505	294433	4588749	4339	4332	44594	117306
建筑业	5619	10288	32621	1064686	25	25	115	240
交通运输、仓储和邮政业	2186	3946	11375	306890	20	20	96	226
信息传输、计算机服务和软件业	2181	4059	14145	270533	511	506	4923	50901
批发和零售业	40735	73905	212736	3341889	1737	1698	5759	15044
住宿和餐饮业	1362	2120	15417	213904	417	397	5067	46428
房地产业	3292	6395	17007	1049143	4	4	14	33
租赁和商务服务业	11512	23402	58226	2468599	283	268	972	3286
居民服务和其他服务业	4631	7328	26223	279417	583	544	5351	15461
卫生、社会保障和社会福利业	25	42	316	17233				
文化、体育和娱乐业	1103	1991	8217	107602	211	211	3198	14552
其他行业	4303	8772	23080	1470539	34	32	176	818

1-18 续表

项目	2. 合伙企业				3. 有限责任公司			
	户数（户）	投资者人数（人）	雇工人数（人）	注册资本（万元）	户数（户）	投资者人数（人）	雇工人数（人）	注册资本（万元）
合计	990	2718	7414	264033	112971	219746	636473	14253050
农、林、牧、渔业	82	206	1195	5576	223	464	1089	45584
工业	342	831	3001	21008	40430	83012	245929	4252645
建筑业	1	3	5	25	5582	10260	32436	1064422
交通运输、仓储和邮政业	4	10	12	145	2159	3914	11252	306019
信息传输、计算机服务和软件业	140	322	867	13980	1514	3222	8254	201319
批发和零售业	85	186	332	3299	38829	71590	206352	3251770
住宿和餐饮业	62	151	736	10400	882	1572	9606	157075
房地产业	4	11	12	30	3279	6373	16965	1032152
租赁和商务服务业	162	697	588	200085	11039	22360	56542	2197088
居民服务和其他服务业	68	164	493	2790	3968	6617	20352	260167
卫生、社会保障和社会福利业					24	42	311	17233
文化、体育和娱乐业	27	62	132	1878	864	1718	4879	91172
其他行业	13	75	41	4817	4178	8602	22506	1376404

注：本表数据来源于市工商局。

1-19 历年总供售电

Gross Electricity Supply over Years

单位：万千瓦时

年 份	总供电量	#网供	总售电量	#工业用电	#农村工业用电	照明用电
1978	16375	16376	14909	10828		1741
1979	19271	19271	17325	12474		2338
1980	21659	21569	19663	13407		3372
1981	22247	22247	19902	14194		4650
1982	26871	26351	23502	14618		6272
1983	31527	31527	27461	17496		8052
1984	32617	28566	28403	18019		9484
1985	38183	33907	33907	22139		9934
1986	39305	35100	35099	25567		10204
1987	64258	45129	57083	38076		16657
1988	94842	66295	84738	60226		22347
1989	120861	76762	108387	80050	60116	26139
1990	180142	111800	161479	119322	70459	39677
1991	240471	139841	216657	157062	99767	56504
1992	320003	180902	288688	210373	144391	25578
1993	436231	242205	393962	287400	205687	103583
1994	585763	393312	530232	416128	297479	110357
1995	680030	384764	616788	487873	386413	125135
1996	800300	506062	727093	569317	423898	153093
1997	949296	612907	866456	702811	519325	180583
1998	1094816	724758	1009086	781811	597601	221750
1999	1327788	973427	1234183	965945	756713	261629
2000	1780290	1349134	1690557	1345766	1104301	337044
2001	2077248	1649458	1965858	1567083	1400915	584700
2002	2585474	2219054	2471342	2070709	1877278	392879
2003	3216468	2846679	2835389	2401970	2071712	424869
2004	3728441	3196454	3502821	2966131	2539962	527332
2005	4156629	3422603	3965892	3303140	2873734	652514
2006	4644506	3676492	4455157	3686266	3234929	759384
2007	5078933	4167125	4825614	3956118	3483474	859851
2008	5073489	4423085	4873204	3928108	3424868	935510
2009	4888467	4318868	4781895	3761046	3292716	1011494
2010	5568902	5473261	5436637	4355690	3841990	1070692
2011	5793482	5699321	5666889	4457615	3919883	1196914
2012	6005828	5911793	5811757	4522891	4316008	1274923

1-20 历年国民经济主要指标人均水平

The Per Capita Level of Main National Economic Indicators over Years

年 份	人均地区生产总值（元）	人均地方财政收入（元）	人均出口总 额（美元）	人均消费品零售额（元）	人均固定资产投资额（元）	人 均用电量（千瓦时）	年末人均储蓄存款余额（元）
1978	553	60	36	192	21	135	49
1979	593	59	48	224	15	155	64
1980	643	60	69	281	21	175	104
1981	802	60	81	354	33	175	178
1982	991	70	94	417	157	204	238
1983	1115	73	102	447	157	235	328
1984	1350	72	110	625	254	240	520
1985	1885	93	146	781	589	283	761
1986	2462	132	191	1004	945	288	1068
1987	3170	163	216	1214	1145	461	1519
1988	4408	215	253	1959	1315	674	1965
1989	4768	250	273	2116	392	848	2529
1990	6173	274	436	2454	576	1239	2592
1991	5095	236	879	1943	732	1154	3074
1992	5038	263	1217	2073	883	1350	3580
1993	5850	385	1318	2615	1345	1617	4131
1994	6357	277	1548	3070	5074	1911	5130
1995	7421	366	2468	3577	1998	1952	6924
1996	8444	268	2553	3489	1879	2021	8300
1997	9747	278	2774	3564	1608	2114	9758
1998	11265	324	2799	3753	1650	2162	10740
1999	12494	344	2851	3806	1662	2322	10890
2000	13679	503	2834	3884	1700	2792	10422
2001	15268	693	2923	4244	1932	3026	12212
2002	18131	845	3626	4907	2926	3775	15297
2003	22174	1030	4275	5645	4876	4329	18788
2004	27554	1261	5369	6506	6940	5344	21836
2005	33287	1585	6240	7719	9106	6047	26343
2006	39173	1922	7062	8934	10516	6641	29364
2007	45057	2658	8588	10301	11994	6881	29577
2008	50471	2851	8931	12008	12869	6641	35146
2009	48988	3009	7180	12482	14239	6224	36950
2010	52798	3455	8653	13777	13863	6760	41179
2011	57470	3799	9506	15368	13099	6877	44956
2012	60557	4307	10282	16372	14267	7025	50700

注：1. 人均指标1991年以前按户籍人口计算，1991年起按常住人口计算；时点数按年末人口计算，时期数按年平均人口计算。
2. 人均指标2006-2010年数据，根据东莞市第六次全国人口普查数据结果重新修订，下同。

主要统计指标解释

Explanatory Notes on Main Statistical Indicators

国内（地区）生产总值 指按市场价格计算的一个国家（或地区）所有常住单位在一定时期内生产活动的最终成果。国内（地区）生产总值有三种计算方法，即生产法、收入法和支出法。三种方法分别从不同的方面反映国内（地区）生产总值及其构成。

增加值 指常住单位生产过程创造的新增价值和固定资产的转移价值。它可以按生产法计算，也可以按收入法计算，按生产法计算，它等于总产出减去中间投入；按收入法计算，它等于劳动者报酬、生产税净额、固定资产折旧和营业盈余之和。

劳动者报酬 指劳动者因从事生产活动所获得的全部报酬，包括劳动者获得的各种形式的工资、奖金和津贴，既包括货币形式的，也包括实物形式的，还包括劳动者所享受的公费医疗和医药卫生费、上下班交通补贴和单位支付的社会保险费、住房公积金等。对于个体经济来说，其所有者所获得的劳动报酬和经营利润不易区分，这两部分统一作为劳动者报酬处理。

生产税净额 指生产税减生产补贴后的差额。生产税指政府对生产单位从事生产、销售和经营活动以及因从事生产活动使用某些生产要素（如固定资产、土地、劳动力）所征收的各种税、附加费和规费。生产补贴与生产税相反，指政府对生产单位的单方面转移支付，因此视为负生产税，包括政策性亏损补贴、价格补贴等。

固定资产折旧 指一定时期内为弥补固定资产损耗按照规定的固定资产折旧率提取的固定资产折旧，或按国民经济核算统一规定的折旧率虚拟计算的固定资产折旧。它反映了固定资产在当期生产中的转移价值。各类企业和企业化管理的事业单位的固定资产折旧是指实际计提的折旧费；不计提折旧的政府机关、非企业化管理的事业单位和居民住房的固定资产折旧是按照统一规定的折旧率和固定资产原值计算的虚拟折旧。

营业盈余 指常住单位创造的增加值扣除劳动者报酬、固定资产折旧和生产税净额后的余额。它相当于企业的营业利润加上生产补贴，但要扣除从利润中开支的工资和福利等。

三次产业 根据社会生产活动历史发展的顺序对产业结构的划分，产品直接取自自然界的部门称为第一产业，初级产品进行再加工的部门称为第二产业，为生产和消费提供各种服务的部门称为第三产业。它是世界上通用的产业结构分类，但各国的划分不尽一致。我国的三次产业划分是：

第一产业：农林牧渔业

第二产业：工业（包括采矿业，制造业，电力、燃气及水的生产和供应业）和建筑业。

第三产业：除第一、二产业以外的其他行业。第三产业包括：交通运输、仓储和邮政业，信息传输、计算机服务和软件业，批发和零售业，住宿和餐饮业，金融业，房地产业，租赁和商务服务业，科学研究、技术服务和地质勘查业，水利、环境和公共设施管理业，居民服务和其他服务业，教育，卫生、社会保障和社会福利业，文化、体育和娱乐业，公共管理和社会组织，国际组织。

发展速度 用以反映社会经济发展程度的相对指标，根据两个时期发展水平的对比而得。由于比较的标准时期不同，发展速度可分为定基发展速度和环比发展速度两种。

增长速度 发展速度 - 1（或 100%）就是增长速度。即增长速度=发展速度 - 1（或 100%）。

平均每年增长速度 我国计算平均增长速度有两种方法，一种是习惯上经常使用的“水平法”，又称几何平均法，是以间隔最后一年的水平同基期水平对比来计算平均每年增长（或下降）的速度；另一种是“累计法”又称代数平均法或方程法，是以间隔年内各年水平的总和同基期水平对比来计算平均每年增长（或下降）的速度。具体计算方法，可参照中国财经出版社出版的《平均增长速度查对表》。

在一般正常情况下，两种方法计算的平均每年增长速度比较接近，但在经济发展不平衡出现大起大落时，两种方法计算的结果差别较大。

本《年鉴》内所列的平均每年增长速度都是用水平法计算的。从某年到某年平均增长速度的年份，均不包基期年在内。如 1981-2012 年平均每年增长速度，是以 1980 年为基期，2012 年为报告期，年份从 1981 年算起，共 32 年。

二、人口与劳动力

Population and Labor Force

2-1 历年总人口数与人口密度

Total Population and Density over Years

单位：万人

年份	户籍人口	按性别分		按农业、非农业分		外来暂住人口	常住人口	人口密度（人/平方公里）
		男	女	农业人口	非农业人口			
1949	68.24	32.87	35.37	56.29	11.95			
1952	71.68	34.53	37.15	58.69	12.99			
1957	77.48	37.50	39.98	62.52	14.96			
1962	79.64	38.07	41.57	64.42	15.22			
1965	86.46	41.83	44.63	70.28	16.18			
1970	98.56	47.91	50.65	81.26	17.30			
1975	107.94	52.70	55.24	90.37	17.57			
1978	111.23	54.34	56.89	92.74	18.29			451
1979	112.04	54.45	57.59	92.86	19.18			455
1980	112.70	54.43	58.27	92.87	19.83			457
1981	114.46	55.36	59.10	94.08	20.38			464
1982	116.19	56.28	59.91	95.32	20.87			471
1983	117.59	57.05	60.54	96.36	21.23			477
1984	118.95	57.80	61.15	96.47	22.48			483
1985	120.85	58.84	62.01	95.36	25.49			490
1986	123.01	59.95	63.06	96.53	26.48	15.62		499
1987	124.86	61.02	63.84	97.20	27.66	25.29		507
1988	126.76	62.09	64.67	97.96	28.80	36.89		514
1989	128.76	63.27	65.49	98.82	29.94	47.19		522
1990	131.85	64.96	66.89	100.99	30.86	65.59	175.62	712
1991	133.65	66.10	67.55	101.79	31.86	80.58	200.01	811
1992	136.06	67.55	68.51	103.35	32.71	114.48	227.78	924
1993	138.92	69.20	69.72	105.18	33.74	121.70	259.41	1052
1994	141.40	70.64	70.76	106.85	34.55	139.09	295.43	1198
1995	143.65	71.97	71.68	108.27	35.38	142.18	336.45	1365
1996	145.25	72.92	72.33	109.11	36.14	143.32	383.17	1554
1997	147.12	74.04	73.08	110.15	36.97	144.68	436.38	1770
1998	148.77	74.99	73.78	110.93	37.84	199.11	496.97	2016
1999	150.82	76.18	74.64	112.09	38.73	244.81	565.98	2296
2000	152.61	77.22	75.39	113.00	39.61	254.72	644.84	2616
2001	153.89	77.94	75.95	113.52	40.37	457.82	654.43	2655
2002	156.19	79.14	77.05	115.17	41.02	433.65	654.84	2657
2003	158.96	80.65	78.31	102.09	56.87	440.45	655.25	2658
2004	161.97	82.25	79.72	100.49	61.48	486.95	655.66	2660
2005	165.65	84.07	81.58	99.81	65.84	584.98	656.07	2662
2006	168.31	85.43	82.88	97.89	70.42	586.76	685.66	2782
2007	171.26	87.00	84.26	97.59	73.67	557.80	717.02	2909
2008	174.86	88.88	85.98	98.06	76.80	552.50	750.60	3045
2009	178.73	90.78	87.95	97.27	81.46	429.96	786.08	3189
2010	181.77	92.27	89.50	89.68	92.09	411.47	822.48	3343
2011	184.77	93.76	91.01	90.31	94.46	413.62	825.48	3356
2012	187.02	94.92	92.10	91.05	95.96	416.74	829.23	3371

注：1. 人口密度1990年以前户籍人口计算，1990年起按常住人口计算。
2. 常住人口2006-2010年数据，根据东莞市第六次全国人口普查数据结果重新修订，下同。

2-2 主要年份户籍人口与劳动力指标

Main Indicators of Household Population and Labor in Main Years

指　　标	单 位	1990年	1995年	2000年	2005年	2010年	2011年	2012年
年末户籍人口	人	1318526	1436525	1526090	1656541	1817709	1847691	1870159
#农业人口	人	1009857	1082703	1130002	998159	896789	903139	910525
人口性别比(女性人口=100)	%	97.1	100.4	102.4	103.1	103.1	103.0	103.1
人口密度	人/平方公里	535	583	619	672	739	751	760
人口出生率	‰	17.1	17.6	12.1	10.6	10.9	10.9	13.3
人口死亡率	‰	4.8	4.8	4.6	4.6	4.7	4.8	5.2
人口自然增长率	‰	12.3	12.8	7.5	6.0	6.2	6.1	8.1
人口净迁移率	‰	1.9	1.9	2.2	16.4	12.0	11.5	6.6
城镇新登记的失业人员人数	人		6536	6524	7080	3207	5545	3153
城镇失业人员安置就业人数	人			5683	6088	3796	11345	10165

2-3 历年户籍人口自然变动情况

Changes of Household Population over Years

年 份	出 生		死 亡		自然增长	
	人 数（人）	出生率（‰）	人 数（人）	死亡率（‰）	人 数（人）	自然增长率（‰）
1978	20728	18.73	5451	4.92	15277	13.81
1979	26931	24.13	5755	5.13	21176	19.00
1980	27428	24.41	5747	5.10	21681	19.31
1981	24828	21.86	6016	5.29	18812	16.57
1982	21991	19.07	5681	4.93	16310	14.14
1983	19573	16.74	6100	5.21	13473	11.53
1984	18380	15.54	5841	4.94	12539	10.60
1985	18432	15.37	5439	4.54	12993	10.83
1986	20049	16.44	5955	4.88	14094	11.56
1987	19962	16.11	5502	4.44	14459	11.67
1988	21077	16.75	5863	4.66	15214	12.09
1989	23457	17.06	5966	4.67	17491	12.39
1990	22238	17.07	6208	4.76	16030	12.31
1991	23771	17.91	6070	4.57	17701	13.34
1992	26040	19.31	6485	4.81	19555	14.50
1993	25270	18.38	6833	4.97	18437	13.41
1994	24152	17.88	6319	4.51	17833	13.37
1995	25312	17.59	6898	4.84	18414	12.75
1996	24635	17.05	7333	5.08	17302	11.97
1997	24106	16.50	6448	4.41	17658	12.09
1998	22563	15.31	6553	4.45	16010	10.86
1999	21673	14.55	6460	4.34	15213	10.22
2000	18260	12.11	6923	4.59	11337	7.52
2001	17083	11.16	6344	4.14	10739	7.01
2002	16029	10.35	6873	4.44	9156	5.91
2003	16204	10.34	7346	4.69	8858	5.65
2004	17312	10.86	7814	4.90	9498	5.96
2005	17301	10.62	7497	4.60	9804	6.02
2006	16819	10.14	7103	4.28	9716	5.86
2007	17482	10.39	7418	4.41	10064	5.98
2008	18382	10.77	7752	4.54	10630	6.23
2009	18584	10.67	7587	4.36	10997	6.31
2010	19509	10.90	8367	4.68	11142	6.23
2011	19884	10.92	8728	4.79	11156	6.13
2012	24712	13.32	9684	5.22	15028	8.10

2-4 历年户籍人口迁移变动情况

Changes of Household Migration over Years

年 份	迁 入		迁 出		总迁移		净迁移	
	人 数（人）	迁入率（‰）	人 数（人）	迁出率（‰）	人 数（人）	总迁移率（‰）	人 数（人）	净迁移率（‰）
1978	10148	9.2	13179	11.9	23327	21.1	-3031	-2.7
1980	13345	11.9	28624	25.5	41969	37.4	-15279	-13.6
1985	19205	16.0	15636	13.0	34841	29.1	3569	3.0
1990	13485	10.4	11061	8.5	24546	18.8	2424	1.9
1991	12628	9.5	12531	9.4	25159	19.0	97	0.1
1992	14622	10.8	11168	8.3	25790	19.1	3454	2.5
1993	10801	7.9	4886	3.6	15687	11.4	5915	4.3
1994	10127	7.2	6406	4.6	16533	11.8	3721	2.7
1995	10312	7.2	7675	5.4	17987	12.6	2637	1.9
1996	9273	6.4	11508	8.0	20781	14.4	-2235	-1.6
1997	10284	7.0	9469	6.5	19753	13.5	815	0.6
1998	12400	8.4	11253	7.6	23653	16.0	1147	0.8
1999	15049	10.0	11497	7.6	26546	17.6	3552	2.4
2000	15618	10.2	12314	8.1	27932	18.3	3304	2.2
2001	15968	10.4	11099	7.2	27067	17.6	4869	3.2
2002	20214	12.9	8033	5.1	28247	18.1	12181	7.8
2003	27143	17.1	7173	4.5	34316	21.6	19970	12.6
2004	29621	18.3	7618	4.7	37239	23.0	22003	13.6
2005	43026	26.0	15798	9.5	58824	35.5	27228	16.4
2006	30710	18.2	11442	6.8	42152	25.0	19268	11.4
2007	26940	15.7	4847	2.8	31787	18.6	22093	12.9
2008	33595	19.2	5974	3.4	39569	22.6	27621	15.8
2009	36387	20.4	7381	4.1	43768	24.5	29006	16.2
2010	28534	15.7	6651	3.7	35185	19.4	21883	12.0
2011	28623	15.5	7425	4.0	36048	19.5	21198	11.5
2012	20698	11.1	8326	4.5	29024	15.5	12372	6.6

2-5 历年外来暂住人口与外来劳动力
Temporary Residents and Labor over Years

单位：人

年 份	外来暂住人口总计	按性别分		按省内省外分						
		男 性	女 性	本 省	外 省	#湖南省	四川省	广 西 自治区	湖北省	江西省
1986	156222									
1987	252895									
1988	368913									
1989	481850									
1990	655902			333180	322722					
1991	805790			360379	445411					
1992	1144753	440500	704253	494278	650475					
1993	1217010	529096	687914	370770	846240					
1994	1390884	547435	843449	380790	1010094	257348	227793	139137	66189	60638
1995	1421754	581304	840450	371816	1023510	253574	223727	149478	84727	67562
1996	1433157	606524	826633	305821	1106749	232329	223315	137933	90528	79730
1997	1446830	554193	892637	298510	1130981	243384	227077	140483	89140	83272
1998	1991122	850266	1140856	402267	1569963	330241	294149	183734	143662	118685
1999	2448134	1084492	1363642	504722	1921206	391491	387730	236936	173787	149000
2000	2547221	1155277	1391944	485889	2041959	377257	319039	240923	196697	157323
2001	4578163	2138218	2439945	731931	3826830	718295	622166	442904	359872	294740
2002	4336453	1973316	2363137	722894	3593034	685311	555569	394088	389735	294086
2003	4404467	2198324	2206143	665549	3720408	663487	591145	432738	443603	339518
2004	4869462	2347115	2522347	747804	4096599	812976	581272	483329	490063	329715
2005	5849785	2746833	3102952	1036417	4747692	844053	642170	574634	514760	376526
2006	5867555	2775718	3091837	1012637	4807064	875904	617644	556961	531987	367094
2007	5577988	2666292	2911696	986062	4551507	816688	553907	497438	521529	355798
2008	5525022	2657712	2867310	1012341	4468505	828779	533496	488226	517519	353738
2009	4299615	2093055	2206560	889160	3367565	604891	441758	396425	391650	269133
2010	4114745	2010869	2103876	791665	3275768	587153	411005	405051	353414	252936
2011	4136177	2054179	2081998	900560	3194930	571601	370717	387198	350490	264965
2012	4167396	2072592	2094804	940956	3183488	587921	387226	398858	352191	236544

2-5 续表

单位：人

年 份			外来劳动力	工 业	农 业	商 业	服务业
	港澳台	国外					
1986			104091	87154	9849	2509	4579
1987			180285	154842	13110	4181	8152
1988			292499	260237	16911	5797	9554
1989			405287	365840	19893	7763	11791
1990			572044	518971	25576	10793	16704
1991			701982	633400	25838	17945	24799
1992			1071048	874149	62324	88087	46488
1993			1126813	933147	40177	88524	64965
1994	21213	2703	1241814	1069478	52146	39869	80321
1995	23729	2699	1265368	1084860	54714	52965	72829
1996	18094	2493	1276626	1084330	64732	61092	66472
1997	16048	1291	1307279	1114235	57214	67242	68588
1998	17557	1335	1831939	1577922	68143	100041	85833
1999	20664	1542	2161487	1609539	113324	282938	155686
2000	17547	1826	2448415	2043270	88195	187015	129935
2001	17975	1427	4496771	3681099	174936	283277	357459
2002	18856	1669	4260142	3573355	127584	300642	258561
2003	16986	1524	4327312	3753904	85109	278632	209667
2004	21700	3359	4733903	4078400	98272	315021	242210
2005	59798	5878	5534248	4676454	107933	420810	329051
2006	44653	3201	5669798	4820388	124942	412180	312288
2007	36321	4098	5389490	4480800	102519	460114	346057
2008	37329	6847	5303008	4227211	97597	560345	417855
2009	35630	7260	4134581	3361306	74982	430183	268110
2010	37665	9647	3912274	3191436	92451	402786	225601
2011	31731	8956	3947135	3277984	82025	358941	228185
2012	34069	8883	3979414	3278448	85557	390327	225082

2-6　主要年份城镇在岗职工年末人数

Number of Employed Persons in Urban Areas at Year-end in Main Years

单位：人

项　　目	1985年	1990年	1995年	2000年	2005年	2010年	2011年	2012年
合　　计	122951	131631	178724	164080	188579	226268	246083	250225
第一产业	2432	2053	620	476	483	625	966	925
第二产业	64525	72993	110885	76153	80596	87136	82164	85582
工　业	60571	68508	105782	68354	79359	84992	80648	82647
采矿业			130	62	59	52	54	55
制造业			99194	62790	71569	77544	72885	76947
电力、热力、燃气及水的生产和供应业			6458	5502	7731	7396	7709	5645
建筑业			5103	7799	1237	2144	1516	2935
第三产业	55994	56585	67219	87451	107500	138507	162953	163718
#金融业	2270	4291	9487	13945	16584	20706	28004	27976
房地产业	1551	2529	73	387	427	488	490	489
公共管理、社会保障和社会组织	5854	7887	9711	15733	28542	41676	43341	47107

注：2000年以前为年末城镇职工人数，下同。

2-7 历年分行业城镇在岗职工人数

Numbers of Employers by Sector in Urban Areas over Years

单位：人

年 份	年末城镇在岗职工人数合计	第一产业	第二产业	#工业	第三产业
1978	81971	2875	41179	38729	37917
1979	96807	3051	44905	42251	48851
1980	98587	2637	47374	44737	48576
1981	106626	2897	52638	50370	51091
1982	114119	2133	56391	52418	55595
1983	115926	1978	58139	53246	55809
1984	117627	1933	59129	54916	56565
1985	122951	2432	64525	60571	55994
1986	132744	2252	73922	65674	56570
1987	136666	2359	76393	69985	57914
1988	127098	2702	69385	64631	55011
1989	131039	2397	73042	68738	55600
1990	131631	2053	72993	68508	56585
1991	145873	2083	84992	79389	58798
1992	154712	2043	89713	82611	62956
1993	176578	1933	107296	92212	67349
1994	160872	621	95378	83322	64873
1995	178724	620	110885	105782	67219
1996	174964	497	98061	91228	76406
1997	164987	616	82513	76619	81858
1998	164047	779	80510	70499	82758
1999	163917	583	76905	68860	86429
2000	164080	476	76153	68354	87451
2001	164226	444	76181	69260	87601
2002	164209	431	75384	68348	88394
2003	165978	522	73357	72118	92099
2004	175415	565	78003	76786	96847
2005	188579	483	80596	79359	107500
2006	199878	483	84618	83328	114777
2007	205640	487	81448	79949	123705
2008	207234	459	77982	76563	128793
2009	225990	477	94365	92943	131148
2010	226268	625	87136	84992	138507
2011	246083	966	82164	80648	162953
2012	250225	925	85582	82647	163718

2-8 主要年份国有单位分行业年末城镇在岗职工人数

Number of Employed Persons in Urban State-owned Units at Year-end by Sector in Main Years

单位：人

指　　标	1985年	1990年	1995年	2000年	2005年	2010年	2011年	2012年
合　　计	56534	63469	71165	78216	94902	121690	137735	145038
按企业、事业、机关单位分								
企业	40201	43538	38022	31988	20401	20348	27928	29299
事业	11362	13072	23147	31506	46382	60310	67531	70120
机关	4971	6859	9996	14722	28119	41032	42276	45619
按国民经济行业分								
第一产业	2264	1956	712	476	483	625	966	925
第二产业	22373	22877	17363	11658	4442	4888	4985	5286
工　业	20919	19390	14610	10119	3471	3638	3735	3728
采矿业	423	72	130	62	59	52	54	55
制造业	19625	16912	12908	6611	1217	981	1007	989
电力、热力、燃气及水的生产和供应业	871	2406	1572	3446	2195	2605	2674	2684
建筑业	1454	3487	2753	1539	971	1250	1250	1558
第三产业	31897	38571	53090	66082	89977	116177	131784	138827
交通运输、仓储和邮政业					3381	2182	5129	5232
信息传输、软件和信息技术服务业					2243	2275	2274	2273
批发和零售业					1582	1790	1641	2440
住宿和餐饮业								
金融业	943	2215	5634	7343	9401	9319	13921	14117
房地产业	138	149	44	98	244	329	336	342
租赁和商务服务业					676	1437	1441	1445
科学研究和技术服务					1496	1928	2075	1936
水利、环境和公共设施管理业					484	542	596	541
居民服务、修理和其他服务业					95	105	157	153
教育					23301	26138	26314	27400
卫生和社会工作					17134	26795	32860	34143
文化、体育和娱乐业					1398	1661	1699	1698
公共管理、社会保障和社会组织	4971	6859	9563	15372	28542	41676	43341	47107
国际组织								

2-9 主要年份集体单位分行业年末城镇在岗职工人数

Number of Employed Persons in Urban Collective-owned Units at Year-end by Sector in Main Years

单位：人

指　　标	1985年	1990年	1995年	2000年	2005年	2010年	2011年	2012年
合　　计	63383	58749	64923	50592	44251	35106	33956	35406
按企业、事业、机关单位分								
企业	58258	54671	63194	49257	43200	34245	33095	34564
事业	4062	3050	1581	974	1051	861	861	842
机关	1063	1028	148	361				
按国民经济行业分								
第一产业	168	97	33					
第二产业	39858	41795	52334	34958	32778	23765	21884	22992
工　业	37358	40979	49984	28698	32527	22879	21626	21623
采矿业		433						
制造业		40458	48600	27268	30772	21497	20540	20560
电力、热力、燃气及水的生产和供应业		88	1384	1430	1755	1382	1086	1063
建筑业	2500	998	2350	6260	251	886	258	1369
第三产业	23357	16857	12556	15634	11473	11341	12072	12414
交通运输、仓储和邮政业					3446	3543	3156	2770
信息传输、软件和信息技术服务业					45	40		
批发和零售业					2078	1818	1859	1909
住宿和餐饮业					307	289	291	291
金融业	1327	2076	3844	3437	4184	4533	5713	6120
房地产业			29	289	183	159	154	147
租赁和商务服务业					843	677	645	914
科学研究和技术服务					16	56	56	56
水利、环境和公共设施管理业					237	112	98	89
居民服务、修理和其他服务业								
教育								
卫生和社会工作					92	64	34	70
文化、体育和娱乐业					42	50	66	48
公共管理、社会保障和社会组织	1063	1028	148	361				
国际组织								

2-10 主要年份其他所有制单位分行业年末城镇在岗职工人数

Number of Employed Persons in Urban Other Ownership Units at Year-end by Sector in Main Years

单位：人

指　　标	1985年	1990年	1995年	2000年	2005年	2010年	2011年	2012年
合　计	3034	9413	42636	35272	49426	69472	74392	69781
按企业、事业、机关单位分								
企业	2312	9413	42597	35272	49426	69472	74392	69781
事业	722		39					
机关								
按国民经济行业分								
第一产业								
第二产业	2294	8321	41188	29537	43376	58483	55295	57304
工　业	2294	8321	41188	29537	43361	58475	55287	57296
采矿业		48						
制造业		8273	37686	28911	39580	55066	51338	55398
电力、热力、燃气及水的生产和供应业			3502	626	3781	3409	3949	1898
建筑业					15	8	8	8
第三产业	740	1092	1448	5735	6050	10989	19097	12477
交通运输、仓储和邮政业					412	702	7112	821
信息传输、软件和信息技术服务业					240	220	220	223
批发和零售业					1530	2607	2788	3089
住宿和餐饮业					678	450	456	450
金融业			9	3165	2999	6854	8370	7739
房地产业	722							
租赁和商务服务业					191	156	151	155
卫生和社会工作								

2-11 工业、建筑业企业年末城镇在岗职工人数（2012年）

Number of Urban Employed Persons in Industrial and Construction Enterprises at Year-end (2012)

单位：人

指　　标	2012年
工业总计	82647
按经济类型分	
国有经济单位	3728
城镇集体经济单位	21623
其他各种经济单位	57296
按工业行业分(大类)	
非金属矿采选业	55
农副食品加工业	402
食品制造业	809
酒、饮料和精制茶制造业	1438
烟草制品业	
纺织业	1304
纺织服装、服饰业	6497
皮革、毛皮、羽毛及其制品和制鞋业	224
木材加工和木、竹、藤、棕、草制品业	
家具制造业	
造纸和纸制品业	1052
印刷和记录媒介复制业	1129
文教、工美、体育和娱乐用品制造业	627
石油加工、炼焦和核燃料加工业	
化学原料和化学制品制造业	1335
医药制造业	2473
化学纤维制造业	
橡胶和塑料制品业	4125
非金属矿物制品业	1122
黑色金属冶炼和压延加工业	
有色金属冶炼和压延加工业	75
金属制品业	662
通用设备制造业	15415
专用设备制造业	1538
汽车制造业	1610
电气机械和器材制造业	10088
计算机、通信和其他电子设备制造业	19745
仪器仪表制造业	5234
其他制造业	2
电力、热力生产和供应业	3998
水的生产和供应业	1647
建筑业总计	2935
国有经济单位	1558
城镇集体经济单位	1369
其他各种经济单位	8

注：2012年起，本表行业分类按《国民经济行业分类》(GB/T4754-2011)进行分类，数据与往年不可比。

2-12 按经济类型分行业城镇在岗职工人数及构成（2012年）

Employed Persons in Urban Areas by Registration Status and Sector (2012)

项　　目	合　计	国有经济单位	城镇集体经济单位	其他经济单位
合　计(人)	250225	145038	35406	69781
第一产业	925	925		
第二产业	85582	5286	22992	57304
工　业	82647	3728	21623	57296
采矿业	55	55		
制造业	76947	989	20560	55398
电力、热力、燃气及水的生产和供应业	5645	2684	1063	1898
建筑业	2935	1558	1369	8
第三产业	163718	138827	12414	12477
交通运输、仓储和邮政业	8823	5232	2770	821
信息传输、软件和信息技术服务业	2496	2273		223
批发和零售业	7438	2440	1909	3089
住宿和餐饮业	741		291	450
金融业	27976	14117	6120	7739
房地产业	489	342	147	
租赁和商务服务业	2514	1445	914	155
科学研究和技术服务	1992	1936	56	
水利、环境和公共设施管理业	630	541	89	
居民服务、修理和其他服务业	153	153		
教育	27400	27400		
卫生和社会工作	34213	34143	70	
文化、体育和娱乐业	1746	1698	48	
公共管理、社会保障和社会组织	47107	47107		
国际组织				
占全部职工人数的比重（%）	100	58	14	28
第一产业	0.37	0.37		
第二产业	34.20	2.11	9.19	22.90
工　业	33.03	1.49	8.64	22.90
采矿业	0.02	0.02		
制造业	30.75	0.40	8.22	22.14
电力、燃气及水的生产和供应业	2.26	1.07	0.42	0.76
建筑业	1.17	0.62	0.55	
第三产业	65.43	55.48	4.96	4.99
交通运输、仓储和邮政业	3.53	2.09	1.11	0.33
信息传输、软件和信息技术服务业	1.00	0.91		0.09
批发和零售业	2.97	0.98	0.76	1.23
住宿和餐饮业	0.30		0.12	0.18
金融业	11.18	5.64	2.45	3.09
房地产业	0.20	0.14	0.06	
租赁和商务服务业	1.00	0.58	0.37	0.06
科学研究和技术服务	0.80	0.77	0.02	
水利、环境和公共设施管理业	0.25	0.22	0.04	
居民服务、修理和其他服务业	0.06	0.06		
教育	10.95	10.95		
卫生和社会工作	13.67	13.64	0.03	
文化、体育和娱乐业	0.70	0.68	0.02	
公共管理、社会保障和社会组织	18.83	18.83		
国际组织				

主要统计指标解释

Explanatory Notes on Main Statistical Indicators

人口数 指一定时点、一定地区范围内的有生命的个人的总和。年度统计的年末人口数是指每年 12 月 31 日 24 时的人口数。

常住人口 包括居住在本乡镇街道、户口在本乡镇街道或户口待定的人；居住在本乡镇街道、离开户口所在的乡镇街道半年以上的人；户口在本乡镇街道、外出不满半年或在境外工作学习的人。

外来暂住人口 指户口登记地在外县、市而目前在本市暂住的人口。

性别比 反映两性人口之间比例的指标。指在总人口中或在各年龄人口中，男性人数与女性人数之比。通常用每 100 个女性人口相应有多少男性人口表示。

出生率（又称粗出生率） 指在一定时期内（通常为一年）平均每千人所出生的人数的比率，一般用千分率表示。

死亡率（又称粗死亡率） 指在一定时期内（通常为一年）一定地区的死亡人数与同期平均人数（或期中人数）之比，一般用千分率表示。

人口自然增长率 指在一定时期内（通常为一年）人口自然增加数（出生人数减死亡人数）与该时期内平均人口数（或期中人数）之比，一般用千分率表示。

总迁移率 是反映人口迁移变动总规模的相对指标，是某地区一定时期内（通常为一年）迁入人数及迁出人数之和与同时期平均人口数之比，一般用千分率表示。

净迁移率 是反映人口迁移变动的相对指标之一，是某地区一定时期内（通常为一年）迁入与迁出相抵销后的余额与同时期平均人口数之比，一般用千分率表示。

在岗职工 指在本单位工作且与本单位签订劳动合同，并由单位支付各项工资和社会保险、住房公积金的人员，以及上述人员中由于学习、病伤产假等原因暂未工作，仍由单位支付工资的人员。

三、农　业

Agriculture

3-1 主要年份农业指标

Main Indicators of Agriculture in Main Years

指　　标	单　位	1978年	1980年	1985年	1990年	1995年	2000年
乡镇从业人员	人	467757	478599	544734	598911	639985	727328
第一产业	人	390585	368322	283425	269460	202138	189349
第二产业	人	51422	94576	167116	228114	283050	362666
第三产业	人	25750	15701	94193	101337	154797	175313
年末耕地面积	亩	1183926	1177400	966725	882602	708595	663304
农业机械总动力	千瓦	248760	354250	667750	1003980	795120	586063
水利建设总投资	万元	413	927	886	5428	16900	35550
化肥施用量(实物量)	吨	113296	100776	150083	235836	124263	103570
农药施用量	吨	4276	3382	2951	3453	1924	1836
农村用电量	万千瓦时	5667	7355	14365	82545	406327	1312931
农业总产值(当年价)	万元	42394	41943	91244	236412	426901	546383
主要农产品产量							
粮　食	吨	532308	529381	488705	494259	227441	204136
糖　蔗	吨	508976	447318	526033	538712	233803	49359
花　生	吨	14157	29015	20963	13411	3724	1960
水　果	吨	26457	23688	189350	282410	243231	129367
水产品	吨	30900	25471	32641	68508	74778	95076
肉　类	吨	26920	27652	33298	62191	97572	179032
#猪 肉	吨	22790	23461	25759	40130	68649	149648
禽　蛋	吨	425	398	2424	6906	5431	4367
森林覆盖率	%			28.6	31.4	29.2	30.6

注：本表乡镇从业人员含部分外来从业人员，下同。

3-1 续表

指　　标	单　位	2005年	2010年	2011年	2012年
乡镇从业人员	人	830705	878912	913251	944317
第一产业	人	110612	72856	58767	60062
第二产业	人	447207	448637	465239	476215
第三产业	人	272886	357419	389245	408040
年末耕地面积	亩	502937	576883	571850	
农业机械总动力	千瓦	229297	367988	379028	391052
水利建设总投资	万元	59437	78308	83436	88453
化肥施用量(实物量)	吨	52749	41445	42307	41026
农药施用量	吨	1090	819	858	763
农村用电量	万千瓦时	2970738	3950486	4319019	4403640
农林牧渔业总产值	万元	420496	283092	306621	320083
主要农产品产量					
粮　食	吨	20004	12482	12890	12476
糖　蔗	吨	450	800	845	
花　生	吨	114	115	78	281
水　果	吨	151255	75540	73866	64916
水产品	吨	67381	76268	78229	76967
肉　类	吨	171737	28830	26010	26726
#猪　肉	吨	159169	22339	19074	19570
禽　蛋	吨	1355	386	643	842
森林覆盖率	%	33.1	36.7	36.9	37.1

注：1. 2010年起，农业机械总动力数据采用农业局统计口径，下同。
　　2. 2011年起，农村用电量数据采用供电局统计口径，下同。

3-2 主要年份农村经济比例和效益指标

Main Indicators of Proportions and Efficiency in Rural Economy in Main Years

指　　标	单　位	1990年	1995年	2000年	2005年	2010年	2011年	2012年
各产业乡镇从业人员比例								
第一产业	%	45.0	31.6	26.0	13.3	8.3	6.4	6.4
第二产业	%	38.1	44.2	49.9	53.8	51.0	50.9	50.4
第三产业	%	16.9	24.2	24.1	32.9	40.7	42.6	43.2
劳动生产条件								
平均每一农业人口用电量	千瓦时	826	3778	11666	29762	44051	47822	48364
每亩耕地农业机械总动力	瓦特	1138	1122	884	455	638	663	
平均每亩耕地化肥施用量	公斤	267	175	156	105	72	74	
平均每亩耕地农药施用量	公斤	3.91	2.72	2.77	2.17	1.42	1.50	
增加值率								
农业增加值率	%		57.8	56.9	51.9	58.5	58.3	58.6
劳动生产率(平均每个劳动力创造或生产的)								
农业总产值	元	3977	6737	7828	5062	3221	3357	3390
农业增加值	元		3892	4453	2627	1886	1958	1986
粮食产量	吨	0.83	0.36	0.29	0.02	0.01	0.01	0.01
蔬菜产量	吨	0.75	0.88	0.94	0.55	0.45	0.43	0.41
糖蔗产量	吨	0.91	0.37	0.07				
水果产量	吨	0.48	0.38	0.19	0.18	0.09	0.08	0.07
畜牧总肉产量	吨	0.10	0.15	0.26	0.21	0.03	0.03	0.03
#猪　肉	吨	0.07	0.11	0.21	0.19	0.03	0.02	0.02
水产品产量	吨	0.12	0.12	0.14	0.08	0.09	0.09	0.08

3-3 主要年份农村集体(经联社、经济社两级)资产负债及收益分配

Assets, Liabilities and Income Distribution of Rural Collective Economy in Main Years

单位：亿元

指　标	2005年	2010年	2011年	2012年
资产负债情况				
资产总额	929.60	1228.20	1234.95	1263.08
负债总额	221.56	292.15	280.42	264.87
资产负债率(%)	23.83	23.79	22.71	20.97
净资产	708.04	936.05	954.53	998.21
收益分配情况				
经营总收入	120.57	143.38	148.48	155.05
#直接经营收入	12.83	14.39	13.38	13.73
物业出租收入	77.02	91.65	96.72	101.87
管理费收入	13.07	7.51	8.10	8.41
结汇收入		3.52	2.95	2.03
农业发包及上交收入	3.17	2.09	2.33	2.44
投资收益	5.07	7.07	7.36	7.63
其他收入	9.40	17.15	17.64	18.93
经营总费用	48.05	66.45	69.47	69.71
#直接经营费用	6.46	8.59	8.50	8.29
租赁费用	24.05	32.62	33.59	34.94
经营税金		1.90	2.11	2.48
管理费用	9.34	12.46	14.34	12.92
其他支出	7.92	10.89	10.93	11.08
经营纯收入	72.52	76.93	79.01	85.33
收益分配总额	64.57	92.79	98.54	101.81
可弥补分配的收益总额	3.29	15.79	17.43	17.52

3-4 历年农产品人均拥有量

Per Capita Possession of Agricultural Products over Years

单位：公斤

年 份	粮 食				蔬 菜	
			# 稻 谷			
	按总人口	按农业人口	按总人口	按农业人口	按总人口	按农业人口
1949	312	378	304	368		
1952	379	463	364	444		
1957	373	463	337	419		
1962	414	514	392	486		
1965	513	632	502	618		
1970	463	562	451	546		
1975	473	565	452	539		
1980	471	570	462	558	111	134
1985	408	510	397	497	260	330
1990	379	495	368	480	337	440
1995	160	211	148	196	388	515
1996	168	224	155	207	411	548
1997	169	225	155	207	436	582
1998	167	224	151	203	450	603
1999	165	222	149	200	443	597
2000	135	181	121	163	431	582
2001	83	113	71	97	459	623
2002	34	54	27	43	418	653
2003	19	30	13	20	352	549
2004	19	30	8	12	329	530
2005	12	20	7	12	278	461
2006	6	10	4	8	212	364
2007	6	10	4	7	200	351
2008	7	12	3	6	224	399
2009	7	12	4	7	224	412
2010	7	14	5	10	216	438
2011	7	14	5	10	211	431
2012	7	14	4	9	207	425

注：本表按户籍人口计算。

3-4 续表

单位：公斤

年 份	水 果		猪 肉		水产品	
	按总人口	按农业人口	按总人口	按农业人口	按总人口	按农业人口
1949					5	6
1952					5	6
1957					5	7
1962					8	10
1965	53	66			12	14
1970	71	87			17	20
1975	34	41			20	24
1980	21	26	21	25	23	27
1985	158	197	21	27	27	34
1990	218	283	31	40	53	69
1995	171	226	48	64	52	70
1996	143	190	58	77	56	76
1997	113	151	68	91	63	84
1998	77	103	84	112	65	88
1999	91	122	87	117	63	84
2000	85	115	97	131	61	82
2001	98	132	109	148	58	79
2002	121	190	106	165	53	82
2003	92	143	85	133	48	74
2004	108	175	79	128	44	71
2005	91	152	96	159	41	68
2006	83	143	18	31	28	48
2007	77	135	9	15	28	48
2008	58	104	10	18	41	74
2009	51	94	11	20	41	75
2010	42	84	12	25	42	85
2011	40	82	10	21	42	87
2012	35	71	10	21	41	85

3-5 主要年份基层组织情况

Basic Statistics on Rural Grassroots Units in Main Years

指　　标	单位	1990年	1995年	2000年	2005年	2010年	2011年	2012年
农村基层组织								
镇街政府	个	33	33	32	32	32	32	32
社区居委会、村委会	个	583	594	593	596	599	594	595
镇街户籍总户数	户	327344	364273	414007	465008	530497	539044	544079
#农业户	户	238221	263669	299576	275988	259691	262105	263144
镇街户籍总人口	人	1318526	1436525	1526090	1656541	1817709	1847691	1870159
#农业人口	人	1009857	1082703	1130002	998159	896789	903139	910525
乡镇从业人员	人	598911	639985	727328	830705	878912	913251	944317
按性别分								
男性	人	289258	315892	364866	427840	475996	490951	506083
女性	人	309653	324093	362462	402865	402916	422300	438234
按行业分								
农、林、牧、渔业	人	269460	190061	174201	110612	72856	58767	60062
工业	人	194485	254999	335545	414017	416197	431269	441850
建筑业	人	33629	28051	27121	33190	32440	33970	34365
交运仓储和邮政业	人	29005	40032	31291	40619	40124	41074	43527
信息传输、计算机服务和软件业	人				16889	31432	33524	37840
批发和零售业	人				65051	82662	87052	92681
住宿和餐饮业	人				32953	48728	51327	53795
其他行业	人				117374	154473	176268	180197

3-6 历年耕地面积

Area of Cultivated Land over Years

单位：亩

年 份	年末实有耕地面积	当 年新增面积	当 年减少面积	粮食占用耕地面积
1949	1398338			1260357
1952	1445016			1283151
1957	1435861			1199575
1962	1214417	15405	75905	1053985
1965	1199611	4142	11473	956906
1970	1203350	11359	8818	944903
1975	1193180	1246	6402	922916
1978	1183926	288	6515	874967
1979	1182292	120	1754	896347
1980	1177400	177	5069	856824
1981	1159963	279	17716	824166
1982	1146458	1086	14591	834028
1983	1121311	216	25363	837642
1984	1077659	664	44316	784763
1985	966725	1655	112589	691895
1986	889780	2350	79295	624471
1987	887369	1986	22271	618066
1988	877308	12374	22435	609332
1989	885694	13885	5499	626334
1990	882602	6991	10083	621564
1991	878980	962	4584	614994
1992	845159	100	33921	532296
1993	753746	6319	97732	391736
1994	718144	11169	46771	382238
1995	708595	12227	21776	394913
1996	674588	6270	40277	391610
1997	663013	6350	17925	382890
1998	663045	156	124	376133
1999	663122	1684	1607	381933
2000	663304	1632	1450	354980
2001	643648	4410	24066	255771
2002	500694		150	116989
2003	492433	1922	10183	81939
2004	489448	625	3610	85988
2005	502937	291	4302	76037
2006	491535		11403	34366
2007	483740		7795	32314
2008	479260	375	4855	40795
2009	516623	9	1212	41561
2010	576883	65649	5362	41922
2011	571850		5033	41461
2012				41282

3-7 历年耕地面积变动情况

Changes of Cultivated Land over Years

单位：亩

年份	当年增加耕地面积	#新开荒	围海造田	当年减少耕地面积	#国家基建占用	种果占用	鱼塘占用
“六五”时期累计	3900	1152		214575	6687	148244	33462
1981	279	91		17716	1275	7577	4507
1982	1086	215		14591	505	3345	8073
1983	216	135		25363	788	19590	2152
1984	664	148		44316	1122	31072	7694
1985	1655	563		112589	2997	86660	11036
“七五”时期累计	33250	2507	600	38017	9587	9138	2698
1986							
1987							
1988	12374	1199		22435	6971	5379	1871
1989	13885	651	100	5499	1433	330	151
1990	6991	657	500	10083	1183	3429	676
“八五”时期累计	30777	569	150	204784	5339	101880	44542
1991	962	95	150	4584	1463	430	57
1992	100	5		33921	1090	17435	3154
1993	6319	270		97732	808	64790	19032
1994	11169	139		46771	645	16031	16162
1995	12227	60		21776	1333	3194	6137
“九五”时期累计	16092	443	175	61383	2824	26550	9637
1996	6270	194	19	40277	532	16382	5597
1997	6350			17925	797	10168	4027
1998	156		156	124	85		
1999	1684	148		1607	128		
2000	1632	101		1450	1282		13
“十五”时期累计	7248			42311	3114	14531	5704
2001	4410			24066	1406	14434	5704
2002				150			
2003	1922			10183	1587		
2004	625			3610	121		
2005	291			4302		97	
“十一五”时期累计	66033	23627		30627			
2006				11403			
2007				7795			
2008	375			4855			
2009	9			1212			
2010	65649	23627		5362			
“十二五”时期累计							
2011				5033			
2012							

3-8 历年乡镇从业人员（按性别、产业分）

Towmship Employees over Years (by Sex and Industry)

单位：人

年 份	合 计	按性别分		按产业分		
		男	女	第一产业	第二产业	第三产业
1978	467757			390585	51422	25750
1979	468059			373438		
1980	478599	227496	251103	368322	94576	15701
1981	484346	231033	253313	367225		
1982	502066	239398	262668	360387	106294	35385
1983	512240	262608	249632	305715	145787	60738
1984	526766	253922	272844	248406	178527	99833
1985	544734	260439	284295	283425	167116	94193
1986	557048	265132	291916	277085	187920	92043
1987	571077	272044	299033	269984	204802	96291
1988	582425	281299	301126	270357	216508	95560
1989	589920	281420	308500	273377	215634	100909
1990	598911	289258	309653	269460	228114	101337
1991	601467	286328	315139	261271	232797	107399
1992	612142	298997	313145	239845	253218	119079
1993	625571	311208	314363	219230	267438	138903
1994	627366	313942	313424	200833	245562	180971
1995	639985	315892	324093	202138	283050	154797
1996	639492	316928	322564	206543	286166	146783
1997	643671	320844	322827	208030	284919	150722
1998	661604	329713	331891	205300	297418	158886
1999	668473	333136	335337	207432	300506	160535
2000	727328	364866	362462	189349	362666	175313
2001	743662	377491	366171	174786	383363	185513
2002	754294	384417	369877	151487	394770	208037
2003	851484	439406	412078	130930	486298	234256
2004	798954	412687	386267	119347	434172	245435
2005	830705	427840	402865	110612	447207	272886
2006	847361	445915	401446	92819	460758	293784
2007	837283	446755	390528	85246	441523	310514
2008	842933	451325	390608	82059	436029	324845
2009	870156	468137	402019	77502	447662	344992
2010	878912	475996	402916	72856	448637	357419
2011	913251	490951	422300	58767	465239	389245
2012	944317	506083	438234	60062	476215	408040

注：本表乡镇从业人员包含部分外来从业人员，下同。

3-9 历年乡镇从业人员（按主要行业分）

Towmship Employees over Years (by Main Sectors)

单位：人

年 份	合 计	#农 业	工 业	建筑业	交通仓储邮电通讯业	商饮业
1978	467757	390585	46651	4771	2515	2441
1979	468059	373438	85306			
1980	478599	368322	94576			
1981	484346	367225	87204			
1982	502066	360387	92860	13434	15580	3158
1983	512240	305715	124791	20996	8129	5916
1984	526766	248406	147324	31203	15804	12808
1985	544734	283425	133685	33431	20142	16970
1986	557048	277085	150136	37784	25049	18417
1987	571077	269984	167354	37448	25832	20919
1988	582425	270357	181234	35274	27280	21698
1989	589920	273377	183107	32527	28491	21582
1990	598911	269460	194485	33629	29005	22652
1991	601467	261271	201152	31645	29787	25813
1992	612142	239845	222722	30496	32777	29991
1993	625571	219230	236994	30444	39612	33629
1994	627366	200833	245562	28425	39479	35798
1995	639985	202138	254999	28051	40032	36974
1996	639492	206543	258227	27939	41092	40166
1997	643671	208030	258432	26487	37375	37702
1998	661604	205300	271099	26319	36939	38880
1999	668473	207432	273914	26592	37323	39284
2000	727328	189349	335545	27121	31291	48088
2001	743662	174786	357527	25836	32153	50512
2002	754294	151487	361418	33352	34919	57997
2003	851484	130930	451920	34378	35517	62978
2004	798954	119347	398596	35576	38406	83901
2005	830705	110612	414017	33190	40619	98004
2006	847361	92819	427500	33258	43295	102259
2007	837283	85246	406910	34613	41687	113141
2008	842933	82059	402895	33134	40827	117545
2009	870156	77502	413929	33733	40299	123631
2010	878912	72856	416197	32440	40124	131390
2011	913251	58767	431269	33970	41074	138379
2012	944317	60062	441850	34365	43527	146476

3-10 历年农林牧渔业总产值及指数

Gross Output Value and Indices of Agriculture over Years

年份	农林牧渔业总产值（万元）	农业	#粮食	水果	林业	牧业	渔业	农林牧渔服务业
农林牧渔业总产值								
1978	42394	29425	21006	1404	312	5665	3149	
1980	41943	28054	17178	1570	238	6313	2878	
1985	91244	57684	19986	1913	759	12652	6219	
1986	122988	79251	18869	34831	2425	18078	8940	
1987	148414	90502	21593	39295	2330	23324	11930	
1988	203685	109531	29776	33939	4732	36915	26500	
1989	221079	117464	35488	30276	4316	45313	28495	
1990	236412	129032	34543	44268	4324	45405	31449	
1991	242587	130986	30256	44250	4038	47839	32640	
1992	271293	148412	28551	56967	5307	57163	38026	
1993	284539	130666	18519	39505	5489	78919	46737	
1994	347451	158315	22426	44798	6735	101117	60263	
1995	426901	194921	29030	59567	8850	128089	68547	
1996	497161	213018	33620	55763	9149	155112	86992	
1997	514373	232721	35329	53483	4383	176254	81573	
1998	536047	220614	34338	29852	5472	193404	93090	
1999	537442	236429	35549	47159	5640	197474	75495	
2000	546383	216318	19893	46423	3649	226293	81118	
2001	559280	228740	12895	48496	5309	245444	72132	
2002	536729	224452	5680	49790	2346	242928	67003	
2003	490206	209739	3377	54346	1414	203477	67276	8300
2004	441912	163246	3489	46992	2247	199912	67272	9235
2005	420496	107174	4194	35130	1746	242534	62639	6403
2006	212632	116110	2232	29801	3101	50638	31968	10815
2007	199782	114389	2446	27434	3238	38354	33562	10239
2008	255307	129962	3326	22551	3585	53221	60296	8243
2009	253077	131924	3170	22986	2232	49982	60642	8297
2010	283092	148151	3389	22804	2937	55499	67958	8547
2011	306621	160161	3562	28917	2109	63758	71450	9143
2012	320083	169305	3349	25163	1675	63278	76427	9398

注：绝对值按当年价格计算，指数按可比价格计算；从2003年起新增农林牧渔服务业，下同。

3-10 续表

年份	农林牧渔业总产值(%)	农业	#粮食	水果	林业	牧业	渔业	农林牧渔服务业
指数(1978=100)								
1978	100.0	100.0	100.0	100.0	100.0	100.0	100.0	
1980	98.0	100.3	98.1	89.0	65.6	81.4	88.3	
1985	138.9	131.3	84.6	719.8	154.2	130.7	127.5	
1986	174.6	158.0	78.8	1159.9	677.2	183.5	166.7	
1987	186.4	160.1	80.0	1354.9	416.9	194.9	241.0	
1988	182.1	143.5	79.8	959.0	476.4	215.1	262.2	
1989	181.9	138.0	84.5	784.5	372.4	225.4	288.4	
1990	195.3	150.6	85.7	1005.4	320.6	238.5	316.2	
1991	199.5	149.4	77.3	961.8	286.4	262.1	335.9	
1992	211.3	163.7	60.0	1255.3	325.7	289.3	356.7	
1993	175.5	115.7	32.9	720.2	281.8	320.1	332.3	
1994	188.4	123.9	32.8	905.8	235.5	364.3	382.1	
1995	207.8	132.8	36.8	1022.0	337.0	410.4	407.0	
1996	216.3	122.6	39.3	791.4	312.7	465.1	467.4	
1997	225.0	129.1	40.0	835.4	167.7	532.0	540.4	
1998	227.3	103.6	39.9	407.7	225.3	612.8	659.7	
1999	242.8	140.2	39.9	981.4	297.4	616.2	686.0	
2000	243.3	111.5	32.9	593.1	214.9	697.5	769.6	
2001	246.3	111.8	20.5	634.6	233.4	750.0	766.0	
2002	263.2	150.9	8.5	1336.5	124.5	730.2	652.5	
2003	209.7	105.7	4.6	654.3	62.1	600.5	666.2	100.0
2004	213.5	118.0	3.3	899.9	123.9	563.1	647.9	108.0
2005	222.2	107.7	2.2	861.4	171.4	662.2	653.8	72.9
2006	121.0	108.3	2.4	683.1	246.6	155.2	590.7	121.2
2007	105.6	102.7	2.3	667.9	261.7	93.6	584.9	111.5
2008	118.3	106.0	3.9	520.6	286.3	109.5	899.5	84.2
2009	122.2	109.4	4.3	507.1	178.9	116.9	929.2	84.8
2010	126.2	107.6	4.6	415.3	205.2	132.2	982.2	84.8
2011	126.1	111.2	4.7	425.7	144.5	121.1	983.2	86.1
2012	126.9	108.8	4.3	352.1	111.7	125.1	1034.3	86.1

3-11 历年农林牧渔业增加值

Added Value of Agriculture over Years

单位：万元

年份	农林牧渔业增加值	农业	林业	牧业	渔业	农林牧渔服务业
1978	27235	18903	200	3639	2023	
1980	26323	17606	149	3962	1806	
1985	61475	38864	511	8524	4190	
1986	81416	52463	1605	11967	5918	
1987	98236	59904	1542	15438	7897	
1988	118888	63932	2762	21547	15468	
1989	126568	67248	2471	25942	16313	
1990	132787	72474	2429	25503	17664	
1991	134523	72636	2239	26528	18100	
1992	144115	78839	2819	30366	20200	
1993	143953	66106	2777	39926	23645	
1994	174796	79645	3388	50870	30317	
1995	214306	97851	4443	64301	34411	
1996	248645	106537	4576	77576	43507	
1997	256388	115999	2185	87853	40660	
1998	259437	106773	2648	93604	45054	
1999	257863	113438	2706	94747	36222	
2000	259087	102575	1730	107305	38465	
2001	260968	106733	2477	114528	33658	
2002	248791	104041	1087	112605	31058	
2003	228165	96676	658	94708	31313	4810
2004	227087	84939	1155	102730	34569	3694
2005	218212	82306	1162	97864	34412	2468
2006	123936	83612	1913	17938	16011	4462
2007	118991	82374	1997	13586	16810	4224
2008	148250	93585	2212	18851	30202	3400
2009	147877	94998	1378	17703	30375	3423
2010	165719	106684	1812	19658	34040	3525
2011	178777	115332	1301	22583	35789	3772
2012	187556	121950	1033	22413	38282	3878

注：绝对值按当年价格计算。

3-12 历年农作物播种面积

Total Sown Area of Farm Crops over Years

单位：亩

年 份	农作物总播种面 积	粮食	#稻谷	薯类	大豆	甘蔗	#糖蔗	花生	蔬菜(瓜)
1978	2859494	2072184	1715230	66400	36764	131200	130676	155021	68743
1979	2585334	1937441	1676936	62537	37993	110580	110123	185434	63959
1980	2436118	1756854	1624873	49665	39261	92397	91908	232541	58550
1981	2267521	1606926	1525072	48999	32143	131453	131103	264903	63768
1982	2204381	1600137	1511345	57188	35450	125787	124431	217612	82982
1983	2193087	1635344	1530918	71430	32029	110684	109283	152335	119370
1984	2165276	1576777	1468801	77105	31718	98449	96224	173198	153636
1985	1950081	1395692	1293847	70997	28982	96627	91884	159918	139795
1986	1791221	1257126	1174464	54993	31469	67920	63729	152214	159100
1987	1795990	1250934	1165554	57850	28471	63655	59637	130292	184744
1988	1792952	1236359	1151493	55368	27929	69694	66505	113882	208930
1989	1834039	1284184	1199979	55964	26200	85238	82666	101077	211217
1990	1848814	1286028	1194153	61281	26444	85977	83246	97808	229532
1991	1791266	1226573	1138043	60107	22785	90137	87356	85537	238418
1992	1561497	963947	889074	51273	20688	76184	72845	67897	318193
1993	1068053	551155	499223	34449	12843	43720	40594	39062	361826
1994	1009468	536191	482051	32615	7542	36346	34621	25344	367122
1995	1078363	598547	527594	43346	7058	28521	26488	24779	379362
1996	1083418	628347	559499	37989	8276	32620	30880	20805	363331
1997	1082610	624091	560506	32629	8190	41427	40166	18490	369113
1998	1101826	624383	558668	34799	7028	48602	47772	16824	385151
1999	1088854	626481	558508	36329	5597	31641	30889	14305	388173
2000	986022	527689	465616	31754	5290	7566	6775	11969	407304
2001	854229	338467	283351	31214	3947	4610	3290	9405	465659
2002	634205	148184	112388	18265	1983	3193	2299	4746	445447
2003	509504	84782	54970	11154	1550	1879	626	2823	380252
2004	462244	81207	31108	24683	816	868	373	1544	350412
2005	410648	62084	34356	9390	1006	950	55	574	315537
2006	333854	34366	25159	4100	183	575	55	556	241070
2007	320500	32314	19534	5330	253	1676	281	340	236490
2008	352222	40352	18781	4381	443	2330	340	586	287618
2009	370740	41421	18629	5047	140	4144	209	838	306270
2010	369257	41922	26124	3192		2944	100	713	300622
2011	366840	41461	26412	4247	418	2395	116	456	297537
2012	372455	41282	23675	8044	901	2434		930	303778

3-13 历年农作物产量

Total Output of Farm Crops over Years

单位：吨

年份	粮食			大豆	甘蔗		花生	蔬菜（瓜）
		#稻谷	薯类			#糖蔗		
1978	532308	501074	6458	1948	511492	508976	14157	135603
1979	535342	516263	6568	1982	366424	364084	19100	127918
1980	529381	518591	5432	2245	449907	447318	29015	124859
1981	447540	439534	6318	1722	678160	676074	35506	132846
1982	543349	532998	8430	2162	707764	699174	29930	123117
1983	561246	548073	11345	1875	553174	553105	19662	168878
1984	558216	545548	10946	1980	569225	554919	23076	230454
1985	488705	476399	10304	1771	556983	526033	20963	314539
1986	455243	443760	9422	2050	382608	354759	20056	427138
1987	462830	451032	10058	1920	378094	349749	17019	414261
1988	460929	448923	9950	1965	420391	400045	15119	412436
1989	487648	474476	11052	2023	528463	511031	13746	410879
1990	494259	479350	12452	2184	557102	538712	13411	444377
1991	473663	458425	12998	1838	619884	601734	11510	446204
1992	368083	354298	11070	1763	543657	523271	9323	523806
1993	202097	192018	7366	1035	343133	326389	5594	572376
1994	202356	189688	7929	668	313851	302669	3678	537442
1995	227441	210876	10758	647	246707	233803	3724	557807
1996	243204	224469	11271	806	285732	274531	3120	597732
1997	246901	227163	11487	811	354420	346469	2879	641403
1998	247194	223938	13916	758	411555	406644	2588	668753
1999	247287	223403	14580	566	242773	238774	2204	668822
2000	204136	183485	9730	610	54095	49359	1960	658196
2001	128366	109881	9920	426	33387	24768	1556	706775
2002	53732	42508	5420	244	20224	15025	865	653272
2003	30500	20423	3415	215	8019	2564	395	560523
2004	30374	12230	9803	138	4763	1437	216	532116
2005	20004	11941	2733	147	4433	450	114	460204
2006	10040	7548	1314	31	3167	379	99	356347
2007	9864	6467	1732	48	10834	1953	73	342703
2008	11902	6007	1381	95	15286	2580	130	391192
2009	11912	6560	1437	19	23044	1249	113	400335
2010	12482	8768	668		15952	800	115	392904
2011	12890	9137	888	53	14239	845	78	389014
2012	12476	8357	1609	162	13032		281	386603

3-14 主要年份农作物播种面积、亩产及总产量

Sown Area, Yield Per Acreage and Total Output of Farm Crops in Main Years

单位：亩、公斤、吨

指　　标	1978年			1985年			1990年		
	播种面积	亩产	总产量	播种面积	亩产	总产量	播种面积	亩产	总产量
粮食作物	2072184	257	532308	1395692	350	488705	1286028	384	494259
按品种分									
稻谷	1715230	292	501074	1293847	368	476399	1194153	401	479350
旱粮	290554	85	24776	30848	65	2002	30594	80	2457
薯类	66400	97	6458	70997	145	10304	61281	203	12452
按季节分									
春收				30978	131	4042	33352	174	5790
夏收	1127790	248	279552	649856	377	244755	614059	399	244890
#早稻	814852	309	251907	620409	389	241413	587821	410	241018
秋收	944394	268	252757	714858	336	239907	638617	381	243579
#晚稻	900378	277	249167	673438	349	234985	606332	393	238332
大豆	36764	53	1948	28982	61	1771	26444	83	2184
经济作物				306406			209120		
#甘蔗	131200	3899	511492	96627	5765	556983	85977	6480	557102
糖蔗	130676	3895	508976	91884	5725	526033	83246	6471	538712
果蔗	524	4802	2516	4743	6525	30950	2731	6734	18390
油料作物				160186	131	20974	97808	137	13411
#花生	155021	91	14157	159918	131	20963	97808	137	13411
其他作物				219001			327222		
#蔬菜	68743	1973	135603	139795	2250	314539	229532	1936	444377

3-14 续表 1

单位：亩、公斤、吨

指　　标	1995年			2000年			2005年		
	播种面积	亩产	总产量	播种面积	亩产	总产量	播种面积	亩产	总产量
粮食作物	598547	380	227441	527689	387	204136	62084	322	20004
按品种分									
稻谷	527594	400	210876	465616	394	183485	34356	348	11941
旱粮	27607	210	5807	30319	360	10921	18338	291	5330
薯类	43346	248	10758	31754	306	9730	9390	291	2733
按季节分									
春收	17880	224	4008	20787	287	5966	9665	312	3019
夏收	282978	388	109914	245110	392	96015	23286	306	7136
#早稻	255886	405	103592	225985	397	89729	14713	351	5164
秋收	297689	381	113519	261792	390	102155	29133	338	9850
#晚稻	271708	395	107284	239631	391	93756	19643	345	6777
大豆	7058	92	647	5290	115	610	1006	146	147
经济作物	62092			35221			18011		
#甘蔗	28521	8650	246707	7566	7150	54095	950	4666	4433
糖蔗	26488	8827	233803	6775	7285	49359	55	8182	450
果蔗	2033	6347	12904	791	5987	4736	895	4450	3983
油料作物	24779	150	3724	11969	164	1960	574	199	114
#花生	24779	150	3724	11969	164	1960	574	199	114
其他作物	410666			417822			329547		
#蔬菜	379362	1470	557807	407304	1616	658196	315537	1458	460204

3-14 续表 2

单位：亩、公斤、吨

指　　标	2010年			2011年			2012年		
	播种面积	亩产	总产量	播种面积	亩产	总产量	播种面积	亩产	总产量
粮食作物	41922	298	12482	41461	311	12890	41282	302	12476
按品种分									
稻谷	26124	336	8768	26412	346	9137	23675	353	8357
旱粮	12606	242	3046	10384	271	2812	8662	271	2348
薯类	3192	209	668	4247	209	888	8044	200	1609
按季节分									
春收	5202	221	1150	4186	242	1015	5917	244	1445
夏收	17948	306	5501	18070	315	5701	17493	316	5523
#早稻	12017	330	3965	12878	339	4367	11468	360	4126
秋收	18772	311	5831	19205	321	6174	17872	308	5508
#晚稻	14107	340	4803	13534	352	4770	12207	347	4231
大豆				418	127	53	901	180	162
经济作物	14084			16924			21281		
#甘蔗	2944	5418	15952	2395	5945	14239	2434	5354	13032
糖蔗	100	8000	800	116	7284	845			
果蔗	2844	5328	15152	2279	5877	13394	2434	5354	13032
油料作物	713	161	115	456	171	78	930	302	281
#花生	713	161	115	456	171	78	930	302	281
其他作物	313251			308455			309892		
#蔬菜	300622	1307	392904	297537	1307	389014	303778	1273	386603

3-15 主要年份农机总动力、水利、化肥、农药及农村用电量

Basic Statistics on Total Power of Agricultural Machinery, Water Conservancy, Consumption of Chemical Fertilizers and Pesticides, and Electricity Consumed in Rural Areas in Main Years

指　　标	单　位	1978年	1990年	1995年	2000年	2005年	2010年	2011年	2012年
农业机械总动力	千瓦	248760	1003980	795120	586063	229297	367988	379028	391052
耕作机械	千瓦	42550	157910	83482	51848	16386	24079	25947	25789
排灌机械	千瓦	104050	178280	112392	91745	36251	99716	104926	105597
收获机械	千瓦	6180	84130	54722	51084	969	2280	2400	600
运输机械	千瓦	16930	322950	397735	184949	41678	12463	14363	14389
水利建设完成土石方	万立方米	957	737	891	927	682	442	742	447
土方	万立方米	932	693	835	864	611	386	569	375
石方	万立方米	25	44	56	63	71	56	173	72
水利建设总投资	万元	413	5428	16900	35550	59437	78308	83436	88453
化肥施用实物量	吨	113296	235836	124263	103570	52749	41445	42307	41026
#氮肥	吨	86371	84642	43441	30214	14439	10214	10653	9930
磷肥	吨	23164	52483	28939	23939	10967	8055	8269	8075
钾肥	吨	3761	26131	16915	14606	6403	5030	5113	4977
复合肥	吨		39098	34968	34811	20940	18146	18272	18044
农药施用量	吨	4276	3453	1924	1836	1090	819	858	763
农村用电量	万千瓦时	5667	82545	406327	1312931	2970738	3950486	4319019	4403640
#农村工业用电量	万千瓦时		70459	386413	1104301	2873735	3841990	3919883	4316008
平均每一农业人口用电量	千瓦时		826	3778	11666	29762	44051	47822	48364

注：农业机械总动力数据从2010年起采用农业局统计口径，数据与往年不可比，下同。

3-16 历年水果面积及产量

Planted Area and Output of Fruits over Years

年份	年末实有水果面积(亩)	#香(大)蕉	荔枝	水果总产量(吨)	#香(大)蕉	荔枝
1978	93245	18828	46678	26457	18867	4959
1979	91021	17977	46697	23346	12165	8667
1980	88444	15582	46743	23688	10894	7884
1981	97468	18042	48230	46909	25513	15599
1982	114730	28439	50669	58196	40872	7042
1983	159260	39749	63349	77225	42079	20724
1984	235311	66506	84183	105851	69186	14714
1985	407416	125998	115428	189350	133503	19304
1986	609347	171168	168820	307743	210439	18577
1987	609569	158874	175366	363085	222826	17439
1988	548482	99256	176979	263710	126655	7699
1989	476598	54867	164782	221418	69410	6165
1990	452729	54185	160355	282410	73555	16994
1991	440442	56481	154456	343155	85702	6201
1992	420661	81331	139584	344751	97986	22972
1993	360130	86299	117557	271346	80982	717
1994	325336	67595	121236	264875	92072	12703
1995	322876	62351	142370	243231	86466	23324
1996	326291	59822	159403	206276	77768	14804
1997	319556	57583	188220	165016	80355	22572
1998	310873	46377	208899	114106	78978	2885
1999	285514	48975	198144	136317	82169	35218
2000	297618	71454	189862	129367	108913	9107
2001	275428	86578	156019	150115	132292	7059
2002	209924	76764	109948	189343	135209	45339
2003	199634	82024	95812	146414	130688	9012
2004	183375	84812	80115	175389	150669	18312
2005	176845	75452	83357	151255	123986	21026
2006	173470	73493	81395	139582	124601	8615
2007	163448	66904	80313	131571	116833	10107
2008	178337	64141	94953	101541	86817	8498
2009	177281	52761	103364	91544	75341	10240
2010	170536	47420	100136	75540	60236	8266
2011	167667	42874	101458	73866	55291	11032
2012	178746	36661	118158	64916	51883	6333

3-17 历年林业生产

Basic Statistics on Forestry Production over Years

年　份	林业用地面积（亩）	#杉	松	桉	当年育苗面积（亩）	当年幼林抚育面积（亩）	当年迹地更新面积（亩）	当年四旁植树（万株）
1978	700570	63994	541492	49008	485	32900	5365	44
1979	705764	67104	543210	50439	880	14900	4745	30
1980	740052	70665	568729	56272	316	9500	3924	15
1981	743697	67236	584674	49994	133	12500	931	12
1982	698715	63730	535072	52925	500	11945	2531	19
1983	769893	67423	574171	56724	361	40464	3193	17
1984	739402	66107	552721	58092	501	106982	5120	16
1985	761460				801	120000	4479	150
1986	706823	61438	510042	60581	33231	210540	16908	22
1987	714664	57824	526254	75498	1728	53759	28007	35
1988	729896	59351	512451	90998	3667	70275	34467	37
1989	691944	53293	490370	103887	2101	64950	31241	58
1990	709240	47054	484397	133706	3464	56647	15782	54
1991	709306	44432	459015	148127	609	53827	22294	63
1992	662919	39326	422527	149944	762	60764	28184	49
1993	628612	36213	400816	144346	677	28511	13318	57
1994	1016138	43815	382482	129473	2492	28127	9689	34
1995	1015223	43661	360591	125133	4273	25130	11140	48
1996	1014972	9654	248288	115878	699	21000	23143	133
1997	1014954	8843	235410	113928	823	23745	22462	218
1998	1014876	8367	222147	112005	387	36000	22273	417
1999	1009965	10890	221585	133500	506	29863	29000	522
2000	1009037	29940	526797	280618	625	47145	13515	425
2001	1007298	9678	189930	133464	705	45000	38000	357
2002	900335	8265	187665	138525	516	46500	13700	98
2003	890877	6540	66206	105666	420	38910	10425	147
2004	980942				255	60000	8472	625
2005	934700	3086	2860	100145	195	61005	3383	253
2006	930162	3716	60890	162125	15	25320	3900	480
2007	926760	3870	62363	149440	255	43320	4701	600
2008	923097	3873	59864	145340	255	49571	4548	610
2009	921000	3719	58375	143690	610	56545	6184	60
2010	909900	3719	56987	142971	285	37278	5889	18
2011	905370	3719	56801	141945	345	41085		22
2012	902927	2934	41480	99353	360	35790		19

3-18 历年畜牧业生产及产品产量

Production of Animal Husbandry and Output of Livestock Products over Years

年 份	耕牛年末存栏量(头)	羊年末存栏量(头)	生猪饲养量(头)	生猪存栏量(头)	生猪出栏量(头)	三鸟饲养量(万只)	三鸟出栏量(万只)	畜牧总肉量(吨)	#猪肉	禽蛋总产量(吨)
1978	53004		1018060	672919	345141	428	219	26920	22790	425
1979	50595		995408	626435	368973	379	187	29209	25647	367
1980	53385		799568	501380	298188	420	209	27652	23461	444
1981	58619		703659	449638	254021	476	252	28011	23387	1284
1982	64067		791518	526106	265412	568	309	33037	27374	679
1983	69117		842198	489887	352311	630	370	35695	28872	1256
1984	70992		784473	458804	325669	652	369	33260	26301	1899
1985	62763		790505	471268	319237	832	414	33298	25759	2424
1986	62874		812102	428545	383557	940	655	43302	30920	5159
1987	58577		781957	396082	385875	1235	862	46120	32588	5478
1988	54723		811945	402035	409910	1400	1020	56125	35067	6734
1989	52713		846598	407317	439281	1565	1136	58563	38270	7109
1990	48760	1559	870782	410875	459907	1592	1188	62191	40130	6906
1991	44121	1396	930377	420919	509458	1806	1336	68844	44702	5924
1992	32259	1068	981698	448586	533112	1889	1419	67983	45492	5845
1993	18688	783	982084	404352	577732	2185	1647	76562	49470	4990
1994	14219	863	1089793	434904	654889	2334	1730	85448	57920	5521
1995	12207	1593	1250597	469355	781242	2501	1881	97572	68649	5431
1996	12945	1806	1407080	490161	916919	2418	1851	116058	83404	5862
1997	12675	2391	1772892	619114	1153778	2608	1863	128992	99300	6295
1998	10522	2159	2217247	776851	1440396	2291	1742	153513	123874	4738
1999	6811	1508	2573310	900285	1673025	2228	1667	159889	130494	4742
2000	5550	1675	2894126	967056	1927070	2362	1784	179032	149648	4367
2001	4618	1851	3255780	1079397	2176383	2226	1683	198423	168353	4441
2002	2919	1931	3075523	927477	2148046	1962	1557	188774	165344	4052
2003	1727	1789	2525252	742101	1783151	1652	1282	154615	135344	3597
2004	1024	1936	2444990	785289	1659701	1396	1048	146184	128286	3435
2005	827	998	2487962	214120	2273842	1314	1072	171737	159169	1355
2006	82	242	530959	110396	420563	485	312	34891	30199	371
2007	399	415	292234	88648	203586	525	341	20257	14862	361
2008	55		454117	195016	259101	758	574	24052	17946	106
2009	94		464727	183904	280823	767	576	25457	19095	515
2010	224	60	511356	174933	336423	761	591	28830	22339	386
2011	200	50	455875	176805	279070	706	547	26010	19074	643
2012	28	80	428781	142454	286327	733	577	26726	19570	842

3-19 历年水产品产量及养殖面积

Output and Cultured Area of Aquatic Products over Years

年 份	水产品产量(吨)	海 水			淡 水			养殖面积(亩)		
		产 量	捕 捞	养 殖	产 量	捕 捞	养 殖		海水养殖	淡水养殖
1978	30900	23307	23307		7593		7593	89040		89040
1979	22309	13878	13878		8431		8431	94916		94916
1980	25471	17069	17069		8402		8402	95549		95549
1981	24905	15669	15669		9236		9236	104069		104069
1982	27695	16120	16120		11575		11575	112586		112586
1983	30292	17330	17330		12962		12962	116943		116943
1984	32465	18025	18025		14440		14440	119456		119456
1985	32641	15422	15214	208	17219		17219	131350	5301	126049
1986	46534	28439	25918	2521	18095		18095	138651	16078	122573
1987	65679	45214	42793	2421	20465		20465	163225	15036	148189
1988	68087	44111	42926	1185	23976	182	23794	137966	9670	128296
1989	62306	37189	35372	1817	25117	1194	23923	123090	10350	112740
1990	68508	41002	38423	2579	27506	2177	25329	136174	19286	116888
1991	69025	39906	37209	2697	29119	2147	26972	131849	18446	113403
1992	73164	42429	38033	4396	30735	2590	28145	134558	20400	114158
1993	64973	33745	28192	5553	31228	3120	28108	143696	25855	117841
1994	67420	31284	24059	7225	36136	2565	33571	144869	26583	118286
1995	74778	32132	24637	7495	42646	2084	40562	162609	27795	134814
1996	81067	33363	25471	7892	47704	1940	45764	172656	27791	144865
1997	91901	35407	26704	8703	56494	5157	51337	184889	30326	154563
1998	96872	33618	24319	9299	63254	3146	60108	192381	29223	163158
1999	94023	31332	24257	7075	62691	2747	59944	167880	19440	148440
2000	95076	33234	24180	9054	61842	3135	58707	167841	25695	142146
2001	89599	30877	23726	7151	58722	2285	56437	155720	27928	127792
2002	82361	30800	23474	7326	51561	2762	48799	142167	26696	115471
2003	75756	30151	22826	7325	45605	2121	43484	126660	27097	99563
2004	71526	29289	22382	6907	42237	3078	39159	125116	25652	99464
2005	67381	28319	21622	6697	39062	1783	37279	102023	23530	78493
2006	47059	21152	15256	5897	25907	1062	24845	71745	6345	65400
2007	47292	21637	15992	5645	25655	857	24797	71100	5925	65175
2008	72282	21297	14322	6975	50985	512	50473	137718	17559	120159
2009	73323	19034	13205	5829	54289		54289	129136	4197	124939
2010	76268	19300	13257	6043	56968	1563	55405	132960	4147	128813
2011	78229	17816	12255	5561	60413	1801	58612	118676	3473	115203
2012	76967	17131	11664	5467	59836	1513	58323	131640	10175	121465

3-20 主要农产品产量与最高年份比较（2012年）

Output of Main Agricultural Products in Comparison with Peak Year (2012)

指　　标	单位	2012年	建国以来最高年份		
			年　份	产　量	2012年为最高年份的%
粮食总产量	吨	12476	1977	563463	2.2
#稻　谷	吨	8357	1973	548073	1.5
#早　稻	吨	4126	1983	279723	1.5
晚　稻	吨	4231	1984	279898	1.5
大　　豆	吨	162	1954	2790	5.8
经济作物					
#甘　蔗	吨	13032	1982	707764	1.8
#糖　蔗	吨		1982	699174	
花　生	吨	281	1981	35506	0.8
其他作物					
#蔬　菜	吨	386603	2001	706775	54.7
水果总产量	吨	64916	1987	363085	17.9
#香(大)蕉	吨	51883	1987	222826	23.3
荔　枝	吨	6333	2002	45339	14.0
水产品	吨	76967	1998	96872	79.5
生猪年末存栏量	头	142454	2001	1079397	13.2
生猪年出栏头数	头	286327	2005	2273842	12.6
猪肉产量	吨	19570	2001	168353	11.6
三鸟饲养量	万只	733	2000	2362	31.0
三鸟出栏量	万只	577	2000	1784	32.3
禽蛋产量	吨	842	1989	7109	11.8

主要统计指标解释

Explanatory Notes on Main Statistical Indicators

耕地面积 指可以用来种植农作物、经常进行耕锄的田地，包括熟地、当年新开荒地、连续撂荒未满三年的耕地和当年的休闲地(轮歇地)，还包括以种植农作物为主并附带种植桑树、茶树、果树和其他林木的土地，以及沿海、沿湖地区已围垦利用的“海涂”、“湖田”等面积。不包括属于专业性的桑园、茶园、果园、果木苗圃、林地、芦苇地、天然或人工草地面积。

农作物播种面积 指实际播种或移植有农作物的面积。凡是实际种植有农作物的面积，不论种植在耕地上还是种植在非耕地上，均包括在农作物播种面积中。在播种季节基本结束后，因遭灾而重新改种和补种的农作物面积，也包括在内。

粮食产量 指全社会的产量。包括国有经济经营的、集体统一经营的和农民家庭经营的粮食产量，还包括工矿企业办的农场和其他生产单位的产量。粮食除包括稻谷、小麦、玉米、高粱、谷子及其他杂粮外，还包括薯类和豆类。其产量计算方法，豆类按去豆荚后的干豆计算；薯类(包括甘薯和马铃薯，不包括芋头和木薯)1963年以前按每4公斤鲜薯折1公斤粮食计算，从1964年开始改为按5公斤鲜薯折1公斤粮食计算。城市郊区作为蔬菜的薯类(如马铃薯等)按鲜品计算，并且不作粮食统计。其他粮食一律按脱粒后的原粮计算。

水产品产量 指人工养殖的水产品和天然生长的水产品的捕捞量。包括海水的鱼类、虾蟹类、贝类和藻类以及内陆水域的鱼类、虾蟹类和贝类，不包括淡水生植物。

猪、牛、羊肉产量 指当年出栏并已屠宰、除去头蹄下水后带骨肉(即胴体重)的重量。

期初(末)畜禽存栏头(只)数 指报告期初(末)农村各种合作经济组织和国营农场、农民个人、机关、团体、学校、工矿企业、部队等单位以及城镇居民饲养的大牲畜、猪、羊、家禽等畜禽的存栏数。

农林牧渔业总产值 指以货币表现的农、林、牧、渔业全部产品的总量，它反映一定时期内农业生产总规模和总成果。农业总产值的计算方法通常是按农林牧渔业产品及其副产品的产量分别乘以各自单位产品价格求得；少数生产周期较长，当年没有产品或产品产量不易统计的，则采用间接方法匡算其产值；然后将四业产品产值相加即为农业总产值。

农业机械总动力 指主要用于农、林、牧、渔业的各种动力机械的动力总和。包括耕作机械、排灌机械、收获机械、农用运输机械、植物保护机械、牧业机械、林业机械、渔业机械和其他农业机械〔内燃机按引擎马力折成瓦(特)计算、电动机按功率折成瓦(特)计算〕。不包括专门用于乡、镇、村、组办工业、基本建设、非农业运输、科学试验和教学等非农业生产方面用的动力机械与作业机械。

四、工　业

Industry

4-1 主要年份工业主要指标

Main Indicators of Industry in Main Years

指　　标	单位	1998年	2000年	2005年	2010年	2011年	2012年
全市企业单位数	个	16406	16975	21868	38273	46413	57808
全市工业增加值	万元	2906904	4304525	11732288	20784479	22884117	22975137
规模以上工业:							
企业单位数	个	1500	1663	4505	5899	4243	4526
年末固定资产原值合计	万元	6257040	7288486	18560858	32162507	33049643	37464516
年末固定资产	万元	4392164	4701886	11052566	17836928	19882642	21560952
年末流动资产	万元	3798813	5298239	18732801	37888251	41732138	45900348
年末资产总额	万元	9267121	11225950	33453291	60017098	66127123	72060215
年末负债总额	万元	4752964	5630399	18580908	35252952	38770617	41895576
所有者权益	万元	4514157	5595551	14872383	24750103	27263562	30043497
工业增加值	万元	1687134	2594352	10624190	17083110	16424508	19781297
主营业务收入	万元	6399088	9889058	39121487	77081695	84549238	96126551
利税总额	万元	447544	841047	1830988	4695854	4833042	5188363
#利润总额	万元	255715	503589	1243516	3523632	3165403	2916748
全员劳动生产率(按增加值计算)	元/人	26688	36101	53340	60854	65087	77666
综合效益指数	%	94.1	114.0	119.9	130.3	128.3	134.4

注：1. 2005年以前数据根据东莞市第一次经济普查取得，2008年数据根据第二次经济普查取得，下同。
2. 规模以上工业企业1997年及以前年份为独立核算工业企业口径,1998-2005年为全部国有工业及年销售收入500万元以上非国有工业企业口径，2006-2010年为年主营业务收入500万元及以上工业企业口径，2011年起为年主营业务收入2000万元及以上的工业企业口径,下同。

4-2 历年工业企业单位数（按经济成份分）

Number of Industrial Enterprises over Years (by Ownership)

单位：个

年份	全市工业企业单位数	国有	集体企业	港澳台投资企业	外商投资企业	其他类型企业
1949	1	1				
1952	23	20	3			
1957	262	76	186			
1962	280	57	223			
1965	260	61	199			
1970	220	57	163			
1975	324	61	263			
1978	1290	64	1226			
1979	1250	63	1187			
1980	1293	64	1229			
1981	1479	64	1415			
1982	1862	66	1796			
1983	1964	68	1896			
1984	2329	69	2109			151
1985	4187	73	2990	79		1045
1986	5949	81	4263	89		1516
1987	8106	74	5123	175		2734
1988	8408	72	5424	241		2671
1989	8757	76	5835	323		2523
1990	9892	78	6165	521	4	3124
1991	10094	77	6404	754	4	2855
1992	11639	72	6400	932	4	4231
1993	12449	75	7129	1388	24	3833
1994	14086	45	7185	2002	191	4663
1995	15215	70	9345	2631	210	2959
1996	15326	40	8958	2128	253	3947
1997	16857	41	9949	2064	315	4488
1998	16406	29	8814	2050	461	5052
1999	16877	29	10325	2627	731	3165
2000	16975	23	10184	2717	893	3158
2001	18094	20	9978	3605	1186	3305
2002	21313	19	198	10830	907	9359
2003	21935	19	200	10969	958	9789
2004	22156	13	211	9450	1422	11060
2005	21868	10	220	10141	2093	9404
2006	22447	10	211	10271	2190	9765
2007	22587	16	151	10041	2528	9851
2008	26372	35	484	5122	2489	18242
2009	31160	26	313	5141	2439	23241
2010	38273	21	262	5417	2447	30126
2011	46413	20	215	6114	2562	37502
2012	57808	20	254	6435	2530	48569

注：本表来源于市工商局，从2002年起集体企业不包括“三来一补”企业。

4-3 主要年份工业企业单位数（按不同类型分）

Number of Industrial Enterprises in Main Years (by Ownership)

单位: 个

指　　标	1998年	2000年	2005年	2010年	2011年	2012年
全市企业单位数	16406	16975	21868	38273	46413	57808
轻工业	14389	14440	12651	20651	24787	30858
重工业	2017	2535	9217	17622	21626	26950
在总计中:						
(一)规模以上工业企业	1500	1663	4505	5899	4243	4526
按轻重工业分						
轻工业	1082	1124	2569	3183	2266	2416
重工业	418	539	1936	2716	1977	2110
按登记注册类型分						
国有	29	16	5	10	9	10
集体	204	248	162	151	81	53
私营	24	44	621	1159	736	922
联营	5	6	2	5	1	3
股份合作	9	6	1	2	1	2
股份有限公司	6	3	18	20	24	25
外商投资	134	201	820	1321	1073	1052
港澳台商投资	1082	1119	2481	2564	1823	1846
其他	7	20	395	667	495	613
按企业规模分						
大型企业	16	28	39	84	206	223
中型企业	27	19	579	1327	1677	1744
小型企业	1457	1616	3887	4488	2256	2500
微型企业					104	59
(二)规模以下工业企业	14906	15312	17363	32374	42170	53282

注：2011年起采用新的企业规模划分标准，共分大型、中型、小型、微型四类企业规模，下同。

4-4 历年工业增加值

Value-added of Industry over Years

年 份	工业增加值	
	绝对值 （万元）	增速 (%)
1986	105398	
1987	142357	25.8
1988	250456	51.4
1989	272185	6.4
1990	391840	30.6
1991	483441	21.8
1992	566316	13.7
1993	828934	38.5
1994	1107729	24.3
1995	1541922	35.3
1996	1878517	16.2
1997	2307863	20.1
1998	2906904	22.2
1999	3495304	20.7
2000	4304525	20.9
2001	5170314	22.0
2002	6218553	23.0
2003	7571849	21.4
2004	9680128	26.5
2005	11732288	20.2
2006	14416864	22.0
2007	16818293	15.0
2008	18192243	6.4
2009	17415347	-0.6
2010	20784479	17.5
2011	22884117	7.7
2012	22975137	6.0

注：本表工业增加值绝对值为当年价，增速按可比价计算。

4-5 规模以上工业企业单位数（2012年）

Number of Industrial Enterprises above Designated Size (2012)

单位：个

项　　目	工业单位数	按登记注册类型分		
		国有及国有控股工业	集体工业	港澳台及外商投资工业
总　计	4526	31	53	2898
按轻重工业分				
轻工业	2416	14	44	1481
重工业	2110	17	9	1417
按企业规模分				
大型企业	223	4	2	186
中型企业	1744	12	21	1320
小型企业	2500	15	27	1361
微型企业	59		3	31
按工业行业分(大类)				
煤炭开采和洗选业				
石油和天然气开采业				
黑色金属矿采选业				
有色金属矿采选业				
非金属矿采选业				
开采辅助活动				
其他采矿业				
农副食品加工业	43	2	1	12
食品制造业	29			12
酒、饮料和精制茶制造业	13	2		8
烟草制品业				
纺织业	134			88
纺织服装、服饰业	338	1	2	139
皮革、毛皮、羽毛及其制品和制鞋业	285	1	5	221
木材加工和木、竹、藤、棕、草制品业	29			15
家具制造业	207			110
造纸和纸制品业	225		4	86
印刷和记录媒介复制业	78	1	1	51
文教、工美、体育和娱乐用品制造业	193	1	2	160
石油加工、炼焦和核燃料加工业	4			3
化学原料和化学制品制造业	160	2		89
医药制造业	10			4
化学纤维制造业	8			5
橡胶和塑料制品业	478	1	2	343
非金属矿物制品业	94	1		46
黑色金属冶炼和压延加工业	29	1		20
有色金属冶炼和压延加工业	68			35
金属制品业	244	2		162
通用设备制造业	181	1		116
专用设备制造业	144	1		98
汽车制造业	45			32
铁路、船舶、航空航天和其他运输设备制造业	18	1		11
电气机械和器材制造业	485	1	3	330
计算机、通信和其他电子设备制造业	818	4	9	601
仪器仪表制造业	70			56
其他制造业	42			33
废弃资源综合利用业	1			
金属制品、机械和设备修理业				
电力、热力生产和供应业	16	5		9
燃气生产和供应业	5			3
水的生产和供应业	32	3	24	

注：2011年起，本表行业分类按《国民经济行业分类》(GB/T4754-2011)进行分类，下同。

4-6 规模以上工业增加值（2012年）

Value-added of Industrial Enterprises above Designated Size (2012)

单位：万元

项　　目	工业增加值	按登记注册类型分		
		国有及国有控股工业	集体工业	港澳台及外商投资工业
总　计	19781297	1684773	211759	14316358
按轻重工业分				
轻工业	9280902	191381	136492	6696852
重工业	10500396	1493392	75267	7619506
按企业规模分				
大型企业	8845460	1232101	40470	6615290
中型企业	7245952	231885	122458	5528088
小型企业	3649428	220787	48698	2146426
微型企业	40458		133	26555
按工业行业分(大类)				
煤炭开采和洗选业				
石油和天然气开采业				
黑色金属矿采选业				
有色金属矿采选业				
非金属矿采选业				
开采辅助活动				
其他采矿业				
农副食品加工业	331303	110058	912	104008
食品制造业	367837			329460
酒、饮料和精制茶制造业	323420	7965		309853
烟草制品业				
纺织业	447078			374345
纺织服装、服饰业	1140689	1565	5787	486216
皮革、毛皮、羽毛及其制品和制鞋业	1120688	4638	29888	917926
木材加工和木、竹、藤、棕、草制品业	39509			18577
家具制造业	516540			292210
造纸和纸制品业	984416		8662	676461
印刷和记录媒介复制业	355826	2793	1758	308620
文教、工美、体育和娱乐用品制造业	736495	997	24200	631639
石油加工、炼焦和核燃料加工业	11405			4003
化学原料和化学制品制造业	434124	20063		309741
医药制造业	57589			4835
化学纤维制造业	14174			5895
橡胶和塑料制品业	1096454	2324	36376	885822
非金属矿物制品业	294001	1596		198317
黑色金属冶炼和压延加工业	35150	1457		24456
有色金属冶炼和压延加工业	88744			58467
金属制品业	672895	1636		487919
通用设备制造业	612503	12102		506788
专用设备制造业	344301	5894		256295
汽车制造业	239269			201903
铁路、船舶、航空航天和其他运输设备制造业	128097	60871		114723
电气机械和器材制造业	1708276	2182	11292	1353910
计算机、通信和其他电子设备制造业	5656693	86344	50477	4748736
仪器仪表制造业	386134			338607
其他制造业	131942			118218
废弃资源综合利用业	2061			
金属制品、机械和设备修理业				
电力、热力生产和供应业	1376283	1322398		214994
燃气生产和供应业	36109			33415
水的生产和供应业	91293	39889	42408	

4-7 规模以上工业企业主要财务指标（2012年）

Main Financial Indicators of Industrial Enterprises above Designated Size (2012)

单位：万元

指　　标	全市总计	按登记注册类型分			按轻重工业分	
		内资企业	港澳台商投资企业	外商投资企业	轻工业	重工业
企业单位数(个)	4526	1628	1846	1052	2416	2110
年末资产						
流动资产合计	45900348	12296223	20192974	13411150	21131162	24769186
#产成品存货	4092588	1162507	1708644	1221437	2032149	2060439
固定资产净值	20640589	6531864	9640962	4467763	7934893	12705696
年末资产总额	72060215	20907895	32094610	19057710	31264481	40795733
年末负债及所有者权益						
年末负债总额	41895576	14060695	17326125	10508756	18076929	23818647
所有者权益合计	30043497	6805798	14736183	8501516	13132553	16910944
损益及分配						
主营业务收入	96126551	27505512	37950587	30670452	39264023	56862527
主营业务成本	86314480	24583192	34137968	27593320	34374642	51939838
主营业务税金及附加	271432	75712	110907	84813	147929	123504
主营业务利润	9540638	2846608	3701711	2992319	4741452	4799185
销售费用	1888957	598874	711616	578466	1184708	704249
管理费用	4608271	1107265	2107687	1393318	2133282	2474989
财务费用	453489	273396	146911	33181	198155	255334
#利息支出	531638	286513	179832	65293	248393	283245
利税总额	5188363	1769916	1772043	1646405	2310120	2878244
利润总额	2916748	905282	999404	1012062	1297846	1618902
亏损企业亏损总额	443282	51625	266680	124977	189325	253957

4-8　规模以上工业企业主要指标（2012年）

Main Indicators of Industrial Enterprises above Designated Size (2012)

单位：万元

项　　目	企业单位数(个)	#亏损企业	工业销售产值	工　业增加值	全部从业人员平均人数(人)
总　　计	4526	691	95234082	19781297	2546960
按轻重工业分					
轻工业	2416	358	38944248	9280902	1347691
重工业	2110	333	56289834	10500396	1199269
按企业规模分					
大型企业	223	20	44662808	8845460	841080
中型企业	1744	275	30805205	7245952	1303585
小型企业	2500	376	19560228	3649428	398947
微型企业	59	20	205841	40458	3348
按工业行业分(大类)					
煤炭开采和洗选业					
石油和天然气开采业					
黑色金属矿采选业					
有色金属矿采选业					
非金属矿采选业					
开采辅助活动					
其他采矿业					
农副食品加工业	43	5	3276839	331303	8015
食品制造业	29	2	919890	367837	15119
酒、饮料和精制茶制造业	13	1	1803768	323420	8450
烟草制品业					
纺织业	134	20	1788975	447078	62021
纺织服装、服饰业	338	34	4285356	1140689	181501
皮革、毛皮、羽毛及其制品和制鞋业	285	53	3116508	1120688	272481
木材加工和木、竹、藤、棕、草制品业	29	6	172861	39509	5750
家具制造业	207	25	2052073	516540	84824
造纸和纸制品业	225	25	5190503	984416	69282
印刷和记录媒介复制业	78	11	1059188	355826	36691
文教、工美、体育和娱乐用品制造业	193	37	2746781	736495	184502
石油加工、炼焦和核燃料加工业	4	1	171281	11405	258
化学原料和化学制品制造业	160	17	2567171	434124	26636
医药制造业	10	2	126735	57589	2519
化学纤维制造业	8		69488	14174	1812
橡胶和塑料制品业	478	70	4281877	1096454	183790
非金属矿物制品业	94	12	1209066	294001	29274
黑色金属冶炼和压延加工业	29	5	390381	35150	4949
有色金属冶炼和压延加工业	68	14	974082	88744	10669
金属制品业	244	33	2528835	672895	91352
通用设备制造业	181	26	4469529	612503	76187
专用设备制造业	144	20	1165069	344301	47813
汽车制造业	45	2	1044868	239269	18296
铁路、船舶、航空航天和其他运输设备制造业	18	2	476022	128097	9527
电气机械和器材制造业	485	75	7870232	1708276	245714
计算机、通信和其他电子设备制造业	818	149	33190769	5656693	759509
仪器仪表制造业	70	15	1234537	386134	58545
其他制造业	42	9	531001	131942	20422
废弃资源综合利用业	1	1	13389	2061	94
金属制品、机械和设备修理业					
电力、热力生产和供应业	16	4	5976835	1376283	25584
燃气生产和供应业	5		268662	36109	668
水的生产和供应业	32	15	261516	91293	4706

4-8 续表 1

(2012年)

单位：万元

项目	年末资产合计	#流动资产合计	#产成品	固定资产合计	年末负债合计
总计	72060215	45900348	4092588	21560952	41895576
按轻重工业分					
轻工业	31264481	21131162	2032149	8438111	18076929
重工业	40795733	24769186	2060439	13122842	23818647
按企业规模分					
大型企业	30303950	17025939	1529716	11460925	16923254
中型企业	25102212	16732249	1624079	6611802	14514833
小型企业	16409916	11966489	926774	3454137	10278819
微型企业	244137	175670	12018	34089	178670
按工业行业分(大类)					
煤炭开采和洗选业					
石油和天然气开采业					
黑色金属矿采选业					
有色金属矿采选业					
非金属矿采选业					
开采辅助活动					
其他采矿业					
农副食品加工业	1740345	1350080	107022	295746	1306397
食品制造业	1033351	752632	36234	234580	342438
酒、饮料和精制茶制造业	1017985	628938	41574	342307	615720
烟草制品业					
纺织业	1788491	1257240	168584	486838	903784
纺织服装、服饰业	3243166	2567734	254309	503818	2077321
皮革、毛皮、羽毛及其制品和制鞋业	1965827	1519358	151864	345227	1340902
木材加工和木、竹、藤、棕、草制品业	211703	155960	12781	40626	153063
家具制造业	1531710	1175683	119781	265228	862882
造纸和纸制品业	5778283	2710590	225826	2827130	3278283
印刷和记录媒介复制业	1125108	798770	49473	269407	524377
文教、工美、体育和娱乐用品制造业	1827690	1417507	209031	349371	1111178
石油加工、炼焦和核燃料加工业	167832	156714	4984	8344	142630
化学原料和化学制品制造业	2096771	1558840	119284	327004	1132010
医药制造业	239218	168569	6243	49430	69622
化学纤维制造业	36549	30643	4959	5443	23668
橡胶和塑料制品业	3650762	2535962	283041	821734	2016992
非金属矿物制品业	1758617	911279	75941	660019	1088631
黑色金属冶炼和压延加工业	360842	278925	25034	48332	231410
有色金属冶炼和压延加工业	671910	546689	66840	89147	454919
金属制品业	2243056	1466533	123414	689560	1115299
通用设备制造业	3013581	2191408	199838	505079	1888347
专用设备制造业	1226709	852650	75896	314006	659708
汽车制造业	770675	480874	39491	217602	305435
铁路、船舶、航空航天和其他运输设备制造业	553180	340936	15985	164095	347356
电气机械和器材制造业	6544142	4904367	400126	1297214	3653810
计算机、通信和其他电子设备制造业	19008579	12739106	1156972	5371249	11450221
仪器仪表制造业	904575	587523	60586	257654	472121
其他制造业	472865	315191	31530	104328	277626
废弃资源综合利用业	8027	6729		164	5235
金属制品、机械和设备修理业					
电力、热力生产和供应业	5839913	1089433	24563	4037382	3200099
燃气生产和供应业	247826	82280	180	119206	140471
水的生产和供应业	980925	321206	1201	513685	703625

4-8 续表 2

(2012年)

单位：万元

项　　目	主营业务收入	主营业务税金及附加	成本费用总额	本年应交增值税	亏损企业亏损总额
总　　计	96126551	271432	94188347	1969193	443282
按轻重工业分					
轻工业	39264023	147929	38535875	856879	189325
重工业	56862527	123504	55652472	1112314	253957
按企业规模分					
大型企业	44766830	104023	43726031	1035916	64663
中型企业	31203268	105223	30573541	538827	248492
小型企业	19923768	61640	19651513	392732	117337
微型企业	232685	547	237263	1717	12790
按工业行业分(大类)					
煤炭开采和洗选业					
石油和天然气开采业					
黑色金属矿采选业					
有色金属矿采选业					
非金属矿采选业					
开采辅助活动					
其他采矿业					
农副食品加工业	3392365	1805	3330265	24296	757
食品制造业	915277	7830	764235	56315	892
酒、饮料和精制茶制造业	1804404	18185	1602461	69488	2005
烟草制品业					
纺织业	1784923	4742	1757546	61300	7535
纺织服装、服饰业	4255506	16896	4081338	129291	20190
皮革、毛皮、羽毛及其制品和制鞋业	3175916	15144	3188414	43167	30312
木材加工和木、竹、藤、棕、草制品业	172419	894	173973	5537	1108
家具制造业	2079615	10371	2072602	51266	17990
造纸和纸制品业	5168949	16023	5490513	136118	22756
印刷和记录媒介复制业	1079128	4667	1004246	28528	6519
文教、工美、体育和娱乐用品制造业	2827947	10805	2786420	18538	8686
石油加工、炼焦和核燃料加工业	169969	204	169148	1368	127
化学原料和化学制品制造业	2569171	7771	2450181	71855	10755
医药制造业	127401	1268	104220	11807	278
化学纤维制造业	69664	204	67442	1724	
橡胶和塑料制品业	4378449	13707	4303596	81527	29849
非金属矿物制品业	1212440	4734	1179930	36045	32565
黑色金属冶炼和压延加工业	445213	637	448949	5345	4317
有色金属冶炼和压延加工业	973672	1891	968064	13761	2718
金属制品业	2541554	8206	2505219	49042	10360
通用设备制造业	4507756	11738	4415577	51891	10965
专用设备制造业	1191969	5597	1149176	37481	2563
汽车制造业	1059173	4019	985815	18380	807
铁路、船舶、航空航天和其他运输设备制造业	477627	2469	455123	19763	71
电气机械和器材制造业	7855388	23058	7643432	130838	37175
计算机、通信和其他电子设备制造业	33539655	65869	32939751	527778	133868
仪器仪表制造业	1245300	3392	1218897	15719	7773
其他制造业	536506	1699	531518	4027	7351
废弃资源综合利用业	13389	16	13886	2278	494
金属制品、机械和设备修理业					
电力、热力生产和供应业	6019916	4409	5869327	249742	17557
燃气生产和供应业	266879	818	236588	857	
水的生产和供应业	269012	2368	280498	14122	14939

4-8 续表 3

(2012年)

项目	利税总额(万元)	人均税收(元)	利润总额(万元)	人均利润(元)
总计	5188363	8919	2916748	11452
按轻重工业分				
轻工业	2310120	7511	1297846	9630
重工业	2878244	10501	1618902	13499
按企业规模分				
大型企业	2702646	13832	1539257	18301
中型企业	1448454	4990	797967	6121
小型企业	1043453	11417	587988	14738
微型企业	-6190	6794	-8465	-25283
按工业行业分(大类)				
煤炭开采和洗选业				
石油和天然气开采业				
黑色金属矿采选业				
有色金属矿采选业				
非金属矿采选业				
开采辅助活动				
其他采矿业				
农副食品加工业	170626	32700	144417	180183
食品制造业	212305	42427	148160	97996
酒、饮料和精制茶制造业	199107	103755	111433	131874
烟草制品业				
纺织业	114861	10650	48809	7870
纺织服装、服饰业	311249	8058	164995	9091
皮革、毛皮、羽毛及其制品和制鞋业	93829	2144	35402	1299
木材加工和木、竹、藤、棕、草制品业	7982	11223	1529	2660
家具制造业	82633	7508	18945	2233
造纸和纸制品业	271441	21999	119028	17180
印刷和记录媒介复制业	130515	9048	97317	26523
文教、工美、体育和娱乐用品制造业	88908	1812	55473	3007
石油加工、炼焦和核燃料加工业	2723	60903	1152	44651
化学原料和化学制品制造业	208784	29902	129137	48482
医药制造业	36072	51908	22996	91291
化学纤维制造业	4520	10639	2592	14306
橡胶和塑料制品业	180772	5188	85422	4648
非金属矿物制品业	65387	13949	24553	8387
黑色金属冶炼和压延加工业	7232	12086	1250	2527
有色金属冶炼和压延加工业	29666	14693	13990	13112
金属制品业	140517	6276	83187	9106
通用设备制造业	199364	8438	135078	17730
专用设备制造业	108346	9012	65256	13648
汽车制造业	98857	12282	76386	41750
铁路、船舶、航空航天和其他运输设备制造业	45111	23360	22856	23991
电气机械和器材制造业	398326	6293	243703	9918
计算机、通信和其他电子设备制造业	1341482	7831	746722	9832
仪器仪表制造业	49892	3303	30556	5219
其他制造业	12507	2808	6772	3316
废弃资源综合利用业	1800	244053	-494	-52553
金属制品、机械和设备修理业				
电力、热力生产和供应业	529434	107569	254228	99370
燃气生产和供应业	35320	25061	33646	503687
水的生产和供应业	8797	35157	-7748	-16464

4-9 规模以上工业企业主要经济效益指标（2012年）

Main Indicators on Economic Benefit of Industrial Enterprises above Designated Size (2012)

项目	工业增加值率(%)	总资产贡献率(%)	资产负债率(%)	流动资产周转率(次/年)	成本费用利润率(%)	全员劳动生产率(元/人)	产品销售率(%)
总计	20.8	7.7	58.1	2.1	3.1	77666	100.3
按轻重工业分							
轻工业	23.8	7.9	57.8	1.9	3.4	68865	99.7
重工业	18.8	7.6	58.4	2.3	2.9	87557	100.8
按企业规模分							
大型企业	19.9	9.4	55.9	2.7	3.5	105168	100.3
中型企业	23.6	6.3	57.8	1.9	2.6	55585	100.2
小型企业	18.8	7.1	62.6	1.7	3.0	91477	100.6
微型企业	19.6	-2.5	73.2	1.4	-3.6	120841	99.6
按工业行业分(大类)							
煤炭开采和洗选业							
石油和天然气开采业							
黑色金属矿采选业							
有色金属矿采选业							
非金属矿采选业							
开采辅助活动							
其他采矿业							
农副食品加工业	10.3	10.9	75.1	2.6	4.3	413353	101.9
食品制造业	40.9	20.1	33.1	1.2	19.4	243294	102.4
酒、饮料和精制茶制造业	18.7	20.8	60.5	2.9	7.0	382745	104.3
烟草制品业							
纺织业	24.4	5.9	50.5	1.4	2.8	72085	97.6
纺织服装、服饰业	25.5	9.8	64.1	1.7	4.0	62848	95.7
皮革、毛皮、羽毛及其制品和制鞋业	35.9	4.9	68.2	2.1	1.1	41129	99.9
木材加工和木、竹、藤、棕、草制品业	22.6	5.2	72.3	1.1	0.9	68712	99.1
家具制造业	25.2	5.8	56.3	1.8	0.9	60896	100.0
造纸和纸制品业	19.0	6.1	56.7	2.1	2.2	142088	100.3
印刷和记录媒介复制业	33.3	11.6	46.6	1.4	9.7	96979	99.2
文教、工美、体育和娱乐用品制造业	26.8	5.4	60.8	2.0	2.0	39918	100.0
石油加工、炼焦和核燃料加工业	7.7	2.9	85.0	1.1	0.7	442035	116.0
化学原料和化学制品制造业	17.0	10.5	54.0	1.7	5.3	162984	100.4
医药制造业	44.2	14.1	29.1	0.8	22.1	228617	97.2
化学纤维制造业	20.3	13.4	64.8	2.3	3.8	78222	99.3
橡胶和塑料制品业	25.5	5.2	55.3	1.7	2.0	59658	99.8
非金属矿物制品业	24.2	4.3	61.9	1.3	2.1	100431	99.4
黑色金属冶炼和压延加工业	9.0	2.4	64.1	1.6	0.3	71024	99.4
有色金属冶炼和压延加工业	10.1	5.0	67.7	1.8	1.5	83179	111.3
金属制品业	26.4	6.7	49.7	1.8	3.3	73660	99.1
通用设备制造业	13.6	6.6	62.7	2.1	3.1	80395	99.4
专用设备制造业	29.1	9.2	53.8	1.4	5.7	72010	98.3
汽车制造业	23.2	13.4	39.6	2.2	7.8	130777	101.3
铁路、船舶、航空航天和其他运输设备制造业	26.6	8.5	62.8	1.4	5.0	134457	98.8
电气机械和器材制造业	21.6	6.4	55.8	1.6	3.2	69523	99.5
计算机、通信和其他电子设备制造业	17.2	7.3	60.2	2.6	2.3	74478	101.2
仪器仪表制造业	31.5	5.7	52.2	2.1	2.5	65955	100.7
其他制造业	25.2	3.0	58.7	1.7	1.3	64608	101.6
废弃资源综合利用业	15.4	22.4	65.2	2.0	-3.6	219298	100.0
金属制品、机械和设备修理业							
电力、热力生产和供应业	23.0	10.8	54.8	5.6	4.3	537947	100.0
燃气生产和供应业	13.4	16.0	56.7	3.2	14.2	540560	100.0
水的生产和供应业	33.4	3.7	71.7	0.9	-2.8	193993	95.6

4-10 规模以上国有及国有控股工业企业主要经济指标（2012年）

Main Indicators of State-owned and State-holding Industrial Enterprises above Designated Size (2012)

项目	企业单位数（个）	#亏损企业	工业增加值（万元）	主营业务收入（万元）	亏损企业亏损总额（万元）
总计	31	4	1684773	7545167	14146
按轻重工业分					
轻工业	14	2	191381	895352	10014
重工业	17	2	1493392	6649815	4133
按企业规模分					
大型企业	4		1232101	5706094	
中型企业	12	3	231885	966938	10164
小型企业	15	1	220787	872135	3983
微型企业					
按销售收入分					
10亿元以上	8		1551637	7007460	
5-10亿元	4		75088	297186	
1-5亿元	6	1	38587	158864	9555
1亿元以下	13	3	19460	81656	4591
按工业行业分(大类)					
煤炭开采和洗选业					
石油和天然气开采业					
黑色金属矿采选业					
有色金属矿采选业					
非金属矿采选业					
开采辅助活动					
其他采矿业					
农副食品加工业	2		110058	652280	
食品制造业					
酒、饮料和精制茶制造业	2		7965	48116	
烟草制品业					
纺织业					
纺织服装、服饰业	1	1	1565	8503	459
皮革、毛皮、羽毛及其制品和制鞋业	1		4638	5506	
木材加工和木、竹、藤、棕、草制品业					
家具制造业					
造纸和纸制品业					
印刷和记录媒介复制业	1		2793	8793	
文教、工美、体育和娱乐用品制造业	1		997	4995	
石油加工、炼焦和核燃料加工业					
化学原料和化学制品制造业	2		20063	97563	
医药制造业					
化学纤维制造业					
橡胶和塑料制品业	1		2324	9214	
非金属矿物制品业	1		1596	6794	
黑色金属冶炼和压延加工业	1		1457	60575	
有色金属冶炼和压延加工业					
金属制品业	2		1636	9181	
通用设备制造业	1		12102	49110	
专用设备制造业	1		5894	15808	
汽车制造业					
铁路、船舶、航空航天和其他运输设备制造业	1		60871	244786	
电气机械和器材制造业	1		2182	10122	
计算机、通信和其他电子设备制造业	4	2	86344	427723	4133
仪器仪表制造业					
其他制造业					
废弃资源综合利用业					
金属制品、机械和设备修理业					
电力、热力生产和供应业	5		1322398	5769503	
燃气生产和供应业					
水的生产和供应业	3	1	39889	116595	9555

4-10 续表

(2012年)

项目	利税总额(万元)	人均税收(元)	利润总额(万元)	人均利润(元)
总计	670956	78486	367499	95049
按轻重工业分				
轻工业	105250	25011	89925	146769
重工业	565706	88555	277574	85310
按企业规模分				
大型企业	384621	85536	139508	48684
中型企业	126186	31344	101138	126565
小型企业	160150	165079	126853	628920
微型企业				
按销售收入分				
10亿元以上	642360	94677	361728	122036
5-10亿元	16800	46656	6587	30092
1-5亿元	10902	21934	1203	2720
1亿元以下	894	12078	-2019	-8370
按工业行业分(大类)				
煤炭开采和洗选业				
石油和天然气开采业				
黑色金属矿采选业				
有色金属矿采选业				
非金属矿采选业				
开采辅助活动				
其他采矿业				
农副食品加工业	90616	4278	90381	1643289
食品制造业				
酒、饮料和精制茶制造业	4782	64062	2501	70258
烟草制品业				
纺织业				
纺织服装、服饰业	-459		-459	-12742
皮革、毛皮、羽毛及其制品和制鞋业	1154	283639	133	37028
木材加工和木、竹、藤、棕、草制品业				
家具制造业				
造纸和纸制品业				
印刷和记录媒介复制业	1208	21287	1007	107170
文教、工美、体育和娱乐用品制造业	206	8383	15	674
石油加工、炼焦和核燃料加工业				
化学原料和化学制品制造业	8252	35137	4264	37567
医药制造业				
化学纤维制造业				
橡胶和塑料制品业	737	2058	666	19246
非金属矿物制品业	189	7158	66	3883
黑色金属冶炼和压延加工业	553	23354	402	61785
有色金属冶炼和压延加工业				
金属制品业	627	12378	358	16507
通用设备制造业	7493	43205	4590	68304
专用设备制造业	640		640	17497
汽车制造业				
铁路、船舶、航空航天和其他运输设备制造业	20516	32215	14008	69347
电气机械和器材制造业	894	9874	422	8833
计算机、通信和其他电子设备制造业	32228	15603	21932	33235
仪器仪表制造业				
其他制造业				
废弃资源综合利用业				
金属制品、机械和设备修理业				
电力、热力生产和供应业	500847	112651	233898	98703
燃气生产和供应业				
水的生产和供应业	472	61158	-7326	-57457

4-11 规模以上国有及国有控股工业企业主要经济效益指标（2012年）

Main Indicators on Economic Benefit of State-owned and State-holding Industrial Enterprises above Designated Size (2012)

项　　目	工业增加值率(%)	总资产贡献率(%)	资　产负债率(%)	流动资产周转率(次/年)	成本费用利润率(%)	全员劳动生产率(元/人)	产　品销售率(%)
总　　计	22.7	11.2	54.1	4.4	5.1	435747	99.0
按轻重工业分							
轻工业	22.0	14.6	71.7	2.7	11.0	312356	92.1
重工业	22.7	10.7	51.7	4.8	4.4	458983	99.9
按企业规模分							
大型企业	21.7	9.2	54.4	8.1	2.5	429963	99.9
中型企业	24.4	11.6	58.8	1.6	11.5	290182	94.2
小型企业	27.4	25.6	42.8	2.2	16.8	1094629	98.4
微型企业							
按工业行业分(大类)							
煤炭开采和洗选业							
石油和天然气开采业							
黑色金属矿采选业							
有色金属矿采选业							
非金属矿采选业							
开采辅助活动							
其他采矿业							
农副食品加工业	17.8	36.3	78.1	3.4	15.9	2001060	90.1
食品制造业							
酒、饮料和精制茶制造业	16.4	13.2	58.4	2.7	5.4	223742	101.9
烟草制品业							
纺织业							
纺织服装、服饰业	17.5	-5.5	37.9	1.0	-5.2	43483	95.0
皮革、毛皮、羽毛及其制品和制鞋业	84.2	13.6	17.3	2.2	2.5	1288417	100.0
木材加工和木、竹、藤、棕、草制品业							
家具制造业							
造纸和纸制品业							
印刷和记录媒介复制业	27.4	15.1	19.6	2.8	10.6	297128	94.6
文教、工美、体育和娱乐用品制造业	25.0	6.1	2.5	2.2	0.3	43938	99.5
石油加工、炼焦和核燃料加工业							
化学原料和化学制品制造业	20.7	5.0	70.0	0.7	4.5	176764	102.1
医药制造业							
化学纤维制造业							
橡胶和塑料制品业	25.1	13.0	79.1	2.1	7.8	67168	100.0
非金属矿物制品业	24.4	4.3	70.2	2.0	0.8	93339	109.0
黑色金属冶炼和压延加工业	29.3	5.0	70.6	5.3	0.7	224123	100.0
有色金属冶炼和压延加工业							
金属制品业	17.9	7.6	70.7	0.9	4.0	75406	101.1
通用设备制造业	25.0	23.9	49.7	2.1	10.6	180082	99.0
专用设备制造业	41.2	1.1	58.0	0.6	4.2	161041	100.0
汽车制造业							
铁路、船舶、航空航天和其他运输设备制造业	24.8	6.1	66.1	1.4	6.0	301343	99.5
电气机械和器材制造业	23.2	7.8	61.6	1.2	4.4	45638	107.6
计算机、通信和其他电子设备制造业	19.5	6.1	32.0	1.6	5.3	130844	98.5
仪器仪表制造业							
其他制造业							
废弃资源综合利用业							
金属制品、机械和设备修理业							
电力、热力生产和供应业	23.1	11.8	51.9	7.9	4.2	558044	100.0
燃气生产和供应业							
水的生产和供应业	31.6	4.1	78.8	1.5	-5.9	312854	92.4

4-12 规模以上集体工业企业主要经济指标（2012年）

Main Indicators of Collective-owned Industrial Enterprises above Designated Size (2012)

项目	企业单位数（个）	#亏损企业	工业增加值（万元）	主营业务收入（万元）	亏损企业亏损总额（万元）
总　　计	53	20	211759	442620	6585
按轻重工业分					
轻工业	44	19	136492	338195	6505
重工业	9	1	75267	104426	79
按企业规模分					
大型企业	2	1	40470	100952	1241
中型企业	21	6	122458	198746	1671
小型企业	27	11	48698	142534	3585
微型企业	3	2	133	388	88
按销售收入分					
10亿元以上					
5-10亿元	1		35339	59851	
1-5亿元	10	3	80903	199471	1490
1亿元以下	42	17	95517	183298	5094
按工业行业分(大类)					
煤炭开采和洗选业					
石油和天然气开采业					
黑色金属矿采选业					
有色金属矿采选业					
非金属矿采选业					
开采辅助活动					
其他采矿业					
农副食品加工业	1		912	3267	
食品制造业					
酒、饮料和精制茶制造业					
烟草制品业					
纺织业					
纺织服装、服饰业	2		5787	7156	
皮革、毛皮、羽毛及其制品和制鞋业	5	4	29888	30697	922
木材加工和木、竹、藤、棕、草制品业					
家具制造业					
造纸和纸制品业	4	1	8662	63165	9
印刷和记录媒介复制业	1		1758	4409	
文教、工美、体育和娱乐用品制造业	2	2	24200	26774	823
石油加工、炼焦和核燃料加工业					
化学原料和化学制品制造业					
医药制造业					
化学纤维制造业					
橡胶和塑料制品业	2		36376	63978	
非金属矿物制品业					
黑色金属冶炼和压延加工业					
有色金属冶炼和压延加工业					
金属制品业					
通用设备制造业					
专用设备制造业					
汽车制造业					
铁路、船舶、航空航天和其他运输设备制造业					
电气机械和器材制造业	3	1	11292	68788	1241
计算机、通信和其他电子设备制造业	9	1	50477	56885	79
仪器仪表制造业					
其他制造业					
废弃资源综合利用业					
金属制品、机械和设备修理业					
电力、热力生产和供应业					
燃气生产和供应业					
水的生产和供应业	24	11	42408	117501	3512

4-12 续表

(2012年)

项目	利税总额(万元)	人均税收(元)	利润总额(万元)	人均利润(元)
总计	25161	1809	15168	2746
按轻重工业分				
轻工业	11379	2714	2191	647
重工业	13782	376	12978	6071
按企业规模分				
大型企业	202	335	-266	-190
中型企业	15720	438	14071	3736
小型企业	9289	23618	1450	4370
微型企业	-50	1269	-88	-2963
按销售收入分				
10亿元以上				
5-10亿元	1362	319	975	802
1-5亿元	12856	1785	9323	4710
1亿元以下	10943	2608	4871	2092
按工业行业分(大类)				
煤炭开采和洗选业				
石油和天然气开采业				
黑色金属矿采选业				
有色金属矿采选业				
非金属矿采选业				
开采辅助活动				
其他采矿业				
农副食品加工业	76	5274	26	2684
食品制造业				
酒、饮料和精制茶制造业				
烟草制品业				
纺织业				
纺织服装、服饰业	398		398	3284
皮革、毛皮、羽毛及其制品和制鞋业	-835	55	-904	-730
木材加工和木、竹、藤、棕、草制品业				
家具制造业				
造纸和纸制品业	2537	18977	334	2876
印刷和记录媒介复制业	161		161	29796
文教、工美、体育和娱乐用品制造业	-813	10	-823	-801
石油加工、炼焦和核燃料加工业				
化学原料和化学制品制造业				
医药制造业				
化学纤维制造业				
橡胶和塑料制品业	1377	298	988	758
非金属矿物制品业				
黑色金属冶炼和压延加工业				
有色金属冶炼和压延加工业				
金属制品业				
通用设备制造业				
专用设备制造业				
汽车制造业				
铁路、船舶、航空航天和其他运输设备制造业				
电气机械和器材制造业	1470	815	1263	4960
计算机、通信和其他电子设备制造业	12735	357	12317	10509
仪器仪表制造业				
其他制造业				
废弃资源综合利用业				
金属制品、机械和设备修理业				
电力、热力生产和供应业				
燃气生产和供应业				
水的生产和供应业	8056	23903	1408	5063

4-13 规模以上集体工业企业主要经济效益指标（2012年）

Main Indicators on Economic Benefit of Collective-owned Industrial Enterprises above Designated Size (2012)

项目	工业增加值率(%)	总资产贡献率(%)	资产负债率(%)	流动资产周转率(次/年)	成本费用利润率(%)	全员劳动生产率(元/人)	产品销售率(%)
总计	49.5	6.4	85.9	1.8	3.6	38335	98.3
按轻重工业分							
轻工业	41.0	4.1	85.6	1.5	0.7	40308	97.9
重工业	79.3	34.1	90.3	4.5	14.0	35210	99.9
按企业规模分							
大型企业	40.1	1.6	78.5	7.9	-0.4	28998	100.0
中型企业	67.8	13.5	136.4	3.6	6.9	32511	97.4
小型企业	33.3	4.5	71.3	0.8	1.0	146726	98.4
微型企业	34.4	-1.5	32.5	0.1	-21.3	4492	100.0
按工业行业分(大类)							
煤炭开采和洗选业							
石油和天然气开采业							
黑色金属矿采选业							
有色金属矿采选业							
非金属矿采选业							
开采辅助活动							
其他采矿业							
农副食品加工业	24.9	11.8	39.3	10.2	0.7	95947	89.4
食品制造业							
酒、饮料和精制茶制造业							
烟草制品业							
纺织业							
纺织服装、服饰业	80.9	12.1	15.1	3.3	5.7	47785	100.0
皮革、毛皮、羽毛及其制品和制鞋业	97.4	-7.0	725.9	2.9	-1.8	24161	85.4
木材加工和木、竹、藤、棕、草制品业							
家具制造业							
造纸和纸制品业	14.1	9.5	59.8	5.3	0.5	74609	100.6
印刷和记录媒介复制业	35.3	3.6	23.7	1.6	3.3	325611	100.0
文教、工美、体育和娱乐用品制造业	90.4	-4.2	70.5	5.3	-3.1	23571	100.0
石油加工、炼焦和核燃料加工业							
化学原料和化学制品制造业							
医药制造业							
化学纤维制造业							
橡胶和塑料制品业	56.9	10.3	88.0	5.4	1.6	27911	100.0
非金属矿物制品业							
黑色金属冶炼和压延加工业							
有色金属冶炼和压延加工业							
金属制品业							
通用设备制造业							
专用设备制造业							
汽车制造业							
铁路、船舶、航空航天和其他运输设备制造业							
电气机械和器材制造业	16.4	20.1	46.2	13.0	3.2	44352	99.9
计算机、通信和其他电子设备制造业	106.2	42.4	100.4	4.7	27.4	43065	99.8
仪器仪表制造业							
其他制造业							
废弃资源综合利用业							
金属制品、机械和设备修理业							
电力、热力生产和供应业							
燃气生产和供应业							
水的生产和供应业	37.5	4.0	71.0	0.7	1.2	152492	97.8

4-14 规模以上外商投资工业企业主要经济指标（2012年）

Main Indicators of Industrial Enterprises above Designated Size with Foreign Funds (2012)

项目	企业单位数(个)	#亏损企业	工业增加值(万元)	主营业务收入(万元)	亏损企业亏损总额(万元)
总　计	1052	208	5725790	30670452	124977
按轻重工业分					
轻工业	444	87	2247649	9746799	49271
重工业	608	121	3478142	20923653	75705
按企业规模分					
大型企业	78	5	2885485	16819061	4723
中型企业	444	82	2027860	8683134	85147
小型企业	518	119	801774	5080274	34875
微型企业	12	2	10672	87983	232
按销售收入分					
10亿元以上	48	1	2637466	17090848	587
5-10亿元	47	7	654128	3247652	14831
1-5亿元	344	59	1617350	7167663	61463
1亿元以下	613	141	816847	3164290	48096
按工业行业分(大类)					
煤炭开采和洗选业					
石油和天然气开采业					
黑色金属矿采选业					
有色金属矿采选业					
非金属矿采选业					
开采辅助活动					
其他采矿业					
农副食品加工业	7	1	51812	840978	331
食品制造业	2		262462	460443	
酒、饮料和精制茶制造业	2		179646	587558	
烟草制品业					
纺织业	16	3	59688	292148	264
纺织服装、服饰业	21	4	70641	216504	1310
皮革、毛皮、羽毛及其制品和制鞋业	75	11	335965	1065250	9529
木材加工和木、竹、藤、棕、草制品业	5	1	7368	31041	148
家具制造业	47	8	126800	572677	8369
造纸和纸制品业	15	2	25686	141465	645
印刷和记录媒介复制业	13	4	99595	222043	804
文教、工美、体育和娱乐用品制造业	44	6	136021	427500	3580
石油加工、炼焦和核燃料加工业	1	1	336	5011	127
化学原料和化学制品制造业	40	8	146734	1043402	9579
医药制造业	1		1813	5796	
化学纤维制造业					
橡胶和塑料制品业	115	27	279738	1156485	17470
非金属矿物制品业	18	5	41453	238325	12159
黑色金属冶炼和压延加工业	11	2	7204	146945	1415
有色金属冶炼和压延加工业	14	5	31837	441991	1687
金属制品业	55	12	138350	715761	4041
通用设备制造业	47	11	268142	2301395	4744
专用设备制造业	43	2	122542	437709	267
汽车制造业	21	2	157041	700016	807
铁路、船舶、航空航天和其他运输设备制造业	8	1	38176	131559	64
电气机械和器材制造业	118	20	450550	2090288	6019
计算机、通信和其他电子设备制造业	279	66	2465523	15469441	39462
仪器仪表制造业	17	2	159687	560582	1081
其他制造业	12	4	16280	75216	1078
废弃资源综合利用业					
金属制品、机械和设备修理业					
电力、热力生产和供应业	2		11289	44189	
燃气生产和供应业	3		33415	248736	
水的生产和供应业					

4-14 续表

(2012年)

项目	利税总额(万元)	人均税收(元)	利润总额(万元)	人均利润(元)
总计	1646405	9187	1012062	14657
按轻重工业分				
轻工业	603609	8254	365754	12692
重工业	1042796	9855	646307	16064
按企业规模分				
大型企业	998806	13144	639323	23376
中型企业	406728	5794	215811	6549
小型企业	237614	9593	154187	17730
微型企业	3257	10193	2740	54045
按销售收入分				
10亿元以上	1095447	21275	708207	38909
5-10亿元	160868	10311	80197	10250
1-5亿元	299075	3842	199821	7735
1亿元以下	91014	3908	23836	1387
按工业行业分(大类)				
煤炭开采和洗选业				
石油和天然气开采业				
黑色金属矿采选业				
有色金属矿采选业				
非金属矿采选业				
开采辅助活动				
其他采矿业				
农副食品加工业	15659	46364	8848	60231
食品制造业	157555	64670	119891	205856
酒、饮料和精制茶制造业	123505	204104	71132	277210
烟草制品业				
纺织业	6306	3878	3266	4167
纺织服装、服饰业	8739	2989	3972	2490
皮革、毛皮、羽毛及其制品和制鞋业	31114	1948	16201	2116
木材加工和木、竹、藤、棕、草制品业	1166	9341	362	4201
家具制造业	15314	5172	3426	1490
造纸和纸制品业	2369	3594	920	2284
印刷和记录媒介复制业	54822	9744	47819	66536
文教、工美、体育和娱乐用品制造业	11724	1396	7196	2217
石油加工、炼焦和核燃料加工业	-112	4688	-127	-39594
化学原料和化学制品制造业	63776	44312	30609	40893
医药制造业	137	2166	96	5150
化学纤维制造业				
橡胶和塑料制品业	32042	3362	15021	2967
非金属矿物制品业	-3267	8629	-7946	-14655
黑色金属冶炼和压延加工业	2715	28380	221	2510
有色金属冶炼和压延加工业	12434	17628	6823	21436
金属制品业	26511	5704	16767	9816
通用设备制造业	76434	9728	49203	17577
专用设备制造业	34445	7274	21310	11801
汽车制造业	77008	17152	59571	58598
铁路、船舶、航空航天和其他运输设备制造业	18309	26240	6312	13806
电气机械和器材制造业	77194	3499	54795	8560
计算机、通信和其他电子设备制造业	728492	11241	411221	14569
仪器仪表制造业	18109	1252	16028	9644
其他制造业	1261	4724	-293	-889
废弃资源综合利用业				
金属制品、机械和设备修理业				
电力、热力生产和供应业	19816	59028	18140	638729
燃气生产和供应业	32828	24915	31279	502873
水的生产和供应业				

4-15 规模以上外商投资工业企业主要经济效益指标（2012年）

Main Indicators on Economic Benefit of Industrial Enterprises above Designated Size with Foreign Funds (2012)

项　　目	工业增加值率 (%)	总资产贡献率 (%)	资　产负债率 (%)	流动资产周转率 (次/年)	成本费用利润率 (%)	全员劳动生产率 (元/人)	产　品销售率 (%)
总　　计	19.2	8.8	55.1	2.3	3.4	82923	101.9
按轻重工业分							
轻工业	23.6	9.1	54.4	2.0	3.9	77997	101.4
重工业	17.1	8.6	55.5	2.5	3.2	86451	102.2
按企业规模分							
大型企业	17.7	12.1	58.0	2.9	4.0	105505	102.4
中型企业	23.8	6.3	54.0	1.9	2.6	61537	100.9
小型企业	16.3	6.3	51.4	1.8	3.1	92197	101.9
微型企业	18.3	6.6	37.1	2.2	3.2	210495	105.6
按工业行业分(大类)							
煤炭开采和洗选业							
石油和天然气开采业							
黑色金属矿采选业							
有色金属矿采选业							
非金属矿采选业							
开采辅助活动							
其他采矿业							
农副食品加工业	6.2	6.4	55.9	3.8	1.1	352699	100.1
食品制造业	58.4	23.6	21.7	1.0	35.6	450656	102.4
酒、饮料和精制茶制造业	41.3	35.8	52.5	2.4	16.8	700100	130.2
烟草制品业							
纺织业	20.8	2.7	49.3	2.1	1.1	76142	102.0
纺织服装、服饰业	33.0	5.5	62.7	1.8	1.9	44289	101.1
皮革、毛皮、羽毛及其制品和制鞋业	31.9	4.4	56.6	2.0	1.6	43873	99.9
木材加工和木、竹、藤、棕、草制品业	22.0	3.9	50.1	0.9	1.2	85570	93.2
家具制造业	22.2	3.2	54.8	1.5	0.6	55166	98.3
造纸和纸制品业	20.7	2.6	51.3	1.6	0.7	63737	100.8
印刷和记录媒介复制业	47.2	25.2	36.0	1.3	27.3	138576	101.8
文教、工美、体育和娱乐用品制造业	32.6	3.8	59.4	1.9	1.7	41916	100.8
石油加工、炼焦和核燃料加工业	7.7	0.2	60.1	0.8	-2.3	105063	115.9
化学原料和化学制品制造业	14.0	9.1	54.2	2.1	3.0	196038	99.9
医药制造业	31.3	6.6	104.0	3.2	1.7	96936	100.0
化学纤维制造业							
橡胶和塑料制品业	24.5	3.2	58.8	1.5	1.3	55263	99.9
非金属矿物制品业	16.6	-0.5	45.7	1.9	-3.2	76454	95.9
黑色金属冶炼和压延加工业	5.0	3.3	47.7	1.7	0.2	81957	101.9
有色金属冶炼和压延加工业	9.4	5.8	58.4	2.5	1.6	100021	131.2
金属制品业	19.3	5.4	49.9	2.1	2.4	80992	100.0
通用设备制造业	11.6	4.6	66.2	2.0	2.2	95792	99.6
专用设备制造业	27.5	8.1	52.2	1.4	5.1	67864	96.5
汽车制造业	23.0	16.8	29.3	2.5	9.3	154477	101.0
铁路、船舶、航空航天和其他运输设备制造业	28.6	14.7	50.0	1.4	5.1	83498	98.4
电气机械和器材制造业	21.7	4.4	55.0	1.7	2.7	70386	99.7
计算机、通信和其他电子设备制造业	16.4	10.4	59.2	3.0	2.7	87351	102.4
仪器仪表制造业	28.8	5.0	51.1	2.3	3.0	96081	100.5
其他制造业	22.2	3.3	42.3	2.3	-0.4	49497	101.2
废弃资源综合利用业							
金属制品、机械和设备修理业							
电力、热力生产和供应业	25.6	13.6	23.7	0.7	30.1	397504	100.0
燃气生产和供应业	13.3	15.7	57.2	3.2	14.2	537217	100.0
水的生产和供应业							

4-16 规模以上港澳台商投资工业企业主要经济指标（2012年）

Main Indicators of Industrial Enterprises above Designated Size with Hong Kong, Macao and Taiwan Funds (2012)

项　　目	企　业单位数(个)	#亏 损企 业	工　业增加值(万元)	主营业务收入(万元)	亏损企业亏损总额(万元)
总　　计	1846	347	8590568	37950587	266680
按轻重工业分					
轻工业	1037	193	4449204	17413958	107105
重工业	809	154	4141364	20536629	159576
按企业规模分					
大型企业	108	13	3729805	17198348	58640
中型企业	876	159	3500228	14162104	137403
小型企业	843	165	1344652	6518851	58410
微型企业	19	10	15883	71283	12227
按销售收入分					
10亿元以上	57	6	3062555	16578863	34913
5-10亿元	57	8	1035990	3820528	38708
1-5亿元	548	84	2921070	11811723	114561
1亿元以下	1184	249	1570953	5739472	78499
按工业行业分(大类)					
煤炭开采和洗选业					
石油和天然气开采业					
黑色金属矿采选业					
有色金属矿采选业					
非金属矿采选业					
开采辅助活动					
其他采矿业					
农副食品加工业	5	1	52196	543450	307
食品制造业	10	1	66998	269387	390
酒、饮料和精制茶制造业	6	1	130207	1127976	2005
烟草制品业					
纺织业	72	12	314657	1203612	7136
纺织服装、服饰业	118	22	415575	1440982	15142
皮革、毛皮、羽毛及其制品和制鞋业	146	33	581961	1566108	19713
木材加工和木、竹、藤、棕、草制品业	10	3	11209	41554	819
家具制造业	63	12	165410	599923	9207
造纸和纸制品业	71	13	650775	3173974	20760
印刷和记录媒介复制业	38	5	209025	696014	5660
文教、工美、体育和娱乐用品制造业	116	27	495618	1531824	4119
石油加工、炼焦和核燃料加工业	2		3667	45866	
化学原料和化学制品制造业	49	8	163006	758280	1066
医药制造业	3	2	3023	10075	278
化学纤维制造业	5		5895	28455	
橡胶和塑料制品业	228	38	606084	2391386	11939
非金属矿物制品业	28	6	156864	563596	20390
黑色金属冶炼和压延加工业	9	3	17252	166123	2903
有色金属冶炼和压延加工业	21	5	26631	213223	771
金属制品业	107	18	349569	1123922	5323
通用设备制造业	69	11	238646	1699767	4651
专用设备制造业	55	13	133753	430713	2130
汽车制造业	11		44862	185723	
铁路、船舶、航空航天和其他运输设备制造业	3		76547	286735	
电气机械和器材制造业	212	38	903360	3906365	21871
计算机、通信和其他电子设备制造业	322	58	2283214	12443190	84570
仪器仪表制造业	39	11	178920	499765	6299
其他制造业	21	3	101939	365109	1733
废弃资源综合利用业					
金属制品、机械和设备修理业					
电力、热力生产和供应业	7	3	203705	637492	17504
燃气生产和供应业					
水的生产和供应业					

4-16 续表

(2012年)

项目	利税总额(万元)	人均税收(元)	利润总额(万元)	人均利润(元)
总计	1772043	5946	999404	7692
按轻重工业分				
轻工业	878718	5684	456383	6142
重工业	893324	6297	543021	9762
按企业规模分				
大型企业	900610	8732	517640	11803
中型企业	489054	3466	242487	3409
小型企业	393390	9653	250845	16988
微型企业	-11011	3179	-11568	-65990
按销售收入分				
10亿元以上	1020137	14830	645597	25563
5-10亿元	156445	5115	79478	5282
1-5亿元	445990	3814	240403	4460
1亿元以下	149470	3234	33926	949
按工业行业分(大类)				
煤炭开采和洗选业				
石油和天然气开采业				
黑色金属矿采选业				
有色金属矿采选业				
非金属矿采选业				
开采辅助活动				
其他采矿业				
农副食品加工业	2075	1256	1949	19413
食品制造业	40159	42767	21085	47275
酒、饮料和精制茶制造业	70296	67625	37424	76987
烟草制品业				
纺织业	92596	12271	39358	9072
纺织服装、服饰业	81521	5236	38012	4574
皮革、毛皮、羽毛及其制品和制鞋业	27370	1251	7852	503
木材加工和木、竹、藤、棕、草制品业	675	5338	-370	-1888
家具制造业	16949	5330	1301	443
造纸和纸制品业	172855	29084	74444	22001
印刷和记录媒介复制业	63610	8417	43010	17574
文教、工美、体育和娱乐用品制造业	46142	1533	26028	1984
石油加工、炼焦和核燃料加工业	2408	81445	1219	83473
化学原料和化学制品制造业	85113	22743	61942	60799
医药制造业	445	20242	18	858
化学纤维制造业	2327	10645	1470	18258
橡胶和塑料制品业	111624	6152	51520	5273
非金属矿物制品业	39446	16296	19178	15420
黑色金属冶炼和压延加工业	1794	7772	-46	-194
有色金属冶炼和压延加工业	4628	8655	1819	5607
金属制品业	51568	3588	33893	6880
通用设备制造业	85732	6040	64936	18860
专用设备制造业	44403	11069	23577	12530
汽车制造业	9336	4563	6973	13461
铁路、船舶、航空航天和其他运输设备制造业	24175	23925	15316	41360
电气机械和器材制造业	200602	6199	116742	8630
计算机、通信和其他电子设备制造业	326406	4029	181822	5067
仪器仪表制造业	8943	1718	2606	707
其他制造业	13685	1677	11089	7164
废弃资源综合利用业				
金属制品、机械和设备修理业				
电力、热力生产和供应业	145158	408747	115238	1574291
燃气生产和供应业				
水的生产和供应业				

4-17 规模以上港澳台商投资工业企业主要经济效益指标（2012年）

Main Indicators on Economic Benefit of Industrial Enterprises above Designated Size with Hong Kong, Macao and Taiwan Funds (2012)

项　　目	工业增加值率 (%)	总资产贡献率 (%)	资　产负债率 (%)	流动资产周转率 (次/年)	成本费用利润率 (%)	全员劳动生产率 (元/人)	产　品销售率 (%)
总　　计	22.7	5.9	54.0	1.9	2.6	66114	99.7
按轻重工业分							
轻工业	25.4	6.0	52.3	1.8	2.6	59876	99.4
重工业	20.3	5.7	55.6	2.0	2.7	74447	99.9
按企业规模分							
大型企业	21.6	6.7	52.0	2.3	3.0	85042	99.3
中型企业	24.8	4.5	54.6	1.8	1.7	49205	99.8
小型企业	20.9	6.9	56.7	1.5	3.9	91063	100.7
微型企业	22.9	-10.1	93.2	1.0	-15.2	90604	94.4
按工业行业分(大类)							
煤炭开采和洗选业							
石油和天然气开采业							
黑色金属矿采选业							
有色金属矿采选业							
非金属矿采选业							
开采辅助活动							
其他采矿业							
农副食品加工业	9.8	1.0	73.1	3.0	0.4	519882	101.9
食品制造业	24.9	16.5	39.6	1.6	8.7	150221	100.2
酒、饮料和精制茶制造业	10.8	13.5	65.3	3.1	3.4	267861	95.1
烟草制品业							
纺织业	25.0	6.2	45.9	1.3	3.3	72528	96.7
纺织服装、服饰业	28.3	7.0	57.7	1.7	2.7	50011	99.6
皮革、毛皮、羽毛及其制品和制鞋业	37.4	2.8	69.8	1.9	0.5	37293	99.4
木材加工和木、竹、藤、棕、草制品业	27.7	2.8	70.0	0.7	-0.8	57278	101.3
家具制造业	27.9	3.3	45.5	1.6	0.2	56344	101.5
造纸和纸制品业	20.5	5.3	51.5	2.0	2.1	192326	100.6
印刷和记录媒介复制业	29.7	8.2	46.5	1.3	6.4	85407	98.9
文教、工美、体育和娱乐用品制造业	32.7	4.2	61.8	1.7	1.7	37782	99.2
石油加工、炼焦和核燃料加工业	7.7	6.4	68.6	0.8	2.7	251171	99.3
化学原料和化学制品制造业	21.8	13.1	41.5	1.6	8.8	159998	100.6
医药制造业	31.3	1.5	122.8	0.5	0.2	143251	98.0
化学纤维制造业	20.4	14.5	51.2	1.9	5.4	73230	99.1
橡胶和塑料制品业	26.0	5.5	48.0	1.7	2.2	62031	99.9
非金属矿物制品业	28.0	4.2	64.0	1.1	3.6	126127	99.7
黑色金属冶炼和压延加工业	10.0	1.3	62.5	1.4	-0.03	72854	97.2
有色金属冶炼和压延加工业	12.4	2.8	66.4	1.7	0.9	82066	99.2
金属制品业	30.7	4.5	41.5	1.6	3.0	70957	99.0
通用设备制造业	14.0	8.4	55.3	2.3	3.9	69313	98.5
专用设备制造业	31.3	9.9	46.2	1.4	5.6	71085	101.2
汽车制造业	24.2	6.8	43.5	1.9	3.9	86606	100.0
铁路、船舶、航空航天和其他运输设备制造业	26.3	6.7	65.0	1.4	5.6	206717	98.3
电气机械和器材制造业	22.8	6.7	54.5	1.7	3.1	66780	99.9
计算机、通信和其他电子设备制造业	18.6	3.9	54.8	2.5	1.5	63631	100.0
仪器仪表制造业	36.6	2.4	51.5	1.9	0.5	48506	101.6
其他制造业	28.4	4.4	38.1	1.8	3.1	65860	102.3
废弃资源综合利用业							
金属制品、机械和设备修理业							
电力、热力生产和供应业	32.1	17.2	64.5	1.4	18.7	2782848	99.9
燃气生产和供应业							
水的生产和供应业							

4-18 规模以上私营工业企业主要经济指标（2012年）

Main Indicators of Private Industrial Enterprises above Designated Size (2012)

项目	企业单位数（个）	#亏损企业	工业增加值（万元）	主营业务收入（万元）	亏损企业亏损总额（万元）
总计	922	62	1982753	9361456	13660
按轻重工业分					
轻工业	531	28	1235559	5527973	6753
重工业	391	34	747195	3833483	6908
按企业规模分					
大型企业	12	1	391184	1488706	59
中型企业	227	13	756685	3583203	7200
小型企业	668	44	826896	4242503	6221
微型企业	15	4	7988	47045	180
按销售收入分					
10亿元以上	5		279977	1143557	
5-10亿元	17		213648	1198124	
1-5亿元	204	13	774062	3729328	7883
1亿元以下	696	49	715066	3290447	5778
按工业行业分(大类)					
煤炭开采和洗选业					
石油和天然气开采业					
黑色金属矿采选业					
有色金属矿采选业					
非金属矿采选业					
开采辅助活动					
其他采矿业					
农副食品加工业	14	1	43326	310197	40
食品制造业	10	1	16874	96841	503
酒、饮料和精制茶制造业	3		5602	40755	
烟草制品业					
纺织业	21		32173	129246	
纺织服装、服饰业	155	5	555953	2163531	3262
皮革、毛皮、羽毛及其制品和制鞋业	31	3	79162	256550	43
木材加工和木、竹、藤、棕、草制品业	8	1	6946	36712	81
家具制造业	57	4	95047	434369	291
造纸和纸制品业	78	5	153007	965455	935
印刷和记录媒介复制业	13	2	15712	70638	56
文教、工美、体育和娱乐用品制造业	19		33888	134844	
石油加工、炼焦和核燃料加工业	1		7401	119092	
化学原料和化学制品制造业	35		44781	235248	
医药制造业	1		3491	6202	
化学纤维制造业	3		8279	41209	
橡胶和塑料制品业	84	3	107022	460380	428
非金属矿物制品业	26	1	64916	284387	16
黑色金属冶炼和压延加工业	4		4483	30922	
有色金属冶炼和压延加工业	20	4	13253	156462	260
金属制品业	50	1	66274	315542	40
通用设备制造业	34	3	52294	278720	108
专用设备制造业	29	2	49405	185672	45
汽车制造业	1		1352	6207	
铁路、船舶、航空航天和其他运输设备制造业	5	1	10597	48669	7
电气机械和器材制造业	88	7	168887	941249	3155
计算机、通信和其他电子设备制造业	117	15	300793	1445522	3799
仪器仪表制造业	8	1	35328	126911	91
其他制造业	6	1	4447	26537	7
废弃资源综合利用业	1	1	2061	13389	494
金属制品、机械和设备修理业					
电力、热力生产和供应业					
燃气生产和供应业					
水的生产和供应业					

4-18 续表

(2012年)

项目	利税总额(万元)	人均税收(元)	利润总额(万元)	人均利润(元)
总　计	643429	11388	351246	13690
按轻重工业分				
轻工业	394880	11497	212371	13378
重工业	248549	11211	138874	14196
按企业规模分				
大型企业	188646	15931	131324	36496
中型企业	222653	8492	118726	9701
小型企业	231538	13329	101088	10329
微型企业	591	14245	108	3177
按销售收入分				
10亿元以上	151098	28927	108739	74260
5-10亿元	95432	14180	63946	28798
1-5亿元	246226	12157	125533	12644
1亿元以下	150673	8107	53027	4403
按工业行业分(大类)				
煤炭开采和洗选业				
石油和天然气开采业				
黑色金属矿采选业				
有色金属矿采选业				
非金属矿采选业				
开采辅助活动				
其他采矿业				
农副食品加工业	32080	40689	23792	116799
食品制造业	4829	11431	1538	5343
酒、饮料和精制茶制造业	523	2205	376	5640
烟草制品业				
纺织业	7139	8214	2460	4317
纺织服装、服饰业	198043	12485	116979	18016
皮革、毛皮、羽毛及其制品和制鞋业	19624	11169	7854	7453
木材加工和木、竹、藤、棕、草制品业	2161	21296	145	1528
家具制造业	24067	10728	6584	4040
造纸和纸制品业	47698	13600	24124	13917
印刷和记录媒介复制业	5518	11800	3184	16098
文教、工美、体育和娱乐用品制造业	4849	5269	1830	3193
石油加工、炼焦和核燃料加工业	427	45900	60	7500
化学原料和化学制品制造业	27629	25492	17881	46761
医药制造业	1466	33529	896	52706
化学纤维制造业	2193	10634	1122	11146
橡胶和塑料制品业	20887	8036	8952	6027
非金属矿物制品业	19646	13993	8033	9680
黑色金属冶炼和压延加工业	1387	13360	337	4289
有色金属冶炼和压延加工业	4906	14274	2063	10354
金属制品业	16996	9505	6901	6497
通用设备制造业	19417	12825	11173	17382
专用设备制造业	16887	9106	11671	20375
汽车制造业	72	1751	36	1811
铁路、船舶、航空航天和其他运输设备制造业	2256	12894	1199	14617
电气机械和器材制造业	53458	13175	24535	11176
计算机、通信和其他电子设备制造业	89353	6887	57193	12249
仪器仪表制造业	16939	24002	10343	37639
其他制造业	1179	5617	480	3861
废弃资源综合利用业	1800	244053	-494	-52553
金属制品、机械和设备修理业				
电力、热力生产和供应业				
燃气生产和供应业				
水的生产和供应业				

4-19 规模以上私营工业企业主要经济效益指标（2012年）

Main Indicators on Economic Benefit of Private Industrial Enterprises above Designated Size (2012)

项目	工业增加值率(%)	总资产贡献率(%)	资产负债率(%)	流动资产周转率(次/年)	成本费用利润率(%)	全员劳动生产率(元/人)	产品销售率(%)
总计	20.9	10.8	69.4	1.9	3.9	77278	98.1
按轻重工业分							
轻工业	21.6	11.9	70.4	2.0	4.0	77833	96.7
重工业	19.8	9.4	68.2	1.8	3.7	76378	100.3
按企业规模分							
大型企业	22.7	17.7	49.9	1.7	9.7	108713	89.1
中型企业	21.2	9.6	68.2	2.0	3.4	61830	100.1
小型企业	19.9	9.3	77.8	1.9	2.4	84489	100.1
微型企业	16.5	2.4	78.4	1.5	0.2	235646	100.0
按工业行业分(大类)							
煤炭开采和洗选业							
石油和天然气开采业							
黑色金属矿采选业							
有色金属矿采选业							
非金属矿采选业							
开采辅助活动							
其他采矿业							
农副食品加工业	13.9	19.0	78.9	2.5	6.9	212693	100.1
食品制造业	19.4	7.6	86.0	1.9	1.6	58611	111.3
酒、饮料和精制茶制造业	14.4	3.8	50.7	8.3	0.9	83987	104.6
烟草制品业							
纺织业	25.2	5.7	62.6	1.4	2.0	56474	98.8
纺织服装、服饰业	23.2	14.0	64.3	1.8	5.7	85625	92.0
皮革、毛皮、羽毛及其制品和制鞋业	32.9	13.4	55.2	2.9	3.2	75121	104.3
木材加工和木、竹、藤、棕、草制品业	18.4	9.9	88.0	1.9	0.4	73348	99.7
家具制造业	22.4	9.7	74.7	1.9	1.6	58325	100.0
造纸和纸制品业	15.5	10.0	74.8	2.5	2.6	88270	99.9
印刷和记录媒介复制业	28.1	11.7	72.5	1.9	4.7	79432	100.9
文教、工美、体育和娱乐用品制造业	24.8	7.7	84.2	2.2	1.4	59131	94.9
石油加工、炼焦和核燃料加工业	7.7	0.8	98.6	1.3	0.1	925150	124.3
化学原料和化学制品制造业	19.8	12.7	55.7	1.3	8.1	117105	105.3
医药制造业	36.3	28.0	71.7	1.4	17.1	205359	63.9
化学纤维制造业	20.2	12.4	76.6	2.7	2.8	82213	99.4
橡胶和塑料制品业	23.5	8.5	81.3	2.1	2.0	72059	99.5
非金属矿物制品业	23.7	10.4	69.5	2.2	2.9	78221	103.8
黑色金属冶炼和压延加工业	15.3	3.4	86.3	2.0	1.1	57036	101.0
有色金属冶炼和压延加工业	8.3	6.8	73.6	2.1	1.3	66533	99.2
金属制品业	20.9	8.9	81.6	1.8	2.2	62399	99.7
通用设备制造业	19.3	10.8	68.3	1.8	4.2	81353	99.3
专用设备制造业	26.9	10.7	65.9	1.6	6.6	86252	95.5
汽车制造业	19.5	1.2	56.9	0.9	0.6	67284	97.1
铁路、船舶、航空航天和其他运输设备制造业	22.5	6.1	83.0	1.3	2.5	129228	103.2
电气机械和器材制造业	18.1	8.4	71.0	1.5	2.7	76931	97.9
计算机、通信和其他电子设备制造业	21.0	9.6	64.3	2.2	4.1	64419	99.5
仪器仪表制造业	27.4	20.2	53.5	2.0	8.8	128557	98.4
其他制造业	18.7	8.3	75.2	2.4	1.8	35751	100.8
废弃资源综合利用业	15.4	22.4	65.2	2.0	-3.6	219298	100.0
金属制品、机械和设备修理业							
电力、热力生产和供应业							
燃气生产和供应业							
水的生产和供应业							

4-20 大中型工业企业主要经济指标（2012年）

Main Indicators of Large and Medium-sized Industrial Enterprises (2012)

项目	企业单位数（个）	#亏损企业	工业增加值（万元）	主营业务收入（万元）	亏损企业亏损总额（万元）
总计	1967	295	16091412	75970098	313155
按轻重工业分					
轻工业	1137	165	7582672	30327683	131497
重工业	830	130	8508740	45642415	181658
按企业规模分					
大型企业	223	20	8845460	44766830	64663
中型企业	1744	275	7245952	31203268	248492
按工业行业分(大类)					
煤炭开采和洗选业					
石油和天然气开采业					
黑色金属矿采选业					
有色金属矿采选业					
非金属矿采选业					
开采辅助活动					
其他采矿业					
农副食品加工业	7		170381	1365424	
食品制造业	9		336960	782979	
酒、饮料和精制茶制造业	7		305998	1703400	
烟草制品业					
纺织业	42	4	355828	1388740	2594
纺织服装、服饰业	178	20	950258	3481328	13102
皮革、毛皮、羽毛及其制品和制鞋业	175	32	970395	2700864	22054
木材加工和木、竹、藤、棕、草制品业	4	2	14134	55499	797
家具制造业	90	10	386295	1525538	16374
造纸和纸制品业	62	5	779212	3827098	18318
印刷和记录媒介复制业	36	4	285534	859590	5692
文教、工美、体育和娱乐用品制造业	134	27	670049	2562080	6998
石油加工、炼焦和核燃料加工业					
化学原料和化学制品制造业	21	2	130681	702709	8624
医药制造业	2		42439	90479	
化学纤维制造业	2		5579	32482	
橡胶和塑料制品业	173	31	710918	2638209	21915
非金属矿物制品业	28	7	201896	807852	30601
黑色金属冶炼和压延加工业	5		17946	70742	
有色金属冶炼和压延加工业	8	1	18383	116916	121
金属制品业	75	11	444922	1540825	4611
通用设备制造业	48	11	463497	3711642	7238
专用设备制造业	44	3	221437	688901	823
汽车制造业	17		156061	713331	
铁路、船舶、航空航天和其他运输设备制造业	12		124498	459376	
电气机械和器材制造业	220	31	1382908	5603308	25131
计算机、通信和其他电子设备制造业	495	78	5262301	31353106	110179
仪器仪表制造业	46	12	349177	1127296	6881
其他制造业	18	2	105871	384741	1505
废弃资源综合利用业					
金属制品、机械和设备修理业					
电力、热力生产和供应业	4		1158513	5325841	
燃气生产和供应业	1		30381	230094	
水的生产和供应业	4	2	38962	119711	9598

4-20 续表

(2012年)

项目	利税总额(万元)	人均税收(元)	利润总额(万元)	人均利润(元)
总计	4151100	8458	2337224	10898
按轻重工业分				
轻工业	1964828	7102	1159125	10217
重工业	2186272	9980	1178100	11663
按企业规模分				
大型企业	2702646	13832	1539257	18301
中型企业	1448454	4990	797967	6121
按工业行业分(大类)				
煤炭开采和洗选业				
石油和天然气开采业				
黑色金属矿采选业				
有色金属矿采选业				
非金属矿采选业				
开采辅助活动				
其他采矿业				
农副食品加工业	105803	27640	96654	292005
食品制造业	202502	54893	142356	129922
酒、饮料和精制茶制造业	193246	111463	110708	149505
烟草制品业				
纺织业	102532	11873	46659	9915
纺织服装、服饰业	281306	7923	161336	10655
皮革、毛皮、羽毛及其制品和制鞋业	85297	1920	37326	1494
木材加工和木、竹、藤、棕、草制品业	2745	9939	510	2266
家具制造业	56496	7426	9046	1416
造纸和纸制品业	228559	25632	110438	23965
印刷和记录媒介复制业	115684	8686	89513	29707
文教、工美、体育和娱乐用品制造业	81153	1718	51518	2987
石油加工、炼焦和核燃料加工业				
化学原料和化学制品制造业	46885	24691	17575	14805
医药制造业	31852	75081	21235	150180
化学纤维制造业	1658	10848	864	11798
橡胶和塑料制品业	105088	4276	45631	3282
非金属矿物制品业	41971	13650	13466	6449
黑色金属冶炼和压延加工业	5656	10449	2932	11245
有色金属冶炼和压延加工业	3960	5981	1676	4391
金属制品业	105232	5499	67882	9994
通用设备制造业	141813	6917	102762	18202
专用设备制造业	67892	7784	42581	13095
汽车制造业	69774	10403	55893	41890
铁路、船舶、航空航天和其他运输设备制造业	44322	24378	22835	25907
电气机械和器材制造业	320606	5545	208325	10289
计算机、通信和其他电子设备制造业	1259276	7988	699310	9976
仪器仪表制造业	43633	3011	27263	5014
其他制造业	13445	1871	10385	6349
废弃资源综合利用业				
金属制品、机械和设备修理业				
电力、热力生产和供应业	361233	100960	118261	49140
燃气生产和供应业	30669	20384	29577	551806
水的生产和供应业	813	52255	-7292	-47015

4-21 大中型工业企业主要经济效益指标（2012年）

Main Indicators on Economic Benefit of Large and Medium-sized Industrial Enterprises (2012)

项目	工业增加值率(%)	总资产贡献率(%)	资产负债率(%)	流动资产周转率(次/年)	成本费用利润率(%)	全员劳动生产率(元/人)	产品销售率(%)
总计	21.4	8.0	56.7	2.3	3.2	75030	100.3
按轻重工业分							
轻工业	25.1	8.6	55.6	1.9	3.9	66836	99.6
重工业	18.9	7.5	57.6	2.6	2.6	84233	100.7
按企业规模分							
大型企业	19.9	9.4	55.9	2.7	3.5	105168	100.3
中型企业	23.6	6.3	57.8	1.9	2.6	55585	100.2
按工业行业分(大类)							
煤炭开采和洗选业							
石油和天然气开采业							
黑色金属矿采选业							
有色金属矿采选业							
非金属矿采选业							
开采辅助活动							
其他采矿业							
农副食品加工业	13.9	17.2	76.8	2.9	7.6	514746	105.3
食品制造业	44.0	22.2	31.1	1.2	22.5	307530	102.3
酒、饮料和精制茶制造业	18.8	22.2	60.6	2.9	7.4	413232	104.5
烟草制品业							
纺织业	24.9	6.6	49.3	1.4	3.4	75616	97.5
纺织服装、服饰业	25.6	10.6	61.2	1.6	4.9	62758	94.8
皮革、毛皮、羽毛及其制品和制鞋业	36.4	5.3	68.6	2.1	1.4	38832	99.6
木材加工和木、竹、藤、棕、草制品业	25.1	5.2	83.6	0.9	0.9	62846	100.0
家具制造业	25.6	5.1	55.0	1.7	0.6	60453	100.1
造纸和纸制品业	20.3	6.2	54.0	2.0	2.7	169089	100.2
印刷和记录媒介复制业	33.7	12.6	44.3	1.4	11.3	94761	99.4
文教、工美、体育和娱乐用品制造业	26.9	5.5	61.1	2.0	2.0	38849	100.3
石油加工、炼焦和核燃料加工业							
化学原料和化学制品制造业	19.1	6.9	57.2	1.5	2.5	110084	102.7
医药制造业	47.0	16.2	8.3	0.7	30.6	300135	100.3
化学纤维制造业	17.7	11.3	75.5	2.4	2.7	76209	100.6
橡胶和塑料制品业	27.4	5.0	55.1	1.8	1.8	51132	100.0
非金属矿物制品业	25.2	3.5	63.0	1.1	1.7	96684	100.3
黑色金属冶炼和压延加工业	25.3	11.4	60.8	1.8	4.3	68837	99.7
有色金属冶炼和压延加工业	15.2	4.6	68.3	1.3	1.4	48149	95.2
金属制品业	28.8	7.9	45.0	2.0	4.5	65502	99.2
通用设备制造业	12.4	6.1	62.7	2.3	2.8	82097	99.3
专用设备制造业	31.8	9.6	54.8	1.5	6.4	68097	98.9
汽车制造业	22.2	13.8	34.9	2.3	8.5	116961	100.7
铁路、船舶、航空航天和其他运输设备制造业	26.8	8.6	63.4	1.4	5.2	141251	98.6
电气机械和器材制造业	24.2	7.1	49.2	1.8	3.8	68297	99.0
计算机、通信和其他电子设备制造业	17.1	7.5	60.3	2.8	2.3	75069	101.1
仪器仪表制造业	31.4	5.6	52.3	2.2	2.5	64216	100.6
其他制造业	28.3	4.5	36.1	2.0	2.8	64721	102.5
废弃资源综合利用业							
金属制品、机械和设备修理业							
电力、热力生产和供应业	21.9	9.5	53.9	9.9	2.3	481390	100.0
燃气生产和供应业	13.2	15.6	56.9	3.0	14.5	566813	100.0
水的生产和供应业	31.8	4.0	83.0	1.2	-5.7	251205	92.0

4-22 主要年份规模以上工业企业经济效益指标

Main Indicators on Economic Benefit of Industrial Enterprises above Designated Size in Main Years

项　　目	单位	1985年	1990年	1995年	2000年	2005年	2010年	2011年	2012年
产品销售率	%	85.6	94.7	98.7	99.8	99.5	99.9	99.6	100.3
成本费用利润率	%	6.5	1.5	5.0	5.4	3.3	4.8	3.7	3.1
产值利税率	%	6.9	6.4	9.8	9.2	4.6	6.1	5.7	5.5
资金利税率	%	9.0	6.3	6.9	7.5	5.5	7.8	7.3	7.8
销售利税率	%	8.2	6.7	9.1	9.2	4.7	6.1	5.7	5.4
每百元固定资产原值实现的产值	元	174.9	133.6	108.7	125.5	212.4	240.6	256.3	253.4
每百元固定资产原值实现的利税	元	14.2	8.5	10.7	11.5	9.9	14.6	14.6	13.8
每百元固定资产原值实现的利润	元	4.4	1.8	5.5	6.9	6.7	11.0	9.6	7.8
每百元流动资产实现的产值	元	210.2	247.8	169.4	178.6	216.3	204.3	203.0	206.8
每百元流动资产实现的利税	元	17.1	15.7	16.6	16.4	10.0	12.4	11.6	11.3
每百元流动资产实现的利润	元	4.9	3.3	8.6	9.8	6.8	9.3	7.6	6.4
亏损企业亏损面	%	7.2	11.1	25.9	31.3	30.1	16.2	16.0	15.3
全部流动资产周转天数	天	173.7	155.6	201.1	189.0	169.8	179.4	177.6	169.9
全员劳动生产率	元/人	2906	6439	13778	36101	53340	60854	65087	77666
人均利税	元	626	1519	5351	11703	9193	16728	19152	20371

注：由于1993年财务会计制度改革，本表中有关财务指标1993年起数字与往年不可比；全员劳动生产率1993年起按增加值计算，以前年份按净产值计算；1993年以前的流动资产按定额资金计算，下同。

4-23 主要年份规模以上国有经济工业企业经济效益指标

Main Indicators on Economic Benefit of State-owned and State-holding Industrial Enterprises above Designated Size in Main Years

项　　目	单位	1985年	1990年	1995年	2000年	2005年	2010年	2011年	2012年
产品销售率	%	89.6	102.0	100.8	98.3	100.0	99.8	100.0	99.8
成本费用利润率	%	8.0	-0.8	15.5	7.0	5.8	3.2	2.7	1.8
产值利税率	%	13.2	9.2	40.6	69.4	11.3	7.3	7.3	6.3
资金利税率	%	20.4	8.3	14.9	21.6	10.6	6.7	7.1	8.1
销售利税率	%	14.8	9.0	20.6	19.2	11.3	7.3	7.3	6.2
每百元固定资产原值实现的产值	元	142.9	85.5	61.1	63.4	105.0	79.0	79.4	85.6
每百元固定资产原值实现的利税	元	21.1	7.8	24.8	44.0	11.8	5.7	5.8	5.4
每百元固定资产原值实现的利润	元	9.6	-0.6	10.8	14.5	5.6	2.4	2.1	1.5
每百元流动资产实现的产值	元	445.1	397.8	96.3	73.4	443.4	794.5	796.5	990.2
每百元流动资产实现的利税	元	65.7	36.4	39.1	50.9	50.0	57.7	58.2	62.1
每百元流动资产实现的利润	元	27.5	-2.4	17.0	16.7	23.8	24.6	20.8	17.6
亏损企业亏损面	%	9.9	16.7	20.9		20.0			10.0
全部流动资产周转天数	天	80.9	88.7	299.8	137.7	83.0	46.1	45.8	35.9
全员劳动生产率	元/人	3641	11253	73910	456736	2320312	405232	450003	458865
人均利税	元	1757	5325	55113	303960	1197862	144620	152273	135757

4-24 主要年份规模以上集体经济工业企业经济效益指标

Main Indicators on Economic Benefit of Collective-owned Industrial Enterprises above Designated Size in Main Years

项　　目	单位	1985年	1990年	1995年	2000年	2005年	2010年	2011年	2012年
产品销售率	%	85.1	92.2	98.0	97.0	100.5	97.4	100.5	98.3
成本费用利润率	%	5.9	3.3	5.2	2.7	3.3	9.7	0.8	3.6
产值利税率	%	9.3	6.9	9.0	5.1	5.8	10.4	4.0	5.9
资金利税率	%	15.1	9.7	6.0	2.9	3.2	9.7	3.2	5.3
销售利税率	%	11.0	7.5	8.7	5.2	5.8	10.7	3.8	5.7
每百元固定资产原值实现的产值	元	236.7	159.4	128.0	99.3	98.1	131.1	139.1	97.2
每百元固定资产原值实现的利税	元	22.1	11.0	11.5	5.0	5.7	13.6	5.5	5.7
每百元固定资产原值实现的利润	元	10.8	4.5	6.4	2.4	3.0	11.5	1.1	3.4
每百元流动资产实现的产值	元	509.0	225.7	179.5	113.8	157.7	214.9	210.5	174.2
每百元流动资产实现的利税	元	47.5	15.6	16.1	5.7	9.1	22.4	8.3	10.2
每百元流动资产实现的利润	元	23.2	6.4	9.0	2.8	4.8	18.8	1.6	6.2
亏损企业亏损面	%	6.6	8.8	12.8	18.6	25.9	22.5	30.9	37.7
全部流动资产周转天数	天	84.3	175.3	197.4	340.1	241.7	175.1	165.8	198.0
全员劳动生产率	元/人	2664	5437	5820	16344	28414	31412	29868	38335
人均利税	元	715	1058	1533	3135	5241	8428	3344	4555

4-25 主要年份大中型工业企业经济效益指标

Main Indicators on Economic Benefit of Large and Medium-sized Industrial Enterprises in Main Years

项　　目	单位	1985年	1990年	1995年	2000年	2005年	2010年	2011年	2012年
产品销售率	%	104.3	103.5	99.7	98.6	99.5	100.6	99.5	100.3
成本费用利润率	%	14.3	2.2	12.9	12.0	3.8	5.1	4.2	3.2
产值利税率	%	16.1	8.7	19.9	21.4	4.7	6.4	6.0	5.5
资金利税率	%	14.8	6.5	14.0	15.3	6.1	8.4	7.7	8.1
销售利税率	%	15.5	8.4	19.8	21.7	4.7	6.4	6.0	5.5
每百元固定资产原值实现的产值	元	106.0	87.1	112.8	98.4	229.8	221.6	243.6	251.4
每百元固定资产原值实现的利税	元	17.1	7.6	22.4	21.1	10.7	14.2	14.6	13.9
每百元固定资产原值实现的利润	元	11.5	1.7	13.1	13.0	8.4	10.9	10.0	7.8
每百元流动资产实现的产值	元	758.8	329.3	174.3	183.4	227.4	220.6	212.4	223.0
每百元流动资产实现的利税	元	122.4	28.6	34.6	39.2	10.6	14.2	12.7	12.3
每百元流动资产实现的利润	元	82.3	6.4	20.2	24.2	8.3	10.9	8.7	6.9
亏损企业亏损面	%		17.2	22.2	12.8	20.1	12.2	14.4	15.0
全部流动资产周转天数	天	46.1	107.1	209.5	210.2	160.8	164.8	170.3	158.1
全员劳动生产率	元/人	6202	16492	81787	280810	72657	66101	63688	75030
人均利税	元	2601	7883	52997	165448	11918	18679	18731	19355

4-26 主要年份规模以上港澳台商投资工业企业经济效益指标

Main Indicators on Economic Benefit of Industrial Enterprises above Designated Size with Hong Kong, Macao and Taiwan Funds in Main Years

项　　目	单位	1990年	1995年	2000年	2005年	2010年	2011年	2012年
产品销售率	%	94.2	99.6	100.8	99.4	99.7	99.6	99.7
成本费用利润率	%	-11.5	2.1	4.6	3.2	5.4	3.6	2.6
产值利税率	%	-9.3	4.9	6.6	4.0	6.3	5.3	4.7
资金利税率	%	-14.3	3.8	5.4	4.6	7.6	6.5	5.9
销售利税率	%	-9.9	4.9	6.5	4.1	6.3	5.3	4.7
每百元固定资产原值实现的产值	元	104.9	114.8	114.5	198.1	216.6	232.0	214.0
每百元固定资产原值实现的利税	元	-9.7	5.6	7.5	8.0	13.6	12.3	10.0
每百元固定资产原值实现的利润	元	-12.6	2.6	5.1	6.0	11.1	8.9	5.6
每百元流动资产实现的产值	元	154.3	165.2	182.2	192.3	189.1	191.0	187.7
每百元流动资产实现的利税	元	-14.3	8.1	12.0	7.8	11.8	10.1	8.8
每百元流动资产实现的利润	元	-18.5	3.7	8.1	5.8	9.7	7.3	4.9
亏损企业亏损面	%	25.0	46.4	36.1	35.1	20.2	18.6	18.8
全部流动资产周转天数	天	251.1	199.1	199.9	191.1	194.1	187.5	187.8
全员劳动生产率	元/人	16962	17478	28933	41933	54793	57058	66114
人均利税	元	-8238	4232	7026	6244	14293	14263	13638

4-27 主要年份规模以上外商投资工业企业经济效益指标

Main Indicators on Economic Benefit of Foreign-funded Industrial Enterprises above Designated Size in Main Years

项　　目	单位	1990年	1995年	2000年	2005年	2010年	2011年	2012年
产品销售率	%	94.2	91.0	99.2	99.4	100.1	99.7	101.9
成本费用利润率	%	-11.5	-2.6	4.7	2.8	4.4	3.6	3.4
产值利税率	%	-9.3	-0.6	5.7	3.2	5.3	5.3	5.5
资金利税率	%	-14.3	-0.5	7.4	4.1	7.5	7.4	9.2
销售利税率	%	-9.9	-0.6	5.7	3.2	5.3	5.3	5.4
每百元固定资产原值实现的产值	元	104.9	155.5	231.2	285.2	286.9	332.4	355.3
每百元固定资产原值实现的利税	元	-9.7	-0.9	13.1	9.2	15.3	17.6	19.6
每百元固定资产原值实现的利润	元	-12.6	-1.9	10.3	7.6	12.1	11.7	12.0
每百元流动资产实现的产值	元	154.3	94.3	251.0	223.6	211.1	204.1	222.5
每百元流动资产实现的利税	元	-14.3	-1.5	14.2	7.2	11.2	10.8	12.3
每百元流动资产实现的利润	元	-18.5	5.5	11.1	5.9	8.9	7.2	7.5
亏损企业亏损面	%	25.0	38.2	31.3	34.5	18.8	21.5	19.8
全部流动资产周转天数	天	251.1	174.1	148.4	164.4	173.0	177.3	156.5
全员劳动生产率	元/人	16962	3646	50318	70722	66212	67335	82923
人均利税	元	-8238	-700	13714	8288	16893	20145	23844

4-28　主要年份规模以上工业产品产量

Output of Main Industrial Products of Industrial Enterprises above Designated Size in Main Years

产品名称	单位	1985年	1990年	1995年	2000年	2005年	2010年	2011年	2012年
食用植物油	吨	5571	4431	6824	5180	181869	1135677	1293312	1847151
糖	吨	51858	61016	7841	17869				
饼　干	吨		45158	26252	21262	38859	142126		
罐　头	吨	924	1352	5982			12890		
饮料酒	千升	4034	2441	1720			493644	595920	575383
软饮料	吨		44061	71566	158599	861853	3142076	3737047	3574273
棉　纱	吨		321	9902	3048	49383	11252	3411	2268
布	万米		82	31045	28139	65669	15794	9958	12410
服　装	万件	108	1835	112177	85635	70054	140556	107297	108932
#衬　衫	万件			2518	3624	2210	6372	8869	10237
西　服	万件			205	1761	555	204	462	264
轻　革	万平方米		5	1076	378	1391	744	574	486
皮　鞋	万双	17	457	27184	23474	31942	43062	31905	23368
人造板	立方米		7100	40666		167088	266113	98777	172487
家　具	万件	815	8657	77501	151374	7974	7390	6418	4759
机制纸及纸板	万吨	3	11	34	62	408	933	1021	1153
玩　具	万元			657936	469792	1354386	827916		
火　柴	万件	19	22	9					
中成药	吨		216	6268	2354	1759	2478	2154	2484
塑料制品	吨	3089	17335	624476	571900	1265865	3998208	2015355	1543048
#塑料薄膜	吨		1928	59128	71394	83954	134737	152599	174255
水　泥	万吨	41	140	283	435	305	249	251	249
砖	万块	159305	296962	252783		2903			
日用陶瓷	万件	561	480	2414	1860	5745	2426		
耐火材料制品	吨	7600	9928	9144			62512	52162	18216
钢　材	吨	4678	1730	19690	14550	1087242	191656		42697
铝　材	吨		881	3536	4080	61510	69933	14808	55990
输送机械	吨		8622	3736		33200			2785

注：2000年以前家具的计量单位为“万元”，输送机械的计量单位为“吨”。

4-28 续表

产 品 名 称	单 位	1985年	1990年	1995年	2000年	2005年	2010年	2011年	2012年
电动手提式工具	万台		1.89	471	357	6	1520	585	1717
滚动轴承	万套	36	373	691	594	1333	4232	10183	3555
民用钢质船	载重吨	1916	841	3620	2894		18186	17934	14155
交流电动机	万千瓦	23	19	43	87		193	163	660
变压器	千伏安				6730	816409	2980343	1705625	1553904
电力电缆	公里		15091	20694	61996	78266	383829	367142	2219568
原电池(折干电池)	万只	12354	7607	63237	69401	214507	417215	390496	252281
吸尘器	万台	0.13	7.35	483	67	464	428	918	613
电风扇	万台		106	474	436	964	2081	1811	1462
房间空调器	台	31		26480	39582	4941		239260	
排油烟机	台			57551					
缝纫机	台			190		504	440		
自行车	辆			95439	185608	885211	1014533	975192	819711
家用电冰箱	台			35336		19360		2707	3205
白炽灯泡	万只			5778	8560	45164	13198	16	14
灯 具	万件		87	42407	25135	14017	22819	18770	22098
电话单机	万部		17	877	1074	3651	4809	4443	3883
移动电话机	万部				619	639	1995	4336	6729
电子计算机	万台				27	180	44	44	100
彩色显像管	万只			210	394				
电子元件	亿只	0.14	2.05	71.93	103.95	4641.67	9184.57	10125.45	11166.06
显示器	万台						157	1	15
打印机	万台						57	77	113
硬盘存储器	万台						30	2	
半导体分立器件	亿只			248.48	3.23	220.32	404.44	475.66	447.74
彩色电视机	万台		1.04	81	134	135	536	541	493
组合音响	万台			1136	1572	2446	3637	2827	5733
照相机	万台		3	374	122	1355	210	185	31
手 表	万只		15	8514	954	1370	2168	1670	1043
钟	万只			1986	984	1193	3776	3656	2415
发电量	亿千瓦时	0.29	93	139	269	344	356	376	338
自来水生产量	万吨			21070	102083	94962	179639	174538	173413

4-29 规模以上五大支柱产业及四个特色产业主要经济指标（2012年）

Main Indicators of Five Pillar Industries & Four Characteristic Industries above Designated Size (2012)

项　　目	企业单位数（个）	#亏损企业	工业增加值（万元）	主营业务收入（万元）	亏损企业亏损总额（万元）
总　计	3470	520	15845093	79100037	321746
按轻重工业分					
轻工业	1981	282	8206706	35405996	147814
重工业	1489	238	7638387	43694042	173932
按企业规模分					
大型企业	202	19	7169821	37784047	52012
中型企业	1441	220	6131648	26772660	191996
小型企业	1789	267	2515513	14393836	71944
微型企业	38	14	28111	149495	5794
按工业行业分(大类)					
五大支柱产业	2828	429	13790703	70374207	277669
电子信息制造业	818	149	5656693	33539655	133868
电气机械及设备制造业	943	140	3418580	16337213	59354
纺织服装鞋帽制造业	757	107	2708455	9216345	58037
食品饮料加工制造业	85	8	1022559	6112046	3654
造纸及纸制品业	225	25	984416	5168949	22756
四个特色产业	642	91	2054390	8725830	44077
玩具及文体用品制造业	193	37	736495	2827947	8686
家具制造业	207	25	516540	2079615	17990
化工制品制造业	164	18	445529	2739140	10882
包装印刷业	78	11	355826	1079128	6519

4-29 续表

(2012年)

项　　目	利税总额（万元）	人均税收（元）	利润总额（万元）	人均利润（元）
总　计	4128357	8006	2394824	11060
按轻重工业分				
轻工业	2102332	7599	1199126	10089
重工业	2026026	8501	1195698	12241
按企业规模分				
大型企业	2199405	11531	1328863	17602
中型企业	1247374	4909	703234	6344
小型企业	682418	10620	364917	12206
微型企业	-841	4635	-2189	-7523
按工业行业分(大类)				
五大支柱产业	3614795	8306	2092800	11421
电子信息制造业	1341482	7831	746722	9832
电气机械及设备制造业	899897	7149	573835	12582
纺织服装鞋帽制造业	519939	5247	249206	4830
食品饮料加工制造业	582037	56366	404010	127916
造纸及纸制品业	271441	21999	119028	17180
四个特色产业	513563	6354	302024	9072
玩具及文体用品制造业	88908	1812	55473	3007
家具制造业	82633	7508	18945	2233
化工制品制造业	211507	30199	130289	48445
包装印刷业	130515	9048	97317	26523

4-30 规模以上电子信息、电气机械及仪器仪表制造业主要指标(2011-2012年)

Main Indicators of Electronic Information，Machinery and Instrument Manufacturing above Designated Size (2011-2012)

指　　标	单位	2011年	2012年
企业单位数	个	1292	1373
#亏损企业单位数	个	231	239
工业增加值	亿元	633.84	775.11
主营业务收入	亿元	3754.40	4264.03
成本费用总额	亿元	3647.55	4180.21
#营业成本及销售费用	亿元	3476.10	3973.63
管理费用	亿元	171.69	198.47
财务费用	亿元	-0.24	8.12
利税总额	亿元	152.61	178.97
#利润总额	亿元	113.66	102.10
应交增值税	亿元	32.39	67.43
亏损企业亏损总额	亿元	16.72	17.88
企业资产总额	亿元	2390.82	2645.73
#流动资产	亿元	1622.67	1823.10
#应收帐款余额	亿元	663.92	729.51
产成品存货	亿元	141.08	161.77
企业负债总额	亿元	1406.50	1557.62
企业资产负债率	%	58.8	58.9
成本费用利润率	%	3.1	2.4

注：本表统计范围为规模以上计算机、通信和其他电子设备制造业、电气机械和器材制造业、仪器仪表制造业。

4-31 规模以上先进制造业企业主要经济指标（2012年）

Main Indicators of Advanced Manufacturing Enterprises above Designated Size（2012）

项目	企业单位数（个）	#亏损企业	工业增加值（万元）	主营业务收入（万元）	亏损企业亏损总额（万元）
总计	1809	283	8343471	47100310	195818
按企业规模分					
大型企业	126	13	4202444	26476955	41054
中型企业	619	100	2638659	11766898	105019
小型企业	1039	165	1486697	8736805	49320
微型企业	25	5	15672	119653	425
按工业行业分					
装备制造业	1586	255	7805732	43669039	179514
金属制品业	204	25	504545	2085694	8815
通用设备制造业	155	21	344451	2096711	7479
专用设备制造业	133	19	314367	1094702	2548
汽车制造业	45	2	239269	1059173	807
铁路、船舶、航空航天和其他运输设备制造业	8	1	76681	298771	64
电气机械和器材制造业	276	49	918226	4669124	27069
计算机、通信和其他电子设备制造业	725	130	5221822	31589097	128176
仪器仪表制造业	40	8	186371	775767	4557
船舶、航空航天器修理					
钢铁冶炼及加工	22	5	14632	361981	4317
炼铁	1		524	4730	
炼钢					
钢压延加工	21	5	14108	357252	4317
铁合金冶炼					
石油及化学	201	23	523107	3069290	11987
石油和天然气开采业					
石油加工、炼焦及核燃料加工业	4	1	11405	169969	127
化学原料和化学制品制造业	160	17	434124	2569171	10755
橡胶制品业	37	5	77578	330151	1105

4-31 续表 1

(2012年)

项目	利税总额(万元)	人均税收(元)	利润总额(万元)	人均利润(元)	工业增加值率(%)
总计	2179026	8521	1265904	11813	18.0
按企业规模分					
大型企业	1198740	10791	714129	15902	16.2
中型企业	517972	5241	275894	5973	22.5
小型企业	458406	11611	272867	17076	17.5
微型企业	3908	10363	3014	34922	17.3
按工业行业分					
装备制造业	1955014	8009	1130934	10992	18.2
金属制品业	97927	5981	56010	7991	24.1
通用设备制造业	120774	9313	79363	17848	16.5
专用设备制造业	103394	9716	61991	14547	28.8
汽车制造业	98857	12282	76386	41750	23.2
铁路、船舶、航空航天和其他运输设备制造业	24946	19636	17459	45787	25.7
电气机械和器材制造业	190969	7132	93363	6822	19.5
计算机、通信和其他电子设备制造业	1284440	8046	728607	10547	16.9
仪器仪表制造业	33706	7270	17754	8092	24.6
船舶、航空航天器修理					
钢铁冶炼及加工	1347	16339	-1880	-9519	4.7
炼铁	45	1283	30	2458	13.5
炼钢					
钢压延加工	1302	17313	-1910	-10294	4.6
铁合金冶炼					
石油及化学	222665	21051	136850	33570	17.3
石油和天然气开采业					
石油加工、炼焦及核燃料加工业	2723	60903	1152	44651	7.7
化学原料和化学制品制造业	208784	29902	129137	48482	17.0
橡胶制品业	11158	3314	6561	4730	23.7

4-31　续表 2

(2012年)

项　　　目	总资产贡献率(%)	资　产负债率(%)	流动资产周转率(次/年)	成本费用利润率(%)	全员劳动生产率(元/人)	产　品销售率(%)
总　　计	7.3	58.8	2.2	2.7	77858	100.8
按企业规模分						
大型企业	8.6	60.5	2.9	2.8	93579	101.6
中型企业	5.7	54.9	1.9	2.4	57127	99.3
小型企业	6.9	60.7	1.5	3.2	93038	100.6
微型企业	4.9	61.3	1.7	2.6	181596	104.5
按工业行业分						
装备制造业	7.2	58.9	2.3	2.6	75866	100.8
金属制品业	5.7	50.1	1.8	2.7	71987	99.0
通用设备制造业	6.3	61.3	1.6	3.9	77462	99.3
专用设备制造业	9.5	53.3	1.4	5.9	73771	98.3
汽车制造业	13.4	39.6	2.2	7.8	130777	101.3
铁路、船舶、航空航天和其他运输设备制造业	6.5	65.3	1.4	6.2	201105	99.7
电气机械和器材制造业	5.6	61.7	1.7	2.0	67090	99.7
计算机、通信和其他电子设备制造业	7.4	60.0	2.7	2.4	75590	101.3
仪器仪表制造业	6.8	60.1	2.1	2.3	84942	101.1
船舶、航空航天器修理						
钢铁冶炼及加工	0.8	64.5	1.6	-0.5	74088	99.4
炼铁	0.8	47.9	1.2	0.6	43692	105.1
炼钢						
钢压延加工	0.8	64.9	1.6	-0.5	76054	99.3
铁合金冶炼						
石油及化学	9.4	56.5	1.6	4.7	128323	101.1
石油和天然气开采业						
石油加工、炼焦及核燃料加工业	2.9	85.0	1.1	0.7	442035	116.0
化学原料和化学制品制造业	10.5	54.0	1.7	5.3	162984	100.4
橡胶制品业	4.6	58.1	1.8	2.0	55928	99.8

4-32 规模以上高技术制造业企业主要经济指标（2012年）

Main Indicators of High-tech Manufacturing Enterprises above Designated Size (2012)

项目	企业单位数（个）	#亏损企业	工业增加值（万元）	主营业务收入（万元）	亏损企业亏损总额（万元）
总计	892	161	6154907	36798578	139219
按企业规模分					
大型企业	107	10	3789102	25666863	32603
中型企业	431	75	1928609	8799388	81844
小型企业	342	73	430630	2277191	24434
微型企业	12	3	6566	55136	337
按工业行业分					
信息化学品制造业					
医药制造业	10	2	57589	127401	278
航空航天器制造业					
电子及通信设备制造业	698	130	4810372	28034692	126101
通信设备制造业	41	4	614348	5509288	1530
雷达及配套设备制造业	2		8324	29335	
广播电视设备制造业	12	3	36878	163772	2344
电子器件制造业	86	20	991313	8147686	44389
电子元件制造业	376	71	2484549	11127055	61337
视听设备制造业	93	19	434870	1950559	5692
其他电子设备制造业	88	13	240090	1106998	10809
电子计算机及办公设备制造业	132	20	1064370	7738103	8268
计算机整机制造业	11	1	97665	424991	175
计算机零部件制造业	65	10	602190	4181070	4187
计算机外围设备制造业	37	8	112335	633379	3404
其他计算机制造业	7		34131	265524	
办公设备制造业	12	1	218049	2233139	502
医疗设备及仪器仪表制造业	51	9	216305	873034	4572
医疗仪器设备及器械制造业	11	1	29934	97267	15
仪器仪表制造业	40	8	186371	775767	4557
公共软件服务制造业					
其他	1		6272	25348	

4-32　续表 1

(2012年)

项　　目	利税总额(万元)	人均税收(元)	利润总额(万元)	人均利润(元)	工业增加值率(%)
总　计	1491284	7973	844253	10404	17.1
按企业规模分					
大型企业	1105740	11299	651087	16181	15.1
中型企业	292897	4397	140751	4067	21.9
小型企业	90795	6395	50772	8112	19.7
微型企业	1852	4330	1643	34095	19.8
按工业行业分					
信息化学品制造业					
医药制造业	36072	51908	22996	91291	44.2
航空航天器制造业					
电子及通信设备制造业	1154627	8469	614832	9647	17.5
通信设备制造业	215633	15760	100507	13759	12.3
雷达及配套设备制造业	1808	12601	765	9238	26.1
广播电视设备制造业	6544	5965	1308	1490	23.0
电子器件制造业	274758	8386	186992	17866	12.1
电子元件制造业	567741	7878	294640	8499	22.6
视听设备制造业	57042	5666	18115	2637	22.1
其他电子设备制造业	31101	5364	12505	3607	23.0
电子计算机及办公设备制造业	258829	5303	182365	12649	14.0
计算机整机制造业	76093	22636	60644	88856	22.7
计算机零部件制造业	82405	3417	52173	5897	14.7
计算机外围设备制造业	20697	3411	13347	6194	18.5
其他计算机制造业	7659	3640	5726	10779	13.1
办公设备制造业	71974	9766	50475	22929	9.7
医疗设备及仪器仪表制造业	38658	6499	21019	7745	25.4
医疗仪器设备及器械制造业	4952	3245	3265	6280	32.5
仪器仪表制造业	33706	7270	17754	8092	24.6
公共软件服务制造业					
其他	3099	1847	3040	94698	25.5

4-32 续表 2

(2012年)

项目	总资产贡献率(%)	资产负债率(%)	流动资产周转率(次/年)	成本费用利润率(%)	全员劳动生产率(元/人)	产品销售率(%)
总计	7.4	60.2	2.6	2.3	75846	101.0
按企业规模分						
大型企业	8.8	61.6	3.0	2.6	94167	101.8
中型企业	5.0	57.6	2.2	1.6	55732	98.7
小型企业	5.5	59.9	1.6	2.3	68803	101.4
微型企业	5.4	50.8	2.0	3.1	136228	100.1
按工业行业分						
信息化学品制造业						
医药制造业	14.1	29.1	0.8	22.1	228617	97.2
航空航天器制造业						
电子及通信设备制造业	7.4	61.5	2.6	2.2	75475	101.4
通信设备制造业	8.1	83.0	2.2	1.9	84102	108.7
雷达及配套设备制造业	17.7	76.6	3.1	2.7	100536	91.9
广播电视设备制造业	6.0	74.3	1.3	0.8	42006	103.2
电子器件制造业	7.5	62.4	3.5	2.4	94717	99.6
电子元件制造业	7.7	51.4	2.4	2.7	71671	99.8
视听设备制造业	5.7	64.1	2.6	0.9	63296	99.4
其他电子设备制造业	4.7	66.4	2.1	1.1	69254	100.3
电子计算机及办公设备制造业	6.8	56.8	3.0	2.4	73824	99.9
计算机整机制造业	34.6	40.8	2.4	16.7	143098	99.2
计算机零部件制造业	3.9	54.2	3.3	1.3	68062	99.6
计算机外围设备制造业	5.5	55.1	2.3	2.2	52130	104.1
其他计算机制造业	5.8	45.8	3.0	2.2	64253	100.7
办公设备制造业	7.5	68.1	2.9	2.3	99050	99.5
医疗设备及仪器仪表制造业	6.5	59.9	2.0	2.5	79700	100.9
医疗仪器设备及器械制造业	5.0	58.9	1.5	3.5	57577	98.8
仪器仪表制造业	6.8	60.1	2.1	2.3	84942	101.1
公共软件服务制造业						
其他	17.8	39.1	1.7	13.7	195377	100.0

4-33 规模以上IT制造业企业主要经济指标（2012年）

Main Indicators of IT Manufacturing Enterprises above Designated Size (2012)

项目	企业单位数(个)	#亏损企业	工业增加值(万元)	主营业务收入(万元)	亏损企业亏损总额(万元)
总计	1016	191	6433394	36152644	147694
按企业规模分					
大型企业	100	11	3650923	23129990	38814
中型企业	492	90	2260829	9739601	83393
小型企业	414	86	517891	3238190	24426
微型企业	10	4	3751	44863	1061
按工业行业分(小类)					
训练健身器材制造	3	1	4946	19929	117
玩具制造	95	23	444802	1164081	5320
信息化学品制造					
照相机及器材制造	7	3	36882	117637	1523
复印和胶印设备制造	7	1	147526	1159447	502
计算器及货币专用设备制造	5		70523	1073692	
医疗诊断、监护及治疗设备制造	2		7526	22420	
微电机及其他电机制造	17	3	226512	757672	7261
电线、电缆制造	126	22	314941	2268999	3379
光纤、光缆制造	2	1	3015	20324	33
锂离子电池制造	18	5	222736	762890	2912
镍氢电池制造	2		9481	37154	
其他电池制造	12		43550	237794	
计算机整机制造	11	1	97665	424991	175
其他计算机制造	7		34131	265524	
通信系统设备制造	13		145963	836705	
通信终端设备制造	28	4	468385	4672583	1530
电视机制造	8	2	95689	319882	656
音响设备制造	62	14	271379	1219042	2349
影视录放设备制造	23	3	67803	411635	2687
电子真空器件制造					
集成电路制造	13	2	232229	2162044	3221
光电子器件及其他电子器件制造	71	18	711563	5788481	41168
电子元件及组件制造	334	61	2298976	10284439	45681
印制电路板制造	42	10	185573	842615	15656
其他电子设备制造	88	13	240090	1106998	10809
电子测量仪器制造	2		5876	27648	
其他未列明制造业	18	4	45636	148016	2716

4-33 续表 1

(2012年)

项目	利税总额(万元)	人均税收(元)	利润总额(万元)	人均利润(元)	工业增加值率(%)
总计	1566691	7689	885081	9985	18.1
按企业规模分					
大型企业	1145217	12254	677264	17736	16.2
中型企业	316607	3794	152765	3537	23.1
小型企业	105532	6874	55852	7728	16.3
微型企业	-666	3418	-800	-20398	16.1
按工业行业分(小类)					
训练健身器材制造	669	8169	253	4971	25.0
玩具制造	31500	1501	13668	1151	38.0
信息化学品制造					
照相机及器材制造	1549	276	1343	1800	31.6
复印和胶印设备制造	57186	13669	37199	25441	12.7
计算器及货币专用设备制造	14789	2046	13276	17960	6.5
医疗诊断、监护及治疗设备制造	577	838	465	3476	33.6
微电机及其他电机制造	76994	23595	30229	15252	30.5
电线、电缆制造	59272	6011	31527	6831	13.9
光纤、光缆制造	1192	14587	715	21872	12.5
锂离子电池制造	81547	3986	72936	33767	28.9
镍氢电池制造	1979	8999	495	3002	21.4
其他电池制造	8110	8379	4746	11819	17.6
计算机整机制造	76093	22636	60644	88856	22.7
其他计算机制造	7659	3640	5726	10779	13.1
通信系统设备制造	35103	3601	26733	11501	18.1
通信终端设备制造	180530	21435	73775	14813	11.1
电视机制造	12824	5256	7810	8187	27.8
音响设备制造	37976	6013	9792	2089	22.6
影视录放设备制造	6242	4661	513	417	15.9
电子真空器件制造					
集成电路制造	62214	14886	32010	15775	10.7
光电子器件及其他电子器件制造	209387	7156	151902	18909	12.2
电子元件及组件制造	551722	8086	291827	9079	22.6
印制电路板制造	16019	5231	2814	1115	22.4
其他电子设备制造	31101	5364	12505	3607	23.0
电子测量仪器制造	883	2930	678	9732	22.1
其他未列明制造业	3576	3333	1502	2414	30.5

4-33 续表 2

(2012年)

项目	总资产贡献率(%)	资产负债率(%)	流动资产周转率(次/年)	成本费用利润率(%)	全员劳动生产率(元/人)	产品销售率(%)
总计	7.6	61.5	2.4	2.5	72577	101.0
按企业规模分						
大型企业	9.9	62.5	2.9	3.0	95607	102.1
中型企业	4.8	59.4	2.0	1.6	52346	98.6
小型企业	4.9	62.5	1.7	1.8	71661	100.4
微型企业	-3.1	65.4	2.3	-1.8	95699	99.4
按工业行业分(小类)						
训练健身器材制造	6.1	72.1	2.2	1.3	97167	88.4
玩具制造	3.5	67.6	1.5	1.2	37448	100.0
信息化学品制造						
照相机及器材制造	1.7	34.0	2.0	1.2	49426	100.6
复印和胶印设备制造	14.4	57.9	3.6	3.3	100893	99.6
计算器及货币专用设备制造	2.5	75.4	2.4	1.3	95404	99.4
医疗诊断、监护及治疗设备制造	8.4	32.4	3.8	2.1	56288	100.0
微电机及其他电机制造	17.4	48.3	2.4	4.1	114284	100.6
电线、电缆制造	4.2	67.6	1.6	1.4	68237	99.9
光纤、光缆制造	6.0	74.3	1.2	3.7	92205	96.7
锂离子电池制造	13.2	49.8	1.7	10.5	103118	98.6
镍氢电池制造	6.4	71.1	1.5	1.4	57495	84.0
其他电池制造	4.8	56.4	2.1	1.9	108467	99.9
计算机整机制造	34.6	40.8	2.4	16.7	143098	99.2
其他计算机制造	5.8	45.8	3.0	2.2	64253	100.7
通信系统设备制造	8.6	69.6	3.0	3.3	62796	101.4
通信终端设备制造	7.9	85.3	2.1	1.6	94046	110.1
电视机制造	9.3	72.4	3.9	2.4	100313	92.9
音响设备制造	6.3	56.3	2.9	0.8	57895	101.9
影视录放设备制造	2.5	75.5	1.6	0.1	55165	97.7
电子真空器件制造						
集成电路制造	7.1	69.2	3.4	1.5	114449	100.7
光电子器件及其他电子器件制造	8.1	60.2	3.6	2.7	88576	99.2
电子元件及组件制造	8.4	52.0	2.5	2.9	71527	99.8
印制电路板制造	2.3	46.2	1.8	0.3	73509	100.5
其他电子设备制造	4.7	66.4	2.1	1.1	69254	100.3
电子测量仪器制造	9.7	65.4	4.1	2.5	84301	103.8
其他未列明制造业	3.7	61.3	1.9	1.0	73334	99.1

主要统计指标解释

Explanatory Notes on Main Statistical Indicators

工业 指从事自然资源的开采，对采掘品和农产品进行加工和再加工的物质生产部门。具体包括：对自然资源的开采，如采矿、晒盐、森林采伐等（但不包括禽兽捕猎和水产捕捞）；对农副产品的加工、再加工，如粮油加工、食品加工、轧花、缫丝、纺织、制革等；对采掘品的加工、再加工，如炼铁、炼钢、化工生产、石油加工、机器制造、木材加工等，以及电力、自来水、煤气的生产和供应等；对工业品的修理、翻新，如机器制造设备的修理、交通运输工具（包括小卧车）的修理等。

轻工业 是指主要提供生活消费品和制作手工工具的工业。按其所使用的原料不同，可分为两大类：以农产品为原料的轻工业，是指直接或以农产品为基本原料的轻工业，主要包括食品制造、饮料制造、烟草加工、纺织、缝纫、皮革和毛皮制作、造纸以及印刷等工业；以非农产品为原料的轻工业，是以工业品为原料的轻工业，主要包括文教体育用品、化学药品制造、合成纤维制造、日用化学制品、日用玻璃制品、日用金属制品、手工工具制造、医疗器械制造、文化和办公用机械制造等工业。

重工业 是指为国民经济各部门提供物质技术基础的主要生产资料的工业。按其生产性质和产品用途，可以分为下列三类：采掘（伐）工业，是对自然资源的开采，包括石油开采、煤炭开采、金属矿开采等工业；原材料工业，指向国民经济各部门提供基本材料、动力和燃料的工业，包括金属冶炼及加工、炼焦及焦炭化学、化学原料、水泥、人造板以及电力、石油和煤炭加工等工业；加工工业，是指对工业原材料进行再加工制造的工业，包括装备国民经济各部门的机械设备制造工业、金属结构、水泥制造等工业，以及为农业提供的生产资料如化肥、农药等工业。

资产总额 是指企业拥有或控制的能以货币计量的经济资源，包括各种财产、债权和其他权利。资产按其流动性（即资产的变现能力和支付能力）划分为：流动资产、长期投资、固定资产、无形资产、递延资产和其他资产，即为企业资产负债表中的资产总计项。

流动资产 是企业资产的重要组成部分，通常是指一年内或超过一年的一个营业周期内可以变现或耗用的资产。其特点是在企业的生产经营或者业务活动中不断地在生产循环中周转，不断改变其形态。其价值一次性消耗、转移或者实现。包括：货币资金、短期投资、应收票据、应收账款、预付账款、其他应收款、存货、待摊费用、待处理流动资产损失、一年内到期的本期债券投资及其他流动资产。

固定资产原价 是指企业在建造、购置、安装、改建、扩建、技术改造某项固定资产时实际支出的全部货币总额。它一般包括买价、包装费、运杂费和安装费等。

固定资产合计 包括固定资产净值、固定资产清理、在建工程、待处理固定资产净损失所占用的资金合计。

固定资产净值 是指固定资产原价减去历年已提折旧额后的净额。

负债 是指企业所承担的能以货币计量，将以资产或劳务偿付的债务。其偿还形式可以用货币，也可以用资产或提供劳务的方式进行。包括流动负债、长期负债和递延税款贷项等，即为企业资产负债表的负债合计项。

实收资本 是指企业实际收到的投资人投入的资本。包括有国家资本、集体资本、法人资本、个人资本、外商资本、港澳台资本等。

主营业务收入 是企业在销售商品、提供劳务及让渡资产使用权等日常活动中所产生的收入。

主营业务税金及附加 是指企业日常活动应负担的税金及附加，包括营业税、消费税、城市维护建设税、资源税、土地增值税和教育费附加等。

主营业务成本 是指企业因销售商品、提供劳务或让渡资产使用权等日常活动而发生的实际成本。

营业利润　是企业生产经营活动所取得的利润，包括主营业务利润和其他业务利润。

利润总额　是指企业在一定时期内生产经营活动的最终的财务成果，是企业的收入减去有关成本与费用后的差额，收入大于相关的成本费用，企业就盈利，反之则亏损。包括营业利润、补贴收入、投资净收益、营业外收支净额、以前年度损失调整。

应交增值税　是指企业按税法规定，从事货物销售或提供加工、修理修配劳务等增加货物价值的活动本期应交纳的税金，即企业在报告期应交的增值税额。计算公式为：

应交增值税 ＝ 销项税额-(进项税额-进项税额转出)-出口抵减内销产品应纳税额-减免税款+出口退税

从业人员平均人数　从业人员指企业工作并取得劳动报酬的全部人员数。包括在岗职工、再就业的离退休人员、民办教师及在企业工作的外方人员和港澳台方人员、兼职人员、借用的外单位人员和第二职业者。不包括离开本单位但仍保留劳动关系的职工。而从业人员平均人数指报告期内每天平均拥有的从业人员人数。其计算公式为：

月平均人数=报告月内每天实有人数之和÷报告月日历日数

季平均人数=季内各月平均人数之和÷3

年平均人数=全年各月平均人数之和÷12

资产利税率　是在一定时期内已实现的利润、税金总额与同期的资产总额之比。计算公式：

$$资产利税率（\%）=\frac{报告期累计实现利税总额}{资产总额}\times 100\%$$

资产利税率反映每单位（通常是每万元）资产所提供的利税金额。它是考察和评价部门或企业资金运用的经济效益，分析资金投入效果的主要分析指标。

产值利税率　是报告期已实现的利润、税金总额（包括利润总额、产品销售税金及附加和应交增值税）占同期全部工业总产值的百分比，计算公式为：

$$产值利税率（\%）=\frac{利税总额}{工业总产值（现价）}\times 100\%$$

工业经济效益综合指数　是现行综合评价工业经济效益总体水平及工业经济运行质量的指数，它是以若干项代表性经济效益指标，分别除以各项指标的标准值，再乘以各自的权数，加总后除以总权数求得。其计算公式为：

$$工业经济效益综合指数=\Sigma（\frac{某项经济效益指标报告期数值}{该项指标标准值}\times 权数）\div 总权数$$

上式总权数为100。

工业产品销售率　是反映工业产品已实现销售的程度，是分析工业产销衔接情况、研究工业产品满足社会需求的指标。计算公式是：

$$产品销售率（\%）=\frac{现价工业销售产值}{现价工业总产值}\times 100\%$$

总资产贡献率　是指企业一定时期内全部资产获利能力，是企业经营业绩和管理水平的集中体现，是评价和考核企业盈利能力的核心指标。计算公式为：

$$总资产贡献率(\%)=\frac{利润总额+税金总额+利息支出}{平均资产总额}\times100\%\times\frac{12}{累计月数}$$

注：税金总额为主营业务税金及附加与应交增值税之和，平均资产总额为期初、期末资产总计的算术平均值。

资本保值增值率 是反映企业净资产变动状况的一个重要指标，是企业发展能力的集中体现。是指期末所有者权益总额与期初所有者权益总额的比率。计算公式为：

$$资本保值增值率(\%)=\frac{期末所有者权益}{期初所有者权益}\times100\%$$

所有者权益等于资产总计减负债总计。

资产负债率 是指反映企业经营风险的大小，反映企业利用债权人提供的资金从事经营活动的能力。计算公式为：

$$资产负债率(\%)=\frac{负债总额}{资产总额}\times100\%$$

资产及负债均为报告期期末数。

流动资产周转率 是指一定时期内流动资产完成的周转次数，反映投入工业企业流动资金的周转速度，一般以一年内周转多少次表示。计算公式为：

$$流动资产周转率(次)=\frac{产品销售收入}{流动资产平均余额}\times\frac{12}{累计月数}$$

成本费用利润率 是指工业企业投入的生产成本及费用的经济效益，同时也反映企业降低成本所取得的经济效益。计算公式为：

$$成本费用利润率(\%)=\frac{利润总额}{成本费用总额}\times100\%$$

注：成本费用总额为产品销售成本、销售费用、管理费用、财务费用之和。

全员劳动生产率 是指反映企业的生产效率和劳动投入的经济效益。一般用平均每人一年创造的工业增加值表示。计算公式为：

$$全员劳动生产率(元/人)=\frac{工业增加值}{全部职工平均人数}\times\frac{12}{累计月数}$$

五、固定资产投资与建筑业

Investment in Fixed Assets and Construction

5-1 主要年份固定资产投资与建筑业主要指标

Main Indicators of Investment in Fixed Assets and Construction in Main Years

项　　目	单　位	1990年	1995年	2000年	2005年	2010年	2011年	2012年
固定资产投资总额	万元	75052	631355	1028914	5972443	11149822	10793144	11803493
#国有单位	万元	50658	106935	197658	686333	1479886	923083	798477
私营个体经济	万元				1027969	2077250	1988277	2243023
港澳台投资经济	万元		10281	130501	1246450	1326063	1460388	1891724
外商投资经济	万元		230409	92699	507322	938943	747677	1050419
新增固定资产	万元				1732967	5778616	5788850	6238451
固定资产交付使用率	%				29.02	51.83	53.63	52.90
房屋竣工面积	万平方米				696.99	686.22	441.43	489.05
房屋面积竣工率	%				21.6	20.7	12.9	14.0
固定资产计划总投资	万元				13905355	45000174	48278061	54498794
固定资产投资建设周期	年				2.32	4.04	4.47	4.62
固定资产投资资金来源	万元	50100	480875	1047861	6717711	18550102	17026442	20156825
#国家预算内资金	万元	3600	10858	10490	536	130717	47949	338356
国内贷款	万元	2900	27439	122561	651723	1882278	1401681	1677214
利用外资	万元	17000	194486	207444	940432	1400920	1237319	1593223
自筹资金	万元	25400	163090	587176	3901138	8390847	8082831	7520432
房地产开发投资	万元		85163	112498	1444277	2989853	3733062	3773210
房地产开发当年房屋施工面积	万平方米		160.74	315.45	1160.17	2060.54	2393.57	2453.93
房地产开发当年房屋竣工面积	万平方米		76.78	103.20	132.88	296.59	242.28	362.47
#住宅	万平方米		68.36	77.97	115.23	256.09	210.85	306.34
商品房销售面积	万平方米		25.42	63.21	321.85	511.25	595.61	639.12
#住宅	万平方米		20.49	51.02	297.19	469.90	540.68	583.38
建筑企业(单位)个数	个	8	8	99	361	431	448	473
建筑企业平均人数	人	6803	22200	64300	79965	57473	59013	61316
建筑企业总产值	万元	12678	94941	404493	843540	1220569	1308530	1575771
劳动生产率(按总产值计算)	元/人	18636	42766	60849	108136	218076	207555	280706
建筑业房屋施工面积	万平方米	66.30	278.72	1218.00	1234.98	733.44	756.01	777.57
建筑业房屋竣工面积	万平方米	29.95	94.99	53.76	707.77	311.94	403.94	389.01

注：1. 本表固定资产投资资金来源1990年前是国有单位数，1995年以后是城镇集体以上单位数；1995年固定资产投资含沙角C厂完成的126374万元，2005年起是全社会固定资产投资单位数。
2. 从2011年起，固定资产投资统计起点由计划投资50万元提高到计划投资500万元，下同。

5-2 历年固定资产投资

Total Investment in Fixed Assets over Years

单位：万元

年份	固定资产投资总额	#民营	#外资	#港澳台	#房地产开发
1978	2319				
1979	1641				
1980	2395				
1981	3756				
1982	18102				
1983	18370				
1984	30050				
1985	70600				
1986	115173				
1987	141856				
1988	165459				
1989	50135				
1990	75052				
1991	137464				
1992	188824				
1993	327630		62600		52110
1994	1407621		1038599		78392
1995	631355		240690		85163
1996	676185		259705		86258
1997	658941		69055		86662
1998	769953		91719	35868	95451
1999	883201		188036	116708	104411
2000	1028914		146887	96112	112498
2001	1254945		224812	181822	148544
2002	1915741		466569	213458	268350
2003	3193889		888664	619193	551184
2004	4548691		1094045	716611	1144195
2005	5972443		1753772	1246450	1444277
2006	7054511	2410417	2297486	1584104	1642398
2007	8412074	2841860	2356983	1136955	2094187
2008	9443426	3240949	2710398	1469186	2714197
2009	10940753	4279669	2038232	1114631	2776623
2010	11149822	4847208	2265006	1326063	2989853
2011	10793144	4438880	2228117	1460388	3733062
2012	11803493	6662441	2942143	1891724	3773210

注：1994、1995、1996年全社会投资总额分别含沙角C厂投资额956758万元、126374万元、102760万元。

5-3 按登记类型和行业分的固定资产投资（2012年）

Total Investment in Fixed Assets by Registration Status and Sector (2012)

单位：万元

项　　目	全市合计	城镇	#房地产	农村
合　　计	11803493	9595487	3773210	2208006
按登记注册类型分				
内资	8861350	7586564	3356422	1274786
国有	798477	789580	13677	8897
集体	1197995	858577	81759	339418
股份合作	42639	42639	23942	
国有联营				
集体联营	657	657		
国有与集体联营				
其他联营				
国有独资公司	342544	342544	51570	
其他有限责任公司	3782937	3382461	2026626	400476
股份有限公司	213468	187344		26124
私营	2051055	1736558	1109477	314497
其他	239610	185968	49371	53642
个体经营：个体户	174128	58334		115794
个人合伙	17840	1902		15938
港澳台商投资	1891724	1278698	274730	613026
#合资经营	336627	244255	50862	92372
合作经营	136868	134367	132443	2501
独资	1332860	826110	91425	506750
股份有限公司	76464	68487		7977
外商投资	1050419	730225	142058	320194
#合资经营	122922	108912	67887	14010
合作经营	10841	10841	8095	
独资	907666	606379	66076	301287
股份有限公司	7978	4093		3885
按国民经济行业分				
第一产业	19710	5800		13910
第二产业	4148885	2620396		1528489
制造业	3826025	2312219		1513806
电力、热力、燃气及水的生产和供应业	320667	306484		14183
建筑业	2193	1693		500
第三产业	7634898	6969291	3773210	665607
交通运输、仓储和邮政业	1278633	1178706		99927
信息传输、软件和信息技术服务业	218614	217394		1220
批发和零售业	195376	136527		58849
住宿和餐饮业	101943	58537		43406
金融业	25898	25898		
房地产业	4419691	4169824	3773210	249867
租赁和商务服务业	25679	16658		9021
科学研究和技术服务业	99097	87634		11463
水利、环境和公共设施管理业	855336	735241		120095
居民服务、修理和其他服务业	8015	8015		
教育	245393	202624		42769
卫生和社会工作	55031	52620		2411
文化、体育和娱乐业	70219	52099		18120
公共管理、社会保障和社会组织	35973	27514		8459

5-4 固定资产投资主要指标（2012年）

Main Indicators of Total Investment in Fixed Assets (2012)

单位：万元

项目	计划总投资	本年完成投资	建筑工程	安装工程	设备工器具购置	其他费用
合计	26348824	8030283	4134383	319846	2866396	709658
按登记注册类型分						
内资	22180688	5504928	3716751	252818	878821	656538
国有	5370807	784800	556023	64062	91936	72779
集体	3797797	1116236	987332	25516	15541	87847
股份合作	117000	18697	15397	2880	420	
国有联营						
集体联营	2075	657				657
国有与集体联营						
其他联营						
国有独资公司	1824943	290974	204681	179	26373	59741
其他有限责任公司	7953442	1756311	1114006	76993	370852	194460
股份有限公司	336739	213468	132307	26396	41501	13264
私营个体	2360149	1133546	591415	40668	285015	216448
其他	417736	190239	115590	16124	47183	11342
港澳台商投资	2868254	1616994	281041	59709	1255084	21160
外商投资	1299882	908361	136591	7319	732491	31960
按国民经济行业分						
第一产业	28755	19710	11711		977	7022
第二产业	7818827	4148885	1222103	78587	2696360	151835
制造业	5808352	3826025	1041199	67886	2589355	127585
电力、热力、燃气及水的生产和供应业	2008209	320667	180904	9649	105978	24136
建筑业	2266	2193		1052	1027	114
第三产业	18501242	3861688	2900569	241259	169059	550801
交通运输、仓储和邮政业	9230025	1278633	987026	9002	31183	251422
信息传输、软件和信息技术服务业	273751	218614	55310	87112	76068	124
批发和零售业	662114	195376	157134	9100	18631	10511
住宿和餐饮业	217332	101943	74967	16163	6204	4609
金融业	65300	25898	21814	3623	420	41
房地产业	2167112	646481	437510	29127	8697	171147
租赁和商务服务业	93387	25679	18126	318	70	7165
科学研究和技术服务业	675027	99097	83063	73		15961
水利、环境和公共设施管理业	3424279	855336	752167	59293	13011	30865
居民服务、修理和其他服务业	27631	8015	3097	800	4118	
教育	754818	245393	180092	18912	7135	39254
卫生和社会工作	423514	55031	53716			1315
文化、体育和娱乐业	290423	70219	56821	3506	2120	7772
公共管理、社会保障和社会组织	196529	35973	19726	4230	1402	10615
按建设性质分						
新建	20447316	4623955	3257311	186147	532065	648432
扩建	1392201	533345	284753	83035	144390	21167
改建和技术改造	2306551	879553	556925	38848	244661	39119
单纯建造生活设施	36779	16523	14078	1594		851
迁建	68703	22036	15518	6518		
恢复	60567	9591	5798	3704		89
单纯购置	2036707	1945280			1945280	

注：本表不含房地产开发投资。

5-4 续表 1

(2012年)

单位：万元

项　　目	本年新增固定资　产	本年施工房屋面积(万平方米)	本年竣工房屋面积(万平方米)	本年资金来源合　计	#上年末结余资金
合　　计	4523549	1028.58	126.58	10151858	908767
按登记注册类型分					
内资	2818264	872.75	120.97	7135418	614740
国有	150572	22.46	1.20	861302	84556
集体	757989	267.55	11.39	1486568	145279
股份合作	15237	2.27	1.40	18697	
国有联营					
集体联营				3383	
国有与集体联营					
其他联营					
国有独资公司				203938	
其他有限责任公司	835359	161.69	24.68	2202232	250845
股份有限公司	66141	36.06	12.33	254734	11109
私营个体	920410	310.01	65.92	1747938	115616
其他	72556	72.72	4.05	356626	7335
港澳台商投资	1008719	102.92	4.57	2068974	264635
外商投资	696566	52.92	1.04	947466	29392
按国民经济行业分					
第一产业	9608	13.00	1.47	19710	31
第二产业	2651691	477.86	75.49	4707369	271504
制造业	2565488	473.92	75.49	4338158	238192
电力、热力、燃气及水的生产和供应业	84010	3.94		367018	33312
建筑业	2193			2193	
第三产业	1862250	537.73	49.62	5424779	637232
交通运输、仓储和邮政业	80219	43.57	1.61	1434296	177350
信息传输、软件和信息技术服务业	196941	4.63		217661	9
批发和零售业	152466	60.89	21.32	244803	43874
住宿和餐饮业	89850	29.42		107742	5399
金融业	23367	16.02	12.33	60847	349
房地产业	499186	172.02	8.41	1499532	208335
租赁和商务服务业	12608	15.79	1.62	30779	991
科学研究和技术服务业	30835	12.49		122241	13764
水利、环境和公共设施管理业	569427	9.05	0.04	934932	81348
居民服务、修理和其他服务业	5601	1.12		22460	12557
教育	83341	136.96	1.04	469319	16587
卫生和社会工作	48119	22.64	1.20	84110	30624
文化、体育和娱乐业	42552	10.06	1.01	73259	9065
公共管理、社会保障和社会组织	27738	3.07	1.04	122798	36980
按建设性质分					
新建	2127238	957.16	119.34	6352195	676491
扩建	362986	37.94	3.89	546586	68828
改建和技术改造	579703	20.29	3.35	1014448	59060
单纯建造生活设施	1858			16523	
迁建	20894	13.20		31167	
恢复	9245			12197	
单纯购置	1421625			2178742	104388

5-4 续表 2

(2012年)

单位：万元

项目	本年资金来源					
	#本年资金来源小计	国家预算内资金	国内贷款	利用外资	自筹资金	其他资金来源
合　　计	9243091	338356	631862	1584720	6266727	421426
按登记注册类型分						
内资	6520678	338356	412585	207277	5228897	333563
国有	776746	220099	86757		415832	54058
集体	1341289	69424	6875	184	1225208	39598
股份合作	18697		50		18647	
国有联营						
集体联营	3383		2000			1383
国有与集体联营						
其他联营						
国有独资公司	203938	47752			156186	
其他有限责任公司	1951387	181	242526	200000	1282168	226512
股份有限公司	243625		45187	4335	193188	915
私营个体	1632322	900	29190	2758	1589527	9947
其他	349291				348141	1150
港澳台商投资	1804339		211997	702344	811984	78014
外商投资	918074		7280	675099	225846	9849
按国民经济行业分						
第一产业	19679			4474	15205	
第二产业	4435865	24573	298081	1569450	2435239	108522
制造业	4099966	900	293497	1569450	2137581	98538
电力、热力、燃气及水的生产和供应业	333706	23492	4584		295758	9872
建筑业	2193	181			1900	112
第三产业	4787547	313783	333781	10796	3816283	312904
交通运输、仓储和邮政业	1256946	120328	199494		702390	234734
信息传输、软件和信息技术服务业	217652				216452	1200
批发和零售业	200929		8700	533	185822	5874
住宿和餐饮业	102343	1892		6500	93036	915
金融业	60498				58948	1550
房地产业	1291197	9820	1967		1277840	1570
租赁和商务服务业	29788	9343			14214	6231
科学研究和技术服务业	108477	113		398	107966	
水利、环境和公共设施管理业	853584	94814	53592	3204	655303	46671
居民服务、修理和其他服务业	9903				9903	
教育	452732	32023	69453	161	347916	3179
卫生和社会工作	53486	19933			31193	2360
文化、体育和娱乐业	64194	18460			37114	8620
公共管理、社会保障和社会组织	85818	7057	575		78186	
按建设性质分						
新建	5675704	301178	325164	386853	4365915	296594
扩建	477758	20746	18633	32761	309779	95839
改建和技术改造	955388	16235	272161	19452	631668	15872
单纯建造生活设施	16523				16523	
迁建	31167			4800	25456	911
恢复	12197	197			12000	
单纯购置	2074354		15904	1140854	905386	12210

5-5 固定资产投资分类情况（2012年）

Basic Statistics on Total Investment in Fixed Assets by Type (2012)

单位：万元

项目	计划总投资	自开始建设累计完成投资	本年完成投资	#住宅	本年新增固定资产
固定资产投资总额	26348824	15779922	8030283	76603	4523549
#基础设施	14129252	7725896	2534206		875747
#基础产业	14284862	7832257	2633353		924673
#城市建设	7710858	4033109	1498263		592448
#原材料	209690	152911	122008		67491
#能源	1352304	869195	268343		59822
#工业合计	7816561	5978122	4146692	3259	2649498
#工业九大产业	4588391	3473158	2909234	2663	2059636
#电子信息业	1909938	1343030	1138870	1200	625888
电气机械及专用设备	1515560	1189642	1023210		902090
石油及化学	97976	75480	50500		38797
纺织及服装	199734	181147	174371	1463	125471
食品饮料	286669	179969	136650		92841
建筑材料	109440	74364	68441		26424
森工造纸	374117	371196	262486		222614
医药	36920	19582	19582		3206
汽车	58037	38748	35124		22305

注:本表不含房地产开发投资。

5-6 房地产开发主要指标

Main Indicators of Real Estate Development

项目	单位	2005年	2006年	2007年	2008年	2009年	2010年	2011年	2012年
本年土地购置面积	万平方米	45	73	58	70	92	136	152	243
本年完成投资额	万元	1444277	1642398	2094187	2714197	2776623	2989853	3733062	3773210
#住宅	万元	1197154	1475181	1860580	2213498	2513852	2504525	3225434	2734249
资金来源	万元	1632570	2120240	2900238	4049833	4281021	6533564	7873335	6593153
#国内贷款	万元	114755	292488	446710	1079194	544169	1271530	786127	1045352
利用外资	万元	2075	10140		27053	105397	75182	3650	8503
自筹资金	万元	867824	677095	905912	1067823	1840753	2025670	2222753	1253705
房屋施工面积	万平方米	1160	1438	1522	1998	2334	2061	2394	2454
#住宅	万平方米	890	1229	1371	1681	2050	1687	1997	1922
房屋竣工面积	万平方米	133	166	137	478	310	297	242	362
#住宅	万平方米	115	114	112	395	268	256	211	306
商品房屋销售额	万元	1193991	1612449	2949939	2885975	3530040	3737742	4596123	5423825
#住宅	万元	1091095	1460425	2736729	2461024	3342466	3341485	4133322	4725186
商品房屋销售面积	万平方米	322	382	573	512	600	511	596	639
#住宅	万平方米	297	353	541	468	579	470	541	583

5-7 房地产开发企业主要经济指标（2012年）

Main Indicators of Real Estate Enterprises (2012)

单位:万元

项　　目	资产总计	负债总计	主营业务收入	主营业务税金及附加	利润总额
合　　计	22439277	17020412	4060786	424942	596082
按登记注册类型分					
#内源型经济	19972982	15172526	3535958	367906	508349
#民营经济	14549272	10648011	2540873	234695	288538
#国有经济	810210	603032	204592	29534	52631
集体经济	766571	560747	91272	9216	-1297
私营个体经济	8015486	5557431	1071347	96954	114855
外源型经济	2466295	1847885	524828	57036	87733
#港澳台商投资	1234286	818351	346392	39155	88221
外商投资	1232009	1029535	178436	17881	-488
按控股情况分					
国有控股	1001570	791250	204592	29534	50933
集体控股	862848	643762	91338	9270	-1972
私人控股	14549272	10648011	2540873	234695	288538
港澳台控股	1241958	821876	346392	39155	87914
外商控股	1267374	1028517	178794	17748	9663
其他控股	3516256	3086997	698798	94541	161007
按资质等级分					
一级	3005311	1794751	208098	25584	31927
二级	2654831	2301142	501148	44513	58843
三级	3820451	3008824	831595	93358	165777
四级	6564153	5286219	1622422	150625	216999
暂定	3790940	3496836	811713	97274	136608
其他	2603592	1132640	85809	13589	-14073

5-8 房地产开发投资情况（2011-2012年）

Investment in Real Estate Development (2011-2012)

项　　目	2011年		2012年	
	房地产开发投资（万元）	住宅	房地产开发投资（万元）	住宅
合　　计	3733062	3225434	3773210	2734249
内资	3465434	3013900	3356422	2420010
国有	38188	30322	13677	10899
集体	52871	45698	81759	53921
国有独资公司	144076	137605	51570	51330
其他有限责任公司	1969654	1783439	2026626	1496825
私营独资	131715	122741	78024	62436
私营有限责任公司	1022016	797132	1029217	681454
私营股份有限公司	28573	27805	220	141
其他(内资企业)	19724	13943	49371	37056
港澳台商投资	172426	117385	274730	186453
外商投资	95202	94149	142058	127786

5-9 房地产开发企业、房屋建筑面积及价值（2011-2012年）

Floor Space and Value of Buildings in Real Estate Development (2011-2012)

项　　目	2011年			2012年		
	房屋建筑面积（平方米）		竣工房屋价值	房屋建筑面积（平方米）		竣工房屋价值
	施工面积	竣工面积	（万元）	施工面积	竣工面积	（万元）
合　　计	23935687	2422825	1112723	24539252	3624675	1619347
内资	21772361	2363626	1078537	21702932	3302256	1472699
国有	798983			346386	205177	67576
集体	571255	87097	46134	909429	51483	14957
国有独资公司	388859			476362	145173	60445
其他有限责任公司	10216029	948612	438179	11767361	2064443	951402
私营独资	432352	98102	46391	383149	172429	41006
私营有限责任公司	8949107	1186300	511667	7287171	498126	213548
私营股份有限公司	114106			312	312	141
其他(内资企业)	117949	18008	9004	371294	122665	113012
港澳台商投资	1849928	59199	34186	2002142	121549	40987
外商投资	313398			834178	200870	105661

5-10 商品房屋销售情况（2012年）

Sale of Commercialized Buildings (2012)

项　目	商品房屋销售建筑面积（平方米）	#住宅	商品房屋销售额（万元）	#住宅
合　计	6391237	5833841	5423825	4725186
内资	5718207	5249391	4738834	4134394
国有	32860	28783	10497	7544
集体	152399	126603	91814	75266
国有独资公司	174632	172550	171563	167850
其他有限责任公司	3376638	3170489	2811557	2511119
私营独资	90257	87779	86943	81874
私营有限责任公司	1715265	1492716	1410141	1136680
私营股份有限公司	4938	4938	2528	2528
其他内资企业	135072	134920	101814	101364
港澳台商投资	446776	364005	495079	418994
外商投资	226254	220445	189912	171798

5-11 建筑施工企业主要指标（2011-2012年）

Main Indicators of Construction Enterprises (2011-2012)

指　标	单　位	2011年		2012年	
		合　计	#国有单位	合　计	#国有单位
企业单位数	个	448	1	473	1
年平均人数	人	59013	1539	61316	1551
自有固定资产原价	万元	266362	15518	270089	16393
自有固定资产净值	万元	145481	7331	141911	7439
自有施工机械设备年末总台数	台	15645	375	13721	384
自有施工机械设备年末净值	万元	57644	2384	61493	3757
自有施工机械设备年末总功率	万千瓦	21	1	23	1
建筑业总产值	万元	1308530	211649	1575771	217799
建筑工程产值	万元	1048214	211527	1327630	217799
安装工程产值	万元	191160	122	215698	
其他产值	万元	69156		32443	
建筑业竣工产值	万元	866997	130724	1144968	157056
建筑业增加值	万元	777901		781228	
房屋建筑施工面积	万平方米	756	11	778	8
房屋建筑竣工面积	万平方米	404	2	389	8
利润总额	万元	49397	1310	56383	1549
利税总额	万元	97110	8981	108708	9037
劳动生产率(按总产值计算)	元/人	207555	1812063	280706	1818022
劳动生产率(按增加值计算)	元/人	130949		139167	
技术装备率	元/人	9768	15491	10029	24223
动力装备率	千瓦/人	3.5	8.1	3.7	8.1
房屋建筑面积竣工率	%	53.4	21.7	50.0	97.8
产值利润率	%	3.8	0.6	3.6	0.7
产值利税率	%	7.4	4.2	6.9	4.1

主要统计指标解释

Explanatory Notes on Main Statistical Indicators

固定资产投资额 是以货币形式表现的在一定时期内建造和购置固定资产的工作量以及与此有关的费用的总称。按构成可分为建筑工程、安装工程、设备工器具购置和其他费用。

房屋建筑施工面积 指报告期内施工的全部房屋建筑面积。包括本期新开工的面积和上期开工跨入本期继续施工的房屋面积，以及上期已停建在本期复工的房屋面积。本期竣工和本期施工后又停缓建的房屋，其建筑面积仍计入本期施工房屋面积中。

房屋建筑竣工面积 指在报告期内房屋建筑按照设计要求已全部完工，达到住人和使用条件，经验收鉴定合格(或达到竣工验收标准)，可正式移交使用的各栋房屋建筑面积的总和。

房屋建筑面积竣工率 指一定时期内房屋竣工面积占同期房屋施工面积的比率。它是从房屋建筑施工速度的角度反映投资效果和建筑业经济效益的指标。

固定资产交付使用率 指一定时期新增固定资产与同期完成投资额的比率。它反映各个时期固定资产动用速度、衡量建设过程中投资效果的一个综合性指标。

六、运输邮电

Transport, Postal and Telecommunication Services

6-1 主要年份运输邮电主要指标

Main Indicators of Transport, Postal and Telecommunication Services in Main Years

项　　目	单　位	1985年	1990年	1995年	2000年	2005年	2010年	2011年	2012年
公路通车里程	公里	1240	1325	2327	2519	2871	4751	4828	4969
#高速公路	公里				89	154	217	251	319
一级公路	公里		6	679	782	1315	2394	2420	2484
内河通航里程	公里	532	598	598	798	664	643	643	643
公路桥梁	座	211	267	338	538	826	1211	1395	1462
民用汽车	辆	7897	19394	88311	153684	406577	920766	1061373	1207044
#载客	辆	1878	7225	25366	69658	268918	772701	906454	1047922
载货	辆	5980	12087	52242	80405	129298	143005	149635	153655
摩托车	辆	11786	47881	255591	482636	775838	423766	352553	276401
机动船	艘	2883	5885	5292	806	467	286	312	333
机动船净载重	吨位	80324	186056	259329	152661	148737	557846	1083217	1280142
邮电局(所)	处	52	53	273	594	702	555	626	595
邮路长度	公里	790	459	685	3550	6835	4667	4283	4070
长途自动交换机容量	路端		2100	15000	42182	510045	419110	419237	237150
局用交换机容量	万门	1.14	6.98	52.29	103.13	286.25	365.02	357.00	364.00
移动电话交换机总容量	万户			4.8	154.2	1059.1	1657.0	2066.0	2219.3
本地电话用户	万户	0.77	4.90	31.57	78.12	384.52	332.42	319.55	330.79
移动电话用户(含充值卡)	万户		0.05	4.77	123.68	1016.41	1607.60	1677.77	1797.75
互联网用户	万户			0.05	13.78	52.90	153.92	190.72	209.59
邮政业务收入	万元						63178	73686	78201
电信业务收入	万元						1490174	1574893	1621418
客运量	万人	2072	5758	10237	30697	33551	77446	80337	79739
#公路	万人	1940	5728	10210	30680	33510	77415	80306	79707
旅客周转量	万人公里	95237	322236	446230	1001906	1185290	1290692	1458811	1568758
#公路	万人公里	90950	320690	444293	1000492	1182000	1288675	1456782	1566652
货运量	万吨	2913	2701	4266	5431	6400	9312	10165	11191
#公路	万吨	1922	1571	2377	3440	4586	7640	8210	8421
货物周转量	万吨公里	171591	184700	264605	404678	424829	1090340	1874802	2967132
#公路	万吨公里	113038	72162	128026	246046	272500	510801	531304	543633
港口货物吞吐量	万吨	276	233	201	746	2280	5657	6848	9228

注：1. 2006年起公路通车里程含专用公路和村道，下同。
2. 2010年起，长途自动交换机容量统计口径有变，与往年不可比，下同。
3. 2010年起，邮政业务相关指标不包括速递物流及邮政储蓄银行独立运营部分，下同。

6-2 历年运输线路长度与公路密度

Length of Transportation Routes and Road Density over Years

年 份	公路通车里 程(公里)	等级公路	#一级	等外公路	高级、次高级路面通车里程(公里)	内河通航里 程(公里)	公路密度(公里/百平方公里)
1978	1259	287		972		530	51.08
1979	1225	355		870		603	49.70
1980	1225	355		870		603	49.70
1981	1225	845		380		415	49.70
1982	1225	845		380		115	49.70
1983	1225	872		353		132	49.70
1984	1240	896		344		132	50.30
1985	1240	490		750	488	132	50.30
1986	1248	977		271		274	50.63
1987	1261	991		270		598	51.16
1988	1302	1068	6	234		598	52.82
1989	1325	1091	6	234		598	53.75
1990	1325	1102	6	223	750	598	53.75
1991	1759	1226	6	533	1137	598	71.36
1992	2055	1431	151	624	1442	599	83.37
1993	2260	1673	315	587	1675	598	91.68
1994	2292	1868	599	424	1773	598	92.98
1995	2327	1930	679	397	1650	598	94.40
1996	2330	2087	689	243	1653	598	94.50
1997	2330	2087	690	243	1563	598	94.50
1998	2429	1897	714	480	1958	598	98.52
1999	2467	1935	717	480	2048	798	100.06
2000	2519	2339	782	91	2253	798	102.15
2001	2570	2393	845	78	2321	798	104.26
2002	2641	2464	908	78	2406	798	107.14
2003	2688	2508	967	75	2472	716	109.05
2004	2759	2609	1148	37	2637	798	111.93
2005	2871	2686	1315	31	2774	664	116.47
2006	3891	3619	1585	117	3823	664	157.85
2007	3924	3650	1591	116	3860	535	159.19
2008	4001	3884	1639	117	3864	643	162.31
2009	4713	4598	2389	115	4643	643	191.21
2010	4751	4637	2394	114	4681	643	192.74
2011	4828	4716	2420	112	4759	643	196.24
2012	4969	4861	2484	108	4800	643	201.98

注：公路密度数据来源于交通运输局，下同。

6-3　主要年份运输线路长度

Length of Transport Routes in Main Years

项　　目	单　位	1980年	1990年	1995年	2000年	2005年	2010年	2011年	2012年
公路通车里程合计	公里	1225	1325	2327	2519	2871	4751	4828	4969
#按等级分									
等级公路	公里	355	1102	1930	2339	2686	4637	4716	4861
高速公路	公里				89	154	217	251	319
一　级	公里		6	679	782	1315	2394	2420	2484
二　级	公里		65	361	684	703	1317	1335	1338
三　级	公里		60	135	310	297	178	182	197
四　级	公里	355	971	755	563	371	532	528	523
等外公路	公里	870	223	397	91	31	114	112	108
#按路面分									
有路面里程	公里		800	1808	2508	2858	4689	4767	4808
#高级、次高级	公里		750	1650	2253	2774	4681	4759	4800
无路面里程	公里		524	519	11	13	62	61	59
桥梁合计	座		267	338	538	826	1211	1395	1462
	延米				39956	112385	162767	224548	236243
公路密度	公里/百平方公里	49.70	53.75	94.40	102.15	116.47	192.74	196.24	201.98
#等级公路密度	公里/百平方公里	14.40	44.71	78.30	94.89	108.97	188.12	191.70	197.59
内河通航里程	公里	603	598	598	798	664	643	643	643

6-4　主要年份运输工具拥有量

Possession of Main Means of Transport in Main Years

项　　目	单　位	1985年	1990年	1995年	2000年	2005年	2010年	2011年	2012年
民用车辆拥有量									
汽车	辆	7897	19394	88311	153684	406577	920766	1061373	1207044
载客汽车	辆	1878	7225	25366	69658	268918	772701	906454	1047922
	客位	23462	66361	302844	560155	2420591	5101240	5810047	6541753
载货汽车	辆	5980	12087	55000	81623	129298	143005	149635	153655
	吨位	20428	38010	133757	332621	243390	253879	270309	275798
其他汽车	辆	39	82	7945	2403	8361	5060	5284	5467
摩托车	辆	11786	47881	255591	482636	775838	423766	352553	276401
挂车	辆				8	2222	2983	3196	3374
民用运输船舶拥有量									
机动船	艘	2883	5885	5292	806	467	286	312	333
	净载重吨位	80323	186056	259329	152661	148737	557846	1083217	1280142
	客位	2056	776	1881	1054	604	902	902	589
#货船	艘	2866	5875	5259	796	465	283	309	331
	净载重吨位	80285	186038	259314	152661	148431	557236	1082607	1279837
客船	艘			26	10	2	3	3	2
	客位			1295	1054	604	902	902	589
期末机动车驾驶员	人	44186	118229	351947	563564	798086	1287738	1486810	1674774
#汽车驾驶员	人	10661	28768	94778	173865	428912	1110932	1334243	1554444

注：2002年起民用汽车拥有量按新的口径分类，部分指标数值与往年不可比。

6-5 历年客货运输量

Passenger and Freight Traffic over Years

年 份	客运量（万人）	公 路	水 运	旅客周转量（万人公里）	公 路	水 运
1978	403	224	179	9425	5097	4328
1979	467	272	195	11162	6354	4808
1980	572	362	210	13584	8285	5299
1981	578	349	229	13845	7943	5902
1982	639	405	234	16026	9683	6343
1983	1281	1071	210	54075	47939	6136
1984	1287	1130	157	62107	56890	5217
1985	2072	1940	132	95237	90950	4287
1986	2304	2224	80	127458	124322	3136
1987	3359	3283	76	159117	156578	2539
1988	3223	3176	47	173335	171575	1760
1989	5288	5254	34	240999	239193	1806
1990	5758	5728	30	322236	320690	1546
1991	6749	6719	30	373284	371720	1564
1992	9267	9247	20	503973	502607	1366
1993	10907	10897	10	577800	576116	1684
1994	11234	11229	5	595134	594100	1034
1995	10237	10210	27	446230	444293	1937
1996	10749	10723	26	477466	476072	1394
1997	11300	11273	27	511592	509614	1978
1998	17485	17463	22	577452	575541	1911
1999	25404	25385	19	804278	802590	1688
2000	30697	30680	17	1001906	1000492	1414
2001	31220	31203	17	1031579	1030192	1387
2002	32100	32081	19	1091821	1090155	1666
2003	32588	32566	22	1126964	1125098	1866
2004	33240	33200	40	1166262	1163010	3352
2005	33551	33510	41	1185290	1182000	3290
2006	35182	35143	39	1213809	1210944	2865
2007	37182	37136	46	1264982	1261777	3205
2008	122468	122431	37	2248521	2246128	2393
2009	73324	73291	33	1053469	1051324	2145
2010	77446	77415	31	1290692	1288675	2017
2011	80337	80306	31	1458811	1456782	2029
2012	79739	79707	32	1568758	1566652	2106

6-5 续表 1

年　份	货运量(万吨)	公　路	#个体及联户	水　运	#个体及联户
1978	394	73		321	
1979	399	68		331	
1980	349	51		298	
1981	317	37		280	
1982	319	35		284	
1983	2366	1519	1515	847	535
1984	2738	1728	1710	1018	718
1985	3110	1922	1906	1188	814
1986	3296	2208	2190	1088	725
1987	2618	1304	1288	1314	928
1988	2685	1374	1358	1311	912
1989	3233	1516	1501	1717	1375
1990	2701	1571	1557	1130	837
1991	2456	1300	1286	1156	282
1992	2895	1703	1688	1192	902
1993	3256	1976	1960	1280	1011
1994	3646	2233	2222	1413	1147
1995	4266	2377	2368	1889	1599
1996	4451	2645	2636	1806	1556
1997	4644	2748	2740	1896	1622
1998	4776	2808	2808	1968	1678
1999	5016	3039	3039	1977	1653
2000	5431	3440	3440	1991	1660
2001	5527	3539	3539	1988	1659
2002	5857	4015	4015	1842	1504
2003	5877	4046	4046	1831	1496
2004	6054	4250	4250	1804	721
2005	6400	4586	4586	1814	1484
2006	5481	4930	4930	551	
2007	5676	5115	1194	561	75
2008	9273	8010	1273	1263	86
2009	8733	6944	1973	1789	159
2010	9312	7640	2080	1672	158
2011	10165	8210	2155	1955	133
2012	11191	8421	2310	2770	84

6-5 续表 2

年份	货物周转量(万吨公里)	公路	#个体及联户	水运	#个体及联户	港口货物吞吐量(万吨)
1978	15148	924		14224		293
1979	15390	636		14654		297
1980	16353	1479		14874		295
1981	15606	304		15302		272
1982	17185	252		16933		253
1983	108634	70723	70572	37911	20317	319
1984	140113	91774	91702	48339	29179	268
1985	171591	113038	113002	58553	31784	276
1986	126898	71392	71358	55506	27916	268
1987	174942	101285	101253	73657	41049	296
1988	169112	69014	68986	100098	82351	320
1989	186626	70942	70921	115684	82351	297
1990	184700	72162	72141	112538	83094	233
1991	194101	82555	82534	111546	82075	267
1992	232752	116698	116673	116054	85084	292
1993	248230	134918	134890	113312	87574	313
1994	273053	151108	148152	121945	93235	370
1995	264605	128026	127928	136579	105099	201
1996	267193	121625	121603	145568	118169	289
1997	278649	126336	126244	152313	122428	338
1998	285889	130378	130378	155511	123343	516
1999	300410	143465	143465	156945	119120	654
2000	404678	246046	246046	158632	119855	746
2001	406247	250121	250121	156126	118112	883
2002	420684	265908	265908	154776	115444	1611
2003	422822	268998	268998	153824	114812	2352
2004	423669	272220	272220	151449	48377	2600
2005	424829	272500	272500	152329	113249	2280
2006	336783	278566	278566	58217		1951
2007	356677	297223	50803	59454	6414	2017
2008	1747489	462797	38398	1284692	5598	3208
2009	1016490	452880	126052	563610	8787	3530
2010	1090340	510801	131929	579539	9399	5657
2011	1874802	531304	138976	1343498	9606	6848
2012	2967132	543633	147604	2423499	5941	9228

6-6 历年主要运输工具年末拥有量

Possession of Main Means of Transport at Year-end over Years

年 份	民用汽车(辆)	#客车	货车	摩托车(辆)	机动船(艘)
1978	623	78	506	134	2169
1979	1115	178	1089	156	2034
1980	2009	516	1457	170	1948
1981	3039	751	2031	517	2107
1982	3419	791	2724	1168	2285
1983	4473	854	3580	1636	2313
1984	6059	1243	4822	7060	2563
1985	7897	1878	5980	11786	2883
1986	8632	2245	6334	18006	4368
1987	9983	2954	6973	21308	4884
1988	13581	3456	8690	26995	4911
1989	16340	4214	10434	36820	4901
1990	19394	7225	12087	47881	5885
1991	20734	5206	15423	65770	4405
1992	32625	5753	25048	106013	4351
1993	48145	8710	35421	153014	4379
1994	61572	11550	43925	200543	4562
1995	88311	25366	55000	255591	5292
1996	90793	29430	54870	249492	5313
1997	103425	40101	62507	287076	5064
1998	113435	47769	64434	382010	456
1999	127007	55715	69470	399324	690
2000	153684	69658	82841	482636	806
2001	183638	89677	91304	560310	536
2002	220134	116783	102253	642034	483
2003	255603	155206	97047	692562	392
2004	319725	210531	105050	687651	417
2005	406577	268918	129298	775838	467
2006	489306	351265	131704	697175	440
2007	608933	466999	134825	567002	393
2008	701600	557359	136295	521118	326
2009	795554	653273	137334	470818	293
2010	920766	772701	143005	423766	286
2011	1061373	906454	149635	352553	312
2012	1207044	1047922	153655	276401	333

6-7 主要年份邮电通信业务基本情况

Basic Statistics on Postal and Telecommunication Services in Main Years

项目	单位	1978年	1990年	1995年	2000年	2005年	2010年	2011年	2012年
邮电通信网									
邮电局、所	处	50	53	273	594	702	555	626	595
邮路长度	公里	513	459	685	3550	6835	4667	4283	4070
农村投递线路长度	公里	1985	1812	2057	8865	19722	13261	12875	16048
邮电通信工具									
邮政汽车	辆		7	10	35	192	131	151	234
长途自动交换机容量	路端		2100	15000	42182	510045	419110	419237	237150
移动电话交换机总容量	万户			4.8	154.2	1059.1	1657.0	2066.0	2219.3
移动电话用户(含充值卡)	万户				123.68	1016.41	1607.60	1677.77	1797.75
移动电话用户(不含充值卡)	万户		0.05	4.77	80.97	176.83	174.04	244.78	442.87
局用交换机容量	万门		6.98	52.29	103.13	286.25	365.02	357.00	364.00
#市话交换机	万门		2.10	16.82	21.84	67.68	94.28	56.43	27.48
本地电话用户	万户	0.20	4.90	31.57	78.12	384.52	332.42	319.55	330.79
市内电话用户	万户	0.04	1.50	9.78	19.69	68.30	85.76	73.37	64.93
农村电话用户	万户	0.16	3.40	21.80	58.43	316.22	246.66	246.18	265.86
数字数据用户(DDN)	端口				2741	2170	1098	388	978
互联网用户	万户			0.05	13.78	52.90	153.92	190.72	209.59
邮电业务量									
邮电业务收入	亿元						155.34	164.86	169.96
#电信业务	亿元						149.02	157.49	162.14
#移动通信业务	亿元						105.78	116.34	121.34
邮政特快专递	万件					292.17	183.00	167.00	148.00
函件	万件		3372	10407	8124	9430	4507	5148	5065
长途电话	万次		1739	21287	66419	159762	135811	152131	104951

6-8 历年邮电通信业务主要指标

Main Indicators of Postal and Telecommunication Services over Years

年 份	邮 电 局、所 (处)	长途自动 交换机容量 (路端)	局 用 交 换机容量 (万门)	本地电话 用 户 (万户)	移动电话 用 户 (万户)	邮电业务 收 入 (亿元)
1978	50			0.20		
1979	50			0.21		
1980	50		0.50	0.31		
1981	50			0.34		
1982	51			0.35		
1983	51			0.39		
1984	52			0.48		
1985	52		1.14	0.77		
1986	53			0.88		
1987	45			1.63		
1988	48			2.52		
1989	50			4.30	0.02	
1990	53	2100	6.98	4.90	0.05	
1991	60		9.82	7.50	0.11	
1992	91	3510	11.07	9.70	0.30	
1993	161	3510	21.24	14.98	0.72	
1994	216	11410	36.37	23.19	2.41	
1995	273	15000	52.29	31.57	4.77	
1996	310	15000	52.79	36.91	8.24	
1997	339	15000	57.76	42.65	15.29	
1998	397	25000	73.09	50.13	26.17	
1999	458	40000	84.79	60.87	51.01	
2000	594	42182	103.13	78.12	123.68	
2001	689	59000	155.29	98.96	295.76	
2002	696	59000	176.94	127.93	412.39	90.56
2003	846	129000	220.28	206.11	660.86	105.12
2004	854	200985	265.66	281.35	856.09	120.78
2005	702	510045	286.25	384.52	1016.41	132.82
2006	560	563071	299.19	461.31	1216.34	146.69
2007	567	713290	329.50	469.17	1408.23	161.90
2008	547	766946	340.71	439.41	1454.29	172.38
2009	546	864970	347.15	378.40	1409.29	156.31
2010	555	419110	365.02	332.42	1607.60	155.34
2011	626	419237	357.00	319.55	1677.77	164.86
2012	595	237150	364.00	330.79	1797.75	169.96

注：本地电话用户含小灵通用户。

6-9 主要年份邮电通信企业财务指标

Main Financial Indicators of Postal and Telecommunication Enterprises in Main Years

单位：万元

指　　标	2005年	2010年	2011年	2012年
职工人数(人)	10730	10050	10276	10394
#固定工	4803	4375	4575	4758
年末资产总额	1465629	1615528	1598573	1725286
年末流动资产合计	181039	261091	157213	165396
#应收帐款净额	67608	53749	60994	63661
年末固定资产合计	1238276	1118833	1198064	1382327
年末固定资产原值合计	1790159	2835390	3130717	3440804
#生产用	1770843	2827527	3121472	2184773
累计折旧	664786	1647586	1865640	2188604
#当年折旧	177293	112848	218732	225508
年末固定资产净值合计	1125360	1187804	1265077	1352201
无形资产及递延资产	42582	63073	63960	73484
其它资产	2198	172531	179336	198869
负债及所有者权益总计	1465629	1615528	1598573	1725286
年末流动资产负债合计	365735	570387	597492	749532
#未交税金	39447	17248	29965	6716
短期借款	3000			
年末长期负债合计		-2635	31522	33844
期末所有者权益合计	1099894	1047776	969559	941911
主营业务收入	1326686	1155820	1723350	1767238
#营业成本	406999	468110	644909	741144
营业税金及附加	41122	32063	51978	53364
其他业务利润	-11316	-1721	-2868	3851
管理费用	99425	34802	53001	54685
财务费用	539	2718	735	439
营业外收入	879	6093	2679	4903
营业外支出	2838	3281	2962	2668
利润总额	716380	496456	748937	690643
利税总额	756757	520173	780934	728737

主要统计指标解释

Explanatory Notes on Main Statistical Indicators

公路里程 指在一定时点上实际达到交通部规定的公路技术等级标准，并经公路主管部门正式验收交付使用的公路里程数。包括大、中城市的郊区公路以及公路通过城镇（指县城、集镇）街道的里程数。但不包括大、中城市街道，厂矿、林区内部生产用道、农业生产用道，以及新建公路尚未进行验收交付使用的路段里程。公路按工程技术等级分为高速、一、二、三、四级公路；按公路是否铺设路面分为有路面和无路面公路；按公路通车情况分为晴雨通车里程和晴通雨阻里程。

货（客）运量 在一定时期内，各运输部门实际运送的货物（旅客）数量。货运按吨计算，客运按人计算。货物不论运输距离长短，货物类型，均按实际重量统计；旅客不论行程远近或票价多少，均按一人一次作为客运量统计。半价票，小孩票也按一人统计。货（客）运量反映运输业为国民经济和人民生活服务的数量，也是制定和检查运输生产计划，研究运输发展规模和速度的重要指标。

货物（旅客）周转量 指在一定时期内，由各种运输工具运输业运送的货物（旅客）数量与其相应运输距离的乘积，通常以吨公里和人公里为计算单位。计算货物周转量通常按发出站与到达站之间的最短距离，也就是计费距离计算。它是反映运输业生产总成果的重要指标，也是编制和检查运输生产计划，计算运输效率，劳动生产率以及核算运输单位成本的主要基础资料。

货物吞吐量 是指经由水运运进、运出港区范围，并经过装卸的货物数量。货物吞吐量分别按国内进口（装卸）、出口（装船），外贸进口、出口统计。货物吞吐量按货物实际重量吨统计，以货物交接清单或货单上记载的重量吨为准。如无实际重量吨，可根据船舶装载情况来推算。在本港区内的水运转口分别按进口和出口各计算一次吞吐量。货物吞吐量是衡量港口生产规模的一个主要数量指标。

邮电业务收入 是指邮电营运企业从事邮政、电信、移动及其他邮电业务所取得的营业收入。

局用交换机容量 指安装在本地电信运营商内用于接读本地固定电话的电话交换机容量，有倍增设备按倍增后的数量计数。包括现用和备用的人工或自动交换全部容量。

本地电话用户 是指接入本地电信运营商固定电话网上的电话用户。包括：住宅电话、单位用户、公用电话用户等。

移动电话用户 是指在移动通信部门办理登记手续，通过移动电话交换机进入移动电话网，占用移动电话号码的电话用户。

邮政局所 指经邮政部门审批许可，有固定的地址，领有上级发给的邮政日戳或邮政戳记，对外营业直接为用户办理邮政业务（至少办理出售邮票和收寄给据函件）的服务机构。邮政局所按经营方式分为自办局所和代办局所；按设置地点分为城市局所和农村局所。

七、国内贸易

Domestic Trade

7-1 历年社会消费品零售总额

Total Retail Sales of Consumer Goods over Years

年　份	社会消费品零售总额	
	绝对值（万元）	增速（%）
1978	21269	
1979	24956	17.3
1980	31595	26.6
1981	40201	27.2
1982	48126	19.7
1983	52255	8.6
1984	73930	41.5
1985	93640	26.7
1986	122420	30.7
1987	150511	23.0
1988	246518	63.8
1989	270354	9.7
1990	319738	18.3
1991	364972	14.2
1992	443464	21.5
1993	636882	43.6
1994	851556	33.7
1995	1130081	32.7
1996	1255311	11.1
1997	1460396	16.3
1998	1751551	19.9
1999	2023008	15.5
2000	2351634	16.2
2001	2757143	17.2
2002	3212436	16.5
2003	3697814	15.1
2004	4264704	15.3
2005	5062917	18.7
2006	5993201	18.4
2007	7224491	20.5
2008	8811519	22.0
2009	9590727	8.8
2010	11080592	15.9
2011	12663109	15.0
2012	13545787	9.3

注：本表1979-2003年数据根据东莞市第一次全国经济普查结果重新核定，2005-2008年数据根据东莞市第二次全国经济普查结果重新核定，2010年、2011年统计口径均有调整，增长速度按同口径计算。

7-2 历年批发零售贸易企业与个体户数

Wholesale and Retail Trades Enterprises and Self-employed Individuals over years

单位：个

年　份	单位数合计	国有经济	集体经济	其他经济	
					私营个体经济
1979	2459	406	1918	135	135
1980	2613	395	1679	539	537
1981	4603	371	1954	2278	2274
1982	3323	373	1838	1112	1107
1983	8723	401	1539	6783	6783
1984	18917	431	6720	11766	11766
1985	16885	670	4543	11672	11671
1986	18547	823	3063	14661	14660
1987	23468	739	4102	18627	18626
1988	26247	665	4405	21177	21176
1989	28453	695	4196	23562	23561
1990	27931	709	3512	23710	23709
1991	29474	678	3934	24862	24862
1992	34465	803	4193	29469	29469
1993	43511	886	7640	34985	34985
1994	49706	633	11396	37677	37677
1995	56339	745	14492	41102	41101
1996	60078	670	15183	44225	44224
1997	48910	811	8477	39622	39546
1998	52543	1064	4046	47433	46615
1999	55925	1056	3843	51026	50172
2000	57474	1024	3581	5289	51914
2001	68909	866	2960	65083	63760
2002	89246	748	2424	86078	84614
2003	113531	530	2068	110933	109236
2004	149067	539	1941	146587	144304
2005	192525	393	1451	190681	188082
2006	236124	283	1090	234751	231930
2007	284109	268	930	282911	279524
2008	301996	288	833	300875	296613
2009	300088	256	744	299088	294753
2010	300668	239	654	299775	295166
2011	288904	223	629	288052	283209
2012	305784	227	594	304963	299666

7-3 批发零售业商品销售总额（2012年）

Total Sales of Commodities in Wholesale and Retail Trades (2012)

单位：万元

项 目	商品销售总额		
		批发额	零售额
合 计	25228935	12888068	12340867
按行业分			
批发业	11945373	11447510	497863
零售业	13283562	1440558	11843004
按规模分			
限额以上企业和个体户	17266937	10991096	6275841
粮油、食品、饮料、烟酒类	1995470	1551583	443886
粮油类	316442	191414	125028
肉禽蛋类	57867	24829	33038
水产品类	15693	682	15012
蔬菜类	33720	21	33699
干鲜果品类	57282	9305	47977
饮料类	181789	116408	65381
烟酒类	850035	802918	47117
服装鞋帽、针纺织品类	1334607	1066370	268237
服装类	908707	714258	194448
鞋帽类	190534	143133	47401
针、纺织品类	235366	208979	26387
化妆品类	61575	11741	49834
金银珠宝类	41539	21021	20518
日用品类	417802	310782	107020
洗涤用品类	178188	117935	60253
儿童玩具类	42919	36351	6569
五金、电料类	294948	282337	12611
体育、娱乐用品类	30534	21664	8870
书报杂志类	13219	3427	9793
电子出版物及音像制品类	1843	223	1619
家用电器和音像器材类	665552	343463	322088
中西药品类	383000	215263	167737
西药	189746	68918	120828
中草药及中成药	80226	42358	37868
文化办公用品类	266641	163444	103197
家具类	686481	681644	4837
通讯器材类	824088	728876	95213
煤炭及制品类	464525	464525	
木材及制品类	26005	26005	
石油及制品类	3596590	1983543	1613046
化工材料及制品类	1064439	1064439	
化肥类	1192	1192	
金属材料类	568475	568475	
建筑及装潢材料类	80294	58557	21737
机电产品及设备类	240273	212171	28102
农机类	512	512	
汽车类	3078198	135517	2942681
种子饲料类	823	823	
棉麻类			
其它	1130018	1075202	54816
限额以下企业和个体户	7961998	1896972	6065026

7-4 限额以上住宿业和餐饮业经营情况（2012年）

Business of Hotels and Catering Services above Designated Size (2012)

项目	法人企业（个）	从业人数（人）	营业额（万元）	客房收入	餐费收入	商品销售收入	其它收入
总计	338	68640	873627	199915	583820	5164	84728
住宿业	189	47715	563015	195913	283434	2320	81348
按登记注册类型分							
内资企业	175	41530	493248	173863	243424	1733	74229
港、澳、台商投资企业	10	4391	47762	16455	26291	586	4430
外商投资企业	4	1794	22004	5594	13720	1	2689
按国民经济行业分							
旅游饭店	153	43747	531211	181526	270418	2248	77019
一般旅馆	31	3608	27133	12368	10469	41	4256
其它住宿服务业	5	360	4672	2020	2547	32	74
餐饮业	149	20925	310612	4002	300386	2844	3380
按登记注册类型分							
内资企业	133	13712	182771	4002	173618	2543	2608
港、澳、台商投资企业	6	1131	18631		17676	301	653
外商投资企业	10	6082	109211		109092		119
按国民经济行业分							
正餐服务业	129	12442	164328	4002	155193	1759	3375
快餐服务业	9	6861	129071		129071		
饮料及冷饮服务业	1	511	1207		122	1085	
其他餐饮服务业	10	1111	16006		16001		5

7-5　限额以上批发和零售企业财务状况（2012年）

Main Financial Indicators of Enterprises above Designated Size in Wholesale and Retail Trade (2012)

单位：万元

项　　目	法　人 企业数 （个）	年末资产负债				
		流动资 产合计	存货	固定资 产原价	累　计 折　旧	本年折旧
总　计	959	9423814	1449546	883423	330670	78619
批发企业	500	6108066	817927	316726	124150	25798
按登记注册类型分						
内资企业	477	5802514	753527	302843	118656	24522
港、澳、台商投资企业	18	263806	60856	7834	2932	945
外商投资企业	5	41746	3545	6049	2562	331
按国民经济行业分						
农、林、牧产品批发业	2	6886	5825	2311	73	73
食品、饮料及烟草制品批发业	42	448754	63023	51192	18309	5649
纺织、服装及家庭用品批发业	62	704616	90938	43123	18617	1833
文化、体育用品及器材批发业	16	143079	41759	6925	3094	876
医药及医疗器材批发业	14	170194	42100	9736	3830	608
矿产品、建材及化工产品批发业	232	3249463	373709	110080	47762	8862
机械设备、五金交电及电子产品批发业	72	922500	120016	59699	21072	5362
贸易经纪与代理	18	145257	4508	6948	3625	1003
其他批发业	42	317317	76049	26713	7767	1532
零售企业	459	3315748	631619	566696	206520	52821
按登记注册类型分						
内资企业	431	3122477	557661	468533	175989	43649
港、澳、台商投资企业	14	87253	39235	47469	10951	4594
外商投资企业	14	106018	34723	50694	19580	4578
按国民经济行业分						
综合零售业	81	329968	80838	172644	52145	14744
食品、饮料及烟草制品专门零售业	12	43992	20125	3362	2018	1085
纺织、服装及日用品专门零售业	8	13798	8767	406	225	81
文化、体育用品及器材专门零售业	3	12346	7072	218	214	
医药及医疗器材专门零售业	28	61152	19516	8258	3903	707
汽车、摩托车、燃料及零配件专门零售业	264	2380778	353774	330713	127880	30875
家用电器及电子产品专门零售业	26	407766	130144	13335	5893	3298
五金、家具及室内装修材料专门零售业	8	9608	2851	5247	3636	435
货摊、无店铺及其他零售业	29	56339	8531	32513	10606	1596

7-5 续表 1

(2012年)

单位: 万元

项目	年末资产负债				损益及分配	
	资产总计	负债合计	所有者权益合计	实收资本	营业收入合计	主营业务收入
总计	10946297	8732627	2213670	837046	20512846	20299682
批发企业	6933709	6116749	816960	463756	13752671	13671833
按登记注册类型分						
内资企业	6612043	5862563	749480	411859	12841457	12762695
港、澳、台商投资企业	270779	232516	38264	35634	794004	792146
外商投资企业	50887	21670	29217	16263	117210	116992
按国民经济行业分						
农、林、牧产品批发业	21550	18256	3294	800	64618	64616
食品、饮料及烟草制品批发业	850209	586915	263295	76288	1514145	1491328
纺织、服装及家庭用品批发业	753008	678744	74264	46825	2858654	2845691
文化、体育用品及器材批发业	167107	141949	25158	18717	173826	173706
医药及医疗器材批发业	181366	155310	26056	13534	236411	236382
矿产品、建材及化工产品批发业	3471383	3229347	242036	205755	5465822	5454832
机械设备、五金交电及电子产品批发业	981405	864506	116899	57621	1988398	1963572
贸易经纪与代理	152307	142223	10085	7596	643453	642922
其他批发业	355374	299500	55875	36622	807345	798786
零售企业	4012588	2615878	1396709	373290	6760175	6627849
按登记注册类型分						
内资企业	3731369	2406682	1324687	285205	5742934	5623655
港、澳、台商投资企业	129150	85015	44135	34578	390110	385363
外商投资企业	152068	124181	27887	53506	627131	618831
按国民经济行业分						
综合零售业	501705	426705	75000	66144	888348	854642
食品、饮料及烟草制品专门零售业	46656	37396	9260	5568	58281	57906
纺织、服装及日用品专门零售业	14847	11802	3044	4110	33869	33782
文化、体育用品及器材专门零售业	16060	14680	1380	4100	7501	6099
医药及医疗器材专门零售业	68219	55038	13180	3759	147010	144093
汽车、摩托车、燃料及零配件专门零售业	2815635	1602781	1212854	226942	4444245	4382538
家用电器及电子产品专门零售业	453997	398801	55196	26086	916716	890576
五金、家具及室内装修材料专门零售业	12059	18910	-6851	7410	25846	24779
货摊、无店铺及其他零售业	83411	49765	33645	29171	238360	233435

7-5　续表 2

(2012年)

单位: 万元

项　　目	损益及分配					
	主营业务成本	营业税金及附加	其他业务利润	销售费用	管理费用	税金
总　计	18777054	64885	141932	750472	272815	9489
批发企业	12898813	48275	40598	351099	147652	5823
按登记注册类型分						
内资企业	12053778	46489	40085	316039	134108	5286
港、澳、台商投资企业	738392	1524	417	31841	11768	371
外商投资企业	106643	262	96	3219	1775	166
按国民经济行业分						
农、林、牧产品批发业	63894	15	-1	132	634	30
食品、饮料及烟草制品批发业	1281399	37972	19436	49430	36446	1052
纺织、服装及家庭用品批发业	2764990	1049	6089	44528	17985	475
文化、体育用品及器材批发业	156154	201	4282	13362	5181	267
医药及医疗器材批发业	215678	338	92	8102	4731	151
矿产品、建材及化工产品批发业	5172811	4304	3723	147910	42336	2271
机械设备、五金交电及电子产品批发业	1855612	2823	4549	63664	26003	574
贸易经纪与代理	631720	88	553	3260	5323	381
其他批发业	756554	1485	1874	20712	9013	622
零售企业	5878242	16610	101334	399373	125162	3666
按登记注册类型分						
内资企业	4971707	14316	86531	319387	106973	3384
港、澳、台商投资企业	353502	835	4630	26566	7529	221
外商投资企业	553033	1460	10172	53420	10661	61
按国民经济行业分						
综合零售业	714291	5614	41694	151479	21397	189
食品、饮料及烟草制品专门零售业	54223	122	9	1391	1333	138
纺织、服装及日用品专门零售业	24169	177	96	8985	814	8
文化、体育用品及器材专门零售业	5779	90	318	543	516	18
医药及医疗器材专门零售业	120743	307	439	11228	8063	128
汽车、摩托车、燃料及零配件专门零售业	3898820	7221	30388	141746	73303	2966
家用电器及电子产品专门零售业	829025	2470	24960	66703	11913	47
五金、家具及室内装修材料专门零售业	20146	145	278	4989	417	48
货摊、无店铺及其他零售业	211046	466	3152	12308	7406	125

7-5 续表 3

(2012年)

单位: 万元

项目	损益及分配				应付职工薪酬	应交增值税
	财务费用	营业利润	利润总额	应交所得税		
总计	157412	199421	219957	67731	318481	246012
批发企业	103446	142219	145864	45119	126072	123175
按登记注册类型分						
内资企业	102910	123675	127479	41968	109909	109789
港、澳、台商投资企业	739	7813	7553	1804	14911	11871
外商投资企业	-203	10730	10832	1347	1252	1516
按国民经济行业分						
农、林、牧产品批发业	158	-235	-188	18	335	145
食品、饮料及烟草制品批发业	23373	117103	119483	27114	27340	34084
纺织、服装及家庭用品批发业	5930	18578	20296	3861	19593	7869
文化、体育用品及器材批发业	1790	5561	5626	186	7417	1653
医药及医疗器材批发业	2611	4945	4034	1052	5724	4516
矿产品、建材及化工产品批发业	59014	-28878	-28260	4613	30277	37258
机械设备、五金交电及电子产品批发业	5501	14837	14772	5747	23778	20378
贸易经纪与代理	1786	1253	1239	317	2198	2533
其他批发业	3283	9055	8863	2212	9409	14739
零售企业	53966	57203	74093	22612	192409	122837
按登记注册类型分						
内资企业	48460	49441	64803	20118	159000	96205
港、澳、台商投资企业	3649	-3114	-2714	777	11471	5530
外商投资企业	1856	10876	12004	1717	21938	21103
按国民经济行业分						
综合零售业	3799	5553	9679	4699	44048	16304
食品、饮料及烟草制品专门零售业	336	510	516	126	1423	1095
纺织、服装及日用品专门零售业	102	-346	-228	114	1500	3293
文化、体育用品及器材专门零售业	88	-630	-629	13	766	200
医药及医疗器材专门零售业	1360	1578	1598	538	9945	2293
汽车、摩托车、燃料及零配件专门零售业	42971	44088	54842	14550	92156	87679
家用电器及电子产品专门零售业	4098	1289	2347	1218	29864	7902
五金、家具及室内装修材料专门零售业	494	-368	141	18	2576	866
货摊、无店铺及其他零售业	719	5528	5828	1336	10131	3205

7-6 限额以上住宿和餐饮企业财务状况（2012年）

Main Financial Indicators of Enterprises above Designated Size in Hotels and Catering Services (2012)

单位：万元

项目	法人企业数（个）	年末资产负债				
		流动资产合计	存货	固定资产原价	累计折旧	本年折旧
总计	338	691853	37738	1036356	485925	65697
住宿业	189	585902	28624	932327	438989	59082
按登记注册类型分						
内资企业	175	496693	25200	789060	349143	54083
港、澳、台商投资企业	10	73548	2758	99442	70209	3940
外商投资企业	4	15662	666	43826	19637	1059
按国民经济行业分						
旅游饭店	153	566980	27415	889348	419787	56942
一般旅馆	31	18557	1151	41881	18476	1877
其它住宿服务业	5	365	59	1098	725	262
餐饮业	149	105951	9114	104029	46936	6615
按登记注册类型分						
内资企业	133	83564	4778	57734	27295	4779
港、澳、台商投资企业	6	7595	284	18220	4982	989
外商投资企业	10	14792	4052	28074	14659	848
按国民经济行业分						
正餐服务业	129	41374	5324	74043	31873	4589
快餐服务业	9	60677	3025	29169	14870	1889
饮料及冷饮服务业	1	621	585	505	87	66
其他餐饮服务业	10	3279	180	313	106	72

7-6　续表 1

(2012年)

单位: 万元

项　　目	年末资产负债				损益及分配	
	资产总计	负债合计	所有者权益合计	实收资本	营业收入	主营业务收入
总　计	1614027	1380943	233083	324895	874040	864531
住宿业	1380529	1257525	123004	246674	563919	558036
按登记注册类型分						
内资企业	1208337	1118190	90147	183464	495846	490080
港、澳、台商投资企业	127247	104735	22512	41908	45748	45718
外商投资企业	44946	34600	10346	21302	22326	22238
按国民经济行业分						
旅游饭店	1330341	1236113	94228	230091	532207	526649
一般旅馆	49130	18950	30180	15783	27041	26716
其它住宿服务业	1059	2461	-1403	800	4672	4672
餐饮业	233497	123419	110079	78221	310121	306495
按登记注册类型分						
内资企业	162090	98599	63491	39671	181993	178492
港、澳、台商投资企业	22085	16020	6065	9347	18583	18576
外商投资企业	49323	8800	40523	29204	109545	109427
按国民经济行业分						
正餐服务业	96837	66677	30159	37920	163475	159854
快餐服务业	131400	54679	76721	38017	129432	129432
饮料及冷饮服务业	1039	287	752	240	1207	1207
其他餐饮服务业	4222	1775	2447	2044	16006	16001

7-6 续表 2

(2012年)

单位: 万元

项目	损益及分配					
	主营业务成本	主营业务税金及附加	其他业务利润	销售费用	管理费用	
						税金
总计	315375	52375	9625	309859	174165	3121
住宿业	163196	35214	8458	215237	145424	2420
按登记注册类型分						
内资企业	143384	31076	8340	192164	124664	2149
港、澳、台商投资企业	11549	2739	29	14913	15746	227
外商投资企业	8264	1398	90	8160	5015	44
按国民经济行业分						
旅游饭店	153705	33210	8136	203118	138519	2378
一般旅馆	7416	1736	322	10426	6266	39
其它住宿服务业	2074	268		1694	639	3
餐饮业	152179	17162	1166	94622	28741	701
按登记注册类型分						
内资企业	94564	10052	705	44588	21795	640
港、澳、台商投资企业	8403	1066	7	7469	1453	61
外商投资企业	49212	6044	454	42565	5492	1
按国民经济行业分						
正餐服务业	83669	9126	767	49825	18457	587
快餐服务业	57270	7199	400	42145	8476	104
饮料及冷饮服务业	855	61		244	13	1
其他餐饮服务业	10385	776		2408	1795	9

7-6 续表 3

(2012年)

单位: 万元

项目	损益及分配				应付职工薪酬
	财务费用	营业利润	利润总额	应交所得税	
总计	30037	-3761	-6239	8119	183076
住宿业	29557	-19368	-12679	4684	128215
按登记注册类型分					
内资企业	24434	-14508	-7868	4606	112764
港、澳、台商投资企业	4096	-3324	-3281	75	11269
外商投资企业	1028	-1536	-1531	2	4181
按国民经济行业分					
旅游饭店	28851	-19440	-12812	4359	120767
一般旅馆	676	107	168	255	6583
其它住宿服务业	30	-34	-35	70	864
餐饮业	480	15607	6440	3436	54862
按登记注册类型分					
内资企业	1062	8176	-464	2486	34984
港、澳、台商投资企业	48	143	145	123	3608
外商投资企业	-630	7288	6759	827	16271
按国民经济行业分					
正餐服务业	931	-262	-350	878	31944
快餐服务业	-453	15178	6105	2487	18865
饮料及冷饮服务业	2	33	33	8	786
其他餐饮服务业		658	652	62	3267

7-7 历年住宿餐饮企业与个体户数

Enterprises and Self-employed Individuals in Hotels and Catering Services over Years

单位：个

年 份	单位数合 计	国有经济	集体经济	其他经济	#私营个体经济
1979	147	22	115	10	10
1980	182	23	121	38	38
1981	622	24	283	315	315
1982	308	24	102	182	182
1983	2069	31	98	1940	1940
1984	4012	31	445	3536	3536
1985	2982	36	389	2557	2557
1986	3268	38	270	2960	2956
1987	2281	35	308	1938	1934
1988	2265	31	296	1938	1934
1989	2850	32	276	2542	2538
1990	3387	30	439	2918	2914
1991	3438	44	225	3169	3165
1992	4456	25	320	4111	4106
1993	7119	12	1851	5256	5232
1994	7819	12	1748	6059	6051
1995	8918	26	1802	7090	7082
1996	9708	9	1900	7799	7789
1997	9968	28	606	9334	9210
1998	11069	102	368	10599	10532
1999	11904	80	337	11487	11392
2000	8335	78	361	7896	7831
2001	9776	67	343	9366	9318
2002	15128	74	265	14789	14740
2003	17615	64	229	17322	17276
2004	19802	39	424	19339	19224
2005	25972	28	315	25629	25522
2006	27108	16	247	26845	26747
2007	38435	11	219	38205	38094
2008	40154	9	177	39968	39687
2009	38220	5	130	38085	37795
2010	36156	4	113	36039	35728
2011	29280	4	91	29185	28825
2012	29381	4	81	29296	28874

7-8 历年限额以上企业商品购进、销售、库存总额

Total Purchases, Sales and Stock of Commercial Enterprises above Designated Size over Years

单位：万元

年 份	商品购进总额	商品销售总额	批 发	零 售	年末库存总额
1978	82347	74936	50207	24729	7576
1979	91074	82878	55528	27350	8378
1980	109147	99324	66547	32777	10041
1981	131797	119936	80357	39579	12125
1982	156730	142615	95552	47063	14418
1983	160485	146042	97848	48194	14764
1984	214364	195072	130698	64374	19721
1985	254458	231557	155143	76414	23410
1986	630988	283945	190243	93702	28706
1987	380242	346021	231834	114187	34982
1988	714661	650342	435729	214613	65749
1989	729163	663539	444570	218969	67083
1990	766549	697560	467365	230195	70523
1991	796488	672666	433991	238675	74092
1992	881697	743990	473014	270976	64939
1993	1141163	1063567	725979	337588	92249
1994	1323263	1296363	912457	383906	177377
1995	1584470	1556882	1044334	512548	143404
1996	1694496	1737121	1117111	620010	166267
1997	1857884	1922001	1212399	709602	175715
1998	779319	863214	696921	166293	91640
1999	1064070	1106048	875799	230249	73620
2000	1232026	1354640	1072929	281711	58304
2001	1312924	1405409	1080688	324721	67415
2002	1588853	1682579	1188961	493618	102657
2003	1712564	1805840	1138496	667344	107996
2004		5406921	3479209	1927712	251427
2005	4798504	5683548	3882222	1801326	322445
2006	5324450	6487742	4215562	227179	335108
2007	6706290	8102415	4875668	3226748	485401
2008	8349926	10772768	6604662	4168106	790691
2009	8689984	10167222	6137228	4029994	839175
2010	12846503	14271362	9046899	5224463	1002940
2011	15777469	18129917	11738336	6391581	1401733
2012	20036523	22307974	15515426	6792549	1699355

7-9 市场分类基本情况（2011-2012年）

Basic Statistics on Market Classification (2011-2012)

单位：个

项　　目	2011年			2012年		
	合　计	城　市	农　村	合　计	城　市	农　村
合　　计	812	181	631	816	186	630
消费品市场	765	167	598	728	213	515
消费品综合市场	162	42	120	120	38	82
农副产品市场	496	100	396	509	135	374
农副产品综合市场	465	96	369	499	132	367
农副产品专业市场	31	4	27	10	3	7
工业品消费市场	72	18	54	65	32	33
工业消费品综合市场	32	11	21	35	24	11
工业消费品专业市场	40	7	33	30	8	22
其他消费品市场	35	7	28	34	8	26
生产资料市场	47	14	33	37	14	23
生产资料综合市场	6	2	4	4	2	2
工业生产资料市场	23	4	19	20	5	15
机动车交易市场	6	2	4	4		4
钢材交易市场	2		2	2	1	1
煤炭交易市场						
木材交易市场	5	1	4	4		4
其他工业生产资料市场	10	2	8	10	4	6
农业生产资料市场						
农业生产资料综合市场						
农业生产资料专业市场						
其他生产资料市场	18	8	10	13	7	6

注：本表数据来源于市工商局。

7-10 历年城乡集市贸易

Statistics on Urban and Rural Trade Fairs over Years

单位：个

年　份	集贸市场 总　数	城　市	农　村
1978	35		35
1979	35		35
1980	35		35
1981	38		38
1982	40		40
1983	41		41
1984	43		43
1985	48		48
1986	57	7	50
1987	63	10	53
1988	66	12	54
1989	69	11	58
1990	73	10	63
1991	75	10	65
1992	53	7	46
1993	155	13	142
1994	162	12	150
1995	189	17	172
1996	219	20	199
1997	241	23	218
1998	252	25	227
1999	286	36	250
2000	308	29	279
2001	375	31	344
2002	495	28	467
2003	576	34	542
2004	610	35	575
2005	665	36	629
2006	812	39	773
2007	845	36	809
2008	871	228	643
2009	883	225	658
2010	792	194	598
2011	812	181	631
2012	816	186	630

注：2008年以前的城市集贸市场数只包括莞城的集贸市场，2008年起包括莞城、东城、南城和万江四大街道办的市场数。

主要统计指标解释

Explanatory Notes on Main Statistical Indicators

社会消费品零售总额 指企业（单位、个体户）通过交易直接售给个人、社会集团非生产、非经营用的实物商品金额，以及提供餐饮服务所取得的收入金额。个人包括城乡居民和入境人员，社会集团包括机关、社会团体、部队、学校、企事业单位、居委会或村委会等。

商品购进总额 指从本企业以外的单位和个人购进（包括从国外直接进口）作为转卖或加工后转卖的商品金额（含增值税）。本指标反映批发和零售业从国内外市场上购进商品的总价。

商品销售总额 指对本单位以外的单位和个人出售的商品金额（包括售给本单位消费用的商品，含增值税），本指标反映批发和零售业在国内市场上销售商品以及出口商品的总量。

期末库存 对于批发和零售业法人企业和个体经营户，是指取得所有权的全部商品金额（含增值税）；对于批发和零售业产业活动单位，是指期末实际在库且归属法人具有所有权的全部商品金额（含增值税）。这个指标反映批发和零售业的商品库存情况，以及对市场商品供应的保证程度。

批发额 指售给国民经济各行业企业（单位）用于生产、经营用的商品金额。

零售额 指售给城乡居民用于生活消费和社会集团用于公共消费的商品金额。

住宿和餐饮业零售额 指住宿和餐饮业单位因为提供就餐服务或销售商品取得的全部收入，包括餐费收入和商品销售收入（含增值税）。

流动资产合计 资产满足以下条件之一应归为流动资产：(1) 预计在一个正常营业周期中变现、出售或耗用，主要包括存货、应收帐款等；(2) 主要为交易目的而持有；(3) 预计在资产负债表日起一年内（含一年）变现；(4) 自资产负债日起一年内，交换其他资产或清偿负债的能力不受限制的现金或现金等价物。包括货币资金、应收票据、应收账款、存货等项目。根据会计“资产负债表”中“流动资产合计”项目的期末余额数填报。

固定资产合计 指企业为生产商品、提供劳务、出租或经营管理而持有的，使用寿命超过一个会计年度的有形资产。包括使用期限超过一年的房屋、建筑物、机器、机械、运输工具以及其他与生产、经营有关的设备、器具、工具等。固定资产合计是时点指标，表示固定资产经过扣减折旧、减值准备等后的期末余额。根据会计“资产负债表”中“固定资产”项目的期末余额数填报。

所有者权益合计 指企业资产扣除负债后由所有者享有的剩余权益。公司的所有者权益又称股东权益。包括实收资本、资本公积、盈余公积、未分配利润等。根据会计“资产负债表”中“所有者权益合计”项目的期末余额数填报。

营业税金及附加 指企业因从事生产经营活动按税法规定缴纳的应从经营收入中抵扣的税金和附加，包括营业税、消费税、城市维护建设税、教育费附加等。根据会计“利润表”中“营业税金及附加”项目的本期金额数填报。

利润总额 指企业在一定会计期间的经营成果，是生产经营过程中各种收入扣除各种耗费后的盈余，反映企业在报告期内实现的亏盈总额。根据会计“利润表”中“利润总额”项目的本期金额数填报。执行 2006 年《企业会计准则》的企业，利润总额为营业利润加上营业外收入，减去营业外支出后的金额；未执行 2006 年《企业会计准则》的企业，利润总额为营业利润加上投资收益、补贴收入、营业外收入，再减去营业外支出后的金额。

应交增值税 指企业按税法规定，从事货物销售或提供加工、修理修配劳务等增加货物价值的活动本期应交纳的税金。指企业在报告期应交增值税额。

计算公式 本年应交增值税＝销项税额－（进项税额-进项税额转出）－出口抵减内销产品应纳税额－减免税款＋出口退税

批发零售贸易、餐饮业统计限额标准

行业类别	统计指标名称	限额标准
批发业	年主营业务收入	2000万元
零售业	年主营业务收入	500万元
住宿业、餐饮业	年主营业务收入	200万元

说明：

1．外贸企业包括在批发业中，其年销售额以外币计量的，应折合成人民币，按批发业标准执行。

2．本限额标准对象为批发和零售业、住宿和餐饮业法人企业和个体经营户、非批发和零售业、住宿和餐饮业法人单位附营的批发和零售业、住宿和餐饮业产业活动单位。

八、价格指数

Price Indices

8-1 历年物价总指数（以上年价格为100）

General Price Indices over Years (Preceding Year=100)

年　份	商品零售价格总指数	#食品	#家用电器及音像器材	居民消费价格总指数	#食品	#服务项目	工业生产者出厂价格指数
1978	100.4	101.6					
1979	102.6	107.1					
1980	110.9	114.5					
1981	109.3	110.3					
1982	101.2	100.8					
1983	99.6	99.5					
1984	98.6	97.5		99.3	97.5	102.0	
1985	106.9	108.7		106.5	108.7	103.3	
1986	104.4	105.0		104.2	105.0	102.3	
1987	112.2	113.6		112.0	113.6	109.6	
1988	132.8	133.9		136.0	133.9	168.0	
1989	122.4	125.7		122.0	127.5	118.8	
1990	94.9	92.8		96.6	92.8	111.0	
1991	101.4	101.1		102.4	101.1	109.8	
1992	107.7	109.0		109.2	109.0	117.9	
1993	119.5	123.7		121.8	123.7	134.6	
1994	118.4	125.9	99.6	123.5	126.4	141.2	
1995	109.7	119.5	95.6	113.9	119.1	128.9	
1996	104.7	108.1	94.5	106.8	107.8	115.0	
1997	99.7	100.0	92.7	101.5	99.4	113.1	
1998	98.7	99.9	93.3	99.9	99.5	108.4	
1999	95.9	95.6	94.9	97.9	95.7	109.5	
2000	100.1	100.3	97.2	101.5	100.4	112.8	
2001	97.8	99.1	97.0	96.6	98.9	101.1	
2002	99.1	100.9	98.0	98.1	99.0	98.7	
2003	101.7	103.6	99.0	100.7	103.5	97.8	
2004	103.2	108.6	98.7	103.0	108.6	99.7	
2005	103.0	106.5	101.1	102.4	106.5	100.4	100.4
2006	102.8	100.1	100.5	101.2	100.1	101.6	100.7
2007	104.2	108.3	98.2	103.1	108.0	100.2	101.4
2008	107.9	115.6	100.4	105.5	115.1	100.1	101.7
2009	95.3	97.9	95.6	96.9	98.1	96.3	96.8
2010	103.2	104.8	95.6	102.8	104.6	102.6	102.6
2011	104.7	111.1	99.3	104.9	111.1	103.0	102.9
2012	102.4	106.4	95.2	102.9	106.1	101.1	99.8

8-2 居民消费价格分类指数（2012年，以上年价格为100）

Consumer Price Indices by Category (2012, Preceding Year=100)

项　　目	指 数	项　　目	指 数
居民消费价格总指数	102.9	袜子	100.3
非食品价格指数	101.3	帽子	92.3
服务项目价格指数	101.1	衣着加工服务费	100.0
扣除鲜菜鲜果总指数	102.4	家庭设备用品及维修服务	101.4
消费品价格指数	103.6	耐用消费品	101.9
食　品	106.1	家具	108.2
粮食	103.7	家庭设备	97.8
大米	103.7	室内装饰品	105.5
粮食制品	104.1	床上用品	95.6
淀粉及制品	97.0	家庭日用杂品	99.1
干豆类及豆制品	100.2	家庭服务及加工维修服务	104.7
油脂	105.0	医疗保健和个人用品	104.8
肉禽及其制品	102.6	医疗保健	105.7
蛋	101.1	中药材及中成药	116.7
水产品	108.3	西药	102.4
菜	124.5	医疗保健服务	99.8
鲜菜	126.9	个人用品及服务	103.1
干菜及菜制品	111.0	化妆美容用品	102.8
调味品	102.4	清洁类化妆品	107.8
糖	105.0	个人饰品	100.7
食糖	104.2	个人服务	99.9
糖果	101.4	交通和通信	98.8
茶及饮料	101.2	交通	99.6
干鲜瓜果	98.4	交通工具	98.0
鲜瓜果	97.3	市区公共交通费	99.8
糕点饼干面包	102.2	城市间交通费	97.6
液体乳及乳制品	104.9	通信	97.3
在外用膳食品	106.3	通信工具	87.0
主食	105.3	通信服务	99.1
炒菜	106.0	娱乐教育文化用品及服务	101.8
地方小吃	107.3	文娱用耐用消费品及服务	94.8
其他食品	100.9	教育	106.5
烟酒	101.4	教材及参考书	101.7
烟草	100.0	学前教育	126.3
酒	103.4	文化娱乐类	100.3
衣着	101.0	文化娱乐用品	101.1
服装	100.2	书报杂志	100.0
衣着材料	92.8	文娱费	99.8
棉布	93.0	旅游	102.8
化纤布	89.4	居住	101.5
毛线	100.0	建房及装修材料	102.4
其他	90.9	住房租金	97.1
鞋袜帽	103.9	自有住房	100.5
鞋	105.0	水、电、燃料	103.6

8-3 居民消费价格分月指数（2012年，以上年同月价格为100）

Consumer Price Indices by Month (2012, Same Month of Preceding Year=100)

项目	1 月	2 月	3 月	4 月	5 月	6 月
居民消费价格总指数	105.0	104.2	104.3	104.0	104.2	103.4
非食品价格指数	101.7	101.8	102.4	102.1	101.1	101.0
服务项目价格指数	104.6	102.8	102.4	102.3	101.6	101.9
扣除鲜菜鲜果总指数	104.9	104.0	104.1	103.7	103.2	102.5
消费品价格指数	105.1	104.8	105.1	104.7	105.3	104.0
食品	112.4	109.5	108.4	108.2	111.2	108.6
#粮食	109.4	108.1	107.5	107.4	108.7	104.7
肉禽及制品	119.2	111.8	110.7	108.3	106.4	102.4
蛋	108.7	105.8	102.5	99.7	97.9	102.8
水产品	119.5	110.8	108.6	109.0	116.0	109.8
菜	110.0	116.7	122.8	129.7	151.2	135.5
烟酒	102.7	102.6	102.6	102.1	102.3	102.3
#烟草	100.0	100.0	100.0	100.0	100.0	100.0
酒	106.5	106.3	106.4	105.1	105.5	105.6
衣着	101.2	103.6	104.8	102.1	99.7	99.7
#服装	99.6	101.7	101.2	100.5	99.8	99.7
家庭设备用品及维修服务	102.3	100.1	100.7	100.8	100.3	101.6
#耐用消费品	102.4	103.0	103.5	103.3	100.3	102.6
医疗保健和个人用品	100.1	102.2	104.2	104.8	104.4	105.0
#医疗保健	98.5	100.7	103.0	104.1	105.0	106.8
个人用品及服务	103.2	105.1	106.6	106.1	103.3	101.6
交通和通信	99.4	99.3	99.3	99.2	98.4	97.9
#交通	102.0	101.6	101.5	101.3	99.7	97.9
通信	95.2	95.6	95.7	95.8	96.3	97.9
娱乐教育文化用品及服务	108.2	102.4	103.2	103.8	102.9	103.0
#文娱用耐用消费品及服务	95.9	95.9	94.8	94.8	94.9	95.6
教育	109.6	109.2	109.2	109.3	109.3	109.9
文化娱乐类	101.3	101.3	101.3	101.1	100.4	99.8
旅游类	123.0	100.3	104.1	106.5	103.4	103.0
居住	99.7	103.1	103.4	102.3	101.1	100.2
#建房及装饰材料	99.0	101.3	103.7	106.3	106.4	101.6
住房租金	96.9	102.4	99.9	97.9	96.3	96.3
自有住房	102.0	105.8	103.1	102.2	101.4	101.4
水、电、燃料	98.3	100.9	104.6	102.2	100.0	99.4

8-3 续表

项目	7月	8月	9月	10月	11月	12月
居民消费价格总指数	102.2	102.0	101.5	100.7	101.1	102.0
非食品价格指数	100.7	101.2	101.1	101.0	101.0	101.3
服务项目价格指数	100.9	101.1	99.9	98.7	98.6	99.1
扣除鲜菜鲜果总指数	101.5	101.2	100.9	100.6	100.8	101.3
消费品价格指数	102.7	102.4	102.1	101.5	102.1	103.1
食品	105.4	103.8	102.3	100.1	101.3	103.5
#粮食	100.2	99.6	100.3	100.0	100.3	99.8
肉禽及制品	97.5	96.6	94.4	93.8	96.8	99.0
蛋	98.7	95.4	98.1	98.2	101.2	105.2
水产品	110.3	107.8	105.8	100.7	99.9	102.1
菜	123.3	132.0	123.4	106.7	117.1	129.9
烟酒	101.3	101.3	101.1	100.4	99.3	99.1
#烟草	100.0	100.0	100.0	100.0	100.0	100.0
酒	103.1	103.2	102.5	101.0	98.4	97.9
衣着	99.7	99.7	99.6	99.8	101.3	101.0
#服装	99.6	99.9	99.4	100.0	100.6	100.5
家庭设备用品及维修服务	101.4	101.8	101.4	102.1	101.8	101.9
#耐用消费品	102.0	102.1	101.0	101.2	100.9	100.8
医疗保健和个人用品	105.2	105.6	106.3	106.7	106.5	106.4
#医疗保健	107.1	107.6	108.5	109.1	109.2	108.6
个人用品及服务	101.6	101.8	102.2	102.4	101.7	102.2
交通和通信	97.3	97.8	98.6	99.6	99.5	99.0
#交通	96.7	97.5	98.7	100.1	99.9	99.0
通信	98.3	98.3	98.4	98.8	99.0	99.1
娱乐教育文化用品及服务	101.9	102.3	99.4	98.6	98.2	98.7
#文娱用耐用消费品及服务	94.7	94.8	94.2	94.2	93.9	93.9
教育	109.8	109.9	100.7	100.8	100.8	101.1
文化娱乐类	99.8	99.7	99.7	99.3	99.9	99.9
旅游类	99.6	101.2	101.4	98.3	96.5	98.2
居住	100.5	101.2	102.0	101.0	101.3	102.4
#建房及装饰材料	102.5	102.2	101.6	102.1	100.8	102.2
住房租金	95.4	96.3	96.3	95.5	94.8	97.6
自有住房	99.8	99.5	99.5	96.9	97.3	97.7
水、电、燃料	102.2	104.2	107.1	107.5	108.3	109.3

8-4 居民消费价格分月指数（2012年，以上月价格为100）

Consumer Price Indices by Month (2012, Preceding Month=100)

项目	1 月	2 月	3 月	4 月	5 月	6 月
居民消费价格总指数	101.8	99.7	100.7	100.3	99.7	99.5
非食品价格指数	100.9	99.8	100.5	100.2	99.5	99.9
服务项目价格指数	102.3	98.6	99.9	99.9	99.9	100.3
扣除鲜菜鲜果总指数	101.5	99.5	100.3	100.3	99.6	99.8
消费品价格指数	101.6	100.2	101.0	100.5	99.6	99.1
食品	103.7	99.5	101.2	100.5	100.0	98.5
#粮食	102.4	99.8	100.0	99.8	99.8	100.0
肉禽及制品	103.2	96.9	99.7	99.6	99.1	99.2
蛋	100.4	96.2	97.9	96.6	99.1	107.6
水产品	109.4	101.1	100.9	101.6	100.3	96.1
菜	112.0	103.0	113.5	102.5	101.3	89.3
烟酒	100.1	100.0	100.2	99.9	100.1	99.9
#烟草	100.0	100.0	100.0	100.0	100.0	100.0
酒	100.3	100.0	100.4	99.8	100.3	99.6
衣着	99.6	99.5	100.3	100.4	99.1	100.1
#服装	99.4	99.4	99.8	100.6	99.7	100.1
家庭设备用品及维修服务	102.9	97.8	100.3	100.3	99.1	100.6
#耐用消费品	100.0	100.2	100.4	99.7	97.2	102.0
医疗保健和个人用品	99.7	101.6	101.5	101.0	100.7	100.6
#医疗保健	99.8	102.1	102.2	101.3	101.0	100.9
个人用品及服务	99.5	100.7	100.1	100.4	100.2	100.0
交通和通信	100.7	99.8	100.0	100.4	99.2	99.1
#交通	101.1	99.8	100.1	100.7	98.7	98.6
通信	100.0	99.8	100.0	99.8	100.0	99.9
娱乐教育文化用品及服务	103.6	96.2	99.4	100.6	99.4	100.9
#文娱用耐用消费品及服务	99.8	99.9	99.0	99.5	98.1	100.3
教育	100.0	100.0	100.0	100.0	100.0	100.6
文化娱乐类	99.9	99.9	100.1	99.9	99.5	100.5
旅游类	114.1	86.5	98.3	102.8	99.4	102.0
居住	99.7	102.5	101.2	99.5	99.5	99.4
#建房及装饰材料	100.6	101.1	100.0	100.7	99.7	100.1
住房租金	97.6	103.9	100.8	97.9	100.0	100.0
自有住房	99.7	102.9	100.7	99.1	100.0	100.0
水、电、燃料	100.0	102.1	102.5	100.1	98.8	98.2

8-4 续表

项目	7 月	8 月	9 月	10 月	11 月	12 月
居民消费价格总指数	100.0	100.3	100.0	99.7	99.9	100.5
非食品价格指数	100.3	100.4	100.2	99.9	99.7	99.8
服务项目价格指数	100.4	100.3	99.7	99.5	98.6	99.6
扣除鲜菜鲜果总指数	100.1	100.2	100.2	99.9	99.8	100.1
消费品价格指数	99.8	100.3	100.1	99.7	100.4	100.8
食品	99.3	100.2	99.4	99.1	100.3	101.9
#粮食	97.6	99.8	100.6	100.1	100.3	99.7
肉禽及制品	99.3	100.3	100.4	99.9	100.5	101.1
蛋	98.0	101.7	104.6	100.5	100.3	102.8
水产品	99.2	98.2	98.2	96.3	98.8	102.7
菜	100.9	106.7	92.0	91.8	104.4	112.7
烟酒	99.7	100.0	99.7	99.8	99.9	99.8
#烟草	100.0	100.0	100.0	100.0	100.0	100.0
酒	99.3	100.1	99.4	99.5	99.7	99.5
衣着	100.1	98.9	101.0	100.3	101.9	99.8
#服装	100.2	98.9	101.3	100.6	100.6	100.0
家庭设备用品及维修服务	100.4	100.3	100.1	99.7	100.4	100.1
#耐用消费品	100.5	100.2	100.3	99.4	100.3	100.7
医疗保健和个人用品	99.9	100.8	100.4	100.3	100.0	99.8
#医疗保健	99.9	100.9	100.5	100.1	100.1	99.5
个人用品及服务	99.8	100.6	100.1	100.7	99.7	100.4
交通和通信	99.4	100.4	100.6	100.5	99.8	99.3
#交通	98.8	100.9	101.1	100.8	99.5	99.0
通信	100.4	99.6	99.8	99.9	100.2	99.7
娱乐教育文化用品及服务	100.9	100.4	99.1	100.1	98.5	99.9
#文娱用耐用消费品及服务	99.4	99.9	99.1	99.7	99.6	99.3
教育	100.0	100.1	100.1	100.0	100.0	100.3
文化娱乐类	100.0	100.0	100.0	99.6	100.5	100.0
旅游类	103.9	101.6	97.3	100.7	94.1	99.7
居住	100.7	100.7	100.5	99.3	99.4	99.8
#建房及装饰材料	99.5	99.6	100.0	99.6	101.0	100.3
住房租金	100.0	101.0	100.0	100.0	96.9	99.5
自有住房	100.0	100.5	100.0	98.1	98.1	98.8
水、电、燃料	102.3	101.5	101.5	100.4	100.8	100.9

8-5 居民消费价格分月指数（2012年，以上年12月价格为100）

Consumer Price Indices by Month (2012, December of Preceding Year=100)

项　　目	1 月	2 月	3 月	4 月	5 月	6 月
居民消费价格总指数	101.8	101.5	102.3	102.6	102.3	101.7
非食品价格指数	100.9	100.8	101.2	101.5	101.0	100.9
服务项目价格指数	102.3	100.9	100.8	100.8	100.6	101.0
扣除鲜菜鲜果总指数	101.5	101.0	101.4	101.6	101.3	101.1
消费品价格指数	101.6	101.8	102.8	103.3	102.9	102.0
食品	103.7	103.1	104.4	104.9	104.9	103.3
#粮食	102.4	102.2	102.2	102.1	101.8	101.8
肉禽及制品	103.2	99.9	99.6	99.2	98.3	97.5
蛋	100.4	96.6	94.6	91.4	90.5	97.4
水产品	109.4	110.6	111.7	113.4	113.8	109.3
菜	112.0	115.3	130.9	134.3	136.0	121.5
烟酒	100.1	100.1	100.3	100.2	100.3	100.2
#烟草	100.0	100.0	100.0	100.0	100.0	100.0
酒	100.3	100.2	100.6	100.4	100.7	100.4
衣着	99.6	99.1	99.4	99.8	99.0	99.0
#服装	99.4	98.8	98.6	99.2	98.8	98.9
家庭设备用品及维修服务	102.9	100.6	100.9	101.1	100.2	100.9
#耐用消费品	100.0	100.2	100.5	100.2	97.5	99.4
医疗保健和个人用品	99.7	101.3	102.8	103.8	104.5	105.2
#医疗保健	99.8	101.9	104.1	105.5	106.5	107.5
个人用品及服务	99.5	100.2	100.3	100.7	100.9	100.9
交通和通信	100.7	100.5	100.5	100.9	100.0	99.1
#交通	101.1	100.9	101.0	101.6	100.3	98.9
通信	100.0	99.8	99.8	99.6	99.6	99.5
娱乐教育文化用品及服务	103.6	99.6	99.0	99.6	98.9	99.8
#文娱用耐用消费品及服务	99.8	99.7	98.8	98.3	96.5	96.8
教育	100.0	100.0	100.0	100.0	100.0	100.6
文化娱乐类	99.9	99.8	99.9	99.8	99.2	99.7
旅游类	114.1	98.8	97.1	99.8	99.2	101.1
居住	99.7	102.2	103.4	102.9	102.5	101.8
#建房及装饰材料	100.6	101.7	101.7	102.4	102.1	102.2
住房租金	97.6	101.5	102.3	100.2	100.2	100.2
自有住房	99.7	102.6	103.3	102.4	102.4	102.4
水、电、燃料	100.0	102.1	104.6	104.7	103.4	101.6

8-5 续表

项目	7月	8月	9月	10月	11月	12月
居民消费价格总指数	101.7	102.0	102.0	101.6	101.5	102.0
非食品价格指数	101.2	101.6	101.9	101.8	101.5	101.3
服务项目价格指数	101.4	101.7	101.4	100.9	99.5	99.1
扣除鲜菜鲜果总指数	101.2	101.4	101.6	101.5	101.3	101.3
消费品价格指数	101.8	102.1	102.2	101.9	102.3	103.1
食品	102.6	102.8	102.2	101.3	101.6	103.5
#粮食	99.4	99.2	99.8	99.8	100.1	99.8
肉禽及制品	96.8	97.1	97.5	97.4	97.9	99.0
蛋	95.5	97.1	101.5	102.0	102.4	105.2
水产品	108.5	106.5	104.5	100.6	99.4	102.1
菜	122.6	130.8	120.4	110.5	115.3	129.9
烟酒	99.9	99.9	99.6	99.4	99.3	99.1
#烟草	100.0	100.0	100.0	100.0	100.0	100.0
酒	99.7	99.7	99.1	98.6	98.4	97.9
衣着	99.2	98.1	99.1	99.4	101.2	101.0
#服装	99.1	98.0	99.3	99.8	100.4	100.5
家庭设备用品及维修服务	101.3	101.5	101.7	101.4	101.8	101.9
#耐用消费品	99.9	100.1	100.4	99.8	100.1	100.8
医疗保健和个人用品	105.0	105.9	106.3	106.6	106.6	106.4
#医疗保健	107.4	108.4	108.9	109.0	109.1	108.6
个人用品及服务	100.8	101.4	101.5	102.2	101.9	102.2
交通和通信	98.5	98.9	99.5	100.0	99.8	99.0
#交通	97.7	98.6	99.7	100.5	100.0	99.0
通信	99.8	99.4	99.2	99.1	99.3	99.1
娱乐教育文化用品及服务	100.7	101.2	100.3	100.3	98.8	98.7
#文娱用耐用消费品及服务	96.2	96.1	95.2	94.9	94.5	93.9
教育	100.6	100.7	100.8	100.8	100.8	101.1
文化娱乐类	99.8	99.8	99.8	99.4	99.9	99.9
旅游类	105.1	106.8	103.9	104.6	98.5	98.2
居住	102.6	103.4	103.9	103.2	102.5	102.4
#建房及装饰材料	101.7	101.4	101.3	100.9	102.0	102.2
住房租金	100.2	101.2	101.2	101.2	98.0	97.6
自有住房	102.4	102.8	102.8	100.9	99.0	97.7
水、电、燃料	104.0	105.5	107.1	107.5	108.3	109.3

8-6 商品零售价格分类指数（2012年，以上年价格为100）

Retail Price Indices by Category (2012, Preceding Year=100)

项目	指数	项目	指数
商品零售价格总指数	102.4	专业音像器材	89.5
食品类	106.4	文化办公用品	97.8
粮食	103.7	日用品	102.1
淀粉及制品	97.0	日用百货	99.6
干豆类及豆制品	100.2	日用杂品	99.0
油脂	105.0	洗涤用品	107.6
肉禽及其制品	102.6	其他日用品	98.0
蛋	101.1	体育娱乐用品	100.7
水产品	108.3	体育用品	99.8
菜	124.5	娱乐用品	101.5
调味品	102.4	交通、通信用品	93.9
糖	105.0	交通运输机械	98.8
干鲜瓜果	98.4	通信器材类	87.2
糕点饼干面包	102.2	家具	108.2
液体乳及乳制品	104.9	化妆品类	106.0
在外用膳食品	106.3	金银珠宝类	103.0
其他食品	100.9	中西药品及医疗保健用品类	107.8
饮料、烟酒	101.4	医疗器具及用品	114.8
茶及饮料	101.2	中药材及中成药	116.7
烟草	100.0	西药	102.4
酒	103.4	保健器具及用品	102.4
服装、鞋帽类	101.1	书报杂志及电子出版物类	101.6
服装	100.2	教材及参考书	101.7
鞋袜帽	103.9	书报杂志	100.0
其他	100.2	电子音像制品	105.0
纺织品类	96.5	燃料类	102.9
衣着材料	92.8	煤炭及制品类	100.0
床上用品	97.6	石油及制品类	102.9
家用电器及音像器材	95.2	建筑材料及五金电料类	100.4
家庭设备	97.8	建筑装璜材料	98.7
文娱用耐用消费品	94.0	五金电料类	104.8

8-7 主要年份食品全社会综合平均价格

Comprehensive Average Prices of Food in Main Years

项目	规格等级	单位	价格（元）							
			1985年	1990年	1995年	2000年	2005年	2010年	2011年	2012年
大米	标二	千克	0.39	0.85	2.93	2.16	2.90	3.57	4.46	4.77
面粉	南方	千克	0.74	1.70	3.11	3.65	2.53	6.36	5.17	5.34
豆类	一等大豆	千克	1.07	2.94	3.77	3.99	5.57	7.18	6.97	6.39
植物油	一级花生油	千克	3.55	7.36	12.53	10.62	11.95	18.50	22.74	27.34
猪肉	鲜上肉	千克	3.55	9.50	15.98	13.78	18.53	21.89	27.30	25.61
瘦猪肉	鲜肉	千克	7.20	13.35	23.73	18.04	25.00	29.40	34.76	31.07
牛肉	去骨统肉	千克	5.60	11.22	22.40	18.61	25.73	44.00	43.13	59.90
白条鸡	开膛	千克		9.21	13.80	14.61	21.82	27.82	23.61	25.77
鸡	上等竹丝鸡	千克	7.20	13.04	22.31	15.77	14.99	17.38	19.29	18.56
鸭	上等番鸭	千克	3.17	5.81	11.65	14.28	14.33	17.01	19.78	17.72
鸡蛋	新鲜鸡蛋	千克	3.63	6.70	7.91	6.21	7.73	12.84	15.54	18.00
再制蛋	皮蛋	千克	2.40	4.52	6.40	5.85	7.05	8.82	10.59	10.00
香肠	本地产中等	千克	11.60	23.75	52.13	53.67	31.67	90.00	91.50	121.74
烧鹅	本地产	千克	8.53	14.41	32.54	30.67	44.49	58.20	62.95	66.53
胖头鱼	中等0.5公斤以上一条	千克	2.91	4.81	9.56	8.80	11.79	14.32	16.52	18.15
红三鱼	冰鲜	千克			9.13	16.20	24.85	34.30	42.88	54.74
虾	罗氏虾	千克				40.06	37.18	74.68	86.68	100.99
草鱼	中等1公斤以上一条	千克	2.69	6.67	13.30	10.18	14.25	20.50	18.02	16.41
精盐	再制盐	千克		0.49	1.20	1.60	1.27	3.25	3.25	4.00
白砂糖	国家机制一级	千克	1.36	2.71	6.10	4.32	5.23	6.50	8.50	13.18
红糖	一级冰片糖	千克		2.95	6.55	4.95	5.70	9.50	10.52	23.25
卷烟	广州双喜	盒	1.12	1.40	4.87	5.92	6.62	6.50	6.50	6.50
白酒	0.5千克装	瓶	2.30	2.40	5.55	6.58	7.25	6.25	6.67	8.50
啤酒	热12度	瓶		1.60	6.40	4.92	4.66	5.00	5.50	5.78
红茶	一级	千克	3.98	12.76	28.95	64.68	6.91	127.50	133.38	156.00
绿茶	一级	千克	8.00	10.34	15.40	59.21	27.40	123.00	123.00	80.00
苹果	一级	千克	2.14	4.89	6.54	5.80	6.44	11.18	11.88	11.94
梨	一级	千克	1.86	4.40	5.46	3.99	3.74	5.18	6.28	5.89
柑	一级	千克	1.75	1.97	3.28	3.27	3.54	4.84	6.96	6.46
香蕉	一级	千克	1.24	2.22	3.90	3.18	3.04	4.68	5.77	5.20
荔枝	桂味/糯米糍	千克	2.57	7.95	20.50	14.93	11.75	14.88	11.94	22.44
面包	中等	千克	2.00	5.09	4.39	15.25	7.39	16.70	17.65	19.54
饼干	一级	千克	2.48	7.88	9.03	22.97	8.80	22.00	22.00	22.33
奶粉	国产	千克	4.80	5.27	25.12	24.55	22.33	32.00	56.98	65.50

8-8 工业生产者出厂价格指数（2012年，以上年价格为100）

Producer Price Index (PPI) for Manufactured Goods (2012,Preceding Year=100)

项　　目	2012年
工业生产者出厂价格指数	99.8
#轻工业	101.0
重工业	98.9
#非金属矿采选业	
农副食品加工业	102.9
食品制造业	102.0
酒、饮料和精制茶制造业	104.8
纺织业	101.5
纺织服装、服饰业	102.6
皮革、皮毛、羽毛及其制品和制鞋业	103.7
木材加工和木、竹、藤、棕、草制品业	99.3
家具制造业	101.9
造纸和纸制品业	96.7
印刷业和记录媒介复制业	102.5
文教、美工、体育和娱乐用品制造业	100.2
石油加工、炼焦和核燃料加工业	103.4
化学原料和化学制品制造业	96.7
医药制造业	103.2
化学纤维制造业	95.5
橡胶和塑料制品业	99.1
非金属矿物制品业	94.1
黑色金属冶炼和压延加工业	90.9
有色金属冶炼和压延加工业	90.8
金属制品业	99.9
通用设备制造业	99.5
专用设备制造业	99.8
汽车制造业	99.6
铁路、船舶、航空航天和其他运输设备制造业	99.9
电气机械和器材制造业	98.7
计算机、通信和其他电子设备制造业	99.2
仪器仪表制造业	105.6
其他制造业	104.4
废弃资源综合利用业	92.4
金属制品、机械和设备修理业	91.5
电力、热力的生产和供应业	103.6
燃气生产和供应业	103.3
水的生产和供应业	103.9

注：2012年起，本表行业分类按《国民经济行业分类》（GB/T4754-2011）进行分类，数据与往年不可比。

主要统计指标解释

Explanatory Notes on Main Statistical Indicators

居民消费价格指数 是度量消费商品及服务项目价格水平随着时间而变动的相对数，反映居民家庭购买的消费品及服务价格水平的变动情况。它是宏观经济分析、决策、调控和价格总水平监测以及国民经济核算的重要指标。其按年度计算的变动率通常被用来作为反映通货膨胀(或紧缩)程度的指标。

商品零售价格指数 是度量市场商品零售价格水平变动趋势和变动程度的相对数，反映商品在流通过程中最后一个环节的价格即工业、商业、餐饮业和其他零售企业向城乡居民、机关团体出售生活消费品和办公用品价格水平的变动趋势。它可以为国家宏观调控和国民经济核算提供参考依据，并在此基础上派生其他价格指数。

工业生产者出厂价格总指数 是反映各工业部门主要工业产品出厂价格变动趋势和程度的相对数。编制该价格指数，用以观察和分析在生产环节中工业品价格变动对企业经济效益及宏观经济运行的影响，并为工业增长速度的科学计算提供重要的依据。

九、对外经济贸易与旅游

Foreign Trade and Tourism

9-1 主要年份对外经济与旅游业主要指标

Main Indicators of Foreign Trade and Economic Cooperation and Tourism in Main Years

指　　标	单 位	1985年	1995年	2000年	2005年	2010年	2011年	2012年
进出口总额	万美元		1539112	3204526	7437150	12133773	13522382	14441587
出口总额	万美元	17545	779867	1715927	4092905	6959751	7832871	8506606
进口总额	万美元		759245	1488599	3344245	5174022	5689511	5934981
新签利用外资协议(合同)数	宗	625	3077	1276	992	875	1325	690
#“三来一补”项目	宗	514	2094	871	219	6	1	
“三资”项目	宗	111	983	405	773	869	1324	690
利用外资增资项目宗数	宗				1138	1059	892	813
合同规定外商投资额	万美元	6815	330920	183633	475238	307282	370189	415522
#增资项目	万美元				187422	180723	181800	301646
#“三来一补”项目	万美元	1870	97428	69302	166363	47542	19353	34491
“三资”项目	万美元	4945	233492	114331	308875	259740	350836	381031
实际利用外资	万美元	2894	105665	164712	375139	316287	321821	371904
“三来一补”项目	万美元	1511	38418	55975	93023	43116	16769	34966
“三资”项目	万美元	1383	67247	108737	282116	273171	305052	336938
本年止累计“三来一补”企业投产宗数	宗	1592	8447	9917	8997	5688	3196	2087
年末“三来一补”企业从业人员	万人	9.82	59.44	72.89	126.49	81.00	61.66	38.90
本年止累计“三资”企业投产数	宗	51	2629	3908	6657	8338	8961	9365
年末“三资”企业从业人员	万人	0.64	25.01	87.17	145.50	163.53	175.97	190.66
当年来料加工企业转为三资或民营企业	家					1250	1122	536
合同规定外商投资额(新口径)	万美元				298029	259740	350836	381031
实际利用外资(新口径)	万美元				146796	273171	305052	336938
全年接待旅游人数	万人次		89	291	1156	2251	2615	2744
#国际及港澳台旅游者	万人次		27	106	169	327	357	415
#外国人	万人次		6	15	70	109	121	135
国内旅客	万人次		62	185	987	1924	2258	2329
国际旅游收入	万美元		5679	7617	28189	67592	90975	126924
星级以上宾馆酒店客房数	间		7568	18024	18258	16631	17899	17254
宾馆酒店客房开房率	%		68.80	61.88	58.90	58.12	60.01	59.85

注：1. 对外经济部分除有注明新口径的以外均为旧口径，旧口径包括“三资”和“三来一补”，新口径不含“三来一补”且以验资作为统计标准，后同。
2. 2002年起旅游业指标采用旅游局口径，与往年数不可比。

9-2 主要年份进出口贸易

Total Imports and Exports in Main Years

单位：万美元

项　　目	1995年	2000年	2005年	2010年	2011年	2012年
进出口总额	1539112	3204526	7437150	12133773	13522382	14441587
出口总额	779867	1715927	4092905	6959751	7832871	8506606
按贸易方式分						
#一般贸易	23180	20937	175502	954098	1341146	1692301
来料加工装配	434646	834347	1611676	1955379	1693479	1216525
进料加工	320186	858409	2304325	3946227	4654300	5398579
其他	1855	2234	1402	104047	143947	199201
按经济类型分						
#国有企业	474304	867501	1139776	1102678	702978	400053
三资企业	305061	835611	2353253	4426236	5428116	6337725
集体企业	122	12259	37893	141561	142343	32296
民营企业			561650	1285124	1556283	1732665
进口总额	759245	1488599	3344245	5174022	5689511	5934981
按贸易方式分						
#一般贸易	5394	72475	236133	755349	988370	1096531
来料加工装配	353138	645562	1216566	1424118	1174341	901512
进料加工	259397	616319	1625629	2457194	2881689	3322199
其他	141316	154243	265917	537362	645110	614739
按经济类型分						
#国有企业	419827	764945	987421	1076821	723370	439990
三资企业	329164	706145	1882393	3028036	3651145	4338969
集体企业	243	10267	32167	78053	85574	20718
民营企业			439521	967472	1172126	1131633
贸易顺差	20622	227328	748660	1785728	2143361	2571625

9-3 历年进出口总额

Total Value of Imports and Exports over Years

单位：万美元

年 份	进出口总 额	出口总额	#一般贸易	来料加工装配	进料加工	进口总额	#一般贸易	来料加工装配	进料加工
1978		3938							
1979		5382							
1980		7737							
1981		9173							
1982		10879							
1983		11890							
1984		12966							
1985		17545							
1986		23280							
1987		26755							
1988		31781							
1989		34868							
1990	108229	56828				51401			
1991	317463	165159				152304			
1992	509007	260272				248735			
1993	675647	321137				354510			
1994	882997	429416				453581			
1995	1539112	779867	23180	434646	320186	759245	5394	353138	259397
1996	1784222	918683	16377	496833	405066	865539	8956	383988	309710
1997	2129885	1136768	18020	582863	535708	993117	7598	445237	420014
1998	2327324	1306055	15409	652853	636822	1021269	10406	462194	463450
1999	2846291	1515391	16347	759638	738191	1330900	51726	584224	582721
2000	3204526	1715927	20937	834347	858409	1488599	72475	645562	616319
2001	3445457	1898924	25945	940908	931766	1546533	68392	684323	656910
2002	4424706	2373646	34848	1171688	1167047	2051060	83522	922916	886699
2003	5210623	2800227	48988	1257934	1492723	2410396	144235	962367	1127404
2004	6451775	3519237	85056	1503757	1929967	2932538	222262	1090197	1402413
2005	7437150	4092905	175502	1611676	2304325	3344245	236133	1216566	1625629
2006	8422107	4737640	265784	1661399	2806910	3684467	259709	1265725	1879233
2007	10687290	6023212	357941	2235125	3398212	4664078	371073	1702595	2196521
2008	11329947	6553738	487193	2428365	3585619	4776209	455447	1712939	2206139
2009	9415458	5516861	571682	1823160	3055047	3898597	456075	1297315	1820882
2010	12133773	6959751	954098	1955379	3946227	5174022	755349	1424118	2457194
2011	13522382	7832871	1341146	1693479	4654300	5689511	988370	1174341	2881689
2012	14441587	8506606	1692301	1216525	5398579	5934981	1096531	901512	3322199

注：出口总额1990年以前为外经贸口径，1990年起为海关口径。

9-4 分国别(地区)进出口总值（2011-2012年）

Total Value of Imports and Exports by Countries (Regions)(2011-2012)

单位：亿美元

国别(地区)	实际出口		进口到货	
	2012年	2011年	2012年	2011年
亚洲	445.11	408.65	513.94	483.79
东南亚联盟	49.76	35.24	78.38	81.81
非洲	6.97	4.98	1.37	1.50
欧洲	138.72	135.86	28.79	31.56
欧盟	131.25	128.17	27.09	29.90
拉美洲	27.48	24.38	16.18	20.40
北美洲	221.89	199.75	29.95	27.32
大洋洲	10.49	9.66	2.98	3.14
美国	210.83	189.20	24.83	21.88
香港	225.24	232.82	3.80	9.05
日本	73.84	69.07	92.44	85.07
荷兰	27.45	26.69	2.57	3.01
德国	29.08	30.30	6.67	8.21
英国	21.57	19.21	3.37	3.65
韩国	56.75	36.26	82.42	63.60
台湾	14.70	11.58	94.96	95.98
法国	10.76	10.71	1.40	1.51
加拿大	11.05	10.52	5.12	5.45
澳大利亚	9.52	8.81	2.17	2.45
新加坡	7.67	7.54	11.26	11.48
马来西亚	8.20	5.44	20.78	23.63

9-5 主要商品类别出口总值（2008-2012年）

Total Export Value by Category of Main Commodities (2008-2012)

单位：亿美元

商品名称	2008年	2009年	2010年	2011年	2012年
机电产品	483.66	387.52	494.83	556.16	607.69
高新技术产品	201.49	159.39	241.95	273.42	297.39
自动数据处理设备及其部件	65.86	42.26	52.82	61.21	61.42
服装及衣着附件	31.92	28.11	38.98	46.13	56.51
录、放像机	11.64	8.41	13.24	16.19	7.70
自动数据处理设备的零件	31.97	26.68	33.31	34.71	37.54
纺织纱线、织物及制品	14.69	13.68	15.21	16.43	16.71
玩具	14.69	12.28	16.32	17.20	18.62
鞋类	27.06	24.57	30.96	30.72	29.89
家具及其零件	27.79	24.26	32.09	34.00	39.58
录音机及收录(放)音组合机(包括整套散件)	10.62	7.46	8.85	9.42	9.95
塑料制品	10.74	9.10	11.37	12.71	14.21
静止式变流器	26.71	23.14	35.98	37.61	35.95
旅行用品及箱包	10.91	11.43	15.65	18.16	19.87
灯具、照明装置及类似品	8.87	7.84	10.37	11.74	14.00
电线和电缆	14.03	10.81	15.22	17.31	21.25
通断及保护电路装置	12.36	10.37	13.40	16.18	19.66
有线电话机	15.37	14.84	16.44	19.26	19.23
电视、收音机及无线电讯设备的零附件	16.21	12.59	16.12	14.42	13.37

9-6 主要商品进口数量与金额（海关口径，2010-2012年）

Main Import Commodities in Volume and Value (Custom Statistics) (2010-2012)

金额单位：万美元

商品名称	数量单位	2010年		2011年		2012年	
		数量	金额	数量	金额	数量	金额
谷物及谷物粉	万吨	5.24	2039	5.01	2338	13.44	6023
#小麦粉	吨						
食用植物油	万吨	4.43	3524	4.08	4612	9.15	9532
食糖	万吨	6.27	2664	4.13	2852	2.22	1255
天然橡胶(包括胶乳)	万吨	2.26	4950	2.39	6747	2.06	4896
合成橡胶(包括胶乳)	万吨	10.09	21424	7.82	20953	6.12	18256
原木	万立方	9.95	4699	10.98	6413	13.85	7493
锯材	万立方	46.71	14312	41.33	13547	42.54	13978
羊毛(包括羊毛条)	吨	832	562	1072	962	1273	1124
纺织用合成纤维	万吨	1.68	3299	1.50	3304	1.05	2459
#聚酯纤维	万吨	1.00	1566	0.91	1521	0.75	1226
人造纤维短纤	吨	17.47	5	8.44	2	8.25	2
成品油	万吨	0.92	1769	5.17	6636	11.71	12830
合成有机染料	吨	1886.80	1213	3116.70	1910	2309.12	1726
初级形状的塑料	万吨	216.71	390243	190.50	378111	179.77	357222
#初级形状的聚乙烯	万吨	17.31	24156	15.68	23223	13.79	20657
初级形状的聚丙烯	万吨	34.10	49226	28.66	45219	27.42	42933
初级形状的苯乙烯聚合物	万吨	69.04	119466	62.58	120047	54.36	105822
初级形状的氯乙烯聚合物	万吨	27.52	28931	24.03	26911	24.42	26028
初级形状的聚酯	万吨	20.22	58565	18.11	57769	16.59	54242
牛皮革及马皮革	万吨	7.18	56696	6.95	57310	5.40	57643
纸及纸板(未切成形的)	万吨	44.87	33999	36.15	32037	34.85	31291
毛纱线	万吨	0.76	5678	0.75	6349	0.61	5125
合成纤维纱线	万吨	5.54	18795	4.60	18891	4.22	17641
棉机织物	万米	13572.82	20279	12674	20175	14690	24979
涂覆浸渍塑料的织物	万吨	3.59	12218	2.94	11515	2.50	11832
针织或钩编织物	万米	24854.37	27468	20028	26893	21304	27307
钢材	万吨	141.82	152727	108.79	133356	94.56	114456
#钢铁板材	万吨	126.45	128706	97.58	110644	78.66	87067
未锻造的铜及铜材	万吨	25.18	174812	20.49	171532	17.73	146832
#铜材	万吨	18.19	122608	13.44	108623	11.46	96604
未锻造的铝及铝材	万吨	8.40	33203	6.98	30002	5.35	24400
#铝材	万吨	4.58	24723	3.76	22133	3.44	19647

9-6 续表

金额单位：万美元

商品名称	数量单位	2010年		2011年		2012年	
		数量	金额	数量	金额	数量	金额
钢材或铝制结构体及其部件	吨	955	377	834	346	924	524
蒸汽锅炉及过热水锅炉	台	2	8			2	32
液泵及液体提升机	台	1108302	1417	899529	1419	1649438	1965
冷冻机和制冷设备	台		283		370		559
机械提升搬运装卸设备及零件	台		5335		4556		4447
制造纸及纸制品用机械及零件	金额		15077		9448		1786
印刷、装订机械及零件	金额		79242		95620		85504
纺织机械及零件	金额		12500		15344		4797
#针织机及缝编机	台	2248	10785	3035	12536	747	2983
纱线织物等后整理机器	台	279	829	204	531	170	894
工业用缝纫机	台	3521	1135	2026	795	1175	465
金属加工机床	台	3687	20131	2426	16884	6169	41686
橡胶或塑料加工机械及零件	金额		11352		9957		8855
型模及金属铸造用型箱	吨		6458		7861		9888
自动数据处理设备及其部件	万台	2646	59022	2430	57192	3552	85773
自动数据处理设备的零件	吨	22515	107192	21254	119062	14724	163255
电动机及发电机	万台	39427	29339	44420	31748	45574	38494
发电机组及旋转式变流机	台	28	471	54	3267	65	1487
电视、收音机及无线电讯设备	吨	7731	85203	7058	88685	5166	101474
通断及保护电路装置及零件	万吨		130794		152710		165054
电视显像管	万只	0.79	7				
#彩色显像管	万只	0.50	6				
二极管、晶体管及类似半导体	亿个	512.09	196257	489.63	191639	446.85	183883
电线和电缆	吨	33507	36761	31479	43402	27267	44791
计量检测分析自控仪器及器具	金额		28444		31634		52516
塑料制品	吨	24384	13805	22345	16460	19808	17253

9-7 主要商品出口数量与金额（海关口径，2010-2012年）

Main Export Commodities in Volume and Value (Custom Statistics) (2010-2012)

金额单位：万美元

商品名称	数量单位	2010年		2011年		2012年	
		数　量	金　额	数　量	金　额	数　量	金　额
活猪(种猪除外)	万头		157	121.66	225	124.61	244
水海产品	万吨	0.02	245	0.04	483	0.14	786
谷物及谷物粉	万吨		1				
蔬菜	万吨	0.16	173	0.72	687	5.36	941
鲜、干水果及坚果	万吨		7		3		
食用植物油(包括棕榈油)	吨	324.35	127	535.75	226	575.68	236
药材	吨	44	8	44	9	22	4
锯材	立方米		1				
成品油	万吨	0.03	54	0.18	259	0.16	205
合成有机染料	吨	199	70	166	77	174	79
医药品	吨	1438	779	966	692	669	682
美容化妆品及护肤品	吨	3476	1449	3856	1955	4185	2204
洗衣粉	吨	17887	1098	25061	1696	24368	1708
烟花、爆竹	吨	416	63	353	60	310	55
初级形状的聚氯乙烯	吨	6000	900	7500	1134	8600	1362
家用或装饰用木制品	吨	9500	1828	10900	2495	11500	3848
纸及纸板(未切成形的)	万吨	3.37	2675	3.07	2479	3.29	2964
纺织纱线、织物及制品	金额		152070		164309		167082
#棉纱线	吨	25928	10422	17616	9831	17487	9544
亚麻及苎麻纱线	万米	43.25	116	36.27	104	12.52	38
棉机织物	万米	2349.16	4058	1804.53	4299	2253.32	5143
玻璃制品	金额		3790		4890		6168
家用陶瓷器皿	吨	26100	4312	23900	5100	19800	4671
钢材	万吨	4.40	5098	4.82	6718	5.22	7547
未锻造的铜及铜材	吨	28597	22750	21625	19640	23952	19054
未锻造的铝及铝材	吨	7600	3191	8700	3971	8800	4128
手用或机用工具	吨	10300	9527	9400	12220	8800	14256

9-7 续表

金额单位：万美元

商品名称	数量单位	2010年		2011年		2012年	
		数量	金额	数量	金额	数量	金额
电扇	万台	11169.81	31980	11320.80	36244	12013.85	37262
纺织机械及零件	金额		2005		2002		2587
金属加工机床	万台	0.16	1488	0.22	2432	0.23	2991
电子计算器	亿台	0.48	12682	0.53	14440	0.47	13151
电动机及发电机	亿台	7.21	60650	5.99	63485	5.50	67785
静止式变流器	亿个	6.94	359806	7.25	376054	6.44	359454
原电池	亿个	13.70	16375	12.36	14580	13.84	15602
蓄电池	亿个	2.35	31218	1.84	38253	0.04	5900
电话机	万个	5011.50	164438	5183.60	192614	5264.04	192299
扬声器	亿个	1.76	50717	1.94	66479	2.06	73599
收音设备（包括收录音组合机）	万台	4124.60	88472	4350.91	94214	4477.39	99482
电视机	万台	518.04	96536	452.45	96155	417.57	92070
#彩色电视机	万台	517.53	96529	452.45	96155	417.57	92070
电视、收音机及无线电讯零附件	万吨	7.20	161166	5.96	144218	5.99	133727
电容器	吨	14790.40	72468	13565.50	80327	13028.39	90991
通断及保护电路装置	亿个		133965		161770		196629
二极管及类似半导体器件	亿个	479.44	54844	553.84	55606	546.76	52403
电线和电缆	万吨	20.79	152169	19.32	173136	19.22	212470
照相机	万架	2582.24	160905	2223.97	129006	1346.15	70132
医疗仪器及器械	金额		12824		14739		17959
手表	亿只	0.53	11268	0.52	13635	0.45	14438
#电动手表	亿只	0.53	11028	0.51	13311	0.45	14091
家具	金额		320917		339959		395838
灯具、照明装置及类似品	金额		103738		117380		140006
箱包及类似容器	金额		156455		181550		198731
服装及衣着附件	金额		389784		461285		565121
#织物制服装	金额		342793		412029		504643
裘皮服装	吨	145.45	1857	124.41	1341	99.39	1026
帽类	万个	15532.20	11470	13634.95	12383	13258.54	15079
鞋	亿双	2.66	297056	2.24	293536	1.91	284088
塑料制品	万吨	51.05	113700	50.64	127124	50.94	142073
玩具	金额		163174		172040		186212
贵金属或包贵金属的首饰	金额		15089		19720		9172

9-8 历年新签利用外资协议(合同)宗数

Number of Signed Agreements or Contracts of Utilization of Foreign Capital over Years

单位：宗

年　份	新签协议(合同)数	"三来一补"企业	"三资"企业
1979	184	184	
1980	415	415	
1981	555	553	2
1982	470	468	2
1983	454	447	7
1984	551	508	43
1985	625	514	111
1986	618	559	59
1987	824	729	95
1988	2048	1839	209
1989	939	779	160
1990	1267	1075	192
1991	1636	1268	368
1992	2232	1374	858
1993	3118	1773	1345
1994	2678	1521	1157
1995	3077	2094	983
1996	1678	1343	335
1997	1685	1492	193
1998	1383	1051	332
1999	1362	1135	227
2000	1276	871	405
2001	1395	705	690
2002	1391	524	867
2003	1524	392	1132
2004	1423	391	1032
2005	992	219	773
2006	786	177	609
2007	790	82	708
2008	588	35	553
2009	601	22	579
2010	875	6	869
2011	1325	1	1324
2012	690		690

9-9 历年新签利用外资协议(合同)规定外商投资额

Amount of Signed Agreements or Contracts of Utilization of Foreign Capital over Years

单位：万美元

年　份	协议(合同)规定外商投资额	“三来一补”企业	“三资”企业
1979	476	476	
1980	1055	1055	
1981	806	784	22
1982	787	771	16
1983	1616	841	775
1984	3217	1013	2204
1985	6815	1870	4945
1986	3398	1593	1805
1987	18513	14082	4431
1988	62173	42507	19666
1989	23365	9268	14097
1990	30180	12346	17834
1991	64483	19348	45135
1992	208825	29720	179105
1993	355515	54823	300692
1994	349703	47700	302003
1995	330920	97428	233492
1996	208861	62811	146050
1997	121351	62114	59237
1998	163677	58709	104968
1999	147247	69756	77491
2000	183633	69302	114331
2001	209779	56833	152946
2002	248914	47285	201629
2003	325633	59538	266095
2004	413216	124089	289127
2005	475238	166363	308875
2006	552758	197836	354922
2007	625088	176903	448185
2008	393701	134952	258749
2009	203040	41420	161620
2010	307282	47542	259740
2011	370189	19353	350836
2012	415522	34491	381031

9-10 历年实际利用外资

Foreign Capital Actually Utilized over Years

单位：万美元

年 份	累计实际利用外 资	当年实际利用外 资	"三来一补"企 业	"三资"企业
1979	173	173	173	
1980	1107	934	934	
1981	1642	535	528	7
1982	2357	715	668	47
1983	3258	901	871	30
1984	5175	1917	1233	684
1985	8069	2894	1511	1383
1986	11111	3042	1553	1489
1987	22370	11259	9185	2074
1988	46496	24126	17717	6409
1989	71445	24949	16559	8390
1990	95764	24319	14309	10010
1991	121918	26154	11478	14676
1992	168510	46592	13716	32876
1993	261938	93428	14181	79247
1994	366750	104812	26938	77874
1995	472415	105665	38418	67247
1996	579979	107564	38061	69503
1997	701406	121427	33467	87960
1998	835219	133813	40780	93033
1999	980951	145732	48620	97112
2000	1145663	164712	55975	108737
2001	1327225	181562	66841	114721
2002	1542073	214848	68980	145868
2003	1798409	256336	80936	175400
2004	2101839	303430	89555	213875
2005	2476978	375139	93023	146796
2006	2910751	433773	98543	180789
2007	3415146	504395	94365	211759
2008	3737716	322570	77902	244668
2009	4031873	294157	34758	259399
2010	4348160	316287	43116	273171
2011	4353694	321821	16769	305052
2012	4725598	371904	34966	336938

9-11 主要年份“三资”企业利用外资

Utilization of Foreign Capital of Enterprises with Foreign Investment in Main Years

项　　目	计量单位	1990年	1995年	2000年	2005年	2010年	2011年	2012年
全部“三资”企业利用外资情况								
当年新签协议宗数	宗	192	983	405	773	869	1324	690
本年止累计执行宗数	宗	591	2807	4012	6657	8338	8961	9365
#已投产	宗	454	2629	3908	5870	7469	7636	8675
项目(协议)终止宗数	宗	24	48	338	193	471	707	286
实际投资总额	万美元	18642	75853	115801	290553	277547	315609	345539
境内资金总额	万美元	8632	8606	7064	8437	4376	10557	8601
中方实际投资	万美元	5515	6448	4445	8337	4376	10557	8601
企业境内借款	万美元	3117	2158	2619	100			
境外资金总额	万美元	10010	67247	108737	282959	273171	305052	336938
外商实际投资	万美元	8934	65416	108468	282116	273171	305052	336938
企业境外借款	万美元	1076	1831	269	842			
引进设备价值	万美元	6619	50267	80215	118401	63822	44106	34853
出口总值	万美元	13439	178351	835600	2353253	4426236	5428116	6337725
期末职工人数	万人	3.81	25.01	87.17	145.50	163.53	175.97	190.66
中外合作企业利用外资情况								
当年新签协议宗数	宗	72	195	19	2			
本年止累计执行宗数	宗	237	730	705	337	184	138	127
#已投产	宗	177	682	700	299	184	138	127
项目(协议)终止宗数	宗	15	12	130	25	23	46	11
实际投资总额	万美元	5072	15159	10045	13529	1345	2836	1915
境内资金总额	万美元	1427	176	1731	860	169	1427	48
中方实际投资	万美元	651	136	1486	860	169	1427	48
企业境内借款	万美元	776	40	245				
境外资金总额	万美元	3645	14983	8314	12669	1176	1409	1867
外商实际投资	万美元	3642	14981	8314	12669	1176	1409	1867
企业境外借款	万美元	3	2					
引进设备价值	万美元	2411	9320	5033	4060	651	266	85
出口总值	万美元	2423	35718	92100	116157	117188	105642	49351
期末职工人数	万人	1.02	5.82	13.57	10.38	3.50	2.84	2.59

注：本表2000年起出口总值是海关口径。

9-11 续表

项目	计量单位	1990年	1995年	2000年	2005年	2010年	2011年	2012年
中外合资企业利用外资情况								
当年新签协议宗数	宗	93	378	29	31	18	24	19
本年止累计执行宗数	宗	338	1590	1690	712	507	447	434
#已投产	宗	251	1498	1650	668	489	423	430
项目(协议)终止宗数	宗	9	31	159	53	99	84	32
实际投资总额	万美元	13070	39659	23966	25672	36342	39481	40539
境内资金总额	万美元	7199	8345	5333	7477	4207	9130	8553
中方实际投资	万美元	4864	6312	2959	7477	4207	9130	8553
企业境内借款	万美元	2335	2033	2374				
境外资金总额	万美元	5871	31314	18633	18195	32135	30351	31986
外商实际投资	万美元	4798	29496	18364	18195	32135	30351	31986
企业境外借款	万美元	1073	1818	269				
引进设备价值	万美元	3920	25557	14365	4060	28850	17757	2366
出口总值	万美元	10934	90357	248800	289344	348622	340366	349158
期末职工人数	万人	2.69	13.51	24.68	17.95	11.60	12.48	8.83
外商独资企业利用外资情况								
当年新签协议宗数	宗	27	410	357	740	851	1300	671
本年止累计执行宗数	宗	16	487	1614	5607	7641	8364	8793
#已投产	宗	8	449	1555	4903	6790	7064	8107
项目(协议)终止宗数	宗		5	49	115	349	577	243
实际投资总额	万美元	500	21035	79113	252194	239860	272534	302731
境内资金总额	万美元	6	85		100			
中方实际投资	万美元							
企业境内借款	万美元	6	85		100			
境外资金总额	万美元	494	20950	79113	252094	239634	272534	302731
外商实际投资	万美元	494	20939	79113	251252	239634	272534	302731
企业境外借款	万美元		11		842			
引进设备价值	万美元	288	15390	58140	91288	34321	26082	32401
出口总值	万美元	82	52276	494700	1947751	3960425	4982107	593216
期末职工人数	万人	0.10	5.67	48.92	117.17	148.43	160.65	179.24

9-12 主要年份分方式、分国别(地区)实际利用外资

Foreign Capital Actually Utilized by Type and Countries(Regions) in Main Years

单位：万美元

项　　目	1990年	1995年	2000年	2005年	2010年	2011年	2012年
按引进方式分							
总　计	10167	68438	164712	375139	316287	321821	371904
外商直接投资	10010	67247	108737	282116	273171	305052	336938
合资经营企业	5871	31314	18865	18195	32135	30351	42452
合作经营企业	3645	14983	8305	12669	1176	1409	13760
外资(独资)经营企业	494	20950	78890	251252	239634	272534	280533
外商投资股份公司			2677		226	758	193
外商其他投资	157	1191	55975	93023	43116	16769	34966
国际租赁							
补偿贸易							
加工装配	157	1191	55975	93023	43116	16769	34966
按国家和地区分							
总　计	10167	67247	164712	375139	316287	321821	371904
香　港	10167	58333	88950	185214	182600	183124	213771
澳　门		13		44	442	653	618
台　湾		3016	23722	130682	82674	84261	82657
日　本		391	7476	25253	12861	18649	29103
泰　国		96	33	20		4	
新加坡		822	3511	3994	6094	3230	3642
德　国		3	1884	487	1488	1373	1101
法　国			89	20	688	1303	230
瑞　士			546		127	58	255
加拿大		46	15	99	568	296	99
美　国		3230	2391	8122	3309	5407	8906
澳大利亚		56	14	48	61	1431	30
韩　国			2362	6958	5955	8907	7845
利比亚			153				
英　国		79		12	277	500	337
其　他		1162	33566	14186	19143	12625	23310

注：1995年分国别地区的外商投资额是外商直接投资额。

9-13 外商直接投资分行业情况（2011-2012年）

Foreign Direct Investment by Sector (2011-2012)

单位：万美元

行业	2011年			2012年		
	项目个数(个)	合同外资金额	实际投资金额	项目个数(个)	合同外资金额	实际投资金额
总计	1325	370189	305052	690	381031	336938
农、林、牧、渔业	1	1580	559		369	318
采矿业						
制造业	1172	293826	259790	503	293911	251960
#纺织业	55	12846	16659	13	4676	8496
化学原料及化学制品制造业	12	2637	2476	7	6354	3348
医药制造业			179		1259	1207
通用设备制造业	30	5808	8814	11	4190	5015
专用设备制造业	32	13806	19921	19	33696	16186
通信设备、计算机及其他电子设备制造业	211	83647	65660	73	75113	60606
电力、燃气及水的生产和供应业	2	2950		4	1192	644
建筑业			2	1	71	3837
交通运输、仓储和邮政业		4064	4052	3	5723	11031
信息传输、计算机服务和软件业	3	200	1045	2	19	90
批发和零售业	102	28232	23568	136	45295	42680
住宿和餐饮业	3	536	764	3	294	598
金融业				1	250	305
房地产业	4	13876	10163	4	16156	7907
#房地产开发经营	3	13825	8093			
租赁和商务服务业	22	1954	1865	25	4304	1932
科学研究、技术服务和地质勘查业	10	779	741	8	1510	246
居民服务和其他服务业	1	252	328		50	295
卫生、社会保障和社会福利业		1275	2012			2008
公共管理和社会组织			15			

9-14 主要年份宾馆酒店接待能力和接待人数

Capacity and Tourists Received by Hotels in Main Years

项目	单位	1990年	1995年	2000年	2005年	2010年	2011年	2012年
三星级以上宾馆(酒店)	家	3	16	30	63	82	77	75
三星级	家	3	16	23	27	35	31	30
四星级	家			6	22	25	25	25
五星级	家			1	14	22	21	20
客房（已评1星以上）	间	3793	7568	18024	18258	16631	17899	17254
床位（已评1星以上）	张	8531	15136	30895	25014	24841	24348	23612
开房率	%	60.2	68.8	61.9	58.9	58.1	60.0	59.9
全年接待人数	万人次	125	89	291	1156	2251	2615	2744
国际及港澳台旅游者	万人次	27	27	106	169	327	357	415
#外国人	万人次	1	6	15	70	109	121	135
港澳台同胞	万人次	26	21	89	99	219	236	280
国内旅客	万人次	98	62	185	987	1924	2258	2329
外出旅游人数	万人次					154	183	185
国内旅游人数	万人次					139	167	168
出国（境）游人数	万人次					15	16	18

9-15 历年旅游业情况

Basic Statistics on Tourism over Years

年份	三星级以上宾馆(酒店)(家)	客房(已评1星以上)(间)	床位(已评1星以上)(张)	开房率(%)	全年接待人数(万人次)	国际及港澳台旅游者	外国人	港澳台同胞	国内游客	国际旅游外汇收入(万美元)
1978										
1979										
1980										
1981										
1982										
1983										
1984										
1985										
1986					80	11		10	69	554
1987					107	19	1	18	87	453
1988		6435	7641	65.8	125	20		19	105	710
1989		3324	7376	64.8	115	18		18	97	504
1990		3793	8531	60.2	125	27	1	26	98	1025
1991		4004	8701	64.9	155	37	1	36	118	2443
1992		4042	8770	72.6	172	47	2	46	125	2473
1993		4258	8517	75.1	169	52	2	50	117	2888
1994		3542	7443	77.6	119	44	4	40	75	3464
1995	16	7568	15136	68.8	89	27	6	21	62	5679
1996	16	13409	26818	50.3	175	36	6	29	139	6464
1997	19	10420	19142	50.6	171	59	5	54	112	6778
1998	20	17428	31987	53.3	216	75	11	63	141	6601
1999	20	17931	25482	63.5	253	97	17	77	156	7055
2000	30	18024	30895	61.9	291	106	15	89	185	7617
2001	48	20572	32789	62.0	327	110	22	88	217	8200
2002	53	9427	14652	69.0	930	108	22	86	822	11847
2003	52	8170	12599	65.0	1086	80	24	56	1006	13825
2004	60	10530	14934	61.2	1131	149	66	83	982	23437
2005	63	18258	25014	58.9	1156	169	70	99	987	28189
2006	71	18258	25014	60.1	1363	193	81	112	1170	33180
2007	74	19023	26132	63.4	1725	248	102	146	1477	42702
2008	77	19510	26864	58.9	1872	268	103	165	1604	45614
2009	80	16332	24389	58.0	2037	286	104	182	1751	51756
2010	82	16631	24841	58.1	2251	327	109	219	1924	67592
2011	77	17899	24348	60.0	2615	357	121	236	2258	90975
2012	75	17254	23612	59.9	2744	415	135	280	2329	126924

注：国际旅游外汇收入1995年以前单位为万元(外汇券)，1995年起为万美元。

主要统计指标解释

Explanatory Notes on Main Statistical Indicators

海关进出口总额 指实际进出我国国境的货物（包括贸易和非贸易）的价值总和。主要包括对外贸易实际进出口货物，来料加工装配、补偿贸易、进料加工进出口货物，国家间及国际组织无偿援助物资和赠送品，华侨、港澳台同胞和外籍华人捐赠品，租赁期满归承租人所有的租赁货物，边境地方贸易及边境地区小额贸易进出口货物（边民互市贸易除外），中外合资、合作经营企业、外商独资经营企业进出口货物和公用物品，到、离岸价格在规定限额以上的进出口货样和广告品（无商业价值、无使用价值和免费提供出口的除外），从保税仓库提取在中国境内销售的进出口货物，以及其他进出口货物。海关进出口总额反映一个国家在对外经济贸易方面实际进出口货物的总规模。

贸易出口 指由外贸进出口公司、工农贸易进出口公司和地方性的进出口公司由国家统一安排的出口、代理出口和自营、联营出口，其中包括进料加工出口，以及各进出口公司在国内以外汇结算方式售给友谊商店、华侨商店、出国人员服务公司和中外合资、合作经营和外资企业等的出口商品。

“三来一补”出口 指来料加工装配出口按工缴费计算，中小型补偿贸易按金额计算。

“三资”企业出口 指三资企业自己出口的本企业产品。不包括委托外贸进出口公司出口的商品。

利用外资 指我国各级政府、部门、企业和其他经济组织通过对外借款、吸收外商直接投资以及向境外发行债券、股票等方式筹措的境外资金。

外资的形式可以是现汇、实物、工业产权或专有技术等有形资本和无形资本。

我国自有外汇如国家外汇、中国银行等金融机构用自有资金发放的外汇贷款等，华侨、港澳同胞的捐赠，联合国或其他国际组织的无偿赠送资金、无偿援建的项目均不属于外资范围。

利用外资的方式有：对外借款，外国（或港澳地区）企业和经济组织或个人在我国境内开办独资企业，与我国境内的企业或组织共同开办合资企业合作经营（企业）项目或合作开发资源，以及补偿贸易、国际租赁等。

外商直接投资 指外国企业和经济组织或个人（包括华侨、港澳同胞以及我在境外注册的企业）按我国有关政策、法规，在我国境内开办外商独资企业，与我国境内的企业或经济组织共同举办中外合资企业、合作经营企业或合作开发资源的投资以及外商从企业得到收益的再投资。

新口径合同利用外资 根据2003年修订的《利用外资统计制度》，明确指出合同外资的统计指外商直接投资（三资企业）企业设立时，根据合同（章程）规定，外方投资者应缴付的注册资本。

国际旅游（外汇）收入 指国内各部门为来我国旅游的外国人、华侨、港澳和台湾同胞提供商品和劳务而得到的外汇收入。包括供应商品、饮食和提供住宿、交通、邮电、文化娱乐、导游等各项服务所得的全部外汇收入。

十、财政、金融与保险

Finance, Banking and Insurance

10-1 主要年份财政收支主要指标

Main Indicators of Government Revenue and Expenditure in Main Years

单位：万元

项　　目	1978年	1980年	1985年	1990年	2000年	2005年	2006年
财政收入							
来源于东莞的财政收入	6604	6710	11118	35719	1035561	3319079	4065412
中央财政收入					617151	1935069	2323977
#关税和海关代征税					273972	483327	526251
省级财政收入					113681	344330	451990
市财政一般预算收入	6604	6710	11118	35719	304730	1039680	1289445
工商税收							
工商税收总额					867584	2923001	3593704
国税(不含关税)					607216	1849818	2208722
地税					260368	1073183	1384982
财政支出							
市财政一般预算支出	1792	2015	4999	22779	336102	1170427	1478955
#基本建设支出					27426	276646	242829
企业挖潜改造支出		88	15	37	1584	9107	9691
科技三项费用支出		7		140	9963	31572	87397
农林水气部门事业费支出		304	1154	3261	40097	62181	64911
工交部门事业费支出		2	7	180	192	20499	18552
城市维护费支出		31	219	1350	41267	162370	205426
科教文卫体事业费支出		1051	2139	7357	86737	210620	291467
#科学事业费				404	936	3956	3874
教育事业费		760	1504	3786	68194	171055	244113
卫生事业费		185	262	743	12083	11469	12826
体育事业费		18	50	827	1517	2860	3266
抚恤和社会福利救济支出		75	132	368	2888	8335	34050
行政管理费支出		293	320	1324	29817	102296	119034
公检法司支出			92	740	46446	166055	225382

注：1. 1995年及以前年份，来源于东莞的财政收入不含关税。
　　2. 从2007年起财政收支按新的分类项目，在10-2表中反映。

10-2 财政收支主要指标（2006-2012年）

Main Indicators of Government Revenue and Expenditure (2006-2012)

单位：万元

指　　标	2006年	2007年	2008年	2009年	2010年	2011年	2012年
来源于东莞的财政收入	4065412	5395362	6010642	6278114	7851003	8385226	8456419
财政总收入	3358095	4574778	5234746	5402140	6542697	7665371	8624762
#中央	1638195	2151906	2476902	2392927	2940745	3422151	3777465
省级	430455	558404	665596	697658	823548	1112580	1284052
市公共财政预算收入	1289445	1864468	2092248	2311555	2778404	3130639	3563245
#增值税	347153	474288	552515	534382	626301	719263	830244
营业税	291122	380958	422427	446884	458712	453341	518165
企业所得税	145739	173566	184478	176786	247986	265919	296278
个人所得税	60518	75765	87895	87313	110441	111982	89047
房产税	51622	63228	65560	75806	92706	106267	131973
契税	80793	355039	113509	157533	186994	230554	246352
罚没收入	75238	81766	79104	72888	78400	83203	113223
市公共财政预算支出	1478955	1930968	2182626	2326216	2898306	3519171	3855844
#一般公共服务	161657	220367	234172	259865	269505	326164	361982
公共安全	233413	324714	365387	367266	388243	478295	494280
教育	293000	412347	499978	553429	653090	832341	927975
科学技术	10593	91232	93518	112506	79830	181369	185411
社会保障和就业	27100	104264	232742	194637	264017	243839	241938
农林水事务	77188	116452	143695	131828	229613	180411	296891
交通运输	14439	54144	49759	73635	90609	252799	332270
税收总额	3593704	4709341	5361733	5475100	6887249	8435699	9391074
#国税	2208722	3057525	3390812	3384667	4394366	5234084	5827273
地税	1384982	1651816	1970921	2090433	2492883	3201615	3563801

注：1. 2009及以前年份，国税不含海关代征税。
2. 2010年及以前年份，地税不含契税和耕地占用税。
3. 2011年起，来源于东莞的财政收入含政府性基金和出口退税。
4. 按照财政部规定，从2012年1月开始，“一般预算收入”与“一般预算支出”分别更名为“公共财政预算收入”和“公共财政预算支出”，下同。

10-3 历年财政收入

Government Revenue over Years

单位：万元

年份	来源于东莞的财政收入	财政总收入	中央财政收入	省级财政收入	市公共财政预算收入	各项税收	工商税收	专项收入	其他收入
1978	6604				6604	6595	5826		9
1979	6634				6634	6625	5725		9
1980	6710				6710	6699	5785		11
1981	6823				6823	6805	5942		18
1982	8103				8103	8068	7184		35
1983	8578				8578	8501	7599		77
1984	8469				8469	8385	7442		84
1985	11118				11118	10998	9708		120
1986	16053				16053	15865	14574	45	143
1987	20221				20221	19989	18551	50	182
1988	27076				27076	26837	25309	76	163
1989	31888				31888	30997	29331	116	775
1990	35719				35719	33544	31911	686	1489
1991	44374				44374	41659	39302	913	1802
1992	56204				56204	52620	48272	1351	2233
1993	93828				93828	88920	83462	1947	2961
1994	130531				76940	70451	60889	2697	3792
1995	180051				115618	106388	95463	4070	5160
1996	283506				96541	85648	74323	4470	6423
1997	335044				114069	96980	85245	4794	12295
1998	472422				151012	123816	106700	5693	21503
1999	717847				182577	159873	134852	8759	13945
2000	1035561				304730	265565	248159	14709	24456
2001	1259961				450163	402668	381660	18356	29139
2002	1678848				552933	489780	467998	26438	36715
2003	2064052				674461	575342	536390	30710	68409
2004	2591086				826389	707954	655571	35273	83162
2005	3319079				1039680	879653	797038	36423	123604
2006	4065412	3358095	1638195	430455	1289445	1077152	990029	49285	163008
2007	5395362	4574778	2151906	558404	1864468	1652620	1291335	55863	155985
2008	6010642	5234746	2476902	665596	2092248	1682270	1555499	60590	349388
2009	6278114	5402140	2392927	697658	2311555	1822650	1618514	60007	428899
2010	7851003	6542697	2940745	823548	2778404	2217675	1950773	72153	488576
2011	8385226	7665371	3422151	1112580	3130639	2433937	2171228	133951	562751
2012	8456419	8624762	3777465	1284052	3563245	2792882	2514813	159582	610780

注：1. 1995年及以前年份，来源于东莞的财政收入不含关税。
2. 2011年起，来源于东莞的财政收入含政府性基金和出口退税。

10-4　历年财政支出

Government Expenditure over Years

单位：万元

年 份	预算内地方财政支出总额	#基本建设支出	科技三项费用	农林水气等部门事业费	城市维护费	科教文卫体育事业费	教育事业费	行政管理费
1978	1792							
1979	1908		20	451	74	852	618	202
1980	2015		7	304	31	1051	760	293
1981	2139		4	341	36	1182	818	246
1982	2612		1	359	141	1346	912	336
1983	2804		1	413	28	1672	1004	287
1984	3013			264	48	1868	1309	340
1985	4999			1154	219	2139	1504	320
1986	9916			2541	1431	2887	1793	330
1987	12512			3479	1624	4759	1871	510
1988	17475		100	4094	1614	6950	3339	888
1989	21623		103	3509	2286	7958	3733	1159
1990	22779		140	3261	1350	7357	3786	1324
1991	27499		30	4938	866	7956	4720	1484
1992	38162		50	5637	567	17505	7682	2348
1993	72910	5400	1289	8882	5737	25716	14427	4002
1994	88984	14575	1496	12835	5254	20725	13552	6158
1995	124173	13736	441	15798	9947	31021	23110	8433
1996	124059	17285	1332	14962	5199	28927	21237	10384
1997	148510	16923	1479	15349	6258	36614	23262	11691
1998	179064	26144	1164	19255	7264	36710	25578	11082
1999	212641	40681	1429	26648	12994	40863	30631	12979
2000	336102	27426	9963	40097	41267	86737	68194	29817
2001	478646	119692	4113	28957	43706	105990	85544	28961
2002	649606	165283	28013	37348	64483	143225	120195	43678
2003	765190	201077	30062	41164	44240	193138	163390	50022
2004	941554	179039	27110	53855	164770	162573	139337	84798
2005	1170427	276646	31572	62181	162370	210620	171055	102296
2006	1478955	242829	87397	64911	205426	291467	244113	119034

注：从2007年起财政支出按新的分类项目，在10-2表中反映。

10-5 税务登记情况及税种征收情况（2011-2012年）

Taxes (2011-2012)

指　　标	国税		地税	
	2011年	2012年	2011年	2012年
税务登记情况(户)	268962	302800	735568	490294
#国有企业	329	341	1523	1122
集体企业	4202	3036	11982	8402
私营企业	37493	41533	39377	41103
港澳台投资企业	7032	7295	22781	12539
外商投资企业	4025	4143	8081	4996
个体经营	165318	182835	559939	318764
工商税收总额(万元)	5234084	5827273	2938906	3563801
#国有企业	10465	11859	42090	37923
集体企业	41910	34661	231496	196852
私营企业	518783	597139	242012	331644
港澳台投资企业	1087092	1250433	479100	549741
外商投资企业	748870	844109	401668	454927
个体经营	421657	417543	271647	433115
#增值税	4218072	4689052		
消费税	43305	50271		
营业税			1054446	1243764
企业所得税	752046	847628	604192	681594
个人所得税	663	183	559247	445051
房产税			106267	131973
印花税			59703	68699
城镇土地使用税			95962	122709
土地增值税			204218	271772
车船税			35188	45944
车辆购置税	218200	238486		
#第一产业	146	124	1642	5512
第二产业	2946786	3402940	1200865	1244295
#采矿业	1201	1024	1926	1240
制造业	2737250	3184200	849824	916765
农副食品加工业	12528	18153	8727	14595
食品制造业	74627	93795	39578	66016
饮料制造业	40675	43899	11953	20198
纺织业	118609	119299	19718	15912
纺织服装、鞋、帽制造业	191676	183380	35730	38818
皮革、毛皮、羽绒及其制品业	88459	171895	24201	32957
木材加工及竹、藤、棕草制品业	12670	15684	3690	3210
家具制造业	101335	137679	21744	22209
造纸及纸制品业	144575	137685	22315	24971

10-5 续表

单位：万元

指标	国税		地税	
	2011年	2012年	2011年	2012年
印刷业、记录媒介的复制	73580	90301	15447	14020
文教体育用品制造业	65234	118834	19440	24037
石油加工、及炼焦业及核燃业	5793	11517	2848	2500
化学原料及化学制品制造业	73940	83620	19486	20352
医药制造业	17160	26312	5642	6252
化学纤维制造业	3703	5364	274	319
橡胶和塑料制品业	203088	243477		61641
非金属矿物制品业	74411	77714	12135	12605
黑色金属冶炼及压延加工业	343	1482	1782	1918
有色金属冶炼及压延加工业	6748	6424	2658	2925
金属制品业	190794	227373	48181	58469
通用设备制造业	94238	119561	21884	21696
专用设备制造业	111724	129462	25667	28179
交通运输设备制造业	58926	84765	16273	17559
电气机械及器材制造业	207154	269953	78273	78049
通信设备、计算机及其他电子设备制造业	589655	664011	261655	266915
仪器仪表及文化、办公用机械制造业	59675	42383	16047	11020
其他制造业	115930	60178	50045	49423
电力、燃气及水的生产和供应业	201080	210482	49841	42236
建筑业	7255	7234	299274	284054
房屋和土木工程建筑业	1109	1183	95382	79098
建筑安装业	1729	2790	163570	153679
建筑装饰业和其他建筑业	4417	3261		51277
第三产业	2287152	2424213	1736399	2313994
#交通运输、仓储及邮政业	11933	10764	104704	122022
信息传输、计算机服务和软件业	4447	11569	59102	92486
批发和零售业	529282	554729	142149	183303
住宿和餐饮业	1774	1585	89879	93542
金融业	140358	180966	250794	304386
房地产业	108582	102902	649545	1034539
租赁和商务服务业	14444	13049	125967	144686
居民服务和其他服务业	17341	12598	209639	211351
教育	169	170	5068	4499
卫生、社会保险和社会福利业	282	794	5185	4368
文化、体育和娱乐业	240	355	25804	24630
公共管理和社会组织	12	58	24682	49144
其他行业	1458288	1533557	43881	45038

10-6 历年金融机构各项人民币存贷款余额

Balance of RMB Deposits and Loans over Years

单位：万元

年 份	各项存款余额	#城乡居民储蓄存款余额	各项贷款余额	#短期贷款	#中长期贷款
1978	10497	5409	19607	19607	
1979	14875	7184	21301	21301	
1980	26093	11718	30797	29669	403
1981	38003	20339	40243	38365	765
1982	45120	27650	45525	44081	690
1983	60547	38597	57618	56063	837
1984	110265	61823	121891	114522	3365
1985	134867	91941	142437	130716	6230
1986	195948	131352	206813	193501	9486
1987	284819	189654	312431	292104	7162
1988	380511	249134	415818	381957	12351
1989	468203	325670	493737	456504	12338
1990	680696	455140	630355	570324	13427
1991	949713	614737	783957	714848	17385
1992	1473354	815404	1059794	935064	23000
1993	1798346	1071715	1343103	923157	237985
1994	2497834	1515445	1734350	1246772	250806
1995	3836761	2329685	2548512	1645696	274157
1996	4896463	3180215	3128076	2053343	353298
1997	6711687	4258238	3826560	2737916	205486
1998	8640053	5337482	4427394	3666563	155295
1999	10408377	6163430	5243735	4628058	328875
2000	12286706	6720704	6308405	5313933	469249
2001	14586491	7991768	7501801	5341925	1436127
2002	17901799	10016909	9334054	5731973	2312883
2003	21267775	12310616	12067237	6918877	3730104
2004	24628693	14316777	14052461	7118671	5222504
2005	29334026	17282760	15005217	7341939	7007138
2006	33656508	20133979	17305554	7792175	8684306
2007	37518345	21207413	21547660	9245906	11427676
2008	43545340	26380433	23803585	10132902	12052974
2009	49866108	29045704	29037984	12604957	14519686
2010	59433885	33868535	33298244	12340319	19675448
2011	66093904	37109919	37160847	14804666	20698930
2012	74304570	42042032	41956074	17567188	22363544

10-7 保险行业主要指标(2006-2012年)

Main Indicators of Insurance (2006-2012)

指　　标	单位	2006年	2007年	2008年	2009年	2010年	2011年	2012年
保险公司	家	26	30	35	37	37	38	46
保险业从业人员	人	11714	17846	24771	27386	27281	28064	33449
保费收入	万元	473835	676062	902986	1150795	1597166	1636513	1776566
寿险类	万元	277769	397962	583983	797192	1129950	1085528	1166113
#传统寿险	万元	51772	57890	61255	63681	72494	72212	79299
分红险	万元	157264	190521	355674	572703	867738	813006	966343
万能险	万元	34050	51114	73233	85142	110035	18650	17032
投连险	万元	1750	60993	38195	18481	18953	805	724
意外险	万元	12382	14490	17188	17143	18718	23730	27899
健康险	万元	20477	22954	38438	40043	42012	57507	74816
财险类	万元	196066	278100	319010	353602	467216	550985	610453
#机动车险	万元	155067	231073	270082	301526	400405	460241	515282
企财险	万元	17160	21254	22626	24276	32123	34107	32135
家财险	万元	3228	3393	1373	1113	1832	1806	1476
货运险	万元	1985	2514	2819	3648	4576	6917	7164
责任险	万元	4179	5477	6571	7273	9772	10516	12930
短健险	万元	1448	271	759	8058	4289	7222	6924
短意险	万元	10536	12945	13145	6184	11073	10271	11959
农业险	万元	23	43	17		55	35	61

主要统计指标解释

Explanatory Notes on Main Statistical Indicators

公共财政预算收入 国家财政参与社会产品分配所取得的收入，是实现国家职能的财力保证，主要包括：

（1）各项税收 包括增值税、营业税、消费税、土地增值税、城市维护建设税、资源税、城市土地使用税、印花税、个人所得税、企业所得税、关税、农牧业税和耕地占用税等。

（2）专项收入 包括征收排污费收入、征收城市水资源费收入，教育费附加收入等。

（3）其他收入 包括基本建设贷款归还收入、基本建设收入、捐赠收入等。

（4）国有企业计划亏损补贴 这项为负收入，冲减财政收入。

公共财政预算支出 国家财政将筹集起来的资金进行分配使用，以满足经济建设和各项事业的需要，主要包括：基本建设支出、企业挖潜改造资金、地质勘探费用、科技三项费用、支援农村生产支出、农林水利气象等部门的事业费用、工业交通商业等部门的事业费、文教科学卫生事业费、抚恤和社会福利救济费、国防支出、行政管理费、价格补贴支出等项目。

银行信贷存款 指企业、机关、团体或居民把货币资金存入银行或其他信用机构保管并取得一定利息的一种信用活动形式。根据存款对象的不同可划分为：企业存款、财政存款、机关团体存款、基本建设存款、城镇居民储蓄存款、农村存款等科目。它是银行信贷资金的主要来源。

银行信贷贷款 银行或其他信用机构根据必须归还的原则，按一定利率，为企业、个人等提供资金的一种信用活动形式。我国银行贷款，分流动资金贷款、固定资产贷款、城乡个体工商户贷款以及农业贷款等科目。

十一、人民生活

People’s Living Conditions

11-1 主要年份人民生活主要指标

Basic Statistics on People's Living Conditions in Main Years

指　　标	单位	1985年	1990年	1995年	2000年	2005年	2010年	2011年	2012年
城镇在岗职工年平均工资	元	1456	3552	9682	14051	28253	46576	50398	57007
国有单位	元	1400	3600	9390	16371	37919	57275	61504	66857
城镇集体单位	元	1501	3507	7507	10475	15958	27391	30549	35977
其他各种单位	元	1571	3525	7891	14218	20882	37803	39591	47726
城市居民家庭每一就业者负担人口	人	1.58	1.70	1.50	1.54	1.58	1.60	1.58	1.60
城市居民家庭人均可支配收入	元	791	2508	9588	14142	22882	35690	39513	42944
城市居民家庭人均总支出	元	718	2152	10049	14193	25822	32140	34978	41663
城市居民家庭人均消费性支出	元	689	2038	9220	12529	21768	25733	27495	31369
食品	元	493	1295	3644	4048	6035	8732	9513	11103
衣着	元	28	95	604	487	1285	1706	1806	2121
居住	元	58	184	1084	1218	1242	2089	2128	2852
家庭设备用品及服务	元	48	153	694	623	1165	1771	1902	2173
医疗保健	元	14	42	258	431	811	1294	1251	1521
交通和通信	元	4	25	1562	3309	7482	5925	6035	6108
教育文化娱乐服务	元	21	113	991	1517	3205	3443	3886	4348
其他商品和服务	元	23	131	383	896	543	773	974	1143
城市居民家庭人均非消费性支出	元		12	829	1664	4054	6407	7483	10294
农民人均纯收入	元	803	1542	4769	8484	13076	20486	22842	24944
全市职工年平均工资	元				7765	10639	16108	21739	25658

注：1. 职工年平均工资从2000年起是城镇在岗职工工资,不含乡镇及以下办企业职工，下同。
2. 全市职工年平均工资统计是根据中央、省、市属各类企事业机关单位，各镇街、村及村以下非农企业,个体私营非农企业以及“三资”、“三来一补”非农企业的在岗从业人员劳动报酬抽样调查计算所得。
3. 城市居民人均可支配收入1997年以前是生活费收入口径，1997年起是可支配收入口径。
4. 农民人均纯收入采用农村住户抽样调查口径，相应调整了往年数，下同。

11-2 历年城镇在岗职工工资总额与平均工资

Total and Average Wage of Employed Persons in Urban Areas over Years

年　份	工　资 总　额 (万元)	国　有 单　位	城镇集 体单位	其　他 单　位	平　均 工　资 (元)	国　有 单　位	城镇集 体单位	其　他 单　位
1978	4485	2911	1574		474	630	325	
1979	5869	3611	2258		650	708	574	
1980	7255	4210	3045		750	867	632	
1981	9416	5000	4416		887	979	801	
1982	11839	6440	5399		1095	1089	1102	
1983	12808	6834	5974		1197	1138	1273	
1984	14963	7002	7961		1383	1333	1431	
1985	17260	7619	9238	403	1456	1400	1501	1571
1986	20980	10336	10026	618	2616	1698	1525	1940
1987	27610	12300	14159	1151	2067	2028	2094	2166
1988	35007	17931	14854	2222	2757	2942	2588	2574
1989	42947	20340	20808	1799	3320	3355	3295	3236
1990	46780	22321	21012	3447	3552	3600	3507	3525
1991	54002	24456	23268	6278	3777	3841	3674	3933
1992	68360	30469	28886	9005	4531	4610	4404	4696
1993	107088	47088	40171	19829	6228	7007	5583	6044
1994	131160	61869	49323	19968	8360	9390	7507	7891
1995	171543	75157	51398	44988	9682	10802	8007	10367
1996	178968	83372	52581	43015	10382	11623	8658	10775
1997	175156	87890	47185	40081	10691	12160	8774	10610
1998	187636	98109	50302	39225	11422	13123	9362	10959
1999	204550	109437	52217	42896	12557	14601	9966	12062
2000	229404	125711	53903	49790	14051	16371	10475	14218
2001	261645	152564	52645	56436	16183	19869	11001	15238
2002	291778	165611	58907	67260	17804	22228	11640	17348
2003	362935	230464	55866	76605	22598	29773	12940	19140
2004	432893	282512	62898	87483	25326	35163	13954	19223
2005	518216	349572	70872	97772	28253	37919	15958	20882
2006	608670	413718	74637	120315	31135	41457	17174	23032
2007	707007	487826	74408	144773	35284	46197	18807	26218
2008	809893	570134	82432	157327	39516	51441	20833	28838
2009	944243	639161	76001	229081	42585	56129	22077	31195
2010	1029873	678673	96664	254537	46576	57275	27391	37803
2011	1229001	826777	104824	297400	50398	61504	30549	39591
2012	1434133	960274	126456	347404	57007	66857	35977	47726

注：2000年以前为年末城镇职工工资总额和平均工资，下同。

11-3 城镇在岗职工工资总额及平均工资(2012年，按经济类型、行业分)

Total and Average Wage of Fully Employed Persons in Urban Areas (2012,by Status of Registration and Sector)

项目	工资总额(万元)	国有单位	城镇集体单位	其他单位	平均工资(元)	国有单位	城镇集体单位	其他单位
总计	1434133	960274	126456	347404	57007	66857	35977	47726
按企业、事业和机关分								
企业	696843	226610	122830	347404	50835	75537	35822	47726
事业	440562	436935	3626		63228	63491	42167	
机关	296729	296729			66215	66215		
按国民经济行业分								
农、林、牧、渔业	4886	4886			51869	51869		
工业	327586	25702	63290	238595	38505	69521	29669	39735
建筑业	11277	6251	5008	18	38540	40302	36637	22000
交通运输、仓储和邮政业	46031	29611	11975	4445	51083	57386	41307	46690
信息传输、软件和信息技术服务业	28527	26427		2101	115729	118559		89008
批发和零售业	37394	8613	7887	20895	50160	36588	39295	67534
住宿和餐饮业	1554		497	1057	23724		24259	23480
金融业	242691	132693	31247	78752	83811	87870	52018	100333
房地产业	3203	2657	547		66049	78834	36939	
租赁和商务服务业	13172	7177	4453	1543	53177	51118	48503	99516
科学研究和技术服务	12460	12248	212		64559	65359	37804	
水利、环境和公共设施管理业	4256	3993	262		68197	75202	28204	
居民服务、修理和其他服务业	943	943			61660	61660		
教育	139563	139563			51849	51849		
卫生和社会工作	244409	243824	585		72984	72960	84783	
文化、体育和娱乐业	11704	11211	494		67655	66652	102813	
公共管理、社会保障和社会组织	304477	304477			65790	65790		
国际组织								

11-4 主要年份各种分组的城镇在岗职工平均工资

Average Wage of Employed Persons in Urban Areas by Item in Main Years

单位：元

项　　目	1985年	1990年	1995年	2000年	2005年	2010年	2011年	2012年
职工平均工资	1456	3552	9682	14051	28253	46576	50398	57007
按企业事业和机关分								
企　业			9316	13501	24152	43121	46249	50835
事　业			10872	15485	32203	46478	51504	63228
机　关			12171	15383	38441	57300	62281	66215
按经济类型分								
国有单位	1400	3600	10802	16371	37919	57275	61504	66857
城镇集体单位	1501	3507	8007	10475	15958	27391	30549	35977
其他单位	1571	3525	10367	14218	20882	37803	39591	47726
按国民经济行业分								
农、林、牧、渔业	1312	3639	12412	14000	37046	61606	50167	51869
工　业	1450	3481	8945	12316	18371	30418	33284	38505
建筑业	2052	3813	9125	9820	18385	31020	32497	38540
交通运输、仓储和邮政业					31989	40809	33950	51083
信息传输、软件和信息技术服务业					71801	110207	116568	115729
批发和零售业					28565	38986	44506	50160
住宿和餐饮业					18257	21955	23658	23724
金融业	1500	3303	13254	20560	40655	94569	89587	83811
房地产业	1779	4414	11184	17993	34805	53939	61490	66049
租赁和商务服务业					29824	47505	52732	53177
科学研究和技术服务					37423	51017	58185	64559
水利、环境和公共设施管理业					34573	51426	57598	68197
居民服务、修理和其他服务业					44853	56776	59924	61660
教育					27255	37734	41166	51849
卫生和社会工作					37991	52867	58145	72984
文化、体育和娱乐业					37710	58317	65900	67655
公共管理、社会保障和社会组织	1519	3666	12347	15424	37888	56817	61665	65790
国际组织								

11-5 各种经济类型分行业城镇在岗职工工资总额、平均工资(2011-2012年)

Total and Average Wage of Employed Persons in Arban Areas by Status of Registration and Sector (2011-2012)

项目	国有经济		城镇集体经济		其他经济类型	
	2011年	2012年	2011年	2012年	2011年	2012年
职工工资总额(万元)	826777	960274	104824	126456	297400	347404
农、林、牧、渔业	4886	4886				
工业	28869	25702	53026	63290	192299	238595
建筑业	4254	6251	805	5008	18	18
交通运输、仓储和邮政业	20554	29611	11581	11975	21128	4445
信息传输、软件和信息技术服务业	26319	26427			2112	2101
批发和零售业	5122	8613	6154	7887	15980	20895
住宿和餐饮业			497	497	1057	1057
金融业	147379	132693	28019	31247	63280	78752
房地产业	2391	2657	585	547		
租赁和商务服务业	7173	7177	3065	4453	1527	1543
科学研究和技术服务	11734	12248	212	212		
水利、环境和公共设施管理业	3641	3993	258	262		
居民服务、修理和其他服务业	941	943				
教育	106538	139563				
卫生和社会工作	185440	243824	217	585		
文化、体育和娱乐业	10968	11211	406	494		
公共管理、社会保障和社会组织	260567	304477				
国际组织						
职工平均工资(元)	61504	66857	30549	35977	39591	47726
农、林、牧、渔业	50167	51869				
工业	78834	69521	24001	29669	33961	39735
建筑业	34193	40302	25961	36637	22000	22000
交通运输、仓储和邮政业	40350	57386	35800	41307	28706	46690
信息传输、软件和信息技术服务业	118394	118559			97782	89008
批发和零售业	31912	36588	33922	39295	59075	67534
住宿和餐饮业			24259	24259	23385	23480
金融业	109372	87870	50357	52018	83230	100333
房地产业	72245	78834	38222	36939		
租赁和商务服务业	51419	51118	44745	48503	101093	99516
科学研究和技术服务	58757	65359	37804	37804		
水利、环境和公共设施管理业	62889	75202	26337	28204		
居民服务、修理和其他服务业	59924	61660				
教育	41166	51849				
卫生和社会工作	58139	72960	63765	84783		
文化、体育和娱乐业	66073	66652	61561	102813		
公共管理、社会保障和社会组织	61665	65790				
国际组织						

11-6 国有企、事业和机关单位城镇在岗职工工资总额及平均工资(2012年)

Total and Average Wage of Employed Persons in Urban State-owned Enterprises, Institutions and Government Agencies (2012)

项　　目	单位从业人员劳动报酬（万元）	在岗职工工资总额	其他从业人员工资总额	在岗职工平均工资（元）
总　计	968104	960274	7830	66857
按企事业机关分				
企　业	228205	226610	1595	75537
#地　方	169528	167950	1577	80022
事　业	440527	436935	3592	63491
#地　方	438303	434712	3592	63365
机　关	299372	296729	2643	66215
#地　方	299372	296729	2643	66215
按行业分				
农、林、牧、渔业	4887	4886	1	51869
工　业	25722	25702	20	69521
建筑业	6251	6251		40302
交通运输、仓储和邮政业	29618	29611	7	57386
信息传输、软件和信息技术服务业	26427	26427		118559
批发和零售业	9646	8613	1033	36588
住宿和餐饮业				
金融业	132966	132693	274	87870
房地产业	2686	2657	29	78834
租赁和商务服务业	7275	7177	99	51118
科学研究和技术服务	12444	12248	196	65359
水利、环境和公共设施管理业	4091	3993	97	75202
居民服务、修理和其他服务业	956	943	13	61660
教育	139745	139563	182	51849
卫生和社会工作	246652	243824	2828	72960
文化、体育和娱乐业	11530	11211	320	66652
公共管理、社会保障和社会组织	307209	304477	2732	65790
国际组织				

11-7 工业、建筑业城镇在岗职工工资总额和平均工资（2012年）

Total and Average Wage of Employed Persons in Urban Industrial and Construction Units (2012)

项　　目	工资总额（万元）	平均工资（元）
工业总计	327586	38505
按经济类型分		
国有单位	25702	69521
城镇集体单位	63290	29669
其他各种单位	238595	39735
按工业行业分(大类)		
非金属矿采选业	318	58926
农副食品加工业	1840	44658
食品制造业	2895	35256
酒、饮料和精制茶制造业	2714	19522
烟草制品业		
纺织业	2006	15857
纺织服装、服饰业	15008	23913
皮革、毛皮、羽毛及其制品和制鞋业	976	45817
木材加工和木、竹、藤、棕、草制品业		
家具制造业		
造纸和纸制品业	3294	29565
印刷和记录媒介复制业	5005	44133
文教、工美、体育和娱乐用品制造业	1179	16986
石油加工、炼焦和核燃料加工业		
化学原料和化学制品制造业	4057	31233
医药制造业	14550	62555
化学纤维制造业	13433	31592
橡胶和塑料制品业		
非金属矿物制品业	2855	24593
黑色金属冶炼和压延加工业		
有色金属冶炼和压延加工业	127	14953
金属制品业	1147	17177
通用设备制造业	59722	36014
专用设备制造业	5516	39458
汽车制造业	9650	59898
电气机械和器材制造业	33611	33408
计算机、通信和其他电子设备制造业	88674	41964
仪器仪表制造业	17948	33194
其他制造业	4	21000
电力、热力生产和供应业	32213	79461
水的生产和供应业	8724	53754
建筑业总计	11277	38540
国有单位	6251	40302
城镇集体单位	5008	36637
其他单位	18	22000

11-8 历年居民收支、农民收入

Income and Expenditure of Urban Households and Net Income of Rural Households over Years

年 份	城市居民人均可支配收入(元)	城市居民人均消费性支出(元)	农民人均纯收入(元)
1978			149
1979			188
1980			272
1981			463
1982			567
1983			618
1984			691
1985	791	689	803
1986	1033	883	951
1987	1247	1174	1142
1988	1778	1583	1325
1989	2282	1980	1424
1990	2508	2038	1542
1991	3068	2481	1673
1992	4026	3901	2290
1993	5970	5533	2903
1994	8270	7270	3769
1995	9588	9220	4769
1996	10824	8585	5554
1997	11032	8309	6132
1998	11506	8644	6830
1999	12954	11348	7704
2000	14142	12529	8484
2001	16938	14669	9383
2002	16949	15157	10178
2003	18471	15446	11033
2004	20526	18426	11941
2005	22882	21768	13076
2006	25320	18995	14313
2007	27025	21545	15747
2008	30275	23208	16904
2009	33045	24270	18098
2010	35690	25733	20486
2011	39513	27495	22842
2012	42944	31369	24944

注：本表城市居民人均可支配收入1997年以前是生活费收入口径，1997年起是可支配收入口径，下同。

11-9 历年城市居民家庭户基本情况

Basic Conditions of Urban Households over Years

年　份	平均每户家庭人口(人)	平均每户家庭就业人口(人)	平均每户住房使用面积(平方米)	平均每户家庭可支配收入(元)	平均每户家庭消费性支出(元)
1985	3.89	2.30	42.79	3077	2680
1986	4.01	2.13	48.12	4142	3541
1987	4.02	2.09	52.26	5013	4719
1988	4.08	2.17	61.20	7254	6459
1989	3.88	2.01	65.96	8854	7682
1990	4.06	2.09	64.96	10182	8274
1991	4.08	2.14	65.28	12517	10122
1992	4.06	2.06	69.02	16346	15838
1993	3.86	2.68	77.20	23044	21357
1994	3.86	2.26	88.78	31922	28062
1995	3.94	2.18	78.80	37777	36327
1996	4.07	2.31	85.47	44054	34941
1997	4.02	2.30	84.42	44349	33402
1998	3.92	2.17	101.92	45104	33884
1999	4.05	2.38	120.29	52464	45959
2000	3.89	2.69	121.10	55012	48738
2001	3.75	2.30	149.59	63518	55009
2002	3.66	2.47	152.99	62033	55475
2003	3.57	2.11	147.73	65941	55142
2004	3.50	2.17	145.53	71841	64491
2005	3.38	2.14	144.26	77341	73576
2006	3.68	2.31	166.23	93178	69902
2007	3.41	2.09	147.11	92155	73468
2008	3.43	1.81	138.06	103843	79603
2009	3.38	2.00	136.59	111692	82033
2010	3.32	2.08	146.23	118491	85434
2011	3.39	2.14	167.59	133948	93209
2012	3.43	2.15	150.37	147298	107596

注：平均每户住房使用面积2002年以前为平均每户居住面积口径。

11-10 历年人均总收入分类

Per Capita Total Income over Years

单位：元

年份	年人均总收入	#工资性收入	经营净收入	财产性收入	转移性收入	可支配收入
1985	837	603				791
1986	1111	974				1033
1987	1364	989				1247
1988	1889	1097				1778
1989	2439	1185				2282
1990	2678	1459	46	30	417	2508
1991	3343	2160	226	55	534	3062
1992	4520	2560	411	175	709	4026
1993	6623	3684	749	889	319	5969
1994	9131	5758	840	553	994	8270
1995	10491	6260	1210	659	1329	9588
1996	11640	8428	1127	455	1273	10824
1997	11063	8024	625	349	1544	11032
1998	11551	8334	884	319	1207	11506
1999	13009	7910	1799	357	1541	12954
2000	14231	8702	2740	895	720	14142
2001	17062	11037	2643	895	1879	16938
2002	17711	13050	1662	1076	1923	16949
2003	19478	15282	1598	1210	1388	18471
2004	21875	17153	1634	1553	1535	20526
2005	24663	18524	2709	1894	1536	22882
2006	27157	18318	4389	2504	1946	25320
2007	29335	18930	3359	4849	2101	27025
2008	31967	20872	4521	3527	3047	30275
2009	35750	23723	4724	4209	3094	33045
2010	38961	26799	4171	4771	3220	35690
2011	43202	27272	4075	7481	4374	39513
2012	47040	30518	3940	9099	3484	42944

注：1. 本表2007年以前采用50户抽样调查的统计口径,2007年起采用250户抽样调查的统计口径，下同。
2. 本表年人均总收入指标2002年以前采用年人均实际收入统计口径，2002年起采用年人均总收入统计口径，下同。

11-11　历年人均消费性支出分类

Per Capita Living Expenditure over Years

单位：元

年　份	年人均消费性支出	食　品	衣　着	居　住	家庭设备用品及服务	医　疗保　健	交通和通　信	教育文化娱乐服务	其他商品和 服 务	恩格尔系　数 (%)
1985	689	493	28	58	48	14	4	21	23	71.6
1986	883	588	43	66	84	15	6	46	35	66.6
1987	1174	709	64	79	128	55	9	106	24	60.4
1988	1583	977	64	136	171	22	12	124	77	61.7
1989	1980	1235	101	156	196	55	24	115	98	62.4
1990	2038	1295	95	184	153	42	25	113	131	63.5
1991	2481	1476	188	254	122	47	47	211	136	59.5
1992	3901	1834	259	369	263	94	587	331	164	47.0
1993	5533	2615	373	333	583	133	855	389	252	47.3
1994	7270	3172	420	761	925	192	850	714	236	43.6
1995	9220	3644	604	1084	694	258	1562	991	383	39.5
1996	8585	3682	706	674	660	225	990	847	802	42.9
1997	8309	3681	594	880	435	415	916	939	449	44.3
1998	8644	3785	457	659	612	455	1025	1074	577	43.8
1999	11348	3712	400	898	601	371	3398	1043	923	32.7
2000	12529	4048	487	1218	623	431	3309	1517	896	32.3
2001	14669	4572	648	1173	746	513	4258	1429	1330	31.2
2002	15157	4818	748	1060	611	529	4303	2660	428	31.8
2003	15446	4804	921	2966	1093	693	2062	2512	395	31.1
2004	18426	5041	1134	2517	925	811	4973	2673	352	27.4
2005	21768	6035	1285	1242	1165	811	7482	3205	543	27.7
2006	18995	6321	1238	2341	1229	809	3531	3001	525	33.3
2007	21545	6966	1213	1903	1342	860	5208	3515	538	32.3
2008	23208	7778	1349	2585	1539	1332	4462	3464	699	33.5
2009	24270	7972	1492	2232	1616	1400	5456	3326	776	32.8
2010	25733	8732	1706	2089	1771	1294	5925	3443	773	33.9
2011	27495	9513	1806	2128	1902	1251	6035	3886	974	34.6
2012	31369	11103	2121	2852	2173	1521	6108	4348	1143	35.4

11-12 不同收入等级年人均可支配收入与消费性支出水平

Per Capita Annual Disposable Income and Consumption Expenditure by Level of Income

单位：元

年　份	年人均可支配收入	#最低收入户	低收入户	高收入户	最高收入户	年人均消费性支出	#最低收入户	低收入户	高收入户	最高收入户
1985	791					689				
1986	1033					883				
1987	1247					1174				
1988	1778					1583				
1989	2282					1980				
1990	2508	1391	1744	3774	4546	2038	1170	1539	2099	4156
1991	3068	1665	2286	4092	4592	2481	1725	1877	2699	3784
1992	4026	2053	2650	5988	7275	3901	1966	2648	4690	6070
1993	5970	2977	4203	8484	9852	5533	3046	3685	6691	6956
1994	8270	4157	5248	12217	14265	7270	4477	5762	10839	8378
1995	9588	4539	5867	13828	18771	9220	4362	6912	12194	19353
1996	11639	5627	7142	15377	19224	8585	5152	6278	11496	10498
1997	11032	5778	7214	16496	22069	8309	5298	5963	15265	12323
1998	11506	6136	7853	16660	21591	8644	4888	6259	11774	14733
1999	12954	5998	7944	18951	23447	11348	4777	7755	18118	26001
2000	14142	6826	7806	19104	28769	12529	6706	7211	10297	25896
2001	16938	7174	10365	25167	33526	14669	6990	7425	18880	29834
2002	16949	6374	9398	23342	45001	15157	7224	8974	29735	21807
2003	18471	4535	9146	27000	48849	15446	6436	7990	25065	26683
2004	20526	8548	11658	31923	39058	18426	8047	9190	30530	45944
2005	22882	9590	13348	35885	43010	21768	10038	8908	31542	31498
2006	25320	13551	15633	37559	51957	18995	8841	11781	32568	39862
2007	27025	12073	16207	39071	55821	21545	12862	14547	31653	36732
2008	30275	11172	17340	46744	66034	23208	10927	14275	37741	53404
2009	33045	13642	19311	47680	71031	24270	12793	13654	27597	42949
2010	35690	18466	23384	48582	69968	25733	14073	15412	39674	46282
2011	39513	18405	22992	56246	86527	27495	13381	14980	43798	54008
2012	42944	21187	28493	59594	86510	31369	18178	21919	39926	58301

注：本表分组数据采用城镇住户抽样调查按相对收入不等距九组分户汇总资料，下同。

11-13 主要年份城市居民家庭基本情况

Basic Conditions of Urban Households in Main Years

项目	单位	1985年	1990年	1995年	2000年	2005年	2010年	2011年	2012年
调查户数	户	50	50	50	50	50	250	250	250
平均每户家庭人口	人	3.90	4.06	3.94	3.89	3.38	3.32	3.39	3.43
平均每户家庭就业人口	人	2.30	2.09	2.18	2.69	2.14	2.08	2.14	2.15
平均每一就业者负担人口	人	1.58	1.70	1.50	1.54	1.58	1.60	1.58	1.60
平均每人每年可支配收入	元	791	2508	9588	14142	22882	35690	39513	42944
#工资性收入	元	603	1459	6260	8702	18524	26799	27272	30518
平均每人每年消费性支出	元	689	2038	9220	12529	21768	25733	27495	31369
食品	元	493	1295	3644	4048	6035	8732	9513	11103
衣着	元	28	95	604	487	1285	1706	1806	2121
居住	元	58	184	1084	1218	1242	2089	2128	2852
家庭设备用品及服务	元	48	153	694	623	1165	1771	1902	2173
#耐用消费品	元	21	93	368	18	425	460	510	770
医疗保健	元	14	42	258	431	811	1294	1251	1521
交通和通信	元	4	25	1562	3309	7482	5925	6035	6108
教育文化娱乐服务	元	21	113	991	1517	3205	3443	3886	4348
#文化娱乐用品	元	13	36	521	532	610	687	698	762
文化娱乐服务	元	5	37	173	286	1112	1691	1673	1937
教育	元	3	40	297	699	1482	1065	1515	1650
其他商品和服务	元	23	131	383	896	543	773	974	1143
平均每人住房使用面积	平方米	10.98	16.61	20.00	31.13	42.68	44.05	49.44	43.84
平均每人每年购买商品									
粮食	元	106	109	74	66	65	466	582	544
油脂类	元	5	5	7	8	8	121	129	156
肉禽及其制品	元	37	48	40	50	72	1692	1898	2104
蛋类	元	6	6	10	9	8	77	96	111
水产品	元	23	29	25	29	22	660	712	765
鲜菜	元	90	100	117	116	114	591	582	674
烟草类	元	3	18	52	94	53	192	231	255
酒和饮料	元	16	25	48	78	132	324	410	524
干鲜瓜果	元	11	84	258	298	344	628	681	875
糕点、奶及奶制品	元		13	42	105	264	484	567	574
服装	元	28	95	434	356	944	1297	1368	1596

注：1. 平均每人住房使用面积2002年以前为平均每人居住面积口径。
2. 粮食、油脂类、肉禽及其制品、蛋类、水产品、鲜菜2008年以前以公斤为计量单位。

11-14 主要年份城市居民人均消费性支出及构成

Consumption Expenditure of Urban Households in Main Years

项目	单位	1985年	1990年	1995年	2000年	2005年	2010年	2011年	2012年
年人均消费性支出	元	689	2038	9220	12529	21768	25733	27495	31369
食品	元	493	1295	3644	4048	6035	8732	9513	11103
衣着	元	28	95	604	487	1285	1706	1806	2121
居住	元	58	184	1084	1218	1242	2089	2128	2852
#住房	元	7	92	725	455	34	482	409	973
水电燃料及其他	元	51	92	358	763	972	1299	1411	1515
家庭设备用品及服务	元	48	153	694	623	1165	1771	1902	2173
#耐用消费品	元	21	93	368	18	425	460	510	770
医疗保健	元	14	42	258	431	811	1294	1251	1521
#药品费	元			109	240	276	466	407	396
滋补保健品	元			46	178	207	434	414	458
交通和通信	元	4	25	1562	3309	7482	5925	6035	6108
交通	元	4	25	1245	2154	6381	4473	4605	4426
通信	元			317	1155	1101	1452	1430	1682
教育文化娱乐服务	元	21	113	991	1517	3205	3443	3886	4348
文化娱乐用品	元	13	36	521	532	610	687	698	762
文化娱乐服务	元	5	37	173	286	1112	1691	1673	1937
教育	元	3	40	297	699	1482	1065	1515	1650
其他商品和服务	元	23	131	383	896	543	773	974	1143
消费性支出构成									
食品	%	71.55	63.54	39.52	32.31	27.72	33.93	34.60	35.40
衣着	%	4.06	4.66	6.55	3.89	5.90	6.63	6.57	6.76
居住	%	8.42	9.03	11.76	9.72	5.71	8.12	7.74	9.09
家庭设备用品及服务	%	6.97	7.51	7.53	4.97	5.35	6.88	6.92	6.93
#耐用消费品	%	43.76	60.78	53.03	2.89	1.95	1.79	1.85	2.45
医疗保健	%	2.03	2.06	2.80	3.44	3.73	5.03	4.55	4.85
交通和通信	%	0.58	1.23	16.94	26.41	34.37	23.02	21.95	19.47
教育文化娱乐服务	%	3.05	5.54	10.75	12.11	14.72	13.38	14.13	13.86
其他商品和服务	%	3.34	6.43	4.15	7.15	2.50	3.00	3.54	3.64

11-15 历年城市居民家庭平均每百户主要耐用消费品拥有量

Ownership of Durable Consumer Goods Owned per 100 Urban Households over Years

年　份	汽车（辆）	电冰箱（台）	洗衣机（台）	空调器（台）	组合音响（套）	彩色电视机（台）	固定电话（部）	移动电话（部）	计算机（台）
1985		22	56			22			
1986		26	66			40			
1987		42	72			52			
1988		52	86			66			
1989		72	96		4	84			
1990		84	54	16	14	92			
1991		98	106	16	14	100			
1992		96	112	12	18	98	64		
1993		108	108	28	34	102	60		
1994		110	114	60	52	114	72		
1995		110	108	82	54	138	82		
1996		104	110	128	68	132	98		
1997		106	108	100	68	116	98		22
1998	2	110	112	122	64	146	96	28	28
1999	10	116	118	130	84	178	100	72	34
2000	12	108	114	150	88	178	100	126	68
2001	16	118	110	184	76	176	100	186	98
2002	24	126	112	204	76	192	100	200	102
2003	26	134	108	226	82	194	104	224	96
2004	32	132	118	258	80	192	112	264	108
2005	42	124	110	264	72	200	112	294	114
2006	44	130	112	280	80	218	116	298	112
2007	52	115	110	271	82	206	115	272	111
2008	47	110	103	200	59	180	108	248	100
2009	63	113	105	233	69	184	105	261	112
2010	68	118	107	259	68	186	110	267	129
2011	80	117	112	272	72	187	106	280	136
2012	86	120	110	297	67	185	107	294	156

11-16 按收入等级分的城市居民家庭基本情况(2012年)

Basic Conditions of Urban Households by Level of Income (2012)

项目	单位	总平均	最低收入户	低收入户	中等偏下户	中等收入户	中等偏上户	高收入户	最高收入户
调查户数	户	250	26	25	50	51	50	23	25
平均每户家庭人口	人	3.43	3.81	3.76	3.56	3.44	3.43	2.96	2.81
平均每户家庭就业人口	人	2.15	1.96	2.34	2.05	2.25	2.20	2.14	2.05
平均每一就业者负担人口	人	1.60	1.94	1.61	1.74	1.53	1.56	1.38	1.37
平均每户就业面	%	62.68	51.44	62.23	57.58	65.41	64.14	72.30	72.95
平均每人总收入	元	47040	23514	31483	37266	45730	54070	65209	94374
平均每人可支配收入	元	42944	21187	28493	34068	41826	49361	59594	86510
平均每人总支出	元	41663	21770	27456	30763	39394	44857	51377	105063
平均每人消费性支出	元	31369	18178	21919	25046	32681	34991	39926	58301
平均每一就业者总收入	元	75045	45708	50588	64716	69916	84300	90196	129361
平均每人住房建筑面积	平方米	58.44	54.43	52.56	53.28	59.25	60.20	64.96	72.03
平均每百户家庭年末主要耐用消费品拥有量									
家用汽车	辆	86	42	76	72	84	104	96	124
洗衣机	台	110	100	112	112	108	112	108	112
电冰箱	台	120	100	124	120	124	120	120	128
彩色电视机	台	185	181	184	166	182	186	196	220
计算机	台	156	112	140	136	171	172	148	204
组合音响	套	67	50	44	58	75	86	72	68
照相机	架	90	58	60	82	86	106	92	140
钢琴	架	4		4	4	4	2	8	4
空调器	台	297	235	264	258	318	314	320	376
淋浴热水器	台	142	142	124	140	143	146	136	164
消毒碗柜	台	88	77	80	86	94	98	88	84
健身器材	套	16	4	20	4	20	18	12	40
固定电话	部	107	100	100	118	102	104	96	124
移动电话	部	294	285	336	278	306	300	252	300

11-17 按收入等级分的城市居民家庭平均每人全年现金收入(2012年)

Per Capita Annual Cash Income of Urban Households by Level of Income (2012)

项目	单位	总平均	最低收入户	低收入户	中等偏下户	中等收入户	中等偏上户	高收入户	最高收入户
平均每户家庭就业人口	人	2.15	1.96	2.34	2.05	2.25	2.20	2.14	2.05
#国有经济单位职工人数	人	0.30	0.17	0.24	0.20	0.33	0.34	0.23	0.59
城镇集体经济单位职工人数	人	0.59	0.31	0.68	0.76	0.51	0.63	0.69	0.40
其它经济类型单位职工人数	人	0.31	0.10	0.32	0.26	0.37	0.31	0.22	0.57
城镇个体或私营企业主人数	人	0.18	0.08	0.24	0.13	0.14	0.19	0.27	0.26
城镇个体或私营企业被雇人数	人	0.62	1.03	0.64	0.58	0.71	0.58	0.68	0.06
其他就业人数	人	0.07	0.08	0.08	0.10	0.08	0.06		0.08
家庭总收入	元	47040	23514	31483	37266	45730	54070	65209	94374
#可支配收入	元	42944	21187	28493	34068	41826	49361	59594	86510
#工资性收入	元	30518	13583	20242	23815	30279	36321	43436	59082
#工资及补贴收入	元	30374	13575	19952	23703	30227	36056	43339	58876
经营净收入	元	3940	615	2077	2025	2160	4450	8919	14316
财产性收入	元	9099	6083	6027	8849	9230	10206	10026	14197
#股息与红利收入	元	2864	2992	2366	3589	2328	3101	2294	2834
出租房屋收入	元	5773	2905	3480	4657	6593	6601	7510	9972
转移性收入	元	3484	3233	3138	2577	4061	3093	2828	6778
#养老金或离退休金	元	1980	2250	1978	1076	2359	1712	1132	4444
捐赠收入	元	861	505	746	896	826	851	1153	1254

11-18 城市居民家庭平均每人全年消费性支出（2012年）

Per Capita Annual Consumption Expenditure of Urban Households (2012)

项目	单位	总平均	最低收入户	低收入户	中等偏下户	中等收入户	中等偏上户	高收入户	最高收入户
平均每人年消费性支出	元	31369	18178	21919	25046	32681	34991	39926	58301
食品	元	11103	8003	8232	9621	12196	12093	13830	15282
粮油类	元	799	687	717	751	870	794	902	918
肉禽蛋水产品类	元	2980	2688	2762	2788	3269	3041	3137	3142
#水产品	元	765	692	695	691	840	779	811	888
蔬菜类	元	739	683	688	702	823	735	788	726
调味品	元	86	80	78	76	94	89	90	102
糖烟酒饮料类	元	856	651	634	615	1033	939	1268	996
干鲜瓜果类	元	875	637	742	788	971	952	1033	1030
糕点、奶及奶制品	元	574	451	459	556	601	608	686	689
其他食品	元	80	59	63	72	90	93	92	83
饮食服务	元	4115	2067	2089	3273	4444	4841	5833	7596
衣着	元	2121	1025	1099	1674	2169	2694	3211	3587
#服装	元	1596	716	825	1244	1654	2035	2423	2735
居住	元	2852	1458	1563	1804	2613	2421	3944	9797
#住房	元	973	19	43	60	713	399	2040	6890
水电、燃料及其它	元	1515	1378	1370	1505	1551	1525	1488	1840
家庭设备用品及服务	元	2173	744	1455	1821	2386	2713	3061	3334
#耐用消费品	元	770	146	549	566	786	1146	897	1392
医疗保健	元	1521	1149	1095	1196	1129	1455	2033	4083
#药品费	元	396	492	328	313	306	310	648	741
滋补保健品	元	458	162	267	298	606	374	458	1374
交通和通信	元	6108	2713	5080	4234	7353	6847	7236	11046
交通	元	4426	1469	3895	2823	5668	4900	5096	8496
通信	元	1682	1244	1185	1411	1686	1948	2141	2550
教育文化娱乐服务	元	4348	2778	2770	3935	3840	5516	4859	7674
文化娱乐用品	元	762	345	356	765	841	823	1015	1288
文化娱乐服务	元	1937	612	763	1206	1897	2829	2728	4399
教育	元	1650	1821	1651	1964	1102	1864	1117	1988
其他商品和服务	元	1143	308	625	760	995	1252	1751	3497

11-19 农村居民人均实际收入与实际支出（2006-2012年）
Per Capita Actual Income and Expenditure of Rural Households (2006-2012)

单位：元

年 份	家庭现金收入	#纯收入	家庭现金支出	#生活消费现金支出	#食品消费支出
2006	17676	14313	12173	9370	3380
2007	19945	15747	13078	10771	3805
2008	20622	16904	13154	10887	3823
2009	22077	18098	14643	10598	3711
2010	22537	20486	16245	11842	4447
2011	26460	22842	18061	14055	5313
2012	27008	24944	19119	16103	5980

11-20 农村居民人均实际收入（2006-2012年）
Per Capita Actual Income of Rural Households (2006-2012)

单位：元

年 份	家庭现金收 入	#工资性收入	家庭经营收入	财产性收入	转移性收入
2006	17676	8522	4195	4171	789
2007	19945	9446	4388	5191	920
2008	20622	9876	4326	5531	889
2009	22077	10442	4517	6210	908
2010	22537	11201	3629	6402	1305
2011	26460	13254	4150	7232	1822
2012	27008	14045	3829	7013	2121

11-21 农村居民人均消费支出（2006-2012年）

Per Capita Consumption Expenditure of Rural Households (2006-2012)

单位：元

年 份	生活消费现金支 出	#食品	衣着	家庭设备及 服 务	医疗保健	交通通讯	教育文化娱乐服务	居住	杂项商品和 服 务
2006	9370	3380	448	474	510	1543	932	1458	625
2007	10771	3805	602	581	494	1953	1029	2001	306
2008	10887	3823	691	622	545	1799	1198	1500	709
2009	10598	3711	633	471	565	1764	1223	1485	746
2010	11842	4447	627	480	569	2120	1082	1877	640
2011	14055	5313	655	574	665	2698	1225	2345	580
2012	16103	5980	751	771	765	2828	1533	2817	659

11-22 每百户农村居民家庭主要耐用消费品拥有量（2006-2012年）

Ownership of Durable Consumer Goods Owned per 100 Rural Households (2006-2012)

项目	单位	2006年	2007年	2008年	2009年	2010年	2011年	2012年
洗衣机	台	101	105	107	103	106	107	107
电冰箱	台	108	111	111	109	110	112	111
空调机	台	210	223	234	209	218	223	230
微波炉	台	37	45	50	46	46	48	49
热水器	台	137	143	142	129	132	133	131
摩托车	辆	134	95	84	83	87	89	91
生活用汽车	辆	49	59	67	53	57	61	64
固定电话机	部	139	137	137	122	120	121	120
移动电话	部	240	251	261	257	268	276	284
彩色电视机	台	175	178	183	160	164	167	165
影碟机	台	92	95	95	74	71	69	67
摄像机	台	15	17	21	13	17	17	15
照相机	架	54	59	64	53	55	58	57
家庭计算机	台	84	97	107	98	104	108	124
中高档乐器	件	8	9	10	10	11	12	12

主要统计指标解释

Explanatory Notes on Main Statistical Indicators

城市居民家庭可支配收入 指调查户可用于最终消费支出和其它非义务性支出以及储蓄的总和，即居民家庭可以用来自由支配的收入。它是家庭总收入扣除交纳的个人所得税、个人交纳的社会保障支出以及调查户的记账补贴后的收入。计算公式为：

可支配收入=家庭总收入-交纳个人所得税-个人交纳的社会保障支出-记账补贴

城市居民家庭消费性支出 指调查户用于本家庭日常生活的全部支出，包括食品、衣着、家庭设备用品及服务、医疗保健、交通和通讯、娱乐教育文化服务、居住、其他商品和服务八大类等，均按商品（服务）的用途分类。

农村居民家庭总收入 是指农村住户年内从各种来源得到的全部实际收入（包括现金收入和实物收入）。由基本收入、转移性收入和财产性收入三部分组成。

农村居民家庭纯收入 是农村常住居民家庭总收入扣除相应的各项费用性支出后，归农民所有的收入。它既可以用于生产、非生产投资、改善物质和文化生活，以及用于再分配的支出和结余的收入。这个指标用来观察农民实际收入水平，以及农民扩大再生产和改善生活的能力。

农村居民家庭生活费支出 是指农民住户年内用于物质生活和精神生活方面的实际支出，直接反映农民的生活水平、研究农民消费结构变化的基本指标。生活消费支出包括食品，衣着、居住，家庭设备，用品及服务，医疗保健，交通和通讯，文化教育娱乐用品及服务，其他商品和服务等消费支出。

职工工资总额 指各单位在一定时期内直接支付给本单位全部职工的劳动报酬总额。工资总额的计算原则应以直接支付给职工的全部劳动报酬为根据。各单位支付给职工的劳动报酬以及其他根据有关规定支付的工资，不论是计入成本的还是不计入成本的，不论是按国家规定列入计征奖金税项目的，还是未列入计征奖金税项目的，不论是以货币形式支付的还是以实物形式支付的，均包括在工资总额内。

职工平均工资 指企业、事业、机关单位的职工在一定时期内平均每人所得的货币工资额。它表明一定时期职工工资收入的高低程度，是反映职工工资水平的主要指标。计算公式为：职工平均工资=报告期实际支付全部职工工资总额/报告期全部职工平均人数

十二、社会事业

Social Undertakings

12-1 主要年份社会事业主要指标

Main Indicators of Social Undertakings in Main Years

项目	单位	1985年	1990年	1995年	2000年	2005年	2010年	2011年	2012年
国有企事业单位科学技术人员数	人	9166	11629	16856		42593	40025	41370	41336
三种专利申请量	件		34	325	1653	6694	21654	24455	29199
三种专利授权量	件		30	262	1399	3114	20397	19353	20900
各类技术合同签订项目数	项		5	46	110	50	90	163	152
各类技术合同签订项目金额	万元		12	1804	3469	4058	18366	31966	14516
在校学生数									
普通高等学校	人			1628	3241	16645	38293	45081	52381
成人高等学校	人	403	531	1254	3642	12665	21703	20497	18759
中等职业技术学校	人	3363	8919	18737	23144	29487	47531	48159	50092
普通中学	人	46596	61188	92481	112418	191044	258276	263076	267918
小学	人	134421	162664	195063	272793	480923	552377	578279	608118
学龄儿童入学率	%	99.8	99.9	100.0	100.0	100.0	100.0	100.0	100.0
小学毕业生升学率	%	79.5	95.4	99.2	99.8	99.9	100.0	100.0	100.0
初中毕业生升学率	%	38.5	43.6	85.4	90.3	94.1	97.9	98.0	97.8
普通高中毕业生升学率	%	26.5	31.2	64.9	70.5	96.5	95.1	94.5	95.9
高考省线入围人数	人	285	224	809	2646	11196	13761	15501	17316
电影放映单位	个	60	114	218	192	70	46	52	59
艺术表演团体	个	1	7	2	1		4	5	6
文化馆(群众艺术馆)	个	1	1	1	1	1	1	1	1
公共图书馆(室)	个	3	5	15	18	473	505	622	723
博物馆	个	2	2	2	3	16	30	31	31
档案馆	个	1	1	1	1	1	1	1	1
《东莞日报》发行量	万份		177	987	1578	2751	4563	3132	4482
广播电台	座		1	1	1	1	1	1	1
电视台	座	1	1	1	1	1	1	1	1
镇街文化广电服务中心	个						28	28	28
病床床位数	张	2323	3866	5798	7081	11972	19980	22814	24617
卫生技术人员数	人	3305	3902	5290	6915	16608	37487	39582	40597
#执业(助理)医师	人	1201	1721	2299	3309	6901	13214	13644	14043
举办全民健身活动	次							174	373
参加全民健身活动人数	万人次							77.30	43.41
执业律师人数	人	6	12	85	130	625	1366	1513	1668
公证人员数	人	6	10	19	20	48	96	106	105
人民调解委员会调解人员数	人	3603	3664	3664	3644	4556	17438	20240	16005
优抚收养单位收养人数	人		19	11	7	8	8	9	6
工业固体废物综合利用率	%	37.5	17.9	18.2	63.8	86.5	95.0	77.9	78.1
城市环境空气质量优良天数	天						357	358	362

注：1. 2010年起，国有企事业单位科学技术人员数只统计在编在岗人员数，与往年数不可比。
2. 中等职业技术学校包含市技工学校，不含一般成人中专。
3. 2004年起，卫生方面包含诊所、卫生所、医务室及村卫生室的数据，与往年数不可比。

12-2 科技活动基本情况（2012年）

Basic Statistics on Scientific and Technological Activities (2012)

项　　目	单位	2012年	项　　目	单位	2012年
科技企业			专利申请数	件	249
企业数	个	4723	获专利授权数	件	168
#国家高新技术企业	个	537	营业收入	万元	161745
省创新型试点企业	个	25	科技园区和基地		
省创新型企业	个	14	国家级高新区	个	1
省创新百强企业	个	8	省级高新区	个	
省民营科技企业	个	1080	专业镇	个	22
重点培育上市后备科技企业	个	76	#工业总产值	万元	68279963
市民营科技企业	个	2983	专业镇科技投入	万元	333278
科技合作			国家高新技术企业数	家	294
国际合作项目立项数	项	5	火炬计划特色产业基地	个	11
#国家立项数	项	1	#工业总产值	万元	15490361
省级立项数	项	4	国家高新技术企业数	家	122
国际科技合作示范基地	个	18	科技企业孵化器/加速器	个	9
#国家级基地	个	3	#建筑场地面积	万平方米	35.58
省级基地	个	15	在孵企业数	个	677
产学研项目立项数	项	73	毕业企业数	个	84
#省部合作	项	64	工程中心		
省院合作	项	9	国家级工程中心	个	1
总投入	万元	26045	省级工程中心	个	45
资助金额	万元	4790	#工程中心职工总数	人	7135
市配套金额	万元		经费收入	万元	100527
省部产学研示范基地	个	31	研究开发课题(项目)	项	365
省部产学研创新联盟	个	10	专利授权数	项	680
科技机构			研究与发展(R&D)人员	人	4677
机构数	个	41	研究与发展经费	万元	100374
从业人员	人	5879	市级工程中心	个	78
#科技活动人员	人	4835	#工程中心职工总数	人	9827
#本科及以上	人	3314	经费收入	万元	143186
#中级及以上职称	人		研究开发课题(项目)	项	734
科技经费筹集额	万元	136615	专利授权数	项	827
#政府拨款	万元	50714	研究与发展(R&D)人员	人	7246
企业自筹	万元	85901	研究与发展经费	万元	132376
科技经费内部支出	万元	97415	科技金融		
项目(课题)数	项	316	科技贷款机构	个	
项目(课题)经费支出额	万元	46409	上市后备企业	个	74
论文数	篇	387	创业风险机构	个	25
科技专著数	篇	5			

12-3 研究与试验发展(R&D)基本情况（2009-2012年）

Basic Statistics on Research and Development (R&D) (2009-2012)

指标	单位	2009年	2010年	2011年	2012年
R&D活动单位数	个	496	492	495	668
#规上工业企业	个	439	436	428	607
R&D研究机构数	个	454	414	482	456
#规上工业企业办机构	个	429	376	468	417
R&D项目(课题)数	个	2508	2583	3208	3850
#规上工业企业	个	1992	1955	2448	3083
R&D活动人员数	人	31334	38330	45123	57333
#规上工业企业	人	28974	36064	39400	51386
#全时人员	人	21914	28655	32008	37032
R&D人员折合全时当量合计	人年	18524	27809	36038	46200
#规上工业企业	人年	17177	26634	31743	44335
#研究人员	人年	3502	5161	6558	7243
R&D经费内部支出	万元	413840	516701	716221	830190
按执行部门分					
规上工业企业	万元	390728	495099	612516	748347
科研机构	万元	14211	12166	92239	68365
高等院校	万元	3542	3528	5556	7569
其他企事业单位	万元	5358	5908	5909	5909
按活动类型分					
基础研究	万元	501	691	50653	23512
应用研究	万元	9572	18253	18719	18165
试验发展	万元	403766	497757	646850	788513
按资金来源分					
政府资金	万元	22055	31237	85894	53970
企业资金	万元	374463	463927	613432	753387
境外资金	万元	6703	10021	3083	5626
其他资金	万元	10619	11516	13810	17207
按使用项目分					
日常性支出	万元	363143	433603	539954	728069
资产性支出	万元	50697	83097	176266	102121
R&D经费内部支出占GDP比重	%	1.10	1.22	1.51	1.66
R&D经费外部支出	万元	15362	12383	14921	29557
R&D产出情况					
专利申请数	件	4932	4994	6060	8384
#发明专利	件	911	1433	1323	2751
专利授权数	件	164	205	112	194
#发明专利	件	16	25	25	73
有效发明专利数	件	828	2044	3457	2367
专利所有权转让及许可数	件	228	170	552	152
专利所有权转让及许可收入	万元	3216	9572	16763	10960
集成电路布图设计登记数	件				
植物新品种权授予数	项	1	2		1
形成国家或行业标准数	项	141	181	63	219
发表科技论文数	篇	1242	1205	1266	1370
出版科技著作数	种	32	26	31	30
工业新产品产值	万元	3041803	5501675	6945494	8643848
工业新产品销售收入	万元	3019395	5391190	6373687	8385864

12-4 主要年份国有企事业单位科学技术人员

Scientific and Technical Personnel in State-owned Enterprises and Institutions in Main Years

单位：人

项目	1990年	1995年	2005年	2010年	2011年	2012年
国有企事业单位科技人员数	11629	16856	42593	40025	41370	41336
#工程技术人员	1084	1718	1839	1438	1427	1426
农业技术人员	432	230	290	172	216	217
卫生技术人员	1430	1988	16188	11171	11117	10762
科学研究人员	21	52	77	16	21	24
教学人员	7524	11553	21717	24010	25084	25412
经济人员	278	329	636	1184	1393	1261
会计人员	581	484	1299	1454	1426	1556
统计人员	170	77	82	91	90	79

注：2010年起，国有企事业单位科技人员为在编在岗人员数。

12-5 主要年份三种专利申请量与授权量

Three Kinds of Patents Application Accepted and Granted in Main Years

单位：件

项目	1990年	1995年	2000年	2005年	2010年	2011年	2012年
申请量	34	325	1653	6694	21654	24455	29199
发　明	1	5	35	245	3143	4214	5568
实用新型	5	70	386	1971	7677	10822	13167
外观设计	28	250	1232	4478	10834	9419	10464
授权量	30	262	1399	3114	20397	19353	20900
发　明	1	8	4	24	442	758	1381
实用新型	4	41	344	1116	7529	7977	10667
外观设计	25	213	1051	1974	12426	10618	8852

12-6 主要年份各类技术合同签订情况

Basic Statistics on Technical Contracts Signed by Type in Main Years

项　　目	1990年	1995年	2000年	2005年	2010年	2011年	2012年
技术合同项目数(项)	5	46	110	50	90	163	152
#技术开发合同	3		1	41	79	126	105
技术咨询合同				2		1	
技术转让合同	2	44	78	1	2	6	5
技术服务合同		2	31	6	9	30	42
技术合同金额(万元)	12	1804	3469	4058	18366	31966	14516
#技术开发合同			1000	1888	6878	14984	11278
技术咨询合同				80		8	
技术转让合同	12	1656	2007	2000	11046	16403	1220
技术服务合同		148	1362	90	442	572	2018
技术合同实现金额(万元)	7	1623	2398	2522	17891	29923	13577
#技术开发合同			700	1427	6402	13962	10339
技术咨询合同				35		8	
技术转让合同	7	1535	1260	1000	11046	15381	1220
技术服务合同		88	438	60	442	572	2018

12-7 主要年份高新科技发展情况

Basic Statistics on High-tech Development in Main Years

项　　目	单 位	1995年	2000年	2005年	2010年	2011年	2012年
高新技术企业							
企业数	个	11	66	247	334	412	526
总产值	亿元	30.55	274.41	925.07	1240.59	1214.43	1368.39
总收入	亿元	26.76	266.49	927.72	1249.50	1261.27	1417.25
出口总额	亿美元	0.54	7.34	71.59	99.08	94.71	94.78
从业人员数	人	6400	36304	171812	246134	227920	245196
#科技活动人员	人	832	8663	34448	72833	53259	53907
高新技术产品							
产品	个	27	177	947	1430	1250	1601
总产值	亿元	31.43	186.00	1062.40	2353.70	2756.86	3323.48
#电子与信息技术	亿元			726.92	1407.39	1650.06	2472.18
生物技术	亿元			8.20	51.93	20.01	25.50
新材料技术	亿元			51.43	115.46	101.25	296.40
光机电一体化技术	亿元			146.94	153.74	149.51	197.90
新能源高效节能技术	亿元			32.71	95.52	124.77	123.22
环保技术	亿元			6.58	4.95	13.58	13.58
其他	亿元			89.63	524.70	697.67	194.69
销售收入	亿元			1033.64	2316.74	2682.64	3278.51
#出口销售收入	亿元			651.99	1510.87	1672.93	2113.31
实现利税	亿元			66.06	116.82	151.31	113.20

注：1. 高新技术企业情况2009年以前为省级高新技术企业情况，2009年起为国家级高新技术企业情况。
2. 高新技术产品情况从2010年起，统计口径为规模以上工业企业。

12-8 主要年份科学技术成果项数

Achievements for Scientific and Technological Research in Main Years

单位：项

项目	1985年	1990年	1995年	2000年	2005年	2010年	2011年	2012年
获省级科技进步奖		1	4	6	3	8	13	9
市级科技进步奖	68	31	22	47	75	87	84	93
农业方面	30	8	3	13	9	7	7	7
一等奖	1	4		2	1	2	2	2
二等奖	3	3		5	3	2	2	3
三等奖	18	1	3	6	5	3	3	2
四等奖	8							
工业方面	32	18	14	24	42	57	46	57
特等奖				1	2			
一等奖	1	3		5	7	13	12	14
二等奖	8	11	5	8	19	21	17	21
三等奖	10	4	9	10	14	23	17	22
四等奖	13							
医药卫生方面	6	5	5	10	25	23	24	29
特等奖								
一等奖			1			5	7	6
二等奖		1		2	4	6	11	9
三等奖	2	4	4	8	19	12	6	14
四等奖	4							
市长奖						5	7	5
技术成果类						1	1	
荣誉类						4	2	5
创新企业奖						4	4	1

12-9 科技创新平台情况（2010-2012年）

Basic Statistics on Technology Innovation Platform (2010-2012)

单位：个

项目	2010年	2011年	2012年
科技创新平台合计	207	224	230
#公共科技创新平台	10	11	13
行业性科技创新平台	34	30	32
#行业性科技创新平台(企业研究院)	11	12	12
专业镇技术创新平台	15	12	12
科技行业技术联盟	8	6	8
企业创新平台	125	124	124
#企业工程技术研究开发中心	125	124	124
#国家级	1	2	1
省级	40	42	45
市级	84	80	78
实验室	28	59	61
#国家级			
省级	5	9	11
市级	23	50	50
#重点实验室		31	31
资助获中国合格评定国家认可委员会认可实验室	10	19	19

12-10 历年国有企事业单位科学技术人员数

Scientific and Technical Personnel in Enterprises and Institutions over Years

单位：人

年份	科学技术人员	工程技术人员	农业技术人员	卫生技术人员	科学研究人员	教学人员	经济人员	会计人员	统计人员
1980	6619	370	190	1076	19	4282		564	99
1981	7473	463	217	1166	23	4978		501	109
1982	7547	468	243	1241	28	4954		509	101
1983	8453	525	315	1699		5257		109	109
1984	9033	615	307	1791		5534		261	201
1985	9166	663	318	2319	6	5129		491	214
1986	9490	768	358	2398	5	5222		501	203
1987	10945	797	378	2426	6	6495		583	222
1988	12495	1014	359	3093	24	7064	72	590	197
1989	11306	960	388	1393	19	7394	281	632	181
1990	11629	1084	432	1430	21	7524	278	581	170
1991	15004	2170	405	3347	13	7843	308	558	153
1992	16809	2522	375	3690	18	8659	313	613	153
1993	18491	2871	264	4074	112	9511	290	916	141
1994	20198	3490	272	4513	57	9949	300	657	112
1995	23104	3944	255	4878	66	11613	329	750	171
1996	24693	4037	263	5356	51	12287	360	740	143
1997	26103	4258	294	5504	48	13371	418	882	280
1998	26582	4321	310	4862	48	14316	376	894	171
1999	28789	4620	288	5246	48	15604	416	946	152
2000									
2001	24677	795	121	5493	31	17309	252	273	40
2002	34168	5261	246	6538	28	18756	555	1319	184
2003	33070	996	159	11145	44	19614	314	741	57
2004	39398	1752	276	14541	141	20905	561	613	74
2005	42593	1839	290	16188	77	21717	636	1299	82
2006	46371	1913	462	18401	70	22434	763	1512	93
2007	49032	2037	492	19528	71	23364	892	1832	92
2008	51729	2375	343	20955	50	24063	1048	1827	100
2009	55097	2302	284	21679	43	26741	1129	1940	122
2010	40025	1438	172	11171	16	24010	1184	1454	91
2011	41370	1427	216	11117	21	25084	1393	1426	90
2012	41336	1426	217	10762	24	25412	1261	1556	79

注：2010年起为在编在岗人员数。

12-11 历年三种专利与技术合同签订情况

Basic Statistics on Three Kinds of Patents and Technical Contracts Signed by Type over Years

年 份	三种专利申请量(件)	#发明	三种专利授权量(件)	#发明	技术合同签订项目数（项）	技术合同签订金额(万元)	技术合同实现金额(万元)
1990	34	1	30	1	5	12	7
1991	70	3	50	1	4	10	10
1992	102	5	78	2	3	23	10
1993	100	3	90	1	2	24	2
1994	104	4	100	2	14	2537	1756
1995	325	5	262	8	46	1804	1623
1996	333	3	312	4	133	4839	3756
1997	725	1	321		78	2036	800
1998					62	3048	2398
1999					20	1124	1077
2000	1653	35	1399	4	110	3469	2398
2001	2914	71	1753	5	89	1335	953
2002	3100	90	2680	10	91	766	730
2003	3865	93	2858	14	58	700	680
2004	4325	185	3167	26	69	4278	2726
2005	6694	245	3114	24	50	4058	2522
2006	9879	553	4872	28	25	13644	13402
2007	13842	876	6752	44	53	8510	8138
2008	14406	1188	8093	115	54	12838	3694
2009	19106	1593	12918	254	60	6996	6264
2010	21654	3143	20397	442	70	15760	15572
2011	24455	4214	19353	758	163	31966	29923
2012	29199	5568	20900	1381	152	14516	13577

12-12 历年科学技术成果项数

Scientific and Technological Achievements over Years

单位：项

年份	获国家级科技进步奖	获省级科技进步奖	获市级科技进步奖	特等奖	一等奖	二等奖	三等奖	四等奖
1979			25			5	4	16
1980			27			2	11	14
1981			35		2	4	11	18
1982			62		1	3	21	37
1983			38		2	6	11	19
1984			35			11	11	13
1985			68		2	11	30	25
1986			86		5	14	27	40
1987			59		2	19	25	13
1988		1	37		6	10	16	5
1989		1	32		4	6	22	
1990		1	31		7	15	9	
1991		4	35	1	3	18	13	
1992		3	19		4	7	8	
1993			18	1	3	8	6	
1994		6	23		4	9	10	
1995		4	22		1	5	16	
1996		3	32		7	6	19	
1997		4	32		7	6	19	
1998		6	38	1	2	11	24	
1999		9	39		6	11	22	
2000		6	47	1	7	15	24	
2001		4	51		4	23	24	
2002		3	47		7	15	25	
2003		4	50		7	14	29	
2004		6	60	1	6	19	34	
2005		3	75	2	10	25	38	
2006		3	70	1	8	24	37	
2007		4	83	1	18	26	38	
2008		10	83		19	28	36	
2009		19	85		22	24	39	
2010		4	87		20	29	38	
2011		13	77		21	30	26	
2012		9	93		22	33	38	

12-13 主要年份各类学校情况

Basic Statistics on Schools by Type in Main Years

项　　目	单位	1985年	1990年	1995年	2000年	2005年	2010年	2011年	2012年
普通高等专业学校									
学校数	所			1	1	4	5	6	6
毕业生数	人			395	985	1439	8105	9463	12625
招生数	人			576	1440	7273	12660	16837	20507
在校学生数	人			1628	3241	16645	38293	45081	52381
教职工数	人			262	293	1761	3192	3542	3805
#专任教师	人			119	161	1081	2174	2435	2729
中等职业技术学校									
学校数	所	3	17	20	23	21	26	26	24
毕业生数	人	234	2210	4641	9554	9062	14028	14774	14099
招生数	人	1508	3866	8697	8759	10971	18477	17812	18269
在校学生数	人	3363	8919	18737	23144	29487	47531	48159	50092
教职员工数	人	217	619	1134	1608	2230	2996	3048	3092
#专任教师	人	150	434	859	1221	1621	2341	2403	2448
普通中学									
学校数	所	106	64	69	77	134	190	199	203
毕业生数	人	12317	18688	24165	30261	48935	73810	76816	79449
#高中生	人	2055	2527	3231	7120	12233	20816	22095	23398
招生数	人	16978	20441	33086	41488	70843	93196	95155	96348
#高中生	个	2915	3389	6099	9048	19540	24668	25647	25758
在校学生数	人	46596	61188	92481	112418	191044	258276	263076	267918
#高中生	人	6304	8572	13653	24677	52283	70398	73644	75851
教职员工数	人	3266	4001	5900	6012	12177	16946	19563	20133
#专任教师	个	2420	2963	4381	5027	9640	14572	15262	15858
小　学									
学校数	所	583	570	595	552	414	330	324	322
毕业生数	人	17901	18262	27257	33684	61173	77429	80463	87733
招生数	人	20264	26158	36702	53786	84784	108900	114763	123290
在校学生数	人	134421	162664	195063	272793	480923	552377	578279	608118
教职员工数	人	7009	7797	9560	9131	21964	28298	28420	28745
#专任教师	人	6017	6785	8060	7946	17478	23733	24787	25379

注：中等职业技术学校包含市技工学校，不含一般成人中专，下同。

12-13 续表

项　　目	单位	1985年	1990年	1995年	2000年	2005年	2010年	2011年	2012年
成人高等专业教育									
当年招生人数	人				1697	6387	6086	6345	5999
在校学生数	人	403	531	1254	3642	12665	21703	20497	18759
#广播电视大学	人	403	531	1254	1362	4169			
学龄儿童入学									
学龄儿童总数	人	103460	133011	177791	247555	423058	511439	539286	567799
已入学学龄儿童数	人	103282	132934	177787	247539	423058	511439	539286	567799
学龄儿童入学率	%	99.8	99.9	100.0	100.0	100.0	100.0	100.0	100.0
小学毕业生升学									
小学毕业生人数	人	17901	18262	27257	33684	61173	77429	80463	87733
已升学人数	人	14235	17413	27166	33627	61095	77429	80463	87733
小学毕业生升学率	%	79.5	95.4	99.2	99.8	99.9	100.0	100.0	100.0
初中毕业生升学									
初中毕业生人数	人	10262	16161	20933	23141	36702	52994	54721	56051
已升学人数	人	3955	7134	17876	20896	34536	51881	53626	54818
初中毕业生升学率	%	38.5	43.6	85.4	90.3	94.1	97.9	98.0	97.8
普通高中毕业生升学									
高考省线入围人数	人	285	224	809	2646	6455	13761	15501	17316
高考录取人数	人	543	759	2095	5017	12461	20099	21358	22127
#高考升本科人数	人	274	250	697	1678	5161	11033	11901	13377
普通高中毕业生升学率	%	26.5	31.2	64.9	70.5	96.5	95.1	94.5	95.9
幼儿园									
幼儿园数	所	83	86	258	452	511	727	749	791
在园幼儿数	人	31382	47040	84263	111763	111330	208373	227656	255657
幼教职工数	人	984	1387	1427	7517	12567	22122	26242	28103
#专任教师	人	841	1160	1160	4618	7002	13947	15232	16689
全国各类大中专院校招生人数									
国家各大(学)专院校在我市招生人数	人				11680	35831	40795	43161	45256
国家各中专学校在我市招生人数	人				3359	2768			
全市教育经费投入总额	亿元				15.5	50.2	94.4	125.1	136.3

12-14 历年各类学校在校学生数

Number of Students Enrollment by Type of School over Years

单位：人

年　份	普通高等学校	中等职业技术学校	#技工学校	普通中学	#高中	小　学	幼儿园
1949		151		1960	318	52781	
1952		543		3394	296	70359	
1957		561		6652	848	88001	
1962		380		9736	1513	119998	
1965		358		10469	1397	160931	
1970				60150	9873	118128	
1975		689		49569	10847	168236	
1978		595		76025	12092	161114	18228
1979		450		62292	7010	158008	12774
1980		386		54829	6909	154871	7630
1981		450		43514	5755	150857	8103
1982		661		41683	4654	144754	14650
1983		967		42777	4798	135440	15436
1984		1070		46488	5766	134567	23702
1985		3363		46596	6304	134421	31382
1986		3891	60	49445	7880	140700	38195
1987		5847	117	54435	8367	144287	42569
1988		7120	229	59268	8201	150097	42845
1989		7878	293	61955	7687	155852	44110
1990		8919	582	61188	8572	162664	47040
1991		10938	915	60146	8725	170064	51051
1992		13161	1277	65171	9711	175203	57537
1993	1079	14176	1516	75305	10297	180114	65310
1994	1451	16084	2025	85827	11409	186244	72552
1995	1628	18737	2404	92481	13653	195063	84263
1996	1771	22614	2567	95150	16887	205957	85709
1997	2025	24821	2598	98005	20609	221838	100059
1998	2171	25588	2291	101202	22490	235787	103585
1999	2241	25073	2001	105518	23084	248759	109773
2000	3241	23144	1746	112418	24677	272793	111763
2001	3802	23638	2039	122115	28232	295384	112963
2002	5144	25363	2152	135256	32398	342804	108898
2003	6884	27664	2564	149656	38143	386890	104832
2004	9104	28487	2559	171336	45050	448296	112538
2005	16645	29487	2618	191044	52283	480923	111330
2006	22005	35403	2905	214638	57662	496828	118683
2007	25178	40429	3063	234578	61151	520684	130932
2008	28656	45419	3238	248442	63962	528644	156362
2009	33992	46538	3268	249464	66750	511160	176249
2010	38293	47531	2955	258276	70398	552377	208373
2011	45081	48159	2915	263076	73644	578279	227656
2012	52381	50092	2833	267918	75851	608118	255657

12-15 历年各类学校当年招收学生数

Number of New Students Enrollment by Type of School over Years

单位：人

年 份	普通高等学校	中等职业技术学校	#技工学校	普通中学	#高中	小 学
1949		102				
1952		285		1666	190	
1957		80		2516	259	
1962		45		3716	566	
1965		134		3656	476	
1970				45069	7919	
1975		188		28329	5930	
1978		250		29788	3436	30152
1979		200		25364	3900	28315
1980		186		24083	3906	26857
1981		266		16808	2594	26461
1982		162		17492	2317	23970
1983		573		18111	2344	19604
1984		1964		16609	2477	17644
1985		1508		16978	2915	20264
1986		1977	60	17944	2781	25867
1987		2883	64	21720	2665	28926
1988		2832	112	23280	2925	29437
1989		2966	124	21877	2686	27539
1990		3866	343	20441	3389	26158
1991		5008	445	21430	3266	27539
1992		5696	487	26161	3751	28804
1993	567	5835	633	29948	3944	31841
1994	569	7064	952	32229	4440	34495
1995	576	8697	996	33086	6099	36702
1996	711	10119	978	33576	7385	39689
1997	750	9718	798	35140	8273	42066
1998	750	9664	852	36423	8118	43802
1999	802	9060	665	38400	8199	47715
2000	1440	8759	527	41488	9048	53786
2001	1597	8850	1116	44729	10727	56521
2002	2190	9417	1153	49881	11852	65066
2003	3104	9809	874	55564	15147	71476
2004	3804	10618	1044	63085	17467	80525
2005	7273	10971	1100	70843	19540	84784
2006	8032	13357	1250	79985	20866	89663
2007	8519	16491	1297	85816	21146	92860
2008	10218	17475	1163	89808	22313	94641
2009	12863	15767	1598	88325	23631	92281
2010	12660	18477	2052	93196	24668	108900
2011	16837	17812	1180	95155	25647	114763
2012	20507	18269	1306	96348	25758	123290

12-16 历年各类学校当年毕业生数

Number of Graduates by Type of School over Years

单位：人

年 份	普通高等学校	中等职业技术学校	#技工学校	普通中学	#高中	小 学
1949				414	83	
1952		48		588	44	14349
1957		87		1365	203	59056
1962		209		2680	468	28418
1965		44		2363	393	32508
1970				15081	1954	26187
1975		374		20842	4937	25009
1978		244		43035	8533	30480
1979		244		33554	8004	28925
1980		250		19578	3096	27294
1981		191		13308	3046	27215
1982				10483	3004	27348
1983		260		10752	1940	26723
1984		230		10969	1404	17870
1985		234		12317	2055	17901
1986		660		13527	1271	17533
1987		819		13895	2296	23183
1988		1323		15322	2966	23054
1989		1960	60	15310	2716	20315
1990		2210	57	18688	2527	18262
1991		2634	112	19820	2559	19186
1992		2126	123	19323	2643	23308
1993	30	2915	390	18363	3020	26893
1994	197	5035	445	20360	2787	28500
1995	395	4641	541	24165	3231	27257
1996	560	5813	753	27675	3483	27156
1997	484	6745	691	28729	3834	27992
1998	556	8316	918	29839	5448	29794
1999	714	9044	796	30109	6585	31426
2000	985	9554	634	31291	7120	33684
2001	1019	7748	684	32409	7553	37077
2002	753	7171	542	34204	8277	40611
2003	1350	7217	509	39031	8784	45599
2004	1506	8630	917	43471	10676	51831
2005	1439	9062	777	48935	12233	61173
2006	2269	9422	677	55856	15486	70474
2007	5096	10061	754	60436	17354	74681
2008	6486	10728	821	66594	19315	78037
2009	7292	11927	962	71811	20550	78027
2010	8105	14028	956	73810	20816	77429
2011	9463	14774	831	76816	22095	80463
2012	12625	14099	993	79449	23398	87733

12-17 历年各级各类学校专任教师数

Number of Full-time Teachers by Level and Type of School over Years

单位：人

年 份	普通高等学校	中等职业技术学校	#技工学校	普通中学	#高中	小 学	幼儿园
1978		34		3641	638	5641	
1979		31		3367	369	6136	
1980		29		2996	370	6022	
1981		32		2343	344	6433	
1982		38		2210	284	6186	
1983		61		2361	296	5830	
1984		63		2352	309	5971	
1985		150		2420	354	6017	841
1986		168	5	2463	407	6515	720
1987		208	7	2709	490	6878	941
1988		306	9	3007	540	7112	967
1989		422	11	2949	462	6743	980
1990		434	12	2963	488	6785	1160
1991		513	15	3019	500	6831	1470
1992		600	17	3198	479	7164	1569
1993	99	737	16	3583	610	7314	1773
1994	113	767	26	4001	710	7610	1920
1995	119	859	34	4381	733	8060	1160
1996	119	924	40	4310	886	7410	2175
1997	123	1151	89	4404	991	7518	2753
1998	125	1338	93	4632	1065	7912	3247
1999	133	1205	92	4699	1149	7198	3715
2000	161	1221	84	5027	1310	7946	4618
2001	231	1286	121	5348	1411	8693	4701
2002	290	1445	125	6373	1769	10880	5351
2003	312	1548	124	7069	1976	12490	5505
2004	560	1531	134	8437	2367	15512	6218
2005	1081	1621	150	9640	2817	17478	7002
2006	1357	1801	122	10953	3215	18717	7919
2007	1569	1965	156	12272	3678	20511	9279
2008	1691	2218	161	12995	3976	21203	11072
2009	1890	2321	160	13598	4178	21130	12419
2010	2174	2341	171	14572	4541	23733	13947
2011	2435	2403	167	15262	4851	24787	15232
2012	2729	2448	180	15858	5026	25379	16689

12-18 历年各类学校入(升)学率与高考入围人数

Number of Passing College Entrance Examination and Proportion of Students Entering Schools over Years

年份	学龄儿童入学率(%)	小学毕业生升学率(%)	初中毕业生升学率(%)	高中毕业生升学率(%)	高考入围人数(人)	省线入围人数
1978	98.36	85.80	14.30	8.14	846	250
1979	98.70	76.00	16.00	6.71	566	166
1980	98.85	73.40	25.40	7.15	222	140
1981	98.72	50.56	27.40	8.64	239	154
1982	99.06	54.40	34.40	8.04	252	115
1983	99.75	57.60	37.40	12.34	245	150
1984	99.65	70.80	29.86	43.32	619	220
1985	99.83	79.52	38.54	26.50	534	285
1986	99.90	84.71	33.89	43.69	595	228
1987	99.94	83.60	40.10	27.09	644	297
1988	99.93	89.88	42.00	30.63	925	315
1989	99.92	96.18	43.30	32.92	977	284
1990	99.94	95.35	43.60	31.20	759	224
1991	99.92	96.18	45.20	26.22	861	268
1992	99.94	97.58	56.00	35.59	994	312
1993	99.95	97.79	68.50	39.23	1102	423
1994	99.96	98.94	79.02	62.75	1823	586
1995	99.99	99.16	85.40	64.90	2095	809
1996	99.98	96.45	86.70	66.80	2160	1093
1997	99.99	99.90	87.35	60.00	2212	1215
1998	99.99	99.86	88.25	47.69	2348	1315
1999	99.99	99.87	89.80	53.15	3501	1790
2000	99.99	99.83	90.30	70.50	5017	2646
2001	100.00	99.77	90.50	74.82	5651	3225
2002	100.00	99.80	91.10	83.00	6873	3759
2003	100.00	99.80	92.10	93.60	9167	4509
2004	100.00	99.90	93.30	96.70	10756	5452
2005	100.00	99.90	94.10	96.50	11196	6455
2006	100.00	100.00	94.80	82.90	11359	7652
2007	100.00	100.00	95.20	89.10	13275	9185
2008	100.00	100.00	96.60	91.00	15047	9987
2009	100.00	100.00	97.00	87.50	17487	12569
2010	100.00	100.00	97.90	95.10	18845	13761
2011	100.00	100.00	98.00	94.50	19588	15501
2012	100.00	100.00	97.80	95.90	22127	17316

12-19 历年文化艺术、文物事业机构数

Number of Institutions in Culture and Cultural Relics over Years

年 份	电影放映单位(个)	#影剧院	艺术表演团体(个)	群众艺术馆(个)	文化站(广电文化中心)(个)	公共图书馆(个)	公共图书馆藏书量(万册)	博物馆(个)	档案馆(座)
1978	167	5	1	1	33	1	11	2	1
1979	157	5	1	1	33	1	15	2	1
1980	65	5	1	1	33	1	16	2	1
1981	75	6	1	1	33	1	17	2	1
1982	53	6	1	1	33	1	19	2	1
1983	49	6	1	1	33	1	19	2	1
1984	65	6	1	1	33	1	24	2	1
1985	60	7	1	1	33	3	30	2	1
1986	61	9	2	1	33	3	30	2	1
1987	70	13	4	1	33	8	30	2	1
1988	78	15	5	1	33	3	30	2	1
1989	102	26	6	1	33	3	30	2	1
1990	114	26	7	1	33	5	30	2	1
1991	126	36	5	1	33	6	31	2	1
1992	150	50	2	1	33	8	37	2	1
1993	163	53	2	1	33	11	47	2	1
1994	193	63	2	1	33	14	58	2	1
1995	218	97	2	1	33	15	68	2	1
1996	225	111	4	1	33	16	73	2	1
1997	229	130	4	1	33	26	84	2	1
1998	233	147	4	1	32	26	106	3	1
1999	210	87	4	1	32	20	133	3	1
2000	192	87	1	1	32	18	97	3	1
2001	145	84	1	1	32	21	99	3	1
2002	162	81	2	1	32	24	109	3	2
2003	107	55	2	1	32	346	289	3	2
2004	88	78		1	32	397	631	6	2
2005	70	31		1	32	473	660	16	2
2006	51	34		1	33	1222	771	21	2
2007	51	34		1	33	1271	896	23	2
2008	40	34	1	1	33	387	515	23	1
2009	40	62	4	1	33	504	599	31	1
2010	46	62	4	1	33	505	701	30	1
2011	52	62	5	1	33	622	771	31	1
2012	59	11	6	1	33	649	1020	31	1

12-20 主要年份广播电视事业发展情况

Basic Statistics on Radio and Television Industry in Main Years

项　　目	单位	1985年	1990年	1995年	2000年	2005年	2010年	2011年	2012年
广播电台	个		1	1	1	1	1	1	1
电视台	个	1	1	1	1	1	1	1	1
镇街文化广电服务中心	个						28	28	28

12-21 主要年份安全生产事故中火灾事故情况

Basic Statistics on Fire of Production Accidents in Main Years

项　　目	单位	1995年	2000年	2005年	2010年	2011年	2012年
发生起数	起	24	60	13	13	7	10
受伤人数	人	8	34	7	8	11	
死亡人数	人	12	31	18	15	14	11
损失折款	万元	1596	1022	22	21	56	4758
平均每起事故损失	万元	66.50	17.03	1.67	1.63	8.00	475.77

注：本表数据来源于市安监局。

12-22 主要年份交通事故发生情况

Basic Statistics on Traffic Accidents in Main Years

项目	单位	1995年	2000年	2005年	2010年	2011年	2012年
发生起数	起	2015	7386	7124	4874	4491	4302
受伤人数	人	2061	8217	8642	5355	4999	4831
死亡人数	人	692	903	921	528	496	492
损失折款	万元	685	1759	934	682	566	561
平均每起事故损失	元	3400	2382	1312	1400	1261	1304

注：本表数据来源于市安监局，含道路和水上交通事故。

12-23 各类卫生事业机构及床位、人员数（2012年）

Number of Health Care Institutions, Beds and Employed Personnel by Type of Institution (2012)

项目	机构数(个)	实有床位数(张)	卫生工作人员(人)	卫生技术人员	
					执业(助理)医师
总计	2222	24617	49353	40597	14043
医疗机构	2218	24617	48987	40279	13964
县及县以上及其他医院	73	24042	36608	29767	9799
#综合医院	54	21457	33111	27217	9026
中医医院	2	1062	1377	1132	317
专科医院	17	1523	2120	1418	456
社区卫生服务中心(站)	387		5277	4027	1552
村(社区)卫生站	1206		3077	3077	1194
门诊部	279		2067	1744	719
诊所、卫生所、医务室	270		744	700	403
妇幼保健院	1	455	948	778	237
专科疾病防治院	1	120	236	169	60
急救中心(站)	1		30	17	
采供血机构	1		110	89	9
疾病预防控制中心	1		157	130	70
卫生监督所	1		99	99	
健康教育所	1				
其他卫生机构					

12-24 主要年份卫生事业机构各类人员数

Number of Personnel in Health Institutions in Main Years

单位：人

项　　目	1980年	1985年	1990年	1995年	2000年	2005年	2010年	2011年	2012年
总　　计	3599	3945	4503	6149	9289	22127	46102	48142	49353
卫生技术人员	2960	3305	3902	5290	6915	18757	37487	39582	40597
执业(助理)医师	980	1177	1724	2326	2819	8130	13214	13644	14043
注册护士	584	643	1164	1751	2673	6303	14689	16217	16914
药剂人员	236	572	546	602	706	1281	2284	2352	2503
检验人员	120	147	152	216	367	781	1412	1427	1504
其　他	1040	766	316	395	350	2262	5888	5942	5633
其他技术人员	8		13	96	174	786	1217	1191	1409
管理人员	299	282	243	432	597	1080	2418	2391	2115
工勤人员	332	358	345	331	453	1504	4980	4978	5231

注：1. 从2002年起卫生技术人员按新口径分类。
2. 2004年起，卫生方面包含诊所、卫生所、医务室及村卫生室的数据，与往年数不可比。

12-25 医疗机构服务情况（2012年）

Services in Medical Institutions (2012)

指标名称	诊疗人数(人次)	门、急诊	入院人数(人)	病死率(%)	健康检查人数(人次)
总　　计	70607139	70368809	838194	0.29	4542522
医院	33801663	33658515	808276	0.30	3382789
#综合医院	31881917	31748308	754000	0.32	3253481
中医医院	1192750	1189531	19542		38873
专科医院	726996	720676	34734	0.02	90435
#民营医院	4740534	4695330	184635	0.40	965003
社区卫生服务中心(站)	14975276	14934600			1125757
村卫生站	14819148	14786072			
门诊部(所)	5587099	5565878			
妇幼保健院(所、站)	1153027	1152818	28643		8171
专科疾病防治院(所、站)	184146	184146	1275		25805

12-26 历年卫生事业机构、床位、人员数

Number of Health Care Institutions, Beds and Personnel over Years

年 份	机构数(个)	实有床位数(张)	卫生工作人员(人)		
				#卫生技术人员	#执业(助理)医 师
1978	82	2257	3242	2636	768
1979	81	2271	3466	2863	971
1980	83	2207	3599	2960	1167
1981	83	2210	3724	3091	1102
1982	83	2292	3886	3253	1097
1983	83	2098	3985	3335	1088
1984	83	2231	4005	3351	1132
1985	87	2323	3945	3305	1201
1986	88	3054	4084	3454	1179
1987	88	3393	4475	3490	1304
1988	87	3640	4582	3829	1537
1989	87	3677	4522	3874	1620
1990	85	3866	4503	3902	1721
1991	85	4085	4578	3946	1755
1992	83	4517	4705	4127	1832
1993	99	4940	5247	4524	2023
1994	98	5365	5689	4930	2221
1995	99	5798	6149	5290	2299
1996	99	5288	6712	5766	2449
1997	151	5505	7286	6283	2605
1998	171	5892	8306	7139	2955
1999	176	6241	8697	7575	3080
2000	174	7081	9289	8065	3309
2001	173	7474	9323	8064	3429
2002	178	8641	10692	9011	3523
2003	172	9820	11584	9807	3758
2004	944	10797	15058	13053	4870
2005	874	11972	22127	18757	8130
2006	1210	13293	27128	22904	8629
2007	1649	15227	34151	28758	10446
2008	2106	16778	40449	33113	11869
2009	2106	18080	43561	35766	12884
2010	2229	19980	46102	37487	13214
2011	2249	22814	48142	39582	13644
2012	2222	24617	49353	40597	14043

注：2004年起本表包含诊所、卫生所、医务室及村卫生室的数据，与往年数不可比。

12-27 历年体育运动情况

Basic Statistics on Sports over Years

年 份	破（超）世界纪录（次）	破（超）亚洲纪录（次）	破（超）全国纪录（次）	在国际比赛中获得金牌总数（枚）	在全国比赛中获得金牌总数（枚）	在省级比赛中获得金牌总数（枚）	市级运动会参赛运动员人数（人）	为国家省输送运动员（人）
1978			9	1	7	26	2500	11
1979	2		2	1	7		2250	18
1980			12		2		2400	14
1981			11	4	19		2500	13
1982			14	4	30	15	2650	9
1983	1		7	5	6		2420	7
1984			1	16	5		2500	33
1985		2	1	5	2		1960	7
1986		7	4	7	4	52	2420	16
1987	1	1	8	35	9		2130	19
1988	3	1	4	14	25		2540	15
1989			27	5	43	92	6430	18
1990	13	5		4	6		2370	25
1991	2	1	8	12	14		4800	16
1992	2	3	21	10	6		15000	30
1993	2	8	5	12	9		10350	16
1994	34	2	24	6	23	157	2720	14
1995	10	1		5	37		1500	14
1996				3	16		7800	13
1997	10	9		1	6	36	6000	74
1998	2	4	28	4	28	87	1560	74
1999				4	33		6000	6
2000			3	4	91		4000	6
2001				13	22	48	8000	5
2002				2	35	58		11
2003		7		2	31	82		6
2004	3	4	4	49	34			18
2005				2	13	46	8564	44
2006				20	21	32	16000	
2007				3	25	46	2740	9
2008				3	16	49	630	17
2009		1	3	8	20	94	1550	17
2010				4	6	40	9895	16
2011				8	27	116	3300	25
2012					10	127	3400	16

12-28 主要年份体育比赛成绩

Basic Statistics on Sports Achievements in Main Years

项　目	单位	1980年	1985年	1990年	1995年	2000年	2005年	2010年	2011年	2012年
破世界纪录	次			13	10					
获得国际赛冠军	个		5	4	5	4		4		
破亚洲纪录	次		2	5	1					
破全国纪录	次	12	1			3				
获国际比赛奖牌										
金牌	枚		5	4	5	4	2	4	8	
银牌	枚			4	3	2	1	2	1	
铜牌	枚						2		3	
获全国比赛金牌	枚	2	2	6	37	91	13	6	27	10

注:“获得国际赛冠军”及“获国际比赛奖牌”含地区赛。

12-29 主要年份群众体育活动情况

Basic Statistics on Activities of Mass Sports in Main Years

项　目	单位	1980年	1985年	1990年	1995年	2000年	2005年	2010年	2011年	2012年
举办市级运动会	次	5	4	9	4	2	4	16	2	12
市级运动会参赛运动员人数	人	2400	1960	2370	1500	4000	8564	9895	3300	3400
举办全民健身活动	次								174	373
参加全民健身活动人数	万人次								77.30	43.41
为国家和省输送运动员人数	人	14	7	25	14	6	47	16	25	16

12-30 主要年份治安案件情况

Basic Statistics on Public Security Cases in Main Years

项　　目	单位	2005年	2010年	2011年	2012年
治安案件受理数	起	13760	44979	50877	50321
扰乱公共秩序	起	2816	198	203	388
妨害公共安全	起	243	630	923	1008
侵犯人身、财产权利	起	6044	24551	25355	27454
#盗窃	起	2599	10513	6909	5629
妨害社会管理秩序	起	4296	19600	24396	21471
#吸毒	起	2697	4455	5297	6225
卖淫、嫖娼	起	153	663	582	601
赌博或为赌博提供条件	起	942	10464	13597	9591
治安案件查处数	起	12490	37818	45133	44932
扰乱公共秩序	起	2797	186	193	380
妨害公共安全	起	237	583	718	703
侵犯人身、财产权利	起	4865	17687	19925	22475
#盗窃	起	2007	5476	3574	3004
妨害社会管理秩序	起	4246	19362	24297	21374
#吸毒	起	2665	4317	5259	6210
卖淫、嫖娼	起	147	659	580	600
赌博或为赌博提供条件	起	938	10408	13587	9575
查处违法人员数	人	20692	42815	48230	49071
扰乱公共秩序	人	4486	363	356	633
妨害公共安全	人	218	618	662	723
侵犯人身、财产权利	人	6769	14145	15578	14772
#盗窃	人	2676	3802	3161	2719
妨害社会管理秩序	人	8201	27689	31634	32943
#吸毒	人	3922	4885	5967	7085
卖淫、嫖娼	人	415	1506	1348	1363
赌博或为赌博提供条件	人	3179	17191	19339	19291

注：本表数据来源于市公安局。

12-31 主要年份刑事案件情况

Basic Statistics on Criminal Cases in Main Years

单位：起

项　　目	2005年	2010年	2011年	2012年
刑事案件立案数	44641	36965	37831	38180
危害公共安全	264	586	849	994
破坏市场经济秩序	451	577	451	1537
侵犯公民人身权利	3748	3587	3107	2913
#杀人	87	69	52	27
伤害	3071	2882	2525	2275
强奸	266	336	288	306
侵犯财产	39657	31251	32156	30986
#抢劫	9144	5045	5168	4536
抢夺	3736	3250	3906	3845
入室盗窃	4150	8779	7134	6863
盗窃机动车	16050	3526	4189	2798
诈骗	897	3203	2681	3070
妨害社会管理秩序	571	963	1266	1746
#毒品犯罪	215	587	826	930
刑事案件破案数	13682	16271	17796	18959
危害公共安全	161	550	829	988
破坏市场经济秩序	439	388	210	1049
侵犯公民人身权利	2037	1933	1644	1811
#杀人	73	61	48	25
伤害	1586	1449	1225	1325
强奸	171	224	195	226
侵犯财产	10598	12534	13935	13500
#抢劫	3582	2531	2797	2612
抢夺	1525	1700	2076	1986
入室盗窃	1081	4182	3970	3091
盗窃机动车	1880	631	1064	525
诈骗	202	536	435	566
妨害社会管理秩序	490	866	1178	1609
#毒品犯罪	210	569	815	909

注：本表数据来源于市公安局。

12-32 主要年份道路交通违法情况

Basic Statistics on Traffic Offense in Main Years

项　目	单位	2005年	2010年	2011年	2012年
处理违法起数	万起	61.04	282.48	278.42	263.31
#机动车	万起		280.44	276.42	258.91
非机动车	万起		1.01	1.11	1.44
行人和乘车人	万起		1.03	0.88	2.96
教育人次	万人次		26.14	27.24	11.34
#机动车	万人次		25.38	26.48	7.96
非机动车	万人次		0.35	0.42	1.06
行人和乘车人	万人次		0.41	0.33	2.32
罚款总额	万元	9991.70	44359.52	45213.47	40037.85
#机动车	万元		44355.07	45210.39	40036.58
非机动车	万元		2.80	1.82	1.28
行人和乘车人	万元		1.65	1.26	

注：本表数据来源于市公安局。

12-33 主要年份律师、公证、基层司法及普法教育

Basic Statistics on Lawyers, Notarization, Grassroots Judicial Work and Law Education in Main Years

项　目	单位	1990年	1995年	2000年	2005年	2010年	2011年	2012年
律师工作								
律师事务所	个	2	8	22	46	115	130	146
律师	人	12	85	221	625	1366	1513	1668
担任常年法律顾问	家	102	364	416	1426	2752	2839	3091
民事诉讼代理	件	145	343	1203	6543	12041	15892	14800
非诉讼法律事务	件	110	1162	2079	13391	19967	16366	21173
刑事辩护及代理	件	295	235	438	2496	2776	2913	3568
国内经济案件诉讼代理	件	107	348	1100	1801	1133	1198	990
涉外及港澳台经济案件诉讼代理	件	165	11	27	160	299	80	87
公证工作								
公证处	个	1	1	1	1	3	3	3
公证人员	人	10	19	20	48	96	106	105
办结公证总数	件	5347	11377	28910	60685	48296	57298	61486
#国内民事公证	件	113	2795	19607	19627	35104	42708	46012
国内经济公证	件	236	898	1776	34015	3536	4266	3669
涉外公证（含港澳台）	件	4998	7684	4809	4607	9656	10324	11805
基层司法工作								
法律服务所	个	24	29	32	32	32	32	32
法律工作人员	人	70	115	117	191	360	378	386
担任法律顾问	家	62	482	695	1208	724	758	666
民事诉讼代理	件	26	568	1221	1790	1090	1207	709
非诉讼代理	件	129	1045	3016	3837	1549	1298	1161
调解工作								
人民调解委员会	个	904	813	750	814	1552	1494	1492
调解人员	人	3664	3466	3644	4556	17438	20240	16005
调解民间纠纷	件	2005	2632	2642	15210	15239	16216	16332
参加普法教育人数	万人	79.9	170	79	571	288	587	570

12-34 历年计划生育情况

Basic Statistics on Family Planning over Years

年 份	已婚育龄妇女人数(人)	女性初婚人数(人)			落实各种节育措施	
			23周岁及以上	不 足20周岁	育龄夫妇(对)	节育率(%)
1978	130438	10974			103414	79.28
1979	134483	11914			104612	77.79
1980	136742	9270	8920		101190	74.00
1981	141079	13714			112956	80.07
1982	142324	8729			115302	81.01
1983	149928	12664			129035	86.06
1984	156444	9579			138785	88.71
1985	159985	11208			142974	89.37
1986	168611	13983	11899		150545	89.30
1987	176868	13492	11252		158857	89.80
1988	183022	12419	10072		164889	90.10
1989	196042	13691	10228	15	172799	88.20
1990	202505	13264	9670	29	177425	87.60
1991	211544	13790	10834	12	184254	87.10
1992	224624	15295	10375	13	190151	84.70
1993	235150	13932	9793	6	200673	85.30
1994	243456	13213	9833	9	208234	85.50
1995	252627	13921	10430	26	215339	85.20
1996	258873	13556	10114	20	221805	85.70
1997	263646	12968	9623	9	226674	85.98
1998	267982	12366	9260	7	233007	86.95
1999	280455	12114	8999	4	249368	88.92
2000	285244	11122	7050	14	249741	87.55
2001	295395	10903	6755	14	260077	88.04
2002	303134	11635	7082	8	268243	88.49
2003	306157	12441	7767	5	266832	87.16
2004	312941	13957	9318	2	273387	87.36
2005	317062	13251	9057	5	275685	86.95
2006	323479	12460	9117	3	279246	86.33
2007	331556	13621	10333	1	293733	85.29
2008	343051	14485	11053	1	291049	84.84
2009	352115	14450	11157	5	297559	84.51
2010	367607	14265	11019	4	309054	84.07
2011	380570	14899	11820	1	320135	84.12
2012	384854	14875	12049	12	320907	83.38

12-34 续表

年　份	领取独生子女证		人口出生率（‰）		政策生育率（%）	多孩率（%）
	累　计（人）	领证率（%）	省计划指　标	实　际完　成		
1978			13.0	18.73		
1979			12.0	24.13		
1980	423	1.84	13.0	24.41	69.72	23.38
1981			11.9	21.86		
1982			18.1	19.07		
1983			17.0	16.74		
1984			15.5	15.54		
1985	1954	1.22	15.3	15.37	88.94	4.27
1986	2029	1.20	16.5	16.44	92.45	2.93
1987	2257	1.28	16.0	16.11	93.16	1.97
1988	2408	1.32	17.0	16.75	93.58	2.14
1989	2116	1.10	17.0	17.06	92.35	2.54
1990	2288	1.13	17.5	17.07	89.08	3.71
1991	2514	1.19	20.0	17.91	89.55	3.65
1992	2335	1.04	19.8	19.31	86.08	4.44
1993	2905	1.24	20.0	18.38	87.29	4.50
1994	3245	1.33	19.2	17.88	86.50	4.71
1995	3389	1.34	19.3	17.76	85.09	4.33
1996	4028	1.63	18.3	17.05	83.83	4.87
1997	4514	1.71	18.0	16.50	83.98	4.68
1998	4971	1.85	16.6	15.31	90.01	2.92
1999	21228	7.57	15.8	14.55	89.31	2.92
2000	30921	10.84	15.3	12.11	90.17	1.77
2001	41636	14.10	14.9	11.16	91.75	1.57
2002	49188	16.23	14.3	10.35	91.80	1.31
2003	51814	16.92	12.5	10.34	92.45	1.24
2004	55425	17.71	12.5	10.86	93.48	1.14
2005	60426	19.06	11.5	10.62	94.32	0.80
2006	69507	21.49	11.6	10.14	94.69	0.71
2007	73766	22.25	11.0	10.39	95.48	0.63
2008	77919	22.71	11.0	10.77	96.28	0.54
2009	80738	22.93	11.0	10.67	96.75	0.75
2010	81736	22.23	11.5	10.90	96.97	0.99
2011	83312	21.89	12.5	10.92	98.65	0.90
2012	81341	21.14	12.0	13.32	84.23	3.42

注：领证率是期末已领取独生子女证人数除以全市已婚育龄妇女人数。

12-35 主要年份优抚和社会救济、福利事业

Basic Statistics on Special Care, Social Relief and Welfare in Main Years

项　　目	单位	1990年	1995年	2000年	2005年	2010年	2011年	2012年
优抚事业								
优抚收养性事业单位数	个	1	1	1	1	1	1	1
优抚收养性单位收养人数	人次	19	11	7	8	8	9	6
优抚事业费用	万元	340	213	412	2400	4555	2761	327
社会救济								
社会救济人数	人次	4433	7273	19914	23886	36516	32584	24732
年末社会散居孤老残幼人数	人	2026	2444	1596	875	11	11	11
#定期救济对象	人	142	569	29	18	11	11	11
社会救济福利事业费	万元		190	993	6955	21199	21629	29309
自然灾害生活救助费	万元	4.6	70	50	744	139	269	274
社会福利								
社会福利事业单位数	个	1	1	3	36	38	38	34
#民政部门办	个	1	1	3	4	3	3	3
社会福利事业单位收养人数	人	363	351	406	2240	2609	2689	2269
#民政部门办	人	363	351	406	893	1715	1816	1560
社会福利企业单位	个	9	15	20	20	10	9	6
安排“四残”人员就业人数	人	199	239	393	351	321	296	351
社会福利事业单位费用支出	万元					9770	10773	18373
敬老院情况								
全市敬老院个数	个			32	31	35	35	31
年末敬老院供养人数	人			833	1347	894	873	709
“五保户”情况								
年末列入“五保户”户数	户			1545	1575	1254	1199	1009
年末列入“五保户”人数	人			1587	1575	1263	1210	1015
全年“五保户”费用支出	万元			2198	1594	1536	1724	1703
城乡基层社会保障								
建立社会保障网络镇街数	个	33	24	32	32	32	32	32

注：“五保户”人数及费用支出含敬老院供养人数及费用支出。

12-36　主要年份婚姻登记情况

Basic Statistics on Marriage Registration in Main Years

项　　目	单位	1985年	1990年	1995年	2000年	2005年	2010年	2011年	2012年
准予登记结婚	对	11870	13668	14170	10535	14293	11415	7025	18292
#涉外、华侨、港澳台同胞	对	638	709	510	213	113	79	144	121
准予登记离婚	对				448	1319	1856	1074	3191
#涉外、华侨、港澳台同胞	对						9	16	35

12-37　主要年份环境保护基本情况

Basic Statistics on Environmental Protection in Main Years

项　　目	单 位	1985年	1990年	1995年	2000年	2005年	2010年	2011年	2012年
废水									
废水排放总量	万吨	3100	5259	9681	40703	69049	87953	102679	100713
#工业废水	万吨	2686	4124	5511	11753	21355	29742	29091	26909
城镇生活废水处理率	%						71.5	84.2	85.6
废气									
工业废气排放量	亿标立方	34	307	556	1318	1695	2340	2686	2929
工业固体废物									
固体废物产生量	万吨	16	112	108	149	284	313	558	544
固体废物处置量	万吨	8	2	1	5	12	15	122	123
固体废物处置率	%	48.2	1.8	0.9	66.9	99.8	4.8	22.1	22.6
固体废物综合利用率	%	37.5	17.9	18.2	63.8	86.5	95.0	77.9	78.1
城市环境质量及污染控制									
空气污染指数	范围值				21-87	24-123	14-108	18-110	17-111
交通干线噪声平均值	db				68.4	67.9	67.7	67.8	67.9
汽车尾气排放达标率	%				81.2	88.1	81.0	83.6	84.0
全市生活垃圾无害化处理率	%						37.3	41.2	54.4

12-38 主要年份社会保险事业情况

Basic Statistics on Social Insurance in Main Years

项　　　目	单 位	1995年	2000年	2005年	2010年	2011年	2012年
参加各种社会保险人数	万人次	149.33	338.33	804.71	2726.37	2464.69	2553.93
#失业保险	万人次	6.49	17.84	177.78	279.90	299.38	312.78
养老保险	万人次	8.46	82.95	182.49	421.84	481.05	513.29
医疗保险	万人次	7.60	88.21	189.40	592.27	602.41	616.86
工伤保险	万人次	126.78	136.53	235.10	469.08	479.44	494.14
社会保险基金总收入	万元	18155	127964	491540	1544112	1793980	2079191
#失业保险	万元	60	2732	28954	27008	32312	35928
养老保险	万元	7697	85245	343429	976257	1248706	1492100
医疗保险	万元	2057	23488	82138	333342	415349	450985
工伤保险	万元	8341	15891	35073	62806	97613	100178
社会保险待遇总支出	万元	10520	40454	217413	547470	732642	743640
#失业保险	万元	16	440	6676	9681	14015	17464
养老保险	万元	7450	24130	135958	194055	229260	276347
医疗保险	万元	1436	3694	51021	299975	426244	378327
工伤保险	万元	1618	11703	22220	41910	63123	71502

注：1. 1997年起养老保险因口径调整，与以前年份不可比。
　　2. 参加各种社会保险总人数包含生育保险人数。

12-39 主要年份最低生活保障情况

Basic Statistics on Minimum Income Relief in Main Years

项　　　目	单 位	2005年	2010年	2011年	2012年
居民最低生活保障线	元/人月	320	440	440	440
村民最低生活保障线	元/人月	300	440	440	440
居民最低生活保障户数	户	1911	1599	3796	3015
居民最低生活保障人数	人	4885	3643	9415	6598
居民最低生活保障金支出	万元	790	673	2001	2942
村民最低生活保障户数	户	6705	12214	8744	7433
村民最低生活保障人数	人	17426	30785	21959	17423
村民最低生活保障金支出	万元	2318	5922	4299	5965

12-40 主要年份市政建设情况

Basic Statistics on Municipal Construction in Main Years

项目	单位	1995年	2000年	2005年	2010年	2011年	2012年
水厂日供水能力	万立方米	66	187	480	700	700	461
年末供水管道总长度	公里	1580	2106	3680	16268	22553	17734
全年供水量	万立方米	18802	70046	155100	165607	173433	164047
#生活用水量	万立方米	7361	21433	51100	28560	39628	39311
园林绿地面积	万平方米	800	1396	10298	33092	36091	39422
#公园绿地面积	万平方米				9075	9837	9956
建成区绿化覆盖面积	万平方米	1885	1364	9436	35571	38035	37628
建成区土地面积	平方公里	82.00	147.68	657.17	798.48	854.3	888.4
公园数	个		273	931	1004	1039	1057
公园面积	公顷		1423	2887	11130	10546	12146

注：公园数和公园面积不含森林公园数及其面积。

12-41 主要年份液化石油气及天然气供应情况

Basic Statistics on Supply of Liquefied Petroleum Gas and Natural Gas in Main Years

项目	单位	1995年	2000年	2005年	2010年	2011年	2012年
年末液化石油气用户数	户	63419	110172	144797	956018	1176076	898589
#家庭用气户数	户	62246	106910	144035	870921	1040167	832792
全年液化石油气供气量	吨	25935	58287	161930	344762	338089	312920
#家庭用量	吨	18948	22104	24354	188108	195508	226562
年末天然气用户数	户			5027	147047	178780	210967
#家庭用气户数	户			5000	116239	177279	197082
全年天然气供气量	万立方米			350	23414	36486	43195
#家庭用量	万立方米			45	1600	2047	2055
年末汽车天然气加气站	个				10	15	19
年末汽车天然气加气站全年供气量	万立方米				5324	7800	8987

注：本表2000-2006年为市喜威液化石油气有限公司与市中液石油气有限公司的业务量，2007年起调整为市城市管理局统计口径。

12-42 历年环境保护基本情况

Basic Statistics on Environmental Protection over Years

年份	降水PH均值	酸雨PH均值	酸雨频率(%)	酸雨占总降水量(%)	交通干线噪声平均值(db)	工业废水排放量(万吨)
1982						1842
1983						2068
1984	6.53					2127
1985						2686
1986					76.8	2416
1987	6.64	5.38		38.4	78.9	3501
1988	4.85	4.72	63.6	75.1	77.6	3029
1989	5.44	5.21	31.0	31.8	74.1	3976
1990	6.15	5.30	29.5	43.3	75.9	4124
1991	5.24	4.78	35.4	30.4	72.2	5506
1992	5.10	4.71	36.8	35.9	76.0	5849
1993	4.93	4.41	22.5	29.1	75.8	6500
1994	5.33	4.81	23.2	25.5	72.6	7057
1995	5.89	5.49	9.2	13.7	70.3	5511
1996	5.83	5.40	14.7	10.9	70.4	6033
1997	4.94	4.84	56.6	76.4	70.6	8930
1998	4.79	4.70	60.3	80.4	70.3	7989
1999	4.97	4.68	40.0	50.5	69.1	11719
2000	4.90	4.67	50.7	56.6	68.7	11753
2001	5.06	4.74	31.6	43.9	68.2	11694
2002	5.47	5.09	29.3	28.8	68.0	25587
2003	4.55	4.44	60.5	77.2	67.9	23389
2004	4.47	4.41	69.6	85.7	68.0	22501
2005	4.07	4.00	65.7	86.2	67.9	21355
2006	3.57-6.57	4.70	50.0	42.4	68.0	24134
2007	5.21	4.36-7.59	54.2	59.2	67.9	91260
2008	4.83	4.65	60.1	63.6	63.6	33359
2009	5.03	4.88	51.8	67.3	63.8	29960
2010	5.11	4.97	52.2	65.3	67.7	29742
2011	5.02	4.59	47.6	31.9	67.8	29091
2012	5.26	4.98	33.7	47.2	67.9	26909

注：2007年工业废水排放量统计口径变更，与往年不可比。

主要统计指标解释

Explanatory Notes on Main Statistical Indicators

工程技术人员 指在国民经济各行业从事工程技术工作的自然科学技术专业人员，包括：高级工程师、工程师、助理工程师、技术员和未评定职称的技术人员。

农业技术人员 指在国民经济各行业从事农业技术工作的自然科学技术专业人员，包括：高级农艺师、农艺师、助理农艺师、技术员和未评定职称的技术人员。

科学研究人员 指在国民经济各行业从事科学技术活动的科学技术专业人员，包括：正副研究员、助理研究员、研究实习员、技术员和未评定职称的技术人员。

专利申请量 指企业当年向国家知识产权局提出专利申请并被受理项数。

专利授权量 指企业当年获国家知识产权局授予专利权的项数。

发明 专利法及其实施细则所称的发明是指对有关产品、方法或其改进所提出的新的技术方案。

实用新型 专利法及其实施细则所称的实用新型是指对产品的形状、构造或者其结合所提出的适于实用的新的技术方案。

外观设计 专利法及其实施细则所称的外观设计是指对产品的形状、图案、色彩或者其结合所作出的富有美感并适于工业上应用的新设计。

毕业生数 毕业生数是指上学年内，具有学籍的学生学完教学计划规定的全部课程，考试及格，实际毕业的学生数。不包括结业生和肄业生。

招生数 招生数是指新学年开始时，按规定实际招收入学的新生数，不包括重读生和复学生（高等教育包括春秋两季招收的学生）。

在校学生数 是指具有学籍的注册学生总数。

学龄儿童入学率 指调查范围内已入小学学习的学龄儿童占校内外学龄儿童总数（包括弱智儿童在内，但不包括盲聋哑儿童）的比重。

电影放映单位 指具有放映机器设备、固定或不固定的放映场所与专职或兼职的放映技术人员，经有关部门登记批准，经常为一定的观众对象放映电影的机构。包括经批准对外开放进行营业，并与电影发行放映管理机构分帐的专用放映单位和军委系统租片单位。

公共图书馆藏书量 是指本馆已编目的古籍、图书、期刊和报纸的合订本、小册子、手稿，以及缩微制品、录像带、录音带、光盘等视听文献资料数量之和。

医疗机构 是指根据《医疗机构管理条例》的规定，经登记取得《医疗机构执业许可证》的机构。包括医院、社区卫生服务中心（站）、卫生院、门诊所、诊疗所、医务室、村卫生室、妇幼保健院（所、站）、专科疾病防治院（所、站）、急救中心、临床检验中心。

医院 指设有固定床位能收容病人住院并能为病人提供医疗、护理服务的医疗机构。包括县及县以上医院、农村乡卫生院、其他医院三部分。按所属性质分为卫生部门、工业及其他部门、集体经济单位三类。其中县及县以上医院按业务性质分为综合医院和专科医院。

实有床位 是指报告期末固定实有床位数，包括正规床、简易床、监护床、正在消毒和修理床位、因扩建或修理而停用的床位，不包括产科新生儿床、待产室待产床、库存床、观察床、临时加床和病人家属陪伴床。

诊疗人数 是指所有诊疗工作的总人数。包括病人来院就诊的门诊、急诊人次和出诊、下地段、赴家庭病床、到工厂、农村、工地、会议、集体活动等外出诊疗的人次数，以及外出进行的单项健康检查及健康咨询指导人次数。并包括本院职工的诊疗的人次数及局部的单项健康检查人数。

卫生技术人员 指卫生事业机构支付工资的全部固定职工和合同制职工中现任职务为卫生技术工作的专业人员。包括中医师、西医师、中西医结合高级医师、护师、中药师、西药师、检验师、其他技师、中医士、西医士、护士、助产士、中药剂士、西药剂士、检验士、其他技士、其他中医、护理员、中药剂员、西药剂员、检验员，其他初级卫生技术人员。

病死率 是指年内住院病人中死亡人数占出院人数的比例。

刑事案件立案 是指实施违反我国刑事法律的行为，构成犯罪的案件。根据《关于公安机关办理刑事案件程序规定》第一百六十二条，公安机关受理案件后，经过审查，认为有犯罪事实需要追究刑事责任，且属于自己管辖的，由接受单位制作《刑事案件立案报告书》，经县级以上公安机关负责人批准，予以立案。

刑事案件破案 根据《关于公安机关办理刑事案件程序规定》第一百六十六条的规定，刑事案件破案应当具备下列条件：（一）犯罪事实已有证据证明；（二）有证据证明犯罪事实是犯罪嫌疑人实施的；（三）犯罪嫌疑人或者主要犯罪嫌疑人已经归案。

治安案件查处 是指触犯了《中华人民共和国治安管理处罚条例》规定，给社会或个人造成一定危害，公安机关依照相关法律、法规和规定，应当给予处罚的行为事件。

律师 指受聘参加法律顾问处工作，担任法律顾问、刑（民）事代理人、刑事辩护人，办理非诉讼事件、解答法律询问，代写法律事务文书等主要从事律师业务的专职法律工作者和兼职律师。

公证人员 指在国家公证机关依法办理公证事务的司法人员。包括公证员、助理公证员和在公证处工作的其他人员。

调解人员 在人民调解委员会担负调解民间一般民事纠纷和轻微违法行为所引起的纠纷的工作人员。包括调解委员会的委员和调解小组的调解员。

社会保险基金收入 是指根据国家规定，由纳入基本社会保险范围的单位，按照国家规定的缴费基数和缴费比例缴纳的社会统筹基金，以及通过其他方式取得的形成基金来源的收入，包括：单位缴纳的社会统筹基金收入、财政补贴收入、利息收入、其他收入。

社会保险基金支出 是指按照国家政策规定的开支范围和开支标准从社会统筹基金中支付给参加基本社会保险人员个人的费用，以及由于保险关系转移、上下级之间调剂资金等原因而发生的支出。

社会福利事业单位 指集中收养社会孤老、残、幼的机构。包括由民政部门管理的社会福利院、儿童福利院、精神病人福利院和城镇集体办的福利院，以及农村集体举办的敬老院。

社会福利事业单位收养人数包括民政部门管理的和城镇及农村集体举办的社会福利事业单位中收养的老人、少年儿童、缺乏生活自理能力的残疾人员和精神病人。

废水排放总量 包括工业废水和生活污水。工业废水指工业企业在生产、科研过程中向企业外部排放的所有排放口的废水量总和。生活污水指居民或职工在饮用、洗涤、烹饪、清洁卫生等过程中排放的污水量。

十三、能　源

Energy

13-1 主要年份能源主要指标

Main Indicators of Energy in Main Years

项　　目	单　位	2005年	2010年	2011年	2012年
地区能源消费总量(等价值)	万吨标准煤	1885.78	2812.65	2896.05	2935.73
地区能源消费总量(当量值)	万吨标准煤	1800.14	2438.84	2512.46	2437.34
电力消耗	亿千瓦时	419.83	562.00	586.07	604.28
单位GDP能耗(等价值)	吨标准煤/万元	0.864	0.691	0.632	0.604
单位GDP能耗(当量值)	吨标准煤/万元	0.825	0.599	0.548	0.501
规模以上工业综合能源消费量(当量值)	万吨标准煤	1203.77	1496.06	1482.56	1385.42
规模以上工业发电量	亿千瓦时	378.81	368.26	384.78	336.28
火力发电转换效率	%	37.05	38.91	39.21	39.79
供热转换效率	%		91.18	86.72	87.06
能源消费比上年增长	%		8.03	2.97	1.37
电力消费比上年增长	%		13.40	4.28	3.11
地区生产总值比上年增长	%		10.27	7.95	6.10
能源消费弹性系数			0.78	0.37	0.22
电力消费弹性系数			1.30	0.54	0.51

注：单位GDP能耗(等价值)和单位GDP能耗(当量值)2006-2010年按2005年可比价计算；2011年开始按2010年可比价计算。

13-2 主要年份综合能源平衡表
Overall Energy Balance Sheet in Main Years

单位：万吨标准煤

项 目	2005年	2010年	2011年	2012年
可供本地区消费的能源量	1885.78	2812.65	2896.05	2935.73
年初库存量	77.54	133.72	115.00	177.25
一次能源生产量		31.61	17.79	15.08
回收能	1.31			
外省调入量	1866.72	2564.50	2361.06	3027.08
进口量	9.31	205.75	509.50	593.71
境内轮船和飞机在境外加油量				
本省调出量(-)		-7.31	-4.47	-701.32
出口量(-)				
境外轮船和飞机在境内加油量(-)				
年末库存量(-)	-69.11	-115.62	-102.83	-176.07
加工转换投入(-)产出(+)量	-0.08	-15.28	-22.63	-22.32
火力发电				
供热		-13.93	-21.36	-21.58
洗选煤				
炼焦				
炼油				
制气				
损失量	63.74	42.12	39.90	60.17
运输和输配损失	63.74	42.12	39.90	60.17
终端消费量	1821.96	2755.25	2833.52	2853.24
第一产业	5.04	6.86	7.42	7.94
农、林、牧、渔业	5.04	6.86	7.42	7.94
第二产业	1334.30	1952.34	1969.34	1957.47
工业	1305.42	1913.74	1932.12	1920.44
建筑业	28.88	38.59	37.21	37.03
第三产业	304.16	483.54	521.94	530.44
交通运输、仓储及邮政业	84.47	139.41	148.88	151.86
批发、零售业和住宿、餐饮业	137.35	198.74	214.63	216.03
其他	82.34	145.39	158.43	162.55
生活消费	178.45	312.51	334.83	357.39
城镇	178.45	312.51	334.83	357.39
乡村				
平衡差额				
消费量合计	1885.78	2812.65	2896.05	2935.73

13-3 主要年份石油平衡表
Petroleum Balance Sheet in Main Years

单位：万吨

项　目	2005年	2010年	2011年	2012年
可供量	413.06	401.11	385.84	373.98
生产量				
外省(区、市)调入量	408.02	394.75	379.21	372.97
进口量	1.82	0.03		43.02
境内轮船和飞机在境外加油量				
本省(区、市)调出量(-)		2.09		42.66
出口量(-)				
境外轮船和飞机在境内加油量(-)				
年初年末库存差额	3.22	8.42	6.63	0.65
年初库存量	18.64	28.29	19.87	16.79
年末库存量(-)	15.42	19.87	13.24	16.14
消费量	413.06	401.11	385.84	373.98
消费量分组一				
农林牧渔业	1.23	2.47	2.42	2.50
工业	249.88	135.08	112.06	97.84
建筑业	14.49	14.55	14.32	13.15
交通运输、仓储和邮政业	54.93	85.15	88.21	87.53
批发、零售业和住宿、餐饮业	28.76	48.56	51.75	50.94
其他	21.91	33.18	34.61	34.82
生活消费	41.86	82.11	82.47	87.20
消费量分组二				
终端消费	266.62	389.49	385.20	373.49
#工业	103.76	123.56	111.52	97.45
加工转换损失	146.12	11.53	0.54	0.39
火力发电	146.12	11.53	0.54	0.39
供热				
炼油损耗				
制气				
损失量	0.32	0.09	0.10	0.10
平衡差额				

13-4 主要年份煤炭平衡表

Coal Balance Sheet in Main Years

单位：万吨

项　　目	2005年	2010年	2011年	2012年
可供量	1596.99	2039.07	2147.51	1967.59
生产量				
外省(区、市)调入量	1582.15	1750.92	1439.79	2245.89
进口量	9.40	287.97	713.18	610.88
本省(区、市)调出量(-)		8.02	9.15	889.17
出口量(-)				
年初年末库存差额	5.44	8.20	3.69	-0.01
年初库存量	70.80	129.63	121.43	212.03
年末库存量(-)	65.36	121.43	117.74	212.04
消费量	1596.99	2039.07	2147.51	1967.59
消费量分组一				
农林牧渔业				
工业	1596.99	2037.77	2146.13	1967.49
建筑业				
交通运输、仓储和邮政业				
批发、零售业和住宿、餐饮业		1.20	1.28	
其他				
生活消费				
消费量分组二				
终端消费	132.22	374.94	385.56	382.01
#工业	132.22	373.74	384.28	382.01
用于加工转换	1464.76	1664.03	1761.85	1585.48
火力发电	1464.76	1448.61	1533.55	1348.24
供热		217.88	235.74	244.21
洗煤损耗				
炼焦				
制气				
型煤加工损耗		-2.46	-7.44	-6.97
损失量	0.01	0.10	0.10	0.10
平衡差额				

13-5 主要年份全社会用电量

Total Consumption of Electricity in Main Years

单位：万千瓦时

项　　目	2005年	2010年	2011年	2012年
全社会用电量总计	4198289	5619996	5860652	6042842
#各行业用电量合计	3855742	5036303	5203144	5330800
#第一产业	9761	10279	12359	13943
第二产业	3397588	4317267	4403326	4486991
第三产业	448393	708757	787459	829866
城乡居民生活用电量合计	342547	583693	657508	712042
各行业用电分类				
农、林、牧、渔业	9761	10279	12359	13943
工业	3374306	4262339	4351290	4429317
#轻工业	1357858	1821542	1801345	1786637
重工业	2016448	2440797	2549945	2642680
#采矿业	8112	8044	6902	5689
制造业	3044575	3953169	4040754	4092221
#电力、燃气及水的生产和供应业	321619	301126	303634	331407
#电力、热力的生产和供应业	240737	183361	193762	231088
#电厂生产全部耗用电量	41656	51096	67171	37014
线路损失电量	190736	132265	126591	194074
燃气生产和供应业	654	1778	2158	1835
水的生产和供应业	80228	115987	107714	98484
建筑业	23282	54928	52036	57674
交通运输、仓储和邮政业	14425	26524	31830	40549
#交通运输业	8614	16173	19913	26932
仓储业	2084	5774	6930	8516
邮政业	3727	4577	4987	5101
信息传输、计算机服务和软件业	15277	35085	40150	46289
批发、零售业和住宿、餐饮业	282238	376037	412597	429271
#批发和零售业	148555	194549	223703	242870
住宿和餐饮业	130153	181488	188894	186401
金融、房地产、商务及居民服务业	65223	117690	131271	133107
#金融业	16158	14156	14977	15580
房地产业	21976	23489	23941	23292
租赁和商务服务、居民服务和其他服务	27089	80045	92353	94235
公共事业及管理组织	71230	153421	171611	180650
#科学研究、技术服务和地质勘查业	4550	2950	2945	2763
#地质勘查业	248	45	10	14
水利、环境和公共设施管理业	26633	56514	67243	67106
#水利管理业	12157	5208	10119	5885
教育、文化、体育和娱乐业	13596	29655	33757	37683
#教育	4793	8615	10548	14111
卫生、社会保障和社会福利业	12151	8964	12051	14444
公共管理和社会组织、国际组织	14300	55338	55615	58654

13-6 规模以上工业综合能源消费量（2012年）

Overall Energy Consumpiton of Industrial Enterprises above Designated Size (2012)

单位：万吨标准煤

指　　标	2012年
合　计	1385.42
采矿业	
煤炭开采和洗选业	
石油和天然气开采业	
黑色金属矿采选业	
有色金属矿采选业	
非金属矿采选业	
开采辅助活动	
其他采矿业	
制造业	833.29
农副食品加工业	20.64
食品制造业	7.18
酒、饮料和精制茶制造业	5.79
烟草制品业	
纺织业	61.18
纺织服装、服饰业	7.02
皮革、毛皮、羽毛及其制品和制鞋业	16.97
木材加工和木、竹、藤、棕、草制品业	2.40
家具制造业	6.98
造纸和纸制品业	441.14
印刷和记录媒介复制业	4.18
文教、工美、体育和娱乐用品制造业	10.93
石油加工、炼焦和核燃料加工业	0.21
化学原料和化学制品制造业	16.28
医药制造业	0.75
化学纤维制造业	0.74
橡胶和塑料制品业	33.77
非金属矿物制品业	61.37
黑色金属冶炼和压延加工业	2.08
有色金属冶炼和压延加工业	2.81
金属制品业	11.05
通用设备制造业	7.75
专用设备制造业	6.72
汽车制造业	3.33
铁路、船舶、航空航天和其他运输设备制造业	1.81
电气机械和器材制造业	24.49
计算机、通信和其他电子设备制造业	67.21
仪器仪表制造业	5.11
其他制造业	3.33
废弃资源综合利用业	0.04
金属制品、机械和设备修理业	0.01
电力、热力、燃气及水生产和供应业	552.13
电力、热力生产和供应业	547.13
燃气生产和供应业	0.02
水的生产和供应业	4.98

注：2012年起，本表行业分类按《国民经济行业分类》(GB/T4754-2011)进行分类，数据与往年不可比。

主要统计指标解释

Explanatory Notes on Main Statistical Indicators

能源生产总量　指一定时期内全国（地区）一次能源生产量的总和，是观察全国（地区）能源生产水平、规模、构成和发展速度的总量指标。一次能源生产量包括原煤、原油、天然气、水电、核能及其他动力能（如风能、地热能等）发电量。不包括低热值燃料生产量、生物质能、太阳能等的利用和由一次能源加工转换而成的二次能源产量。

能源消费总量　指一定时期内全国（地区）生产和生活消费的各种能源的总和，是观察能源消费水平、构成和增长速度的总量指标，能源消费总量包括原煤和原油及其制品、天然气、电力等。能源消费总量分为三部分，即终端能源消费量、能源加工转换损失量和损失量。

(1)终端能源消费量　指一定时期内全国（地区）生产和生活消费的各种能源在扣除了用于加工转换二次能源消费量和损失量以后的数量。

(2)能源加工转换损失量　指一定时期内全国（地区）投入加工转换的各种能源数量之和与产出各种能源产品之和的差额。它是观察能源在加工转换过程中损失量变化的指标。

(3)能源损失量　指一定时期内能源在输送、分配、储存过程中发生的损失和由客观原因造成的各种损失量。不包括各种气体能源放空、放散量。

能源生产弹性系数　是研究能源生产增长速度与国民经济增长速度之间关系的指标。计算公式：

$$能源生产弹性系数=\frac{能源生产总量增长速度}{国民经济增长速度}$$

国民经济增长速度，可根据不同的目的或需要，用国民生产总值，国内生产总值等指标来计算，本资料是采用国内生产总值指标计算的。

电力生产弹性系数　是研究电力生产增长速度与国民经济增长速度之间关系的指标。计算公式：

$$电力生产弹性系数=\frac{电力生产量增长速度}{国民经济增长速度}$$

能源消费弹性系数　是反映能源消费增长速度与国民经济增长速度之间比例关系的指标。计算公式：

$$能源消费弹性系数=\frac{能源消费量增长速度}{国民经济增长速度}$$

电力消费弹性系数　是反映电力消费增长速度与国民经济增长速度之间比例关系的指标。计算公式：

$$电力消费弹性系数=\frac{电力消费量增长速度}{国民经济增长速度}$$

能源加工转换效率　指一定时期内能源经过加工、转换后，产出的各种能源产品的数量与同期内投入加工转换的各种能源数量的比率。它是观察能源加工转换装置和生产工艺先进与落后、管理水平高低等的重要指标。计算公式：

$$能源加工转换效率=\frac{能源加工、转换产出量}{能源加工、转换投入量}\times 100\%$$

十四、镇街主要指标

Main Indicators of Towns

14-1 镇街生产总值

Gross Domestic Product by Town

单位：万元

镇街	(1991年) 地区生产总值	第一产业	第二产业	第三产业	(1992年) 地区生产总值	第一产业	第二产业	第三产业
全市	959073	134523	503220	321330	1108922	144115	592701	372106
莞城	22046	174	16612	5260	28881	108	22263	6510
石龙	25154	907	17669	6578	29467	1026	21163	7278
虎门	44900	10059	16412	18429	56539	10336	24781	21422
东城	23500	7179	13793	2528	32770	7362	21392	4016
万江	18518	3874	11653	2991	27997	3968	18928	5102
南城	13339	2219	8181	2939	18147	1973	12681	3493
中堂	14889	3300	9065	2524	19902	4360	10669	4873
望牛墩	11950	2794	7394	1762	13789	2854	8683	2252
麻涌	24449	10489	11478	2482	26907	9797	14294	2816
石碣	12556	2686	7660	2210	16967	2888	11140	2939
高埗	11546	3352	5163	3031	14295	4017	6503	3775
道滘	15659	4540	9542	1577	19009	4805	12003	2201
洪梅	6492	3879	1872	741	6906	2441	3435	1030
沙田	12616	6467	4552	1597	16779	6511	7850	2417
厚街	31303	5679	22403	3221	38272	6064	28528	3680
长安	24850	7961	13185	3704	36298	8980	21883	5435
寮步	23700	9030	8979	5691	30083	9256	12627	8200
大岭山	10557	5918	3123	1516	16175	6342	4928	4905
大朗	19481	11277	4870	3334	24694	10104	9836	4754
黄江	20403	2765	15888	1750	28355	3244	22864	2247
樟木头	10515	10515	2107	6426	13972	2212	8536	3224
清溪	8673	2076	4428	2169	12742	2405	6936	3401
塘厦	17826	6128	9049	2649	30454	6300	19988	4166
凤岗	8676	2698	5550	428	12119	3257	8146	716
谢岗	9472	2019	5197	2256	7178	2339	4236	603
常平	38008	13134	14511	10363	45046	11625	20103	13317
桥头	14030	4083	8114	1833	22099	5429	10336	6334
横沥	11125	2499	6349	2277	15673	2710	9342	3621
东坑	16245	3544	11393	1308	22332	3368	17294	1670
企石	16155	3731	9575	2849	21159	4699	13097	3363
石排	16123	2350	10727	3046	18091	2704	11839	3548
茶山	13328	3385	7146	2797	16377	4160	8782	3435

注：各镇街合计不等于全市数，下同。

14-1 续表 1

单位：万元

镇街	(1993年)				(1994年)			
	地区生产总值	第一产业	第二产业	第三产业	地区生产总值	第一产业	第二产业	第三产业
全市	1570491	143953	873114	553424	2170340	174796	1194928	800616
莞城	41307		32838	8469	55021		43120	11901
石龙	34182	582	21188	12412	48891	216	32738	15937
虎门	74808	11281	37710	25816	103070	14350	51597	37123
东城	37567	4379	25901	7287	44963	5223	30065	9675
万江	39317	4818	26939	7561	45953	5499	31186	9268
南城	23341	2767	16312	4262	46416	2811	38511	5094
中堂	31352	7282	16982	7089	34819	6271	19472	9076
望牛墩	15717	2642	10196	2879	18449	2796	11974	3679
麻涌	34553	9305	22223	3025	42676	9160	27917	5599
石碣	23877	2542	16311	5024	34401	2816	24582	7003
高埗	17843	4751	8347	4745	22368	5495	10877	5996
道滘	24306	5086	15471	3749	37062	5698	27835	14072
洪梅	8069	2265	4292	1512	9020	2406	4756	1858
沙田	24446	6574	14434	3438	31950	6196	20646	5107
厚街	57912	6707	44408	6796	101289	7615	77637	16037
长安	49862	9995	31962	7905	68914	11024	46939	10951
寮步	46311	9423	21926	14962	63089	12428	30205	20456
大岭山	22611	6717	7660	8234	27722	6725	11258	9739
大朗	32720	10237	15152	7331	46550	13958	21052	11540
黄江	37008	3021	30171	3816	47096	3254	39031	4811
樟木头	18265	1361	13994	2910	23438	1680	18008	3750
清溪	19533	3299	12076	4158	30510	4230	20391	5889
塘厦	41635	4353	31001	6281	80870	6396	65620	8854
凤岗	16961	3282	12778	901	24520	4166	19054	1300
谢岗	12063	2367	8997	699	16093	3365	11143	1585
常平	67921	12564	34518	20839	100294	13561	62109	24624
桥头	27654	5023	15085	7546	40632	6225	22445	11962
横沥	23825	23825	2604	13815	33565	3922	17444	12198
东坑	33565	4073	25007	4485	36161	4245	26665	5251
企石	28573	5167	17684	5722	34915	6545	21854	6516
石排	25462	2992	17949	4521	31920	3699	21172	7049
茶山	21196	4908	12096	4192	30233	6017	18221	5995

14-1 续表 2

单位：万元

镇街	(1995年)				(1996年)			
	地区生产总值	第一产业	第二产业	第三产业	地区生产总值	第一产业	第二产业	第三产业
全市	2962892	214306	1669723	1078863	3617502	248645	1994826	1374031
莞城	69318		52710	16608	72335		50523	21812
石龙	70501	318	46550	23633	72190	303	36303	35584
虎门	130282	18388	68784	43110	158257	25193	85444	47620
东城	85114	6208	57257	21649	100581	6744	66136	27701
万江	55648	6705	37884	11059	63649	8488	40934	14227
南城	83707	2938	63407	17362	103785	3667	79347	20771
中堂	41537	6593	23358	11585	50533	7418	28908	14206
望牛墩	21961	3197	14061	4703	25963	3440	16512	6011
麻涌	47340	11783	28584	6973	49764	15494	26884	7386
石碣	46831	3332	33206	10293	66081	3495	45532	17054
高埗	28324	6213	14403	7708	36274	6945	19348	9981
道滘	47605	5698	27835	14072	55596	6031	35931	13634
洪梅	15209	2667	6923	5619	16733	2908	7657	6168
沙田	42922	7741	29376	5806	49023	10655	32354	6015
厚街	118353	9670	90642	18041	140036	10906	83151	45979
长安	93323	12505	65233	15585	131672	12882	97066	21724
寮步	75398	14727	32311	28360	85876	15651	37022	33203
大岭山	39228	8485	17265	13478	49383	9773	21083	18527
大朗	66807	17319	25844	23644	78506	16982	29641	31883
黄江	61098	3708	46392	10998	63391	3929	46558	12904
樟木头	31914	2662	24710	4543	41323	3443	32232	5647
清溪	52550	5721	35627	11202	82953	6083	55419	21451
塘厦	112158	6909	90588	14661	139903	9900	112916	17087
凤岗	37051	4767	30135	2149	48015	5521	39670	2824
谢岗	18872	4356	12655	1861	25536	5213	18242	2081
常平	135315	18444	87856	29015	146594	19303	86033	41258
桥头	54012	7206	30626	16180	64694	8418	38393	17883
横沥	44663	4484	23559	16620	54922	4717	29045	21161
东坑	34654	5179	19727	9748	50965	5274	32218	13473
企石	44588	7760	28861	7967	54066	8947	35535	9584
石排	34349	4898	20547	8904	37946	5718	21459	10769
茶山	41484	6017	18221	5995	51339	7159	24892	9433

14-1 续表 3

单位：万元

镇街	(1997年)				(1998年)			
	地区生产总值	第一产业	第二产业	第三产业	地区生产总值	第一产业	第二产业	第三产业
全市	4485981	256388	2432816	1796777	5579965	259437	3056779	2263749
莞城	80298		49962	30336	110076		49677	60399
石龙	95560	293	48361	46906	133953	116	77910	55927
虎门	246823	25799	130963	90061	362826	29535	176729	156562
东城	125730	5850	78959	40921	161819	5246	105142	51431
万江	69516	8749	42333	18434	82239	9424	50075	22922
南城	130392	3490	103126	23776	160524	3933	128850	27741
中堂	61741	7610	35991	18140	76980	7727	45359	23894
望牛墩	30854	3780	19390	7684	36531	3941	22769	9821
麻涌	52217	15965	29345	6907	62531	16443	35485	10603
石碣	85990	3782	54674	27534	109255	3852	70872	34531
高埗	46630	7586	26579	12465	60242	8235	36383	15624
道滘	69424	6383	47525	15516	80887	6756	54039	20092
洪梅	20052	4501	7602	7949	23134	4607	9569	8958
沙田	54881	11342	36602	6936	71203	16829	42167	12207
厚街	184205	11448	96880	75877	247177	12150	146229	88798
长安	180377	13111	134235	33031	245676	13562	183031	49083
寮步	103656	17341	45112	41203	129731	18768	60452	50511
大岭山	65246	10538	31884	22824	83268	9134	45040	29094
大朗	95301	19093	38996	37212	122409	15008	53085	54316
黄江	67618	4139	47073	16406	83585	4244	58492	20849
樟木头	55682	4725	43020	7936	71299	5333	51615	14351
清溪	120961	7519	84276	29166	160483	7802	115314	37367
塘厦	178757	11467	140870	26420	230580	12121	177569	40890
凤岗	63066	5925	51486	5655	79286	6187	65440	7659
谢岗	29488	6379	20521	2588	34881	6958	24888	3035
常平	185390	20195	98068	67127	231059	19811	131252	79995
桥头	79685	8523	51919	19243	96661	9712	61140	25809
横沥	67894	6411	34892	26591	81263	5364	45427	30472
东坑	63718	4810	44682	14226	78576	5726	54359	18491
企石	62625	9562	42240	10823	72065	9827	47551	14687
石排	43477	6463	23530	13484	53842	6606	28932	18304
茶山	63955	9321	39524	15110	77319	9878	47785	19656

14-1 续表 4

单位：万元

镇　街	(1999年) 地区生产总值	第一产业	第二产业	第三产业	(2000年) 地区生产总值	第一产业	第二产业	第三产业
全　市	6672386	257863	3670519	2744004	8202531	259087	4507072	3436372
莞　城	131005		58104	72901	184225		67030	117195
石　龙	157715	349	86171	71195	184256	189	98240	85827
虎　门	442633	31013	213607	198014	532946	30479	263928	238539
东　城	207432	4126	125159	78147	262854	4233	153667	104954
万　江	97379	9435	59636	28308	138724	11604	85526	41594
南　城	198820	2756	149678	46386	233013	3119	171413	58481
中　堂	94412	7001	57217	30194	123213	7032	76571	39610
望牛墩	43303	4012	26738	12553	51516	4072	31399	16045
麻　涌	75449	12466	44768	18215	90816	12213	45965	32638
石　碣	137148	3866	88152	45130	175180	4021	111038	60121
高　埗	78709	8792	50131	19786	102516	9155	67888	25473
道　滘	93751	7151	61687	24913	109999	7569	67841	34589
洪　梅	26118	4162	11872	10084	29921	4383	14095	11443
沙　田	86339	12167	53505	20667	109128	12714	71503	24911
厚　街	300721	12412	171495	116814	405317	12705	221947	170665
长　安	332335	13820	240690	77825	419347	14256	299650	105441
寮　步	161782	19944	82582	59256	202379	20732	110577	71070
大岭山	108469	9238	67662	31569	138789	9742	89991	39056
大　朗	156427	16699	69193	70535	201504	17826	94065	89613
黄　江	97621	4410	67206	26005	123331	5243	83748	34340
樟木头	94385	4225	64138	26021	147697	4639	71921	71138
清　溪	206524	8790	151219	46515	303131	9984	231303	61844
塘　厦	288110	12783	217897	57430	363971	13486	272234	78251
凤　岗	100753	6267	61392	33094	128298	6336	79138	42824
谢　岗	42142	3610	29017	9515	50174	3975	35779	10420
常　平	302805	15703	166347	120755	395318	16116	218229	160974
桥　头	111892	9062	69595	33235	130380	9093	82261	39026
横　沥	97209	6178	55276	35756	116749	8593	62314	45842
东　坑	101287	5363	65010	30913	118430	6241	76250	35940
企　石	85313	10000	51789	23524	99467	11339	58897	29231
石　排	69030	6772	37874	24384	87817	6913	48532	32372
茶　山	90250	9514	55468	25268	105432	10712	64726	29994

14-1 续表 5

单位：万元

镇街	(2001年)				(2002年)			
	地区生产总值	第一产业	第二产业	第三产业	地区生产总值	第一产业	第二产业	第三产业
全市	9918905	260968	5405092	4252845	11869374	248791	6488109	5132474
莞城	222233		80203	142030	312742		76890	235852
石龙	215738	150	115691	99897	248664	144	135163	113357
虎门	618557	30469	304781	283307	717425	26838	350636	339951
东城	342044	3785	188628	149631	466960	2110	232502	232348
万江	175693	13015	90857	71821	213919	11026	106945	95948
南城	286473	2929	211622	71922	350029	2711	262431	84887
中堂	153366	7155	95677	50533	194263	5908	122819	65536
望牛墩	60921	3540	36872	20509	73104	3591	43299	26214
麻涌	127061	12298	74806	39957	173557	1002	120426	43079
石碣	243163	4139	150613	88411	340162	4141	209830	126191
高埗	133362	9477	90730	33155	173004	9701	120415	42888
道滘	128327	8011	76692	43624	153201	8479	87039	57683
洪梅	34245	4587	16543	13115	41756	4793	21676	15287
沙田	142060	13641	92266	36153	182363	13912	119778	48673
厚街	483117	13088	253149	216880	583689	13976	297707	272006
长安	529219	14496	371263	143460	679022	14622	469032	195368
寮步	252526	21246	143824	87456	314871	20276	182688	111907
大岭山	194021	10089	133489	50443	251078	5741	178811	66526
大朗	264929	17764	128283	118882	341930	15525	181234	145171
黄江	154595	5176	98438	50981	199781	5288	122001	72492
樟木头	176062	4460	84195	87407	210845	5545	101237	104063
清溪	393471	10517	302613	80341	501941	11106	382584	108251
塘厦	457175	13796	335872	107507	573947	13603	425078	135266
凤岗	162854	6400	97540	58914	205006	2035	126903	76068
谢岗	58323	4115	41585	12623	71092	5665	40790	24637
常平	493419	16451	272983	203985	557039	16077	310537	230425
桥头	151979	8366	98054	45559	179442	7245	118564	53633
横沥	140251	9252	74148	56851	168932	9380	90576	68976
东坑	132805	6013	84256	42535	149147	5438	92587	51122
企石	115314	12403	63421	39490	127616	9088	68807	49721
石排	107585	6925	61859	38801	131394	6967	75798	48629
茶山	123931	9801	75341	38789	153215	9801	91916	51498

14-1 续表 6

单位：万元

镇街	(2003年) 地区生产总值	第一产业	第二产业	第三产业	(2004年) 地区生产总值	第一产业	第二产业	第三产业
全市	14525187	228165	7981954	6315068	18060258	227087	10160382	7672789
莞城	415993		80802	335191	552370		94035	458335
石龙	287713	116	167126	120471	317521	51	186652	130820
虎门	905165	27106	462105	415954	1139827	27168	598000	514659
东城	652408	1657	314094	336657	897727	900	411172	485655
万江	269593	9622	129625	130346	329849	5617	156431	167801
南城	452911	2743	314752	135416	741609	1869	349496	390244
中堂	256251	7013	162945	86292	338808	5956	206693	126159
望牛墩	87872	3520	50846	33506	106086	3550	59709	42827
麻涌	234612	8769	177540	48303	292911	8664	226131	58116
石碣	463023	4253	290495	168275	590604	3649	381862	205093
高埗	224078	9891	157949	56238	282716	9943	202317	70456
道滘	178954	8975	100566	69413	217400	9499	119688	88213
洪梅	53960	5113	29668	19179	76686	4770	41140	30776
沙田	236769	13944	155438	67387	310921	13975	202383	94563
厚街	721188	12275	374482	334431	878666	12341	454284	412041
长安	887947	14863	603308	269776	1162826	15040	759582	388204
寮步	394322	13167	234806	146349	498253	5327	303435	189491
大岭山	322872	4937	226565	91370	447412	4571	313857	128984
大朗	443891	10640	240983	192268	574604	6986	325826	241792
黄江	258682	4567	152903	101212	331432	3294	187369	140769
樟木头	250877	4863	119145	126869	291893	4350	139729	147814
清溪	645553	11218	495035	139300	848426	9610	660589	178227
塘厦	710030	13565	526730	169735	882099	13700	653816	214583
凤岗	284608	2048	170574	111986	373309	2015	220434	150860
谢岗	91482	4266	51312	35904	119007	4328	69024	45655
常平	657385	12627	377679	267079	796109	10792	468642	316674
桥头	213712	5419	134937	73356	264849	4495	144282	116072
横沥	205872	9602	117554	78716	253887	9075	153884	90928
东坑	181394	8423	113270	59701	230057	7943	145998	76116
企石	142717	5216	72284	65217	167279	3848	80461	82970
石排	157729	7144	92020	58565	190127	7259	109953	72915
茶山	195098	8607	118895	67596	268473	7413	161070	99990

14-1 续表 7

单位：万元

镇街	(2005年)				(2006年)			
	地区生产总值	第一产业	第二产业	第三产业	地区生产总值	第一产业	第二产业	第三产业
全市	21831961	205546	12278624	9347791	26279791	120089	15065985	11093717
莞城	617849		153367	464482	712319		230144	482174
石龙	349301	141	194749	154411	384329	35	213392	170902
虎门	1283052	22937	668632	591483	1492628	11446	763086	718096
东城	1049758	480	473888	575389	1264850	427	571728	692694
万江	375471	4209	164099	207164	440346	4711	187932	247702
南城	1016644	1900	440431	574313	1229016	1995	508223	718798
中堂	424212	6122	276399	141691	507968	6428	332766	168774
望牛墩	126751	3511	73191	50049	156949	3480	87638	65831
麻涌	387211	8588	310275	68348	494018	7106	398466	88445
石碣	728816	3782	491498	233535	868731	3091	588622	277018
高埗	366593	10020	254017	102556	456695	6552	320225	129918
道滘	255589	8753	143285	103551	301036	9568	174820	116648
洪梅	102660	3939	61138	37583	123863	4082	77274	42507
沙田	364800	13695	240822	110283	442784	12585	293854	136345
厚街	1033929	11722	531019	491188	1199117	6929	609223	582965
长安	1339428	9492	917732	412204	1539236	7505	1042139	489592
寮步	598969	7765	364261	226943	739610	1136	451671	286803
大岭山	547734	4102	370108	173524	675091	2329	431260	241502
大朗	707369	14112	411161	282096	850356	1491	499588	349277
黄江	364377	3065	220654	140658	441152	741	276062	164349
樟木头	330537	3463	157434	169640	393688	600	185556	207532
清溪	984943	9036	761281	214626	1097986	8012	828219	261755
塘厦	1057175	13661	771724	271790	1186644	12312	830537	343794
凤岗	517427	1762	320177	195488	623929	1750	373375	248804
谢岗	148917	4467	91026	53424	192841	4795	118714	69332
常平	951464	10062	556932	384470	1119659	6338	644544	468777
桥头	287240	4495	168473	114271	388604	1387	210763	176454
横沥	304870	8593	195659	100619	373304	7274	242406	123624
东坑	261238	11543	165441	84254	295233	5703	194653	94877
企石	200581	3129	102183	95269	244027	2266	129255	112506
石排	234709	7268	128132	99308	294009	7283	154259	132467
茶山	305183	6652	190620	107911	384988	3215	245078	136695

14-1 续表 8

单位：万元

镇街	(2007年)				(2008年)			
	地区生产总值	第一产业	第二产业	第三产业	地区生产总值	第一产业	第二产业	第三产业
全市	31600489	118991	17546573	13934924	37036004	148251	19016068	17871685
莞城	897597		298250	599347	1015311		294311	721000
石龙	427216	10	235821	191385	475742	7	239943	235792
虎门	1846638	10373	936639	899626	2153489	11940	1093014	1048535
东城	1559123	377	699730	859017	1816793	339	773623	1042831
万江	520636	3405	221314	295917	604659	3702	262498	338459
南城	1425257	2015	583496	839747	1632407	1285	618209	1012913
中堂	588085	6553	379181	202351	659949	6760	419455	233734
望牛墩	193635	3462	105983	84190	236495	3359	127759	105377
麻涌	651344	5985	537412	107947	834681	7564	693959	133158
石碣	994532	3096	670790	320646	1082524	2795	694349	385380
高埗	568276	6530	384637	177109	690604	6526	442377	241701
道滘	362268	8202	211240	142826	439328	7218	240510	191600
洪梅	163384	4281	110958	48145	206785	4381	147969	54435
沙田	515106	12403	327706	174997	588063	12863	337140	238060
厚街	1420026	7270	719643	693113	1616483	7971	797404	811108
长安	1770272	7746	1152474	610052	2029075	4979	1158887	865209
寮步	886584	1118	531815	353650	1038493	2141	584767	451585
大岭山	822554	2241	502679	317634	960138	2248	554712	403178
大朗	1025864	2098	592111	431655	1100875	877	688340	411658
黄江	556305	740	347972	207593	721414	724	438204	282486
樟木头	461719	505	228647	232567	507743	311	253050	254382
清溪	1266762	6207	924401	336153	1417816	5170	966538	446108
塘厦	1365736	11206	903107	451422	1602945	10447	980030	612468
凤岗	747757	1752	409163	336843	901696	1725	472782	427189
谢岗	239771	5178	143093	91500	273944	9273	160217	104454
常平	1311744	6665	747353	557726	1495652	6058	796227	693366
桥头	467790	1326	242928	223536	536868	2692	254438	279737
横沥	443014	4350	275399	163265	522130	6972	300380	214778
东坑	320991	4532	204804	111654	372361	4017	231268	137076
企石	291765	2868	150052	138844	320630	2314	159252	159064
石排	360806	7308	187787	165711	417073	7313	216033	193727
茶山	476010	3131	293991	178888	593265	4327	353036	235902
松山湖					618635		297419	321216

14-1 续表 9

单位：万元

镇街	(2009年)				(2010年)			
	地区生产总值	第一产业	第二产业	第三产业	地区生产总值	第一产业	第二产业	第三产业
全市	37639142	147877	18230836	19260428	42464527	165719	21608153	20690656
莞城	1054949		318447	736502	1138887		328434	810453
石龙	502973	6	249848	253119	559487	14	301186	258287
虎门	2437582	13180	1213679	1210723	2728626	17635	1299038	1411953
东城	1989067	386	742171	1246510	2282606	391	926086	1356129
万江	611916	3578	241005	367333	685201	3590	268049	413562
南城	1841809	1235	706141	1134433	2005491	1173	524640	1479678
中堂	662727	6965	396592	259170	669207	7035	396336	265836
望牛墩	288697	3395	162960	122342	306900	3498	166207	137195
麻涌	932351	8332	788621	135398	1070116	9248	895934	164934
石碣	1094432	2667	641983	449782	1001406	2954	656042	342410
高埗	609392	6228	387053	216111	697532	6350	452412	238770
道滘	449115	8024	234381	206710	515731	8181	289160	218390
洪梅	253003	4612	186637	61754	341015	4626	263103	73286
沙田	614104	12894	360064	241146	674850	12903	417895	244052
厚街	1695963	8373	880274	807316	1918700	9108	1000759	908833
长安	2083662	4532	1196987	882143	2371479	4959	1450285	916235
寮步	1120641	1866	630705	488070	1335015	2395	774425	558195
大岭山	975717	2255	505238	468224	1060202	2407	524440	533355
大朗	1160519	1242	675946	483331	1352689	1352	807882	543455
黄江	768073	720	419897	347456	860211	745	463492	395974
樟木头	524759	378	251340	273041	550388	404	234874	315110
清溪	1363307	5410	873074	484823	1438135	5864	907020	525251
塘厦	1713803	11448	1059192	643163	1790583	11713	1120627	658243
凤岗	1013446	1220	513090	499136	1114665	1222	543805	569638
谢岗	294969	9452	166712	118805	358653	8230	216560	133863
常平	1516942	6725	799850	710367	1615270	7102	790276	817892
桥头	535223	3546	251952	279725	583924	5738	277615	300571
横沥	538610	6294	326010	206306	576143	3982	321902	250259
东坑	387579	2118	237522	147939	416762	1760	250523	164479
企石	318197	1974	172565	143658	327900	1648	184444	141808
石排	438939	7500	243190	188249	507685	7520	299884	200281
茶山	620174	4327	360862	254985	641962	2878	346959	292125
松山湖	810599		343700	466899	1009096		362442	646654

14-1 续表 10

单位：万元

镇街	2011年				2012年			
	地区生产总值	第一产业	第二产业	第三产业	地区生产总值	第一产业	第二产业	第三产业
全市	47353949	178776	23662018	23513155	50101727	187556	23756366	26157806
莞城	1288562		387954	900608	1323607		382515	941092
石龙	622168	13	329569	292586	662926	16	344166	318744
虎门	3100010	17434	1352694	1729882	3480905	17927	1526167	1936811
东城	2553050	400	978519	1574131	2729294	430	937223	1791641
万江	769132	4034	296564	468534	806632	3332	294829	508471
南城	2328755	1170	597078	1730507	2606318	1051	624986	1980282
中堂	740823	7895	430871	302057	737173	7873	411137	318163
望牛墩	360982	3786	198059	159137	372240	4108	187177	180955
麻涌	1205818	11411	967151	227256	1077177	12780	800453	263944
石碣	1098260	3008	717595	377657	1074157	3060	688971	382126
高埗	798981	6351	519762	272868	833584	6707	535360	291517
道滘	582510	9247	316509	256754	610742	10033	318099	282610
洪梅	372907	5001	281752	86154	326380	4506	227057	94817
沙田	724112	15098	423611	285403	711774	16940	368149	326685
厚街	2170463	9736	1149481	1011246	2535484	10077	1445170	1080237
长安	2564370	4522	1550789	1009059	2429495	4368	1369172	1055955
寮步	1471407	2029	841514	627864	1574932	13635	880005	681292
大岭山	1221652	2463	575529	643660	1325413	2558	636324	686531
大朗	1469179	1555	855609	612015	1564995	1872	895278	667844
黄江	962019	765	488300	472954	1079436	842	554519	524076
樟木头	623121	445	259066	363610	647297	357	264182	382758
清溪	1522825	6550	899945	616330	1530352	7470	870284	652598
塘厦	2025381	12255	1204708	808418	2070280	14303	1193834	862143
凤岗	1305676	1370	629700	674606	1388729	1566	637064	750100
谢岗	416269	10748	255645	149876	467190	14028	288711	164451
常平	1823461	7851	892551	923059	2000198	8372	934772	1057054
桥头	651918	4900	296495	350523	750036	5253	374632	370151
横沥	638887	5177	339962	293748	683498	5232	355688	322578
东坑	519150	2236	329596	187318	527614	2379	320175	205060
企石	364218	1817	196388	166013	385851	1941	202636	181274
石排	527052	7558	289733	229761	529243	8006	282664	238572
茶山	722124	3341	360722	358061	765976	3822	403755	358399
松山湖	1354180		397200	956980	1549087		665679	883408

14-2 镇街第三产业增加值（2012年）

Value-added of the Tertiary Industry by Town (2012)

单位：万元

镇 街	第三产业增加值	#交通运输及仓储业	批发和零售业	住宿和餐饮业	金融业	房地产业
全 市	26157806	1360939	5021959	1679436	1999080	4653249
莞 城	941092	77289	245441	34264	149504	211477
石 龙	318744	15342	74684	29544	39821	51652
虎 门	1936811	64769	561557	143958	121066	163838
东 城	1791641	70093	224084	147615	190546	487687
万 江	508471	27671	70363	42625	40310	86161
南 城	1980282	44860	266921	84129	387507	321172
中 堂	318163	9865	86887	33833	29278	40952
望 牛 墩	180955	50135	24909	9488	16127	14572
麻 涌	263944	80370	24784	9743	19433	21580
石 碣	382126	14811	71038	28681	33548	52286
高 埗	291517	29952	58097	30625	19290	48435
道 滘	282610	13340	38365	19549	21835	85239
洪 梅	94817	12846	13988	11139	6135	15535
沙 田	326685	48067	45154	29402	19373	47091
厚 街	1080237	26863	168473	116322	84768	177491
长 安	1055955	18309	289383	112581	80660	103754
寮 步	681292	58854	106251	68494	62822	122232
大 岭 山	686531	19821	254009	50730	41988	89338
大 朗	667844	8874	114780	83787	53723	124477
黄 江	524076	15478	102150	58470	49153	105442
樟 木 头	382758	10892	76349	33371	36767	91229
清 溪	652598	16667	73227	64116	47025	146423
塘 厦	862143	23689	90996	99343	65666	180440
凤 岗	750100	12199	96403	82504	57139	192404
谢 岗	164451	9369	23459	21835	15585	35884
常 平	1057054	31630	169183	153589	83038	204328
桥 头	370151	14499	30378	43809	21383	48739
横 沥	322578	4575	95227	12724	27659	61423
东 坑	205060	1350	39011	22205	18996	43758
企 石	181274	8822	18822	14702	12393	36612
石 排	238572	10051	45181	24784	24391	59429
茶 山	358399	28455	61900	39602	28120	79065
松 山 湖	883408	493	29694	12881	7826	289986

14-3 镇街户籍户数与人口数（2012年）

Population of Household by Town (2012)

单位：人

镇街	户数（户）			人口数	按性别分		按农业、非农业分		总人口中未落户籍的人口数
		农业户	非农业户		男	女	农业人口	非农业人口	
全市总计	544079	263144	280935	1870159	949194	920965	910525	959634	3890
莞城	39271	1	39270	176960	91122	85838	3184	173776	
石龙	21586	2380	19206	71444	35502	35942	8930	62514	940
虎门	35232		35232	129798	65651	64147	2	129796	2
东城	25841		25841	92474	47202	45272		92474	11
万江	25028		25028	79967	40676	39291		79967	246
南城	21506		21506	76937	39897	37040		76937	14
中堂	22111	15561	6550	75952	38636	37316	56411	19541	19
望牛墩	11885	10114	1771	46823	23306	23517	40402	6421	1010
麻涌	21988	17713	4275	73368	36755	36613	62929	10439	314
石碣	15193	11451	3742	45360	23075	22285	37731	7629	27
高埗	11471	10759	712	38401	19351	19050	35435	2966	87
道滘	17019	12565	4454	56384	28264	28120	44601	11783	6
洪梅	6674	6136	538	22559	11394	11165	21162	1397	263
沙田	12817	11498	1319	41789	20996	20793	37079	4710	20
厚街	29422	23616	5806	98557	49486	49071	85196	13361	44
长安	13714		13714	45956	23820	22136		45956	
寮步	21548	13599	7949	71758	36334	35424	43614	28144	1
大岭山	13465	11346	2119	46047	23215	22832	39501	6546	
大朗	19082	16503	2579	71994	37233	34761	63016	8978	5
黄江	8361	6004	2357	25917	13075	12842	18716	7201	1
樟木头	8217		8217	28458	14403	14055		28458	5
清溪	11749	9266	2483	36656	18281	18375	29649	7007	
塘厦	18039		18039	48272	24380	23892		48272	39
凤岗	7273	4962	2311	25535	12414	13121	17757	7778	4
谢岗	5381	4243	1138	20797	10393	10404	17415	3382	162
常平	25114	17982	7132	75681	39038	36643	58514	17167	7
桥头	11875	4970	6905	36522	18372	18150	16512	20010	202
横沥	11779	8873	2906	37765	19349	18416	30927	6838	5
东坑	10816	9040	1776	30551	15714	14837	27357	3194	211
企石	13401	11271	2130	42801	21901	20900	37342	5459	21
石排	13137	11552	1585	43788	22064	21724	39558	4230	207
茶山	13611	11739	1872	45276	22777	22499	37576	7700	17
松山湖	470		470	9603	5109	4494		9603	

14-4 镇街户籍人口自然变动情况（2012年）

Population Household by Town (2012)

镇街	出生		死亡		自然增长	
	人数（人）	出生率（‰）	人数（人）	死亡率（‰）	人数（人）	自然增长率（‰）
全市总计	24712	13.32	9684	5.22	15028	8.10
莞城	1782	10.31	1022	5.92	760	4.40
石龙	613	8.60	367	5.15	246	3.45
虎门	1545	11.95	755	5.84	790	6.11
东城	1035	11.32	347	3.79	688	7.52
万江	969	12.21	407	5.13	562	7.08
南城	1386	18.36	203	2.69	1183	15.67
中堂	1078	14.23	462	6.10	616	8.13
望牛墩	706	15.15	248	5.32	458	9.83
麻涌	1084	14.82	423	5.78	661	9.04
石碣	659	14.62	226	5.01	433	9.60
高埗	526	13.82	177	4.65	349	9.17
道滘	709	12.60	347	6.17	362	6.43
洪梅	312	13.92	118	5.26	194	8.65
沙田	676	16.27	248	5.97	428	10.3
厚街	1260	12.79	511	5.19	749	7.60
长安	652	14.33	199	4.37	453	9.96
寮步	954	13.45	412	5.81	542	7.64
大岭山	847	18.52	220	4.81	627	13.71
大朗	980	13.71	431	6.03	549	7.68
黄江	372	14.47	123	4.79	249	9.69
樟木头	432	15.24	114	4.02	318	11.22
清溪	552	15.17	208	5.72	344	9.45
塘厦	744	15.57	239	5.00	505	10.57
凤岗	358	14.16	79	3.13	279	11.04
谢岗	309	15.08	109	5.32	200	9.76
常平	861	11.51	421	5.63	440	5.88
桥头	550	15.10	206	5.66	344	9.44
横沥	501	13.30	196	5.20	305	8.10
东坑	345	11.39	161	5.31	184	6.07
企石	685	16.03	231	5.41	454	10.63
石排	584	13.38	229	5.25	355	8.13
茶山	516	11.42	242	5.36	274	6.06
松山湖	130	13.38	3	0.31	127	13.07

14-5 镇街人口迁移变动情况（2012年）

Population Migration by Town (2012)

单位：人

镇　　街	迁移总计	省　内	省　外	迁入总计	省内迁入	省外迁入	迁出总计	迁往省内	迁往省外
全市总计	29024	10509	18515	20698	7253	13445	8326	3256	5070
莞　　城	5400	972	4428	3620	637	2983	1780	335	1445
石　　龙	841	408	433	593	308	285	248	100	148
虎　　门	906	383	523	615	264	351	291	119	172
东　　城	1970	700	1270	1609	570	1039	361	130	231
万　　江	1172	334	838	1029	290	739	143	44	99
南　　城	3325	1239	2086	2511	917	1594	814	322	492
中　　堂	329	174	155	220	128	92	109	46	63
望 牛 墩	140	71	69	109	53	56	31	18	13
麻　　涌	559	200	359	398	150	248	161	50	111
石　　碣	654	207	447	488	159	329	166	48	118
高　　埗	143	62	81	117	53	64	26	9	17
道　　滘	189	83	106	135	59	76	54	24	30
洪　　梅	123	47	76	105	42	63	18	5	13
沙　　田	299	114	185	238	95	143	61	19	42
厚　　街	486	182	304	343	153	190	143	29	114
长　　安	1216	239	977	939	161	778	277	78	199
寮　　步	1348	515	833	1245	498	747	103	17	86
大 岭 山	588	176	412	467	143	324	121	33	88
大　　朗	552	187	365	421	151	270	131	36	95
黄　　江	412	170	242	354	146	208	58	24	34
樟 木 头	604	196	408	465	150	315	139	46	93
清　　溪	569	192	377	390	160	230	179	32	147
塘　　厦	1453	642	811	1171	568	603	282	74	208
凤　　岗	626	264	362	514	224	290	112	40	72
谢　　岗	156	82	74	107	66	41	49	16	33
常　　平	718	257	461	546	201	345	172	56	116
桥　　头	211	94	117	146	80	66	65	14	51
横　　沥	288	83	205	222	72	150	66	11	55
东　　坑	138	45	93	78	31	47	60	14	46
企　　石	299	117	182	205	106	99	94	11	83
石　　排	288	101	187	164	83	81	124	18	106
茶　　山	291	93	198	149	65	84	142	28	114
松 山 湖	2723	1876	847	977	466	511	1746	1410	336

注：本表按户籍人口统计。

14-6 镇街土地面积和人口密度（2012年）

Land Area and Population Density by Town (2012)

镇　街	土地面积 (平方公里)	人口密度（人/平方公里）	
		户籍人口	常住人口
莞　城	11.2	15800	14884
石　龙	13.8	5177	10355
虎　门	166.5	780	3863
东　城	105.1	880	4737
万　江	48.5	1649	5078
南　城	56.6	1359	5244
中　堂	59.9	1268	2346
望牛墩	31.6	1482	2712
麻　涌	87.2	841	1368
石　碣	36.2	1253	6884
高　埗	34.6	1110	6292
道　滘	54.3	1038	2641
洪　梅	33.2	679	1771
沙　田	78.8	530	2279
厚　街	125.7	784	3513
长　安	89.4	514	7478
寮　步	72.5	990	5815
大岭山	95.5	482	2948
大　朗	97.5	738	3218
黄　江	92.9	279	2515
樟木头	118.8	240	1129
清　溪	140.1	262	2248
塘　厦	128.2	377	3792
凤　岗	82.4	310	3899
谢　岗	91.0	229	1101
常　平	103.3	733	3763
桥　头	56.0	652	3000
横　沥	44.7	845	4624
东　坑	23.7	1289	5895
企　石	58.2	735	2105
石　排	48.7	899	3333
茶　山	45.4	997	3463
松山湖	58.1	165	668

注：土地面积数据来源于市国土局，不包括海域面积。

14-7 镇街常住人口（2011-2012年）

Permanent Population by Town (2011-2012)

单位：万人

镇　　街	2011年	2012年	镇　　街	2011年	2012年
莞　　城	16.43	16.67	寮　　步	42.04	42.16
石　　龙	14.24	14.29	大 岭 山	28.04	28.15
虎　　门	64.07	64.32	大　　朗	31.22	31.38
东　　城	49.57	49.79	黄　　江	23.23	23.36
万　　江	24.63	24.63	樟 木 头	13.35	13.41
南　　城	29.20	29.68	清　　溪	31.34	31.49
中　　堂	14.04	14.05	塘　　厦	48.40	48.61
望 牛 墩	8.53	8.57	凤　　岗	32.00	32.13
麻　　涌	11.88	11.93	谢　　岗	9.97	10.02
石　　碣	24.80	24.92	常　　平	38.80	38.87
高　　埗	21.79	21.77	桥　　头	16.73	16.80
道　　滘	14.34	14.34	横　　沥	20.55	20.67
洪　　梅	5.84	5.88	东　　坑	13.92	13.97
沙　　田	17.82	17.96	企　　石	12.23	12.25
厚　　街	43.97	44.16	石　　排	16.10	16.23
长　　安	66.58	66.85	茶　　山	15.70	15.72
松 山 湖	3.83	3.88			

14-8 镇街外来暂住人口数（2011-2012年）

Migrant Population by Town (2011-2012)

单位：人

镇街	2011年			2012年		
	外来暂住人口	男	女	外来暂住人口	男	女
全市总计	4136177	2054179	2081998	4167396	2072592	2094804
莞城	56323	28555	27768	52273	26762	25511
石龙	52046	24892	27154	53941	22300	31641
虎门	415700	203170	212530	379688	185639	194049
东城	211983	106339	105644	230626	120202	110424
万江	65386	33670	31716	65766	33870	31896
南城	133878	72898	60980	136390	74920	61470
中堂	48370	25421	22949	48386	24982	23404
望牛墩	37165	17632	19533	38136	16707	21429
麻涌	34843	19354	15489	34855	19636	15219
石碣	100445	45561	54884	100312	48733	51579
高埗	128551	76216	52335	129656	77062	52594
道滘	53961	22197	31764	54110	24692	29418
洪梅	24467	12052	12415	25649	12290	13359
沙田	68568	36591	31977	71264	39392	31872
厚街	297025	138609	158416	298832	139706	159126
长安	388226	187817	200409	395581	193057	202524
寮步	177889	96346	81543	183360	95294	88066
大岭山	99160	53390	45770	100086	51408	48678
大朗	111964	52904	59060	120000	56701	63299
黄江	148650	81245	67405	149500	81670	67830
樟木头	114395	65201	49194	108812	62307	46505
清溪	136616	54094	82522	140002	50250	89752
塘厦	362173	167486	194687	328321	151816	176505
凤岗	148377	77990	70387	158884	79319	79565
谢岗	44200	21005	23195	44005	21651	22354
常平	207803	97350	110453	215502	104289	111213
桥头	61808	26586	35222	73083	33062	40021
横沥	100629	58113	42516	100843	60168	40675
东坑	67751	34503	33248	71493	33058	38435
企石	36742	18330	18412	37387	19316	18071
石排	92018	44250	47768	92262	44386	47876
茶山	77792	34891	42901	78006	37348	40658
其他单位	31273	19521	11752	50385	30599	19786

14-9 镇街计划生育情况（2012年）

Basic Statistics on Family Planning by Town (2012)

镇　　街	已婚育龄妇女人数（人）	女性初婚人数（人）	#23周岁及以上	落实各种节育措施 育龄夫妇（对）	节育率（%）	领取独生子女证 累　计（人）	领证率（%）	政　策生育率（%）	多孩率（%）
全市总计	384854	14875	12049	320907	83.38	81341	21.14	84.23	3.42
莞　　城	34819	1085	1000	28880	82.94	9260	26.59	88.44	1.63
石　　龙	13094	426	369	10743	82.05	3715	28.37	79.93	3.26
虎　　门	26352	1002	827	21030	79.80	4946	18.77	84.53	3.43
东　　城	14126	660	535	12161	86.09	3056	21.63	89.05	1.58
万　　江	8474	446	356	7109	83.89	1605	18.94	80.45	5.10
南　　城	17129	681	590	14712	85.89	4238	24.74	76.99	3.10
中　　堂	9335	383	285	7705	82.54	2192	23.48	86.95	3.03
望 牛 墩	7373	360	285	6085	82.53	1478	20.05	83.84	6.27
麻　　涌	13818	679	560	11666	84.43	3552	25.71	90.50	1.48
石　　碣	10217	490	423	8620	84.37	1552	15.19	91.41	2.45
高　　埗	9094	364	267	7769	85.43	2117	23.28	89.05	2.81
道　　滘	10365	418	310	8647	83.42	2088	20.14	77.01	4.65
洪　　梅	4404	177	140	3752	85.20	887	20.14	82.69	2.24
沙　　田	19028	678	555	16296	85.64	3274	17.21	80.32	4.76
厚　　街	19852	897	804	16033	80.76	3330	16.77	82.25	1.80
长　　安	20542	665	573	16523	80.44	3689	17.96	81.35	2.42
寮　　步	14795	529	404	12550	84.83	2917	19.72	84.07	4.61
大 岭 山	10168	450	331	8614	84.72	1873	18.42	89.85	2.83
大　　朗	14958	542	397	12572	84.05	3418	22.85	83.88	4.59
黄　　江	6129	219	170	5215	85.09	1475	24.07	81.45	4.30
樟 木 头	6773	248	191	5480	80.91	966	14.26	77.78	4.17
清　　溪	8314	293	231	6962	83.74	1470	17.68	87.86	3.62
塘　　厦	10371	455	384	8269	79.73	2188	21.10	85.48	3.76
凤　　岗	6055	227	183	5001	82.59	835	13.79	87.99	2.23
谢　　岗	4494	158	119	3781	84.13	781	17.38	81.88	2.91
常　　平	15247	504	392	13145	86.21	3987	26.15	87.57	3.25
桥　　头	7693	282	212	6579	85.52	2005	26.06	77.09	5.82
横　　沥	7744	254	188	6751	87.18	1749	22.59	83.23	3.39
东　　坑	5755	237	177	4902	85.18	1331	23.13	88.12	3.77
企　　石	9052	373	264	7704	85.11	1554	17.17	80.29	6.13
石　　排	8965	326	241	7348	81.96	1839	20.51	82.88	4.97
茶　　山	8998	301	223	7670	85.24	1695	18.84	78.68	5.81
松 山 湖	1321	66	63	633	47.92	279	21.12	96.92	1.54

14-10 镇街农林牧渔业总产值（2012年）

Gross Output Value of Agriculture by Town (2012)

单位：万元

镇　　街	农林牧渔业总产值	农业	林业	牧业	渔业	农林牧渔服务业
石　　龙	54				54	
虎　　门	28317	8281	139	6512	13385	
东　　城	2528	1686	316		525	
万　　江	7055	6040	3		1013	
南　　城	2000	1834	5		161	
中　　堂	13894	10983		1326	1586	
望 牛 墩	6962	5035		1308	619	
麻　　涌	17053	13908	9	333	2804	
石　　碣	4895	3835			467	593
高　　埗	10377	9285			1092	
道　　滘	17212	7010	9	7078	3051	65
洪　　梅	9437	1853		5343	2240	
沙　　田	29762	9239	1	3507	16782	234
厚　　街	16243	13000	44	135	3063	
长　　安	8556	704	15	1520	6318	
寮　　步	7178	5702	1		1475	
大 岭 山	4794	3535	83	11	1165	
大　　朗	3642	2709	7	229	697	
黄　　江	1523	1149	39	18	317	
樟 木 头	639	391	27	174		47
清　　溪	13373	12966	167		240	
塘　　厦	25054	14309	11	7144	757	2833
凤　　岗	2818	2532	11		275	
谢　　岗	25708	10579	39	8119	6971	
常　　平	22418	9730	29	10648	2011	
桥　　头	8398	3951	5	2777	1665	
横　　沥	7520	2262		3777	1481	
东　　坑	1461	835			626	
企　　石	5086	3061	9	703	1313	
石　　排	11032	4510	1		6522	
茶　　山	6429	2175		1812	2442	

14-11 镇街主要农产品生产及产品产量（2012年）

Production and Output of Main Agricultural Products by Town (2012)

镇街	粮食播种面积（亩）	粮食总产量（吨）	稻谷播种面积（亩）	稻谷产量（吨）	蔬菜播种面积（亩）	蔬菜产量（吨）	水果总面积（亩）	水果总产量（吨）
石龙								
虎门	908	297	768	266	20417	21986	4830	1660
东城	1375	594	1375	594	2909	4895	216	246
万江	546	179	256	95	11479	18182	121	188
南城	470	92			240	198	1836	139
中堂	2435	719	1663	566	18621	26096	4848	7387
望牛墩	509	170	401	143	3082	4300	5750	9533
麻涌	10700	3406	10041	3287	11204	11605	20834	25483
石碣	713	186	30	13	10800	13579	412	419
高埗	1662	535	882	362	21418	30331	90	182
道滘	1560	585	1560	585	11381	23811	46	116
洪梅	3089	987	2385	846	603	726	2477	3599
沙田	3068	1062	2606	934	18146	19867	1950	2189
厚街	1150	233			41450	45827	11468	925
长安					1059	957	2000	414
寮步	189	42			1957	1851	1627	577
大岭山	603	144			7155	8083	6685	905
大朗	701	127			3963	3482	18074	1041
黄江	575	115			1560	2224	14220	514
樟木头	505	143			540	767	5120	75
清溪	863	187			12550	13429	11420	632
塘厦	1038	303	23	11	26762	32114	11950	925
凤岗	480	99			4910	5007	13997	1095
谢岗	1105	380	475	186	18000	25200	14550	3945
常平	1280	257			16719	28792	10507	138
桥头	1246	383	298	129	7160	10406	1972	324
横沥	820	202			6970	6250	3072	77
东坑	110	24			1418	1311	1457	436
企石	1877	586	562	192	4576	7478	3020	472
石排	881	269	350	148	10717	12019	962	910
茶山	824	170			6012	5830	3235	370

14-11 续表 1

(2012年)

镇　街	香(大)蕉面积(亩)	香(大)蕉产量(吨)	荔枝面积(亩)	荔枝产量(吨)	林业用地面积(亩)	当年种植面积(亩)	生猪年末存栏量(头)	肉猪出栏量(头)
石　龙					150			
虎　门	250	205	3000	540	31193		16900	28356
东　城	10	20	86	51	10914			
万　江	87	164	7	6				
南　城			1075	91	15431			
中　堂	4719	7302	22	30			2030	8509
望牛墩	5666	9400					5980	8424
麻　涌	19524	24346						266
石　碣	361	411	51	8				
高　埗								
道　滘	46	116					44792	45043
洪　梅	2477	3599					16413	35323
沙　田	1458	2039	40	15	450		3304	3810
厚　街	158	26	9245	546	55007	1500		
长　安			1802	302	19425	1500	24471	9699
寮　步	20	60	979	233	14148	400		
大岭山			5808	532	54092	1000		
大　朗	30	5	16165	801	33801			
黄　江			13140	300	71442	3300		
樟木头			4461	50	53870	815		
清　溪	80	4	9140	336	71672	3300		
塘　厦	38	63	10842	642	35804	800	8238	15500
凤　岗			10383	798	41412	2450		
谢　岗	1050	3600	13000	330	61740	1300		40214
常　平			8747	75	30038		3760	41422
桥　头	40	32	772	20	10248			17900
横　沥	13	11	2956	56	6150		11000	24000
东　坑	30	8	1139	353	5186			
企　石	377	452	2323	8	9293	100	3766	4561
石　排	218	14	45	10	767			
茶　山	9	6	2930	200	9945		1800	3300

注：林业用地面积、当年种植面积指标采用林业局数据。

14-11 续表 2

(2012年)

镇街	三鸟年末存栏量(只)	三鸟出栏量(只)	畜牧总肉量(吨)	#猪肉	禽蛋产量(吨)	淡水养殖面积(亩)	水产品产量(吨)	#淡水产量
石龙						94	75	53
虎门	130000	596555	2900	1938	12	8025	11977	4319
东城						1410	637	637
万江						1950	925	925
南城						322	184	184
中堂	8913	8841	601	587		3510	1887	1741
望牛墩	27400	27880	591	575	8	2265	703	703
麻涌	53983	93000	118	18	29	3824	1946	1944
石碣						930	580	580
高埗						2983	1349	1349
道滘	66795	114647	3200	3083	70	6701	3169	3169
洪梅	27599	37205	2433	2414		4013	1990	1935
沙田	223730	945256	1361	261	15	16858	13581	7079
厚街						5534	1890	1890
长安	6830	25836	686	662		2636	4441	442
寮步						1875	1475	1475
大岭山						1875	1680	1680
大朗	23680	39586	55			3521	910	910
黄江						4545	410	410
樟木头	5000	48129	63					
清溪						788	268	268
塘厦	448646	1405734	2521	1053	652	2816	1253	1253
凤岗						360	276	276
谢岗	100087	722000	3818	2735		16290	9220	9220
常平	393136	1569232	4421	2831	30	4095	2489	2489
桥头	7990	31200	1260	1223	18	3820	2300	2300
横沥	15000	50000	1703	1640	8	2461	1476	1476
东坑						3120	689	689
企石			320	319		3045	1607	1607
石排						7494	4183	4183
茶山	19200	53200	675	231		4305	3137	3137

14-12 镇街农机总动力、机耕面积及农村用电量（2012年）

Basic Statistics on Total Power of Agricultural Machinery, Area of Tractor Ploughing and Electricity Consumption in Rural Areas by Town (2012)

镇 街	农机总动力（千瓦）	#耕作机械	排灌机械	农村用电量（万千瓦时）	化肥施用实物量（吨）	农药使用量（吨）
石龙				1824		
虎门	31033	154	1209	472223	1731	69
东城	9411	345	7060	63410	204	1
万江	550	27	225	105309	1552	9
南城				7000	80	2
中堂	7712	517	2713	140500	2867	30
望牛墩	2280	379	382	7036	1945	21
麻涌	3477	1174	250	13996	7326	53
石碣	1810	196	1414	161785	798	21
高埗	13063	4162	2004	112290	1325	38
道滘	1569	329	378	117427	1566	8
洪梅	439	132	271	961	1729	22
沙田	37066	1737	1646	54159	2160	75
厚街	901		424	325508	3721	87
长安	174			516451	60	2
寮步	130	4	126	22518	391	6
大岭山	8876	3782	407	26407	552	23
大朗	817	536	144	236263	1255	36
黄江	31	8	3	70611	216	27
樟木头				95677	81	9
清溪	686	396	192	236726	960	73
塘厦	378	76	135	337225	2299	33
凤岗	363	123	210	221561	226	10
谢岗	2783	1098	1600	5000	1998	45
常平	268		58	188419	816	10
桥头	2121	185	1865	107486	1651	8
横沥	10275	600	7105	115513	386	5
东坑				89178	544	
企石	492	412	80	81478	364	
石排	3355	216	1567	117840	1287	38
茶山	3050	970	680	132917	936	2

14-13 镇街农村集体(经联社、经济社两级合计)经济收益分配（2012年）

Income Distribution of Rural Economy by Town (2012)

单位：万元

镇　街	经营总收入	经营总费用	经营纯收入
全市总计	1550471	697127	853345
莞　城	16884	5239	11645
石　龙	18295	9359	8936
虎　门	151402	68016	83386
东　城	102789	47845	54945
万　江	52507	27369	25138
南　城	56340	24146	32195
中　堂	54008	15422	38586
望牛墩	9151	3520	5631
麻　涌	17571	7169	10402
石　碣	64965	30380	34585
高　埗	26063	9253	16810
道　滘	22659	8981	13678
洪　梅	5980	3234	2746
沙　田	24967	10800	14166
厚　街	118030	61434	56596
长　安	158446	68406	90040
寮　步	72486	34202	38283
大岭山	39848	16118	23731
大　朗	61577	29891	31685
黄　江	23641	8846	14795
樟木头	20763	17391	3372
清　溪	52984	22889	30095
塘　厦	63264	23731	39533
凤　岗	70133	20726	49407
谢　岗	8910	3533	5377
常　平	69953	32204	37750
桥　头	31132	15771	15361
横　沥	25409	16304	9105
东　坑	22820	11067	11754
企　石	15899	9583	6316
石　排	31767	13905	17863
茶　山	39829	20394	19435

14-14 镇街规模以上工业企业主要经济指标（2012年）

Main Indicators of Industrial Enterprises above Designated Size by Town (2012)

单位：万元

镇　街	企业单位数（个）	亏损企业	工业销售产值	主营业务收入
莞　城	29	4	1122440	1129977
石　龙	52	12	1943489	1960523
虎　门	330	38	4621191	4610835
东　城	201	25	3390942	3397304
万　江	89	14	1005175	1001366
南　城	59	17	2557894	2563363
中　堂	110	16	1922044	1941028
望牛墩	85	12	787684	854086
麻　涌	75	15	5547983	5583694
石　碣	119	17	3590374	3611356
高　埗	118	20	1707417	1721971
道　滘	120	14	1325969	1343853
洪　梅	48	7	1725861	1747304
沙　田	98	11	1546336	1553566
厚　街	229	35	6909252	7092198
长　安	261	55	7225971	7291721
寮　步	191	31	4391497	4463745
大岭山	178	19	3215545	3223230
大　朗	250	28	2751402	2741443
黄　江	117	23	3015094	3112632
樟木头	82	15	914415	916097
清　溪	212	32	4217992	4172889
塘　厦	348	66	5271471	5238068
凤　岗	166	31	2318695	2291229
谢　岗	90	11	762684	771226
常　平	225	36	3554643	3584577
桥　头	120	15	1701324	1738647
横　沥	111	16	1242184	1328459
东　坑	71	9	1737755	1764281
企　石	79	9	671121	726151
石　排	88	16	695359	719462
茶　山	125	13	1480545	1542192
松山湖	44	9	4663948	4648098

14-14 续表 1

(2012年)

单位：万元

镇街	资产总额			负债总额
		流动资产	固定资产净值	
莞城	1082775	460442	431018	617525
石龙	1088826	823730	201737	516900
虎门	3824970	2753363	788132	2251518
东城	2881345	1976590	782329	1401786
万江	921397	596896	173390	619501
南城	2134385	1436943	392724	1269452
中堂	1916602	1097824	600651	1316903
望牛墩	579144	432702	120985	410644
麻涌	5323340	2692660	2223230	3141542
石碣	1958513	1380647	469360	1073364
高埗	1244412	851753	309757	736332
道滘	1014207	750075	197215	479789
洪梅	1907954	1101840	725993	974455
沙田	1012777	712270	231288	584695
厚街	3162919	2386867	621698	1845399
长安	5005840	3287035	1394546	3270373
寮步	2649774	1852013	624467	1553631
大岭山	2573955	1918021	509262	1773381
大朗	2406770	1840154	420341	1651857
黄江	2067611	1103795	659575	976544
樟木头	780388	530822	202756	450269
清溪	3182171	2270753	768457	1615016
塘厦	3948340	2919619	749095	2170352
凤岗	2077560	1277539	649381	1056732
谢岗	611726	409205	164275	392490
常平	3057683	2328778	627606	1807466
桥头	1194734	868070	210974	772212
横沥	1053225	781537	248820	667222
东坑	1037328	701377	289796	686202
企石	718383	591857	95272	503283
石排	563060	398176	128467	297426
茶山	1209151	822004	302414	671252
松山湖	2940294	1833962	753626	1826426

14-14 续表 2

(2012年)

单位：万元

镇　　街	主营业务税金及附加	利润总额	利税总额	本年应交增值税	全部从业人员平均人数（人）
莞　　城	4246	62023	129339	62391	19615
石　　龙	7188	124694	180074	48180	36418
虎　　门	19750	151387	257213	85774	169807
东　　城	24847	226490	355501	104154	115957
万　　江	4215	14712	40096	21167	31967
南　　城	9024	116497	177807	52123	48409
中　　堂	10116	36235	84571	38214	35962
望 牛 墩	3188	38682	65050	23042	21993
麻　　涌	8609	191252	355941	156000	42590
石　　碣	6511	92876	132459	33052	89403
高　　埗	4024	36947	60372	18956	103711
道　　滘	4344	53901	85222	26973	36320
洪　　梅	1456	45517	64188	17214	20751
沙　　田	4545	41181	69969	24233	35268
厚　　街	20155	267084	339566	52065	169691
长　　安	21438	197463	335953	116985	222428
寮　　步	9344	117825	341673	214447	125165
大 岭 山	8950	48085	144050	86699	92942
大　　朗	6937	41280	140725	92475	86892
黄　　江	7698	45422	99168	46024	79502
樟 木 头	3241	10034	22003	8728	38038
清　　溪	10608	78170	118868	29869	132461
塘　　厦	14891	121576	208540	66098	182590
凤　　岗	7817	57599	103621	38123	97632
谢　　岗	2065	4449	43089	36574	28924
常　　平	9392	99680	150463	41307	121593
桥　　头	3549	42083	69280	23508	53887
横　　沥	3902	51824	70644	14876	56968
东　　坑	2599	47016	77053	27435	72012
企　　石	2736	8530	22708	11407	28292
石　　排	2168	20080	28744	6443	40408
茶　　山	5696	43952	76815	27080	43417
松 山 湖	12408	147545	234971	74439	42033

14-15 镇街规模以上工业企业主要经济效益指标（2012年）

Main Indicators on Economic Benefit of Industrial Enterprises above Designated Size by Town (2012)

镇　街	工业增加值率 (%)	总资产贡献率 (%)	资　产负债率 (%)	流动资产周 转 率 (次/年)	成本费用利 润 率 (%)	全员劳动生 产 率 (元/人)	产　品销售率 (%)
莞　城	24.6	13.8	57.0	2.5	5.7	140162	100.3
石　龙	18.9	16.6	47.5	2.4	6.8	101413	99.6
虎　门	23.0	6.9	58.9	1.7	3.4	66386	94.4
东　城	31.2	12.4	48.7	1.7	7.1	92655	98.5
万　江	24.5	5.5	67.2	1.7	1.5	74610	103.2
南　城	22.6	9.0	59.5	1.8	4.9	108191	110.5
中　堂	16.3	6.4	68.7	1.8	1.9	83395	104.6
望 牛 墩	22.2	12.1	70.9	2.0	4.7	81523	97.6
麻　涌	18.0	7.5	59.0	2.3	3.3	239081	98.2
石　碣	18.7	6.8	54.8	2.6	2.6	75167	99.8
高　埗	32.9	5.6	59.2	2.0	2.1	54174	100.1
道　滘	21.2	8.7	47.3	1.8	4.2	75669	102.4
洪　梅	15.0	3.8	51.1	1.6	2.7	121368	102.8
沙　田	19.1	7.4	57.7	2.3	2.7	84334	99.3
厚　街	15.2	11.0	58.3	3.0	3.9	61613	100.5
长　安	20.3	6.8	65.3	2.2	2.8	66596	99.0
寮　步	23.3	13.5	58.6	2.4	2.7	81503	100.1
大 岭 山	20.5	6.5	68.9	1.7	1.5	69693	101.9
大　朗	22.4	6.1	68.6	1.5	1.5	70809	100.2
黄　江	17.1	5.0	47.2	2.8	1.5	65454	99.3
樟 木 头	23.4	4.0	57.7	1.7	1.1	56043	100.4
清　溪	19.4	3.7	50.8	1.9	1.9	60777	101.6
塘　厦	21.7	5.5	55.0	1.8	2.4	63633	98.6
凤　岗	24.0	5.3	50.9	1.8	2.5	57164	99.9
谢　岗	23.9	7.7	64.2	1.9	0.6	63593	99.2
常　平	21.1	5.1	59.1	1.6	2.8	61211	100.5
桥　头	21.7	6.1	64.6	2.0	2.5	70112	97.8
横　沥	22.9	7.0	63.4	1.7	4.0	49644	100.5
东　坑	25.6	7.7	66.2	2.5	2.7	59151	104.6
企　石	19.2	4.0	70.1	1.2	1.2	45902	99.2
石　排	24.8	5.7	52.8	1.8	2.9	42466	100.5
茶　山	21.3	7.1	55.5	1.9	2.9	71946	100.7
松 山 湖	13.7	8.5	62.1	2.6	3.3	142947	106.3

14-16 镇街规模以上工业企业R&D人员情况（2012年）

R&D Personnel of Industrial Enterprises above Designated Size by Town (2012)

镇　街	有R&D活动的工业企业数（个）	R&D人员合计（人）	#参加项目人员	#女性	#研究人员	#全时人员	非全时人员
全市总计	607	51386	47287	7746	6807	34858	16528
莞　城	6	761	689	217	154	576	185
石　龙	16	1411	1298	319	121	726	685
虎　门	39	2498	2346	409	383	1504	994
东　城	29	3509	3305	491	363	2679	830
万　江	16	1237	1189	274	173	706	531
南　城	15	1523	1444	188	141	1045	478
中　堂	12	476	455	136	73	211	265
望牛墩	11	244	239	26	27	67	177
麻　涌	26	2223	2127	160	350	1568	655
石　碣	21	7974	7255	517	774	5577	2397
高　埗	11	384	351	38	72	246	138
道　滘	14	431	387	63	63	318	113
洪　梅	8	680	653	103	68	415	265
沙　田	18	540	468	126	101	377	163
厚　街	21	1915	1776	372	316	1245	670
长　安	36	4170	3921	596	384	3056	1114
寮　步	40	1803	1683	218	372	1210	593
大岭山	25	1063	973	177	321	934	129
大　朗	26	2105	1991	534	189	1733	372
黄　江	17	1383	1321	168	208	628	755
樟木头	10	412	385	178	75	347	65
清　溪	11	1044	1002	173	72	677	367
塘　厦	48	4303	3699	736	500	1848	2455
凤　岗	19	1014	918	168	208	892	122
谢　岗	7	217	206	17	24	133	84
常　平	18	1507	1220	376	252	1150	357
桥　头	11	404	373	51	76	268	136
横　沥	18	859	808	129	109	430	429
东　坑	8	377	331	60	29	202	175
企　石	5	901	882	69	148	853	48
石　排	8	510	487	77	28	382	128
茶　山	10	271	249	36	85	147	124
松山湖	27	3237	2856	544	548	2708	529

14-17 镇街规模以上工业企业R&D人员全时当量情况（2012年）

R&D Personnel Full-time-equivalent of Industrial Enterprises above Designated Size by Town (2012)

镇 街	有R&D活动的工业企业数（个）	R&D人员全时当量（人年）	#研究人员	#应用研究人员	#试验发展人员
全市总计	607	44335	5999	34	44301
莞 城	6	683	138		683
石 龙	16	1360	111		1360
虎 门	39	2047	322		2047
东 城	29	2814	321		2814
万 江	16	1040	146		1040
南 城	15	1264	132		1264
中 堂	12	357	56		357
望 牛 墩	11	183	18	12	171
麻 涌	26	2029	324		2029
石 碣	21	7808	745		7808
高 埗	11	289	56		289
道 滘	14	403	57		403
洪 梅	8	626	64		626
沙 田	18	483	89		483
厚 街	21	1528	294		1528
长 安	36	3076	306	5	3071
寮 步	40	1438	317		1438
大 岭 山	25	946	290		946
大 朗	26	1860	183		1860
黄 江	17	1071	194		1071
樟 木 头	10	397	72		397
清 溪	11	983	65		983
塘 厦	48	3498	409	10	3488
凤 岗	19	890	154		890
谢 岗	7	170	20		170
常 平	18	1341	185		1341
桥 头	11	387	71		387
横 沥	18	753	98		753
东 坑	8	313	21		313
企 石	5	880	145		880
石 排	8	444	24		444
茶 山	10	233	75		233
松 山 湖	27	2739	494	6	2733

14-18 镇街规模以上工业企业R&D经费情况（2012年）

The R&D Funds of Industrial Enterprises above Designated Size by Town (2012)

镇　　街	R&D经费内部支出合　计（万元）	按活动类型分组			按资金来源分组			
		基础研究支出	应用研究支出	试验发展支出	政府资金	企业资金	境外资金	其他资金
全市总计	748347		348	747999	16789	720243	5626	5690
莞　　城	14288			14288	132	14155		
石　　龙	16686			16686	1736	14950		
虎　　门	45786			45786	317	45419	50	
东　　城	45728			45728	1500	44228		
万　　江	12506			12506	667	11474		365
南　　城	25913			25913	2655	22916		342
中　　堂	8478			8478	55	8370		53
望 牛 墩	7081		80	7001	31	6859		192
麻　　涌	67475			67475	544	64210	2520	202
石　　碣	78309			78309	98	77113	1098	
高　　埗	7701			7701	527	7174		
道　　滘	7913			7913	266	7471		177
洪　　梅	21359			21359	14	21345		
沙　　田	10866			10866	414	10346		105
厚　　街	28643			28643	119	28238		286
长　　安	59872		67	59805	81	59618		173
寮　　步	24660			24660	962	23698		
大 岭 山	22439			22439	332	21808		298
大　　朗	22632			22632	627	21772		232
黄　　江	19128			19128	391	18556		182
樟 木 头	5571			5571	1	5570		
清　　溪	9083			9083	237	8846		
塘　　厦	48479		69	48410	1029	46057	324	1069
凤　　岗	12329			12329	367	10935	69	959
谢　　岗	4322			4322	20	3025	1277	
常　　平	21234			21234	496	19787		951
桥　　头	4760			4760	22	4344	289	106
横　　沥	10488			10488	6	10482		
东　　坑	6518			6518		6518		
企　　石	5659			5659	39	5620		
石　　排	7292			7292	20	7272		
茶　　山	5913			5913	151	5762		
松 山 湖	59238		133	59105	2934	56304		

14-18 续表

(2012年)

镇　街	按使用项目分		R&D经费外部支出合计(万元)	对境内研究机构支出	对境内高等院校支出	对境外支出
	经常性支出	资产性支出				
全市总计	676645	71702	28331	4437	2980	1245
莞　城	13429	859	395	33	362	
石　龙	15620	1066	1521	1227	294	
虎　门	42270	3516	268	193	75	
东　城	43783	1945	149	130	19	
万　江	11398	1108	416	2	411	
南　城	21177	4736	597	562	32	
中　堂	6918	1560	2	1		
望牛墩	6661	421				
麻　涌	64974	2501	1112	1045	66	
石　碣	70382	7926	119	71	48	
高　埗	7083	619	13		13	
道　滘	6463	1450	4	4		
洪　梅	17961	3398	16	11	5	
沙　田	8226	2640	79	25	30	23
厚　街	27038	1605	72	13	13	
长　安	54789	5082	19842	465	28	119
寮　步	23479	1181	135	83	40	
大岭山	19838	2601	61		45	
大　朗	20330	2301	1385	2	425	946
黄　江	17786	1343	152			
樟木头	4603	968				
清　溪	7171	1913	56	17	39	
塘　厦	43948	4531	225	5	219	
凤　岗	11314	1016				
谢　岗	4143	179				
常　平	16851	4383	249	60	79	20
桥　头	4695	65				
横　沥	9901	587	31		31	
东　坑	5646	872	153	83	70	
企　石	5081	579				
石　排	6811	481	19	19		
茶　山	4400	1513	14		14	
松山湖	52478	6760	1250	386	622	137

14-19 镇街规模以上工业企业全部R&D项目情况（2012年）

Basic Statistics on R&D Projects of Industrial Enterprises above Designated Size by Town (2012)

镇　　街	项目数（个）	参加项目人员（人）	项目人员折合全时当量（人年）	全部项目经费内部支出（万元）
全市总计	3083	47287	40669	695671
莞　　城	159	205	617	13480
石　　龙	69	1298	1251	13894
虎　　门	217	2501	1925	44024
东　　城	126	3824	2651	44343
万　　江	85	1189	1000	10372
南　　城	81	1444	1195	24348
中　　堂	33	455	342	7724
望 牛 墩	36	239	179	6549
麻　　涌	132	2127	1939	65588
石　　碣	152	7255	7104	70512
高　　埗	34	351	261	7097
道　　滘	47	387	360	6929
洪　　梅	50	653	601	20862
沙　　田	53	468	421	9121
厚　　街	150	1766	1397	26341
长　　安	255	3921	2920	56712
寮　　步	156	1688	1338	23175
大 岭 山	114	973	868	20832
大　　朗	140	2007	1761	22192
黄　　江	63	1321	1017	17775
樟 木 头	24	385	370	5127
清　　溪	70	1002	943	8064
塘　　厦	204	3699	2946	44277
凤　　岗	83	918	805	11479
谢　　岗	16	1220	161	4304
常　　平	88	206	1065	16428
桥　　头	25	373	363	4696
横　　沥	75	808	711	9986
东　　坑	79	331	272	5967
企　　石	17	882	863	4581
石　　排	38	487	425	7135
茶　　山	25	249	214	5478
松 山 湖	187	2655	2383	56279

14-20 镇街规模以上工业企业办科技机构情况（2012年）

Basic Statistics on Scientific and Technological Institutions of Industrial Enterprises above Designated Size by Town (2012)

镇街	有科技机构的工业企业数（个）	机构数（个）	机构人员合计（人）	#博士毕业	#硕士毕业	#本科毕业	机构经费支出（万元）
全市总计	321	417	27060	251	1160	10890	440568
莞　城	1	2	64		1	48	1002
石　龙	7	8	728	11	20	236	8069
虎　门	17	20	1181	9	30	430	22237
东　城	23	28	3527	11	50	1208	51812
万　江	11	14	576	6	28	312	7925
南　城	6	12	406	12	49	192	11819
中　堂	4	4	141	3	13	86	1766
望牛墩	7	7	118	2	6	42	5513
麻　涌	13	18	965	15	70	517	19816
石　碣	8	8	2322	1	45	1137	26633
高　埗	6	6	265	6	6	126	4813
道　滘	7	8	387		9	90	5344
洪　梅	4	4	114	3	6	36	1740
沙　田	9	11	400	2	8	133	6467
厚　街	8	8	616	4	11	289	18449
长　安	16	21	1878	9	93	928	35213
寮　步	12	14	585	1	23	178	6088
大岭山	15	19	538	1	12	175	10827
大　朗	17	18	733	13	20	523	13375
黄　江	11	12	1181	5	35	234	15597
樟木头	7	7	167	3	2	46	3451
清　溪	12	29	1710	16	15	423	19832
塘　厦	25	37	2805	35	88	1256	43248
凤　岗	12	14	638	3	26	289	7378
谢　岗	1	1	10			10	172
常　平	11	16	745	21	47	129	13386
桥　头	5	6	101		3	42	1878
横　沥	5	8	199	5	7	53	2112
东　坑	7	7	215	2	8	70	5196
企　石	7	10	352	3	21	163	4826
石　排	4	4	371	2	8	109	4380
茶　山	9	10	259	2	13	139	6509
松山湖	14	26	2763	45	387	1241	53697

14-21 镇街规模以上工业企业高新技术产品情况（2012年）

Basic Statistics on High-tech Products of Industrial Enterprises above Designated Size by Town (2012)

镇　街	高新产品个数（个）	高新产品产值（万元）	高新产品销售收入（万元）	#高新产品出口销售收入	高新产品实现利税（万元）
全市总计	1601	33234826	32785071	21133130	1131971
莞　城	17	255880	254619	105458	18266
石　龙	45	1766878	1681915	1403334	134435
虎　门	91	932592	895217	392524	49813
东　城	74	1087496	986762	265225	20086
万　江	40	225445	207304	32155	17525
南　城	37	594038	701220	427292	27866
中　堂	24	73102	70069	14863	1884
望牛墩	28	240818	241720	81548	6728
麻　涌	43	350062	325793	142427	22287
石　碣	98	2256274	2251087	1769658	88730
高　埗	25	425739	420748	309946	40036
道　滘	33	283801	284416	97512	9026
洪　梅	18	109494	110309	42429	7971
沙　田	42	672561	664581	107700	30601
厚　街	36	3356297	3342421	3227113	33276
长　安	172	2339771	2304323	2081100	35733
寮　步	86	2608079	2566101	2250944	71006
大岭山	91	1691658	1709665	846151	73489
大　朗	51	468309	459145	295469	18792
黄　江	28	1785911	1756198	1529095	27740
樟木头	23	243837	243634	114561	4550
清　溪	52	1593982	1584758	1382292	30505
塘　厦	71	1256790	1211107	780534	35410
凤　岗	45	395903	398333	213611	20720
谢　岗	28	209617	201586	119162	-4438
常　平	78	1506045	1501358	598420	61677
桥　头	32	697971	694616	624140	20399
横　沥	36	205379	201273	117199	12274
东　坑	45	636948	648059	421794	7461
企　石	10	46207	45806	3256	2695
石　排	16	140249	84263	43900	2783
茶　山	35	407228	408521	137963	6981
松山湖	51	4370469	4328145	1154359	195662

14-22 镇街固定资产投资总额（2012年）

Total Investment in Fixed Assets by Town(2012)

单位：万元

镇　　街	固定资产投资	#第二产业	#工　业	第三产业	#民营
莞　　城	255912	62198	60505	193714	187962
石　　龙	176316	34706	34706	141610	47741
虎　　门	783984	127568	127568	656416	588629
东　　城	558062	120610	120610	437452	384380
万　　江	253466	40663	40663	212803	224281
南　　城	930321	363113	363113	567208	468264
中　　堂	221050	130183	130183	90867	221050
望 牛 墩	139326	94484	94484	44842	117568
麻　　涌	306933	167907	167907	139026	222714
石　　碣	169443	132614	132614	36829	88422
高　　埗	224168	145044	145044	79124	111479
道　　滘	149517	71772	71772	77745	149517
洪　　梅	136677	118757	118757	17920	25895
沙　　田	187391	64999	64999	122392	105890
厚　　街	438116	109877	109877	328239	278135
长　　安	570966	184204	184204	386762	434369
寮　　步	348518	161571	161571	185647	230313
大 岭 山	279367	132710	132710	146657	186399
大　　朗	350221	138985	138985	211236	273439
黄　　江	189121	79661	79661	109460	103043
樟 木 头	151849	9207	8707	142642	109718
清　　溪	253966	195341	195341	58625	71480
塘　　厦	557124	18524	18524	538600	499615
凤　　岗	374920	224526	224526	150394	167168
谢　　岗	101716	62299	62299	39417	52431
常　　平	337942	68065	68065	269877	282657
桥　　头	216209	184092	184092	27617	73776
横　　沥	85627	18617	18617	67010	73625
东　　坑	146520	70513	70513	66602	95704
企　　石	70788	32280	32280	38508	51024
石　　排	133998	85352	85352	48646	128753
茶　　山	129621	92518	92518	32598	78062
松 山 湖	744006	341937	341937	402069	426337

14-23 镇街邮电局、所通信能力及服务网点（2011-2012年）

Communication Capacity and Service Establishments of Telecommunication Offices by Town (2011-2012)

镇　街	邮电局(所、综合营业厅)(处)		服务网点(含报刊亭)(处)		固定电话用户(含小灵通)(户)	
	2011年	2012年	2011年	2012年	2011年	2012年
全市总计	626	595	2970	2961	3113665	2665142
市　区	87	64	508	499	578751	510296
石　龙	14	11	51	40	69760	62112
虎　门	46	47	239	210	242557	208132
中　堂	11	12	57	29	59637	54115
望 牛 墩	6	5	25	22	28478	23869
麻　涌	8	7	22	29	39573	35385
石　碣	27	17	89	127	87882	67077
高　埗	14	11	55	50	53555	48158
道　滘	8	6	41	37	49052	41666
洪　梅	5	5	17	14	19196	15199
沙　田	9	8	49	50	48750	42908
厚　街	36	33	170	209	188486	157082
长　安	47	44	265	162	237493	197985
寮　步	24	21	101	133	127669	103125
大 岭 山	17	24	90	110	83923	65700
大　朗	21	26	116	96	136709	119193
黄　江	17	18	85	95	80886	71413
樟 木 头	17	14	83	78	81121	70538
清　溪	27	25	120	155	95081	73680
塘　厦	34	40	150	159	145496	129211
凤　岗	24	26	86	91	104682	83006
谢　岗	8	4	45	37	37577	29530
常　平	41	39	179	169	164472	146299
桥　头	14	15	68	94	62205	50788
横　沥	17	17	57	75	70272	55539
东　坑	11	10	41	44	43492	36113
企　石	9	10	47	29	46010	37642
石　排	12	12	64	64	64510	54674
茶　山	15	21	50	53	66390	59428
松 山 湖		3		1		15279

注：市区指莞城、南城、东城、万江四个街道。

14-24 镇街商贸情况（2012年）

Statistics on Commerce by Town (2012)

单位：万元

镇　　街	社会消费品零售总额	批发和零售业销售额	住宿和餐饮业营业额
莞　　城	1048870	2807720	53291
石　　龙	259993	464500	35225
虎　　门	1359300	1543493	183743
东　　城	930290	2492591	129551
万　　江	352765	509837	50129
南　　城	1409882	3948434	136219
中　　堂	203574	700559	39546
望 牛 墩	59614	174088	8058
麻　　涌	107167	175305	15295
石　　碣	207739	674991	25672
高　　埗	173452	322919	22145
道　　滘	114507	197594	18287
洪　　梅	42485	41365	12521
沙　　田	143955	932630	24938
厚　　街	898006	1051059	127429
长　　安	616812	909875	99468
寮　　步	1462348	1636636	49566
大 岭 山	466828	555141	51687
大　　朗	513769	720637	52030
黄　　江	244274	350204	41093
樟 木 头	406894	761301	40101
清　　溪	324513	316904	43540
塘　　厦	564833	813426	76056
凤　　岗	282636	431823	41129
谢　　岗	93253	225892	14367
常　　平	737046	927318	133705
桥　　头	175143	184920	39899
横　　沥	194295	194328	25868
东　　坑	145548	144007	14612
企　　石	110913	126020	13343
石　　排	191819	207690	19799
茶　　山	214575	334254	23497
松 山 湖	30856	841900	21983

14-25 镇街注册工商企业及个体户数（2012年）

Registered Industrial & Commercial Enterprises and Self-employed Individuals by Town (2012)

单位：户

镇 街	总户数	国有集体	三资企业	三来一补	私营企业	个体户
全市总计	541321	13264	11974	3231	122703	388932
莞 城	16866	637	204	10	4578	12279
石 龙	9569	246	115	16	1117	8057
虎 门	44700	644	791	117	8547	35472
东 城	36533	1023	640	106	10045	25506
万 江	16700	366	206	18	5034	12042
南 城	26957	1132	590	23	10905	15072
中 堂	9253	306	97	23	1615	7209
望 牛 墩	3350	138	102	13	711	2384
麻 涌	5010	222	81	14	776	3902
石 碣	14741	288	245	92	2667	12417
高 埗	8091	202	165	26	1365	6323
道 滘	6626	188	167	22	1578	4666
洪 梅	2357	97	81	3	465	1708
沙 田	7284	338	219	13	1596	5102
厚 街	35603	492	625	120	5763	29500
长 安	47545	801	1105	461	14101	31943
寮 步	23934	622	453	71	5954	17795
大 岭 山	20875	392	358	51	4811	16229
大 朗	24449	509	450	138	4580	19732
黄 江	12542	336	367	116	3197	8506
樟 木 头	13073	317	239	67	3281	9137
清 溪	13190	290	662	191	2881	9200
塘 厦	25703	514	972	323	6817	18082
凤 岗	17108	421	540	379	3285	12466
谢 岗	5402	134	218	66	879	4098
常 平	23686	608	672	236	5150	17816
桥 头	10033	285	339	88	1923	7387
横 沥	11284	301	387	135	2356	8098
东 坑	6040	277	155	64	1066	4474
企 石	6885	273	178	57	1334	5039
石 排	11050	314	240	85	1855	8555
茶 山	11041	316	240	87	1951	8441
松 山 湖	1122	235	71		520	295

注：本表数据来源于市工商局。

14-26 镇街集市贸易市场数及私营个体户注册资金额(2011-2012年)

Fair Trades and Registered Capital of Private Enterprises & Self-employed Individuals by Town (2011-2012)

镇　　街	集市贸易市场数(个)		个体工商户注册资金额(万元)		私营企业注册资金额(万元)	
	2011年	2012年	2011年	2012年	2011年	2012年
全市总计	812	616	844417	909237	12923645	16568945
莞　　城	28	10	19675	22190	825275	988735
石　　龙	12	6	11817	14041	166174	224938
虎　　门	78	42	72813	75790	830717	1007664
东　　城	60	50	44068	49369	1369788	1701895
万　　江	33	31	25361	25815	492141	613181
南　　城	30	19	27980	30654	1784213	2569999
中　　堂	27	23	18699	20862	234739	279646
望 牛 墩	7	6	6698	7176	94050	120701
麻　　涌	14	14	8078	9157	168695	189476
石　　碣	23	17	22353	25520	173739	201287
高　　埗	13	12	13945	15573	173189	225014
道　　滘	12	10	11792	12582	194886	234829
洪　　梅	4	4	3220	4146	115503	125070
沙　　田	21	19	13419	14495	202082	262097
厚　　街	50	29	57759	62546	687918	793682
长　　安	49	23	74430	70328	856293	1183414
寮　　步	37	29	32359	37059	597742	704160
大 岭 山	18	17	34889	33989	302663	384527
大　　朗	24	21	41876	51924	402316	524932
黄　　江	27	21	19605	21185	239116	298096
樟 木 头	24	15	22633	22044	190898	234481
清　　溪	20	19	21013	24052	223926	267151
塘　　厦	26	24	33736	36063	590987	773129
凤　　岗	22	18	27435	30767	242252	320936
谢　　岗	8	8	10393	11031	78688	103969
常　　平	41	34	51501	57443	445332	572884
桥　　头	18	18	17355	19501	177973	226723
横　　沥	18	16	20791	22616	158922	206338
东　　坑	15	12	11764	12656	127995	157685
企　　石	14	13	16644	16958	162085	225512
石　　排	18	15	27739	27015	131541	169931
茶　　山	21	19	21810	22641	180158	228329
松 山 湖		2	768	2046	301649	448535

注:本表数据来源于市工商局。

14-27 镇街来料加工装配签约宗数、出口值及引进设备价值(2012年)

Contracts of Processing and Assembling of Import Materials, Export Value and Value of Equipments Imported by Town (2012)

镇　街	累计投产宗数(宗)	出口值(万美元)	引进设备价值(万美元)
莞　城	1	695	
石　龙	5	1269	
虎　门	20	3577	1
东　城	38	7722	897
万　江	10	1277	50
南　城	11	2369	
中　堂	11	2835	17
望牛墩	1	240	
麻　涌	11	334	
石　碣	47	3864	105
高　埗	7	38928	623
道　滘	4	1364	
洪　梅	2	77	
沙　田	6	121	
厚　街	32	29480	421
长　安	416	181908	25119
寮　步	8	4028	1
大岭山	15	41802	136
大　朗	100	7072	174
黄　江	34	133328	1682
樟木头	27	24265	1
清　溪	141	38914	2253
塘　厦	132	36372	2329
凤　岗	228	19425	238
谢　岗	39	3216	54
常　平	75	23905	161
桥　头	52	41329	172
横　沥	44	8980	31
东　坑	53	26848	22
企　石	22	1798	6
石　排	49	4289	
茶　山	43	10086	1

注：本表为外经贸局口径。

14-28 镇街“三资”企业签约、实际利用外资及出口值(新口径)(2012年)

Contracts, Foreign Capital Actually Utilized and Export Value of Enterprises with Foreign Investment by Town (2012)

镇　　街	签约宗数(宗)	投产企业宗数(宗)	协议(合同)规定外商投资总额(万美元)	外　　商实际投资总　　额(万美元)	出口值(万美元)
莞　　城	10	56	4436	4436	42719
石　　龙	7	55	11013	2256	209898
虎　　门	17	671	11509	13954	244252
东　　城	21	321	12528	16398	242167
万　　江	4	140	950	2522	24257
南　　城	33	220	8464	10220	109457
中　　堂	4	75	490	2173	22232
望 牛 墩	2	85	3623	1933	18930
麻　　涌	5	47	12702	23916	186515
石　　碣	21	214	6332	6639	342278
高　　埗	8	114	14180	9098	69716
道　　滘	3	148	984	2027	38717
洪　　梅	3	60	14749	18810	26816
沙　　田	7	144	4243	3962	77477
厚　　街	14	429	12290	17243	863727
长　　安	97	787	38206	26563	533871
寮　　步	40	356	18968	11923	472337
大 岭 山	6	272	7313	7987	155718
大　　朗	30	372	16285	14213	103903
黄　　江	24	306	16464	12956	302448
樟 木 头	17	166	3923	4306	60551
清　　溪	34	530	13411	17845	475178
塘　　厦	42	747	28770	24580	359271
凤　　岗	74	415	42108	19682	178756
谢　　岗	7	185	2577	4496	58209
常　　平	53	389	17622	13828	410272
桥　　头	25	304	12909	6025	199336
横　　沥	12	315	5137	5989	120892
东　　坑	11	139	5546	7273	147302
企　　石	7	138	1588	1819	31381
石　　排	17	203	7024	4075	48859
茶　　山	16	188	9011	8395	53561
松 山 湖	13	68	12300	2713	69014

注：本表为外经贸局口径。

14-29 镇街进出口总额（2011-2012年，海关口径）

Total Value of Exports and Imports by Town (2011-2012, Custom Statistics)

单位：万美元

镇街	2011年			2012年		
	进出口总额	进口	出口	进出口总额	进口	出口
莞城	130292	52478	77814	157692	55381	102311
石龙	292834	99404	193430	313865	101864	212000
虎门	406401	125370	281031	456103	149110	306993
东城	440514	160343	280171	478619	162194	316425
万江	55402	18150	37251	54198	16589	37609
南城	605897	354801	251096	689396	403807	285589
中堂	79593	54429	25164	78318	50693	27625
望牛墩	34484	12534	21950	41385	14363	27022
麻涌	424246	237857	186389	425166	229300	195866
石碣	625090	263346	361745	589283	234907	354376
高埗	193181	67643	125537	188227	68299	119928
道滘	78317	37504	40812	80532	37723	42808
洪梅	183742	154650	29091	164186	131932	32254
沙田	201115	115324	85791	172701	88309	84391
厚街	1091690	409634	682056	1456166	555626	900540
长安	1293144	556790	736354	1344774	588376	756397
寮步	936140	384449	551692	998126	413331	584795
大岭山	417185	159259	257927	405647	177603	228044
大朗	316273	122372	193901	346862	103819	243043
黄江	697213	276594	420618	743228	296952	446276
樟木头	144227	53010	91218	139752	52146	87607
清溪	877523	345420	532103	886849	361672	525177
塘厦	631511	225157	406354	680063	234018	446045
凤岗	339311	131653	207658	422685	135274	287411
谢岗	83831	28061	55770	89379	27559	61820
常平	669186	273346	395840	757750	292037	465714
桥头	274104	109570	164534	442764	194726	248038
横沥	200574	67492	133081	196809	63328	133482
东坑	272314	108121	164194	312791	119844	192947
企石	54998	14990	40008	55217	15003	40214
石排	85760	21756	64004	91900	21656	70244
茶山	106482	47181	59300	125198	55372	69826

14-30 镇街实际利用外资（2011-2012年）

Foreign Capital Actually Utilized by Town (2011-2012)

单位：万美元

镇　街	2011年	2012年	镇　街	2011年	2012年
莞　城	3932	4436	寮　步	10769	11923
石　龙	7649	2256	大岭山	6285	7987
虎　门	12166	13954	大　朗	12538	14213
东　城	14457	16398	黄　江	12233	12956
万　江	1765	2522	樟木头	6623	4306
南　城	8923	10220	清　溪	17724	17845
中　堂	2512	2173	塘　厦	19390	24580
望牛墩	2697	1933	凤　岗	17171	19682
麻　涌	21444	23916	谢　岗	6297	4496
石　碣	5695	6639	常　平	11610	13828
高　埗	3342	9098	桥　头	4389	6025
道　滘	2599	2027	横　沥	9701	5989
洪　梅	9240	18810	东　坑	6315	7273
沙　田	2497	3962	企　石	2780	1819
厚　街	15121	17243	石　排	3560	4075
长　安	25963	26563	茶　山	7534	8395

14-31 镇街税收总额（2011-2012年）

Taxes by Town (2011-2012)

单位：万元

镇街	2011年			2012年		
	税收总额	国税	地税	税收总额	国税	地税
莞城	292371	98065	194306	302851	91700	211150
石龙	123514	61653	61861	132656	67751	64905
虎门	459405	265608	193797	527904	304203	223701
东城	542514	234234	308280	593748	264421	329327
万江	131670	70341	61329	158779	79999	78780
南城	704044	177713	526331	807018	206267	600752
中堂	96315	70200	26115	102838	75571	27267
望牛墩	54623	42680	11943	61850	48717	13133
麻涌	200026	121792	78235	227307	136172	91134
石碣	159240	95436	63804	181699	116252	65447
高埗	100190	65170	35020	115219	78065	37154
道滘	98325	62386	35940	111857	81534	30324
洪梅	50354	33464	16890	48811	30460	18351
沙田	100419	52466	47953	107652	61792	45860
厚街	298739	175006	123733	343628	189838	153790
长安	475890	301728	174162	543804	344862	198943
寮步	257789	153564	104225	313820	188881	124939
大岭山	185403	108635	76768	201407	126852	74555
大朗	190037	108691	81345	213319	129680	83639
黄江	132963	73767	59196	152092	86166	65926
樟木头	100226	52396	47830	101657	56253	45404
清溪	199573	129846	69727	209261	140064	69197
塘厦	354541	182560	171981	393748	213454	180293
凤岗	198149	95729	102420	223793	113716	110077
谢岗	48026	32000	16025	53799	37307	16492
常平	231640	112911	118729	267518	133404	134114
桥头	76990	47495	29495	89934	57135	32799
横沥	96333	66896	29436	109473	78061	31412
东坑	68883	39957	28926	77527	47621	29907
企石	56114	38015	18099	64986	44201	20785
石排	59751	40945	18806	73222	49255	23967
茶山	94026	62403	31623	105216	69371	35846
松山湖	214408	94215	120193	251682	107291	144391

14-32 镇街本级可支配财政收入和财政支出（2011-2012年）

Disposable Government Revenue and Expenditure by Town (2011-2012)

单位：万元

镇　　街	可支配财政收入		财政支出	
	2011年	2012年	2011年	2012年
莞　　城	74397	74510	70110	60273
石　　龙	59100	62806	58700	62160
虎　　门	204919	212576	217572	226753
东　　城	156688	173810	156182	171503
万　　江	59429	62575	55840	62846
南　　城	182904	186636	160794	142371
中　　堂	61553	63418	59502	63571
望 牛 墩	36518	40963	42208	40933
麻　　涌	59049	66006	59049	66002
石　　碣	46618	52212	46773	51725
高　　埗	44580	48425	44440	48371
道　　滘	55149	59527	54923	59400
洪　　梅	31808	32013	31762	32098
沙　　田	46450	52030	47312	52802
厚　　街	111564	123424	111542	121066
长　　安	143187	164838	140384	157446
寮　　步	96075	106652	95620	106355
大 岭 山	85017	90534	84879	89780
大　　朗	71613	78580	73053	81033
黄　　江	109517	59705	109422	58051
樟 木 头	135913	62979	117988	73006
清　　溪	73694	77113	73623	76060
塘　　厦	144351	185205	133532	143720
凤　　岗	98898	174725	98582	177810
谢　　岗	33325	36954	34097	35030
常　　平	105796	116451	102758	116041
桥　　头	50320	54656	49908	54512
横　　沥	47857	46362	47213	45897
东　　坑	57213	62103	56670	61692
企　　石	37957	36054	37958	35991
石　　排	37118	40171	54835	49058
茶　　山	50299	55568	50257	55189
松 山 湖	322107	94192	203129	247746

14-33 镇街资产负债总额（2011-2012年）

Total Assets and Liabilities by Town (2011-2012)

单位：万元

镇街	资产总额		负债总额	
	2011年	2012年	2011年	2012年
莞城	345680	357083	88549	65744
石龙	320716	355782	153949	188176
虎门	1363193	1431599	496173	471627
东城	560597	628780		
万江	288370	338905	172694	174298
南城	565154	656642	29500	44350
中堂	364470	383765	181465	189693
望牛墩	225888	235643	131163	134874
麻涌	297008	312339	94631	94142
石碣	469384	452883	228668	232313
高埗	314721	307883	158030	133097
道滘	245832	256525	108648	106341
洪梅	161183	165892	110297	114483
沙田	368876	379515	104650	97217
厚街	502602	545383	141112	134078
长安	882359	957227	106953	89492
寮步	654380	691332	184964	175619
大岭山	380666	445982	130371	179655
大朗	378577	380465	82981	86613
黄江	417072	418606	128761	122987
樟木头	330991	320163	160193	151224
清溪	615378	595968	272175	273491
塘厦	995413	1046260	351496	407126
凤岗	472454	481009	187447	177389
谢岗	183623	188030	107276	108989
常平	723404	737796	218684	175510
桥头	355750	348871	184400	179256
横沥	326248	332697	211612	216607
东坑	236824	247179	107406	98993
企石	259268	262500	164279	168152
石排	374235	365186	318498	309695
茶山	417809	426612	113974	117685

14-34 镇街各项人民币存贷款余额与城乡居民储蓄存款余额（2011-2012年）

Balance of Deposits and Loans by Town and Savings Deposit of Urban and Rural Household (2011-2012)

单位：万元

镇街	年末各项存款余额		年末各项贷款余额		年末城乡居民储蓄存款余额	
	2011年	2012年	2011年	2012年	2011年	2012年
莞城	7992828	7117739	5563564	4923345	2381163	2042360
石龙	1478689	1638987	702449	718905	967071	1099302
虎门	5095656	5698477	2287280	2399723	3786685	4339299
东城	4920611	6551515	2719125	3279644	2863771	3514174
万江	1390694	1566635	950306	1006237	947985	1126144
南城	11085024	13090077	8255747	11363772	2535995	3144829
中堂	893370	1014080	670244	711278	640589	725728
望牛墩	414961	464089	186087	201224	299294	339125
麻涌	752735	751678	338336	377787	396647	460410
石碣	1443871	1550487	510145	539173	1021382	1117585
高埗	753088	793558	214772	233340	520735	572138
道滘	669816	746099	266967	314251	476429	546933
洪梅	267100	285099	163564	175669	163577	187044
沙田	903968	975296	400293	420377	485443	548784
厚街	3275691	3740688	2378858	2553781	2337351	2605903
长安	4426131	4896289	1888415	2011226	2960784	3231036
寮步	1534544	1761472	771382	823839	1092838	1265691
大岭山	1229280	1343366	667149	753876	831686	946612
大朗	2050908	2311450	1038020	1100017	1461741	1662900
黄江	1159845	1423686	485417	557874	856638	997188
樟木头	1075966	1197803	688798	705600	842036	944625
清溪	1355190	1543268	512255	494608	935645	1063674
塘厦	2448716	2830320	1327144	1499029	1571874	1778630
凤岗	1519195	1760256	782655	992493	1052569	1204962
谢岗	422040	485903	166667	194376	306742	354097
常平	2611639	3067656	1117455	1283902	1888320	2177611
桥头	787852	884573	344831	390202	639719	723422
横沥	796707	923448	337889	352797	641452	732887
东坑	558823	623736	225108	242756	415415	473887
企石	536811	650221	339291	396185	418246	508259
石排	776940	885986	281036	292776	589370	686226
茶山	941346	1059588	285467	293318	695206	797082
松山湖	523866	671048	294132	352691	85521	123483

注：本表为人民银行东莞支行口径。

14-35 镇街普通中学情况（2012年）

Basic Statistics on Regular Secondary Schools by Town (2012)

镇街	学校数(所)	毕业生数(人)	#普通高中	招生数(人)	#普通高中	在校学生数(人)	#普通高中	教职工数(人)	#专任教师
全市总计	203	79449	23398	96348	25758	267918	75851	20133	15858
莞城									
石龙	4	1417		1453		4419		305	264
虎门	8	3604	340	4462	351	11683	1011	1233	796
东城	11	3127		3666		9657		717	538
万江	7	3412	789	3725	673	10302	1935	642	550
南城	7	3040	703	3418	722	9431	2105	792	550
中堂	7	2057	143	2561	208	7341	559	565	397
望牛墩	3	1370		1389		4181		268	227
麻涌	2	1155		960		2883		241	219
石碣	8	1772	307	2196		6174	308	471	332
高埗	5	932		1232		3218		235	193
道滘	4	1805	493	2013	455	5550	1407	453	310
洪梅	1	298		152		569		76	59
沙田	4	1168	287	1897	500	4917	1366	588	369
厚街	10	2302		2966		7892		674	453
长安	5	2214		2778		7454		415	350
寮步	7	2489		3250		8640		559	473
大岭山	6	1803	346	2102	265	5984	905	446	336
大朗	7	2747	529	3689	514	9923	1557	639	495
黄江	3	770		1079		2930		217	173
樟木头	3	745		1102		3052		233	170
清溪	6	1129		1729		4776		379	280
塘厦	4	2232	145	3242	473	8405	1190	522	423
凤岗	9	2020	274	3019	332	7676	863	588	417
谢岗	3	757		821		2376		164	138
常平	11	2140		3193		8727		582	423
桥头	5	1787	444	2184	476	5886	1354	596	369
横沥	4	811		1311		3352		229	202
东坑	5	844		1365		3550		356	204
企石	3	895		1258		3471		225	193
石排	5	1082		1237		3300		255	221
茶山	7	2039	631	2285	413	6371	1465	435	350
松山湖	2	126		371		723		68	54

14-36 镇街小学情况（2012年）

Basic Statistics on Primary Schools by Town (2012)

镇 街	学校数（所）	毕业生数（人）	招生数（人）	在校学生数（人）	教职工数（人）	#专任教师
全市总计	322	87733	123290	608118	28745	25379
莞 城	9	2317	1974	12673	828	778
石 龙	5	1484	1732	9536	472	412
虎 门	23	5632	7584	37610	1949	1754
东 城	14	5859	7031	34690	1511	1423
万 江	16	3964	5166	26264	1152	1084
南 城	10	3256	4814	23283	1105	1044
中 堂	9	2358	3011	15117	764	721
望 牛 墩	4	1099	1214	6214	390	367
麻 涌	8	1370	1015	5874	468	426
石 碣	8	2794	4448	20392	835	769
高 埗	6	1752	2292	10964	500	463
道 滘	6	1723	1940	10759	461	429
洪 梅	3	336	261	1693	141	121
沙 田	4	1320	2082	9470	416	391
厚 街	15	3527	6456	30132	1356	1243
长 安	22	4609	8699	39318	1727	1486
寮 步	16	3836	5625	28264	1225	1068
大 岭 山	9	2149	3418	18093	769	700
大 朗	18	4548	6797	31907	1319	1103
黄 江	9	1566	2740	13262	657	511
樟 木 头	7	1739	2385	12726	570	468
清 溪	9	2266	3649	18400	886	766
塘 厦	13	4527	6109	30163	1389	1201
凤 岗	15	3693	5573	26697	1208	1112
谢 岗	3	1099	1141	6096	274	247
常 平	17	4300	6263	30891	1289	1177
桥 头	7	2140	2711	13671	626	577
横 沥	6	1861	3050	14492	650	600
东 坑	5	1726	2764	12970	538	485
企 石	7	1576	2301	10400	487	427
石 排	8	2184	2837	13676	673	614
茶 山	7	2417	3454	16637	789	720
松 山 湖	2	426	648	3362	192	176

14-37 镇街卫生事业机构、床位及人员数（2012年）

Number of Health care Institutions, Beds and Personnel by Town (2012)

镇街	机构数(个)	#医院	病床床位(张)	卫生工作人员(人)	#卫生技术人员	#执业(助理)医师	注册护士	药剂人员	检验人员
全市总计	2222	73	24617	49353	40597	14043	16914	2503	1504
莞城	54	4	387	1091	857	306	306	59	26
石龙	24	3	1678	2410	1934	606	845	135	61
虎门	186	7	1933	4309	3593	1186	1495	244	148
东城	159	6	2767	4971	3995	1289	1789	262	183
万江	66	4	2802	4775	4111	1391	1973	241	144
南城	96	4	1053	3134	2617	860	1058	114	99
中堂	48	2	855	937	821	245	351	41	26
望牛墩	32	1	120	320	256	78	81	26	9
麻涌	32	2	422	510	420	142	172	30	19
石碣	39	1	270	889	752	273	336	71	25
高埗	62	2	320	752	569	213	222	34	19
道滘	58	1	160	502	422	149	136	48	21
洪梅	12	1	139	318	264	66	93	30	13
沙田	48	2	197	525	441	170	139	32	18
厚街	132	2	1075	2400	2044	782	903	96	70
长安	110	5	1217	2692	2197	837	943	130	74
寮步	122	2	948	1777	1420	499	591	81	44
大岭山	88	2	360	1101	920	335	371	69	36
大朗	113	3	1100	1685	1350	498	544	76	42
黄江	52	2	650	1270	1024	371	387	77	48
樟木头	34	2	510	1097	870	276	360	41	35
清溪	69	1	514	1204	981	361	364	54	48
塘厦	81	3	708	1985	1600	606	619	106	61
凤岗	57	2	999	1626	1305	443	578	78	57
谢岗	21	1	120	321	272	111	82	16	7
常平	132	2	1209	1976	1606	609	625	82	44
桥头	57	1	380	839	726	252	296	33	21
横沥	64	1	420	863	694	223	275	48	21
东坑	48	1	250	580	495	170	189	19	18
企石	36	1	448	808	663	196	256	41	17
石排	43	1	306	853	687	242	271	42	21
茶山	44	1	300	695	592	212	233	39	20
松山湖	3			138	99	46	31	8	9

14-38 镇街优抚和社会救济基本情况（2012年）

Basic Statistics on Special Care and Social Relief by Town(2012)

镇　街	敬老院个数（个）	敬老院供养人数（人）	最低生活保障户数（户）	最低生活保障人数（人）	最低生活保障费支出（万元）
全市总计	31	709	10277	23598	4331.0
莞　城	1	27	320	735	128.8
石　龙	1	8	279	656	165.9
虎　门	1	15	313	748	176.0
东　城	1	19	43	114	18.8
万　江	1	39	826	1713	342.1
南　城		5	63	151	29.2
中　堂	1	4	666	1665	316.9
望牛墩	1	60	449	1150	323.7
麻　涌	1	11	1235	2530	55.0
石　碣	1	33	79	218	35.0
高　埗	1	16	265	731	124.6
道　滘	1	41	466	1107	263.3
洪　梅	1	30	630	1203	271.7
沙　田	1	19	981	1780	281.1
厚　街	1	28	462	1259	192.0
长　安	1	22	7	18	4.1
寮　步	1	29	223	569	77.2
大岭山	1	21	184	510	95.8
大　朗	1	25	281	510	167.0
黄　江	1	29	113	250	53.5
樟木头	1	50	81	191	48.1
清　溪	1	29	167	405	82.7
塘　厦	1	16	116	251	50.5
凤　岗	1	7	19	37	9.4
谢　岗	1	14	177	562	86.2
常　平	1	19	207	418	90.4
桥　头	1	28	128	309	45.1
横　沥	1	4	235	593	128.2
东　坑	1	23	243	633	112.8
企　石	1	13	312	793	157.7
石　排	1	6	495	1212	308.0
茶　山	1	19	212	577	90.2

14-39 镇街专利申请与授权数（2012年）

Basic Statistics on Patents Application Accepted and Granted by Town (2012)

单位：件

镇 街	专 利 申请数	#发明	实用新型	外观设计	专 利 授权数	#发明	实用新型	外观设计
全市总计	29199	5568	13167	10464	20900	1381	10667	8852
莞 城	609	270	232	107	346	71	203	72
石 龙	178	24	78	76	139	24	59	56
虎 门	1084	161	582	341	887	45	482	360
东 城	3404	416	1402	1586	1867	160	957	750
万 江	697	106	393	198	631	47	379	205
南 城	1424	242	743	439	1053	148	519	386
中 堂	210	38	123	49	186	21	76	89
望牛墩	179	24	100	55	95	6	58	31
麻 涌	147	40	83	24	122	24	78	20
石 碣	740	75	265	400	556	25	194	337
高 埗	224	55	135	34	240	27	128	85
道 滘	531	73	278	180	366	23	163	180
洪 梅	162	20	102	40	158	14	90	54
沙 田	400	56	137	207	284	6	96	182
厚 街	1539	72	438	1029	1259	40	367	852
长 安	3181	1304	1455	422	1515	97	1045	373
寮 步	1166	159	623	384	1052	66	575	411
大岭山	1674	103	348	1223	1471	36	331	1104
大 朗	674	96	377	201	480	16	311	153
黄 江	890	86	493	311	502	34	279	189
樟木头	449	45	212	192	326	21	146	159
清 溪	777	104	459	214	738	28	517	193
塘 厦	1389	197	834	358	1085	55	620	410
凤 岗	626	56	346	224	434	14	234	186
谢 岗	121	22	71	28	65	2	49	14
常 平	948	93	550	305	854	58	461	335
桥 头	378	38	173	167	323	10	161	152
横 沥	600	59	345	196	632	11	308	313
东 坑	446	38	223	185	591	32	373	186
企 石	356	49	140	167	315	21	149	145
石 排	795	57	271	467	568	16	228	324
茶 山	614	96	309	209	444	25	267	152
松山湖	2553	1284	828	441	1263	161	751	351

14-40 镇街总用电量和总供水量（2011-2012年）

Gross Electicity Comsumption and Water Supply by Town (2011-2012)

镇街	总用电量（万千瓦时）		总供水量（万吨）	
	2011年	2012年	2011年	2012年
莞城	51232	50841	17707	17100
石龙	74417	73289	2504	2237
虎门	396924	400650	12098	11994
东城	277307	286361	7130	7130
万江	122094	122396	4849	4639
南城	102740	106594	4461	4915
中堂	138213	140500	2867	2954
望牛墩	63971	65607	1772	1652
麻涌	127540	125995	2526	2374
石碣	157717	161785	4063	3985
高埗	135668	126855	3052	2936
道滘	115905	117427	2984	3003
洪梅	52409	53847	1408	1361
沙田	104589	107365	3480	3144
厚街	328340	325508	10796	10351
长安	547109	561952	13758	13175
寮步	234053	241804	4980	4795
大岭山	171397	178777	4197	4192
大朗	223665	239833	7857	7522
黄江	163041	163953	5042	4597
樟木头	94807	95677	1751	1630
清溪	232950	236726	6047	5774
塘厦	324518	337223	10090	9002
凤岗	215910	221561	5119	5292
谢岗	71273	76158	1970	1992
常平	276345	281088	9522	9276
桥头	133769	143005	3172	3206
横沥	124903	131186	3552	3520
东坑	81416	88115	2292	2301
企石	77172	81478	1942	2067
石排	114265	119915	2724	2728
茶山	131220	132917	4283	4183
松山湖	42655	60236	1369	1716

十五、村（居）委会主要指标

Main Indicators of Villagers' (Neighborhood) Committees

15 村(居)委会主要指标（2012年）

Main Indicators of Villagers'(Neighborhood) Committees (2012)

村(居)委会	土地面积(平方公里)	户籍人口(人)	外来暂住人口(人)	全部企业及个体户数(个)	#工业企业	资产总额(万元)	负债总额(万元)	资产负债率(%)	村组两级经营纯收入(万元)
莞　城									
市桥社区	0.9	31905	1495	2683	2	486	13	2.7	
东正社区	1.7	21321	3150	594	39	560	5	0.9	
罗沙社区	1.8	15055	4880	1806	17	249	54	21.7	
西隅社区	0.6	11979	262	181	3	889	210	23.6	
北隅社区	1.1	28613	9956	1570	4	779	103	13.2	
博厦社区	1.0	9104	1010	255		297	67	22.6	
兴塘社区	2.6	13194	7465	3984	21	247	93	37.7	
创业社区	1.5	23216	9687	2572	31	275	15	5.5	
罗沙联合社						24154	1094	4.5	8157
博厦联合社						6214	253	4.1	1109
细村联合社						16773	1337	8.0	2379
石　龙									
忠维村	0.8	1003	3530	100	10	12026	6252	52.0	400
林屋村	0.7	663	1650	105	29	4756	1436	30.2	494
新维村	0.6	551	2300	485	43	16354	4231	25.9	1944
蒲溪村	0.7	638	358	10		3144	453	14.4	516
西湖村	3.5	2845	4500	600	85	79316	5992	7.6	
王屋洲村	3.2	1600	7007	263	15	13287	586	4.4	536
黄家山村	2.5	1952	3700	158	6	12875	11394	88.5	172
中山东社区	0.5	18251	15982	255	11	1542	743	48.2	
中山西社区	0.5	19971	4095	548	23	1919	473	24.6	
兴龙社区		18502	7688	1546	11	1936	1006	52.0	
虎　门									
树田社区	4.0	1492	8250	462	427	11677	3791	32.5	1042
怀德社区	13.8	6281	27503	879	229	42340	2670	6.3	7076
居岐社区	1.8	1308	13300	581	57	14131	2195	15.5	1620
村头社区	1.3	814	6372	212	62	12566	4680	37.2	828
陈村社区	1.3	784	4138	45	35	6350	1002	15.8	442
黄村社区	0.9	567	4613	86	31	2968	751	25.3	365
大宁社区	5.4	2738	25800	540	206	63866	5350	8.4	6386
北栅社区	5.9	4560	24800	2078	341	33586	8572	25.5	4057
龙眼社区	3.0	2822	45000	909	349	99886	5811	5.8	7047
赤岗社区	7.5	4342	4600	203	80	29278	8829	30.2	941
博涌社区	5.9	7181	40000	3207	305	64269	16981	26.4	8240
新联社区	4.0	1168	7800	441	65	6987	1035	14.8	636
白沙社区	7.8	7203	12663	937	202	50123	13701	27.3	3112
镇口社区	1.8	3161	12563	427	125	17336	1142	6.6	2515
金洲社区	4.8	3942	25000	1550	85	78696	17685	22.5	6071

15 续表 1

(2012年)

村(居)委会	土地面积(平方公里)	户籍人口(人)	外来暂住人口(人)	全部企业及个体户数(个)	#工业企业	资产总额(万元)	负债总额(万元)	资产负债率(%)	村组两级经营纯收入(万元)
小捷滘社区	2.0	907	6122	335	93	15113	4555	30.1	1018
南栅社区	8.2	5379	51621	1430	312	96265	22206	23.1	8782
东风社区	2.8	1781	7600	307	51	14907	5130	34.4	922
宴岗社区	1.3	1115	6772	195	25	7994	1773	22.2	932
路东社区	5.6	3181	19640	880	222	51576	5837	11.3	6413
沙角社区	11.2	5763	19500	1114	364	42632	14656	34.4	3307
虎门寨社区	2.0	7599	10500	6955	28	22511	2195	9.8	7421
九门寨社区	2.6	1474	7300	32	30	13858	4935	35.6	967
南面社区	7.3	2773	3630	120	25	20097	1766	8.8	1146
北面社区	5.5	2589	3999	75	51	9212	3607	39.2	942
武山沙社区	2.9	2296	4331	185	60	7204	3579	49.7	538
东方社区	0.7	9205	2781	717	9	516	84	16.3	2
则徐社区	1.2	15786	10812	2094	52	1319	133	10.1	13
新湾社区	1.0	10878	3650	203	24	5926	1219	20.6	621
东　城									
温塘社区	11.6	9625	28000	625	65	23636	2078	8.8	11098
桑园社区	4.0	3707	29000	445	125	11398	891	7.8	3241
周屋社区	2.8	2372	8000	363	60	6206	436	7.0	1986
余屋社区	2.0	1656	3690	285	65	5244	214	4.1	1218
鳌峙塘社区	2.0	1045	2378	152	72	4433	1120	25.3	509
峡口社区	1.6	1219	2500	207	80	7123	1318	18.5	1723
柏洲边社区	1.0	1093	3850	217	58	5882	192	3.3	1317
上桥社区	1.0	1383	3000	203	42	3367	198	5.9	1600
下桥社区	2.0	2448	6123	923	46	7092	1331	18.8	2529
樟村社区	3.0	3109	4000	530	43	15792	1437	9.1	2613
梨川社区	1.0	1644	1080	596	91	5818	354	6.1	2455
堑头社区	1.5	3100	1580	291	32	9345	368	3.9	3641
主山社区	6.6	6066	28020	596	58	15495	245	1.6	7178
石井社区	6.7	2041	2980	145	60	11780	4904	41.6	2548
同沙社区	4.6	2453	4700	396	125	12364	832	6.7	1940
光明社区	1.9	1431	2320	150	34	9115	108	1.2	995
牛山社区	11.0	4135	7815	818	83	13357	3180	23.8	2924
立新社区	2.5	3231	5300	525	44	5159	333	6.5	2861
火炼树社区	1.2	1369	7000	485	403	7561	3227	42.7	2477
岗贝社区	1.7	13570	9800	2822		1331	259	19.5	92
花园新村社区	0.8	1293	1350	742		2226	355	15.9	
东泰社区	1.4	14997	10193	1226		4131	243	5.9	
星城社区	2.7	8652	23000			250	23	9.2	
万　江									
万江社区	2.6	4199	3372	80	64	13871	2783	20.1	17276
石美社区	2.5	4105	3660	227	74	14104	2671	18.9	
莫屋社区	1.0	1481	1799	165	83	5724	1026	17.9	14342
拔蛟窝社区	1.3	2266	1963	210	65	20742	3818	18.4	17997

15　续表 2

(2012年)

村(居)委会	土地面积(平方公里)	户籍人口(人)	外来暂住人口(人)	全部企业及个体户数(个)	#工业企业	资产总额(万元)	负债总额(万元)	资产负债率(%)	村组两级经营纯收入(万元)
黄粘洲社区	0.3	789	983	38	21	4296	705	16.4	142
蚬涌社区	2.0	2018	2312	243	99	4973	1387	27.9	1549
谷涌社区	2.0	3095	1339	167	24	21288	767	3.6	2214
小享社区	3.8	5018	2741	205	119	16757	672	4.0	1429
滘联社区	2.1	3443	1732	80	36	6689	5247	78.4	23
金泰社区	1.0	2148	2714	131	30	5073	1309	25.8	1429
曲海社区	1.2	1576	600	30	3	15015	155	1.0	825
牌楼基社区	1.6	1620	2093	178	40	18169	796	4.4	1144
大莲塘社区	0.8	1018	809	70	37	8779	308	3.5	549
水蛇涌社区	1.5	2389	1555	150	40	15136	1847	12.2	422
共联社区	1.3	1982	6036	176	53	6001	749	12.5	
新谷涌社区	1.4	2178	1399	88	40	12024	1373	11.4	801
坝头社区	1.4	1561	1413	18	13	12807	3462	27.0	1223
胜利社区	0.9	936	6178	30	26	2813	239	8.5	861
官桥滘社区	1.9	1687	1749	49	51	9655	630	6.5	
简沙洲社区	1.6	1714	2830	136	114	3980	3950	99.2	-38
新和社区	3.7	2745	6870	157	116	9022	887	9.8	2075
上甲社区	1.4	2445	1315	78	69	8414	2408	28.6	486
严屋社区	1.0	1112	666	39	31	4742	1102	23.2	
大汾社区	2.6	3409	1626	185	67	14554	769	5.3	1167
新村社区	5.8	8235	1860	280	168	15085	2878	19.1	1212
流涌尾社区	2.5	2333	1130	60	49	4973	1246	25.1	916
万江墟社区	1.0	7205	1679	246	23	4016	2242	55.8	
新城社区		7014	2427	596		559	167	29.9	
南　　城									
胜和社区	4.0	6647	19018	3210	5	48039	30416	63.3	5632
亨美社区	0.5	1857	3563	48	10	26813	7284	27.2	1117
三元里社区	0.4	1117	863	31	9	33458	1674	5.0	1954
篁村社区	1.0	3045	6974	769	14	27109	2072	7.6	2528
新基社区	2.0	2807	6803	1587	36	101595	576	0.6	2944
周溪社区	5.0	3970	6628	196	23	46388	3564	7.7	3143
袁屋边社区	2.0	1954	4526	360	12	52272	342	0.7	2087
白马社区	4.0	3333	6746	1332	41	35711	3239	9.1	3285
石鼓社区	2.0	1807	6530	254	24	35207	5458	15.5	2491
蛤地社区	8.0	2775	6053	122	26	25909	7667	29.6	2028
西平社区	3.9	3829	15035	708	12	63148	41780	66.2	1722
水濂社区	6.0	2072	4252	104	30	16230	9017	55.6	959
雅园社区	1.8	2348	15085	135	55	21891	1078	4.9	1422
元美社区	0.4	2647	2450	269	14	10307	2305	22.4	883
鸿福社区		13312	42326						
宏远社区	1.0	12973	20121	983	3				
新城社区	4.5	2703	2450	2735					

15　续表 3

(2012年)

村(居)委会	土地面积(平方公里)	户籍人口(人)	外来暂住人口(人)	全部企业及个体户数(个)	#工业企业	资产总额(万元)	负债总额(万元)	资产负债率(%)	村组两级经营纯收入(万元)
中　堂									
潢涌村	9.3	9419	5797	958	108	216774	9830	4.5	24835
三涌村	4.0	3797	1989	370	80	9385	5349	57.0	1126
湛翠村	1.8	2354	969	152	51	4671	1969	42.2	116
袁家涌村	4.0	5616	2165	469	124	7581	2442	32.2	715
吴家涌村	3.4	2754	1583	376	84	9523	3088	32.4	1234
凤冲村	1.3	1649	692	91	38	2516	1595	63.4	81
鹤田村	2.2	2239	1793	389	106	3350	1715	51.2	364
东泊社区	2.9	3772	3785	729	186	18782	5675	30.2	939
中堂村	1.1	1957	965	210	59	1689	449	26.6	541
一村村	0.7	1804	7585	292	29	6176	202	3.3	956
东向村	2.4	3285	1672	338	97	3404	610	17.9	801
斗朗社区	2.5	2622	973	257	47	9426	4170	44.2	797
江南社区	2.1	2443	3873	744	187	13173	351	2.7	1578
蕉利村	4.6	4949	3071	560	160	6826	2323	34.0	1243
槎滘村	9.4	10170	2419	658	180	29193	2683	9.2	2284
下芦村	1.3	1192	405	90	37	3151	1368	43.4	168
马沥村	1.9	1995	472	68	19	8992	1535	17.1	389
四乡村	4.2	3212	279	56	11	2598	1352	52.0	345
红锋社区	0.1	789	78	32	5	1389	849	61.1	75
中心社区	0.7	8929	7821	1697	22	1855	1328	71.6	-6
望牛墩									
李屋村	0.6	643	1380	75	34	2071	973	47.0	171
望东村	1.4	2076	2200	209	19	2254	1064	47.2	276
扶涌村	0.6	896	1600	58	10	2509	828	33.0	167
赤滘村	1.9	2989	2880	48	36	9752	4250	43.6	541
五涌村	1.4	1559	1200	68	43	2649	993	37.5	242
下漕村	3.5	4322	4012	100	42	4922	3372	68.5	358
上合村	1.9	2993	1950	46	34	3442	2182	63.4	358
聚龙江村	0.7	1005	1900	180	24	7249	1220	16.8	301
望联村	2.8	5146	3104	429	21	3622	1072	29.6	390
洲湾村	1.6	1914	850	38	14	3041	1303	42.8	160
洲涡村	1.9	2611	682	25	17	3841	929	24.2	233
寮厦村	1.4	1440	942	36	23	4501	1772	39.4	384
官桥涌村	0.7	968	1150	22	15	3479	310	8.9	316
芙蓉沙村	0.8	1057	450	24	17	2700	1163	43.1	341
杜屋村	1.8	2413	1500	90	35	6341	1075	17.0	335
横沥村	1.8	2271	350	37	8	3443	1362	39.6	156
福安村	0.6	1077	320	35	5	3639	654	18.0	177
官洲村	1.0	1074	500	40	13	2386	1487	62.3	161
石排村	0.4	634	492	16	7	1933	821	42.5	178
朱平沙村	2.7	3391	2800	55	15	8577	3596	41.9	231
锦涡村	2.2	1574	870	35	8	4315	765	17.7	155
望牛墩社区		4770							

15 续表 4

(2012年)

村(居)委会	土地面积(平方公里)	户籍人口(人)	外来暂住人口(人)	全部企业及个体户数(个)	#工业企业	资产总额(万元)	负债总额(万元)	资产负债率(%)	村组两级经营纯收入(万元)
麻　　涌									
麻一村	4.0	4118	670	263	32	4526	2153	47.6	304
麻二社区	6.8	3630	516	124	9	13046	5012	38.4	778
麻三村	3.7	3811	1344	1043	26	9765	1139	11.7	554
麻四村	4.5	4849	800	203	13	13728	8658	63.1	313
大步村	10.7	7262	3082	668	34	26820	1195	4.5	1264
东太村	4.8	4552	1311	295	5	6901	993	14.4	520
新基村	4.4	5695	3419	367	35	9321	421	4.5	1006
川槎村	3.0	3995	2073	258	29	703	554	78.8	727
鸥涌村	2.8	3832	4264	297	17	764	360	47.1	798
黎滘村	1.3	1332	613	64	14	1825	584	32.0	345
华阳村	5.5	5296	940	178	12	10711	1815	16.9	443
南洲村	3.4	2812	1486	195	25	12447	814	6.5	608
大盛村	6.9	2869	12198	627	13	20324	7714	38.0	2102
漳澎村	29.6	12476	2139	302	10	40733	24035	59.0	722
麻涌社区		6802							
石　　碣									
唐洪村	1.0	1812	2952	413	43	12036	2663	22.1	1210
水南村	2.8	3580	5767	1290	150	20114	5949	29.6	3990
石碣村	4.6	5316	11920	1545	238	18489	6439	34.8	6108
刘屋村	4.9	4569	4904	507	105	10229	3219	31.5	2601
横滘村	1.6	1989	4680	611	112	11438	5026	43.9	2083
鹤田厦村	2.5	1939	4584	300	25	10257	3150	30.7	1311
四甲村	4.0	4732	6896	866	134	15334	2906	19.0	4342
沙腰村	4.0	3573	3595	313	68	16525	3686	22.3	2084
梁家村	2.0	2459	2159	180	73	13882	6839	49.3	728
桔洲村	1.2	1458	8630	448	76	36201	1303	3.6	3296
单屋村	2.3	1326	2498	179	97	15244	2347	15.4	771
涌口村	1.6	1755	3780	496	140	20128	7479	37.2	536
西南村	2.6	2011	6500	1048	83	45449	5047	11.1	4410
黄泗围村	1.2	713	1935	391	81	11168	629	5.6	1115
城中社区		8128	5826	1816	37	7295	8901	122.0	-30
高　　埗									
冼沙村	7.5	7507	33149	452	136	13601	9880	72.6	2698
卢溪村	2.3	1712	5267	55	35	4224	520	12.3	
宝莲村	0.7	1043	1422	35	16	1471	322	21.9	74
塘厦村	2.7	1935	3522	102	19	2181	497	22.8	696
草墩村	0.8	814	1708	25	22	3822	1555	40.7	339
护安围村	1.9	1131	2394	42	30	4861	658	13.5	370
保安围村	2.3	2379	3410	72	32	24346	15927	65.4	1817

15 续表 5

(2012年)

村(居)委会	土地面积(平方公里)	户籍人口(人)	外来暂住人口(人)	全部企业及个体户数(个)	#工业企业	资产总额(万元)	负债总额(万元)	资产负债率(%)	村组两级经营纯收入(万元)
三联村	2.1	1372	2617	25	5	2871	1679	58.5	260
横滘头村	0.9	1087	2168	16	8	4528	1169	25.8	404
低涌村	2.2	2885	21466	400	21	5859	2679	45.7	1309
朱磡村	1.0	1486	927	28	18	1636	780	47.7	281
欧邓村	0.7	949	7435	25	9	3318	1886	56.8	229
芦村	1.3	1719	4104	56	19	2574	603	23.4	
高埗村	2.1	3291	48498	281	53	7124	4280	60.1	
凌屋村	1.2	1251	7282	41	8	4949	2044	41.3	246
上江城村	1.9	2338	18148	112	13	8685	3727	42.9	
下江城村	1.5	1504	6755	125	25	5673	2493	43.9	2823
新联村	1.3	1669	1598	148	9	1653	822	49.7	684
新创社区		2329	7431						
道滘									
南城村	7.1	4361	3407	606	112	17691	1727	9.8	1908
闸口村	5.2	2827	4442	457	41	13801	1553	11.3	1184
北永村	6.3	3739	3429	250	117	20857	2522	12.1	1257
永庆村	3.1	1654	2581	163	105	9211	524	5.7	821
厚德村	4.2	2486	4746	183	46	11728	1547	13.2	534
蔡白村	5.5	4751	3727	305	75	19182	3548	18.5	651
南丫村	6.8	4161	12202	398	139	27405	4864	17.7	2043
九曲村	4.6	3137	2466	165	59	6916	1595	23.1	428
大罗沙村	4.5	2929	3713	55	20	8380	1775	21.2	482
小河村	6.1	5744	3574	215	70	6369	1538	24.1	
昌平村	3.8	3443	2598	167	41	2614	1611	61.6	993
大岭丫村	4.1	3636	4270	290	91	25797	6582	25.5	1768
大鱼沙村	1.7	1727	1612	213	38	4640	343	7.4	
兴隆社区		11783	1343			276	224	81.2	
洪梅									
洪屋涡村	14.1	6889	2756	149	145	16562	3296	19.9	585
新庄村	1.0	870	680	36	20	3274	1461	44.6	323
梅沙村	3.5	4092	2250	76	28	7381	2397	32.5	583
金鳌沙村	2.3	1355	520	30	10	3876	1735	44.8	285
乌沙村	3.7	2200	2600	35	21	9222	1064	11.5	501
尧均村	0.9	608	2620	70	11	2445	1216	49.7	105
夏汇村	1.0	717	210	6	6	2270	1451	63.9	234
氹涌村	1.6	1925	2500	63	9	4839	2143	44.3	156
黎洲角村	1.6	2658	3450	349	10	9177	1937	21.1	371
洪梅社区	5.0	1094	2673	217					
沙田									
中围村	0.9	1772	237	21	1	16228	3388	20.9	626
和安村	0.8	3248	146	63	5	12003	3029	25.2	502

15　续表 6

（2012年）

村(居)委会	土地面积(平方公里)	户籍人口(人)	外来暂住人口(人)	全部企业及个体户数(个)	#工业企业	资产总额(万元)	负债总额(万元)	资产负债率(%)	村组两级经营纯收入(万元)
大流村	0.5	2079	340	54	1	10337	3603	34.9	364
泥洲村	0.3	3903	254	30	1	18606	11084	59.6	1228
杨公洲村	3.9	1935	12432	557	343	9306	2615	28.1	1194
阇西村	5.4	2251	13335	510	75	34204	11461	33.5	1748
民田村	5.2	2602	13564	792	139	11680	3278	28.1	904
大泥村	4.4	1876	15443	949	271	9802	1911	19.5	739
福禄沙村	3.5	1979	3719	199	69	7674	2797	36.4	621
西大坦村	0.9	2125	264	6	1	9535	2708	28.4	365
穗丰年村	5.9	2765	4206	281	117	21780	6151	28.2	1570
齐沙村	3.8	2067	15920	957	163	15216	2532	16.6	1368
稔洲村	4.7	2496	22333	1462	262	10428	3238	31.1	911
义沙村	5.1	1924	11690	386	149	10726	2154	20.1	838
西太隆村	4.5	2040	12590	526	356	7765	3717	47.9	797
横流社区	1.0	4687	11017	1425	48	6303	1708	27.1	328
先锋村	0.4	2040	322	40	11	6075	2746	45.2	65
厚街									
厚街村	8.0	9106	24149	3301	880	44219	15704	35.5	2060
珊美村	2.1	2489	15396	3365	92	38324	12485	32.6	1730
寮厦村	2.5	2413	10542	2128	270	28791	4364	15.2	2689
河田村	9.1	6296	23903	2383	356	41602	9978	24.0	3428
汀山村	4.3	1960	20326	1254	496	36944	4421	12.0	1208
环冈村	4.2	2095	8949	502	102	21247	6633	31.2	446
三屯村	4.5	2676	19884	1913	352	84936	12663	14.9	6168
宝屯村	3.0	2584	10241	1448	555	32187	11585	36.0	2545
陈屋村	2.0	1527	9718	1638	271	26817	3252	12.1	2965
赤岭村	5.3	3644	28768	1823	433	67032	30044	44.8	3732
桥头村	10.0	7990	14764	2189	580	70364	9225	13.1	4031
南五村	1.6	1525	7753	740	221	16337	4099	25.1	953
溪头村	4.1	3838	20391	1038	218	67120	12288	18.3	4601
沙塘村	1.5	2065	4754	290	101	16621	5341	32.1	1453
宝塘村	1.7	1568	8027	620	171	25056	4038	16.1	1867
下汴村	2.2	1769	8060	803	264	20228	2882	14.2	1719
白濠村	5.3	5357	23918	1958	752	51633	8069	15.6	4545
新塘村	4.4	5688	17944	1816	377	59151	14079	23.8	3917
双岗村	4.2	6913	7704	1273	408	25199	6503	25.8	2387
涌口村	4.0	5573	15553	1507	320	51593	6589	12.8	3217
大迳村	11.8	3629	3344	260	106	12460	2567	20.6	707
新围村	15.1	4491	3572	359	132	9845	2435	24.7	228
竹溪社区		13361	6178	1		5094	358	7.0	
长安									
涌头社区	3.8	1748	12818	1168	202	28138	12480	44.4	3453

15 续表 7

(2012年)

村(居)委会	土地面积(平方公里)	户籍人口(人)	外来暂住人口(人)	全部企业及个体户数(个)	#工业企业	资产总额(万元)	负债总额(万元)	资产负债率(%)	村组两级经营纯收入(万元)
霄边社区	7.5	3479	32335	2120	71	129840	9431	7.3	6071
咸西社区	4.0	1280	12847	1111	97	73594	11229	15.3	1443
锦厦社区	8.2	4361	54464	2236	283	117739	17084	14.5	16805
新安社区	8.5	3463	68818	2204	177	45083	3035	6.7	6909
乌沙社区	11.3	3889	30567	3402	510	52417	9293	17.7	23067
新民社区	2.4	943	22712	917	156	37917	21163	55.8	1682
沙头社区	13.4	6334	55049	3681	301	132014	67823	51.4	7429
上沙社区	7.2	2886	42362	2918	367	66313	12650	19.1	7135
厦岗社区	8.7	3235	22509	1892	425	47470	1851	3.9	5419
厦边社区	4.7	2516	17247	2420	276	24834	4977	20.0	5482
上角社区	3.2	1326	16090	1243	200	54806	20381	37.2	5144
长盛社区	0.8	7833	7763	3624	6	18010	8129	45.1	
寮 步									
塘边社区	0.7	1671	3000	250	30	8903	5373	60.4	2624
西 溪 村	4.5	4649	8500	378	182	16930	2750	16.2	1492
凫 山 村	4.0	6000	7500	515	78	10858	2854	26.3	3840
石 步 村	4.7	4559	4500	313	82	14603	1568	10.7	1873
良 边 村	2.7	3250	3500	430	268	6091	1233	20.2	2121
富竹山村	3.5	1980	2650	74	39	12890	2766	21.5	1250
塘 唇 村	3.4	2322	2931	121	54	27900	7900	28.3	2442
向 西 村	2.9	2595	4050	241	86	9935	4341	43.7	617
下岭贝村	1.8	1571	6918	232	28	13098	1852	14.1	2065
岭厦社区	0.9	1031	4000	190	59	19120	2281	11.9	1575
新旧围社区	1.4	1010	2000	208	212	8390	662	7.9	482
霞 边 村	1.3	889	1500	102	19	7223	564	7.8	517
横坑社区	5.9	4899	18650	501	406	96911	7555	7.8	6003
竹 园 村	1.5	903	1380	130	33	6917	2634	38.1	281
上 屯 村	4.5	3394	3950	411	45	14572	1694	11.6	1667
石龙坑村	1.9	3702	5000	392	210	9922	237	2.4	1532
牛杨社区	1.2	1553	6000	112	48	11587	4574	39.5	1259
泉塘社区	2.3	1569	5000	52	29	6596	1841	27.9	1054
坑口社区	1.6	1205	3650	277	32	13658	1743	12.8	934
浮竹山村	3.4	1532	3000	140	30	15392	4983	32.4	736
上 底 村	2.0	1491	1400	95	11	3689	1737	47.1	249
刘屋巷村	1.6	575	1125	45	29	5940	1074	18.1	327
药 勒 村	2.4	1154	3000	125	40	9247	1200	13.0	976
陈家埔村	1.6	938	1900	63	16	6675	810	12.1	520
缪边社区	1.6	1220	3000	165	35	13179	1321	10.0	920
寮步社区	1.7	8608	4500	2500	17	4724	1054	22.3	
小 坑 村	1.5	822	1500	50	20	5565	294	5.3	700

15　续表 8

(2012年)

村(居)委会	土地面积(平方公里)	户籍人口(人)	外来暂住人口(人)	全部企业及个体户数(个)	#工业企业	资产总额(万元)	负债总额(万元)	资产负债率(%)	村组两级经营纯收入(万元)
长坑村	1.5	950	500	25	10	8080	2476	30.6	
井巷村	1.1	933	1500	35	25	6774	1951	28.8	534
大岭山									
马蹄岗村	0.8	2227	4100	172	46	6375	2431	38.1	1126
大塘朗村	3.0	1630	4500	60	42	4721	1999	42.3	635
新塘村	2.0	2229	6500	270	102	9282	1366	14.7	1773
元岭村	0.3	986	1094	54	3	14860	403	2.7	422
金桔村	4.3	3689	9000	540	62	24975	6457	25.9	1734
鸡翅岭村	4.5	1333	1973	181	16	5943	2231	37.5	716
大沙村	3.0	1864	2056	238	207	8645	3066	35.5	872
旧飞鹅村	3.1	463	1100	10	8	3995	91	2.3	322
连平村	7.2	2928	12500	275	76	5131	2028	39.5	1468
梅林村	1.5	570	6800	135	52	3945	1030	26.1	954
下高田村	0.5	482	835	62	44	2775	478	17.2	168
大环村	2.0	615	1200	35	25	3608	1152	31.9	326
太公岭村	2.2	1708	4900	198	58	3862	781	20.2	881
百花洞村	4.8	1315	6500	88	61	12091	5929	49.0	58
大片美村	2.6	1023	6000	175	17	4263	262	6.1	778
矮岭冚村	5.5	3706	9300	834	118	15308	7229	47.2	2253
大岭村	7.0	2401	820	75	60	4717	1431	30.3	502
农场社区	1.0	760	3720	455	14	6882	332	4.8	1601
水朗村	4.5	1376	2810	25	15	15262	340	2.2	1022
大塘村	8.5	3324	20000	210	200	12402	3218	25.9	1704
杨屋村	12.0	4949	14800	645	148	10998	1528	13.9	3756
颜屋村	3.0	757	6680	160	76	5960	1073	18.0	336
大岭山社区	10.0	3991	6300	553	19	904	461	51.0	324
领居社区		1711	10000			93	10	10.8	
大朗									
竹山社区	1.3	1651	2601	292	153	12110	914	7.5	476
高英村	1.7	1831	3856	375	166	16176	5342	33.0	437
巷头社区	3.5	4459	13350	3004	555	77320	13403	17.3	3607
巷尾社区	1.6	1991	5867	1088	299	35908	2008	5.6	1947
求富路社区	1.4	1449	5799	705	142	21635	3341	15.4	2074
长塘社区	2.7	4798	9867	2076	305	68552	24009	35.0	4227
大井头社区	4.1	5812	7066	2826	440	62663	3637	5.8	2818
圣堂社区	0.9	1594	2342	1580	56	26956	636	2.4	1848
蔡边村	6.1	4244	4668	1432	469	44083	12712	28.8	702
水口村	3.3	2989	6217	959	346	26639	4690	17.6	1650
洋乌村	2.1	1696	2654	491	269	4756	842	17.7	1168
洋坑塘村	1.1	1087	5215	464	218	11521	1406	12.2	576
松柏朗村	2.5	4185	4430	740	223	16126	9288	57.6	501

15 续表 9

(2012年)

村(居)委会	土地面积(平方公里)	户籍人口(人)	外来暂住人口(人)	全部企业及个体户数(个)	#工业企业	资产总额(万元)	负债总额(万元)	资产负债率(%)	村组两级经营纯收入(万元)
黄草朗社区	1.5	2384	4349	943	461	16575	8086	48.8	438
黎贝岭村	1.9	2274	3232	601	257	14185	1129	8.0	694
佛子凹村	1.1	2436	966	262	102	8047	926	11.5	377
佛新社区	0.6	882	562	251	130	13467	5355	39.8	527
松木山村	2.7	2657	6794	844	418	20283	3475	17.1	1462
犀牛陂村	8.0	3337	7674	1419	854	17698	2546	14.4	2292
水平村	7.9	1929	4277	576	249	18425	3843	20.9	829
屏山社区	2.3	531	369	76	43	4763	610	12.8	176
宝陂村	0.5	721	109	45	15	12802	5658	44.2	447
石厦村	8.0	3027	4733	906	469	18639	1371	7.4	789
杨涌村	1.5	1381	3506	467	182	4243	364	8.6	432
沙步村	3.1	2303	3163	851	444	1410	1124	79.7	587
新马莲村	6.6	1617	3515	475	185	2981	1610	54.0	603
大朗社区	0.3	6456	2219	669	14	2375	343	14.4	376
长富社区	1.5	2273	600						
黄江									
田美社区	11.4	4583	145163	1157	368	32722	4322	13.2	4374
宝山社区	4.9	2713	20390	265	196	31986	2268	7.1	3320
北岸社区	5.9	1590	15057	276	65	9512	1009	10.6	1450
三新社区	16.0	2869	13004	714	59	16293	1142	7.0	1428
梅塘社区	18.2	4855	31250	881	265	38492	4502	11.7	2964
长龙社区	18.0	2530	8000	270	65	9146	2321	25.4	1083
新市社区	1.6	6777	8051	2050		866	182	21.0	175
樟木头									
圩镇社区	4.3	10609	11537	2982	187	18280	13019	71.2	-425
樟罗社区	6.8	3537	12496	2225	69	35718	13116	36.7	1988
百果洞社区	2.4	908	7100	1260	26	15922	5763	36.2	14
樟洋社区	13.5	2446	26953	1369	42	15870	5112	32.2	364
石新社区	7.3	2331	10800	1750	139	43781	26564	60.7	492
柏地社区	6.6	1424	7100	923	90	21126	7039	33.3	154
官仓社区	3.0	1123	3500	339	37	8196	2919	35.6	144
裕丰社区	10.0	2052	8205	520	60	10498	5246	50.0	373
金河社区	14.0	1737	11700	915	205	9882	2925	29.6	268
清溪									
罗马村	7.0	1874	7400	342	52	3561	1664	46.7	1507
长山头村	4.3	1159	6200	75	32	13481	4970	36.9	1346
荔横村	3.4	1534	12000	276	60	10551	9637	91.3	2859
浮岗村	3.0	1952	7500	530	49	13857	4747	34.3	1535
松岗村	3.9	1256	3940	81	44	2223	1199	53.9	902
上元村	4.3	938	3500	225	29	3659	1456	39.8	920
重河村	8.4	2683	5362	350	26	8697	1255	14.4	2650

15 续表 10

(2012年)

村(居)委会	土地面积(平方公里)	户籍人口(人)	外来暂住人口(人)	全部企业及个体户数(个)	#工业企业	资产总额(万元)	负债总额(万元)	资产负债率(%)	村组两级经营纯收入(万元)
清厦村	2.3	1566	5685	570	40	7607	5197	68.3	1155
铁松村	5.6	2558	9875	174	87	12462	4922	39.5	1743
铁场村	7.4	798	280	23	6	6363	3168	49.8	614
九乡村	7.5	1707	3000	200	62	6788	5578	82.2	959
大埔村	1.8	729	2500	94	31	2994	761	25.4	231
大利村	9.6	2674	12556	935	65	14085	3834	27.2	2913
渔樑围村	2.5	1093	18900	341	67	10664	2664	25.0	2007
三星村	2.5	1085	4800	112	23	3556	2937	82.6	815
厦垠村	1.7	894	6395	343	28	10090	6618	65.6	710
土桥村	1.2	588	7200	328	51	9999	5496	55.0	866
谢坑村	3.2	794	4550	100	50	5637	1837	32.6	816
三中村	9.0	1794	58310	670	137	10930	4554	41.7	2995
青皇村	6.5	1145	3190	56	34	2625	348	13.3	1319
清溪社区	7.0	7835	13321	2033	20	5095	3398	66.7	1235
塘厦									
林村社区	21.0	5527	44398	1836	246	71632	8442	11.8	8085
莲湖社区	9.0	2215	20948	560	208	19664	5912	30.1	2325
石潭埔社区	6.8	1625	10000	140	65	16623	675	4.1	
横塘社区	4.0	1123	8310	118	89	10718	1301	12.1	1270
莆心湖社区	6.1	2111	17000	190	69	27857	1158	4.2	2115
诸佛岭社区	2.4	1137	10934	293	50	28795	5196	18.0	
振兴围社区	2.4	978	12000	220	62	16793	1152	6.9	1372
四村社区	4.0	1091	12100	450	290	16899	4532	26.8	1388
蛟乙塘社区	4.9	1454	9998	325		21738	970	4.5	1529
沙湖社区	4.0	601	7645	98	85	11695	1342	11.5	1091
大坪社区	13.0	1389	11682	84	64	36502	4632	12.7	1813
田心社区	4.5	874	9875	97	95	16846	2335	13.9	
龙背岭社区	8.2	986	10000	252	71	12452	569	4.6	
石鼓社区	6.4	2570	16500	338	119	29145	1563	5.4	3227
石马社区	2.7	495	5160	172	61	5617	1724	30.7	376
清湖头社区	4.1	1397	17550	193	147	21670	2307	10.6	3369
平山社区	4.8	788	8360	136	92	18605	1227	6.6	1673
桥陇社区	2.8	1019	11275	159	67	12254	4532	37.0	1144
凤凰岗社区	3.5	1337	9351	365	80	14882	3825	25.7	
塘厦社区	0.9	16693	49100	2180	350	2158	211	9.8	799
三局社区		2754							
凤岗									
雁田村	21.8	3759	36532	3579	422	270624	55439	20.5	23959
官井头村	10.4	1929	15441	1082	160	104703	4512	4.3	5989
油甘埔村	6.9	2019	17046	690	458	38720	11850	30.6	4278
凤德岭村	3.4	1279	5271	453	146	15187	5451	35.9	2468

15　续表 11

(2012年)

村(居)委会	土地面积(平方公里)	户籍人口(人)	外来暂住人口(人)	全部企业及个体户数(个)	#工业企业	资产总额(万元)	负债总额(万元)	资产负债率(%)	村组两级经营纯收入(万元)
塘沥村	6.7	1931	26157	287	80	6673	1441	21.6	3620
黄洞村	11.7	2245	12508	241	134	13201	1684	12.8	692
竹塘村	5.7	1292	11448	385	133	7016	2233	31.8	2843
竹尾田村	1.5	749	5304	155	15	8143	399	4.9	985
三联村	3.4	1504	7068	865	40	5404	1301	24.1	2850
五联村	5.6	1356	10679	222	182	17253	8259	47.9	2095
天堂围村	4.2	1112	8491	341	126	20988	3258	15.5	1569
凤岗社区	1.1	6360	2939	396	20				652
谢岗									
黎村村	12.8	3791	3751	157	51	10092	1893	18.8	1241
南面村	31.6	1514	788	31	20	3397	447	13.2	121
窑山村	1.0	529	1680	52	28	2381	493	20.7	146
大龙村	5.9	1042	2150	54	38	2456	1440	58.6	175
大厚村	6.3	1027	6870	112	55	4424	213	4.8	507
谢山村	3.9	611	2380	157	25	4809	273	5.7	302
谢岗村	10.4	2958	2708	110	70	8815	1016	11.5	851
赵林村	7.1	1685	5121	138	73	6129	1391	22.7	677
曹乐村	7.1	2189	5816	215	172	5394	645	12.0	843
五星村	1.8	1312	3783	53	25	1509	1511	100.1	180
稔子园村	2.4	653	1991	65	39	2416	179	7.4	333
泰园社区	0.8	3486	6967	660	82	579	776	134.0	20
常平									
常平社区	4.0	16396	23312	879	38	466	131	28.1	
下墟村	0.4	853	2050	140	35	24528	6970	28.4	615
岗梓村	2.7	2564	5000	104	70	8942	5385	60.2	841
桥梓村	2.0	2501	6021	211	92	21914	5016	22.9	1414
塘角村	1.1	974	3320	150	120	9997	1884	18.8	818
苏坑村	4.0	3633	4869	272	223	8227	1824	22.2	1301
袁山贝村	5.0	3589	7500	620	330	20006	4052	20.3	
金美村	3.0	2466	9180	310	148	28588	4714	16.5	5492
还珠沥村	5.5	2826	17190	395	153	13479	5408	40.1	1459
朗贝村	4.0	1984	7500	295	85	6016	299	5.0	20376
板石村	3.4	1984	11282	650	44	4673	915	19.6	2055
桥沥村	9.8	3521	36000	755	260	12898	1677	13.0	3412
卢屋村	3.0	848	627	199	99	2205	1264	57.3	10212
土塘村	8.7	2846	31326	1094	145	26123	1876	7.2	7235
麦元村	2.4	1103	3012	188	25	9350	773	8.3	922
九江水村	9.0	1456	6058	280	68	24975	539	2.2	1078
朗洲村	4.1	624	1376	114	29	4004	1138	28.4	
陈屋贝村	2.2	1121	5863	180	41	10753	880	8.2	
司马村	8.1	2824	11493	502	84	21079	3857	18.3	

15 续表 12

(2012年)

村(居)委会	土地面积(平方公里)	户籍人口(人)	外来暂住人口(人)	全部企业及个体户数(个)	#工业企业	资产总额(万元)	负债总额(万元)	资产负债率(%)	村组两级经营纯收入(万元)
霞坑村	1.6	744	4550	229	23	8575	2332	27.2	458
漱旧村	2.0	1133	4280	142	29	4623	337	7.3	588
漱新村	2.4	1271	6300	591	130	6626	1989	30.0	
黄泥塘村	1.0	900	1876	123	59	2653	1579	59.5	123
元江元村	1.9	1483	5160	192	59	8396	1808	21.5	489
横江厦村	5.0	2801	3200	211	85	8057	3124	38.8	563
田尾村	2.1	1565	3000	56	36	4048	1987	49.1	
白花沥村	1.0	700	232	10	10	2555	1014	39.7	
沙湖口村	1.4	1021	3180	91	20	4679	2601	55.6	261
白石岗村	5.0	3749	6051	107	99	6863	4004	58.3	1010
松柏塘村	3.8	2371	5753	84	34	7040	3402	48.3	369
上坑村	1.3	929	2800	120	43	10221	3372	33.0	
木棆村	3.5	2112	1123	506	60	33268	2820	8.5	26600
桥头									
东江村	4.8	2389	2240	185	42	7658	3936	51.4	509
山和村	2.5	972	3608	56	24	6243	1713	27.4	
屋厦村	2.0	701	1458	101	35	5693	1606	28.2	
岗头村	0.6	491	2145	50	30	3746	1204	32.1	134
李屋村	2.3	1615	2992	58	40	16898	5629	33.3	253
邓屋村	2.7	1877	10450	55	38	23201	4188	18.1	1674
朗厦村	4.1	1604	5600	98	78	17836	3954	22.2	1048
邵岗头村	1.3	853	1080	41	35	5184	2324	44.8	388
桥头社区	1.0	1345	4893	297	48	22350	1248	5.6	2429
迳联社区	1.5	1773	3239	112	49	23869	6600	27.7	1103
田新社区	2.2	2196	3620	415	230	20676	5962	28.8	918
岭头社区	1.3	1175	6408	255	55	14369	1425	9.9	
石水口村	7.8	4555	7500	529	132	32945	9927	30.1	2646
大洲社区	4.6	3258		152	81	19635	4333	22.1	
禾坑村	1.5	992	3243	75	23	6339	1437	22.7	
田头角村	1.2	756	1983	78	49	6357	1533	24.1	
莲城社区	14.6	9780	55650						
横沥									
石涌村	3.7	1792	5938	793	152	15597	4029	25.8	1157
隔坑村	2.2	2715	6191	731	70	13579	6138	45.2	1270
半仙山村	2.2	1622	2919	894	22	18468	13433	72.7	70
横沥村	4.6	2939	3200	895	51	14757	7385	50.0	1200
田头村	4.1	2541	4286	906	56	12346	3103	25.1	1036
田坑村	4.8	2848	3644	1147	70	7502	2436	32.5	1404
村头村	3.5	2351	4430	622	83	11341	2723	24.0	317
长巷村	2.1	1659	1096	83	23	4961	1935	39.0	
田饶步村	2.8	1856	1725	278	60	14441	7152	49.5	-118

15　续表 13

(2012年)

村(居)委会	土地面积(平方公里)	户籍人口(人)	外来暂住人口(人)	全部企业及个体户数(个)	#工业企业	资产总额(万元)	负债总额(万元)	资产负债率(%)	村组两级经营纯收入(万元)
六甲村	1.4	1100	3117	219	45	7156	2971	41.5	171
村尾村	2.7	1496	3560	491	45	11539	3763	32.6	290
水边村	4.0	2794	6942	341	32	7211	3236	44.9	236
新四村	2.9	2064	6149	419	111	2097	1835	87.5	1126
山厦村	2.3	1071	2800	244	48	12132	794	6.5	423
月塘村	0.5	1115	1200	138		13076	1473	11.3	223
张坑村	1.0	624	1500	83	33	7379	1863	25.2	184
恒泉社区	0.2	7062	1984	1813	26	1334	762	57.1	49
东坑									
东坑村	2.0	3061	7099	380	37	19279	6845	35.5	1825
黄麻岭村	0.8	1086	1419	273	21	6012	3252	54.1	166
长安塘村	1.3	1877	6962	223	24	11360	6472	57.0	603
寮边头村	0.8	1593	5690	246	31	6363	2928	46.0	
塔岗村	2.1	1782	3604	174	28	8483	1683	19.8	372
坑美村	2.2	1948	4538	154	27	8750	924	10.6	491
新门楼村	2.1	1702	1909	248	24	13535	5317	39.3	855
井美村	1.9	2488	7517	546	30	10461	3448	33.0	
初坑村	2.8	2506	19877	556	50	1976	748	37.9	2160
凤大村	0.3	744	866	131	8	4755	1629	34.3	286
丁屋村	1.1	1085	2809	118	12	3766	1143	30.4	
彭屋村	2.1	1899	3987	222	18	4852	890	18.3	1051
黄屋村	2.0	1978	4642	587	25	10250	2380	23.2	
角社村	2.4	3410	5524	322	29	24759	1571	6.3	877
草塘社区	0.1	3017	1000	161					
骏达社区	0.1	164	49750	60	60				
企石									
铁岗村	5.7	2522	2910	45	31	11028	3517	31.9	
深巷村	4.1	2289	2465	125	55	6176	2811	45.5	96
湖美村	1.0	799	576	31	15	4192	1998	47.7	143
博夏村	6.7	3569	873	53	19	7898	1193	15.1	133
上洞村	5.3	2690	1094	135	23	5418	951	17.6	
清湖村	4.6	2022	1939	42	32	7009	2638	37.6	542
江边村	5.0	2993	1318	50	23	5042	1021	20.2	105
旧围村	3.8	1963	1228	62	32	4190	868	20.7	
东平村	1.5	737	1820	212	32	3806	2731	71.8	
上截村	0.8	1165	1158	51	10	5715	4218	73.8	
下截村	1.2	1462	1042	45	18	7255	3412	47.0	
东山村	6.2	4368	5814	423	101	29685	9368	31.6	
铁炉坑村	3.4	3176	2287	111	64	9201	3012	32.7	
企石村	1.5	1405	494	39	18	6527	2018	30.9	65
杨屋村	0.8	660	512	51	11	3960	2007	50.7	
莫屋村	1.0	1234	587	46	27	2583	1279	49.5	49
霞朗村	1.0	910	1962	253	32	12888	4456	34.6	1010

15 续表 14

(2012年)

村(居)委会	土地面积(平方公里)	户籍人口(人)	外来暂住人口(人)	全部企业及个体户数(个)	#工业企业	资产总额(万元)	负债总额(万元)	资产负债率(%)	村组两级经营纯收入(万元)
新南村	2.8	2124	1759	325	45	8412	2438	29.0	
南坑村	1.5	1237	1283	83	27	7456	191	2.6	139
宝石社区	0.5	5455	6266	440		116	67	57.8	
石　排									
石排村	2.4	3676	9635	602	60	3271	1516	46.3	1470
下沙村	3.4	2617	4000	489	120	4226	1693	40.1	2228
庙边王村	3.7	2413	8072	638	203	4547	858	18.9	
福隆村	5.6	5949	10038	1111	322	17214	6794	39.5	1663
沙角村	3.4	2583	4893	138	35	4003	960	24.0	
黄家壆村	2.4	1938	3000	145	30	11247	260	2.3	
赤坎村	3.2	1427	4500	157	45	8906	2211	24.8	782
向西村	2.0	1202	6132	494	63	6537	1107	16.9	691
水贝村	3.5	3253	4203	338	83	6099	806	13.2	1414
田寮村	3.3	1984	1630	130	53	5307	420	7.9	
横山村	3.8	2041	6350	168	45	2803	920	32.8	1033
谷吓村	3.0	1880	4270	131	65	4220	1650	39.1	1028
埔心村	2.2	1454	11000	676	606	9452	454	4.8	2019
塘尾村	0.9	1093	3500	212	55	7819	489	6.3	460
李家坊村	0.9	932	2700	195	60	5480	1328	24.2	278
田边村	4.2	2119	3150	172	68	3862	2398	62.1	772
中坑村	3.2	2310	2120	136	29	11491	1468	12.8	645
燕窝村	4.3	1762	4720	481	90	8354	874	10.5	1124
太和社区		286				1416	875	61.8	
茶　山									
上元村	5.1	3185	7381	204	94	2737	1149	42.0	1083
茶山村	2.3	1729	4850	538	52	12326	3979	32.3	1101
下朗村	1.8	1411	1666	69	30	14473	2067	14.3	1067
横江村	4.3	3109	5755	136	79	14286	3071	21.5	691
卢边村	3.6	2744	2050	145	100	11996	2074	17.3	645
寒溪水村	1.3	968	1570	43	41	3543	836	23.6	340
增埗村	6.3	7247	13508	650	405	10973	6434	58.6	3396
南社村	4.1	3604	10436	182	100	29729	2312	7.8	1635
塘角村	2.8	2977	8495	341	119	13061	1756	13.4	3448
京山村	4.2	2465	5800	339		17307	4379	25.3	2438
博头村	0.9	647	1600	34	15	4963	559	11.3	301
冲美村	0.7	770	1080	90	39	8002	1066	13.3	692
粟边村	2.3	1994	3125	180	62	7100	1250	17.6	586
刘黄村	1.5	993	3134	258	70	7351	2529	34.4	601
孙屋村	0.8	717	910	46	25	2491	946	38.0	120
超朗村	3.3	2942	3061	180	78	15145	562	3.7	1291
茶山圩社区	0.3	7774	3585						

十六、历年国民经济和社会发展主要指标

Main Indicators of National Economy and Social Development over Years

16 历年国民经济和社会发展主要指标

Main Indicators of National Economy and Social Development over Years

年　份	户 籍 人 口 (万人)	常 住 人 口 (万人)	外来暂 住人口 (万人)	户籍人口 自然增长率 (‰)	外来暂住 从业人员 (万人)	城镇在岗 职工人数 (万人)	城镇在岗 职工平均 工资(元)
1949	68.24						
1952	71.68						
1957	77.48					3.90	400
1962	79.64					2.93	552
1965	86.46			29.60		3.17	524
1970	98.56			20.60		3.29	534
1975	107.94			14.51		3.80	577
1978	111.23			13.81		8.20	474
1979	112.04			19.00		9.68	650
1980	112.70			19.31		9.86	750
1981	114.46			16.57		10.66	887
1982	116.19			14.14		11.41	1095
1983	117.59			11.53		11.59	1197
1984	118.95			10.60		11.76	1383
1985	120.85			10.83		12.30	1456
1986	123.01		15.62	11.56	10.41	13.27	2616
1987	124.86		25.29	11.67	18.03	13.67	2067
1988	126.76		36.89	12.09	29.25	12.71	2757
1989	128.76		47.19	12.39	40.53	13.10	3320
1990	131.85	175.62	65.59	12.31	57.20	13.16	3552
1991	133.65	200.01	80.58	13.34	70.20	14.59	3777
1992	136.06	227.78	114.48	14.50	107.10	15.47	4531
1993	138.92	259.41	121.70	13.41	112.68	17.66	6228
1994	141.40	295.43	139.09	13.37	124.18	16.09	8360
1995	143.65	336.45	142.18	12.75	126.54	17.87	9682
1996	145.25	383.17	143.32	11.97	127.66	17.50	10382
1997	147.12	436.38	144.68	12.09	130.73	16.50	10691
1998	148.77	496.97	199.11	10.86	183.19	16.40	11422
1999	150.82	565.98	244.81	10.22	216.15	16.39	12557
2000	152.61	644.84	254.72	7.52	244.84	16.41	14051
2001	153.89	654.43	457.82	7.01	449.68	16.42	16183
2002	156.19	654.84	433.65	5.91	426.01	16.42	17804
2003	158.96	655.25	440.45	5.65	432.73	16.60	22598
2004	161.97	655.66	486.95	5.96	473.39	17.54	25326
2005	165.65	656.07	584.98	6.02	553.42	18.86	28253
2006	168.31	685.66	586.76	5.86	566.98	19.99	31135
2007	171.26	717.02	557.80	5.98	538.95	20.56	35284
2008	174.87	750.60	552.50	6.23	530.30	20.72	39516
2009	178.73	786.08	429.96	6.31	413.46	22.60	42585
2010	181.77	822.48	411.47	6.23	391.23	22.63	46576
2011	184.77	825.48	413.62	6.13	394.71	24.61	50398
2012	187.02	829.23	416.74	8.10	397.94	25.02	57007

注：城镇在岗职工人数与平均工资1952—1975年是全所有制单位资料，1978—1999年为城镇职工资料，2000年起为城镇在岗职工资料。

16 续表 1

年　份	地区生产总值(亿元)	第一产业	第二产业			第三产业	人均地区生产总值(元)
				工　业	建筑业		
1949							
1952							
1957							
1962							
1965							
1970							
1975							
1978	6.11	2.72	2.68			0.71	553
1979	6.62	2.65	2.92			1.05	593
1980	7.22	2.63	3.33			1.26	643
1981	9.11	3.28	4.30			1.54	802
1982	11.43	3.73	5.81			1.89	991
1983	13.03	3.98	6.90			2.15	1115
1984	15.96	4.57	7.81			3.59	1350
1985	22.60	6.15	11.66			4.80	1885
1986	30.02	8.14	13.57	10.54	3.03	8.30	2462
1987	39.29	9.82	17.72	14.24	3.49	11.74	3170
1988	55.46	11.89	28.28	25.05	3.23	15.29	4408
1989	60.92	12.66	27.97	27.22	0.75	20.29	4768
1990	80.44	13.28	40.53	39.18	1.34	26.63	6173
1991	95.91	13.45	50.32	48.34	1.98	32.13	5095
1992	110.89	14.41	59.27	56.63	2.64	37.21	5038
1993	157.05	14.40	87.31	82.89	4.42	55.34	5850
1994	217.03	17.48	119.49	110.77	8.72	80.06	6357
1995	296.29	21.43	166.97	154.19	12.78	107.89	7421
1996	361.75	24.86	199.48	187.85	11.63	137.40	8444
1997	448.60	25.64	243.28	230.79	12.50	179.68	9747
1998	558.00	25.94	305.68	290.69	14.99	226.37	11265
1999	667.24	25.79	367.05	349.53	17.52	274.40	12494
2000	820.25	25.91	450.71	430.45	20.25	343.64	13679
2001	991.89	26.10	540.51	517.03	23.48	425.28	15268
2002	1186.94	24.88	648.81	621.86	26.96	513.25	18131
2003	1452.52	22.82	798.20	757.18	41.01	631.51	22174
2004	1806.03	22.71	1016.04	968.01	48.03	767.28	27554
2005	2183.20	20.55	1227.86	1173.23	54.63	934.78	33287
2006	2627.98	12.01	1506.60	1441.69	64.91	1109.37	39173
2007	3160.05	11.90	1754.66	1681.83	72.83	1393.49	45057
2008	3703.60	14.83	1901.61	1819.22	82.38	1787.17	50471
2009	3763.91	14.79	1823.08	1741.53	81.55	1926.04	48988
2010	4246.45	16.57	2160.82	2078.45	82.37	2069.07	52798
2011	4735.39	17.88	2366.20	2288.41	77.79	2351.32	57470
2012	5010.17	18.76	2375.64	2297.51	78.12	2615.78	60557

注：1. 本表按当年价格计算。
　　2. 人均生产总值1990年及以前年份按年平均户籍人口计算，1991年起按年平均常住人口计算。

16　续表 2

上年＝100

年　份	地区生产总值指数	第一产业	第二产业	工　业	建筑业	第三产业	人均地区生产总值指数
1949							
1952							
1957							
1962							
1965							
1970							
1975							
1978							
1979	99.5	86.5	107.0			146.4	98.6
1980	102.7	90.3	117.3			113.9	102.0
1981	116.6	115.0	122.1			110.8	115.4
1982	116.9	105.3	131.0			117.6	115.1
1983	110.4	104.8	115.7			111.3	108.9
1984	114.2	109.0	107.0			140.9	112.9
1985	132.3	118.9	144.5			132.7	130.5
1986	126.1	111.9	110.3			174.7	124.0
1987	122.5	111.6	127.7	125.8	147.0	126.0	120.5
1988	115.7	90.6	143.7	151.4	77.9	103.0	114.0
1989	107.1	99.8	106.2	106.4	103.7	113.7	105.5
1990	123.2	104.4	127.6	130.6	76.4	128.0	120.8
1991	117.5	103.1	121.5	121.8	113.2	118.6	108.8
1992	108.3	100.0	112.6	113.7	78.0	105.1	92.6
1993	127.9	79.4	139.2	138.5	168.1	129.0	104.8
1994	122.5	107.2	124.7	124.3	138.5	122.3	96.3
1995	127.4	110.5	135.1	135.3	128.3	116.8	108.9
1996	117.5	109.4	115.5	116.2	91.2	123.5	109.5
1997	119.6	104.5	119.8	120.1	106.1	121.8	111.3
1998	121.8	100.9	122.1	122.2	115.1	124.5	113.1
1999	119.7	102.3	120.6	120.7	115.2	120.3	111.0
2000	119.7	99.8	120.7	120.9	110.5	120.0	106.6
2001	119.9	103.0	121.6	122.0	113.0	118.9	110.7
2002	120.5	97.6	122.6	123.0	114.1	119.1	119.6
2003	120.5	90.2	122.3	121.4	143.5	119.7	120.4
2004	121.0	90.0	125.6	126.5	106.8	115.8	120.9
2005	119.5	102.3	120.0	120.2	113.5	119.3	119.4
2006	119.2	58.9	121.9	122.0	118.7	117.1	116.6
2007	118.3	89.9	114.8	115.0	108.7	123.3	113.1
2008	114.0	110.6	106.1	106.4	100.9	124.0	109.0
2009	105.3	102.3	99.7	99.4	104.7	111.4	100.5
2010	110.3	101.6	116.7	117.5	97.1	104.1	105.3
2011	108.0	100.5	107.0	107.7	87.8	109.0	105.4
2012	106.1	100.0	105.8	106.0	98.5	106.5	105.7

注：本表按可比价格计算。

年 份	固定资产投资总额(亿元)	地方公共财政预算收入(亿元)	地方公共财政预算支出(亿元)	居民消费价格指数(上年=100)	商品零售价格指数(上年=100)	农林牧渔业总产值(亿元)	农林牧渔业总产值指数(1978年=100)
1949						0.54	
1952		0.28	0.02			0.66	
1957		0.32	0.04			0.78	
1962		0.31	0.07			0.76	
1965		0.47	0.07			1.28	
1970		0.48	0.08			1.47	
1975		0.65	0.11			2.53	
1978	0.23	0.66	0.18		100.4	4.24	100.0
1979	0.16	0.66	0.19		102.6	4.15	96.5
1980	0.24	0.67	0.20		110.9	4.19	98.0
1981	0.38	0.68	0.21		109.3	5.04	102.1
1982	1.81	0.81	0.26		101.2	5.59	117.6
1983	1.84	0.86	0.28		99.6	5.64	117.4
1984	3.01	0.85	0.30	99.3	98.6	7.02	126.7
1985	7.06	1.11	0.50	106.5	106.9	9.12	138.9
1986	11.52	1.61	0.99	104.2	104.4	12.30	174.6
1987	14.19	2.02	1.25	112.0	112.2	14.84	186.4
1988	16.55	2.71	1.75	136.0	132.8	20.37	182.1
1989	5.01	3.19	2.16	122.0	122.4	22.11	181.9
1990	7.51	3.57	2.28	96.6	94.9	23.64	195.3
1991	13.75	4.44	2.75	102.4	101.4	24.26	199.5
1992	18.88	5.62	3.82	109.2	107.7	27.13	211.3
1993	32.76	9.38	7.29	121.8	119.5	28.45	175.5
1994	140.76	7.69	8.90	123.5	118.4	34.75	188.4
1995	63.14	11.56	12.42	113.9	109.7	42.69	207.8
1996	67.62	9.65	12.41	106.8	104.7	49.72	216.3
1997	65.89	11.41	14.85	101.5	99.7	51.44	225.0
1998	77.00	15.10	17.91	99.9	98.7	53.60	227.3
1999	88.32	18.26	21.26	97.9	95.9	53.74	242.8
2000	102.89	30.47	33.61	101.5	100.1	54.64	243.3
2001	125.49	45.02	47.86	96.6	97.8	55.93	246.3
2002	191.57	55.29	64.96	98.1	99.1	53.67	263.2
2003	319.39	67.45	76.52	100.7	101.7	49.02	209.7
2004	454.87	82.64	94.16	103.0	103.2	44.19	213.5
2005	597.24	103.97	117.04	102.4	103.0	42.05	222.2
2006	705.45	128.94	147.90	101.2	102.8	21.26	121.0
2007	841.21	186.45	193.10	103.1	104.2	19.98	105.6
2008	944.34	209.22	218.26	105.5	107.9	25.53	118.3
2009	1094.08	231.16	232.62	96.9	95.3	25.31	122.2
2010	1114.98	277.84	289.83	102.8	103.2	28.31	126.2
2011	1079.31	313.06	351.92	104.9	104.7	30.66	126.1
2012	1180.35	356.32	385.58	102.9	102.4	32.01	126.9

注：农林牧渔总产值1952－1970年按1957年不变价计算，1975年按1970年不变价计算，1978年起按当年价计算。

年 份	农作物总播种面积(千公顷)	#粮食	粮食产量(万吨)	油料产量(万吨)	水果产量(万吨)	肉类产量(万吨)	水产品产量(万吨)
1949	141.26	127.26	21.07	0.15			0.32
1952	167.61	149.68	26.95	0.35			0.34
1957	188.98	165.53	28.80	0.33			0.42
1962	155.97	138.18	33.12	0.38			0.63
1965	158.97	121.64	43.71	0.72	4.54		0.99
1970	174.60	127.25	45.08	0.96	6.95		1.62
1975	202.00	137.03	50.72	1.11	3.68		2.19
1978	190.63	138.15	53.23	1.42	2.65	2.69	3.09
1979	172.36	129.16	53.53	1.91	2.33	2.92	2.23
1980	162.41	117.12	52.94	2.90	2.37	2.77	2.55
1981	151.17	107.13	44.75	3.55	4.69	2.80	2.49
1982	146.96	106.68	54.33	2.99	5.82	3.30	2.77
1983	146.21	109.02	56.12	1.97	7.72	3.57	3.03
1984	144.35	105.12	55.82	2.31	10.59	3.33	3.25
1985	130.01	93.05	48.87	2.10	18.94	3.33	3.26
1986	119.41	83.81	45.52	2.01	30.77	4.33	4.65
1987	119.73	83.40	46.28	1.70	36.31	4.61	6.57
1988	119.53	82.42	46.09	1.51	26.37	5.61	6.81
1989	122.27	85.61	48.76	1.37	22.14	5.86	6.23
1990	123.25	85.74	49.43	1.34	28.24	6.22	6.85
1991	119.42	81.77	47.37	1.15	34.32	6.88	6.90
1992	104.10	64.26	36.81	0.93	34.48	6.80	7.32
1993	71.20	36.74	20.21	0.56	27.13	7.66	6.50
1994	67.30	35.75	20.24	0.37	26.49	8.54	6.74
1995	71.89	39.90	22.74	0.37	24.32	9.76	7.48
1996	72.23	41.89	24.32	0.31	20.63	11.61	8.11
1997	72.17	41.61	24.69	0.29	16.50	12.90	9.19
1998	73.46	41.63	24.72	0.26	11.41	15.35	9.69
1999	72.59	41.77	24.73	0.22	13.63	15.99	9.40
2000	65.73	35.18	20.41	0.20	12.94	17.90	9.51
2001	56.95	22.56	12.84	0.16	15.01	19.84	8.96
2002	42.28	9.88	5.37	0.09	18.93	18.88	8.24
2003	33.97	5.65	3.05	0.04	14.64	15.46	7.58
2004	30.82	5.41	3.04	0.02	17.54	14.62	7.15
2005	27.38	4.14	2.00	0.01	15.13	17.17	6.74
2006	22.26	2.29	1.00	0.01	13.96	3.49	4.71
2007	21.37	2.15	0.99	0.01	13.16	2.03	4.73
2008	23.48	2.72	1.20	0.01	10.15	2.41	7.23
2009	24.72	2.77	1.19	0.01	9.15	2.55	7.33
2010	24.62	2.79	1.25	0.01	7.55	2.88	7.63
2011	24.46	2.76	1.29	0.01	7.39	2.60	7.82
2012	24.83	2.75	1.25	0.03	6.49	2.67	7.70

16 续表 5

年 份	工业企业单位数(个)	工业增加值(亿元)	工业增加值指数(上年=100)	规模以上工业增加值(亿元)	总供电量(亿千瓦时)	总售电量(亿千瓦时)	建筑业总产值(亿元)	建筑业增加值(亿元)
1949	1							
1952	23							
1957	262							
1962	280				0.08	0.07		
1965	260				0.36	0.32		
1970	220				0.71	0.60		
1975	324				1.24	1.11		
1978	1290				1.64	1.49		
1979	1250				1.93	1.73		
1980	1293				2.17	1.97		
1981	1479				2.22	1.99		
1982	1862				2.69	2.35		
1983	1964				3.15	2.75		
1984	2329				3.26	2.84		
1985	4187				3.82	3.39		
1986	5949	10.54		6.96	3.93	3.51		3.03
1987	8106	14.24	125.8	8.68	6.43	5.71		3.49
1988	8408	25.05	151.4	15.03	9.48	8.47		3.23
1989	8757	27.22	106.4	15.54	12.09	10.84	1.03	0.75
1990	9892	39.18	130.6	23.76	18.01	16.15	1.27	1.34
1991	10094	48.34	121.8	31.54	24.05	21.67	2.19	1.98
1992	11639	56.63	113.7	38.21	32.00	28.87	3.19	2.64
1993	12449	82.89	138.5	59.08	43.62	39.40	5.39	4.42
1994	14086	110.77	124.3	78.43	58.58	53.02	7.99	8.72
1995	15215	154.19	135.3	111.02	68.00	61.68	9.49	12.78
1996	15326	187.85	116.2	140.89	80.03	72.71	9.66	11.63
1997	16857	230.79	120.1	177.71	94.93	86.65	28.73	12.50
1998	16406	290.69	122.2	240.22	109.48	100.91	35.92	14.99
1999	16877	349.53	120.7	292.58	132.78	123.42	40.73	17.52
2000	16975	430.45	120.9	360.11	178.03	169.06	40.45	20.25
2001	18094	517.03	122.0	410.67	207.72	196.59	50.13	23.48
2002	21313	621.86	123.0	542.03	258.55	246.97	65.84	26.96
2003	21935	757.18	121.4	673.59	321.65	283.54	76.48	41.01
2004	22156	968.01	126.5	826.58	372.84	350.28	77.01	48.03
2005	21868	1173.23	120.2	979.34	415.66	396.59	84.35	58.61
2006	22447	1441.69	122.0	1186.20	464.45	445.52	94.58	64.91
2007	22587	1681.83	115.0	1388.34	507.89	482.56	112.87	72.83
2008	25656	1819.22	106.4	1602.98	507.35	487.32	108.81	82.38
2009	31160	1741.53	99.4	1453.37	488.85	478.19	99.40	81.55
2010	38273	2078.45	117.5	1708.31	556.89	543.66	122.06	82.37
2011	46413	2288.41	107.7	1642.45	579.35	566.69	130.85	77.79
2012	57808	2297.51	106.0	1978.13	600.58	581.18	157.58	78.12

16 续表 6

年 份	公路通车里程(公里)	民用汽车拥有量(万辆)	旅客周转量(万人公里)	货物周转量(万吨公里)	邮电业务收入(万元)	本地电话用户(万户)	移动电话用户(万户)
1949	204	0.002					
1952	219	0.002	1350	139			
1957	373	0.005	2100	195			
1962	598	0.007	4120	293			
1965	882	0.010	4725	457			
1970	1134	0.012	2800	900			
1975	1173	0.025	3890	694			
1978	1259	0.06	9425	15148	686	0.20	
1979	1225	0.11	11162	15290	790	0.21	
1980	1225	0.20	13584	16353	927	0.31	
1981	1225	0.30	13845	15606	962	0.34	
1982	1225	0.34	16026	17185	940	0.35	
1983	1225	0.45	54075	108634	1018	0.39	
1984	1240	0.61	62107	140113	1263	0.48	
1985	1240	0.79	95237	171591	1560	0.77	
1986	1248	0.86	127458	126898	2015	0.88	
1987	1261	1.00	159117	174942	3410	1.63	
1988	1302	1.36	173335	169112	5728	2.52	
1989	1325	1.63	240999	186626	9620	4.30	0.02
1990	1325	1.94	322236	184700	17555	4.90	0.05
1991	1759	2.07	373284	194101	27733	7.50	0.11
1992	2055	3.26	503973	232752	42155	9.70	0.30
1993	2260	4.81	577800	248230	65699	14.98	0.72
1994	2292	6.16	595134	273053	102238	23.19	2.41
1995	2327	8.83	446230	264605	152761	31.57	4.77
1996	2330	9.08	477466	267193	207573	36.91	8.24
1997	2330	10.34	511592	278649	284278	42.65	15.29
1998	2377	11.34	577452	285889	376708	50.13	26.17
1999	2467	12.70	804278	300410	515916	60.87	51.01
2000	2518	15.37	1001906	404678	724593	78.12	123.68
2001	2570	18.36	1031579	406247	1225474	98.96	295.76
2002	2641	22.01	1091821	420684	1816802	127.93	412.39
2003	2688	25.56	1126964	422822	1051220	206.11	660.86
2004	2759	31.97	1166262	423669	1207778	281.35	856.09
2005	2871	40.66	1185290	424829	1328172	384.52	1016.41
2006	3891	48.93	1213809	336783	1466871	461.31	1216.34
2007	3924	60.89	1264982	356677	1619048	469.17	1408.23
2008	4001	70.16	2248521	1747489	1723829	439.41	1454.29
2009	4713	79.56	1053469	1016490	1563077	378.40	1409.29
2010	4751	92.08	1290692	1090340	1553352	332.42	1607.60
2011	4828	106.14	1458811	1874802	1648579	319.55	1677.77
2012	4969	120.70	1568758	2967132	1699619	330.79	1797.75

注：1. 公路通车里程2006年起含专用公路和村道。
2. 邮电业务收入2003年以前为邮电业务总量，按1990年不变价计算，2003年起为邮电业务收入。

16 续表 7

年 份	社会消费品零售总额(亿元)	进出口总额(亿美元)	出口额	进口额	协议(合同)规定外商投资额(亿美元)	实际利用外资(亿美元)	#外商直接投资
1949							
1952							
1957			0.02				
1962			0.04				
1965			0.08				
1970			0.10				
1975			0.25				
1978	2.13		0.39				
1979	2.50		0.54		0.05	0.02	
1980	3.16		0.77		0.11	0.09	
1981	4.02		0.92		0.08	0.05	0.001
1982	4.81		1.09		0.08	0.07	0.005
1983	5.23		1.19		0.16	0.09	0.003
1984	7.39		1.30		0.32	0.19	0.07
1985	9.36		1.75		0.68	0.35	0.14
1986	12.24		2.33		0.34	0.45	0.15
1987	15.05		2.68		1.85	1.32	0.21
1988	24.65		3.18		6.22	2.99	0.64
1989	27.04		3.49		2.34	2.73	0.84
1990	31.97	10.82	5.68	5.14	3.02	2.56	1.00
1991	36.50	31.75	16.52	15.23	6.45	2.83	1.47
1992	44.35	50.90	26.03	24.87	20.88	4.81	3.29
1993	63.69	67.56	32.11	35.45	35.55	10.49	7.92
1994	85.16	88.30	42.94	45.36	34.97	11.95	7.79
1995	113.01	153.91	77.99	75.92	33.09	11.58	6.72
1996	125.53	178.42	91.87	86.55	20.89	13.10	6.95
1997	146.04	212.99	113.68	99.31	12.14	15.16	8.80
1998	175.16	232.73	130.61	102.13	16.37	15.48	9.30
1999	202.30	284.63	151.54	133.09	14.72	17.89	9.71
2000	235.16	320.45	171.59	148.86	18.36	19.54	10.87
2001	275.71	344.55	189.89	154.65	20.98	20.29	11.47
2002	321.24	442.47	237.36	205.11	24.89	23.48	14.59
2003	369.78	521.06	280.02	241.04	32.56	27.72	17.54
2004	426.47	645.18	351.92	293.25	41.32	33.47	21.39
2005	506.29	743.72	409.29	334.42	47.52	42.48	14.68
2006	599.32	842.21	473.76	368.45	55.28	50.04	18.08
2007	722.45	1068.73	602.32	466.41	62.51	60.07	21.18
2008	881.15	1132.99	655.37	477.62	39.37	47.09	24.47
2009	959.07	941.55	551.69	389.86	20.30	42.12	25.94
2010	1108.06	1213.38	695.98	517.40	30.73	31.63	27.32
2011	1266.31	1352.24	783.29	568.95	37.02	32.18	30.51
2012	1354.58	1444.16	850.66	593.50	41.55	37.19	33.69

注：1. 出口总额1990年起为海关口径，1990年以前为外经贸口径。
2. 外商直接投资2004年起为新口径，是以验资作为统计标准，与往年数不可比。

16 续表 8

年　份	国际及港澳台旅游者(万人次)	国际旅游外汇收入(万美元)	接待国内游客人次(万人次)	旅　游总收入(亿元)	各项人民币存款余额(亿元)	城乡居民储蓄存款余额	各项人民币贷款余额(亿元)
1949							
1952						0.003	0.004
1957						0.02	0.26
1962					0.08	0.04	0.75
1965					0.16	0.09	0.81
1970					0.39	0.16	0.87
1975					0.96	0.41	1.39
1978					1.05	0.54	1.96
1979					1.49	0.72	2.13
1980					2.61	1.17	3.08
1981					3.80	2.03	4.02
1982					4.51	2.77	4.55
1983					6.05	3.86	5.76
1984					11.03	6.18	12.19
1985					13.49	9.19	14.24
1986	11	554	69		19.59	13.14	20.68
1987	19	453	87		28.48	18.97	31.24
1988	20	710	105		38.05	24.91	41.58
1989	18	504	97		46.82	32.57	49.37
1990	27	1025	98		68.07	45.51	63.04
1991	37	2443	118		94.97	61.47	78.40
1992	47	2473	125		147.34	81.54	105.98
1993	52	2888	117		179.83	107.17	134.31
1994	44	3464	75		249.78	151.54	173.44
1995	27	5679	62		383.68	232.97	254.85
1996	36	6464	139		489.65	318.02	312.81
1997	59	6778	112		671.17	425.82	382.66
1998	75	6601	141		864.01	533.75	442.74
1999	97	7055	156		1040.84	616.34	524.37
2000	106	7617	185		1228.67	672.07	630.84
2001	110	8200	217	39.80	1458.65	799.18	750.18
2002	108	11847	822	72.51	1790.18	1001.69	933.41
2003	80	13825	1006	79.92	2126.78	1231.06	1206.72
2004	149	23437	982	85.70	2462.87	1431.68	1405.25
2005	169	28189	987	90.72	2933.40	1728.28	1500.52
2006	193	33180	1170	96.01	3365.65	2013.40	1730.56
2007	248	42702	1477	118.88	3751.83	2120.74	2154.77
2008	268	45614	1604	128.69	4354.53	2638.04	2380.36
2009	286	51756	1751	151.49	4986.61	2904.57	2903.80
2010	327	67592	1924	191.32	5943.39	3386.85	3329.82
2011	357	90975	2258	249.37	6609.39	3710.99	3716.08
2012	415	126924	2329	306.35	7430.46	4204.20	4195.61

年份	在校学生数（万人）			小学学龄儿童入学率(%)	高考入围人数(人)	#省线入围人数	医疗机构病床床位数(张)
	普通高等学校	普通中学	小学				
1949		0.20	5.28				219
1952		0.34	7.04				179
1957		0.67	8.80				403
1962		0.97	12.00				1376
1965		1.05	16.09				1308
1970		6.02	11.81				1476
1975		4.96	16.82				1970
1978		7.60	16.11	98.36	846	250	2257
1979		6.23	15.80	98.70	566	166	2271
1980		5.48	15.49	98.85	222	140	2207
1981		4.35	15.09	98.72	239	154	2210
1982		4.17	14.48	99.06	252	115	2292
1983		4.28	13.54	99.75	245	150	2098
1984		4.65	13.46	99.65	619	220	2231
1985		4.66	13.44	99.83	534	285	2323
1986		4.94	14.07	99.90	595	228	3054
1987		5.44	14.43	99.94	644	297	3393
1988		5.93	15.01	99.93	925	315	3640
1989		6.20	15.59	99.92	977	284	3677
1990		6.12	16.27	99.94	759	224	3866
1991		6.01	17.01	99.92	861	268	4085
1992		6.52	17.52	99.94	994	312	4517
1993	0.11	7.53	18.01	99.95	1102	423	4940
1994	0.15	8.58	18.62	99.96	1823	586	5365
1995	0.16	9.25	19.51	99.99	2095	809	5798
1996	0.18	9.52	20.60	99.98	2160	1093	5288
1997	0.20	9.80	22.18	99.99	2212	1215	5505
1998	0.22	10.12	23.58	99.99	2348	1315	5892
1999	0.22	10.55	24.88	99.99	3501	1790	6241
2000	0.32	11.24	27.28	99.99	5017	2646	7081
2001	0.38	12.21	29.54	100.00	5651	3225	7474
2002	0.51	13.53	34.28	100.00	6873	3759	8641
2003	0.69	14.97	38.69	100.00	9167	4509	9820
2004	0.91	17.13	44.83	100.00	10756	5452	10797
2005	1.66	19.10	48.09	100.00	11196	6455	11972
2006	2.20	21.46	49.68	100.00	11359	7652	13293
2007	2.52	23.46	52.07	100.00	13275	9185	15227
2008	2.87	24.84	52.86	100.00	15047	9987	16778
2009	3.40	24.95	51.12	100.00	17487	12569	18080
2010	3.83	25.83	55.24	100.00	18845	13761	19980
2011	4.51	26.31	57.83	100.00	19588	15501	22814
2012	5.24	26.79	60.81	100.00	22127	17316	24617

16　续表 10

年　份	卫生机构技术人员数(万人)	#执业(助理)医师	每万人口拥有		年末参加基本养老保险人数(万人)	年末参加基本医疗保险人数(万人)	城镇居民最低生活保障人数(人)
			床位数(张)	执业(助理)医师（人)			
1949	0.02		3.21				
1952	0.01		2.50				
1957	0.03		5.20				
1962	0.13		17.28				
1965	0.16		15.13				
1970	0.17		14.98				
1975	0.23		18.25				
1978	0.26	0.08	20.29	6.90			
1979	0.29	0.10	20.27	8.67			
1980	0.30	0.12	19.58	10.35			
1981	0.31	0.11	19.31	9.63			
1982	0.33	0.11	19.73	9.44			
1983	0.33	0.11	17.84	9.25			
1984	0.34	0.11	18.76	9.52			
1985	0.33	0.12	19.22	9.94			
1986	0.35	0.12	24.83	9.58			
1987	0.35	0.13	27.17	10.44			
1988	0.38	0.15	28.72	12.13			
1989	0.39	0.16	28.56	12.58			
1990	0.39	0.17	22.01	9.80			
1991	0.39	0.18	20.42	8.77			
1992	0.41	0.18	19.83	8.04			
1993	0.45	0.20	19.04	7.80			
1994	0.49	0.22	18.16	7.52	7.55	7.77	
1995	0.53	0.23	17.23	6.83	8.46	7.60	
1996	0.58	0.24	13.80	6.39	9.16	7.65	
1997	0.63	0.26	12.62	5.97	7.53	8.29	
1998	0.71	0.30	11.86	5.95	7.84	9.05	
1999	0.76	0.31	11.03	5.44	8.35	9.95	
2000	0.81	0.33	10.98	5.13	82.95	88.21	1825
2001	0.81	0.34	11.42	5.24	83.01	84.99	2003
2002	0.90	0.35	13.20	5.38	103.19	105.19	2711
2003	0.98	0.38	14.99	5.74	104.13	105.90	2876
2004	1.31	0.49	16.47	7.43	104.44	105.95	4968
2005	1.88	0.69	18.25	10.52	182.49	189.40	4885
2006	2.29	0.86	22.21	12.58	204.08	212.16	6091
2007	2.88	1.04	21.24	14.57	227.98	236.32	3129
2008	3.31	1.19	22.35	15.81	262.63	513.25	3653
2009	3.58	1.29	23.00	16.39	315.81	536.57	3770
2010	3.75	1.32	24.29	16.07	421.84	592.27	3643
2011	3.96	1.36	27.64	16.53	481.05	602.41	9415
2012	4.06	1.40	29.69	16.93	513.29	616.86	6598

注：每万人口拥有床位数、执业(助理)医师数按常住人口计算。

16 续表 11

年 份	专 利 申请量 (件)	专 利 授权量 (件)	城市居民 人均可支 配收入 (元)	农 民 人 均 纯收入 (元)	城镇人均 住房使用 面 积 (平方米)	农村人均 生活用房 使用面积 (平方米)
1949						
1952						
1957						
1962						
1965						
1970						
1975						
1978				149		
1979				188		
1980				272		
1981				463		
1982				567		
1983				618		
1984				691		
1985			791	803	11	
1986			1033	951	12	
1987			1247	1142	13	
1988			1778	1325	15	
1989			2282	1424	17	
1990	34	30	2508	1542	16	
1991	70	50	3068	1673	16	
1992	102	78	4026	2290	17	
1993	100	90	5970	2903	20	
1994	104	100	8270	3769	23	
1995	325	262	9588	4769	20	
1996	333	312	10824	5554	21	20
1997	725	321	11032	6132	21	41
1998	890	709	11506	6830	26	43
1999	1221	819	12954	7704	29.7	46
2000	1653	1399	14142	8484	31.1	47
2001	2914	1753	16938	9383	39.9	48
2002	3100	2680	16949	10178	41.8	55
2003	3865	2858	18471	11033	41.4	58
2004	4325	3167	20526	11941	41.6	65
2005	6694	3114	22882	13076	42.7	65
2006	9879	4872	25320	14313	45.2	60
2007	13842	6752	27025	15747	43.1	59
2008	14406	8093	30275	16904	40.3	55
2009	19106	12918	33045	18098	40.4	56
2010	21654	20397	35690	20486	44.1	52
2011	24455	19352	39513	22842	49.4	52
2012	29199	20900	42944	24944	43.8	50

十七、东莞与全国、全省、三角洲城市主要指标比较

Comparison of Main Indicators between Dongguan and China, Guangdong Province, the Cities of the Pearl River Delta

17-1 主要年份全国国民经济与社会发展指标

Main Indicators on National Economy and Social Development of China

指　　　标	单 位	1980年	1990年	1995年	2000年	2005年	2010年	2011年	2012年
人口与劳动力									
年末总人口	万人	98705	114333	121121	126743	130756	134091	134735	135404
年末从业人员人数	万人	42361	64749	68065	72085	74647	76105	76420	76704
#城镇从业人员	万人	10525	17041	19040	23151	28389	34687	35914	37102
经济总量									
国内生产总值	亿元	4546	18668	60794	99215	184937	401513	473104	519322
第一产业增加值	亿元	1372	5062	12136	14945	22420	40534	47486	52377
第二产业增加值	亿元	2192	7717	28680	45556	87598	187383	220413	235319
第三产业增加值	亿元	982	5888	19979	38714	74919	173596	205205	231626
人均国内生产总值	元	463	1644	5046	7858	14185	30015	35198	38449
农业									
主要农产品产量									
粮食	万吨	32056	44624	46662	46218	48402	54678	57121	58958
水果	万吨	679	1874	4215	6225	16120	21401	22768	24057
肉类	万吨		2857	5260	6014	6939	7926	7958	8387
水产品	万吨	450	1237	2517	3706	4420	5373	5603	5906
工业									
工业增加值	亿元	1997	6858	24951	40034	77231	160722	188470	199860
主要工业产品产量									
机制纸及纸板	万吨	535	1372	2812	2487	5404	9833	11011	11375
彩电	万台	3	1033	2058	3936	8283	11830	12231	12823
发电量	亿千瓦时	3006	6212	10070	13556	24747	42072	47130	49378
钢材	万吨	2716	5153	8980	13146	39692	80277	88620	95318
运输邮电									
货运量	亿吨	54.65	97.06	123.49	135.87	186.21	324.18	369.70	412.00
货物周转量	亿吨公里	12027	26208	35909	44321	80258	141837	159324	173145
客运量	亿人	34.18	77.27	117.26	147.86	184.70	326.95	352.63	379.00
旅客周转量	亿人公里	2281	5628	9002	12261	17467	27894	30984	33369
邮电业务总量	亿元	39	156	989	4793	12029	31979	13334	15022
年末程控电话用户	万户	214	685	4071	14483	35045	29434	28510	27815
年末移动电话用户	万户		1.8	363	8453	39341	85900	98625	111216

注：城镇从业人员1998年起为城镇在岗职工人数。

17-1 续表

指　　标	单　位	1980年	1990年	1995年	2000年	2005年	2010年	2011年	2012年
固定资产投资									
固定资产投资总额	亿元	911	4517	20019	32918	88774	278122	311485	364835
#房地产开发	亿元		253	3149	4984	15909	48259	61797	71804
商业									
社会消费品零售总额	亿元	2140	8300	20620	39106	67177	156998	183919	210307
物价总指数									
商品零售价格指数	上年=100	106.0	102.1	114.8	98.5	100.8	103.1	104.9	102.0
居民消费价格指数	上年=100	107.5	103.1	117.1	100.4	101.8	103.3	105.4	102.6
外贸外经									
海关进出口总额	亿美元	381	1154	2809	4743	14219	29740	36419	38668
进口额	亿美元	200	533	1321	2251	6599	13962	17435	18178
出口额	亿美元	181	621	1488	2492	7620	15778	18984	20489
实际利用外资	亿美元		35	375	407	603	1057	1160	1117
财政、金融									
公共财政收入	亿元	1160	2937	6242	13395	31649	83102	103874	117210
公共财政支出	亿元	1229	3084	6824	15887	33930	89874	109248	125712
各项人民币存款余额	亿元		13943	53882	123804	287170	718238	809368	917555
各项人民币贷款余额	亿元		17511	50544	99371	194690	479196	547947	629910
人民生活									
在岗职工人均工资	元	762	2140	5500	9371	18364	37147	42452	47593
城市居民人均可支配收入	元	478	1510	4283	6280	10493	19109	21810	24565
农民人均纯收入	元	191	686	1578	2253	3255	5919	6977	7917
城乡居民人民币储蓄存款余额	亿元	400	7120	29662	64332	141051	303302	343636	399551
教育									
在校学生数									
普通高等学校	万人	114	206	291	556	1562	2232	2309	2391
普通中学	万人	5508	4586	5371	7369	8581	7703	7519	7230
小学	万人	14627	12241	13195	13013	10864	9941	9926	9696
卫生									
医院床位数	万张	120	187	206	217	245	339	371	403
卫生技术人员	万人	280	390	426	449	456	588	620	650
#执业（助理）医师	万人	115	176	192	208	204	241	247	252

注：实际利用外资不含对外借款，2005年起为实际使用外商直接投资口径。

17-2 主要年份广东省国民经济与社会发展指标

Main Indicators on National Economy and Social Development of Guangdong Province

指标	单位	1980年	1990年	1995年	2000年	2005年	2010年	2011年	2012年
人口与劳动力									
年末常住人口	万人		6347	7387	8650	9194	10441	10505	10594
年末从业人员人数	万人	2368	3118	3551	3989	5023	5752	5961	5966
#城镇从业人员	万人	564	785	912	759	904	1119	1238	1304
经济总量									
地区生产总值	亿元	250	1559	5933	10741	22557	46013	53210	57068
第一产业增加值	亿元	83	385	864	986	1428	2287	2665	2847
第二产业增加值	亿元	103	616	2900	5000	11357	23015	26447	27701
第三产业增加值	亿元	64	559	2168	4755	9773	20712	24098	26520
人均地区生产总值	元	481	2484	8129	12736	24647	44736	50807	54095
农业									
主要农产品产量									
粮食	万吨	1682	1896	1803	1822	1395	1317	1361	1396
水果	万吨	29	329	415	644	832	1129	1205	1279
肉类	万吨	63	202	305	324	384	441	435	443
水产品	万吨	63	208	354	593	695	729	762	790
工业									
工业增加值	亿元	90	523	2449	4463	10490	21463	24650	25810
主要工业产品产量									
机制纸及纸板	万吨	31	104	288	260	691	1435	1496	1582
彩电	万台	1	262	764	1532	4090	4495	4862	5810
发电量	亿千瓦时	109	344	821	1293	2163	3101	3607	3593
成品钢材	万吨	45	134	247	406	1366	2919	3177	2993
运输邮电									
货运量	万吨	14201	85809	111063	119216	133992	205034	234978	266359
货物周转量	亿吨公里	1413	2599	4643	3065	3917	5934	7113	9781
客运量	万人	21444	78046	130998	164791	161357	467049	522095	586299
旅客周转量	亿人公里	114	453	936	1219	2043	3342	3852	4372
邮电业务总量	亿元	2	26	205	757	2122	4833	1918	2175
年末程控电话用户	万户		113	591	1415	3443	3169	3147	3136
年末移动电话用户	万户		1	99	1357	6407	9710	10793	12468

注：2010年年末人口数为第六次全国人口普查数据。

17-2 续表

指　　标	单 位	1980年	1990年	1995年	2000年	2005年	2010年	2011年	2012年
固定资产投资									
固定资产投资总额	亿元	38	381	2327	3234	7164	16113	16844	19308
#房地产开发	亿元		33	564	859	1592	3660	4810	5353
商业									
社会消费品零售总额	亿元	118	667	2478	4380	7916	17415	20247	22677
物价总指数									
商品零售价格指数	上年=100	108.5	95.6	111.6	99.9	101.8	103.3	105.1	102.2
居民消费价格指数	上年=100		97.5	114.0	101.4	102.3	103.1	105.3	102.8
外贸外经									
海关进出口总额	亿美元	26	419	1040	1701	4280	7849	9133	9839
进口额	亿美元	4	197	474	782	1898	3317	3815	4099
出口额	亿美元	22	222	566	919	2382	4532	5318	5741
实际利用外资	亿美元	2	20	121	146	152	210	223	241
财政、金融									
地方公共财政预算收入	亿元	38	131	382	911	1807	4517	5515	6229
地方公共财政预算支出	亿元	27	151	526	1070	2289	5422	6712	7388
各项人民币存款余额	亿元		1577	7090	16908	35784	78286	86849	97463
各项人民币贷款余额	亿元		1704	5496	11204	20745	46099	52167	58541
人民生活									
在岗职工人均工资	元	789	2929	8250	13823	23959	40358	45152	50577
城市居民人均可支配收入	元	473	2303	7439	9762	14770	23898	26897	30227
农民人均纯收入	元	274	1043	2699	3654	4690	7890	9372	10543
城乡居民人民币储蓄存款余额	亿元	30	752	3885	8667	19051	36219	39725	44803
教育									
在校学生数									
#普通高等学校	万人	4	10	15	30	87	143	153	162
中等职业教育学校	万人	6	45	67	66	71	155	152	150
普通中学	万人	252	234	339	461	612	709	699	668
小学	万人	749	747	883	930	1067	849	822	808
卫生									
医院及卫生院床位数	万张	8	11	14	16	19	28	30	32
卫生技术人员	万人	14	19	23	26	30	45	48	51
#执业(助理)医师	万人	6	8	10	11	12	17	18	19

17-3 主要经济指标东莞占全国、全省的比重（2012年）

Proportion of Main Indicators of Dongguan to China and Guangdong Province (2012)

指　　标	单 位	绝 对 值			东莞占全国的比重(%)	东莞占全省的比重(%)
		全 国	全 省	东 莞		
人口						
年末常住人口	万 人	135404	10594	829.23	0.61	7.83
经济总量						
地区生产总值	亿 元	519322	57068	5010.17	0.96	8.78
第一产业增加值	亿 元	52377	2847	18.76	0.04	0.66
第二产业增加值	亿 元	235319	27701	2375.64	1.01	8.58
第三产业增加值	亿 元	231626	26520	2615.78	1.13	9.86
工业						
工业增加值	亿 元	199860	25810	2297.51	1.15	8.90
主要工业产品产量						
发电量	亿千瓦时	49378	3593	337.68	0.68	9.40
机制纸及纸板	万 吨	11375	1582	1152.91	10.14	72.88
彩电	万 台	12823	5810	493.04	3.84	8.49
农业						
主要农产品产量						
粮食	万 吨	58958	1396	1.25	0.002	0.09
水果	万 吨	24057	1279	6.49	0.03	0.51
肉类	万 吨	8387	443	2.67	0.03	0.60
水产品	万 吨	5906	790	7.70	0.13	0.98
固定资产投资额						
固定资产投资总额	亿 元	364835	19308	1180.35	0.32	6.11
运输邮电						
货物周转量	亿吨公里	173145	9781	296.71	0.17	3.03
旅客周转量	亿人公里	33369	4372	156.88	0.47	3.59
本地电话用户	万 户	27815	3136	318.68	1.15	10.16
年末移动电话用户	万 户	111216	12468	1797.75	1.62	14.42
财政、金融						
公共财政收入	亿 元	117210	6229	356.32	0.30	5.72
公共财政支出	亿 元	125712	7388	385.58	0.31	5.22
各项人民币存款余额	亿 元	917555	97463	7430.46	0.81	7.62
各项人民币贷款余额	亿 元	629910	58541	4195.61	0.67	7.17
外经外贸						
进出口总额	亿美元	38668	9839	1444.16	3.73	14.68
进口总额	亿美元	18178	4099	593.50	3.26	14.48
出口总额	亿美元	20489	5741	850.66	4.15	14.82
实际利用外资	亿美元	1117	241	33.69	3.02	13.98
商业、物价						
社会消费品零售总额	亿 元	210307	22677	1354.58	0.64	5.97
商品零售价格指数	上年=100	102.0	102.2	102.4		
居民消费价格指数	上年=100	102.6	102.8	102.9		
人民生活						
在岗职工人均工资	元	47593	50577	57007		
城市居民人均可支配收入	元	24565	30227	42944		
农民人均纯收入	元	7917	10543	24944		
城乡居民人民币储蓄存款余额	亿 元	399551	44803	4204.20	1.05	9.38

17-4 主要经济指标东莞占全国、全省的比重（2011年）

Proportion of Main Indicators of Dongguan to China and Guangdong Province (2011)

指标	单位	绝对值			东莞占全国的比重(%)	东莞占全省的比重(%)
		全国	全省	东莞		
人口						
年末常住人口	万人	134735	10505	825.48	0.61	7.86
经济总量						
地区生产总值	亿元	473104	53210	4735.39	1.00	8.90
第一产业增加值	亿元	47486	2665	17.88	0.04	0.67
第二产业增加值	亿元	220413	26447	2366.20	1.07	8.95
第三产业增加值	亿元	205205	24098	2351.32	1.15	9.76
工业						
工业增加值	亿元	188470	24650	2288.41	1.21	9.28
主要工业产品产量						
发电量	亿千瓦时	47130	3607	376.00	0.80	10.42
机制纸及纸板	万吨	11011	1496	1021.32	9.28	68.27
彩电	万台	12231	4862	541.00	4.42	11.13
农业						
主要农产品产量						
粮食	万吨	57121	1361	1.29	0.002	0.09
水果	万吨	22768	1205	7.39	0.03	0.61
肉类	万吨	7958	435	2.60	0.03	0.60
水产品	万吨	5603	762	7.82	0.14	1.03
固定资产投资额						
固定资产投资总额	亿元	311485	16844	1079.77	0.35	6.41
运输邮电						
货物周转量	亿吨公里	159324	7113	187.48	0.12	2.64
旅客周转量	亿人公里	30984	3852	145.88	0.47	3.79
年末程控电话用户	万户	28510	3147	305.97	1.07	9.72
年末移动电话用户	万户	98625	10793	1677.77	1.70	15.55
财政、金融						
公共财政收入	亿元	103874	5515	313.06	0.30	5.68
公共财政支出	亿元	109248	6712	351.92	0.32	5.24
各项人民币存款余额	亿元	809368	86849	6609.39	0.82	7.61
各项人民币贷款余额	亿元	547947	52167	3716.08	0.68	7.12
外经外贸						
进出口总额	亿美元	36419	9133	1352.23	3.71	14.81
进口总额	亿美元	17435	3815	568.95	3.26	14.91
出口总额	亿美元	18984	5318	783.29	4.13	14.73
实际利用外资	亿美元	1160	223	30.51	2.63	13.68
商业、物价						
社会消费品零售总额	亿元	183919	20247	1266.31	0.69	6.25
商品零售价格指数	上年=100	104.9	105.1	104.7		
居民消费价格指数	上年=100	105.4	105.3	104.9		
人民生活						
在岗职工人均工资	元	42452	45152	50398		
城市居民人均可支配收入	元	21810	26897	39513		
农民人均纯收入	元	6977	9372	22842		
城乡居民人民币储蓄存款余额	亿元	343636	39725	3710.99	1.08	9.34

17-5 主要经济指标人均水平东莞与全国、全省的比较（2012年）

Comparison of Per Capita Level of Main Economic Indicators between Dongguan and China, Guangdong Province (2012)

指　　标	单 位	人 均 水 平			东莞相当于全国(%)	东莞相当于全省(%)
		全 国	全 省	东 莞		
生产总值	元	38449	54095	60557	157.5	111.9
财政收入	元	8678	5905	4307	49.6	72.9
出口总额	美元	1517	5442	10282	677.8	188.9
各项人民币存款余额	元	67764	91998	89607	132.2	97.4
居民储蓄存款余额	元	29508	42291	50700	171.8	119.9
固定资产投资总额	元	27011	18302	14267	52.8	77.9
社会消费品零售总额	元	15570	21496	16372	105.2	76.2
实际利用外资	美元	83	229	407	492.4	178.2
在岗职工人均工资	元	47593	50577	57007	119.8	112.7
城市居民可支配收入	元	24565	30227	42944	174.8	142.1
农民人均纯收入	元	7917	10543	24944	315.1	236.6
粮食产量	公斤	436	132	2	0.3	1.1
水产品产量	公斤	44	75	9	21.3	12.4
水果产量	公斤	178	121	8	4.4	6.5
工业发电量	千瓦时	3656	3406	4085	111.8	119.9
医院卫生院床位数	张/千人	2.98	3.06	2.90	97.4	94.6
卫生技术人员数	人/千人	4.80	4.81	4.90	102.0	101.7

注：本表人均指标时点数按年末常住人口计算，时期数按年平均常住人口计算。

17-6 主要经济指标人均水平东莞与全国、全省的比较（2011年）

Comparison of Per Capita Level of Main Economic Indicators between Dongguan and China, Guangdong Province (2011)

指　　标	单 位	人 均 水 平			东莞相当于全国(%)	东莞相当于全省(%)
		全 国	全 省	东 莞		
生产总值	元	35083	50807	57470	163.8	113.1
财政收入	元	7718	5265	3799	49.2	72.2
出口总额	美元	1413	5079	9506	673.0	187.2
各项人民币存款余额	元	60071	82674	80067	133.3	96.8
居民储蓄存款余额	元	26122	38463	44956	172.1	116.9
固定资产投资总额	元	23139	16168	13104	56.6	81.0
社会消费品零售总额	元	13683	19333	15368	112.3	79.5
实际利用外资	美元	86	213	370	429.1	173.9
在岗职工人均工资	元	41799	45152	50398	120.6	111.6
城市居民可支配收入	元	21810	26897	39513	181.2	146.9
农民人均纯收入	元	6977	9372	22842	327.4	243.7
粮食产量	公斤	425	130	2	0.4	1.2
水产品产量	公斤	42	73	9	22.8	13.0
水果产量	公斤	169	116	9	5.3	7.8
工业发电量	千瓦时	3497	3444	4563	130.5	132.5
医院卫生院床位数	张/千人	2.73	2.86	2.70	98.8	94.5
卫生技术人员数	人/千人	4.60	4.57	4.80	104.2	104.9

注：本表人均指标时点数按常住人口计算，时期数按年平均常住人口计算。

17-7 珠江三角洲国民经济和社会发展主要指标（2012年）

指　　标	单 位	广州市	深圳市	珠海市
综合				
行政区域土地面积	平方公里	7287	1953	1654
年末常住人口	万人	1283.89	1054.74	158.26
年末户籍人口	万人	822.30	299.15	106.55
地区生产总值	亿元	13551.21	12950.06	1503.76
第一产业增加值	亿元	213.76	6.30	39.02
第二产业增加值	亿元	4720.65	5737.64	776.36
#工业增加值	亿元	4264.16	5355.85	720.25
第三产业增加值	亿元	8616.79	7206.12	688.38
人均生产总值(按常住人口计算)	元	105909	123247	95471
农村经济				
农林牧渔业总产值	亿元	377.34	14.13	69.80
粮食产量	万吨	44.97	5.00	4.43
水果产量	万吨	40.28	0.27	6.26
水产品产量	万吨	46.02	2.87	21.50
工业				
规模以上工业企业数	个	4373	5835	927
规模以上工业增加值	亿元	3945.18	5107.24	664.93
规模以上工业企业主营业务收入	亿元	14595.82	20990.98	3467.34
规模以上工业企业利润总额	亿元	825.60	1135.83	164.38
规模以上工业产品销售率	%	98.6	97.8	98.0
固定资产投资				
固定资产投资总额	亿元	3758.39	2314.43	787.62
#房地产开发投资额	亿元	1370.45	736.84	242.08
商品房屋销售面积	万平方米	1333.13	525.83	251.22
商品房屋销售额	亿元	1754.75	1030.10	268.48
交通、邮电				
民用汽车拥有量	万辆	204.16	221.40	27.34
年末固定电话用户数	万户	590.73	570.38	82.94
年末移动电话用户数	万户	2367.39	2464.43	290.75
全年总用电量	亿千瓦时	694.13	714.01	117.47
#工业用电量	亿千瓦时	358.95	423.24	72.58

Main Indicators of National Economy and Social Development of the Pearl River Delta Economic Zone (2012)

佛山市	惠州市	肇庆市	江门市	东莞市	中山市
3848	11356	14822	9541	2460	1800
726.18	467.40	398.23	448.27	829.23	315.50
377.65	341.91	427.59	391.80	187.02	152.01
6613.02	2367.55	1462.35	1880.39	5010.17	2441.04
130.53	124.56	238.63	149.51	18.76	62.17
4113.34	1377.23	669.31	960.82	2375.64	1353.64
3976.10	1296.40	616.23	913.78	2297.51	1291.41
2369.16	865.76	554.41	770.06	2615.78	1025.24
91259	50873	36864	42028	60557	77527
257.43	206.60	370.43	272.18	32.01	106.37
9.73	62.66	115.11	96.92	1.25	7.75
5.01	63.41	118.93		6.49	16.01
57.71	14.94	35.86	71.24	7.70	35.46
5950	1430	1046	1851	4526	3192
3302.10	1173.97	664.99	576.13	1978.13	1227.06
13980.37	5503.05	2745.09	2464.21	9612.66	5203.63
1140.50	219.32	192.20	127.96	291.67	283.77
97.5	99.5	98.2	97.3	100.3	95.3
2128.33	1208.68	852.60	850.41	1180.35	893.43
638.46	482.17	145.45	144.49	377.32	346.41
802.17	826.72	373.60	351.12	639.12	654.16
646.25	478.42	175.82	193.65	542.38	359.81
119.76	35.77	19.92	36.12	120.70	48.26
278.25	129.24	78.39	132.69	318.68	115.93
1050.68	477.04	264.64	392.09	1754.10	547.55
506.95	227.36	131.03	196.14	604.28	206.49
369.91	160.18	97.17	136.62	452.29	136.63

17-7 续表

(2012年)

指　　标	单 位	广州市	深圳市	珠海市
金融、贸易、财政				
年末金融机构人民币存款余额	亿元	28270.68	25910.24	2987.35
#城乡居民储蓄存款余额	亿元	11174.68	8132.16	1196.27
年末金融机构人民币贷款余额	亿元	17554.90	17305.47	1651.85
社会消费品零售总额	亿元	5977.27	4008.78	635.20
地方公共财政收入	亿元	1102.40	1482.08	162.60
地方公共财政支出	亿元	1343.65	1569.01	212.20
对外经济				
海关进口总额	亿美元	582.52	1954.47	240.44
海关出口总额	亿美元	589.15	2713.56	216.37
外商直接投资项目	个	1095	2428	253
合同利用外资金额	亿美元	68.02	62.62	21.90
实际利用外商直接投资	亿美元	45.75	52.29	14.47
人民生活、物价				
在岗职工年平均工资	元	63752	59010	48486
城市居民年人均可支配收入	元	38054	40742	32978
城市居民年人均消费支出	元	30490	26728	24083
农民人均纯收入	元	16788		13399
居民消费价格总指数(以上年为100)	%	103.0	102.8	102.8
教育、卫生				
学校数				
高等学校	所	79	10	
中等职业技术学校	所	85	15	8
普通中学	所	478	302	63
小学	所	941	333	114
在校学生数				
高等学校	万人	93.92	7.56	12.30
中等职业技术学校	万人	24.01	3.21	2.27
普通中学	万人	55.07	35.96	9.50
小学	万人	82.26	68.31	12.85
医院医疗机构数	个	2415	2623	482
#医院	个	224	121	35
医院床位数	张	62194	26124	6103
执业(助理)医师	人	37101	23973	4733

佛山市	惠州市	肇庆市	江门市	东莞市	中山市
9734.79	2497.37	1319.93	2800.20	7430.46	3212.63
5155.01	1349.23	851.29	1852.48	4204.20	1747.90
6078.40	1483.72	868.63	1329.71	4195.61	1774.51
2019.50	754.15	433.39	807.21	1354.58	809.33
384.08	200.88	103.81	135.03	356.32	201.89
433.96	274.08	176.49	188.12	385.58	215.32
209.08	202.90	25.71	58.02	593.50	88.78
401.50	292.04	37.81	129.70	850.66	246.44
155	327	154	153	690	193
33.05	26.55	29.13	13.65	38.10	13.19
23.50	17.28	11.52	8.70	33.69	8.04
46203	41506	39151	37983	57007	55480
34580	29665	21754	27017	42944	31130
26164	22279	15729	18448	31369	22288
15684	12415	10366	11345	24944	19347
102.6	102.8	102.8	102.7	102.9	102.3
3				6	
38	27	23	24	24	11
189	214	170	183	203	101
411	472	293	321	322	207
4.58			4.45	5.24	3.63
7.98	6.99	6.91	5.23	4.73	2.55
31.86	29.66	30.25	24.19	26.79	15.69
45.28	42.11	33.46	29.13	60.81	24.61
1039	984	726	727	2222	482
83	61	47	36	73	48
22140	11056	8603	10974	24042	11213
13171	8564	5176	7409	14043	5635

17-8 长江三角洲国民经济和社会发展主要指标（2012年）

指　　标	单 位	上海市	南京市	苏州市	无锡市	常州市	镇江市
综合							
行政区域土地面积	平方公里	6341	6582	8488	4788	4375	3847
年末常住人口	万人	2380.43	816.10	1054.91	646.55	468.68	315.50
年末户籍人口	万人	1426.93	638.48	647.81	470.07	364.80	271.40
地区生产总值	亿元	20101.33	7201.57	12011.65	7568.15	3969.75	2630.10
第一产业增加值	亿元	127.80	184.64	195.08	137.22	126.30	116.70
第二产业增加值	亿元	7912.77	3170.78	6502.25	4012.03	2100.76	1419.50
第三产业增加值	亿元	12060.26	3846.15	5314.32	3418.90	1742.69	1093.80
农村经济							
农林牧渔业总产值	亿元	320.76	318.55	337.70	224.15	219.60	177.80
工业							
规模以上工业增加值	亿元	6446.14	2571.98	5879.93	3056.90	1967.32	1427.91
规模以上工业企业主营业务收入	亿元		11149.85	28538.30	14161.53	8980.30	5950.80
规模以上工业企业利润总额	亿元	2131.33	551.27	1217.23	824.19	428.18	358.10
固定资产投资							
固定资产投资总额	亿元	5254.38	4683.45	5266.49	3618.07	2760.10	1500.70
＃房地产开发投资额	亿元	2381.00	1015.76	1263.00	974.37	597.00	205.50
交通、邮电							
民用汽车拥有量	万辆	212.86	117.75	239.27	137.08	72.70	28.80
年末固定电话用户数	万户	902.90	288.92		213.64	161.60	113.50
年末移动电话用户数	万户	3008.30	1153.10	1555.00	896.74	519.40	338.00
金融、贸易、财政							
年末金融机构本外币存款余额	亿元	63555.25	16540.43	18796.06	10740.38	5789.88	2903.48
＃城乡居民储蓄存款余额	亿元	20247.24	4532.02	5845.91	3763.82	2489.97	1308.93
年末金融机构本外币贷款余额	亿元	40982.48	13079.32	14877.84	8024.00	4018.21	2128.23
社会消费品零售总额	亿元	7387.32	3080.58	3240.97	2427.94	1404.53	761.70
地方公共财政收入	亿元	3743.71	733.02	1204.30	658.03	378.99	215.50
地方公共财政支出	亿元	4184.02	769.81	1113.47	648.61	384.10	233.60
对外经济							
海关进口总额	亿美元	2299.51	233.34	1310.01	294.61	90.70	36.80
海关出口总额	亿美元	2068.07	319.01	1746.89	413.14	199.60	77.37
实际利用外商直接投资	亿美元	151.85	41.30	91.65	40.10	33.61	22.14
人民生活、物价							
城市居民年人均可支配收入	元	40188	36322	37531	35663	33587	30045
城市居民年人均消费支出	元	26253	23493	25157	23000	20519	17897
农民人均纯收入	元	17401	14786	19396	18509	16737	14518
居民消费价格总指数(以上年为100)	%	102.8	102.7	102.7	102.5	102.5	102.4

注：1.湖州、绍兴、舟山固定电话含小灵通。

Main Indicators on National Economy and Social Development of the Yangtze River Delta Economic Zone(2012)

南通市	扬州市	泰州市	杭州市	宁波市	嘉兴市	湖州市	绍兴市	舟山市	台州市
8001	6634	5793	16596	9817	3915	5818	8256	1440	9411
729.70	446.72	462.98	880.20	763.90	454.40	290.50	494.30	114.00	600.50
765.20	458.42	506.35	700.52	577.70	344.52	261.38	440.83	97.18	590.95
4558.70	2933.20	2701.67	7803.98	6524.70	2884.94	1661.97	3620.10	851.95	2927.34
319.10	203.86	191.75	255.93	270.00	150.05	123.31	184.72	83.05	201.12
2414.10	1555.78	1434.53	3626.88	3516.70	1620.82	888.20	1949.07	385.42	1435.04
1825.50	1173.56	1075.39	3921.17	2738.00	1114.07	650.46	1486.31	383.48	1291.18
548.90	368.58		384.34	420.50	253.85	208.48		163.71	348.99
2273.20	1770.37	1737.58	2393.59	2132.50	1115.09	555.55	1411.11	223.63	705.23
9592.20	6980.70	6824.60	12404.24		5606.55	3341.76		1486.00	
751.80	471.90	519.94	751.75	520.30	255.91	158.79	437.38	10.12	168.77
2886.50	1783.65	1454.59	3722.75	2901.40	1642.31	970.73	1722.56	600.81	1242.56
481.70	235.84	234.48	1597.36	884.40	415.88	211.17	467.71	158.94	357.38
184.80	83.13	34.09	226.70			33.89	100.56	8.55	79.33
259.60	138.00		346.19		155.89	101.70	195.06	53.43	165.07
809.10	487.07	406.81	1358.03		544.82	324.26	497.61	154.29	782.99
6477.80	3365.22	3076.17	20148.77	11980.50	4597.34	2285.66	5923.60	1389.97	4509.17
3605.70	1705.76	1550.76	6089.98	4208.81	2155.49	1082.79	2503.32	508.59	2385.14
4006.50	2042.98	2080.66	18090.90	11961.00	3670.52	1912.40	5129.15	1295.83	3893.16
1708.70	967.87	737.60	2944.63	2329.30	1084.74	703.87	1158.66	290.54	1304.30
419.70	225.00	233.25	859.99	725.50	257.73	138.55	265.76	85.56	220.42
513.00	268.48	294.79	786.28	828.44	260.70	167.51	278.71	155.22	287.93
75.20	20.30	34.23	204.22	351.30	91.41	13.40	65.41	61.32	33.83
187.90	81.72	69.47	412.62	614.40	196.03	73.96	255.57	92.24	172.39
22.10	21.38	14.50	49.61	28.50	17.86	10.26	9.54	1.83	4.75
28292	28001	26574	37511	37902	35696	32987	36911	34224	33979
17858	17750	16499	22800	22887	21720	19898	22204	20958	20643
13231	12686	12493	17017	18475	18636	17188	17706	18208	14567
102.5	102.6	101.7	102.5	101.7	102.2	102.0	102.0	101.7	102.0

2.苏州、南通、杭州民用汽车拥有量为机动车拥有量,无锡为全社会拥有车辆数。

第三部分　基本单位情况

Part Three　Basic Units

1-1 按行业分的法人单位、产业活动单位数（2012年）

Number of Corporate Units and Industrial Establishments by Sector (2012)

项目	法人单位数（个）	单产业法人单位	多产业法人单位	产业活动单位数（个）	多产业法人单位的产业活动单位
合计	93634	91805	1829	103621	11816
采矿业	15	15		15	
煤炭开采和洗选业					
石油和天然气开采业	1	1		1	
黑色金属矿采选业					
有色金属矿采选业	5	5		5	
非金属矿采选业	6	6		6	
开采辅助活动	2	2		2	
其他采矿业	1	1		1	
制造业	44009	43784	225	44146	362
农副食品加工业	222	219	3	230	11
食品制造业	353	347	6	356	9
酒、饮料和精制茶制造业	75	70	5	76	6
烟草制品业					
纺织业	1482	1472	10	1489	17
纺织服装、服饰业	2759	2739	20	2772	33
皮革、毛皮、羽毛及其制品和制鞋业	2360	2351	9	2364	13
木材加工和木、竹、藤、棕、草制品业	400	395	5	403	8
家具制造业	1403	1390	13	1412	22
造纸和纸制品业	2173	2167	6	2175	8
印刷和记录媒介复制业	1629	1627	2	1630	3
文教、工美、体育和娱乐用品制造业	1884	1878	6	1888	10
石油加工、炼焦和核燃料加工业	47	46	1	48	2
化学原料和化学制品制造业	1144	1132	12	1145	13
医药制造业	51	49	2	52	3
化学纤维制造业	84	84		84	
橡胶和塑料制品业	5479	5468	11	5492	24
非金属矿物制品业	736	731	5	743	12
黑色金属冶炼和压延加工业	208	208		209	1
有色金属冶炼和压延加工业	285	284	1	286	2
金属制品业	5124	5116	8	5132	16
通用设备制造业	2198	2177	21	2198	21
专用设备制造业	2865	2853	12	2871	18
汽车制造业	173	171	2	174	3

1-1 续表 1

(2012年)

项目	法人单位数(个)	单产业法人单位	多产业法人单位	产业活动单位数(个)	多产业法人单位的产业活动单位
铁路、船舶、航空航天和其他运输设备制造业	102	102		107	5
电气机械和器材制造业	3158	3130	28	3176	46
计算机、通信和其他电子设备制造业	5455	5427	28	5472	45
仪器仪表制造业	543	538	5	545	7
其他制造业	1345	1342	3	1343	1
废弃资源综合利用业	31	31		32	1
金属制品、机械和设备修理业	241	240	1	242	2
电力、燃气及水的生产和供应业	165	161	4	192	31
电力、热力生产和供应业	35	35		37	2
燃气生产和供应业	26	25	1	30	5
水的生产和供应业	104	101	3	125	24
建筑业	3168	3126	42	3449	323
房屋建筑业	348	343	5	443	100
土木工程建筑业	168	162	6	221	59
建筑安装业	808	795	13	872	77
建筑装饰和其他建筑业	1844	1826	18	1913	87
批发和零售业	21052	20747	305	24293	3546
批发业	10983	10877	106	11791	914
零售业	10069	9870	199	12502	2632
交通运输、仓储和邮政业	1633	1583	50	2199	616
铁路运输业	9	9		10	1
道路运输业	589	571	18	698	127
水上运输业	61	60	1	65	5
航空运输业	11	11		18	7
管道运输业	1	1		2	1
装卸搬运和运输代理业	726	703	23	845	142
仓储业	126	126		130	4
邮政业	110	102	8	431	329
住宿和餐饮业	1331	1220	111	1892	672
住宿业	643	565	78	681	116
餐饮业	688	655	33	1211	556
信息传输、软件和信息技术服务业	935	910	25	1198	288
电信、广播电视和卫星传输服务	92	86	6	299	213
互联网和相关服务	185	180	5	204	24
软件和信息技术服务业	658	644	14	695	51
金融业	421	375	46	1957	1582
货币金融服务	93	78	15	1282	1204
资本市场服务	115	113	2	160	47
保险业	88	59	29	385	326

1-1 续表 2

(2012年)

项　　目	法　人单位数(个)	单产业法人单位	多产业法人单位	产业活动单位数(个)	多产业法人单位的产业活动单位
其他金融业	125	125		130	5
房地产业	3044	2944	100	3323	379
房地产业	3044	2944	100	3323	379
租赁与商务服务业	9076	8927	149	10178	1251
租赁业	152	152		158	6
商务服务业	8924	8775	149	10020	1245
科学研究、技术服务业	997	977	20	1071	94
研究和试验发展	181	180	1	187	7
专业技术服务业	651	633	18	715	82
科技推广和应用服务业	165	164	1	169	5
水利、环境和公共设施管理业	376	368	8	417	49
水利管理业	63	63		67	4
生态保护和环境治理业	77	76	1	95	19
公共设施管理业	236	229	7	255	26
居民服务、修理和其他服务业	2272	2242	30	2480	238
居民服务业	687	676	11	805	129
机动车、电子产品和日用产品修理业	396	392	4	418	26
其他服务业	1189	1174	15	1257	83
教育	1660	1619	41	1990	371
教育	1660	1619	41	1990	371
卫生和社会工作	547	492	55	902	410
卫生	500	446	54	852	406
社会工作	47	46	1	50	4
文化、体育和娱乐业	1293	1286	7	1383	97
新闻和出版业	14	14		14	
广播、电视、电影和影视录音制作业	63	62	1	66	4
文化艺术业	125	124	1	128	4
体育	66	65	1	72	7
娱乐业	1025	1021	4	1103	82
公共管理、社会保障和社会组织	1640	1029	611	2536	1507
中国共产党机关	54	54		56	2
国家机构	582	531	51	1309	778
人民政协、民主党派	11	11		11	
社会保障	5	5		5	
群众团体、社会团体和其他成员组织	372	364	8	478	114
基层群众自治组织	616	64	552	677	613
国际组织					
国际组织					

1-2 按注册类型分的法人单位、产业活动单位数（2012年）

Number of Corporate Units and Industrial Establishments by Registration Status (2012)

项目	法人单位数（个）	单产业法人单位	多产业法人单位	产业活动单位数（个）	多产业法人单位的产业活动单位
合计	93634	91805	1829	103621	11816
内资	81693	80019	1674	90923	10904
国有	1470	1355	115	3104	1749
集体	2187	2096	91	2862	766
股份合作	373	369	4	911	542
国有联营	11	11		13	2
集体联营	63	62	1	73	11
国有与集体联营	20	18	2	56	38
其他联营	52	50	2	65	15
国有独资公司	53	53		60	7
其他有限责任公司	23340	23042	298	25441	2399
股份有限公司	1127	1081	46	2185	1104
私营独资	10973	10924	49	11187	263
私营合伙	3109	3096	13	3158	62
私营有限公司	30176	29744	432	31595	1851
私营股份有限公司	1507	1490	17	1563	73
其他	7232	6628	604	8650	2022
港澳台商投资	8520	8437	83	8913	476
与港澳台商合资经营	414	402	12	503	101
与港澳台商合作经营	340	338	2	364	26
港澳台商独资	7500	7432	68	7763	331
港澳台商投资股份有限公司	236	235	1	252	17
其他港、澳、台商投资	30	30		31	1
外商投资	3421	3349	72	3785	436
中外合资经营	255	240	15	350	110
中外合作经营	116	113	3	143	30
外资企业	2891	2839	52	3119	280
外商投资股份有限公司	132	130	2	145	15
其他外商投资	27	27		28	1

1-3 按地域分的法人单位、产业活动单位数（2012年）

Number of Corporate Units and Industrial Establishments by District (2012)

项目	法人单位数（个）	单产业法人单位	多产业法人单位	产业活动单位数（个）	多产业法人单位的产业活动单位
全市	93634	91805	1829	103621	11816
东城街道	5131	4977	154	5821	844
南城街道	4369	4206	163	4918	712
万江街道	3221	3157	64	3477	320
莞城街道	4520	4336	184	5191	855
石碣镇	2832	2787	45	3113	326
石龙镇	1032	990	42	1326	336
茶山镇	1897	1864	33	2103	239
石排镇	1918	1883	35	2112	229
企石镇	1015	983	32	1164	181
横沥镇	2060	2030	30	2281	251
桥头镇	2270	2238	32	2525	287
谢岗镇	1164	1145	19	1279	134
东坑镇	1165	1130	35	1341	211
常平镇	5273	5188	85	5896	708
寮步镇	5055	4973	82	5410	437
樟木头镇	2919	2872	47	3238	366
大朗镇	5304	5234	70	5765	531
黄江镇	2236	2205	31	2426	221
清溪镇	2953	2909	44	3213	304
塘厦镇	5387	5332	55	5708	376
凤岗镇	2411	2368	43	2619	251
大岭山镇	3583	3540	43	3830	290
长安镇	6435	6350	85	7100	750
虎门镇	5804	5726	78	6440	714
厚街镇	3900	3854	46	4360	506
沙田镇	2018	1975	43	2202	227
道滘镇	1802	1763	39	1976	213
洪梅镇	648	629	19	748	119
麻涌镇	1090	1058	32	1264	206
望牛墩镇	705	681	24	809	128
中堂镇	1765	1726	39	2004	278
高埗镇	1248	1208	40	1400	192
松山湖	381	366	15	424	58
虎门港	120	119	1	132	13
东莞生态园	3	3		6	3

1-4 营业收入超5000万元的内资企业（2012年）

Domestic-funded Enterprises with Business Revenue over RMB 50 Million (2012)

单位名称	所属镇街	联系电话	主要产品(或服务)
农副食品加工业			
东莞市樟木头食品有限公司	樟木头镇	87718596	牲猪
东莞市新泰粮食有限公司	樟木头镇	87123620	加工粮食
东莞市真功夫餐饮料生产有限公司	长安镇	85534622	肉制品及副产品
东莞市双胞胎饲料有限公司	大岭山镇	82760188	饲料
东莞市东糖中轻糖业有限公司	中堂镇	88118099	单晶冰糖
东莞市日隆食品有限公司	虎门镇	85564450	麦片
东莞市汇美淀粉科技有限公司	麻涌镇	88287968	纺织HM391、HM328变性淀粉
东莞市太粮米业有限公司	樟木头镇	87703313	大米
东莞市海大饲料有限公司	麻涌镇	88237100	畜禽饲料
中储粮油脂工业东莞有限公司	麻涌镇	88236688	豆油
东莞市制糖厂有限公司	中堂镇	88812123	制糖
东莞市益华油脂工业有限公司	樟木头镇	87787111	食用油
广东煌上煌食品有限公司	洪梅镇	88430678	肉制品
东莞市广利饲料有限公司	大岭山镇	83352060	混合饲料
东莞东美食品有限公司	高埗镇	88872108	淀粉
东莞市穗丰食品有限公司	麻涌镇	88224098	小麦粉
广东康达尔农牧科技有限公司	麻涌镇	22236928	饲料
东莞鲁花食用油有限公司	麻涌镇	85656822	花生油
中纺粮油(东莞)有限公司	麻涌镇	88235183	豆油
东莞市沙田顺发畜禽实业有限公司	沙田镇	88686610	饲料添加剂
东莞市国丰粮油有限公司	麻涌镇	88231433	粮食加工
食品制造业			
东莞市金富士食品有限公司	东城街道	22621998	饼干
东莞市华美食品有限公司	茶山镇	86643036	饼干
东莞市金娃食品工业有限公司	谢岗镇	87636739	果冻
东莞市今麦郎食品有限公司	中堂镇	88118372	方便面
东莞市百味佳食品有限公司	寮步镇	83285888	鸡精
东莞市鸿兴食品有限公司	寮步镇	83266492	百利面包粮
广东广益科技实业有限公司	中堂镇	88886882	脱氧保鲜剂、外控型食品保鲜剂
广东一品鲜生物科技有限公司	中堂镇	22613911	酵母抽提物
广东金苹果食品有限公司	寮步镇	86311128	糕点
内蒙古伊利实业集团股份有限公司东莞分公司	道滘镇	88835173	冰淇淋
广东丹宝利酵母有限公司	中堂镇	88812123	高活性干酵母
东莞市来一口食品有限公司	谢岗镇	87637375	果冻
酒、饮料和精制茶制造业			
东莞爱维蒸馏水有限公司	虎门镇	85519666	蒸馏水
东莞市珠江啤酒有限公司	常平镇	83553033	啤酒
东莞市莞怡食品饮料有限公司	大朗镇	81061221	瓶装水
东莞市福地饮用水有限公司	南城街道	22404191	饮用水
广东东鹏维他命饮料有限公司	道滘镇	82630711	饮料
纺织业			
东莞市新阳织造有限公司	常平镇	81898833	毛织加工
东莞市汇得佳纺织制衣有限公司	中堂镇	88129398	服装
东莞市洪梅和田织造厂	洪梅镇	88432938	棉纱线、化纤、织造布料

1-4 续表 1

(2012年)

单位名称	所属镇街	联系电话	主要产品（或服务）
东莞市宝丰服装实业有限公司	寮步镇	83216003	毛织品
东莞市清溪康成针织厂	清溪镇	87316438	毛衫半成品
东莞市福轩针织有限公司	寮步镇	38832777	针织品
东莞市普莱雅纺织科技有限公司	寮步镇	83288000	针强服装
东莞市伊韵儿服饰实业有限公司	虎门镇	85183089	针梳织服装服饰
东莞市惠琪针织有限公司	寮步镇	88909698	毛衣
东莞市汇达纺织有限公司	中堂镇	88110468	布料、织布
东莞市科纺纺织有限公司	中堂镇	88115588	牛仔布、弹力牛仔布
东莞市中玲实业有限公司	万江街道	22175828	纺织品服装
东莞市信远无纺布有限公司	寮步镇	88951008	无纺布
东莞市孚泰针织有限公司	大朗镇	83310801	针织品
东莞市明威包装材料有限公司	高埗镇	84996493	绳、索、缆
东莞市悠派户外用品制造有限公司	茶山镇	84596111	帐篷、车顶帐篷、折叠帐篷
东莞市宜雁纺织有限公司	中堂镇	88416209	牛仔布
东莞市德广隆制衣洗水有限公司	麻涌镇	81206362	服装
东莞市琪然电脑刺绣有限公司	虎门镇	85726660	刺绣、服装辅料
东莞市汇星染织有限公司	洪梅镇	81336122	布匹针织品
东莞市硕源电子材料有限公司	万江街道	88098086	无尘布
东莞市兆鸿纺织有限公司	中堂镇	88182060	牛仔布
东莞市成林服饰有限公司	大朗镇	83116232	毛衣
东莞市雅路家用纺织品有限公司	凤岗镇	87509191	床褥单类
纺织服装、服饰业			
东莞市浩兴毛织有限公司	大朗镇	81068333	毛衣
东莞市润达实业有限公司	茶山镇	81373868	服装
东莞金顺服饰有限公司	大朗镇	89009588	服装
东莞市甲虫屋服装有限公司	虎门镇	85115118	服装
东莞市红番仔实业有限公司	寮步镇	83030893	童装
东莞市经纬制衣实业有限公司	中堂镇	88411698	牛仔裤
东莞市俊颖针织服装有限公司	桥头镇	81027713	针织服装
东莞市康圣针织制造有限公司	常平镇	83996177	棉、化纤针织品及编织品
东莞市原野服装有限公司	虎门镇	85226693	纺织服装
东莞市大朗伟航针织制衣厂	大朗镇	83128091	针织品
东莞市威驰针织有限公司	大朗镇	82811332	针织服装
东莞市星达实业有限公司	虎门镇	88620008	服装
东莞市高颖针织有限公司	常平镇	83759388	针织服装、毛衣
东莞市天之裔服饰有限公司	大朗镇	82231858	针织衫
东莞盈豪嘉实制衣实业有限公司	寮步镇	88902688	服装
东莞市鸿锦服饰有限公司	虎门镇	86091828	制衣
东莞市时艺时装制衣有限公司	虎门镇	85260068	针梳织服装
东莞市中盛针织实业有限公司	横沥镇	83716818	毛衫
东莞市汇盛针织时装有限公司	大朗镇	83010618	针织毛衫
东莞市翔兴针织有限公司	大朗镇	83186788	毛衣
东莞市金泽服装有限公司	大朗镇	83181322	针织服装
东莞市力豪针织服饰有限公司	大朗镇	83017168	针织服装
东莞市颖祺实业有限公司	大朗镇	83180838	针织服装

1-4 续表 2

(2012年)

单位名称	所属镇街	联系电话	主要产品（或服务）
东莞市搜于特服装股份有限公司	道滘镇	88320269	设计服装
东莞市天元制衣有限公司	大朗镇	83195363	针织服装
东莞市斌斌时装有限公司	虎门镇	88923858	服装
东莞市锦隆服饰有限公司	大朗镇	83132838	毛织品
东莞市新远宏制衣有限公司	虎门镇	82889188	针织类服装
东莞市广兄隆电脑针织有限公司	大朗镇	82970668	针织服装
东莞市美东针织制衣有限公司	大朗镇	83186260	毛衣
东莞市新腾服饰有限公司	茶山镇	86645108	服饰
东莞市大朗翔联服饰厂	大朗镇	82226892	服装
东莞市稳发制衣有限公司	中堂镇	88881891	棉梳织服装
东莞市鸥漫服饰有限公司	大朗镇	83139358	服装
东莞市兆沣服饰有限公司	大朗镇	83185898	毛衣
东莞市栢嘉制衣有限公司	大朗镇	83187678	毛衣
东莞市新思路内衣有限公司	虎门镇	85509188	服装
东莞市泽志服饰有限公司	大朗镇	83203138	棉纺织品
东莞市安盛针织制衣有限公司	大朗镇	83137868	毛织品
东莞市超翔服饰有限公司	大朗镇	38879801	针织服装
东莞市大朗雅骏服饰厂	大朗镇	83488798	毛衣
东莞市锦程服装有限公司	望牛墩镇	88559168	商务、时尚休闲裤、牛仔裤等
东莞市合众信德制衣有限公司	常平镇	83986198	服装服饰
东莞市泽和纺织制衣有限公司	中堂镇	88189970	牛仔服装
东莞市瑞麟毛织有限公司	寮步镇	83280312	毛针织
东莞市永丰弘业织造有限公司	常平镇	83826398	针织服装
东莞市金广电脑针织有限公司	大朗镇	82236282	针织品
东莞市双塬实业有限公司	大朗镇	81231008	针织品
东莞市凫山新兴发针织有限公司	寮步镇	83288868	毛衫
东莞市众达针织制衣有限公司	大朗镇	83109181	毛衫
东莞市华轩针织制衣有限公司	大朗镇	83181838	针织服装
东莞市常平满利针织有限公司	常平镇	83977300	毛衣
东莞市建盛针织有限公司	大朗镇	83110188	针织服装
东莞市辉骏针织时装有限公司	大朗镇	83183029	针织时装
东莞市入世丰针织有限公司	东坑镇	88905668	针织衫
东莞市金松针织有限公司	大朗镇	83311811	针织服装
东莞市格林诗缔服饰有限公司	常平镇	82201777	毛织制品
东莞市永豪制衣实业有限公司	寮步镇	83327589	针织服装
东莞市长源毛织制衣有限公司	大朗镇	83200838	针织服装
东莞市百思特服饰有限公司	虎门镇	85709002	服装
东莞市天润服装有限公司	茶山镇	81831883	服装
东莞市欧佳特服饰有限公司	大朗镇	86262988	毛衣
东莞市凯纳德针织服饰有限公司	大朗镇	83110775	毛衣
东莞市盈邦针织有限公司	大朗镇	83482998	针织服装
东莞市圣隆制衣有限公司	厚街镇	81638100	牛仔服装
东莞市广昌隆毛织时装有限公司	大朗镇	83197153	毛织服装
东莞市茶山伟博纺织服装厂	茶山镇	86648311	服装
东莞市东城嘉文制衣厂	东城街道	22267333	梳织服装

1-4 续表 3

(2012年)

单位名称	所属镇街	联系电话	主要产品（或服务）
东莞市盛泰针织制衣有限公司	大朗镇	83206828	针织服装
东莞市大朗华达针织制衣厂	大朗镇	83185358	毛衫
东莞市业联制衣有限公司	大朗镇	81069908	牛仔服装
东莞市乐祺针织有限公司	大朗镇	83190778	毛织服装
东莞市环宇织造有限公司	大朗镇	83112688	毛织服装
东莞市晶晖针织有限公司	大朗镇	83116573	针织服装
东莞市国泰华纺织有限公司	大朗镇	86264568	毛衣
东莞市都维尔服饰有限公司	大朗镇	83482608	毛衣
东莞市恒帮针织有限公司	大朗镇	83186389	毛织品
东莞市英伟实业有限公司	大朗镇	83102266	针织服装
东莞市愉丰制衣有限公司	厚街镇	85986966	服装
东莞市源源制衣有限公司	中堂镇	88126801	服装
东莞市以纯集团有限公司	虎门镇	85520146	纺织服装
东莞市顺光制衣有限公司	东坑镇	83863716	毛织服装
东莞市恩基儿服饰有限公司	大朗镇	83129077	针织衫
东莞市金坚制衣有限公司	清溪镇	82997765	服装
东莞市闽盈服饰有限公司	大朗镇	83107020	服装
东莞市必利服饰有限公司	虎门镇	82261818	服装
东莞市锦盈织造有限公司	大朗镇	83103588	针织品
东莞市大朗民源生毛织制衣有限公司	大朗镇	83186260	针织服装
东莞市海龙针织时装有限公司	大朗镇	82814531	针织时装
东莞市大朗骏松服饰厂	大朗镇	81119288	针织品
东莞市兴业针织有限公司	大朗镇	83311479	针织服装
广东金盾服装公司	南城街道	22404168	警察服装
东莞市天伊毛织时装有限公司	大朗镇	83318017	针织衫
东莞市美姬服饰有限公司	大朗镇	83310268	针织毛衣
东莞市添翔服饰有限公司	万江街道	22277218	服装 针织布
东莞市骏佳纺织服装有限公司	中堂镇	82781769	牛仔服装
东莞市瑞锋服饰有限公司	大朗镇	86260003	针织毛衣
东莞市富士达针织有限公司	大朗镇	83319826	毛衫
东莞市胜兴针织有限公司	大朗镇	83189100	针织女毛衫
东莞市凯浚服饰有限公司	大朗镇	83182889	毛织服装
东莞市薏莎实业有限公司	大朗镇	83138999	针织品
东莞市成功针织制衣厂	东城街道	22265157	纺织服装
东莞市极奇制衣有限公司	企石镇	86664648	衣服
东莞市松鹰实业有限公司	虎门镇	85561999	棉织服装
东莞市茶山聚兴服饰织造厂	茶山镇	86413588	服装
东莞市逸朗毛织有限公司	大朗镇	82220960	毛织制品
东莞市盛丰制衣有限公司	万江街道	22658892	服装
东莞市协欣时装有限公司	大朗镇	83193268	毛衣
东莞市高邦毛衣有限公司	大朗镇	83119628	毛衣
东莞市尚景服装有限公司	石排镇	86557028	纺织服装
东莞市卓越实业有限公司	石排镇	86550111	针织服装
东莞市东林制衣有限公司	寮步镇	83238080	毛织品
东莞市众圣针织有限公司	大朗镇	83111739	毛衫

1-4 续表 4

(2012年)

单位名称	所属镇街	联系电话	主要产品（或服务）
东莞市颖和祺服饰有限公司	大朗镇	81125303	毛衣
东莞市圣旗路时装有限公司	常平镇	89851115	针织品
皮革、毛皮、羽毛及其制品和制鞋业			
东莞市锦兔皮具有限公司	望牛墩镇	81167888	皮具制品
东莞黄江裕成制鞋厂	黄江镇	83363017	运动鞋
东莞市佰鸿鞋材有限公司	洪梅镇	81330969	塑料鞋
东莞市石碣东英塑胶制品厂	石碣镇	86631490	塑胶鞋底
东莞市优秀鞋业有限公司	厚街镇	83088530	女鞋
东莞市琪胜鞋业有限公司	厚街镇	88632999	皮鞋
东莞三元鞋业有限公司	万江街道	22181972	皮鞋
广东宾豪旅行用品有限公司	东坑镇	82800000	拉杆箱
东莞市盛旺鞋材有限公司	洪梅镇	81130969	纺织面料鞋
东莞市国立科技有限公司	道滘镇	88389362	TPR、EVA、SBS、TR改性塑料
东莞尚科思工艺制品有限公司	寮步镇	81192118	工艺制品、手机袋、电脑包
东莞市顺琦手袋实业有限公司	厚街镇	88639898	手袋、皮具
东莞市日泰鞋材有限公司	万江街道	23036108	鞋材
东莞市正宇鞋业有限公司	东城街道	83211528	鞋
东莞市新虎威实业有限公司	虎门镇	85198313	皮鞋
东莞市东辰鞋材有限公司	万江街道	87076238	纺织面料鞋材
东莞市联展鞋业有限公司	东城街道	22669571	各种鞋类产品
东莞市利盈皮革有限公司	麻涌镇	88822413	皮革
东莞市永鸿手袋有限公司	黄江镇	82605681	手袋
东莞市华迩美实业有限公司	虎门镇	85564492	皮革
东莞市振国皮革制品有限公司	厚街镇	38897558	皮革制品
广东万里马投资实业有限公司	长安镇	85355198	皮具制品
东莞市佳荣鞋材有限公司	厚街镇	85893107	鞋材类
东莞市龙运鞋业有限公司	厚街镇	85933911	鞋类制品
东莞市合怡实业有限公司	中堂镇	88185511	手袋
东莞长安霄边兴鹏鞋厂	长安镇	85531541	男女装皮鞋
东莞市莎米特箱包有限公司	樟木头镇	87712545	旅行包袋
东莞市键霖手袋有限公司	厚街镇	85996109	手袋
木材加工和木、竹、藤、棕、草制品业			
东莞市中成木业有限公司	道滘镇	88331338	夹板
东莞市易辉纤维板有限公司	桥头镇	81039118	纤维板
东莞市森宝康木业有限公司	洪梅镇	88439626	中密度竹斑板
东莞市中意厨房设备有限公司	塘厦镇	82061888	家具
东莞市冠宇木业有限公司	中堂镇	81163188	木制品
东莞市德曼木业有限公司	桥头镇	81037666	木门
家具制造业			
东莞市耀震五金家具有限公司	虎门镇	85550956	家具
东莞市荣圣家具有限公司	凤岗镇	87842272	办公椅
东莞市伊莲娜家具有限公司	常平镇	83826528	床垫
东莞市华腾塑钢家具有限公司	洪梅镇	88439399	家具
东莞市中之美家具有限公司	洪梅镇	85927900	木质家具
东莞市宝居乐家居股份有限公司	石碣镇	86384018	家具

1-4 续表 5

(2012年)

单位名称	所属镇街	联系电话	主要产品（或服务）
东莞市创意生活家具有限公司	大岭山镇	85632008	木质家具
东莞市兆生家具实业有限公司	厚街镇	85921466	家具
东莞市远大家具有限公司	大岭山镇	85617870	木制家具
东莞市慕思寝室用品有限公司	厚街镇	85058288	沙发
东莞市恒兆实业有限公司	大岭山镇	85627198	家具
东莞市美迪家具有限公司	洪梅镇	88843128	木质家具
东莞市姻美儿家具有限公司	道滘镇	81333273	五金家具
东莞市裕隆钢管制品有限公司	塘厦镇	87883188	各种铁管、五金家具等
东莞市广纳家具制造有限公司	大朗镇	83136198	家具
东莞市利普家具有限公司	厚街镇	83082222	家居配套用品
东莞市艾伯特家具有限公司	大岭山镇	83356531	沙发家具
东莞市星港家具有限公司	南城街道	22901327	家具
东莞市城市之窗家具有限公司	厚街镇	89982000	家具
东莞市博一家具有限公司	塘厦镇	86855570	家具及配件
东莞市艺源家具制品有限公司	石碣镇	86381818	家具
东莞市德美家具有限公司	大岭山镇	85606228	玻璃酒柜茶机餐台
东莞市广丰家具有限公司	厚街镇	87012199	家具
东莞市桥新家私有限公司	桥头镇		木制家具
东莞市光润家具制造有限公司	东城街道	86216333	办公家具
东莞市元宗家具有限公司	大岭山镇	85610588	家具
东莞市瑞豪家具制造有限公司	高埗镇	88702123	塑胶家具
东莞市华晟家具制造有限公司	东城街道	22653163	家具
东莞市富宝沙发制造有限公司	大岭山镇	85611985	家具
东莞市佳森家具有限公司	大岭山镇	85611222	咖啡桌
东莞市嘉梦家具有限公司	常平镇	83826528	床垫、床上用品
广东大公馆家具制造有限公司	厚街镇	88913333	家具
东莞市森盛家具有限公司	厚街镇	85593555	套房家具
东莞市欣格家具有限公司	石碣镇	86334766	金属家具、五金制品、厨具用品
东莞市时兴家具制造有限公司	高埗镇	88872168	家具
东莞市雅舍家具有限公司	南城街道	22403431	家具
东莞市洋臣家具有限公司	大岭山镇	85788812	家具配件
东莞市创源家具有限公司	大岭山镇	21992308	木质家具
东莞市卓之神家具厂	高埗镇	88704226	木家具
东莞润丰金属塑胶有限公司	寮步镇	83320898	五金家具
东莞市凯晟家具有限公司	大岭山镇	85785581	家具
东莞市兴晟家具制造有限公司	东城街道	22673483	家具
东莞市华辉家具实业有限公司	厚街镇	85592833	家具
东莞市银通家具有限公司	沙田镇	88686466	玻璃家具
东莞市好好家具有限公司	寮步镇	81120825	木器家具
东莞市宏艺木业有限公司	寮步镇	38800208	家具
东莞市同创家具有限公司	大朗镇	85655078	家具
东莞市和晟家具有限公司	东城街道	22673483	家具
东莞佳居乐厨柜有限公司	大岭山镇	85650999	木厨柜、木器制品
东莞市艾慕寝室用品有限公司	厚街镇	85058288	家具
东莞市舒涞家具有限公司	东城街道	22668079	家具

1-4 续表 6

(2012年)

单位名称	所属镇街	联系电话	主要产品（或服务）
造纸和纸制品业			
东莞市轩潼纸业有限公司	中堂镇	88028808	生活用纸、纸制品
东莞市美盈森环保科技有限公司	桥头镇	86938888	轻型环保包装制品
东莞市沣源纸品厂	高埗镇	89910121	纸品
东莞市永源卫生材料科技有限公司	洪梅镇		纸和纸板容器
东莞市义恒包装制品有限公司	洪梅镇	81207666	纸制品
东莞市建盈纸品有限公司	中堂镇	81163988	纸板
东莞市盈泰纸品厂	望牛墩镇	88552289	生活用纸
东莞市天全纸品有限公司	高埗镇	81338828	纸板
东莞市道滘东发纸品有限公司	道滘镇	88839018	机制纸及纸板
东莞市振诚包装制品有限公司	东城街道	22618027	纸板纸箱
东莞市银利纸品有限公司	塘厦镇	87816636	纸板
东莞市珠江特种纸业有限公司	中堂镇	88890808	瓦楞纸
东莞市上合旺盈印刷有限公司	东城街道	23111888	印刷服务
东莞市同舟纸品有限公司	企石镇	81928888	纸品
广东百顺纸品有限公司	茶山镇	86456233	纸制品
东莞市鸿旭包装印刷有限公司	石排镇	88936668	印刷纸板
东莞市瑞兴纸制品有限公司	桥头镇	88282999	纸制品
东莞市达林纸业有限公司	中堂镇	88887388	生活用纸
东莞市大裕纸业有限公司	清溪镇	86812555	纸箱
东莞市茂源纸品有限公司	高埗镇		纸制品
东莞市景辉纸品有限公司	道滘镇	81166138	纸板
东莞市上盈纸品有限公司	道滘镇	88832088	纸箱及其他纸制品
东莞市桐昌纸业有限公司	谢岗镇	82797999	纸制品
东莞市清埔纸业有限公司	清溪镇	81289988	纸制品
东莞市恩赐纸品有限公司	寮步镇	82391550	纸箱
东莞市大发纸品有限公司	桥头镇	83344848	纸箱
东莞市顺丰纸品制造有限公司	茶山镇	86176968	纸板
东莞市道窖东发造纸厂	道滘镇	88839018	瓦楞纸
东莞市振兴造纸有限公司	高埗镇	88949288	高强芯纸
东莞市天荣纸品有限公司	大岭山镇	85631665	纸板
东莞市易创实业有限公司	寮步镇	81118021	纸制品
东莞市建桦造纸有限公司	中堂镇	88887988	箱板纸
东莞市大田包装有限公司	虎门镇	85269998	纸板
东莞市银兴纸品厂	塘厦镇	87816636	纸板
东莞市常联造纸厂有限公司	常平镇	83337837	机制瓦楞纸
东莞市顺通纸品有限公司	道滘镇	88388266	纸和纸板容器
东莞市高安纸品有限公司	高埗镇	88787311	纸板
东莞市伟联纸业有限公司	道滘镇	88382688	机制纸及纸板
东莞市胜源纸品厂	高埗镇	89910165	其他纸制品
东莞市晋邦纸业有限公司	大朗镇	81123388	纸板
东莞市骏业纸业有限公司	道滘镇	88830822	机制纸及纸板
东莞市利泰纸业有限公司	望牛墩镇	88554828	纸板及纸制品
东莞市智达纸业制品有限公司	沙田镇	88862222	纸箱
东莞市天盛特种纸品有限公司	虎门镇	85169458	无碳复写纸

1-4 续表 7

(2012年)

单位名称	所属镇街	联系电话	主要产品（或服务）
东莞市潢涌银洲纸业有限公司	中堂镇	88899113	挂面箱板纸、瓦楞纸、白板纸
东莞市上隆纸业有限公司	中堂镇	88187688	瓦楞纸
东莞市明天纸业有限公司	望牛墩镇	81310788	纸箱用纸
东莞市顺兴造纸有限公司	道滘镇	88328608	机制纸及纸板
东莞市达成纸品有限公司	麻涌镇	88289898	纸制品
东莞市东创纸品制造有限公司	黄江镇	82601888	纸板
东莞清溪现代纸品厂	清溪镇	87295802	纸箱
东莞市华兴纸业实业有限公司	万江街道	22279169	纸制品
东莞市凤岗新达纸品有限公司	凤岗镇	87750288	机制纸及纸板
东莞市有利纸业有限公司	中堂镇	88412438	瓦楞纸、挂面纸、收购废纸
东莞市金田纸业有限公司	万江街道	22280688	灰板纸
广东玉兰装饰材料有限公司	东城街道	22652789	墙纸
东莞市华通包装有限公司	道滘镇	81332988	纸制品
东莞市建航纸业有限公司	中堂镇	88129488	包装纸
东莞市强安造纸有限公司	高埗镇	88876118	造纸
东莞市华利纸品有限公司	高埗镇	88703832	纸板
东莞市致泰纸业有限公司	麻涌镇	88825682	包装用纸
东莞市宝力造纸厂	洪梅镇	88846388	造纸、瓦楞纸
东莞市骏利纸制品有限公司	塘厦镇	87922558	纸箱
东莞市泰昌纸业有限公司	望牛墩镇	88852607	仿牛卡纸
东莞市永安造纸有限公司	望牛墩镇	88818068	瓦楞纸、挂面纸
东莞市兆丰造纸有限公司	中堂镇	81163172	瓦楞纸
东莞东兴纸品厂	南城街道	86228785	瓦楞纸板、瓦楞纸箱
东莞市天赐纸品有限公司	高埗镇	88734233	纸板
东莞市雄东纸业有限公司	洪梅镇	88844928	造纸
东莞市银桦纸品有限公司	中堂镇	81163388	纸板
东莞市旭丰纸业有限公司	中堂镇	88121293	瓦楞原纸
东莞市道滘兴隆造纸厂	道滘镇	88381933	制浆
东莞市宝华造纸有限公司	道滘镇	88336328	机制纸及纸板
东莞市瑞安纸品实业有限公司	东城街道	22660198	纸箱
东莞市东保纸业有限公司	高埗镇	88786298	瓦楞纸挂面纸
东莞市贝辉装饰材料有限公司	大朗镇	83199339	装饰材料（浸渍纸）
东莞市双洲纸业有限公司	中堂镇	88182618	瓦楞纸、挂面纸、高强瓦楞纸
东莞市白天鹅纸业有限公司	万江街道	22172128	纸制品
东莞市华立实业股份有限公司	常平镇	83333239	纸塑、木塑、塑胶
东莞市恒伟纸业有限公司	道滘镇	88323168	机制纸及纸板
东莞市横通纸品有限公司	横沥镇	83378968	纸板
东莞市新富发纸业有限公司	万江街道	22711928	灰纸板
东莞市高埗东保纸品厂	高埗镇	88734233	纸板
东莞市永顺纸品有限公司	望牛墩镇	88551655	纸制品
东莞市祥兴纸业有限公司	中堂镇	88815238	瓦楞纸、挂面纸
东莞市大步纸业有限公司	麻涌镇	88286883	机制纸及纸制品
东莞市同力纸业有限公司	中堂镇	88881892	瓦楞纸
东莞市龙腾实业有限公司	麻涌镇	88826898	纸制品
东莞市裕杨纸品实业有限公司	茶山镇	86411555	纸箱

1-4 续表 8

(2012年)

单位名称	所属镇街	联系电话	主要产品（或服务）
东莞市厚威包装有限公司	大朗镇	82228320	纸箱
东莞市旗峰纸业有限公司	道滘镇	88328212	纸
东莞市深联造纸有限公司	中堂镇	88818778	瓦楞芯纸
东莞市鸿业造纸有限公司	中堂镇	88814848	机制纸
东莞市同兴纸品有限公司	高埗镇	81303788	瓦楞纸板
东莞市伟虹纸业有限公司	望牛墩镇	88558198	造纸
东莞市南翔纸业有限公司	洪梅镇	88844399	纸制品
印刷和记录媒介复制业			
东莞市泰达包装制品有限公司	望牛墩镇	88518999	包装装潢及其他印刷
广东天元印刷有限公司	清溪镇	89151000	运单、快递袋
广东正博精密印刷有限公司	洪梅镇	81202128	包装装潢印刷品
东莞斯道拉恩索正元包装有限公司	高埗镇	81306698	说明书印刷
东莞市金凌印刷有限公司	塘厦镇	87881585	丝印染精
东莞市二轻包装彩印厂有限公司	东城街道	22699213	玩具包装
东莞市天华创展印刷有限公司	凤岗镇	87862122	出版物印刷
东莞市东彩印刷包装有限公司	厚街镇	85820822	包装装潢印刷品印刷
东莞市新广联数码科技有限公司	大朗镇	88289688	只读类光盘复制
东莞日报印刷厂	寮步镇	83303302	报纸印刷
东莞市虹桥印刷有限公司	凤岗镇	87566913	包装装潢印制品
文教、工美、体育和娱乐用品制造业			
东莞市恒生数码制品有限公司	凤岗镇	82069833	数码电子玩具
东莞市星月实业有限公司	常平镇	86836199	塑料制品
东莞市星鼎实业有限公司	东城街道	86212555	户外运动用品
东莞市开普特健身器材有限公司	麻涌镇	88239873	健身器材
东莞市永熹金属制品有限公司	塘厦镇	87913154	秋千
东莞市智高文具有限公司	石碣镇	86634176	文具
东莞市华瀚儿童用品有限公司	清溪镇	87867129	婴儿车
东莞市冠艺金属彩印包装有限公司	横沥镇	83371255	文具盒
东莞市丰泽文具有限公司	虎门镇	85506636	文件夹
东莞市金叶珠宝有限公司	厚街镇	85822216	珠宝首饰
东莞市金龙珠宝首饰有限公司	厚街镇	81636092	黄金饰品
东莞市天宇玩具制品有限公司	桥头镇	83429729	塑胶玩具
东莞市智乐堡儿童玩具有限公司	石排镇	86550188	玩具
东莞市昌晖印染器材有限公司	虎门镇	85555020	印刷、印染机械
石油加工、炼焦和核燃料加工业			
东莞市安美化学有限公司	松山湖	83210707	润滑油
东莞市晔联道路改性沥青有限公司	洪梅镇	88439822	储存改性石油沥青
化学原料和化学制品制造业			
东莞市领创环保材料科技有限公司	长安镇	82281189	环氧大豆油
东莞市伍山建材实业有限公司	沙田镇	81560755	混凝土系列外加剂
东莞市九丰化工有限公司	虎门港	82279292	二甲醚
东莞市上洲塑胶科技有限公司	常平镇	83291333	LCP、PPS等加阡防火、耐热环保产品
东莞市迪生塑胶五金工模有限公司	大岭山镇	81600138	五金
东莞市新秀电子有限公司	塘厦镇	38898900	塑胶制品生产、硅胶等碳纤维制品
东莞市罗孚化工有限公司	洪梅镇	88439999	万能胶

1-4　续表 9

(2012年)

单位名称	所属镇街	联系电话	主要产品（或服务）
东莞市东晖化学工业有限公司	沙田镇	82793166	化工产品
广东信力材料科技有限公司	麻涌镇	88220800	橡胶制品
东莞市英科水墨有限公司	茶山镇	86481155	水性墨
东莞市四辉表面处理科技有限公司	大岭山镇	85628748	抛光腊、麻轮
东莞市汉维新材料科技有限公司	桥头镇	86935888	塑胶新材料
东莞市大兴化工有限公司	谢岗镇	87768860	油墨、油漆
东莞市立顿洗涤用品实业有限公司	望牛墩镇	88999999	肥皂及合成洗涤剂
东莞市保得生物工程有限公司	南城街道	22886693	微生物制剂（生物有机肥）
东莞市贝特利新材料有限公司	麻涌镇	88283198	合成橡胶
东莞市成铭胶粘剂有限公司	石碣镇	86319710	胶粘剂
东莞市芙蓉化工有限公司	望牛墩镇	88857923	分散松香胶、机性涂料
东莞市盛和化工有限公司	黄江镇	87132012	苯酐
东莞市竣成化工有限公司	厚街镇	85595702	胶水
东莞市安美润滑科技有限公司	松山湖	83213232	环保清洗溶剂和润滑材料
东莞市威亮实业有限公司	中堂镇	88886988	合成洗衣粉
东莞市千色有机玻璃有限公司	虎门镇	81611738	有机玻璃
东莞市汶乐实业有限公司	中堂镇	22278388	洗涤用品
东莞市瑞德丰生物科技有限公司	大岭山镇	83359225	农药复配、塑胶瓶
东莞市高旭新材料有限公司	中堂镇	88110096	重质碳酸钙、轻质碳酸钙
东莞市冠盈涂料有限公司	清溪镇	87317533	丙烯酸烘漆
东莞市威一霸涂料有限公司	黄江镇	38942749	涂料
东莞市汇诚塑胶金属制品有限公司	长安镇	87086188	塑胶制品
东莞市阳光树脂制品有限公司	石碣镇	86633666	胶粘剂
东莞市广华化工有限公司	道滘镇	88328668	酸性蚀刻液
广东省福利龙复合肥有限公司	高埗镇	88739816	复合肥料
广东中成化工股份有限公司	麻涌镇	88822402	保险粉
东莞市杉杉电池材料有限公司	南城街道	22035233	锂离子电池材料
东莞长联新材料科技有限公司	寮步镇	81259388	印花染色粘合剂
医药制造业			
广东华南药业集团有限公司	石龙镇	86611718	片剂、硬胶囊剂、混悬剂等药品
广东众生药业股份有限公司	石龙镇	86100111	片剂、硬胶囊剂、颗粒剂等药品
东莞市亚洲制药有限公司	洪梅镇	22388273	君泰双黄连口服液、心力丸等
化学纤维制造业			
东莞市源丰纤维制品有限公司	茶山镇	86645703	涤纶短纤
东莞市拓展实业有限公司	茶山镇	86485888	涤纶纤维
东莞市盈丰纤维制品有限公司	茶山镇	86414618	纤维制品
橡胶和塑料制品业			
东莞市时进实业有限公司	桥头镇	82556000	家居用品
东莞市华源包装有限公司	茶山镇	86646996	塑料包装袋
东莞市创迅精密五金有限公司	樟木头镇		塑料制品
东莞市金隆纸塑制品有限公司	望牛墩镇	88516555	纸塑制品
东莞市旭通达模具塑胶有限公司	凤岗镇	87758888	橡胶零件
东莞市锦力包装制品有限公司	寮步镇	83285620	包装材料
东莞清溪三钢电器制造厂	清溪镇	87732437	五金塑胶制品
东莞市丸万塑料包装有限公司	东城街道	22024286	塑料制品

1-4 续表 10

(2012年)

单位名称	所属镇街	联系电话	主要产品(或服务)
东莞市正新包装制品有限公司	东城街道	22650889	塑料制品
东莞市江顺箱包袋配件有限公司	塘厦镇	87912965	包、箱、袋配件
东莞市常平盈景塑胶制品有限公司	常平镇	83815163	塑胶加工
深圳市航天远东实业有限公司东莞分公司	凤岗镇	82100375	塑胶制品
东莞市信诺橡塑工业有限公司	长安镇	81585111	塑胶粒PC
东莞市以诺塑胶制品有限公司	塘厦镇	86957888	塑料制品
东莞市松燊塑料科技有限公司	厚街镇	85816271	塑胶
东莞市日源盛橡胶绝缘制品有限公司	石碣镇	86289365	绝缘材料
东莞市诠盛塑料有限公司	虎门镇	85556378	塑胶制品
东莞市利源塑胶有限公司	桥头镇	81025718	塑胶制品
东莞市鸿响塑胶制品有限公司	桥头镇	83452678	塑胶制品
东莞市大博塑料有限公司	清溪镇	86819111	塑料制品
东莞联记塑胶原料有限公司	常平镇	83335992	塑胶
东莞市瑞年塑胶科技有限公司	寮步镇	83266789	玻璃贴膜
东莞市链州日用品有限公司	洪梅镇		日用塑料制品
东莞市东力包装制品有限公司	中堂镇	88886028	泡沫
东莞市博美包装制品有限公司	塘厦镇	86255725	小型包装制品
东莞市永超塑胶科技有限公司	黄江镇	83364226	塑胶制品
东莞市长利鞋材有限公司	寮步镇	83223808	纸用鞋材
东莞市泰至塑料五金有限公司	茶山镇	81821668	PVC管材
东莞市永迪泡绵有限公司	大朗镇	83011091	泡棉海绵
东莞市铭丰包装品制造有限公司	万江街道	22171188	首饰盒
东莞市虎门铭锋五金塑胶制品厂	虎门镇	38835099	模具五金塑胶运动器材
东莞市伟捷包装实业有限公司	万江街道	22172183	包装材料封箱胶带
东莞市冠炜塑胶五金制品有限公司	常平镇	83981763	塑胶制品
东莞市兄奕塑胶制品有限公司	樟木头镇	87792188	塑胶制品
东莞市富利时塑胶制品有限公司	东城街道	22653193	玩具
东莞市合鑫电子厂	石排镇	86537079	塑胶
东莞市兆威光电有限公司	黄江镇	83535098	塑胶制品
东莞市庆盈实业有限公司	茶山镇	86178922	塑料
东莞市港源胶粘带制品有限公司	寮步镇	81111360	胶粘带
东莞市惠德丽实业有限公司	企石镇	86728338	塑料制品
东莞市川林再生塑料制品有限公司	凤岗镇	87552765	塑料包装盒
东莞市荣辉塑料粒有限公司	虎门镇	85154933	塑料粒
东莞南城添迪制品厂	南城街道	22417969	电脑磁头臂
东莞市汇泓模具塑胶制品有限公司	长安镇	85353863	模具
东莞市晓铭实业有限公司	长安镇	85390608	塑胶制品
东莞市广海大橡塑科技有限公司	樟木头镇	82022622	橡塑保健用品
东莞市凤岗油甘埔利联塑胶金属制品厂	凤岗镇	87774139	五金纽扣
东莞凤岗五联威达利塑胶制品厂	凤岗镇	87753728	吸塑罩
东莞市汇美实业有限公司	长安镇	85412223	DVD、VCD塑胶面壳
东莞市泰和塑胶制品有限公司	桥头镇	83450238	药品包装复合膜(袋)、食品袋等
东莞市巨祺包装有限公司	常平镇	81093697	塑料瓶盖
东莞市朝阳实业有限公司	企石镇	86763266	其他塑料制品
东莞市悠悠美居家居制品有限公司	石排镇	86598000	PVC台布

1-4 续表 11

(2012年)

单位名称	所属镇街	联系电话	主要产品(或服务)
东莞市晟美包装制品有限公司	南城街道	86228778	塑料制品
东莞市冠宏包装实业有限公司	望牛墩镇	88518756	BOPP封箱皮、双面胶、包装带
东莞市天逸皮业有限公司	道滘镇	88318565	皮革
非金属矿物制品业			
广东唯美陶瓷有限公司	高埗镇	22600290	建筑陶瓷
东莞市伟业水泥有限公司	中堂镇	81165666	水泥
东莞市唯美装饰材料有限公司	东城街道	22650006	陶瓷
东莞市金太阳研磨有限公司	大岭山镇	85613339	砂纸
东莞市建安管桩有限公司	望牛墩镇	88519268	高强度预应力管桩
东莞市华辉玻璃制品有限公司	石排镇	86656791	玻璃镀银镀铝
东莞市联发铸造有限公司	寮步镇	83261788	金属铸片
东莞市鸿旺包装制品有限公司	清溪镇	87737422	胶袋、复合袋、厚片制品
东莞市通州预制件有限公司	高埗镇	88733388	预制件水泥管桩
东莞市虎门摩天建材实业公司	虎门镇	85561768	加气混凝土
东莞市拓为塑料五金制品有限公司	寮步镇	84572099	保湿器皿、塑料制品等
东莞市东成石材有限公司	厚街镇	85596328	大理石、花岗岩的切割
东莞市隆泰美东镜业有限公司	石龙镇	86310690	玻璃制品、货物进出口
东莞市宇虹高分子材料有限公司	塘厦镇	82168490	玻璃纤维
东莞南玻陶瓷科技有限公司	麻涌镇	88288111	陶瓷玻璃
东莞市富家石建材有限公司	桥头镇	81026310	人造大理石
东莞市华佳能玻璃有限公司	桥头镇	81029258	钢化玻璃
东莞市东上板业有限公司	中堂镇	88128816	硅酸钙板
东莞市银通玻璃有限公司	沙田镇	88868988	玻璃制品
东莞市唯美陶瓷工业园有限公司	高埗镇	81133333	马可波罗瓷砖
东莞市建东水泥制品有限公司	中堂镇	88121288	预制桩
东莞市茶山和兴粉磨站	茶山镇	86404633	粉磨水泥
东莞市金洲羊城管桩厂	中堂镇	88885288	水泥预制管桩、预制件、预砖
黑色金属冶炼和压延加工业			
东莞市东上钢材股份有限公司	中堂镇	88890107	钢材
东莞市日月不锈钢有限公司	常平镇	83606259	不锈钢
东莞市勤上金属制品有限公司	常平镇	83395678	铁线
东莞市三联机械有限公司	寮步镇	83321381	铸铁件
东莞市莱钢钢结构有限公司	黄江镇	83666666	钢结构件
东莞市清辉金属有限公司	望牛墩镇	88560326	金属材料
东莞市宝特模具钢加工有限公司	望牛墩镇	88516020	金属制品、模具钢加工
东莞市中一合金科技有限公司	大朗镇	83206618	银铜复合带
东莞市宏顺金属材料有限公司	企石镇	86764001	电镀锌钢板
东莞市千岛金属锡品有限公司	塘厦镇	87880129	锡线
东莞市亿鑫钢业有限公司	企石镇	86768769	钢结构材料
东莞市永铖铝业有限公司	万江街道	22175338	铝挤型材
东莞市华昌铝合金制品厂	东城街道	22265108	铝材加工
东莞市宝拓来金属有限公司	大朗镇	83486377	焊锡品
东莞市东联铝业有限公司	东城街道	22291760	铝制品
东莞市泊卡华铜业有限公司	常平镇	82826666	铜材、铜板
东莞市华昌铝业有限公司	东城街道	22265108	铝材加工

1-4 续表 12

(2012年)

单位名称	所属镇街	联系电话	主要产品（或服务）
东莞市星马焊锡有限公司	东城街道	27384959	无铅锡条
东莞市宏发钢铁结构材料有限公司	企石镇	86737153	钢结构材料
东莞市金达铝业有限公司	道滘镇	88328886	铝型材
东莞市华雨金属材料有限公司	黄江镇	83131757	铝棒延压
东莞市华轩幕墙材料有限公司	谢岗镇	82333588	幕墙材料
东莞市铝美铝型材有限公司	厚街镇	83090188	铝制品
东莞市东城东联金属制品厂	东城街道	22291760	铝制品
东莞市杰夫阻燃材料有限公司	大朗镇	83101593	三氧化二锑（阻燃材料）
东莞市奥达铝业有限公司	大岭山镇	81621188	铝材制品
金属制品业			
东莞市饰成实业有限公司	高埗镇		金属片制作
东莞市金利怡卫浴有限公司	东坑镇	81013337	卫生器具
东莞竹田金属制品有限公司	塘厦镇	38996398	金属冲压产品
东莞市恩绮金属制品有限公司	清溪镇	87325058	五金制品
东莞添迪电子五金实业有限公司	南城街道	22417969	五金、液压、软管元件、切割工具
东莞市灿煜金属制品有限公司	塘厦镇	87814601	不锈钢
广东蓝盾门业有限公司	桥头镇	82366989	金属门窗
东莞市天宝五金塑胶制品有限公司	塘厦镇	87914500	五金铁钗
东莞市锦上钢材有限公司	中堂镇	88186778	PC钢棒
东莞永安科技有限公司	塘厦镇	82077878	金属制品
东莞市广成五金塑胶实业有限公司	桥头镇	81023992	五金塑胶制品
广东华宇钢结构工程有限公司	寮步镇	83218928	金属结构工程、网架工程制作
东莞市坚宜佳五金制品有限公司	塘厦镇	89890388	不锈钢制品
东莞市键颖实业有限公司	常平镇	81898898	钮扣
东莞市石排品佳五金加工厂	石排镇	88935678	五金制品
东莞市金瑞五金制品有限公司	道滘镇	88325501	金属制日用品
东莞市怡丰锁业有限公司	樟木头镇	87795983	五金
东莞市荣杰五金制品有限公司	大朗镇	88609837	五金制品
东莞市泓旭五金制品有限公司	塘厦镇	82064666	五金制品
东莞市银基重工有限公司	麻涌镇	88285559	金属结构
东莞市通旺达五金制品有限公司	凤岗镇	87561911	五金配件
东莞市盈福五金制品有限公司	企石镇	82216633	圣诞灯串
东莞市合莱旅安防盗系统有限公司	寮步镇	23128628	锁
东莞市人本五金有限公司	塘厦镇	86856789	金属制品
东莞市林成精密五金有限公司	樟木头镇	87709512	五金配件
东莞市钲锟精密五金有限公司	茶山镇	81853698	五金制品
东莞特迪五金科技有限公司	清溪镇	86814789	五金配件、散热片
东莞振华特种包装有限公司	麻涌镇	88828115	特种包装铁桶
东莞市汇昌金属制品厂	寮步镇	83307988	铝制品
东莞市东兴铝材制造有限公司	中堂镇	88813671	铝合金型材、铝制品
东莞市协力钢构工程有限公司	厚街镇	85919838	钢购件
东莞市科力钢铁线材有限公司	望牛墩镇	88557276	金属丝绳及其制品
广东坚朗五金制品股份有限公司	塘厦镇	87943311	点支撑幕墙配件
东莞市宏力实业有限公司金属结构加工厂	沙田镇	88861110	空心导轨
东莞市铁生辉制罐有限公司	企石镇	86710633	金属包装制品

1-4　续表 13

(2012年)

单位名称	所属镇街	联系电话	主要产品（或服务）
东莞市精丽制罐有限公司	石排镇	81702261	日用不锈钢制品
东莞市华茂电子有限公司	长安镇	85319118	五金制品零件
通用设备制造业			
东莞瑞雄实业有限公司	洪梅镇		铸造机械
东莞市科光实业有限公司	长安镇	87085877	金属制品
东莞市圣吉川工业自动化设备有限公司	企石镇	81928111	流水线设备
东莞市仁海电子有限公司	企石镇	86663966	散热风扇
东莞市邦泽电子有限公司	沙田镇	89191288	碎纸机
东莞市亿杰五金制品有限公司	黄江镇	83623308	金属紧固件
东莞市国祥空调设备有限公司	道滘镇	22496848	恒温恒湿机
东莞市快意施耐德电梯有限公司	清溪镇	87736443	电梯
东莞市森中冈金属工业有限公司	大岭山镇	85607016	精密金属棒材
东莞市大岭山长虹弹簧厂	大岭山镇	85612812	拉线材、弹簧、塑胶五金制品
东莞市台冠起重机械设备有限公司	大朗镇	83019666	桥式起重机
快意电梯股份有限公司	清溪镇	87731075	电梯
广东大族粤铭激光科技股份有限公司	万江街道	22771433	激光雕刻机
东莞市庆新安制冷设备配件有限公司	桥头镇	83341457	空调贮液器
东莞市银朗电梯配件有限公司	中堂镇	88861110	TK5A空心导轨
东莞市澳星视听器材有限公司	塘厦镇	82037888	影视录放设备
东莞市永强物流设备有限公司	寮步镇	82313315	仓储物流设备
东莞元晖光电照明有限公司	洪梅镇	81336800	LED照明灯
东莞市妙达电动工具制造有限公司	虎门镇	89966022	电动工具
东莞市科达机电设备有限公司	万江街道	22188788	蒸发式降温换气机组
东莞市寮步兆峰轴承有限公司	寮步镇	83328819	轴承
东莞市三洋电梯有限公司	厚街镇	85884455	电梯
东莞市东城永强弹簧厂	东城街道	22261357	弹簧
东莞市乔锋机械有限公司	常平镇	82328091	设备
东莞市晟邦机电有限公司	大朗镇	81129292	减速马达
东莞瑞柯电子科技股份有限公司	清溪镇	87899858	空压机
东莞市富士电梯有限公司	东城街道	23062593	电梯
东莞市TR轴承有限公司	莞城街道	22461784	滚动轴承
东莞市得鑫五金有限公司	大朗镇	81124006	螺丝
东莞市世丰机械有限公司	道滘镇	88380088	金属成形机床
东莞市中海光电材料有限公司	南城街道	22906675	太阳能组件
东莞市达成机械设备制造有限公司	寮步镇	83217777	高度调节板
东莞市南星电子有限公司	沙田镇	88663139	数码相机
广东通鑫起重机科技有限公司	大朗镇	81230999	起重机
专用设备制造业			
东莞市骏朗机械设备制造有限公司	洪梅镇	22706123	设备
东莞市新泽谷机械制造股份有限公司	寮步镇	83286900	电子精密机械
东莞瑞升电子有限公司	黄江镇	83633303	印刷电路板
东莞捷荣模具制造工业有限公司	长安镇	82387988	模具
东莞市华兴隆模具钢材有限公司	凤岗镇	82588888	模具钢材
东莞市洲全塑胶五金制品有限公司	长安镇	86067988	模具
东莞市鸿富纸品有限公司	企石镇	82218806	纸板

1-4 续表 14

(2012年)

单位名称	所属镇街	联系电话	主要产品（或服务）
东莞市隆泰实业有限公司	石龙镇	86323479	普通、煤矿机械、环保设备等
东莞科威医疗器械有限公司	东城街道	21985698	膜式氧合器
东莞市华之力电子有限公司	虎门镇	85186742	器具开关
东莞市拓斯普达机械科技有限公司	长安镇	85390821	五金模具机械
东莞市冠佳电子设备有限公司	塘厦镇		电子设备
东莞市泰康电子科技有限公司	长安镇	85322066	电子连接器
东莞市盛星电脑科技有限公司	大朗镇	81065816	电脑毛织机械机
东莞市塘厦赞扬机械厂	塘厦镇	87721583	立式注塑机
东莞市胜蓝电子有限公司	长安镇	87094988	电子连接器
东莞市三和兴模具钢材有限公司	塘厦镇	82016100	模具钢材
东莞市鑫鹰环保科技有限公司	中堂镇	88893398	高频振动筛
东莞晓达模具科技有限公司	大岭山镇	81881522	模具
东莞市方达实业有限公司	长安镇	85338842	PVC排水器材
东莞市南兴家具装备制造股份有限公司	厚街镇	88803333	木工机械、木工刀具
东莞市虎门机械厂	虎门镇	85711932	B24小型拉伸机、S20B微型拉伸机
东莞市凯格精密机械有限公司	东城街道	22767281	全自动印刷机
东莞市精铁机械有限公司	虎门镇	85556166	电线电缆设备
东莞市建升压铸科技有限公司	东坑镇	89300953	五金模具
汽车制造业			
东莞爱玛车业有限公司	东坑镇	83880000	汽车、摩托车
东莞市佳雅汽车座椅有限公司	中堂镇	88188598	汽车座椅、海绵
东莞市绿通高尔夫观光车有限公司	洪梅镇	88435388	电瓶车
东莞市万码电子科技有限公司	樟木头镇	87182168	汽车GPS卫星定位系统
东莞市旗丰消声器有限公司	东城街道	22658795	汽车及摩托车消声器
东莞市永强汽车制造有限公司	寮步镇	83307688	罐式车
东莞市祥鑫汽车模具制品有限公司	长安镇	87089899	汽车模具
铁路、船舶、航空航天和其他运输设备制造业			
东莞市宏运船舶工程有限公司	洪梅镇	88843299	船舶修理及拆船
东莞市大裕摩托车有限公司	中堂镇	88883627	摩托车
广东锐新船舶工程有限公司	麻涌镇	81297100	船舶
广东雅迪科技发展有限公司	大岭山镇	82761311	助动自行车
电气机械和器材制造业			
东莞市金源电池科技有限公司	石碣镇	86386888	锂离子电池
广东华达电缆有限公司	大岭山镇	83357868	电线
东莞市通成实业股份有限公司	道滘镇	81315688	灯饰
东莞市金达照明有限公司	万江街道	22284761	水晶灯
东莞市高能电气股份有限公司	东城街道	22291876	绝缘体
东莞市开关厂有限公司	寮步镇	83300801	高低压开关屏
东莞市三友联众电器有限公司	塘厦镇	85914551	继电器研发、制造
广东中德电缆有限公司	东坑镇	89610888	电缆
东莞市正德连接器有限公司	长安镇	87085816	连接器
东莞市雄丰配电设备有限公司	茶山镇	86647816	高压配电柜
东莞市奥维漆包线有限公司	茶山镇	81810183	漆包绕线组
康达新能源设备股份有限公司	寮步镇	88996233	燃气发电机组
东莞市民兴电缆有限公司	凤岗镇	87510316	电线、电缆

1-4　续表 15

(2012年)

单位名称	所属镇街	联系电话	主要产品(或服务)
东莞市前锋电子有限公司	石碣镇	86633990	电磁炉
广东科旺电源设备有限公司	南城街道	22900009	稳压器
东莞市科慧电子有限公司	清溪镇	87326186	高频变压器
东莞市康德威变压器有限公司	道滘镇	88321002	整流器和电感器
广东洛贝电子科技有限公司	松山湖	22895186	家用厨房电器具
东莞市有同电器有限公司	南城街道	22401688	电子变压器用铁心电
东莞市春发电子照明有限公司	谢岗镇	82105188	发光二极管
东莞市越洋电线电缆有限公司	虎门镇	85167777	电线电缆
东莞市昶泰五金制品有限公司	大朗镇	83107188	灯饰
东莞市擎洲光电科技有限公司	横沥镇	89110666	电子变压器
东莞华旭电线电缆有限公司	虎门镇	85526356	电线电缆、插头
东莞市迈科科技有限公司	大朗镇	83015380	镍氢电池
东莞市凌力电池有限公司	万江街道	22271791	干电池
广东美林电线电缆有限公司	虎门镇	88920098	电线、电缆
广东志成冠军集团有限公司	塘厦镇	87722374	变压器、整流器
东莞市百利电器有限公司	望牛墩镇	88859188	商用冷柜
东莞市时唛特电器有限公司	塘厦镇	87987070	家用厨房电器具
东莞市联升电线电缆有限公司	虎门镇	85253317	电线、铜线、插头电源线
东莞市凌力电池有限公司麻涌电池厂	麻涌镇	88822642	干电池
东莞市石碣志业电子有限公司	石碣镇	86318226	电脑周边设备、汽车等连接线
东莞市欧雷玛电源有限公司	塘厦镇	87865169	铅酸蓄电池
东莞市旭业光电科技有限公司	石排镇	86341888	光学镜头
东莞市稳畅电子制品有限公司	虎门镇	85521148	电子
广东宏磊达光电科技有限公司	寮步镇	87070008	LED塑胶产品及高科技光学产品
东莞市生命动力按摩器材有限公司	石排镇	86658583	健身器材
东莞市莱尔照明电器有限公司	茶山镇	88930200	照明灯具
东莞市金鸿盛电器有限公司	横沥镇	87060166	空调配件
广东省东莞电机有限公司	麻涌镇	22810778	交流电动机
东莞市梅兰电器有限公司	寮步镇	83300022	高、低压成套开关设备
广东五星太阳能股份有限公司	万江街道	22176388	太阳能热水器
广东康菱动力科技有限公司	松山湖	22895555	发电机及发电机组
东莞勤上光电股份有限公司	常平镇	83395678	LED路灯
东莞市益达实业有限公司	茶山镇	86412628	漆包绕组线
领亚电子科技股份有限公司	松山湖	85510688	电线
东莞市勤上企业有限公司	横沥镇	81107158	烧烤炉
东莞市迈科新能源有限公司	大朗镇	83197555	锂离子电池
东莞市理士奥电源技术有限公司	塘厦镇	87925180	阀控式蓄电池
东莞清溪光荣电业制品厂	清溪镇	87300000	吸尘器
东莞市吉铼升电机有限公司	塘厦镇	82076688	微型电机
东莞市宸裕照明有限公司	企石镇	86788470	灯泡、灯饰
东莞市绿雅家用电器有限公司	万江街道	88991088	电扇
东莞市力宇燃气动力有限公司	虎门镇	85015288	发电机
东莞市通宝电线电缆有限公司	大朗镇	83315034	电线
东莞市力王电池有限公司	塘厦镇	87885755	碱性锌锰电池
东莞市华达电缆厂	大岭山镇	85617836	电缆

1-4 续表 16

(2012年)

单位名称	所属镇街	联系电话	主要产品(或服务)
东莞市凯晟灯头实业有限公司	企石镇	86787878	铜、铁、铝等灯头
东莞厚街科技电业厂	厚街镇	82728888	电钻、电锯
东莞市中亚电缆有限公司	中堂镇	88115798	电线、电缆
东莞市亿丰电池有限公司	万江街道	22179288	干电池
东莞市百分百科技有限公司	东城街道	88754800	塑胶塑胶开关
东莞塘厦新联电器厂	塘厦镇	87910170	电风筒、电台灯、增湿机
东莞市民康电子科技有限公司	茶山镇	88931788	电线
东莞市国登电子有限公司	东城街道	22080805	电子配件
东莞市昊恩装饰品有限公司	道滘镇	88328732	照明灯具
东莞市新时代新能源科技有限公司	大岭山镇	85653393	空气能热水器
东莞市日新传导科技股份有限公司	桥头镇	85425888	电子电器配件
东莞市安德丰电池有限公司	大朗镇	82231000	电池
东莞安尚光源有限公司	道滘镇	88311915	电光源
东莞市锐升电线电缆有限公司	虎门镇	86092388	电线
东莞市亿富灯饰艺品有限公司	高埗镇	81300379	灯饰
东莞市博通电气设备工程有限公司	东坑镇	22789656	配电箱
东莞市科菱电线有限公司	虎门镇	85231398	电线
高达粤电安信电力检修安装有限公司	虎门镇	85561893	机电设备安装
东莞市博伦光电科技有限公司	企石镇	86760086	手电筒、节能灯、应急灯
东莞市瑞桥电器有限公司	企石镇	81358668	电器及连接线、电源适配器等
东莞格力良源电池科技有限公司	塘厦镇	82991177	锂电池
东莞市利赛奥新能源科技有限公司	凤岗镇	82527858	研发锂高子电池
东莞市通宁实业有限公司	大朗镇	83315034	裸铜线
东莞市鸿华电器有限公司	黄江镇	83535800	家用小电器
广东特发信息光缆有限公司	寮步镇	86056605	光缆
深圳市特发信息股份有限公司东莞分公司	寮步镇	86056688	光缆
广东宾士动力科技有限公司	寮步镇	88992216	柴油发电机组
广东亨通光电科技有限公司	松山湖	88755088	光缆
东莞博力威电池有限公司	东城街道	27282038	锂电子充电电池
广东高标电子科技有限公司	松山湖	22899968	防盗器
东莞市振华新能源科技有限公司	凤岗镇	82695120	锂离子电池
东莞市钜大电子有限公司	南城街道	22810105	电池
计算机、通信和其他电子设备制造业			
广东迅扬电脑科技股份有限公司	东坑镇	82800888	电脑机箱、电源
东莞市泓莞电子有限公司	黄江镇	83621009	移动电源
东莞市瑞云电子科技有限公司	长安镇	85092088	电子产品
东莞信恒电子科技有限公司	松山湖	33330999	手机主板
东莞市若美电子科技有限公司	企石镇	82211111	线路板
广东长盈精密技术有限公司	松山湖	23078725	电子元件
东莞金卓通信科技有限公司	大岭山镇	89296666	通信终端设备
东莞市涛森电子科技有限公司	长安镇	81153267	广播电视接收设备及器材
东莞市嘉田电子科技有限公司	凤岗镇	87774386	电脑机箱
东莞龙光电子集团有限公司	长安镇	85338787	机箱
东莞市扬明精密塑胶五金电子有限公司	长安镇	85338940	塑胶五金电子制品
东莞认知电子有限公司	塘厦镇	38961639	TFT-LCD平板显示屏

1-4 续表 17

(2012年)

单位名称	所属镇街	联系电话	主要产品（或服务）
东莞市嘉龙海杰电子科技有限公司	清溪镇	87319065	电子零配件
东莞市煜弘电子制造有限公司	虎门镇	85014888	音箱电脑
东莞市恒兴电子五金有限公司	石碣镇	86321888	铝材板五金材料
东莞市维峰五金电子有限公司	长安镇	85358920	电脑连接器
东莞市塘厦克琛达塑胶电子厂	塘厦镇	86851777	电子元件
东莞市欧珀电子工业有限公司	长安镇	85545555	影碟机
郡懋电子（东莞）有限公司	塘厦镇	87282000	微晶合金
东莞市盈聚电子有限公司	石碣镇	86327382	电子配件变压器整流器
东莞市金众电子有限公司	大岭山镇	86077018	线路板
东莞市庭丰电子有限公司	塘厦镇	87926702	电子制品
东莞伟易达电子通讯设备厂	寮步镇	85581806	室内无线电话
东莞市金培电子有限公司	桥头镇	81026999	电子产品
东莞伟易达电子元器件制造厂	寮步镇	85581806	电子元件
东莞市凯运电子有限公司	虎门镇	86232178	电子工线材
东莞市法拉欧电器有限公司	东坑镇	82802688	DVD播放器
东莞市漫步者科技有限公司	松山湖	23075158	多媒体音箱
东莞清溪显讯电子制品厂	清溪镇	87893556	电子
东莞市飞尔液晶显示器有限公司	大朗镇	83106619	电子元器件
东莞市慧诚电子科技有限公司	厚街镇	85828371	电脑电源
东莞市雷洋电子科技有限公司	长安镇	85391369	电子设备
东莞市方达电子工业有限公司	长安镇	85410922	电子产品
东莞市知音电子有限公司	塘厦镇	89893999	通讯设备、手机外壳
东莞市欧谛特光电科技有限公司	塘厦镇	87985588	光电产品
东莞市合权电子有限公司	塘厦镇	87983209	硬盘
广东天誉飞歌电子科技有限公司	横沥镇	38837633	LED会议系统
东莞市海聚电子有限公司	石碣镇	81398232	小型变压器
东莞市汇兴电子科技有限公司	塘厦镇	87869181	电子产品
东莞市凯昶德电子科技有限公司	塘厦镇		电脑连接线
东莞市耐福电子有限公司	清溪镇	38981500	散热风扇
东莞市荣烨五金制品有限公司	清溪镇	87316268	电子元件
东莞市洪业祥实业有限公司	大岭山镇	82788736	机械设备
东莞市新兆电科技有限公司	清溪镇	87330168	电子计算机外部设备
广东欧华电子有限公司	横沥镇	88971888	汽车电子产品
东莞市乐科电子有限公司	塘厦镇	87289666	电线、电缆
东莞市亚力通电子科技有限公司	塘厦镇	82080288	电子元件
东莞市楚东电子科技有限公司	塘厦镇	82133122	电子元件
广东易事特电源股份有限公司	松山湖	22897777	不间断电源
东莞市亚星半导体有限公司	大岭山镇	82755888	电子产品
东莞市霖玖玖电子科技有限公司	横沥镇	83723861	电脑机箱
东莞轩朗实业有限公司	塘厦镇	82612568	扩散片
东莞市智谦电子有限公司	虎门镇	86235815	手机充电器
东莞华贝电子科技有限公司	松山湖	38960680	GSM手机
东莞市亿盛通讯科技有限公司	塘厦镇	33269150	电池
东莞市五株电子科技有限公司	石碣镇	81321318	线路板
东莞市卓润电子科技有限公司	塘厦镇	82019899	电子产品

1-4 续表 18

(2012年)

单位名称	所属镇街	联系电话	主要产品(或服务)
东莞市古德尔实业有限公司	塘厦镇	38833068	通讯产品
东莞市拓瀚电子科技有限公司	塘厦镇	82108395	电子产品
东莞市龙健电子有限公司	大岭山镇	81159988	音响设备
广东星星光电科技有限公司	石排镇	86921688	视窗防护屏
广东省广播电视网络股份有限公司东莞桥头分公司	桥头镇		广播电视接收设备及器材
东莞市隆锐行电子有限公司	望牛墩镇	88512858	塑胶专用模具及其配件
东莞市艾炜特电子有限公司	东坑镇	83020666	液晶显示器
东莞市铭庆电子有限公司	石排镇	86921000	磁性元器件
东莞市巨电电子科技有限公司	塘厦镇	89029666	电子产品
东莞市威而肯通讯科技有限公司	塘厦镇	81001855	手机的研发等
东莞市金帕特电子科技有限公司	常平镇		电子元件及组件
东莞市华荣通信技术有限公司	东坑镇	89868688	程控交换设备机柜
金龙机电(东莞)有限公司	塘厦镇	82861555	电容式触摸屏
东莞市永晋达通讯科技有限公司	凤岗镇	82695999	通信终端设备
东莞市德瑞精密设备有限公司	东城街道	88999088	电池设备
东莞东石材料开发有限公司	松山湖	26649080	卫星天线
东莞市奕东电子有限公司	东城街道	22200329	电子连接器
东莞市海铭诺信息科技有限公司	清溪镇	86810828	研发计算机产品
东莞市长田电子有限公司	塘厦镇	87947610	电子产品
东莞市东方科技有限公司	厚街镇	85586389	电脑周边设备
东莞市东阳光电容器有限公司	长安镇	85315188	电容器
东莞市兴奇宏电子有限公司	企石镇	86731868	电脑主机
东莞市威力固电路板设备有限公司	石碣镇	81321366	电子工业专用设备
东莞市金铭电子有限公司	大岭山镇	89296666	手机
东莞南城白马荣科电子厂	南城街道	22401145	精密金属部件及汽车配件
东莞市群跃电子材料科技有限公司	道滘镇	89955188	电子产品
东莞市铭基电子有限公司	塘厦镇	83096688	电脑连接线
广东明家科技股份有限公司	横沥镇	87061828	插座
东莞市金业电子科技有限公司	寮步镇	83261111	VCD机
东莞市福地电子材料有限公司	南城街道	22406025	LED芯片
广东步步高电子工业有限公司	长安镇	85545555	手机
步步高教育电子有限公司	长安镇	85540888	语言复读机
东莞市龙本电子科技有限公司	塘厦镇	87818033	网卡、交换机、路由器
东莞市京硕电子有限公司	塘厦镇	87886667	充电器
东莞市竞跃电子有限公司	寮步镇	88900999	电子元器件
东莞市金河田实业有限公司	厚街镇	85585691	其他电脑外部设备
东莞市金翔电器设备有限公司	万江街道	22704478	电脑机箱
东莞市微索电子科技有限公司	黄江镇	82118666	鼠标键盘
东莞市凯华电子有限公司	塘厦镇	87915858	电子开关
东莞市众誉电子有限公司	虎门镇	85554168	鼠标键盘
东莞市意兆电子科技有限公司	长安镇	85399156	电子产品
东莞铭普光磁股份有限公司	石排镇	81701560	网络变压器
东莞市卡能电子有限公司	东城街道	23148846	耳机
东莞市金盈电子有限公司	石碣镇	86326328	电源变压、整流器、塑胶制品
东莞市美声五金塑胶制品有限公司	东坑镇	83661114	电视机外壳及其五金金属结构件

1-4 续表 19

(2012年)

单位名称	所属镇街	联系电话	主要产品(或服务)
东莞市奇声电子实业有限公司	麻涌镇	88231648	音响
东莞市奥莱克电子有限公司	麻涌镇	88226006	组合音响
东莞市大忠电子有限公司	东城街道	22630563	电子产品
东莞市亿辉电子科技有限公司	塘厦镇	87981885	光电子器件及其他电子器件
东莞长安日华电子厂	长安镇	85536840	电子配件
东莞市元圆源电子有限公司	企石镇	82216301	音响器材
东莞市润星机械科技有限公司	桥头镇	82820008	数控机械
东莞市光普实业发展有限公司	清溪镇	87339849	电脑机箱
东莞市华康电脑科技有限公司	横沥镇	83723860	电脑机箱
东莞市慧衍电子有限公司	塘厦镇	87885098	五金制品
东莞市汇电电子科技有限公司	长安镇	86240798	电子产品及配件
东莞市德生通用电器制造有限公司	东城街道	23167118	收音机
东莞市锐嘉精密机械制造有限公司	寮步镇	88908188	通讯网络用机箱
东莞黄江达裕科技电子厂	黄江镇	83531877	液晶显示器
东莞市鸿瀚电子材料有限公司	东城街道	81381535	手机镜片、MP3屏幕镜片
东莞市森特电子有限公司	石碣镇	86329018	电脑机箱
东莞市石碣东诚电子有限公司	石碣镇	83548862	电子材料配件
东莞市茵莉电子有限公司	石碣镇	86314889	变压器、整流器电源开关
东莞厚街下汴电子厂	厚街镇	85591388	CD电唱盘及收音机
东莞市奕联实业有限公司	长安镇	86064988	连接线、连接器
东莞市佳禾电子有限公司	石排镇	86596918	耳机
东莞市石龙富华电子有限公司	石龙镇	86022222	LED驱动电源、医疗及通信类电源等
广东粤林电气科技股份有限公司	清溪镇	87890888	电脑机箱
史博森电子-东莞有限公司	桥头镇	83437761	电力、电子器件
东莞市奥源电子科技有限公司	长安镇	81589595	电子产品及配件
东莞市亿达音响制造有限公司	大朗镇	22665300	组合音箱
东莞市数字印数码科技有限公司	凤岗镇	87510868	数码音乐播放器
东莞市佰利电子有限公司	高埗镇	88708002	发光二极管
东莞市步步高通信设备有限公司	长安镇	85540688	有绳电话机
东莞长安上角康扬塑胶五金电子厂	长安镇	85305187	电脑塑胶配件
华为机器有限公司	松山湖	22898612	通信产品
东莞市宏奥五金制品有限公司	常平镇	83557838	五金制品、铝散热片
东莞市大朗涌韵音膜厂	大朗镇	83138601	振动膜
东莞市旭田电子有限公司	石碣镇	86300036	键盘鼠标、移动硬盘
仪器仪表制造业			
广东万濠精密仪器股份有限公司	长安镇	85316127	投影仪
东莞市远峰科技有限公司	大朗镇	83482500	计算机零件
东莞市华兰海电子有限公司	麻涌镇	88823105	便携式轴重台
东莞市中控电子技术有限公司	塘厦镇	82109991	指纹识别设备
东莞长安新民冠利精密钟表厂	长安镇	85387288	钟表
东莞市立旺电子塑胶有限公司	大朗镇	83117758	3D眼镜
广东正业科技股份有限公司	松山湖	88985666	精密检测仪器设备及电子材料
其他制造业			
东莞市钮成服装辅料有限公司	东城街道	22625327	钮扣
东莞市电力燃料有限公司	万江街道	22475222	石油及制品

1-4 续表 20

(2012年)

单位名称	所属镇街	联系电话	主要产品（或服务）
东莞太平电镀元件厂	虎门镇	85511047	拉链
废弃资源综合利用业			
东莞市裕丰化建有限公司	石碣镇	86384818	危险废物处理
金属制品、机械和设备修理业			
东莞市硕泰实业有限公司	大岭山镇	81516875	收缩膜、胶袋等
电力、热力生产和供应业			
东莞市基宁发电有限公司	虎门镇	85136442	火力发电
东莞市三联热电有限公司	中堂镇	88812123	火力发电
东莞市挚能再生资源发电有限公司	厚街镇	85835918	焚烧垃圾发电
广深沙角B电力有限公司沙角B火力发电厂	虎门镇		火力发电
燃气生产和供应业			
东莞市高埗新奥燃气有限公司	高埗镇	83072020	管道燃气投资
东莞市厚街新奥燃气有限公司	厚街镇	89981018	供应天然气
水的生产和供应业			
东莞市东江自来水有限公司	莞城街道	22214443	自来水供应
东莞市东城自来水公司	东城街道	22612699	自来水供应
东莞市大朗镇自来水公司	大朗镇	83318306	自来水供应
东莞市横沥镇自来水公司	横沥镇	83375146	自来水供应
东莞市清溪自来水有限公司	清溪镇	87733362	自来水供应
东莞市塘厦自来水公司	塘厦镇	87724614	自来水供应
东莞市虎门水务投资有限公司	虎门镇	85525510	自来水供应
东莞市长安镇自来水公司	长安镇	85535689	自来水供应
东莞市沙田自来水厂	沙田镇	88862620	自来水供应
东莞市东江水务有限公司	东城街道	22609238	自来水供应
东莞常平粤海水务有限公司	常平镇	83335588	自来水供应
房屋建筑业			
东莞市方中建筑工程有限公司	莞城街道	86222001	建筑工程施工
东莞市正大建筑工程有限公司	莞城街道	28821822	建筑工程
东莞市福华建筑工程有限公司	沙田镇	88866688	房屋建筑
东莞市光大建筑劳务分包有限公司	东城街道	22986086	房屋工程建筑
东莞市宏泰建筑工程有限公司	南城街道	22813338	建筑施工
东莞市虎门建设发展有限公司	虎门镇	85188631	建筑
东莞市诚峰建筑工程有限公司	塘厦镇	22209083	房屋建筑
东莞市华固建造工程有限公司	南城街道	23023558	房屋建筑工程
东莞市百分百建设工程有限公司	东城街道	88754008	房屋建筑工程施工
东莞市驰宏建设发展有限公司	虎门镇	85128989	房屋工程建筑
东莞市裕欣国建筑工程有限公司	高埗镇	88781698	房屋工程建筑
广东宏达建设工程有限公司	莞城街道	26888888	房屋建筑工程
东莞市城区市政工程公司	莞城街道	22225634	建筑房屋
东莞市南粤建筑工程有限公司	万江街道	22020079	房屋建筑施工
东莞市石龙第二建筑工程有限公司	石龙镇	86615291	房屋建筑工程总承包
东莞市金斗建造工程有限公司	寮步镇	83300000	工业与民用建筑施工
东莞市华源建筑工程有限公司	厚街镇	85596888	建筑工程
东莞市健升建筑工程有限公司	南城街道	22302222	房屋建筑工程施工
东莞市凤岗建筑工程公司	凤岗镇	87860335	房屋工程建筑

1-4 续表 21

(2012年)

单位名称	所属镇街	联系电话	主要产品(或服务)
东莞市中厚建筑工程公司	厚街镇	85582766	房屋工程建筑
东莞市建工集团有限公司	南城街道	22427888	房屋建筑工程施工承包
东莞市东城建筑公司	东城街道	22319001	房屋建筑
广东鸿高建设集团有限公司	企石镇	86664882	房屋工程建筑
东莞市企石深巷建筑工程公司	企石镇	86711321	房屋建筑
东莞市樟木头建筑工程公司	樟木头镇	87798332	房屋建筑工程施工承包
东莞市腾飞建筑工程有限公司	南城街道	22425528	建筑房屋、住宅小区
土木工程建筑业			
东莞市茗鑫路桥建设养护有限公司	莞城街道	82399288	公路路桥建设养护
东莞市芊艺园林绿化有限公司	东城街道	22851298	市政公用工程施工
东莞市高业建设工程有限公司	高埗镇	88788633	水利工程建筑
广东省水利水电第三工程局	塘厦镇	87721441	水利、水电工程施工
东莞市锦新园林绿化有限公司	南城街道	23664092	市政公用工程
东莞市园林绿化工程有限公司	东城街道	22493809	园林绿化
岭南园林股份有限公司	东城街道	22000888	园林景观工程
建筑安装业			
东莞市健升安装工程有限公司	南城街道	22177111	净化空调工程
东莞市力丰钢结构有限公司	厚街镇	85916822	钢结构加工安装
东莞市输变电工程公司	寮步镇	83237889	高、低压电器工程安装、技术咨询
东莞市高宝电气安装工程有限公司	高埗镇	88786869	安装电力设备
东莞市建安集团有限公司	东城街道	22986086	房屋建筑
东莞市塘厦水电空调设备安装工程有限公司	塘厦镇	87913322	机电设备工程安装
东莞市顺安电力消防工程有限公司	莞城街道	22481077	消防设施工程专业承包
东莞市安利来电气安装有限公司	大朗镇	83010013	电力设施承装
东莞市景安电器安装工程有限公司	长安镇	81762299	电器安装
东莞市锐凯机电安装有限公司	万江街道	22271038	安装电器
湖南望新建设集团股份有限公司东莞分公司	南城街道	22999910	建筑
广东集明电力工程有限公司	南城街道	22492728	电力工程安装
东莞市广安电器安装工程有限公司	东城街道	82266666	电器工程安装
广东宏泰照明科技有限公司	南城街道	22880111	房屋工程建筑
建筑装饰和其他建筑业			
东莞市星光建设有限公司	企石镇	86788068	房屋建造
东莞市东电发变电修试有限公司	寮步镇	83223301	发、变、送、配电工贸技术更新改造
东莞市小杨装饰工程有限公司	清溪镇		建筑装饰业
东莞市良友装饰工程有限公司	高埗镇	88876098	建筑装饰业
东莞市堃烨装饰工程有限公司	塘厦镇	87933378	装饰工程
东莞市名雕装饰有限公司	莞城街道	22029268	室内装饰
东莞市东塘电气安装有限公司	塘厦镇	87905273	承装电力设施
东莞市黄江镇建筑工程有限公司	黄江镇	83363938	房屋工程建筑
东莞市金业河建筑基础工程有限公司	南城街道	22985988	各类地基与基础工程施工
东莞市江桦装饰有限公司	寮步镇	83323628	室内装饰
东莞市广强建筑基础工程有限公司	东城街道	22464088	建筑基础工程
东莞市东方动力拆迁有限公司	南城街道	22991778	建筑拆迁
东莞市国贸水电安装工程有限公司	东城街道	22760555	水电安装
东莞市附城东城装修设计工程有限公司	东城街道	22618888	装饰装修

1-4 续表 22

(2012年)

单位名称	所属镇街	联系电话	主要产品(或服务)
东莞市凤安电力工程有限公司	凤岗镇	82082968	电力设施工程
东莞市信维环保工程有限公司	莞城街道	22318089	环保工程
批发业			
东莞市南丰进出口有限公司	南城街道	26189999	家具进出口
东莞市石碣唐洪东城加油站有限公司	石碣镇	86638899	石油气
东莞市华康进出口贸易有限公司	南城街道	22880833	货物进出口
东莞市昌隆进出口有限公司	大岭山镇	82785398	五金
东莞市迅安贸易有限公司	莞城街道	22321232	轻纺品
东莞市江名塑料化工有限公司	黄江镇	86916768	化工材料
东莞市雅安贸易有限公司	黄江镇	83600977	塑胶原料
深圳市女人心百年内衣有限公司	清溪镇	84276676	内衣、服装
东莞市森鼠城堡服装有限公司	虎门镇	82262388	服装
东莞市裕恒医药有限公司	厚街镇	21662900	药品
东莞市同富实业投资有限公司	高埗镇	88739100	化工产品
东莞市永隆废纸回收有限公司	望牛墩镇	88818068	废纸回收
东莞市永盛贸易有限公司	长安镇	85545555	手机
东莞市晟世欣兴格力贸易有限公司	东城街道	23052938	空调
东莞市中力实业投资有限公司	望牛墩镇	88555688	铅
维沃通信科技有限公司	长安镇	85540688	手机
东莞市盛丰废纸回收有限公司	望牛墩镇	88552906	废纸回收
东莞市南北贸易有限公司	麻涌镇	88224098	粮食
东莞市泰安医药有限公司	东城街道	22670921	药品
广东中砼新型建筑材料股份有限公司	洪梅镇	88849633	建材
东莞市洪元进出口有限公司	厚街镇	81211402	鞋类
广东舜荣钢铁有限公司	洪梅镇		金属及金属矿
东莞市蒙自源实业有限公司	寮步镇	88903332	预包装食品
东莞市中天进出口有限公司	东城街道	22385163	体育用品
东莞卓烨能源有限公司	洪梅镇	88436783	重油、罐装润滑油
东莞市宝鑫钢铁有限公司	洪梅镇		金属矿
东莞市澳鹏电子贸易有限公司	石碣镇	86302199	电子元件
东莞市兄弟铝业有限公司	万江街道	87076903	铝材
东莞市盈浚建材有限公司	寮步镇	82930638	水泥
东莞市东孚石油化工有限公司	寮步镇	82316938	石油产品
东莞市扬润机电设备有限公司	中堂镇	22883192	螺纹钢
东莞市恒力机电有限公司	麻涌镇	88821566	机械设备
东莞市扬华贸易有限公司	中堂镇	88186213	钢材
东莞市泛豪贸易有限公司	沙田镇	88666887	化学产品
东莞市盛鑫汽车商贸有限公司	樟木头镇		汽车
广东东泊化工有限公司	中堂镇	81165678	烧碱
东莞市旺盆贸易有限公司	中堂镇	81696189	水泥
广东中塑化工投资管理有限公司	黄江镇	82606666	塑胶原料
东莞市盛峰石化有限公司	樟木头镇	82119253	石油化工
东莞市泓源石油化工有限公司	樟木头镇	82119262	塑胶原料及制品、橡胶制品、化工产品
东莞市隆诚塑胶原料有限公司	樟木头镇	87198230	塑胶及化工原料、塑胶机械及制品等
东莞市金红辉贸易有限公司	中堂镇	88816976	塑胶

1-4 续表 23

(2012年)

单位名称	所属镇街	联系电话	主要产品（或服务）
东莞市易辰化工有限公司	洪梅镇		化工产品
东莞市华铝铝业有限公司	寮步镇	89161633	铝
东莞市长正电子科技有限公司	莞城街道		电子产品
中储粮东莞米业有限公司	麻涌镇	88231030	粮食收购
东莞市木森服装有限公司	虎门镇	82262388	服装
东莞市天保废纸回收有限公司	高埗镇	88786298	废纸回收
东莞市通源实业投资有限公司	高埗镇	88870290	化学产品
东莞市巨锋金属材料有限公司	望牛墩镇	88855782	金属材料
东莞市伟盛饮料有限公司	莞城街道	22200005	饮料、食品
广东中顺电器有限公司	南城街道	23663230	空调器
东莞市利穗达金属材料有限公司	望牛墩镇	88557896	金属材料
东莞市巨骥进出口有限公司	东城街道	23030939	进出口服装
东莞市莞丰能源有限公司	长安镇	82855789	煤炭
东莞市万江昌强贸易有限公司	万江街道	22286228	煤炭
东莞市润兴进出口有限公司	东城街道	23399728	家具进出口贸易
东莞市久久发塑胶化工有限公司	黄江镇	86918298	塑胶原料
东莞市崇泰纸业有限公司	长安镇	82387588	纸制品
东莞市伟力地坪材料有限公司	企石镇		地称材料
东莞市国惠贸易有限公司	桥头镇	83347888	化工产品
东莞市广招贸易有限公司	中堂镇	88893567	锌锭、铝锭
广东新动力能源有限公司	樟木头镇	87188777	石油及制品
东莞市创辉进出口贸易有限公司	寮步镇	81106328	毛织品
东莞市新南泰机电有限公司	寮步镇	22307777	机电设备
东莞市光辉有色金属贸易有限公司	石排镇	86526926	有色金属
东莞市恒旭达塑胶贸易有限公司	樟木头镇	87794418	塑胶原料
东莞市顺镱贸易有限公司	道滘镇	88316989	天然乳胶
东莞市美的日用家电销售有限公司	虎门镇	22666432	美的电饭煲
东莞市永钰精密机械有限公司	厚街镇	85085781	数据机床配件
东莞美的暖通设备销售有限公司	虎门镇	81518680	家用电器
东莞市华升进出口有限公司	寮步镇	82879118	纺织品
东莞市森三冈金属材料有限公司	大岭山镇	82785253	钢材
东莞市创维电器发展有限公司	东城街道	22292742	家用电器
东莞市中实建材贸易有限公司	沙田镇	88802555	建筑材料
东莞市岭南进出口有限公司	寮步镇	81197620	电脑配件
东莞市宜新贸易有限公司	东城街道	22317361	塑料原料
东莞市东宝能源有限公司	望牛墩镇	88566888	煤批发
东长集团有限公司	望牛墩镇	88566888	重油
东莞市东长石油化工有限公司	望牛墩镇	88565388	重油
永恩投资(集团)有限公司广东经销部	厚街镇	83085323	服装
东莞市希贤贸易有限公司	洪梅镇		金属矿
东莞市振乾钢铁贸易有限公司	洪梅镇	89618039	金属矿
东莞市展博钢铁有限公司	洪梅镇	21683544	建材
东莞市上钢钢铁有限公司	洪梅镇	81336369	金属矿
东莞市宝鼎建材有限公司	洪梅镇		建材
东莞市麻涌利南废纸回收有限公司	麻涌镇	88234888	废纸收购

1-4 续表 24

(2012年)

单位名称	所属镇街	联系电话	主要产品(或服务)
东莞市麻涌新奥燃气有限公司	麻涌镇	89981030	燃气供应
东莞市惠欧进出口贸易有限公司	莞城街道	22762777	化工产品
东莞市丰能化工有限公司	大岭山镇	85619555	石油化工产品
东莞市同展五金有限公司	石排镇	81829221	锌合金
东莞市盈邦能源物资有限公司	沙田镇	81631398	重油
东莞市银河化工有限公司	东坑镇	38800999	批发
东莞市金洲化工有限公司	东坑镇	83380111	化工产品
东莞市铭骏实业投资有限公司	洪梅镇		建材
东莞市茂晟石化贸易有限公司	中堂镇	81252099	石油及制品
东莞市际通进出口贸易有限公司	石排镇	81393888	进出口贸易
东莞市宝丰食品贸易有限公司	寮步镇	22800606	预包装食品
东莞市诺信燃料油有限公司	石龙镇	81823808	重油、润滑油、有色金属矿石等
东莞市云金锡业有限公司	塘厦镇	87989620	锡锭制品
东莞市宝力金属材料有限公司	洪梅镇		建材
广东城景贸易有限公司	万江街道	22700318	建筑材料
东莞市森升化工有限公司	洪梅镇	22309778	化工产品
东莞市龙翔纺织品有限公司	寮步镇	83226588	布料
东莞市汇富进出口贸易有限公司	南城街道	22389322	批发家具
东莞市中信化工有限公司	黄江镇	86918388	塑胶粒
东莞市东钢金属贸易有限公司	虎门镇	82887122	钢材
东莞市中堂物资供销有限公司	中堂镇	88815898	钢材
东莞市东江石油化工有限公司	万江街道	87076081	石油及制品
东莞市东糖集团有限公司	东城街道	22613931	成品糖
东莞市虎门粮食有限公司	虎门镇	85511250	粮油
东莞市创兴糖业贸易有限公司	万江街道	22784583	糕点、糖果及糖
广东广浩机电设备有限公司	中堂镇	81312908	五金机电
东莞市中堂废旧物资回收有限公司鸿业分公司	中堂镇	88120732	废纸收购
广东宁兴特钢贸易有限公司	大朗镇	81069989	金属
东莞市悦海实业投资有限公司	寮步镇	81254225	服装出口
黑龙江中盟龙新化工有限公司东莞谢岗分公司	谢岗镇	82121261	MMA、PMMA、ACR、有机板、硫酸等
东莞市鸿基煤炭有限公司	麻涌镇	88280186	煤炭
东莞市广利食品进出口有限公司	莞城街道	22223344	食品
广东大地通讯连锁服务有限公司	莞城街道	23066666	通讯设备
广东省东莞畜产进出口有限公司	东城街道	22206023	五金
东莞市华锐塑胶实业投资有限公司	黄江镇	83608800	塑胶原料
东莞市百维食品化工原料实业有限公司	寮步镇	83263989	食品添加剂
东莞市华丰盛塑料有限公司	中堂镇	88411688	PC塑料
东莞市广联通信器材有限公司	石排镇		手机
上海凯群贸易有限公司东莞分公司	厚街镇	85750312	塑胶、塑样原料及制品
东莞市华辉金属材料有限公司	莞城街道	22468979	金属材料
东莞市亿丰行洗涤产品有限公司	茶山镇	86311487	洗涤用品
中铝洛阳铜业有限公司东莞分公司	虎门镇	85562885	有色金属
东莞市星辰塑胶有限公司	常平镇	86991286	塑胶原料
东莞市华闽金属材料有限公司	横沥镇	83792951	马口铁
东莞市力洲能源有限公司	塘厦镇	82776388	燃料油

1-4 续表 25

(2012年)

单位名称	所属镇街	联系电话	主要产品（或服务）
东莞市三宝贸易有限公司	莞城街道	22361988	食品、奶粉
东莞市华发纸张有限公司	茶山镇	86313868	白纸板
东莞市祥源燃料有限公司	麻涌镇	81210602	煤炭
东莞市美钻廊珠宝有限公司	厚街镇	81696979	黄金制品
东莞市裕兴废纸回收有限公司	望牛墩镇	38831696	废纸回收
东莞市利兴糖业贸易有限公司	万江街道	22784583	糕点、糖果及糖
东莞市环球工艺进出口贸易有限公司	南城街道	22802312	出口家具
东莞市乘风实业有限公司	石排镇	86615001	购销包
东莞市东安石油化工有限公司	塘厦镇	88865128	汽油
东莞市广济医药器械有限公司	南城街道	22906161	药品
东莞市建华贸易有限公司	清溪镇	87733209	日用品
东莞市裕光进出口贸易有限公司	东城街道	22615090	货物进出口
广东钻石世家国际珠宝有限公司	南城街道	22028888	钻石
东莞市精骏包装材料有限公司	中堂镇	88180800	电镀锡薄钢板
东莞市朝阳药业有限公司	道滘镇	88327952	中药
东莞市中港石油化工有限公司	清溪镇	87387218	润滑油、重油、石油化工产品
东莞市中彦进出口有限公司	大朗镇	83315888	服装
广东省东莞市海东石油有限公司	麻涌镇	88232325	油品
东莞市润泰纸业有限公司	长安镇	85499268	纸张
广东省东莞包装进出口有限公司	南城街道	22802861	纺织品进出口
东莞市海华五金矿产进出口有限公司	莞城街道	22243170	进出口代理
东莞市日之泉物流有限公司	中堂镇	88815015	钢材
东莞市彬源塑胶贸易有限公司	厚街镇	85904198	塑胶
东莞市日之泉食品综合贸易有限公司	中堂镇	88815898	啤酒
东莞市立诚立信贸易有限公司	黄江镇	86919417	塑胶
东莞市超捷实业有限公司	麻涌镇	88228979	重油
东莞市辉明石化产品有限公司	谢岗镇	23183527	石脑油
东莞市欢盈投资有限公司	东城街道	22348888	空调
东莞市泓海贸易有限公司	莞城街道	22340699	纺织品染料
东莞市大洋电机工程有限公司	塘厦镇	87928888	电机设备
东莞市群兴贸易有限公司	中堂镇	88815898	钢材、塑料
东莞市道滘珠洲石油气有限公司	道滘镇	88389233	石油及制品
东莞市鑫泉石油化工有限公司	谢岗镇	89978192	化工产品
东莞市日之泉贸易有限公司	中堂镇	88815015	钢材
东莞市瑞峰纸业有限公司	东城街道	22623952	纸张
东莞市顺安废纸回收有限公司	望牛墩镇	88851243	废纸回收
东莞市华润涂料有限公司	东城街道	22363331	油漆
东莞市卓远发展经贸有限公司	黄江镇	87132056	苯酐
东莞市鸿甲五金材料有限公司	凤岗镇	82039544	五金材料
东莞市明旺贸易有限公司	南城街道	22022722	塑胶原料
东莞市森和纸业有限公司	厚街镇	85588818	纸制品
东莞市南腾贸易有限公司	中堂镇	88122189	有机溶剂
东莞市天泰控股集团有限公司	东城街道	23138888	成品油
东莞市同舟化工有限公司	沙田镇	22365733	甲苯
东莞市鼎鑫贸易有限公司	东城街道	22314016	贸易

1-4 续表 26

(2012年)

单位名称	所属镇街	联系电话	主要产品（或服务）
东莞市先锋特殊钢有限公司	凤岗镇	87777097	钢材
东莞市糖酒集团丰裕贸易有限公司	南城街道	22481231	食品
东莞市东物剧毒化学物品有限公司	莞城街道	22383672	化工产品
东莞市万华皮革有限公司	厚街镇	85876266	皮革
东莞市励骏实业有限公司	厚街镇	21123920	皮鞋
东莞市华健医药器械有限公司	莞城街道	22687306	医疗器械药品
东莞市建安贸易有限公司	莞城街道	22321232	轻纺产品服装
东莞市成泰化工有限公司	南城街道	22884548	化工原料、EVA、石油树脂等
东莞市富励贸易有限公司	凤岗镇	87508888	化工产品
东莞市金仙峰实业有限公司	南城街道	22416577	白砂糖
东莞市能信贸易有限公司	中堂镇	88819933	煤炭
东莞市东源投资实业有限公司	南城街道	22855416	煤炭
东莞市丰源石油有限公司	沙田镇	88686693	罐装润滑油
东莞市宇兴贸易有限公司	大朗镇	83109968	毛衣
广东省东莞国药集团仁济堂药业有限公司	莞城街道	22484521	中药材
东莞市源源钢铁贸易有限公司	大朗镇	83130830	钢材材料
中国石油天然气股份有限公司广东东莞销售分公司	南城街道	22022155	成品油
东莞市中堂废旧物资回收有限公司金洲分公司	中堂镇	88120732	废纸收购
东莞市海丽商贸有限公司	松山湖	22508760	架桥剂
东莞市瑞腾贸易有限公司	莞城街道	22223639	农副产品
东莞市百业进出口有限公司	南城街道	22421328	一般贸易
东莞市中堂废旧物资回收有限公司有利分公司	中堂镇	88120732	废纸收购
东莞市洋通饮料贸易有限公司	茶山镇	86110722	啤酒
东莞市创力网络科技有限公司	莞城街道	22333968	电脑
东莞市顺凯纸业有限公司	中堂镇	88818226	高强瓦楞纸
东莞市凯佳塑胶贸易有限公司	樟木头镇	82059076	塑胶原料
广东省东莞市虎门供销社	虎门镇	85513008	家用电子类
东莞市豪景商贸有限公司	石龙镇	86118181	机电产品
东莞市信立实业有限公司	大岭山镇	85633333	农产品贸易
东莞市对外贸易发展有限公司	东城街道		代理进出口
东莞市中堂废旧物资回收有限公司振桦分公司	中堂镇	88120732	废纸收购
东莞市汉森金属材料有限公司	中堂镇	88123433	金属材料
东莞市全方圆纸制品有限公司	万江街道	87076226	纸制品
东莞市长成纸张有限公司	虎门镇	85269985	纸张
东莞市景福贸易有限公司	万江街道	22787068	其他化工产品
东莞市达明发展有限公司	东城街道	22363006	出口家具
东莞市广弘医药有限公司	万江街道	88899033	中药材及中成药
东莞市东孚商贸有限公司	万江街道	22777823	化妆品及卫生用品
东莞市嘉宝石油化工有限公司	樟木头镇	87711087	甲基苯
东莞市荣兴纸业有限公司	石碣镇	86013903	纸类
东莞市巨行实业有限公司	中堂镇	88812373	硅酸钠、食用淀粉
东莞市中堂废旧物资回收有限公司汇达分公司	中堂镇	88120732	废纸收购
东莞市信佳贸易有限公司	南城街道	23186737	热轧卷板
广东蔚欣实业有限公司	樟木头镇	87703399	塑胶原料
东莞市丰和贸易有限公司	万江街道	23179871	商业贸易

1-4 续表 27

(2012年)

单位名称	所属镇街	联系电话	主要产品(或服务)
东莞市力宏贸易有限公司	中堂镇	88411005	化工产品
东莞市捷锐线缆有限公司	寮步镇	83303990	电线、电缆
东莞市彩虹塑胶颜料有限公司	凤岗镇	87777113	塑胶颜料
东莞市龙宫纺织有限公司	中堂镇	88188870	绵纱
东莞市柏百顺石油化工有限公司	樟木头镇	87781216	化工燃料及产品
东莞市中堂废旧物资回收有限公司深联分公司	中堂镇	88120732	废纸收购
东莞市众生医药贸易有限公司	石龙镇	86188276	中成药、中药材、中药饮片等
东莞市瑞展皮革贸易有限公司	厚街镇	85825996	皮革
东莞市永联化工贸易有限公司	大朗镇	83112349	过氧化氢
东莞市合润进出口贸易有限公司	南城街道	22827028	镇流器出口
东莞市澳洁贸易有限公司	常平镇	83750888	日用百货
东莞市庆华能源有限公司	中堂镇	88819933	煤炭
东莞市常平好必来塑胶贸易有限公司	常平镇	86992038	塑胶原料
东莞市万红贸易有限公司	东城街道	22316751	针织品贸易
东莞市开闳贸易有限公司	清溪镇	82995958	铁材
东莞市允新贸易有限公司	寮步镇	83039670	模具钢
东莞市世发贸易有限公司	南城街道	22800368	化工原料
东莞市健宇塑胶原料有限公司	常平镇	86991001	塑胶原料
广东省东莞医药保健品进出口有限公司	南城街道	22802920	出口服装
广东省盐业集团东莞有限公司	莞城街道	22380236	盐产品
东莞市广通贸易有限公司	南城街道	22407968	汽车轮胎
广东烟草东莞市有限公司	东城街道	22210936	烟草
东莞市中堂废旧物资回收有限公司双洲分公司	中堂镇	88120732	废纸收购
东莞市联大特殊金属材料有限公司	樟木头镇	87123992	五金
东莞市巨树食品有限公司	万江街道	22422166	玉米淀粉、木薯粉、白砂糖等
广东省东莞市谢岗食品公司	谢岗镇	87687328	生猪、肉及制品、禽蛋制品
东莞市南洋计算机软件有限公司	东城街道	22505550	计算机应用软件
东莞市永盛燃料有限公司	万江街道	22287225	石油及制品
广东省东莞快宜外经发展有限公司	南城街道	22421003	商品进出口
东莞市惠民贸易有限公司	万江街道	22785333	米、面制品
东莞市创丰科技发展有限公司	南城街道	22855300	自动化设备
东莞市隆兴纸业有限公司	石龙镇	86088777	纸张、造纸材料、印刷器材
东莞市天锐贸易有限公司	长安镇	85545555	电子元件
东莞市汇众进出口有限公司	大朗镇	83209503	针织制品
东莞市伟业石油化工有限公司	望牛墩镇	88850666	柴油、重油、罐装润滑油
东莞市科大贸易有限公司	沙田镇	88867777	钢材
东莞市中堂废旧物资回收有限公司建晖分公司	中堂镇	88120732	废纸收购
东莞市东益实业投资有限公司	中堂镇	88815898	钢材、塑料、实业投资
东莞市文彬贸易有限公司	望牛墩镇		五金批发
东莞市糖酒集团美宜佳便利店有限公司	南城街道	22465830	小食品
东莞市佳森能源有限公司	麻涌镇	88235233	煤炭
东莞市辉煌能源有限公司	麻涌镇	86313666	煤炭
东莞市名加石油有限公司	东城街道	81823808	汽油、柴油、煤油
东莞市雄峰特殊钢有限公司	凤岗镇	87559810	模具钢材
东莞市高力信塑料有限公司	中堂镇	88411688	塑胶原料

1-4　续表 28

(2012年)

单位名称	所属镇街	联系电话	主要产品(或服务)
东莞市精工轴承有限公司	莞城街道	22451028	轴承
东莞市顺盈钢材贸易有限公司	中堂镇	38858085	钢材、五金
东莞市德盛化工有限公司	望牛墩镇	88853358	水性涂料
东莞市新珠江土方工程有限公司	中堂镇	88815015	钢材
东莞市锦茂进出口有限公司	东城街道	22339829	电脑电源、机箱、毛衣等
东莞市华麟贸易有限公司	莞城街道	22313101	食用香精料
东莞市真映切削工具有限公司	大朗镇	83111711	螺纹切削工具
东莞市海川进出口有限公司	大朗镇	83113663	服装
东莞市锦多宝能源有限公司	樟木头镇	87780788	汽油、重油、润滑
东莞市同汇贸易有限公司	东城街道	23360488	化工产品
东莞市昱方钢材有限公司	长安镇	85349788	模具钢材
东莞市恒生进出口有限公司	南城街道	23181991	泡棉加工机进出口
广东振东泰捷医药物流有限公司	寮步镇	22323888	药品
东莞市众富贸易有限公司	莞城街道	22812638	人造革出口
东莞市昌盛铝业有限公司	塘厦镇	85096555	金属制品
东莞市金钥匙进出口贸易有限公司	东城街道	22039888	进出口贸易
东莞市汇福轮胎有限公司	石龙镇	86180598	汽车轮胎、钢圈、橡胶制品
广东省东莞国药集团药材有限公司	莞城街道	22239530	中药材
东莞市德凯经贸有限公司	南城街道	23027769	服装出口贸易
东莞市糖酒集团东方配销有限公司	南城街道	22184011	奶粉、休闲食品、副食品
东莞市文一实业有限公司	道滘镇	88327025	文具
东莞市年丰饮料有限公司	东城街道	22256391	饮料
东莞市银图贸易有限公司	中堂镇	88412888	塑料
东莞市汇鸿纸业有限公司	石碣镇	86010920	纸张
东莞市中堂废旧物资回收有限公司东江分公司	中堂镇	88120732	废纸收购
东莞市合联进出口贸易有限公司	大朗镇	83125556	出口贸易
东莞市岳化贸易有限公司	谢岗镇	87762745	环已酮、盐酸
东莞市金庆五金建材贸易有限公司	南城街道	85189630	五金制品
深圳市庆鹏石油化工经销有限公司东莞分公司	沙田镇	88864889	成品油
东莞市长安利源石油有限公司	长安镇	85416068	石油
东莞市宏川化工供应链有限公司	松山湖	22893998	化工产品
广东省东莞机械进出口有限公司	莞城街道	22222040	机电产品
东莞中茂石油化工贸易有限公司	塘厦镇	89088387	甲醇
东莞市港源贸易有限公司	南城街道	22488703	工艺品
广东省东莞轻工业品进出口有限公司	莞城街道	22212413	各类电器
东莞市利士石油化工有限公司	高埗镇	88731368	石油
东莞市科虹金属有限公司	石碣镇	86309328	铜材
东莞市华树电脑有限公司	莞城街道	22313954	电子计算机及其配件
东莞市中堂废旧物资回收有限公司	中堂镇	88811203	收购废品
东莞市海通工业煤炭销售有限公司	莞城街道		煤炭
东莞市中凯进出口有限公司	大朗镇	83101855	毛衫
东莞市中堂废旧物资回收有限公司珠江分公司	中堂镇	88120732	废纸收购
东莞市溢安贸易有限公司	麻涌镇	88280993	重油
东莞市君科进出口贸易有限公司	南城街道	22299128	货物及技术出口
东莞市百胜能源有限公司	石龙镇	86113029	煤炭、危险化学品等

1-4　续表 29

(2012年)

单位名称	所属镇街	联系电话	主要产品（或服务）
东莞市旗峰对外贸易有限公司	东城街道	22633592	进出口业务
东莞市惠顺贸易有限公司	东城街道	22491688	建材
东莞市明盛能源有限公司	石碣镇	86313666	煤炭
东莞市新技术进出口有限公司	南城街道	22428678	各类商品和技术的进出口
东莞市友华机电工程有限公司	莞城街道	23050801	中央空调
东莞拓驰信息科技有限公司	莞城街道	23066666	通讯器材
东莞市美德石化产品有限公司	谢岗镇	87682025	化工产品
东莞市一君医药有限公司	高埗镇	81306988	中成药
东莞市溢源对外贸易有限公司	东城街道	22201203	各种商品的进出口业务及代理
东莞市银洲燃料有限公司	中堂镇	88181366	煤炭
东莞市万和化工有限公司	万江街道	22273288	洗涤原料用品
东莞市毅达纺织品有限公司	寮步镇	83232555	纺织品
东莞市同兴涂料有限公司	高埗镇	88739118	二甲苯
东莞市伟明贸易有限公司	南城街道	23033918	泡棉全棉涂色布
广东文一朝阳集团有限公司	道滘镇	88327222	报刊
广东省东莞化工进出口有限公司	莞城街道	22231118	进出口代理
东莞福鸿纺织贸易有限公司	莞城街道	22503832	出口服装
东莞市中堂废旧物资回收有限公司中联分公司	中堂镇	88120732	废纸收购
东莞市健宝塑胶化工有限公司	黄江镇	86918999	塑胶
东莞市中堂废旧物资回收有限公司同力分公司	中堂镇	88120732	废纸收购
东莞市智丰贸易有限公司	大朗镇	83015809	服装
东莞市祥兴针车有限公司	石龙镇	86882006	缝纫、整烫设备、服装配料等
东莞市科裕钢铁贸易有限公司	沙田镇	88867777	钢材
东莞市华银贸易有限公司	道滘镇	88311866	煤炭
东莞市天昌塑胶原料有限公司	常平镇	86992933	塑胶原料
东莞市东建浆纸有限公司	莞城街道	22623930	纸张
东莞市永祥贸易有限公司	大岭山镇	85787618	燃料油
东莞市宇阳科技发展有限公司	凤岗镇	87507866	电容
东莞市中堂废旧物资回收有限公司银洲分公司	中堂镇	88120732	废纸收购
广东省东莞纺织品进出口有限公司	莞城街道	22233804	服装进出口
东莞市东宇化工有限公司	麻涌镇	88228828	碱
东莞市仲源化工有限公司	谢岗镇	82528528	化工产品
东莞市文成酒业有限公司	东城街道	22110939	酒类
东莞市诚昌纸业有限公司	长安镇	85311598	文具
东莞市恒泰石油制品贸易有限公司	长安镇	85322068	重油
东莞市德利石油化工有限公司	松山湖	85516299	石油及制品
东莞市金马经贸有限公司	莞城街道	22307188	进出口代理
东莞市凯盈贸易有限公司	南城街道	23188808	机电产品
东莞市建筑材料进出口有限公司	莞城街道	22816022	鞋帽
东莞市宝信实业有限公司	高埗镇	88731100	服装
东莞市泰昌石油化工贸易有限公司	樟木头镇	87711232	罐装润滑油
东莞市东伟石油化工有限公司	望牛墩镇	88855108	油、仓储油、中转油
东莞市大洲进出口有限公司	大朗镇	83032998	服装
东莞市新元素能源有限公司	莞城街道	22761448	重油
东莞市凤岗东晟和电子工具有限公司	凤岗镇	87773289	五金产品

1-4 续表 30

(2012年)

单位名称	所属镇街	联系电话	主要产品(或服务)
东莞市鸿越实业有限公司	虎门镇	85261330	粉煤灰渣
东莞市正诚贸易有限公司	东城街道	22680808	进出口业务
东莞市富松机械设备有限公司	大朗镇	83200373	机械设备
东莞市东辉贸易有限公司	黄江镇	83364788	化工原料
广东省东莞市厚街供销社	厚街镇	85581485	日用百货建材
东莞市麒麟机械有限公司	莞城街道	22473938	轴承
东莞市中堂废旧物资回收有限公司建桦分公司	中堂镇	88120732	废纸收购
广东省东莞五金矿产进出口有限公司	莞城街道	22227420	进出口代理
广东省东莞国药集团有限公司	莞城街道	22337200	药品
东莞市建晖燃料有限公司	莞城街道	22348877	煤炭
东莞市建森废纸回收有限公司	中堂镇	88121098	废纸回收
东莞市基业能源有限公司	虎门港	22480768	水煤浆、研发及技术咨询
东莞市萃华商贸有限公司	桥头镇	83342322	贸易管理
东莞市亿阳信通集团有限公司	中堂镇	88813288	塑料ABS
国药控股东莞有限公司	南城街道	22036911	医药
东莞市加利石油产品有限公司	沙田镇	88689922	润滑油
东莞市银河废纸回收有限公司	中堂镇	88188108	废纸回收
东莞市拓顺贸易有限公司	莞城街道	23032773	五金配件
东莞市兴隆金属实业有限公司	万江街道	22770202	钢材
东莞市虎泰能源有限公司	虎门镇	83817777	重油
东莞美的制冷设备销售有限公司	虎门镇	81518680	家电设备
东莞市明泰贸易有限公司	南城街道	22824398	国际商业贸易
东莞市瀚裕贸易有限公司	万江街道	2173993	服装
东莞市铭鼎贵金属有限公司	高埗镇	88876255	贵金属
东莞市恒镒钢铁有限公司	中堂镇	88189477	钢材
东莞市源来废纸回收有限公司	中堂镇	88117972	废纸
东莞市海天药品有限公司	东城街道	22608998	药品
东莞市兴盛废纸回收有限公司	中堂镇	88881402	废纸回收
东莞市虎门煤气有限公司	虎门镇	85111140	燃气
东莞市双丰废纸回收有限公司	中堂镇	88182628	废纸回收
东莞市瑞丰石油化工有限公司	松山湖	22893255	成品油产品
东莞市金汇废纸回收有限公司	中堂镇		废纸回收
东莞市博耐特精密模具有限公司	南城街道	88777000	模具及其五金配件
广东省东莞丝绸进出口有限公司	南城街道	22482892	服装
东莞市日之泉集团有限公司	中堂镇	88815015	五金钢材
广东鸿程油库有限公司	万江街道	88016809	石油及制品
东莞市天牛塑胶原料有限公司	常平镇	86998877	塑胶原料
东莞市永信药业有限公司	南城街道	22421165	中成药
广东铂利度能源发展有限公司	万江街道	22719554	重油
东莞市东普贸易有限公司	石碣镇	86604338	钢材
零售业			
东莞市华美乐建材超市有限公司	南城街道	22901188	瓷砖
东莞市南方汽车博览有限公司	樟木头镇	87707666	汽车
上海嘉定乐购生活购物有限公司东莞市虎门分公司	虎门镇	81613268	百货
东莞市渝州长安汽车销售有限公司	南城街道	23194316	汽车

1-4 续表 31

(2012年)

单位名称	所属镇街	联系电话	主要产品（或服务）
东莞市永怡汽车贸易有限公司	南城街道	22904057	汽车
东莞市永升汽车贸易有限公司	寮步镇	81128180	汽车
东莞市大通电脑有限公司	东城街道	23071386	计算机软硬件
东莞市华力冷气工程有限公司	莞城街道	23067567	制冷电器
东莞市怡安百货有限公司	长安镇	88612888	服装
东莞市金杯供销有限公司	南城街道	22409128	汽车
东莞市奇旺商贸有限公司	东坑镇	83887138	服装
东莞市顺利汽车贸易有限公司	寮步镇	83305998	商用汽车
东莞市常平石油供应有限公司	常平镇	83022221	汽油煤油
东莞市百力恒丰田汽车销售服务有限公司	长安镇	81603800	汽车
中域电讯连锁集团股份有限公司	南城街道	22888888	手机通讯产品
东莞市广物正安汽车贸易有限公司	长安镇	81608999	汽车配件
东莞市虎门镇嘉燃加油站	虎门镇	85110933	汽油
东莞市东城加成加油站有限公司	东城街道	22489229	汽油、柴油、罐装润滑油
东莞市东瑞汽车有限公司	南城街道	22905208	奇瑞汽车
东莞市桥南加油站有限公司	厚街镇	85882970	汽油
东莞市鸿泰汽车销售服务有限公司	厚街镇	89187788	汽车
东莞市聚成汽车技术服务有限公司	南城街道	22406200	汽车
东莞市和盛佳汽车销售服务有限公司	南城街道	22900106	汽车
东莞市鸿燕贸易有限公司	南城街道	23303318	汽车
东莞市志诚志远汽车销售服务有限公司	常平镇	83226599	克莱斯勒品牌汽车
东莞市车友汽车服务有限公司	寮步镇	83220559	奇端品牌汽车及售后服务
东莞市永奥汽车贸易有限公司	寮步镇	83261895	汽车
东莞市东达汽车有限公司	厚街镇	85935999	汽车
东莞市津丰汽车贸易有限公司	寮步镇	83030313	国产汽车
东莞市英利数控设备有限公司	长安镇	85317431	数控设备
东莞市厚龙燃气有限公司	厚街镇	85817336	液化石油气
东莞市丰华汽车销售服务有限公司	樟木头镇	87193088	汽车
东莞市大朗镇松木山加油站	大朗镇	83128021	汽油、柴油
东莞市东富实业有限公司	寮步镇	83220559	汽车
中海油销售深圳有限公司东莞大朗加油站	大朗镇	83191686	汽油、柴油
东莞市南城海雅百货有限公司	南城街道	23027222	服装
东莞市万昌燃气有限公司	凤岗镇	87510100	生活用燃料
东莞市常平供销社	常平镇	83331117	超级市场
广东省东莞国药集团虎门医药有限公司	虎门镇	85511364	药品
东莞市大兴汽车贸易有限公司	东城街道	22662646	汽车
东莞市寮步横坑加油站有限公司	寮步镇	83301011	汽油
东莞市东鑫汽车销售服务有限公司	塘厦镇	82089077	汽车
东莞市冠骏汽车销售服务有限公司	寮步镇	83230777	汽车
深圳市国美电器有限公司东莞市分公司	莞城街道	22807391	家用电器
东莞市志和汽车销售服务有限公司	寮步镇	81103801	汽车
东莞龙华丰田汽车销售服务有限公司	万江街道	22773388	汽车
东莞市志祥汽车销售服务有限公司	寮步镇	83226530	汽车
东莞市遂通汽车销售服务有限公司	南城街道	22850555	汽车
东莞市凤岗中深天堂围加油站	凤岗镇	87759638	柴油

1-4 续表 32

(2012年)

单位名称	所属镇街	联系电话	主要产品（或服务）
东莞市永丰行汽车服务有限公司	东城街道	22656866	汽车服务
东莞市金美汽车销售服务有限公司	常平镇	83553927	汽车
东莞市通利华汽车贸易有限公司	寮步镇	83260006	东风微型汽车
东莞市冠丰汽车有限公司	寮步镇	83525630	汽车
东莞市愉康超市有限公司	长安镇	85536488	百货
东莞市华康空调电器有限公司	莞城街道	22348888	空调
东莞市骏标汽车销售有限公司	南城街道	22850962	小轿车
东莞市黄江镇江南加油站有限公司	黄江镇	83629433	成品油
东莞市虎门石油公司虎威加油站	虎门镇	85109138	柴油
东莞市路通汽车贸易有限公司	寮步镇	83232099	商用车
东莞市东城中油柏洲边加油站	东城街道	22263969	汽油
东莞市天虹商场有限公司	莞城街道	22765287	百货
东莞市加仑石油化工有限公司	万江街道	88016889	润滑油
东莞市银星实业发展有限公司	清溪镇	87737539	汽柴油
东莞市宏宝汽车销售服务有限公司	寮步镇	81106028	汽车
东莞市年年丰粮油有限公司	东坑镇	82200455	食用油
东莞市福丰汽车有限公司	南城街道	22850001	长安福特品牌汽车
东莞市彩怡百货有限公司	莞城街道	22497688	百货
上海嘉定乐购生活购物有限公司东莞市常平分公司	常平镇	81896969	百货
东莞市大岭山联英加油站	大岭山镇	83351606	柴油
东莞市加南石油供应有限公司	中堂镇	88815477	油品、副食品、日用百货
东莞市常平木椈加油站	常平镇	83988331	机动车燃料
东莞市南城区加油站	南城街道	22417222	汽油
东莞市中堂镇东泊加油站	中堂镇	88885838	柴油
东莞市新东联汽车贸易有限公司	寮步镇	83527292	汽车
东莞市中维商贸有限公司	东坑镇	83887138	西装
东莞市黄江新奥燃气有限公司	黄江镇	82309398	天然气
东莞市常平石油供应有限公司陈屋贝加油站	常平镇	83391105	机动车燃料
中国石油化工股份有限公司广东东莞石油分公司	莞城街道	22506200	汽油
东莞市华隆加油站有限公司	松山湖	22367236	汽油、柴油
东莞市金实力油料有限公司	清溪镇	87737298	重油
东莞市永濠汽车销售服务有限公司	南城街道	22904888	汽车
东莞市大朗镇长塘加油站	大朗镇	83319244	柴、汽油、润滑油
东莞市嘉荣超市有限公司	南城街道	22808810	家用百货
东莞市昊安汽车有限公司	长安镇	85223818	汽车
东莞市东仁汽车销售服务有限公司	南城街道	86228588	汽车
东莞市合禾汽车销售服务有限公司	常平镇	82201168	丰田汽车
东莞市塘厦明华加油站有限公司	塘厦镇	87882837	成品油
广东省东莞市医药有限公司	莞城街道	22507881	西药
东莞市骏鸣汽车销售服务有限公司	寮步镇	81112813	汽车
东莞市渝庆汽车销售服务有限公司	寮步镇	83300138	汽车
东莞东风南方东益汽车销售服务有限公司	虎门镇	85133806	汽车
东莞市正欣科技有限公司	南城街道	22023588	软件设计
东莞市通益汽车销售服务有限公司	寮步镇	81191306	汽车
东莞市凯润东成汽车销售服务有限公司	寮步镇	82223988	广州本田品牌汽车

1-4 续表 33

(2012年)

单位名称	所属镇街	联系电话	主要产品（或服务）
东莞市永虹汽车贸易有限公司	南城街道	22985675	汽车
东莞市大参林连锁药店有限公司	南城街道	22884901	药品
东莞市君通汽车贸易有限公司	寮步镇	83226599	汽车
东莞家乐福商业有限公司	东城街道	22201897	百货
东莞市虎门镇东风加油站	虎门镇	85566666	汽油
东莞中汽南方汽车销售服务有限公司	南城街道	86225930	汽车
东莞东风南方大新汽车销售服务有限公司	东城街道	22672268	汽车
东莞市兴华燃料贸易有限公司	大朗镇	83132700	液化石油汽
东莞市大朗世达汽车有限公司	大朗镇	81116716	汽车
广州市好又多（天利）百货商业有限公司世博分公司	东城街道	22763201	百货超市场
东莞市聚星行汽车销售服务有限公司	厚街镇	82319818	汽车
东莞市东悦汽车销售服务有限公司	大朗镇	81069990	整车
东莞市永成加油站有限公司	厚街镇	85588949	汽油
东莞市中油西溪加油站有限公司	寮步镇	83327859	汽油
东莞市虎门威远加油站有限公司	虎门镇	85040678	机动车燃料
东莞市海雅百货有限公司	东城街道	22031333	百货
东莞市恒波商业连锁有限公司	大朗镇	83018679	通讯产品
东莞市南城丰田汽车销售服务有限公司	南城街道	22987090	汽车
东莞市新大地汽车贸易有限公司	莞城街道		汽车
东莞市同庆汽车贸易有限公司	寮步镇	89162688	汽车
东莞市桥头加桥加油站有限公司	桥头镇	22367236	机动车燃料
东莞市时尚电器有限公司	莞城街道	22342220	家用电器
东莞市广物正通达汽车贸易有限公司	寮步镇	83269019	长安品牌汽车
东莞市东城丰田汽车销售服务有限公司	东城街道	22019999	汽车
东莞市国贸超级市场有限公司	莞城街道	22117591	副食品
东莞市兴隆汽车贸易有限公司	寮步镇	82315618	汽车
东莞市和盈商贸有限公司	万江街道	22422218	日用品
东莞市骏丰汽车有限公司	寮步镇	83229371	汽车
东莞市会通汽车贸易有限公司	南城街道	22853998	汽车配件
东莞华多利汽车有限公司	寮步镇	83523000	汽车
深圳市海王星辰健康药房连锁有限公司东莞分公司	莞城街道	22366079	药品
东莞市天和商贸有限公司	樟木头镇	22508941	百货
东莞市汇天源汽车销售服务有限公司	寮步镇	83528753	汽车
东莞市星高达汽车销售服务有限公司	寮步镇	81105588	斯柯达品牌汽车
东莞市厚街涌口加油站有限公司	厚街镇	85050598	柴油
东莞市长久汽车贸易有限公司	东城街道	22663933	汽车
东莞市骏捷汽车贸易有限公司	厚街镇	83080019	东风本田汽车
东莞市石排燕窝加油站	石排镇	86524520	汽油
东莞市羚丰汽车贸易有限公司	南城街道	22981618	汽车
东莞市通力贸易有限公司	南城街道	22987359	饮料
东莞市华安加油站有限公司	东城街道	22298698	成品油
东莞市捷达通贸易有限公司	南城街道	22971218	汽车
东莞市汉阳电器有限公司	东城街道	22670397	电器
东莞市周通泰汽车贸易有限公司	常平镇	83333390	汽车
东莞市常平液化石油气供应有限公司	常平镇	83337820	液化石油气

1-4 续表 34

(2012年)

单位名称	所属镇街	联系电话	主要产品(或服务)
东莞市东奥汽车服务有限公司	寮步镇	83266998	汽车
东莞市顺昌贸易有限公司	凤岗镇	87755668	机动车燃料
上海嘉定乐购生活购物有限公司东莞市厚街分公司	厚街镇	88913888	百货
东莞市广物君豪实业投资有限公司	万江街道	22703999	汽车
东莞市中油迅兴实业有限公司	中堂镇	88885838	柴油
东莞市骏宇汽车贸易有限公司	南城街道	22851778	汽车及配件
东莞市东部丰田汽车销售服务有限公司	寮步镇	83285989	汽车丰田品牌车
东莞市三益汽车有限公司	寮步镇	83526653	汽车
东莞市长安乌沙长盛加油站	长安镇	85548808	石油
东莞市鸿鹰汽车销售服务有限公司	南城街道	22981108	汽车
东莞市南方亚飞汽车有限公司	樟木头镇	87193666	汽车、汽车维修
东莞市天下行丰田汽车销售服务有限公司	常平镇	83558216	汽车
东莞市中油国威油品销售有限公司	厚街镇	22022152	汽柴油
东莞市南城区农机服务站宏伟加油站	南城街道	22404202	汽油
东莞市同鸿汽车贸易有限公司	寮步镇	83030208	商用车
东莞市南菱汽车销售服务有限公司	南城街道	22909591	汽车
东莞市江铃汽车销售有限公司	寮步镇	83220527	汽车
东莞市合宝汽车销售服务有限公司	南城街道	22851228	宝马轿车
东莞市塘厦镇诸佛岭加油站	塘厦镇	87926329	机动车燃料
东莞市寮步农机加油站	寮步镇	82310777	汽油
东莞宝信汽车销售服务有限公司	常平镇	89306466	汽车
东莞市汇丰加油站有限公司	望牛墩镇	88552338	汽油、柴油
东莞市海川化工有限公司	樟木头镇	87139999	塑胶、化工原料等
东莞市东之捷汽车销售服务有限公司	寮步镇	88952999	汽车
东莞市亚太进出口有限公司	大朗镇		日用品
东莞市世沃汽车销售服务有限公司	寮步镇	81259999	汽车
东莞市坤华实业投资有限公司	万江街道		实业投资
东莞市南菱博通汽车销售服务有限公司	寮步镇	82392536	汽车
东莞市世奥汽车销售服务有限公司	南城街道	21688006	汽车
东莞市华熙汽车销售有限公司	寮步镇	81191508	进口汽车
东莞捷运行汽车销售服务有限公司	寮步镇	81118911	汽车
东莞市红彤汽车贸易有限公司	寮步镇	82871888	汽车
东莞市宝昌汽车销售服务有限公司	虎门镇	88629290	汽车
东莞市庄丰钢铁有限公司	洪梅镇	88438222	五金
东莞市深港钢铁贸易有限公司	洪梅镇		五金
东莞市跃宝钢铁贸易有限公司	洪梅镇		五金
东莞市永佳丰田汽车销售服务有限公司石排分公司	石排镇	81722166	汽车
东莞市曾光金属材料有限公司	洪梅镇		五金
东莞市骅宝汽车销售服务有限公司	厚街镇	89980000	宝马牌轿车
东莞市鸿众汽车销售服务有限公司	常平镇	81913972	汽车
东莞市宝瑞汽车销售服务有限公司	厚街镇	85037293	进口大众汽车
东莞市铸亿实业有限公司	洪梅镇		五金
东莞市贵和汽车服务有限公司	寮步镇	82819068	汽车服务、年审、季审
东莞市君尚百货有限公司	莞城街道	22765287	百货
东莞市实铭精密模具有限公司	清溪镇	87380221	精密模具

1-4 续表 35

(2012年)

单位名称	所属镇街	联系电话	主要产品（或服务）
深圳市华德石油化工股份有限公司东莞分公司	沙田镇	88866342	石油化工产品
中油碧辟石油有限公司东莞周溪加油站	南城街道	22403634	汽油
东莞龙华英菲尼迪汽车销售服务有限公司	寮步镇	82311999	汽车
东莞市塘厦新奥燃气有限公司	塘厦镇	82019831	燃气供应
东莞市粤美特加油站有限公司	大岭山镇	85780222	汽油、柴油润滑油
东莞市城区中穗加油站有限公司	莞城街道	22255930	汽油
东莞市兴华燃料贸易有限公司大朗高英供应站	大朗镇	83187988	液化石油气
东莞市美兴汽车有限公司	寮步镇	82316254	汽车
东莞市志诚汽车销售服务有限公司	寮步镇	83228331	汽车
东莞市广物东捷汽车销售服务有限公司	寮步镇	83269019	商用车（不含乘用车）
东莞市南天大新集团有限公司	桥头镇	89208888	超市百货
中国石油天然气股份有限公司广东东莞石碣新城加油站	石碣镇	86632870	汽车用汽油
东莞市新日和泰隆贸易有限公司	莞城街道	22489993	水果、食品
东莞市中昌贸易有限公司	大朗镇	81123383	汽车
东莞市骐骏汽车销售服务有限公司	樟木头镇	87711038	汽车
东莞市万江国威加油站	万江街道	22275846	机动车燃料
东莞市新天地汽车销售服务有限公司	寮步镇	83523008	汽车
东莞东美丰田汽车销售服务有限公司	塘厦镇	82087662	汽车
东莞市塘厦林村加油站	塘厦镇	87902608	成品油
东莞市龙成汽车销售服务有限公司	万江街道	22779999	汽车
东莞市新华利汽车贸易有限公司	寮步镇	81112303	吉利牌桥车
东莞市广泰汽车有限公司	虎门镇	85223301	汽车
东莞市博雅贸易有限公司	常平镇	81090360	长安福特品牌汽车
东莞市百丰百货商贸有限公司	石碣镇	81816888	用品、食品、生鲜
东莞市永佳丰田汽车销售服务有限公司	厚街镇	81691107	汽车维修
东莞市苏宁电器有限公司	莞城街道	22320266	家用电器
东莞凯润丰田汽车销售服务有限公司	虎门镇	85133988	汽车
广东省东莞国药集团长安医药有限公司	长安镇	85308840	药品
东莞市万里合众汽车经销服务有限公司	莞城街道	22337006	汽车
东莞市嘉祥通讯有限公司	南城街道	88777888	手机
东莞市华升汽车有限公司	虎门镇	85246601	汽车
东莞东风南方东升汽车销售服务有限公司	厚街镇	85089656	东风日产品牌汽车
东莞东风南方汽车销售服务有限公司	南城街道	22985916	东风日产品牌汽车
东莞市安信丰田汽车销售服务有限公司	大岭山镇	81870333	汽车
东莞市沪江五金有限公司	寮步镇	83526022	五金材料
东莞市合信汽车销售服务有限公司	南城街道	23188228	汽车
东莞市华美汽车销售服务有限公司	虎门镇	85017927	汽车
东莞市恒信汽车销售服务有限公司	东城街道	22767228	汽车
道路运输业			
东莞市储邦钢铁贸易有限公司	洪梅镇		道路货物运输
东莞市正泰运输服务有限公司	麻涌镇	88222278	货物中转
东莞市高步客运站有限公司	高埗镇	88706363	客运
东莞市畅安货物运输服务有限公司	洪梅镇		道路货物运输
东莞市新通运输有限公司	寮步镇	82812022	道路客运
东莞市华悦客运集团有限公司	莞城街道	27231596	小汽车

1-4 续表 36

(2012年)

单位名称	所属镇街	联系电话	主要产品（或服务）
东莞市嘉达快运服务有限公司	东城街道	22981833	货物快递
东莞东泰水泥有限公司	厚街镇	81694271	水泥
东莞市长城客运有限公司	莞城街道	22461975	公路客运
东莞市交通集团有限公司	万江街道	22701663	交通运输服务
东莞市飞马物流有限公司	黄江镇	86916838	普通货运
东莞市城巴运输有限公司	莞城街道	22492259	交通运输
东莞市汽车运输有限公司	莞城街道	22463079	道路旅客运输
东莞市公共汽车有限公司	莞城街道	22211806	交通运输
东莞市玖龙运输有限公司	麻涌镇	88234888	公路货运运输
东莞市裕鹏贸易有限公司	洪梅镇	81330009	道路货物运输
水上运输业			
东莞市虎门港集装箱港务有限公司	虎门港	88809999	货运港口
东莞市海昌船务有限公司	麻涌镇	86018810	货物运输
东莞市丰海海运有限公司	塘厦镇	87926329	港澳航线运输业务
广州港集团新沙港务有限公司	麻涌镇	82159033	货物装卸堆存
装卸搬运和运输代理业			
东莞市盛远报关服务有限公司	麻涌镇	82159347	报关服务
东莞市万高贸易有限公司	洪梅镇		运输代理服务
东莞市南城南方物流有限公司	南城街道	22986935	运输
东莞市三和物流有限公司	寮步镇	83214617	普通货运
东莞市德邦货运有限公司	南城街道	22907828	货运代理
东莞市一速百优货运代理有限公司	高埗镇	88700684	货运代理
仓储业			
中央储备粮东莞油脂直属库	麻涌镇	88236688	储备粮油管理
东莞市九丰能源有限公司	虎门港	88866301	液化石油汽及化工品的仓储
东莞市新溢泰谷物处理有限公司	麻涌镇	88231089	粮食中转输运搬运
中央储备粮广东新沙港直属库	麻涌镇	88231111	粮食储备
东莞市业荣威通贸易有限公司	洪梅镇	88431919	石化产品仓储
东莞市百安石化仓储有限公司	虎门港	88666030	化工品仓储
邮政业			
东莞市邮政局	莞城街道	22330782	特快专递等
住宿业			
东莞市厚街国际大酒店有限公司	厚街镇	85088888	餐饮
东莞市常平逸豪国际大酒店	常平镇	82828888	旅业
东莞市富盈酒店有限公司	厚街镇	85888888	餐饮
东莞市松山湖酒店有限公司	松山湖	22891234	酒店管理
东莞市尼罗河酒店有限公司	万江街道	22706666	旅游饭店
东莞市景福酒店有限公司	石碣镇	86366666	旅业服务
东莞市帝豪花园酒店有限公司	大朗镇	83122222	住宿服务
东莞市华南国际大酒店有限公司	东城街道		星级酒店
东莞市长安国际酒店有限公司	长安镇	85333333	餐饮服务
东莞市汇景酒店有限公司	洪梅镇	88848888	餐饮
东莞市太子酒店有限公司	黄江镇	83363333	住宿、餐饮
广东嘉华酒店有限公司	厚街镇	85928888	餐饮
东莞市樟木头三正半山酒店有限公司	樟木头镇	87799333	餐饮、住宿、娱乐

1-4　续表 37

(2012年)

单位名称	所属镇街	联系电话	主要产品（或服务）
东莞市华尔登国际酒店有限公司	桥头镇	81028888	住宿餐饮
东莞市名冠金凯悦大酒店有限公司	凤岗镇	87759888	饭店服务
东莞市悦莱花园酒店有限公司	寮步镇	81118888	餐饮
东莞市丰泰花园酒店有限公司	虎门镇	85708888	旅业
东莞市龙泉国际大酒店	虎门镇	85188688	餐饮
东莞市塘厦三正半山酒店有限公司	塘厦镇	87299333	旅游饭店
东莞市会展国际大酒店	南城街道	22889999	旅游饭店
东莞市昌明实业有限公司喜来登酒店	厚街镇	85988888	饮食服务
东莞市宏远酒店有限公司	南城街道	22418888	餐饮
东莞市石龙名冠金凯悦大酒店有限公司	石龙镇	86188888	酒店住宿
东莞市凯景酒店有限公司	中堂镇	88883333	旅业
东莞宾馆有限公司	莞城街道	22222222	正餐服务
东莞市汇华饭店	常平镇	83938888	旅游饭店
餐饮业			
真功夫餐饮管理有限公司	松山湖	38792952	快餐饮食服务
电信、广播电视和卫星传输服务			
中国网络通信集团公司东莞市分公司	南城街道	89826085	通讯服务
中国铁通集团有限公司东莞分公司长安营业厅	长安镇	86249800	电信业务
中国铁通集团有限公司东莞分公司	莞城街道	86272388	电话
中国电信股份有限公司东莞分公司	南城街道	22808888	固定电话服务
广东省广播电视网络股份有限公司东莞洪梅分公司	洪梅镇	88430100	有线广播电视传输服务
广东省广播电视网络股份有限公司东莞大朗分公司	大朗镇	83019778	广播电视网络规划建设等
广东省电信实业集团东莞市有限公司	莞城街道	22482870	电信业务
广东省广播电视网络股份有限公司东莞南城分公司	南城街道		广播电视网络规划建设等
互联网和相关服务			
东莞市传奇网吧	桥头镇		互联网上网服务
东莞市海潮网络服务有限公司	樟木头镇	87796897	互联网上网服务
软件和信息技术服务业			
广东力优环境系统股份有限公司	松山湖	23076888	冷冻空调
东莞市泰阳实业有限公司	虎门镇	85136389	计算机网络工程
货币金融服务			
中国工商银行股份有限公司东莞分行	南城街道	22481728	金融业务
招商银行股份有限公司东莞分行	东城街道	22303888	金融业务
广东发展银行股份有限公司东莞分行	莞城街道	22477888	金融业务
交通银行股份有限公司东莞分行	莞城街道	22505643	金融业务
中信银行股份有限公司东莞分行	东城街道	22667876	金融业务
东莞农村商业银行股份有限公司	莞城街道	22103131	金融业务
中国农业银行股份有限公司东莞分行	南城街道	23305742	金融业务
中国建设银行股份有限公司东莞市分行	南城街道	22816118	金融业务
东莞农村商业银行股份有限公司石碣西南分理处	石碣镇	86631724	金融业务
中国银行股份有限公司东莞分行	南城街道	22819888	金融业务
兴业银行股份有限公司东莞分行	南城街道	22809988	金融业务
东莞银行股份有限公司	莞城街道	22118010	金融业务
中国邮政储蓄银行有限责任公司东莞分行	莞城街道	22116366	金融业务
中国工商银行股份有限公司东莞厚街富怡支行	厚街镇	85596311	金融业务

1-4 续表 38

(2012年)

单位名称	所属镇街	联系电话	主要产品(或服务)
资本市场服务			
东莞证券有限责任公司	莞城街道	22119350	证券经纪业务
广发证券股份有限公司东莞虎门证券营业部	虎门镇	85521178	证券经纪与交易
保险业			
中国太平洋财产保险股份有限公司东莞分公司	南城街道	22807699	财产、车辆、人身意外险等
天平汽车保险股份有限公司东莞分公司	南城街道	22992063	车辆保险
中国人寿保险股份有限公司东莞分公司	莞城街道	22488488	人寿保险
中国平安财产保险股份有限公司东莞分公司	南城街道	23035258	财产保险
中国人民财产保险股份有限公司东莞市分公司	东城街道	22313601	人寿保险
泰康人寿保险股份有限公司东莞中心支公司	南城街道	22994019	人寿保险
中国大地财产保险股份有限公司东莞中心支公司	东城街道	22361158	财产保险
永安财产保险股份有限公司东莞中心支公司	南城街道	22996100	企业财产损失保险
中华联合财产保险股份有限公司东莞中心支公司	莞城街道	22605888	财产保险经营
中国太平洋人寿保险股份有限公司东莞中心支公司	莞城街道	22321518	各种人身保险
太平人寿保险有限公司东莞中心支公司	南城街道	23188161	人寿保险
中国人民人寿保险股份有限公司东莞市中心支公司	东城街道	22306285	人寿和意外伤害保险等
新华人寿保险股份有限公司东莞中心支公司	莞城街道	22498243	寿险营销
太平保险有限公司东莞中心支公司	莞城街道	22476688	财产保险
中国人民健康保险股份有限公司东莞中心支公司	东城街道	22328887	保险、保险咨询及健康管理
中国平安人寿保险股份有限公司东莞中心支公司	南城街道	21683205	人寿保险
阳光人寿保险股份有限公司东莞中心支公司	南城街道	88981959	人寿保险
其他金融业			
东莞农村商业银行股份有限公司樟木头支行	樟木头镇	87719188	金融服务
东莞信托有限公司	莞城街道	22366101	信托业务
房地产业			
中惠熙元房地产集团有限公司	东城街道	22360398	房地产开发经营
东莞市丰源投资发展有限公司	莞城街道	23133138	投资房地产
东莞市沙田镇房地产开发公司	沙田镇	81522888	房地产开发经营
东莞市东沙港建设发展有限公司	中堂镇	88661823	房地产开发
东莞市三元盈晖投资发展有限公司	万江街道		房地产项目经营
东莞市瀚森房地产开发有限公司	横沥镇	81010511	房地产开发
东莞市金众房地产有限公司	南城街道	82922145	房地产开发经营
东莞市泰安房地产咨询服务有限公司	东城街道	22470531	房地产开发
东莞市丰泰建设房地产有限公司	虎门镇	85221133	房地产开发
东莞市新世纪丽江豪园商住开发有限公司	茶山镇	86409800	房地产开发经营
东莞市粤海村(单项)房地产开发有限公司	东城街道	22611621	房地产开发
东莞市中信康华房地产开发有限公司	南城街道	22482388	房地产开发
东莞市广源房地产开发有限公司	南城街道	22800222	房地产开发经营
中信华南东莞有限公司	东城街道	22482388	其他房地产
东莞市金泓地产有限公司	大朗镇	88286933	房地产开发
东莞市富怡房地产开发有限公司	厚街镇	85832206	房地产开发经营
东莞市捷利物业投资有限公司	虎门镇	85124488	房地产开发经营
东莞市金贤房地产开发有限公司	厚街镇	85936698	房地产开发
东莞市同方房地产开发有限公司	东城街道	22483998	房地产开发
广东宏远集团房地产开发有限公司	南城街道	22411028	城市综合开发
广东鼎峰地产集团有限公司	企石镇	86666016	房地产开发
东莞市中惠香樟绿洲房地产开发有限公司	樟木头镇	22360398	房地产开发

1-4 续表 39

(2012年)

单位名称	所属镇街	联系电话	主要产品(或服务)
东莞市深业房地产有限公司	南城街道	28055128	房地产开发
东莞市三正房地产开发有限公司	塘厦镇	87299333	房地产开发
东莞市石龙镇房地产公司	石龙镇	86116822	房地产综合开发等
东莞市龙泉房地产开发有限公司	长安镇	85112323	房地产开发
东莞市陶然居房地产开发有限公司	长安镇	85533868	房地产开发
东莞市雍景香江房地产开发有限公司	洪梅镇		房地产开发
东莞市中惠沁林山庄房地产开发有限公司	大岭山镇	85784666	房地产项目开发经营
东莞市长佳长安花园开发有限公司	长安镇	85338777	房地产项目开发
东莞市聚龙物业投资发展有限公司	石龙镇	86116908	物业投资、建筑材料
东莞市东田丽园房地产开发有限公司	常平镇	83989677	开发经营
东莞市黄河集团房地产开发有限公司	虎门镇	85222222	实业投资
东莞市丰泰华园山庄建造有限公司	虎门镇	85188896	房地产开发
东莞市龙泽实业发展有限公司	樟木头镇	85122611	房地产开发
东莞市新世纪科教拓展有限公司	凤岗镇	87555552	房地产活动
东莞市麻涌镇房地产开发公司	麻涌镇	88233288	房地产开发经营
东莞市碧水天源物业有限公司	大朗镇	83131976	房地产开发
东莞市致富物业管理有限公司	沙田镇	88868218	物业管理
东莞市富麟实业有限公司	凤岗镇	87568889	房地产开发
东莞市世纪城商住开发有限公司	南城街道	22983333	房地产开发
东莞市星河传说商住区有限公司	东城街道	22031328	房地产开发
东莞市万顺花园建造有限公司	东坑镇	83699833	房地产开发经营
东莞市聚豪名轩商住开发有限公司	石龙镇	86088001	聚豪名轩项目开发经营
东莞市万科物业服务有限公司	莞城街道	88013333	物业管理
东莞市永江集团有限公司	凤岗镇	87840888	实业投资
东莞市万科阳光房地产开发有限公司	常平镇	83916852	房地产开发经营
东莞市玉泉投资开发有限公司	凤岗镇	87508188	土地开发
东莞市盈丰房地产开发有限公司	厚街镇	85873818	房地产开发
东莞市松山湖房地产有限公司	松山湖	22892336	房地产开发
东莞市花样年房地产投资有限公司	寮步镇	81126988	房地产投资
东莞市新世纪房地产开发有限公司(领居)	大岭山镇	83053693	其他房地产
东莞市龙城房地产开发有限公司	石龙镇	82290028	房地产开发、装饰及设计
东莞市新世纪房地产有限公司	大朗镇	88237666	房地产开发
东莞市福都花园开发有限公司	大朗镇	83138085	房地产开发
东莞市樟木头镇物业管理公司	樟木头镇	87713517	物业管理
东莞市翠云轩房地产开发有限公司	寮步镇	22679733	其它房地产活动
东莞市商业中心发展有限公司	南城街道	22422888	房地产开发经营
东莞市塘厦镇房地产开发公司	塘厦镇	87722361	房地产开发
东莞市领居房地产开发有限公司	大岭山镇	83053692	房地产开发
东莞市利丰房地产投资有限公司	石排镇	86555829	房地产开发
东莞市新世纪怡岛花园商住开发有限公司	道滘镇	88638888	房地产开发经营
东莞市康联房地产开发有限公司	厚街镇	85753088	房地产开发
东莞市汇盈豪苑房地产开发有限公司	厚街镇	22388601	房地产开发
东莞市碧湖花园有限公司	常平镇	83981809	房地产开发经营
中信华南(集团)东莞有限公司	东城街道	22482388	房地产开发
东莞市山水雅居房地产开发有限公司	常平镇	82206266	房地产开发经营
东莞市合盛房地产开发有限公司	虎门镇	85705222	房地产开发

1-4 续表 40

(2012年)

单位名称	所属镇街	联系电话	主要产品(或服务)
东莞市合盛房地产开发有限公司	虎门镇	85705222	房地产开发
东莞市广盈服务有限公司企石分公司	企石镇	86666698	房地产开发
广东三正集团有限公司	桥头镇	82470333	房地产开发
东莞市山语湖房地产投资有限公司	常平镇	22032016	房地产综合开发等
东莞市尚峰物业投资有限公司	南城街道	22219180	房地产开发
东莞市清华居建造有限公司	南城街道	23121662	房地产开发
东莞市龙泰房地产开发有限公司	南城街道	22482388	房地产开发
东莞市星城国际房地产开发有限公司	寮步镇	26276301	房地产项目开发经营
东莞市中润投资实业有限公司	万江街道	28631999	房地产项目开发
东莞市盈盛房地产开发有限公司	石龙镇	22801111	物业投资、建筑材料
东莞市新通实业投资有限公司	南城街道	23013547	开发经营
东莞市华凯帝庭园开发建造有限公司	东城街道	22880098	实业投资
东莞市盈泰房地产开发有限公司	南城街道	22801111	房地产开发
东莞市凯沣房地产策划有限公司	东城街道	23110366	房地产开发
东莞市松湖居置业有限公司	松山湖	23013547	房地产活动
东莞市中信广场建造有限公司	东城街道	23282506	房地产开发经营
东莞市罗马假日房地产开发有限公司	寮步镇	22319555	房地产开发
东莞市常平房地产开发实业公司	常平镇	83334075	物业管理
东莞市新万房地产开发有限公司	塘厦镇	25568039	房地产开发
东莞市鸿海物业投资有限公司	清溪镇	87362291	房地产开发
东莞市昌明酒店管理有限公司	厚街镇	85988888	房地产开发
深圳市彩生活物业管理有限公司东莞江山花园分公司	黄江镇	82737277	房地产开发经营
保利(东莞)房地产开发有限公司	松山湖	82059383	聚豪名轩项目开发经营
东莞市光大房地产开发有限公司	东城街道	22986086	物业管理
东莞市长银房地产开发有限公司	塘厦镇	87287398	实业投资
东莞市德洲房地产开发有限公司	塘厦镇	82093666	房地产开发经营
东莞市篁城开发有限公司	南城街道	22113388	土地开发
东莞市高田房地产开发有限公司	万江街道	22386908	房地产开发
东莞市新世纪明上居商住开发有限公司	大朗镇	22306868	房地产开发
东莞市丰泰建设房地产有限公司(丰泰城)	寮步镇	85188701	房地产投资
东莞市深城投实业投资有限公司	万江街道	23185306	其他房地产
东莞市莞都可苑房地产开发有限公司	中堂镇	22211908	房地产开发、装饰及设计
东莞市新世纪润城实业投资有限公司	塘厦镇	88991899	房地产开发
东莞市东城区房地产开发公司	东城街道	22470531	房地产开发
东莞市东城区房地产开发公司	东城街道	22483788	物业管理
东莞市精英世家建造有限公司	南城街道	22413668	其它房地产活动
东莞市阳龙房地产有限公司	长安镇	88436188	房地产开发经营
东莞市新世纪房地产开发有限公司	东城街道	22382251	房地产开发
东莞市瀚森投资集团有限公司	莞城街道	22333488	房地产开发
东莞市丰盛房地产开发有限公司	南城街道	38786333	房地产开发
东莞市田禾房地产投资有限公司	莞城街道	23030787	房地产开发经营
东莞市大绿地房地产开发有限公司	清溪镇	87388810	房地产开发
东莞市天利房地产开发有限公司	南城街道	23190110	房地产开发
东莞市铭可达商住中心开发有限公司	莞城街道	22309112	房地产开发经营
东莞市凯东实业投资有限公司	大岭山镇	85609718	房地产开发
东莞市松山居置业有限公司	松山湖	22303989	房地产开发经营

1-4　续表 41

(2012年)

单位名称	所属镇街	联系电话	主要产品(或服务)
东莞市佳兆业房地产开发有限公司	南城街道	22801111	房地产开发
东莞市富通实业投资有限公司	万江街道	23290515	房地产项目开发经营
东莞市阳光海岸实业有限公司	虎门镇	81615333	房地产
东莞市世海房地产开发有限公司	石龙镇	22498499	房地产开发经营
东莞市振庭贸易有限公司	东坑镇	83699833	房地产开发、投资
东莞市盈锋房地产开发有限公司	莞城街道	22495555	房地产开发
东莞市幸福花苑开发有限公司	万江街道	23129388	项目开发经营
东莞宏远工业区股份有限公司	南城街道	22414228	开发经营工业区
东莞市桃源商住建造有限公司	松山湖	22986086	房地产开发
东莞市塘盛房地产开发有限公司	塘厦镇	87917238	房地产开发
东莞市丰华房地产开发有限公司	莞城街道	22629333	房地产开发
商务服务业			
东莞市沙田对外经济开发总公司	沙田镇	88689966	对外资用地办理立项
东莞市国际旅行社有限公司	莞城街道	22458168	旅业服务
东莞市盈丰报关服务有限公司	寮步镇	81100932	代理报关服务
东莞市瑞中会计税务服务有限公司石碣分公司	石碣镇	81812200	代理记帐
东莞市瑞翔旅行社有限公司	东城街道	88996666	旅业服务
东莞市山凉劳务派遣有限公司	桥头镇	82366539	劳务派遣服务
东莞市永特利实业投资有限公司	高埗镇	88878778	租赁和商务服务
广东华强三洋集团有限公司	塘厦镇		投资、管理属下企业
东莞市凯信知识产权代理有限公司	莞城街道	89810912	商标申请代理
东莞市新龙报关服务有限公司	寮步镇		代理报关业务
东莞市信鸿实业投资有限公司	南城街道	22408991	实业及企业投资、会计咨询等
东莞市五益劳务派遣有限公司	桥头镇	83428422	劳务派遣
东莞市博众劳务派遣有限公司	樟木头镇	82120282	劳务
广东凯顺律师事务所	桥头镇	82829123	律师法律服务
东莞市虎门镇资产经营管理有限公司	虎门镇	85522409	镇属资产产权的管理
东莞市南城区资产经营管理有限公司	南城街道	22417250	管理区属资产
东莞市中国旅行社有限公司	南城街道	22218288	旅游业
东莞市清溪对外经济发展有限公司	清溪镇	87732058	外引内联企业咨询
东莞市常平镇资产经营管理有限公司	常平镇	83331431	企业资产管理
东莞市松山湖工业发展有限公司	松山湖	22891044	房产管理
东莞市虎门名铺城	虎门镇	85113665	商铺管理
东莞市智能市场管理服务有限公司	清溪镇	87738170	市场管理
上沙股份经济联合社	长安镇	85547208	合作社经济管理
东莞市石碣镇石碣股份经济联合社	石碣镇	86632553	合作社经济管理
东莞市凤岗镇资产经营有限公司	凤岗镇	87759398	资产管理
东莞市南枫佳誉保险代理有限公司	南城街道	22995015	代理保险产品
东莞市桥头镇资产经营管理有限公司	桥头镇	83342135	企业管理服务
东莞市合鑫膳食管理服务有限公司	东城街道	23111916	膳食管理
东莞市石碣镇桔洲股份经济联合社	石碣镇	86332030	经联社经济管理
广东石东实业(集团)公司	沙田镇	88662678	仓储
东莞市虎门城郊供电公司	虎门镇	85527786	电力供应管理
东莞市塘厦镇资产经营有限公司	塘厦镇	82087792	资产经营管理
东莞市丰华集团有限公司	莞城街道	22629333	酒店投资
东莞市寮步经济发展总公司	寮步镇	83328387	经济贸易咨询

1-4 续表 42

(2012年)

单位名称	所属镇街	联系电话	主要产品（或服务）
东莞市华源集团有限公司	厚街镇	85928888	企业管理服务
东莞市石龙镇西湖股份经济联合社	石龙镇	86113078	合作社经济管理
东莞市鸿信实业有限公司	东坑镇	83383786	投资实业
东莞市长安镇综合市场	长安镇	85535310	农贸市场管理
城区资产办	莞城街道	22102722	政府内资产物业管理
东莞市长安镇咸西经济联合社	长安镇	85533868	合作社经济管理
东莞市沙田经济发展总公司	沙田镇	88861003	机构商务代理服务
东莞市大朗供电公司	大朗镇	83316187	电力供应管理
东莞市宏图工业开发公司	南城街道	22415322	宏图工业区内土地开发
东莞市高埗供电公司	高埗镇	88781518	电力供应管理
东莞市常平供电公司	常平镇	83399778	电力供应管理
东莞市寮步供电公司	寮步镇	81113608	电力供应
东莞市桥头供电公司	桥头镇	83341212	电力供应
东莞市东城供电公司	东城街道	22669826	电力供应管理
东莞市天纬企业管理咨询服务有限公司	莞城街道	22482678	劳务派遣
东莞市万通实业投资有限公司	东坑镇	83383786	投资实业
东莞市桥头镇邓屋股份经济联合社	桥头镇	83341073	合作社经济管理
东莞市南城区工业发展公司	南城街道	22415322	开办厂场业务
东莞市塘厦镇林村股份经济联合社	塘厦镇	87721501	企业管理咨询
东莞市石碣镇经济发展总公司	石碣镇	86631048	进出口服务
广东宏远集团有限公司	南城街道	22414228	经营和代理各类商品的进出口
东莞市横沥镇经济联合总社	横沥镇	83717663	企业管理咨询
东莞市长安镇霄边经济联合社	长安镇	81882222	合作社经济管理
东莞市寮步镇横坑股份经济联合社	寮步镇	83301024	企业管理咨询
东莞市桥头镇田新股份经济联合社	桥头镇	83341032	合作社经济管理
东莞市樟木头资产经营管理有限公司	樟木头镇	87188978	镇属资产产权管理
东莞市虎门镇北栅经济联合社	虎门镇	85551481	资产管理
东莞市桥头镇桥头股份经济联合社	桥头镇	83342308	合作经济管理
东莞市厚街经济发展总公司	厚街镇	85990333	物业租赁
东莞市集源资产经营管理有限公司	黄江镇	83633322	出租房屋
东莞康辉国际旅行社有限公司	莞城街道	22001168	国内旅游
东莞市万江区资产经营管理有限公司	万江街道	22273273	投资与资产管理
东莞市东城实业发展总公司	东城街道	22331385	实业投资
东莞市长安供电公司	长安镇	85313828	电力供应管理
东莞市桥光实业集团公司	桥头镇	83341012	外引内联企业的咨询
东莞市企石振华开发总公司	企石镇	86765688	外引内联企业的咨询洽谈等
东莞市望牛墩资产经营管理有限公司	望牛墩镇	88853008	镇属资产产权管理
东莞市清溪镇经济联合总社	清溪镇	87733292	咨询服务
东莞市虎门镇虎门寨股份经济联合社	虎门镇	85509032	合作经济管理
东莞市大朗镇长塘股份经济联合社	大朗镇	83318030	合作社经济管理
富盈集团有限公司	厚街镇	81568888	企业管理服务
东莞市虎门镇路东经济联合社	虎门镇	85567032	合作社经济管理
东莞市景鸿物业管理有限公司	莞城街道	22381011	劳务派遣
东莞市福临门企业咨询服务有限公司	石碣镇	86330555	代办企业登记
东莞市明煜管理咨询有限公司	南城街道	22408845	企业管理服务
东莞市新远高速公路发展有限公司	东城街道	22083200	投资

1-4　续表 43

（2012年）

单位名称	所属镇街	联系电话	主要产品（或服务）
东莞市群策外商投资服务有限公司	南城街道	22813652	企业登记代理咨询服务
东莞市凤岗供电公司	凤岗镇	87756877	电力供应
东莞市大岭山镇资产经营管理有限公司	大岭山镇	85788362	经济管理
东莞市石碣镇西南股份经济联合社	石碣镇	86632116	经联社经济管理
东莞市昌明实业有限公司	厚街镇	85598888	实业投资
东莞市石排供电公司	石排镇	86550387	电力供应
东莞市虎门镇南栅股份经济联合社	虎门镇	85561938	合作社经济管理
东莞市江南市场经营管理有限公司	中堂镇	88128088	市场管理服务
东莞市石碣镇发展实业公司	石碣镇	86631030	企业咨询
东莞市麻涌镇经济发展总公司	麻涌镇	88239336	管理服务
东莞市东城资产经营管理有限公司	东城街道	22331385	资产管理
东莞市松山湖控股有限公司	松山湖	22898178	产业投资
东莞市清溪经济发展公司	清溪镇	87366293	企业管理
广东智通人才连锁股份有限公司	莞城街道	87078157	人才信息咨询
东莞市凤岗镇雁田经济联合社	凤岗镇	87771631	合作社经济管理
东莞市虎门镇龙眼股份经济联合社	虎门镇	85553988	投资和资产投资
东莞市万江供电公司	万江街道	22788971	企业管理机构
东莞市中堂镇潢涌股份经济联合社	中堂镇	88881002	合作社经济管理
东莞市电化实业集团公司	莞城街道	22461466	实业投资
东莞市黄江供电公司	黄江镇	83361290	电力供应管理
东莞市桥头镇石水口股份经济联合社	桥头镇	83428823	企业管理咨询
东莞市长安镇长实发展总公司	长安镇	85310368	企业管理
东莞市中堂资产经营管理有限公司	中堂镇	88811116	镇属资产经营管理
东莞市大莹物业管理有限公司	虎门镇	85151566	市场管理
东莞市东坑镇经济联合总社	东坑镇	83889698	企业管理机构
东莞市中之进出口有限公司	南城街道	23182111	各类商品和技术的进出口
东莞市长安镇锦厦经济联合社	长安镇	85301960	企业管理
研究和试验发展			
东莞市万科建筑技术研究有限公司	松山湖	22890188	建筑技术开发
专业技术服务业			
东莞市清溪工业开发有限公司	清溪镇	87732058	工业开发
东莞市公路桥梁开发建设总公司	东城街道	22083269	规划建设公路桥梁
东莞市绿宝石景观建造有限公司洪梅分公司	洪梅镇	22403567	专业技术服务
科技推广和应用服务业			
东莞市方达环宇环保科技有限公司	长安镇	89998656	环保技术的开发转让服务培训
（日本）广濑感应科技株式会社东莞代表处	常平镇	82984991	其他技术推广服务
水利管理业			
东莞市万江区水利管理所	万江街道	22275920	水利工程管理
公共设施管理业			
东莞市家宝园林绿化有限公司	厚街镇	85088699	清洁服务
东莞市松山湖公用事业有限公司	松山湖	23306078	园林绿化维护
居民服务业			
东莞市青年国际旅行社有限公司桥头营业部	莞城街道	22239388	旅游
东莞市星光劳务派遣有限公司	桥头镇		劳务派遣
东莞市东保押运有限公司	寮步镇	83528016	贵重物品押运
东莞市大朗天域康体中心	大朗镇		公共浴室（桑拿）

1-4　续表 44

(2012年)

单位名称	所属镇街	联系电话	主要产品（或服务）
东莞市大华沐足保健中心	莞城街道	23010799	足浴保健
东莞市大岭山名星阁美发形象设计中心	大岭山镇	81883298	美发护理
机动车、电子产品和日用产品修理业			
东莞市卓越电子技术有限公司	寮步镇	83327999	家用电器维修
东莞市华东汽车维修服务有限公司	莞城街道	89776883	汽车维修
其他服务业			
（香港）弘阳国际贸易有限公司东莞代表处	虎门镇		业务联络
东莞市虎门大宁企业发展公司	虎门镇	85553188	办理开办厂场业务
东莞市塘厦林村工业发展公司	塘厦镇	87722262	外引内联企业的咨询及洽谈
东莞市桥供废品回收有限公司	桥头镇	83341037	废旧物资回收
教育			
东莞市新民实业投资有限公司	石碣镇	86638529	教育投资
东莞市东华小学	东城街道	22659823	初等教育
东莞市黄江镇中心小学	黄江镇	83601630	初等教育
东莞市东华高级中学	东城街道	22637808	普通高中教育
东莞市东方明珠学校	沙田镇	88685700	高中教育
东莞市东华初级中学	东城街道	22659333	初中教育
东莞市先进电脑横机技术推广中心	常平镇	89851116	咨询与指导
东莞市第一中学	东城街道	22666280	高中教育
东莞市通圣机动车驾驶员培训有限公司	高埗镇		职业技能培训
卫生			
东莞市南城医院	南城街道	22415129	非盈利性医疗服务
东莞市长安医院	长安镇	85531104	医疗服务
东莞市黄江医院	黄江镇	83636323	综合医院
东莞市茶山医院	茶山镇	86642066	基本医疗
东莞康华医院有限公司	南城街道	22823018	医疗事业服务
东莞广济医院	凤岗镇	87866333	医疗服务
东莞市樟木头镇石新医院	樟木头镇	87710449	医疗服务
东莞市桥头医院	桥头镇	81037663	医疗护理保健服务
东莞东华医院有限公司	东城街道	22333333	医疗服务
东莞市寮步医院	寮步镇	83321545	医疗卫生
东莞市东城医院	东城街道	22213790	综合医院
东莞市厚街医院	厚街镇	81529815	综合医疗
东莞市太平人民医院	虎门镇	85111525	医疗服务
东莞市石龙博爱医院	石龙镇	86118320	综合医院
东莞市光华医院有限公司	寮步镇	22668800	医疗、保健、科研
东莞市石排医院	石排镇	86556333	从事诊疗
东莞市企石医院	企石镇	86661371	综合医院
东莞市石龙人民医院	石龙镇	81368808	医疗保健
东莞市凤岗医院	凤岗镇	87510815	综合医院
新闻和出版业			
东莞日报社	南城街道	23126688	报纸采写编
广播、电视、电影和影视录音制作业			
东莞市桥头镇文化广播电视服务中心	桥头镇	83341352	文化
娱乐业			
东莞市滨河游乐有限公司	樟木头镇	82022562	体育和娱乐业
东莞市朝星娱乐有限公司	沙田镇	89360888	娱乐场

1-5 营业收入超5000万元的外资企业（2012年）

Foreign-funded Enterprises with Business Revenue over RMB 50 Million (2012)

单位名称	所属镇街	联系电话	主要产品（或服务）
农副食品加工业			
东莞兴业生物科技有限公司	东城街道	22652130	预混合配合饲料
东莞益海嘉里粮油食品工业有限公司	麻涌镇	88238760	饲料蛋白
东莞市飞亚达益富可华南油脂有限公司	麻涌镇	88230055	棕榈油精炼
岭南油脂工业（东莞）有限公司	麻涌镇	81210333	精炼棕榈油脂
东莞四洲肉类制品有限公司	高埗镇	81339710	禽类罐头
东莞欧陆食品有限公司	长安镇	86246898	西式肉类食品
金钱饲料(东莞)有限公司	麻涌镇	26898096	植物油
东莞嘉吉饲料蛋白科技有限公司	麻涌镇	88225888	豆油
中粮新沙粮油工业(东莞)有限公司	麻涌镇	88825601	豆油
东莞光华饲料有限公司	中堂镇	88817756	猪、禽、浓缩饲料
东莞顶志食品有限公司	麻涌镇	88238262	芝麻油
东莞嘉吉粮油有限公司	麻涌镇	88236732	豆油
食品制造业			
广东太阳神集团有限公司	黄江镇	83621288	保健养生营养食品等
东莞荣华饼家有限公司	石碣镇	86633692	月饼、蛋卷、曲奇
彩乐糖果(东莞)有限公司	常平镇	83552285	糖果
东莞福满多食品有限公司	麻涌镇	88230290	粮食制品
东莞波仔食品有限公司	清溪镇	82950888	速冻盒饭
东莞领驰食品有限公司	樟木头镇	82127116	味千系列食品饮料
东莞锦泰食品有限公司	南城街道	22400818	饼干
东莞万好食品有限公司	横沥镇	81016222	点心、食品
华嘉食品有限公司	南城街道	22464101	饼干
百利佳糖果玩具礼品(东莞)有限公司	石排镇	86533119	糖果、玩具
东莞徐记食品有限公司	东城街道	22259888	糖果
酒、饮料和精制茶制造业			
东莞捷荣食品有限公司	横沥镇	88971111	咖啡
可口可乐装瓶商生产(东莞)有限公司	南城街道	22401678	茶饮料及果汁饮料
东莞雀巢有限公司	南城街道	22404088	速溶咖啡
东莞日之泉蒸馏水有限公司	中堂镇	88815015	蒸馏水
广东加多宝饮料食品有限公司	长安镇	85331688	罐装加多宝
华润雪花啤酒广东有限公司	东城街道	88772999	啤酒
东莞石龙津威饮料食品有限公司	石龙镇	86625388	布丁、啫喱及葡锌乳酸菌饮料
金威啤酒(东莞)有限公司	松山湖	22898999	啤酒
纺织业			
东莞市立成针织有限公司	清溪镇	87316688	针织毛衫
东莞明海整染厂有限公司	道滘镇	38831553	棉印染、精加工
东莞中永纺织有限公司	洪梅镇	88841581	缝纫线、鞋材针织布
东莞合诚毛织有限公司	清溪镇	87386888	毛织品
东莞拔萃针织有限公司	常平镇	83399650	毛衫
东莞通盈纺织制衣有限公司	中堂镇	88188015	梳织布、针织布及成衣
东莞百宏实业有限公司	沙田镇	88745111	粘扣带、鞋带、反光材料等
东莞欣意医疗保健制品厂	黄江镇	83361381	医疗用品
东莞东美线业有限公司	道滘镇	88339333	缝纫线、涤纶短纤维线
东莞贰发毛绒有限公司	樟木头镇	87718080	静电毛绒

1-5 续表 1

(2012年)

单位名称	所属镇街	联系电话	主要产品(或服务)
得福(东莞)制衣有限公司	中堂镇	88121628	服装
东莞永联弹力织物有限公司	望牛墩镇	88852801	橡根带
海杰制衣(东莞)有限公司	虎门镇	85237905	针梳织服装
东莞南友运动用品有限公司	寮步镇	83268325	护具
东莞合迅服装设计有限公司	长安镇	86244388	针织化纤胸围
东莞勤达针织制衣有限公司	虎门镇	85013599	针织成品
东莞怡力制衣有限公司	横沥镇	81011666	服装
东莞念辉家饰用品有限公司	常平镇	83392366	桌巾
东莞升佳纺织有限公司	沙田镇	88860306	布匹染整
东莞福泰整染有限公司	道滘镇	88834068	布料整染
东莞台新纤维制品有限公司	清溪镇	87311541	汽车地毯
东莞广成线业有限公司	长安镇	85428511	织线产品
东莞三江汇聚服装有限公司	横沥镇	83721616	梳织服装
东莞明辉商标织造有限公司	樟木头镇	87797688	布商标
东莞永达利纺织有限公司	厚街镇	85588751	全棉针织布
东莞超盈纺织有限公司	麻涌镇	88231808	双拉布
东莞东兴商标织绣有限公司	长安镇	85545888	商标
宏达纺织(东莞)有限公司	塘厦镇	87982238	灯芯绒坯布、全棉坯布
东莞福井制衣有限公司	长安镇	85440871	服装
东莞南太时装针织有限公司	万江街道	87073200	丝针织服装
东莞方皓汽车配件有限公司	塘厦镇	87725576	索具、拖车绳、其他起重装卸设备
东莞乐升植绒有限公司	企石镇	86668899	棉、化纤印染精加工
远梦家居用品股份有限公司	厚街镇	85991010	床上用品
东莞碳盈复合材料有限公司	塘厦镇	82076301	炭纤维布
东莞立春纺织有限公司	沙田镇	88742007	粘扣带
东莞安居家饰有限公司	清溪镇	87306597	窗帘
东莞海星服装有限公司	长安镇	85300702	各类服装
东莞富山纺织漂染有限公司	洪梅镇	88841755	学纤维布、漂染针织布、梳织布
东莞南大时装针织有限公司	樟木头镇	87782971	针织毛衫
东莞嘉鹏纺织有限公司	麻涌镇	88826666	毛纺织
东莞虎门科艺纺织印花有限公司	虎门镇	85561798	丝绸印花
东莞百和织造有限公司	沙田镇	88862371	粘扣带
东莞德永佳纺织制衣有限公司	麻涌镇	88821738	棉、针织染整布
东莞联庆纺织有限公司	企石镇	86784606	棉、化纤纺织
东莞联达毛纺有限公司	横沥镇	83374688	毛纺织品
东莞沙田丽海纺织印染有限公司	沙田镇	88866583	印染布
东莞裕源织染有限公司	沙田镇	88863433	针织色布
东莞中联定型厂有限公司	虎门镇	88921118	针织布定型
广东联发毛纺织有限公司	东城街道	22262232	毛纱、混纺纱及毛织品
东莞宝达日用品制造有限公司	大朗镇	83311690	布手套
东莞润达弹性织造有限公司	厚街镇	85593366	织带
东莞联德毛纺有限公司	麻涌镇	88287782	羊毛纱
纺织服装、服饰业			
东莞亮智服装有限公司	寮步镇	83305288	梭织服装
东莞美商制衣有限公司	常平镇	22902688	服装

1-5 续表 2

(2012年)

单位名称	所属镇街	联系电话	主要产品(或服务)
东莞胜德织造有限公司	高埗镇	88738293	毛织品
东莞绰荣制衣有限公司	常平镇	83936788	针梳织服装
东莞邦西纺织制衣有限公司	茶山镇	88655083	针织服装
东莞星华制衣有限公司	万江街道	22179181	梳织服装
乐活制衣(东莞)有限公司	横沥镇	83729200	成衣
东莞茂志针织有限公司	大朗镇	83209838	针织服装
东莞市都市丽人实业有限公司	凤岗镇	86806666	服装
东莞嘉顺针织有限公司	寮步镇	81112666	针织毛衫
东莞高高制衣有限公司	高埗镇	88876660	内衣
东莞益豪时装有限公司	石龙镇	86618323	针梭织服装
东莞绰豪制衣有限公司	长安镇	85317168	服装
东莞中玉服装有限公司	常平镇	86997999	毛衫
东莞宝升制衣有限公司	长安镇	85549971	衣服
东莞盈富制衣有限公司	道滘镇	88838386	机织服装
东莞菲力制衣有限公司	高埗镇	88786698	各式内衣
东莞通威服装有限公司	凤岗镇	86808613	成衣
沛恒制衣(东莞)有限公司	石龙镇	86617980	胸围、内衣、内裤、睡衣、泳衣
东莞达生制衣有限公司	常平镇	83919226	泳衣
东莞精致针织有限公司	常平镇	86836260	各类服装
联业制衣(东莞)有限公司	清溪镇	87738280	衬衫、西裤
东莞宏大制衣有限公司	高埗镇	88468668	各类针织衣服
东莞永嘉盛针织有限公司	南城街道	22407788	纺织毛衫
东莞冠丽时装有限公司	石碣镇	86016001	服装
东莞福百威制衣有限公司	企石镇	86667111	棉衣、洗水休闲服装、童装等
东莞三骏时装有限公司	长安镇	85326098	针梳织服装
东莞联泰制衣有限公司	凤岗镇	86808117	服装
东莞宏宇制衣有限公司	高埗镇	88462208	针织服装
东莞励发制衣厂	厚街镇	85822228	T恤
东莞洋得服饰有限公司	寮步镇	83288888	手套
东莞众信制衣有限公司	道滘镇	88318125	机织服装
东莞时利制衣有限公司	虎门镇	85709662	服装
东莞澳思制衣有限公司	常平镇	83332225	毛衣及针梭织服装
东莞福怡服装有限公司	沙田镇	88666620	服装
东莞福泉制衣有限公司	沙田镇	88666698	棉针织服装
东莞天翔制衣有限公司	万江街道	88751099	梳织、针织服装
东莞达利盛时装有限公司	凤岗镇	87756188	服装
东莞光晖针织有限公司	大朗镇	83112278	针织毛衫
东莞成笑服装有限公司	高埗镇	88709991	服装
东莞忆凯制衣有限公司	大朗镇	83185898	全棉婴儿毛衫
东莞市东方叶杨实业有限公司	东城街道	22634282	羊绒衣服
东莞业基工业有限公司	常平镇	83915577	服装
东莞四海时装有限公司	虎门镇	85113514	服装
东莞高芬制衣有限公司	高埗镇	88876660	胸围
东莞润田服装工艺制品有限公司	石碣镇	86633899	儿童服装、用品、工艺品、玩具
东莞奇兴服装有限公司	东坑镇	83382968	服装

1-5 续表 3

(2012年)

单位名称	所属镇街	联系电话	主要产品（或服务）
东莞市小猪班纳服饰有限公司	樟木头镇	87125086	针织服装
东莞丰泰制衣有限公司	茶山镇	86179848	纺织服装
东莞市清溪立成针织厂	清溪镇	87316688	针织毛衫
东莞大明制衣有限公司	虎门镇	85192121	服装
东莞亿城服装有限公司	长安镇	85311107	各类纺织品服装
东莞胜丰针织有限公司	高埗镇	88879742	纺织服装
东莞励进制衣有限公司	厚街镇	85822228	针梳织服装
东莞富坊制衣有限公司	虎门镇	85159988	针织服装
东莞金巴伦服装有限公司	高埗镇	88738843	成衣、布料、拉链、线等
东莞晶苑毛织制衣有限公司	常平镇	83982212	纺织品
东莞德福制衣有限公司	常平镇	83335273	毛衣针织
东莞迅捷环球制衣有限公司	长安镇	85441918	服装
东莞世丽纺织有限公司	洪梅镇	88843806	全棉针织色布
东莞富阳针织有限公司	大朗镇	88603688	毛衣
东莞高文内衣制品有限公司	横沥镇	83792939	海棉、脯棉
东莞如成服装有限公司	虎门镇	88709991	针织服装
东莞茶山永联织造厂	茶山镇	88655088	婴儿服装
东莞东浩制衣有限公司	东城街道	22265009	梭织类休闲时装
联亚制衣(东莞)有限公司	凤岗镇	82081818	梭织服装
智诚国际(东莞)实业有限公司	万江街道	23175238	服装
东莞泰富服装有限公司	道滘镇	88830780	服装
东莞利来远东针织有限公司	南城街道	22851333	服装
东莞泉泰服饰有限公司	凤岗镇	86808062	衣服
东莞茶山增步成衣一厂	茶山镇	86869888	服装
东莞厚宏制衣有限公司	桥头镇	83341382	针织服装
皮革、毛皮、羽毛及其制品和制鞋业			
东莞裕祥鞋材有限公司	黄江镇	83364958	橡胶靴鞋
东莞卫仕手袋有限公司	厚街镇	85581084	手袋
东莞合雄鞋业有限公司	清溪镇	87734666	人造皮男鞋
东莞佳泰鞋业有限公司	寮步镇	83213089	皮鞋
东莞精博旅行用品有限公司	东坑镇	83695168	箱包
永捷手袋（东莞）有限公司	东城街道	22652968	箱包、手袋
东莞星骏手袋有限公司	塘厦镇	82093198	手袋
东莞成优鞋业有限公司	厚街镇	85583038	鞋类
东莞市百丽鞋业有限公司	虎门镇	86098888	皮鞋
东莞宝悦皮具有限公司	长安镇	85417333	皮制品
东莞美丽华鞋业有限公司	东城街道	88995100	鞋类产品、半成品
科赋尔设计（东莞）有限公司	东城街道	88999988	鞋类产品
东莞捷铃箱包有限公司	东城街道	88753068	手袋
东莞胜艺手袋有限公司	横沥镇	83739245	手袋
东莞裕盛鞋业有限公司	黄江镇	83363017	成品鞋
东莞协和鞋业有限公司	厚街镇	85595058	人革童鞋
东莞永信鞋业有限公司	厚街镇	85918310	运动鞋
东莞安阳鞋业有限公司	大朗镇	83318919	牛皮鞋
东莞欧非雅有限公司	望牛墩镇	88569688	真皮手袋、公文包、票夹

1-5 续表 4

(2012年)

单位名称	所属镇街	联系电话	主要产品（或服务）
东莞纬达皮革有限公司	洪梅镇	88841856	牛皮
东莞昌健鞋业有限公司	厚街镇	85581860	鞋类
东莞忠利手袋有限公司	茶山镇	86486422	手袋
东莞德州鞋业有限公司	长安镇	85531584	鞋
东莞大正鞋业有限公司	厚街镇	88633888	鞋
东莞胜乔鞋业有限公司	塘厦镇	87887018	各类鞋
东莞佳展手袋有限公司	高埗镇	88871735	手袋
东莞南华户外用品有限公司	洪梅镇	88849281	旅游背袋
东莞美商新力鞋业有限公司	寮步镇	83261991	运动鞋
东莞东禾鞋业有限公司	东城街道	22662588	鞋类产品
东莞好利包袋制品有限公司	塘厦镇	87906032	皮箱、包（袋）
东莞超丰手袋有限公司	东城街道	22627688	手袋
东莞胜百吉鞋业有限公司	长安镇	81608888	成品鞋
东莞声宝鞋业有限公司	厚街镇	82275500	鞋
东莞雅建工艺制品有限公司	塘厦镇	86957222	手袋
东莞龙门皮箱有限公司	虎门镇	88625888	箱包
东莞博励图鞋业有限公司	寮步镇	83266168	女鞋
东莞瑞恩鞋业有限公司	横沥镇	83733253	女装皮鞋
东莞朝冠鞋业有限公司	厚街镇	85588915	皮鞋
东莞麦斯鞋业有限公司	横沥镇	83375950	皮鞋
东莞瑞邦鞋业有限公司	横沥镇	83712518	女装皮鞋
东莞亮华鞋业有限公司	厚街镇	87013388	女装鞋
华台鞋业(东莞)有限公司	厚街镇	85917001	皮革鞋、靴
东莞建成鞋业有限公司	清溪镇	87734968	运动鞋
东莞大邦鞋业有限公司	石排镇	23066010	成品鞋
东莞时代皮具制品厂有限公司	厚街镇	85911900	手袋
东莞宏业制鞋有限公司	塘厦镇	86859812	运动鞋、皮鞋
东莞市怡捷手袋有限公司	望牛墩镇	88569888	手袋、钱包
东莞高登鞋材有限公司	道滘镇	88830578	塑料鞋
东莞恒辉鞋业有限公司	厚街镇	85594972	人造革运动鞋
东莞黄江宝亮鞋材厂	黄江镇	83367386	PU人造皮
东莞绿洲鞋业有限公司	厚街镇	85880975	女装皮鞋
东莞加能鞋材有限公司	南城街道	22400092	鞋材
东莞东昌鞋业有限公司	东城街道	23052402	运动休闲鞋
东莞兴泰鞋材有限公司	大岭山镇	85623238	鞋底
东莞澳利高太平洋手袋有限公司	常平镇	83824000	手袋
东莞长明复合材料有限公司	大岭山镇	85655922	鞋材、运动器材及其零配件
东莞中岳旅行用品有限公司	塘厦镇	87925791	运动防护用具、服装、箱包等
东莞华南皮革有限公司	茶山镇	86642187	轻革
东莞钜盛鞋业有限公司	寮步镇	83214345	皮鞋
东莞高埗裕元制造厂第一分厂	高埗镇	88874202	运动鞋、休闲鞋和慢跑鞋
东莞万鑫鞋业有限公司	南城街道	86226699	皮鞋
东莞莱得利皮具有限公司	虎门镇	85554590	皮具
东莞奥天奴皮草服装有限公司	企石镇	86786993	皮草服装
东莞力凯鞋业制造有限公司	厚街镇	85583101	运动鞋

1-5　续表 5

(2012年)

单位名称	所属镇街	联系电话	主要产品（或服务）
东莞福聚皮革有限公司	道滘镇	88326331	皮革鞣制加工
东莞市汉皇鞋业有限公司	横沥镇	83790019	鞋类
东莞环艺实业有限公司	东城街道	88755578	手袋
东莞卫仕皮具有限公司	道滘镇	88386228	皮箱、包（袋）
威华(东莞)鞋业有限公司	清溪镇	86816868	各类鞋
东莞源亨皮具制品有限公司	大朗镇	83312003	手袋
东莞金莹鞋业有限公司	厚街镇	85900471	皮鞋
东莞富程鞋业有限公司	东城街道	22265418	布面鞋
东莞雅威鞋业有限公司	塘厦镇	82061966	皮鞋
宏盛皮具(东莞)有限公司	东城街道	22665668	皮箱
东莞台昌鞋业有限公司	厚街镇	85980666	女装皮鞋
东莞富华鞋业有限公司	高埗镇	88788166	鞋类制品
东莞邦荣鞋业有限公司	厚街镇	85835991	各类鞋及鞋面
东莞台威运动用品有限公司	长安镇	85534587	运动鞋、滑板
东莞朗福皮鞋有限公司	谢岗镇	87761380	皮鞋
东莞汇博鞋业有限公司	厚街镇	85826256	成品鞋
东莞斯杰皮革制品有限公司	横沥镇	83375950	皮革及皮革制品
东莞颖龙皮件制品有限公司	高埗镇	88730366	皮箱
东莞朝代鞋业有限公司	厚街镇	85588915	皮鞋
东莞瑞辉鞋业有限公司	东城街道	22656056	女装羊皮鞋
东莞兴昂鞋业有限公司	大岭山镇	85631888	男、女高级休闲皮鞋
安迈特提箱(东莞)有限公司	大岭山镇	83356051	旅行箱包
东莞丽宝鞋业有限公司	道滘镇	86308999	皮鞋
东莞爱莉莎皮具有限公司	沙田镇	88868969	皮箱、包袋
东莞伯产合成皮革有限公司	麻涌镇	88820807	PU合成皮革
东莞台育鞋业有限公司	石碣镇	86323168	皮鞋、胶水鞋
东莞泰亿袋业有限公司	凤岗镇	87862228	皮箱
东莞永益鞋业有限公司	厚街镇	85825298	各类鞋
东莞星浩手袋有限公司	塘厦镇	87939288	各类手袋
东莞茂德塑胶制品有限公司	虎门镇	85015628	塑胶制品
东莞聚美手袋有限公司	长安镇	85374168	手袋
东莞裕元制造厂	高埗镇	88874202	运动鞋
东莞诚达鞋业有限公司	沙田镇	88806888	休闲鞋
东莞巨辉皮具制品有限公司	厚街镇	89988988	皮具
东莞大田鞋业有限公司	清溪镇	87732488	皮鞋
东莞邦胜鞋业有限公司	厚街镇	85835990	各类鞋及鞋面
东莞泽荣箱包有限公司	寮步镇	83228386	旅行袋
东莞庆桦皮具有限公司	洪梅镇	88840700	皮具手袋
东莞新桥鞋业有限公司	万江街道	22184688	橡胶鞋底
东莞嘉应制鞋有限公司	石碣镇	86631175	皮鞋
东莞威腾皮革有限公司	厚街镇	85080096	皮革
东莞利威鞋业有限公司	南城街道	22009999	成品鞋
东莞兆成鞋业有限公司	厚街镇	81693311	皮鞋
东莞鼎力鞋业有限公司	厚街镇	85586102	运动鞋
东莞捷希皮革制品有限公司	横沥镇	83731678	手袋鞋

1-5 续表 6

(2012年)

单位名称	所属镇街	联系电话	主要产品(或服务)
东莞宝基鞋业制造有限公司	厚街镇	85582985	鞋
东莞昌润皮革制品有限公司	望牛墩镇	88854078	皮革压花
东莞华宝鞋业有限公司	南城街道	22908300	鞋
东莞威霖鞋业有限公司	厚街镇	83093999	运动鞋
东莞宏国制鞋有限公司	虎门镇	85559400	皮鞋
东莞圣皇鞋材有限公司	厚街镇	81691206	鞋材
东莞飞达鞋业有限公司	桥头镇	83344547	运动鞋、皮鞋
圣马可(东莞)制革皮草有限公司	中堂镇	88124610	皮革
金进鞋业(东莞)有限公司	厚街镇	83085185	皮鞋
东莞绿扬鞋业有限公司	厚街镇	85876969	皮鞋及鞋材
东莞大森鞋材有限公司	厚街镇	85901546	鞋材
东莞旭冠皮具有限公司	东城街道	22251741	手袋
东莞永盛鞋业有限公司	厚街镇	85918310	运动鞋
东莞上杰鞋业有限公司	长安镇	81663185	鞋
东莞诠立鞋业有限公司	厚街镇	85992586	女装便鞋
木材加工和木、竹、藤、棕、草制品业			
东莞中南木业有限公司	黄江镇	83627777	木器、家具制品
亚泰(东莞)木业有限公司	大朗镇	83189106	木制礼品
合和胶板(东莞)有限公司	道滘镇	88381666	装饰防火胶板
耐帆包装工程(东莞)有限公司	大岭山镇	83784130	可折叠木包装箱
东莞乡源木器业有限公司	大岭山镇	83355145	纤维板、刨花板、原木大宗进口
家具制造业			
瑞丰木业(东莞)有限公司三中分公司	清溪镇	87310180	家具
东莞爱迪家私有限公司	大岭山镇	83051999	书架
东莞震兴家私有限公司	虎门镇	85551784	家具
东莞美时家具有限公司	塘厦镇	82031091	办公家具
东莞三发钢木家具有限公司	大岭山镇	85622137	餐桌椅
宇谦木器(东莞)有限公司	大岭山镇	85611718	家具
东莞崧崴电子科技有限公司	大岭山镇	86979988	木质家具
东莞汇川金属家具制造有限公司	谢岗镇	87767778	灯饰、家具、五金工艺品
世楷家具(东莞)有限公司	常平镇	82826209	办公家具
东莞厨博士家居有限公司	桥头镇	82825288	整体浴柜
东莞茂德木器钟业有限公司	大岭山镇	82789990	木质家具
东莞上丰家具有限公司	寮步镇	83221455	电视架
东莞瑞鸿家用品有限公司	洪梅镇	88385855	家具
励泰家具(东莞)有限公司	沙田镇	81697222	家具
东莞华新五金家具有限公司东坑黄屋分公司	东坑镇	83385013	五金家具
东莞谦华五金厂有限公司	长安镇	85537869	焊管、冷轧钢带等
东莞振德家具有限公司	大岭山镇	83359011	木制家具
东莞朝阳家俱有限公司	黄江镇	83621515	家具
瑞丰木业(东莞)有限公司	清溪镇	86810555	家具
东莞欣仪五金塑胶制品有限公司	桥头镇	83439116	五金塑胶制品、户外休闲旅箱用品
东莞源宝家具有限公司	清溪镇	87365898	餐椅
东莞群晔五金制品有限公司	厚街镇	85589170	烤漆家具、电镀家具

1-5 续表 7

(2012年)

单位名称	所属镇街	联系电话	主要产品（或服务）
东莞宜庆家具有限公司	东城街道	22632705	家具
东莞创达家具有限公司	桥头镇	83346406	咖啡桌
东莞豪文塑胶五金制品有限公司	清溪镇	87316206	办公家具
东莞威捷家具制品有限公司	塘厦镇	87943088	家具配件
东莞莱富家具有限公司	桥头镇	83432299	咖啡茶几桌
普林斯家具(东莞)有限公司	桥头镇	83455777	五金铁艺制品
东莞超信金属有限公司	寮步镇	83320898	铁制家具
东莞新兴钢具厂有限公司	高埗镇	88872618	办公家具
东莞琪创家具有限公司	黄江镇	83602123	家具
东莞柚隆木业有限公司	大岭山镇	83358666	木制家具等
东莞天山金属家具有限公司	寮步镇	83305743	金属家具
东莞承达木材制品有限公司	樟木头镇	87712640	木门
东莞米德兰五金塑胶制品有限公司	清溪镇	87312071	金属椅子
东莞宏展家具有限公司	桥头镇	83433133	家私
东莞雄伟木业有限公司	大岭山镇	83352804	木制家具等
东莞鑫固家具有限公司	大朗镇	83100350	五金家具
东莞雅克沙发有限公司	厚街镇	85087789	沙发
东莞永鹏家具有限公司	大岭山镇	85617546	家具
东莞诺华家具有限公司	道滘镇	88313444	木制家具
东莞益新家私装饰有限公司	大岭山镇	85658912	木制家私
东莞欧达家具有限公司	大岭山镇	83353408	沙发
东莞欣鼎五金塑胶制品有限公司	清溪镇	87338888	沙滩桌椅
东莞汉平家具有限公司	清溪镇	86814555	木制家具
东莞拓洋家具有限公司	桥头镇	83420011	木家具
东莞长欣电子科技有限公司	沙田镇	89985666	金属家具配件
东莞盛家家私制造有限公司	黄江镇	83663291	家具
京木木制品（东莞）有限公司	石排镇	86516096	木制家具
东莞富运家私有限公司	大岭山镇	83055888	家俱
东莞台升家具有限公司	大岭山镇	83355396	木制家具
东莞大欣家具有限公司	东城街道	23160288	沙发
东莞华欣木制品有限公司	寮步镇	83300835	木制家具等
优先家具（东莞）有限公司	东城街道	22691495	其他家具
东莞泰冠时钟有限公司	清溪镇	87730352	婴儿床
东莞巨千家具有限公司	石碣镇	86306168	铁制家具
东莞超艺家具有限公司	凤岗镇	87555491	家具和家具
亿丰（东莞 ）制帘有限公司	常平镇	83988300	木制百叶窗
东莞华新五金家具有限公司	东坑镇	83385013	五金家具制品
东莞迪信家具厂有限公司	厚街镇	85583448	木餐椅
富鼎木业（东莞）有限公司	大岭山镇	83357899	家具
东莞劲伟木业有限公司	长安镇	85414770	木器制品
东莞达艺家私有限公司	大岭山镇	83351335	木制家私、装饰材料
东莞宝峰金属制品有限公司	谢岗镇	87136078	铁制品、木制品
灿荣五金(东莞)有限公司	石碣镇	88488118	电视、喇叭架、音响
东莞明昌家俱有限公司	沙田镇	88687918	金属家具
东莞铭晋家具有限公司	东城街道	22653362	木质家具

1-5 续表 8

(2012年)

单位名称	所属镇街	联系电话	主要产品(或服务)
广东鼎盛家具有限公司	大岭山镇	83355351	家具
东莞明辉家私有限公司	大岭山镇	83351928	木制家具
东莞悦佳家具有限公司	万江街道	89028330	家具
名隆家具东莞有限公司	大岭山镇	85615322	餐椅
造纸和纸制品业			
伟兴纸业(东莞)有限公司	望牛墩镇	88559318	纸板
东莞永联工艺包装有限公司	长安镇	86064889	纸制品
东莞广发印刷钉装有限公司	道滘镇	88339316	书籍
东莞骏成纸业有限公司	凤岗镇	87505300	其他纸制品
东莞合意印刷有限公司	樟木头镇	87138221	纸制品
东莞天星纸品有限公司	黄江镇	83665636	纸板
东莞荣辉印刷有限公司	清溪镇	87321128	纸制品
东莞吉宝包装有限公司	寮步镇	82810888	彩盒
东莞市弘安纸品包装有限公司	凤岗镇	82100813	纸箱
广东大宝祥旺纸品包装印刷有限公司	洪梅镇	88498822	纸和纸板容器
东莞群盛纸品有限公司	虎门镇	85558520	纸箱
东莞华智彩印包装有限公司	清溪镇	82098710	包装装潢印刷品
正隆(广东)纸业有限公司	厚街镇	82273288	纸板
泓达纸业(东莞)有限公司	黄江镇	83633276	纸板
东莞耀晖纸制品有限公司	清溪镇	87732397	贺卡、精装书及所有纸制品
台华纸业(东莞)有限公司	塘厦镇	87885611	纸板
东莞勤和纸品有限公司	长安镇	85544224	纸制品
广东理文造纸有限公司	洪梅镇	88432168	造纸
东莞中兴造纸厂有限公司	道滘镇	88323518	机制纸及纸板
泓达包装纸品(东莞)有限公司	黄江镇	83360902	纸箱
东莞华成纸业有限公司	塘厦镇	87988111	纸和纸板容器
东莞天兴纸业有限公司	虎门镇	85700268	大型彩箱、纸箱、等包装产品印刷
东莞黄氏锦辉纸品有限公司	常平镇	82200732	纸板
东莞地龙纸业有限公司	麻涌镇	88234888	牛卡纸
东莞华南印刷有限公司	清溪镇	82098700	纸盒
东莞大华纸品有限公司	塘厦镇	87885611	瓦楞纸制品
新华柏纸品(东莞)有限公司	中堂镇	88110888	彩盒纸类包装用品
东莞骏佳纸业有限公司	樟木头镇	87712467	纸类制品
东莞万诚彩印包装有限公司	大岭山镇	83355238	纸张印刷包装，彩盒、彩卡
安姆科国际容器(广东)有限公司	寮步镇	83303343	包装纸箱
东莞天龙纸业有限公司	麻涌镇	88234888	牛卡纸
东莞江南纸业有限公司	中堂镇	88184305	包装用纸、瓦楞纸
东莞龙成纸业有限公司	大朗镇	81125111	瓦楞纸板
东莞顺诚纸品有限公司	中堂镇	88180388	纸板、纸箱及其他纸制品
东莞高昇纸品有限公司	塘厦镇	87983362	瓦楞纸品
东莞建晖纸业有限公司	中堂镇	88888363	涂布白板纸
东莞新丰印刷有限公司	凤岗镇	87752030	书、报、刊印刷
怡高纸品印刷(东莞)有限公司	大朗镇	83122188	纸箱
东莞顺益纸品制造有限公司	茶山镇	86641635	纸箱
东莞大新彩印纸品有限公司	清溪镇	87736060	纸制品

1-5 续表 9

(2012年)

单位名称	所属镇街	联系电话	主要产品(或服务)
永丰余纸业(东莞)有限公司	凤岗镇	87566668	高档纸
东莞瑞麒婴儿用品有限公司	石龙镇	88492212	成人、婴儿纸尿裤
东莞佳木纸品有限公司	横沥镇	83375868	纸板
东莞中世拓实业有限公司	厚街镇	85033228	数码打印纸
东莞正隆纸制品有限公司	黄江镇	83630032	纸箱
东莞海龙纸业有限公司	麻涌镇	88234888	灰底白板纸
东莞长安昌众造纸有限公司	长安镇	85534024	铜板纸
东莞忠柏彩印工艺制品有限公司	东城街道	22024071	纸浆
东莞谦泰纸业有限公司	长安镇	85537598	纸品
东莞金洲纸业有限公司	中堂镇	88181288	瓦楞纸、牛皮纸箱、板纸、白卡纸
东莞顺裕纸业有限公司	望牛墩镇	88560003	瓦楞纸
利丰雅高包装印刷(东莞)有限公司	大岭山镇	85630000	纸板、纸箱、啤盒等
东莞玖龙纸业有限公司	麻涌镇	88234888	牛卡纸
东莞建隆纸制品有限公司	黄江镇	83849909	纸和纸板容器
东莞洪通电脑绣花有限公司	塘厦镇	87722437	标签
东莞洛艺文具厂有限公司	桥头镇	83343998	相簿
坚碧包装制品东莞有限公司	大岭山镇	85780088	包装制品
东莞诚发纸品有限公司	塘厦镇	87886328	纸箱
东莞顺盈纸业有限公司	中堂镇	88812123	瓦楞原纸
永固(东莞)纸业有限公司	塘厦镇	87932383	纸箱
东莞浩文纸品有限公司	樟木头镇	87198718	坑纸
东莞振兴纸品有限公司	高埗镇	88871188	纸板
东莞理文纸品有限公司	中堂镇	88888168	纸板、纸箱
东莞理文造纸厂有限公司	中堂镇	88888168	纸及纸制品
斯默菲石东包装(东莞)有限公司	道滘镇	81331300	瓦楞芯纸
东莞台聚包装有限公司	长安镇	85353369	鞋盒、彩盒、卡牌等包装纸品
东莞进益纸品有限公司	凤岗镇	87758302	纸箱
东莞旭明纸业有限公司	大岭山镇	85615218	纸箱半成品
东莞大宝杰松印刷有限公司	洪梅镇	88844488	纸板、纸箱、包装装潢印刷品印刷
印刷和记录媒介复制业			
东莞信越聚合物有限公司	东坑镇	83699000	打印机橡胶滚轴
东莞中编印务有限公司	大朗镇	83314723	书籍印刷
东莞恒华印刷有限公司	清溪镇	89821895	纸箱印刷
安量彩印制盒(东莞)有限公司	长安镇	85415265	彩盒、贺卡、礼品盒、说明书等
东莞东平彩印包装有限公司	虎门镇	85555615	印刷、彩盒、彩卡、手工盒
东莞富阳彩印有限公司	厚街镇	85824620	彩盒
东莞派克奇包装有限公司	茶山镇	85585950	纸制品
永发印务(东莞)有限公司	大岭山镇	85650898	包装装潢印刷品
东莞市智源彩印有限公司	望牛墩镇	88556888	包装装潢印刷
东莞新扬印刷有限公司	东城街道	22259209	印刷成品书
东莞高绮印刷有限公司	大岭山镇	83355498	铭板
东莞佳艺包装制品有限公司	万江街道	22285667	彩色包装印刷品
东莞永洪印刷有限公司	樟木头镇	87711961	彩色纸盒
东莞明彩纸品有限公司	樟木头镇	87713003	纸袋、包装盒、说明书和坑纸板等
东莞隽思印刷有限公司	樟木头镇	87712112	彩色纸箱

1-5 续表 10

(2012年)

单位名称	所属镇街	联系电话	主要产品（或服务）
东莞杰福瑞包装印刷有限公司	虎门镇	86099000	包装装潢印刷
敬业（东莞）印刷包装厂有限公司	虎门镇	85551734	纸盒
光明（东莞）柯式印务纸品厂有限公司	虎门镇	85553368	彩盒
东莞恒业印刷制品有限公司	长安镇	85099366	包装装潢印刷
东莞冠文彩印有限公司	万江街道	22278166	纸板印刷
东莞晨光印刷有限公司	石排镇	86551928	纸张、塑料工艺商标印刷品
东莞新洲印刷有限公司	大岭山镇	85625222	包装印刷
东莞当纳利印刷有限公司	寮步镇	81126499	印刷服务
东莞明泰彩色包装印刷有限公司	长安镇	85326668	说明书印刷
东莞虎彩印刷有限公司	虎门镇	85252189	包装印刷品
东莞金杯印刷有限公司	常平镇	83394888	印刷书刊
东莞昌明印刷有限公司	大岭山镇	83356851	包装物
东莞永达彩印有限公司	道滘镇	88830968	印刷彩盒、说明书等
有余纸品（东莞）有限公司	大岭山镇	85630000	纸箱、纸板、彩盒
东莞市凯成环保科技有限公司	桥头镇	81027999	包装装潢印刷品印刷
文教、工美、体育和娱乐用品制造业			
东莞成乐电子有限公司	横沥镇	83713213	电子产品
东莞龙鑫运动用品有限公司	塘厦镇	86851318	运动器材
东莞保辉电子有限公司	塘厦镇	87727701	电子玩具
东莞桥头中星电器厂	桥头镇	83344504	电器配件
东莞塘厦童园玩具厂	塘厦镇	87913892	玩具
东莞贯新幼童用品有限公司	清溪镇	86818999	婴幼儿车及制品
东莞硕仕儿童用品有限公司	清溪镇	82038270	童车
东莞达宇运动器材有限公司	东坑镇	83882808	运动器材
东莞飞达玩具制造有限公司	桥头镇	83341136	塑胶玩具
东莞开达电子有限公司	中堂镇	88811559	玩具
东莞威赢高尔夫用品有限公司	长安镇	85389925	高尔夫球捍握把
东莞兴华玩具有限公司	石排镇	81818839	玩具
东莞银辉玩具有限公司	虎门镇	85551910	玩具
东莞鑫达玩具礼品有限公司	横沥镇	83375750	合金塑胶玩具
东莞塘厦保发珠宝首饰厂	塘厦镇	82621838	18K镶钻石首饰
东莞御丰文具有限公司	虎门镇	85154611	文具
东莞东发玩具厂有限公司	长安镇	85540413	玩具
安杰玩具（东莞）有限公司	茶山镇	81822333	玩具
东莞大扬运动器材有限公司	厚街镇	85594466	棒球
东莞宇源精密金属实业有限公司	黄江镇	86968798	金属工艺品
联志玩具礼品（东莞）有限公司	横沥镇	83737875	塑胶玩具
东莞华兴塑胶制品有限公司	清溪镇	87369935	塑胶电子玩具
东莞柏辉玩具有限公司	沙田镇	88861619	玩具
东莞联弘玩具有限公司	横沥镇	83376123	玩具
东莞键辉五金塑胶玩具有限公司	清溪镇	87739230	塑胶玩具
东莞冠贺运动器材有限公司	虎门镇	85551210	球类产品及用具
东莞宝柏新威玩具有限公司	东坑镇	83384113	玩具
展恒玩具电子（东莞）有限公司	石排镇	86655372	玩具
东莞富龙运动用品有限公司	塘厦镇	87813201	高尔夫球杆

1-5　续表 11

(2012年)

单位名称	所属镇街	联系电话	主要产品（或服务）
东莞南栅利高文具制品厂有限公司	虎门镇	85561878	五金文件夹
东莞源泰运动器材有限公司	塘厦镇	87722669	网球拍、壁球拍、高尔夫球杆
东莞太联运动器材有限公司	长安镇	85535757	曲根球中管、曲根球球杆
东莞建林实业有限公司	厚街镇	81560369	各种高档笔类产品及笔类零件
东莞凯元高尔夫用品有限公司	东城街道	22699619	高尔夫球袋
东莞宏溢塑胶玩具有限公司	大岭山镇	81879388	塑胶玩具
东莞顺联玩具有限公司	万江街道	22279238	电子塑胶玩具
东莞韬略运动器材有限公司	茶山镇	88658666	运动头盔
东莞大伟成记玩具有限公司	黄江镇	86963888	电子玩具
东莞好景塑胶制品有限公司	长安镇	85411083	汽车模具
东莞市乐福塑胶电子有限公司	大岭山镇	88968988	塑胶制品
东莞英德玩具塑胶电子有限公司	东城街道	22295251	塑胶制品
东莞大发玩具厂有限公司	长安镇	85315256	玩具
东莞巨佑体育用品有限公司	沙田镇	85582170	运动鞋
东莞峰达电子有限公司	中堂镇	88811559	玩具
伟易达（东莞）电子产品有限公司	厚街镇	85581806	电子玩具
东莞兴利玩具有限公司	石排镇	86516288	玩具
东莞仁景五金塑胶制品有限公司	长安镇	86064789	玩具
东莞冠越玩具有限公司	虎门镇	89968888	塑胶玩具
东莞大德电子有限公司	长安镇	85544242	各类玩具
东莞威保运动器材有限公司	寮步镇	88953278	运动手套、护具
东莞明月工艺美术有限公司	横沥镇	81010665	塑胶动漫制造
东莞超雅玩具有限公司	清溪镇	87312838	布绒填充玩具
东莞百进五金塑料有限公司	石碣镇	81382666	模具塑料玩具
明珠高尔夫制品（东莞）有限公司	清溪镇	87336186	高尔夫球
东莞虎门南栅国际文具制造有限公司	虎门镇	85561686	文具夹
东莞广声五金塑胶制品有限公司	长安镇	86061888	木制玩具
富国运动器材（东莞）有限公司	虎门镇	85252033	运动器材
东莞长安美泰玩具二厂	长安镇	85312683	塑胶玩具
高仕文具(东莞)有限公司	厚街镇	85585588	文具
东莞胜辉健身器材有限公司	清溪镇	82098838	训练健身器材
东莞盈利幼童用品有限公司	清溪镇	87736157	儿童三轮车
明安运动器材(东莞)有限公司	虎门镇	85555321	高尔夫球类用品
东莞安泰玩具有限公司	樟木头镇	87790368	塑胶玩具
长荣玩具(东莞)有限公司	清溪镇	87314418	玩具
东莞稳健高尔夫球用品有限公司	清溪镇	87739826	高尔夫球用品
东莞钜丰运动器材有限公司	凤岗镇	87758887	球拍
东莞华登塑胶制品有限公司	清溪镇	87387555	塑胶电子玩具
东莞怡迪电子塑胶制品有限公司	凤岗镇	87777708	塑胶玩具产品
东莞建力体育器材有限公司	清溪镇	87739848	高尔夫球具
东莞上泰高尔夫制品有限公司	塘厦镇	87919854	高尔夫球头
东莞旭科电子制品有限公司	塘厦镇	87932700	电子玩具
宝钜(中国)儿童用品有限公司	清溪镇	87893231	婴儿手推车
东莞德源塑胶制品有限公司	虎门镇	85566181	塑胶制品
东莞永湖复合材料有限公司	塘厦镇	82035151	棒球棒

1-5　续表 12

(2012年)

单位名称	所属镇街	联系电话	主要产品（或服务）
东莞利达运动用品有限公司	沙田镇	88806900	运动用品
锦美运动用品（东莞）有限公司	清溪镇	87333971	高尔夫球具
东莞易达文具有限公司	常平镇	81032000	文件夹类文具
东莞东耀玩具有限公司	虎门镇	81619866	塑胶及毛绒玩具
山打根实业(东莞)有限公司	万江街道	22272416	塑胶电子玩具
东莞祥兴玩具有限公司	长安镇	85541020	塑胶玩具
东莞西文商标织绣有限公司	长安镇	81767999	商标织绣
东莞龙昌数码科技有限公司	常平镇	86836266	玩具
东莞仁美玩具制品有限公司	大岭山镇	83051388	玩具
东莞登富鞋业有限公司	清溪镇	87736010	运动鞋
东莞宝熊渔具有限公司	塘厦镇	87722967	渔具
东莞浩昌实业有限公司	塘厦镇	87297780	电子玩具
东莞司贸文教赠品有限公司	厚街镇	85598898	文具
盛昌布艺制品（东莞）有限公司	望牛墩镇	88516028	塑胶电子、填充、无线玩具
东莞联欣运动器材有限公司	虎门镇	85259998	溜冰鞋
东莞康贝童车玩具有限公司	塘厦镇	87720591	童车
东莞镇扬玩具有限公司	清溪镇	87736471	玩具（电子塑胶）
东莞佳畅玩具有限公司	塘厦镇	86856166	塑胶玩具
东莞乐迪卡游戏机制造厂有限公司	虎门镇	85159455	游戏机、电子液晶体显示器
东莞玮丰实业有限公司	大朗镇	83319092	塑胶玩具
东莞华源玩具有限公司	东坑镇	88455176	玩具
东莞育童幼儿用品有限公司	塘厦镇	87925551	儿童推车
东莞富美高文具制品有限公司	清溪镇	87898682	文具
东莞广达塑胶制品有限公司	大朗镇	83318515	塑胶玩具
东莞普克运动用品有限公司	塘厦镇	87728352	运动用品
石油加工、炼焦和核燃料加工业			
东莞太平洋博高润滑油有限公司	麻涌镇	88823886	发动机油
东莞泰和沥青产品有限公司	沙田镇	88687798	普通沥青
东莞东交沥青有限公司	沙田镇	88807929	改进沥青
化学原料和化学制品制造业			
东莞新东方科技有限公司	黄江镇	83639068	硅橡胶
东莞宝丽美化工有限公司	常平镇	83392980	印染助剂
东莞高宝化工有限公司	常平镇	83392980	印染助剂
高宝化妆品（中国）有限公司	常平镇	83392980	护肤品
东莞市雄林新材料科技有限公司	道滘镇	86166013	TPU薄膜
东莞大宝化工制品有限公司	大岭山镇	83352051	涂料
东莞冠昱实业有限公司	东城街道	22258668	橡胶粒
东莞清溪联合橡胶制品有限公司	清溪镇	87896278	橡胶制品
东莞铧冠橡塑制品有限公司	厚街镇	85876868	复合橡胶
东莞誉展化工有限公司	凤岗镇	87509919	涂料油漆
东莞杜邦华佳高性能涂料有限公司	万江街道	22288858	涂料
东莞市优诺电子焊接材料有限公司	大岭山镇	85653068	电子焊接材料
东莞普立万氯乙烯聚合体有限公司	厚街镇	85878800	乙稀昱化合物
东莞中瀛涂料有限公司	茶山镇	86636630	丙烯酸清漆
东莞鸥哈希化学涂料有限公司	大朗镇	83317997	塑胶涂料

1-5 续表 13

(2012年)

单位名称	所属镇街	联系电话	主要产品(或服务)
阿克苏诺贝尔涂料(东莞)有限公司	大岭山镇	85630747	工业涂料
东莞毅兴塑胶原料有限公司	厚街镇	85588755	精色粉
东莞广丰兴塑胶有限公司	塘厦镇	87727051	塑胶色母料
东莞大洋硅胶制品有限公司	樟木头镇	87712088	硅胶制品
东莞大通电线有限公司	大朗镇	83132896	PVC塑料粒(电线接口用)
东莞大日化工厂有限公司	虎门镇	85556675	ABS粒
东莞瑞安高分子树脂有限公司	长安镇	85533620	聚丙烯树脂
集美化妆品(东莞)有限公司	樟木头镇	86905801	化妆品
鲁道夫化工(东莞)有限公司	高埗镇	88466888	纺织品助剂
东莞立茂化工有限公司	道滘镇	88330956	无机盐
东莞优立化工有限公司	塘厦镇	87727642	电泳涂料
罗门哈斯电子材料(东莞)有限公司	东城街道	86225511	增导电性盐
舒尔曼塑料(东莞)有限公司	桥头镇	83422777	工程塑料
东莞宏德化学工业有限公司	长安镇	85533620	丙烯酸酯、聚氨酯树和UV光固化树脂
东莞市爱粤金属粉末有限公司	道滘镇	88385804	环氧聚酯型粉末涂料
东莞宏石功能材料科技有限公司	沙田镇	88808241	树脂
广东银禧科技股份有限公司	虎门镇	88922988	PVL胶粒和阻燃ABS胶粒等
维布络安舍(广东)日用品有限公司	东城街道	22253908	合成洗涤剂
德家朗骆驼涂料(东莞)有限公司	凤岗镇	86801888	粉末涂料
日立化成工业(东莞)有限公司	茶山镇	86413898	线路板专用光致抗蚀工膜
东莞万泰橡胶有限公司	道滘镇	88833021	橡胶靴、鞋
田村化研(东莞)有限公司	石碣镇	88487888	锡膏、助焊剂、热硬化导电性粘合剂
欧利生东邦涂料(东莞)有限公司	茶山镇	81866000	化工涂料
银禧工程塑料(东莞)有限公司	道滘镇	38855188	初级形态塑料及合成树脂
东莞威威日用品有限公司	石碣镇	86632080	合成洗涤剂、洗衣粉
东莞扬泰电子有限公司	常平镇	83820380	橡胶件
东莞井上五金橡塑有限公司	沙田镇	88863344	印刷机部件
东莞英铭化工有限公司	常平镇	83919189	聚合树脂
东莞秉顺制漆有限公司	凤岗镇	86801888	油漆
东莞宏柏鞋材制造有限公司	万江街道	22176636	橡胶添加剂
东莞三星道达尔工程塑料有限公司	大岭山镇	82781999	尼龙塑胶
东莞丽利涂料有限公司	大岭山镇	83353187	钢、木家具涂料
益海(东莞)油化工业有限公司	麻涌镇	88238729	皂粒
东莞富宏塑胶原料有限公司	凤岗镇	87280088	PVC塑吸原料料
医药制造业			
东莞保斯医疗器材有限公司	凤岗镇	87756433	手腕固定套
化学纤维制造业			
东莞方德泡绵制品厂	寮步镇	88908889	海绵
东莞联丰巨川纤维膊棉有限公司	黄江镇	86914666	人造纤维制品
东莞东港化纤有限公司	东城街道	89505888	塑胶制品
橡胶和塑料制品业			
东莞金金碧电子有限公司	横沥镇	87574026	塑胶制品
东莞进升塑料制品有限公司	长安镇	85357081	CD袋
东莞冠晖塑胶制品有限公司	南城街道	22404249	塑胶充气制品
东莞黄江福泰塑料厂	黄江镇	83363017	鞋材

1-5 续表 14

(2012年)

单位名称	所属镇街	联系电话	主要产品（或服务）
东莞凡进工业模具有限公司	常平镇	81895181	塑胶模具
晋伦塑料科技（东莞）有限公司	塘厦镇	87929958	尼龙复合塑胶粒
亚化(东莞)胶粘制品有限公司	长安镇	85312270	胶粘带
东莞常平美泰塑胶电子制品厂	常平镇	83919988	塑胶配件
东莞良佳五金塑胶制品有限公司	塘厦镇	87725096	五金塑胶制品
东莞伟士塑胶制品有限公司	望牛墩镇	88853722	烧烤炉手拖车、水桶
东莞华宇塑胶制品有限公司	凤岗镇	87753066	其他塑料制品
东莞华庆塑料有限公司	东城街道	22295808	泡沫塑料
优利（东莞）塑胶材料有限公司	桥头镇	83453008	HIP胶粒
东莞善慕康科技有限公司	谢岗镇	82121900	手机外壳
东莞天盈塑料管材有限公司	洪梅镇	88438128	PE管材
东莞劲胜精密组件股份有限公司	长安镇	82288188	塑胶制品
东莞丰佳塑胶有限公司	厚街镇	85999799	PCC胶粒
东莞新亚华电子材料有限公司	石碣镇	86316960	电子绝缘材料
东莞亚锋电脑零配件有限公司	塘厦镇	87727888	橡胶电脑零配件
东莞贺捷塑胶有限公司	常平镇	83392512	旅行箱塑胶配件
东莞高埗彰元鞋材厂	高埗镇	88872837	鞋材
东莞荣泰塑化材料有限公司	茶山镇	86869211	PVC塑胶粒
东莞宇光鞋业有限公司	凤岗镇	87753066	其他塑料制品
东莞喜益塑胶有限公司	常平镇	83913222	过胶尼龙布
赫比(东莞)电子科技有限公司	长安镇	81886111	模具、塑胶制品
东莞康佳包装材料有限公司	凤岗镇	86202288	泡沫胶袋
东莞洲进电子塑胶五金有限公司	虎门镇	85724011	塑胶配件
东莞捷邦实业有限公司	大朗镇	81238666	模具
康扬塑胶(东莞)有限公司	长安镇	85305187	塑胶配件类
东莞联全鞋材有限公司	东城街道	22250887	鞋材塑胶
东莞保利文塑胶制品有限公司	常平镇	83989198	胶花
东莞宝狮塑胶五金制品有限公司	凤岗镇	87755030	塑料板、管、棒等
东莞三阳塑胶有限公司	凤岗镇	87515998	塑胶浴帘
东莞信柏塑胶有限公司	塘厦镇	82016888	塑料原料加工
东莞增立塑料制品有限公司	沙田镇	88680500	PVC人造革
东莞东锋达电脑零配件有限公司	塘厦镇	87987390	其他塑料制品
东莞市佑忠电子有限公司	塘厦镇	87886100	发泡胶
东莞亚华胶粘带有限公司	石碣镇	86316960	橡胶带
成行精密部件(东莞)有限公司	塘厦镇	87282609	精密部件
东莞井上高分子材料有限公司	茶山镇	86176861	聚氨酯橡胶
品翔电子塑胶制品(东莞)有限公司	石碣镇	86636668	电子塑胶制品
昌煜塑胶(东莞)有限公司	凤岗镇	87750453	塑胶产品
东莞衍青塑胶五金制品有限公司	清溪镇	87733701	水杯
东莞家宝生活用品有限公司	企石镇	86666668	塑料披覆、包装袋及铁制品
东莞莞井橡胶制品有限公司	塘厦镇	87925725	塑料零件
东莞伟嘉塑胶电子制品有限公司	麻涌镇	88232838	塑胶制品
东莞东洋塑胶制品有限公司	塘厦镇	87880688	精密塑胶模具
东莞百瑞立塑胶五金有限公司	长安镇	85414633	塑胶制品外壳
东莞仟麒塑胶五金有限公司	石碣镇	86317056	塑胶制品、模具五金配件

1-5 续表 15

(2012年)

单位名称	所属镇街	联系电话	主要产品（或服务）
东莞厚街创机塑胶制品厂	厚街镇	82728888	塑料制品
信国五金电子(东莞)有限公司	石碣镇	86316760	其他电脑零配件
东莞三和塑胶制品有限公司	常平镇	83392589	手握箱
东莞百信塑胶制品有限公司	桥头镇	83456081	塑胶制品
东莞高成精密注塑科技有限公司	黄江镇	83632679	工程塑料及塑料合金
鸿特利塑胶制品（东莞）有限公司	清溪镇	87738200	塑胶制品
东莞兴发玩具厂有限公司	东城街道	22201697	塑胶玩具
永塑（东莞）塑料有限公司	清溪镇	87331245	塑胶粒
东莞大岭山永盛玩具有限公司	大岭山镇	83352625	塑胶五金玩具
东莞航升实业有限公司	黄江镇	83668283	家用电器
东莞华心塑胶制品厂	凤岗镇	87775513	PVC袋
登迈塑胶(东莞)有限公司	大岭山镇	85613040	PVC吹气产品
东莞同成塑胶五金制品有限公司	茶山镇	86640256	塑胶五金配件
东莞大泰光电科技有限公司	虎门镇	85503858	照相机配件
东莞南星塑胶有限公司	樟木头镇	87713408	聚乙烯胶袋(筒)
东莞竞业塑胶五金制品厂有限公司	中堂镇	88812843	塑料餐具及厨具、餐桌等
东莞维鸿化工有限公司	桥头镇	83342979	聚素胶树脂成型粉
兆丰（东莞）制帘有限公司	企石镇	86716666	门框形百叶窗
东莞怡发塑胶制品有限公司	常平镇	83392238	电话充电器胶件
东莞塘厦三局建钛塑胶制品厂	塘厦镇	87911516	文件夹
东莞立新塑胶有限公司	石排镇	86658588	塑胶五金制品
东莞伟迪电子有限公司	高埗镇	88788261	塑胶配件
东莞泛昌窗帘制品有限公司	常平镇	8399789	塑胶百叶窗帘
东莞嘉德电子科技有限公司	桥头镇	83025777	塑胶配件
东莞大银塑胶制品有限公司	长安镇	85412001	塑料制品
东莞苏扬电器有限公司	常平镇	83391502	圣诞灯串
东莞富增泡棉塑胶有限公司	高埗镇	88462258	塑胶泡棉
东莞三洲物产电子有限公司	茶山镇	86178561	自粘胶纸
东莞荣光技研电子有限公司	桥头镇	83436463	开关
东莞依科聚合物有限公司	厚街镇	82275897	聚氨酯泡沫
东莞怡高塑胶五金电子制品有限公司	常平镇	83394988	汽车CD收放机
东莞鹏远塑胶有限公司	黄江镇	83638000	塑胶粒
东莞骆恒塑胶制品有限公司	清溪镇	87312310	精密成型钢模
东莞长安乌沙新永塑胶零件模具厂	长安镇	85548081	塑胶制品
东莞光群雷射科技有限公司	大岭山镇	85601301	镭射膜、烫金膜、镭射纸
东莞荣成塑胶五金制品有限公司	茶山镇	81811503	塑胶五金配件
东莞丽骏塑胶制品有限公司	塘厦镇	87811708	塑胶制品
东莞富利达塑胶制品有限公司	凤岗镇	87750770	PVC薄膜
金旺塑胶制品（东莞）有限公司	凤岗镇	87515170	窗帘配件
东莞三荣日化容器有限公司	茶山镇	86415046	塑料容器瓶
东莞嘉盈电子有限公司	厚街镇	85812455	电脑塑胶配件
东莞华通发泡塑料制品有限公司	企石镇	86789888	泡沫包装和薄膜
雄进塑料制品(东莞)有限公司	寮步镇	83320081	PVC造革
东莞绿树塑胶制品有限公司	东城街道	22765001	塑胶配件
新崧塑胶(东莞) 有限公司	长安镇	85079188	精密塑胶零部件、模具

1-5 续表 16

(2012年)

单位名称	所属镇街	联系电话	主要产品（或服务）
东莞颖利电子有限公司	谢岗镇	87769809	收录机机芯、耳机
东莞穗联包装制品有限公司	凤岗镇	87559119	塑胶瓶
东莞卓荣实业有限公司	东坑镇	83698138	塑胶衣架
东莞永捷塑胶制品有限公司	石排镇	86920526	塑胶玩具
东莞嘉多利塑胶制品有限公司	凤岗镇	87504968	PVC薄膜
中侨路易塑胶制品(东莞)有限公司	东城街道	22655287	塑胶袋
东莞景丰塑胶制品有限公司	长安镇	85412789	塑胶外壳
东莞康耀录像盒带制品有限公司	樟木头镇	87711691	录像带空盒
东莞新洋电子有限公司	茶山镇	86171021	手机外壳
东莞德宝发包装制品有限公司	塘厦镇	87721296	包装制品
中星婴儿用品（东莞）有限公司	石排镇	86652872	婴儿用品
东莞捷讯橡胶有限公司	企石镇	86724551	橡胶制品
诠立电子科技（东莞）有限公司	清溪镇	86814718	硅胶、橡胶、塑胶
东莞协宇塑胶制品有限公司	长安镇	85495868	塑胶制品
东莞顺兴电子有限公司	寮步镇	83039160	模具
东莞佑茂五金塑胶有限公司	谢岗镇	87686300	电脑五金塑胶配件
品基电子(东莞)有限公司	塘厦镇	87910231	电子元件及组件
星海丰电子有限公司	虎门镇	85196313	橡胶制品
东莞塘厦永东电子制品厂	塘厦镇	87903685	电子制品
希比希真空电子(东莞)有限公司	长安镇	82389200	数码相机零配件
东莞永佑电子胶带有限公司	望牛墩镇	88560201	电子胶带
东莞利富高塑料制品有限公司	石龙镇	86106920	塑料制品
东莞优威王电子塑胶五金有限公司	虎门镇	85701800	计算机用PC塑胶配件
东莞虎邦五金塑胶制品有限公司	长安镇	85544660	运动器材塑胚配件
东莞厚街溪头塑料厂	厚街镇	85599076	新塑胶粒
东莞辰泰实业有限公司	清溪镇	87737400	塑胶产品
东莞井上福坤五金橡塑有限公司	沙田镇	88804002	汽车内装饰材料
泰原塑胶制品(东莞)有限公司	石碣镇	86318157	连接器外壳
东莞山技光电科技有限公司	清溪镇	87388658	扩散膜
东莞宇光塑胶制品有限公司	凤岗镇	87753066	吸塑罩
东莞合旺塑胶颜料有限公司	凤岗镇	87758710	颜料塑胶鞋、ABS胶鞋、HIPS胶鞋
比安斯（东莞）热固性复合材料有限公司	桥头镇	83433844	热固性复合材料
东莞敬记容器有限公司	虎门镇	85151012	塑料制品
东莞好而优塑胶制品有限公司	塘厦镇	87949595	塑胶玩具
东莞华美人造皮厂有限公司	道滘镇	88839163	塑料人造革、合成革
睦龙塑胶(东莞)有限公司	长安镇	85395001	塑胶制品
东莞木村塑胶制品有限公司	沙田镇	88865581	打印机塑胶配件
港龙包装制品(东莞)有限公司	塘厦镇	87903336	塑料薄膜
东莞珂维斯日用品有限公司	东城街道	22089885	美容工具
东莞高富达塑料制品有限公司	东城街道	22636148	塑胶材料
东莞鸿华泡绵制品有限公司	清溪镇	87314688	泡棉
杰斯比塑料(东莞)有限公司	松山湖	88011818	发泡聚丙烯粒子EPP
海格五金（东莞）有限公司	石排镇	86920088	五金制品
东莞第一精工模塑有限公司	长安镇	85358671	各种精密塑胶件
东莞凯钛塑胶制品有限公司	东城街道	22622027	化妆品器具

1-5 续表 17

(2012年)

单位名称	所属镇街	联系电话	主要产品(或服务)
东莞怡昌塑胶制品有限公司	横沥镇	82320888	PVC硬质胶布
东莞普隆塑胶制品有限公司	石碣镇	88181588	塑胶地砖(软体)
东莞建航精密模具塑胶五金有限公司	寮步镇	81199678	塑料零件
东莞宝建鞋材有限公司	黄江镇	83631221	PU树脂
东莞吉田塑料制品有限公司	常平镇	83395533	机芯塑料件
东莞晨彩塑胶制品有限公司	樟木头镇	38957888	塑胶制品
东莞圣纪电子科技有限公司	塘厦镇	82616688	办公用品、塑胶壳
东莞日富纤维科技有限公司	常平镇	83813091	打字色带
东莞南部塑料有限公司	凤岗镇	87750023	打印机、复印机、塑料制品
东莞艾菲卡塑胶制品有限公司	洪梅镇	81202992	再生橡胶
东莞石碣联盛塑胶有限公司	石碣镇	86321416	塑胶粒(PVC)
大东大明(东莞)电子有限公司	常平镇	83825030	塑胶制品
东莞福仓鞋材有限公司	黄江镇	83368777	PU人造皮
东莞华高塑胶电子有限公司	凤岗镇	87754286	塑胶制品
东莞市意艾斯帝静电有限公司	东坑镇	81015393	手机保护膜
东莞新安和兴塑胶有限公司	长安镇	85538501	塑胶制品
东莞益德泡绵制品有限公司	塘厦镇	87811862	海绵制品
东莞南泰绝缘材料有限公司	塘厦镇	87911538	硅橡胶
东莞美都塑胶五金制品有限公司	洪梅镇	88557012	塑料零件
东莞金富包装材料有限公司	虎门镇	85182565	塑料制品
腾翔精密塑胶(东莞)有限公司	黄江镇	83368096	塑胶制品
东莞益卓电子科技有限公司	大朗镇	86263266	塑胶外壳
伟易达(东莞)塑胶制品有限公司	厚街镇	85581806	塑胶制品
东莞一化精密注塑模具有限公司	石龙镇	86186078	精密塑胶配件、五金配件、轴承等
东莞骏威电子制品有限公司	大朗镇	81119390	遥控门铃、PIR感应灯等
东莞天祥塑胶有限公司	东城街道	88990909	电视机外壳
东莞英树电子科技有限公司	中堂镇	86638757	塑胶制品
台翰模具制品(东莞)有限公司	长安镇	87087888	模具、电脑外壳
东莞汇景塑胶制品有限公司	长安镇	85546080	打印机塑胶外壳
东莞钨珍电子科技有限公司	谢岗镇	82126950	手机配件
东莞市翔和塑胶电子有限公司	黄江镇	83056968	塑胶制品
东莞友成精密模具有限公司	桥头镇	83457238	五金塑胶制品
东莞三联热缩材料有限公司	寮步镇	81120158	热缩套管
东莞卓越光像薄膜有限公司	常平镇	83395440	光像薄膜
东莞钱锋特殊胶粘制品有限公司	寮步镇	89160056	胶粘带
东莞日新塑胶制品有限公司	常平镇	83391824	塑胶机械件
东莞宝顺硅胶制品有限公司	清溪镇	82068800	日用塑料品
东莞永柏塑胶制品有限公司	桥头镇	82368088	饰物包装品
东莞骏伟塑胶五金有限公司	东城街道	22293199	塑胶制品
东莞三韩电子有限公司	谢岗镇	82111124	手机外壳
东莞盈彩塑胶电子有限公司	塘厦镇	87849988	塑料胶制品
关西毡子电子(东莞)有限公司	石龙镇	86117447	绝缘材料和液晶显示屏部件
东莞金百升塑胶电子有限公司	常平镇	83391096	塑胶制品
基利连塑胶工艺(东莞)有限公司	常平镇	83363868	PVC圣诞树
协隆(东莞)塑胶电子有限公司	塘厦镇	87916200	其他金属加工机械

1-5 续表 18

(2012年)

单位名称	所属镇街	联系电话	主要产品(或服务)
东莞南新塑胶制品有限公司	常平镇	83996222	塑胶玩具制品
东莞晋原电子有限公司	大岭山镇	85601899	塑胶制品、配件、新型显示器件
东莞联华鑫精密橡胶有限公司	万江街道	22709712	电解、电容器橡胶盖
东莞奇妙包装有限公司	大朗镇	83034888	塑料软包装(塑料袋)
东莞兴宝密封件有限公司	东城街道	22666410	橡胶密封件
东莞万善美耐皿制品有限公司	桥头镇	86936888	美耐皿制品
东莞誉铭电业科技有限公司	长安镇	85373322	塑胶制品
东莞汉星鞋材有限公司	东城街道	88772678	鞋材
丽宾电子通讯(东莞)有限公司	寮步镇	81112051	耳机线材
东莞钜升塑胶电子制品有限公司	长安镇	88611111	手机模型
富裕注塑制模(东莞)有限公司	横沥镇	83378570	塑胶外壳
东莞恒骏吸塑制品有限公司	长安镇	85350072	塑胶盖
东莞东洋佳嘉复合材料有限公司	东城街道	23116651	海绵复合品
东莞美哲塑胶制品有限公司	中堂镇	88181588	塑胶地砖
东莞远展包装制品有限公司	大岭山镇	83354716	发泡胶
东莞市安德固塑料包装物有限公司	东城街道	22259888	塑胶制品
东莞行特电子有限公司	清溪镇	87388642	连接器
东莞普能塑料科技实业有限公司	高埗镇	88735183	塑料再生胶粒
东莞太洋橡塑制品有限公司	樟木头镇	87197979	硅胶制品
晋德塑料科技(东莞)有限公司	塘厦镇	87929956	工程塑料
东莞隆捷塑胶制品有限公司	企石镇	86762711	塑胶制品
泽冠塑胶电子(东莞)有限公司	厚街镇	83086666	塑胶配件
东莞中央化学有限公司	企石镇	86788666	塑料包装容器
东莞玮锋电子包装材料有限公司	长安镇	85381227	塑料型材
非金属矿物制品业			
东莞南玻工程玻璃有限公司	麻涌镇	88288656	中空玻璃
东莞泰升玻璃有限公司	沙田镇	85557608	玻璃
东莞利冠光学电子有限公司	石碣镇	86387600	镜片、塑胶电子配件、特种玻璃
东莞市森泰玻璃制品有限公司	常平镇	81082261	玻璃制品
京瓷光电科技(东莞)有限公司	石龙镇	86186216	光学镜片、组装镜头、光学零件
信义光伏产业(安徽)控股有限公司东莞分公司	虎门镇	85266666	钢化及非钢化玻璃
吉城光学(东莞)有限公司	石龙镇	86109217	光学、研磨液晶玻璃、治具等
东莞泰广玻璃纤维有限公司	道滘镇	88384898	玻璃纤维
环球石材(东莞)有限公司	长安镇	85392177	石材
东莞金鲤水泥有限公司	麻涌镇	81206633	水泥
宏达光电玻璃东莞有限公司	大岭山镇	81625988	TFT-LCD显示屏材料
东莞鸿辉建筑材料制品有限公司	沙田镇	88868880	水泥预制件
东莞华润混凝土有限公司	道滘镇	88326100	水泥制品
信义超白光伏玻璃(东莞)有限公司	虎门镇	85266666	超白光伏玻璃
信义汽车玻璃(东莞)有限公司	虎门镇	85266666	汽车玻璃
东莞美艺宝玻璃制品有限公司	常平镇	83390685	玻璃马赛克
台玻华南玻璃有限公司	洪梅镇	88841000	浮法玻璃
东莞金晶铸造材料有限公司	洪梅镇	88841888	造制覆腊砂
东莞住秀电子有限公司	凤岗镇	87552682	钕铁硼磁铁
东莞华润丰诚混凝土有限公司	茶山镇	88326100	预拌商品混凝土

1-5 续表 19

(2012年)

单位名称	所属镇街	联系电话	主要产品(或服务)
信义汽车部件(东莞)有限公司	虎门镇	85266666	汽车玻璃
力美有机玻璃东莞有限公司	塘厦镇	87885398	玻璃纤维增强塑料制品
东莞普世饰品有限公司	桥头镇	81176666	塑胶
信义超薄玻璃(东莞)有限公司	虎门镇	85266666	玻璃
东莞艺华弧形钢化玻璃有限公司	桥头镇	83346884	玻璃
东莞华润水泥厂有限公司	沙田镇	88867510	水泥
广东可耐福新型建筑材料有限公司	麻涌镇	88222708	环保石膏板
信义玻璃工程(东莞)有限公司	虎门镇	85266666	建筑玻璃
东莞南玻太阳能玻璃有限公司	麻涌镇	88281785	光伏发电盖板玻璃
黑色金属冶炼和压延加工业			
东莞大雅电子科技有限公司	长安镇	85448999	光磁盘驱动器
东莞珂霓钢制品有限公司	长安镇	85417742	不锈钢棒
东莞璋泰五金制品有限公司	清溪镇	87734183	铁制品
东莞侨元金属制品有限公司	大朗镇	87080988	马口铁、电脑配件
东莞力雄五金电器塑胶制品有限公司	凤岗镇	82030633	电箱
东莞顶锋金属制品有限公司	常平镇	83394631	钢材
东莞宇新钢材制品有限公司	清溪镇	87313331	电镀锌铁(钢)板
广东澳洋顺昌金属材料有限公司	寮步镇	81112045	金属材料剪切
东莞华联有成实业股份有限公司	凤岗镇	87773483	钢材分条
东莞雄罐印铁制罐有限公司	寮步镇	83226869	马口铁制品、铁罐
朋胜五金制品(东莞)有限公司	清溪镇	88098988	冷轧铁板、热轧铁板
东莞三星钢材加工有限公司	大朗镇	81129215	电镀锌板、冷轧板、铝板等的深加工
东莞君雄精密五金制造有限公司	企石镇	86710187	钢铁铸件
东莞大洲钢铁有限公司	虎门镇	85557451	五金铁片
东莞川电钢板制品有限公司	长安镇	85543073	矽钢片
东莞住金物产金属制品有限公司	洪梅镇	88439668	铝材、钢材
合胜五金制品(东莞)有限公司	清溪镇	87383625	五金制品
有色金属冶炼和压延加工业			
阪和钢板加工(东莞)有限公司	茶山镇	81821038	电镀锌钢板
东莞东记金属制品有限公司	塘厦镇	87725811	高档建筑五金件
三铃制线(东莞)有限公司	常平镇	83395435	铜线
倍亿得热传科技(东莞)有限公司	横沥镇	83377088	电脑散热器
东莞同亚金属制品有限公司	塘厦镇	82081380	铜片
东莞沙田三和磁材有限公司	沙田镇	88866641	磁材制品
东莞雄福五金有限公司	横沥镇	83723390	数码相机零配件
东莞铁和金属制品有限公司	南城街道	22903361	镀钢板
东莞合立五金制品有限公司	虎门镇	85520161	家具、五金配管、铸铁管
东莞日线线缆有限公司	桥头镇	83344845	通信及电子网络用电缆
东莞钜弦电子科技有限公司	虎门镇	85248941	五金制品
东莞东钜有色金属制品有限公司	茶山镇	86402606	铝合金
东莞华艺铜业有限公司	常平镇	83918628	铜杆
同朋金属制品(东莞)有限公司	塘厦镇	87903150	铜带片
东莞新文钦金属有限公司	中堂镇	88810666	铝合金条
东莞东峰铝型材制品有限公司	塘厦镇	87913344	铝型材
东莞汉华金属制品有限公司	大朗镇	83188845	铜线

1-5 续表 20

(2012年)

单位名称	所属镇街	联系电话	主要产品（或服务）
东莞瑞城压铸制品有限公司	凤岗镇	87511225	铝合金制品
东莞泛亚金属制造有限公司	虎门镇	82888138	铝合金接头
东莞中瑞吉电工材料有限公司	桥头镇	83425961	铜型材料
元生有色金属(东莞)有限公司	寮步镇	38870288	铝合金管材
东莞华巨特殊线材有限公司	道滘镇	88389008	电线、电缆
东莞全良铜铝制品有限公司	虎门镇	85700075	铜制品
东莞新隆漆包线有限公司	茶山镇	86415025	漆包线
东莞铿利五金制品有限公司	樟木头镇	87790560	五金配件
东莞杜邦电子材料有限公司	南城街道	22852951	电子浆料
东莞佳得佳铝箔制造有限公司	黄江镇	83624698	电容器铝箔
东莞巨丰铜线有限公司	东城街道	22266314	漆包线
东莞升洋焊锡材料有限公司	谢岗镇	82126112	无铅锡制品
金属制品业			
东莞承光五金制品有限公司	厚街镇	85926110	五金零配件
东莞宜安科技股份有限公司	清溪镇	87737777	镁铝合金精密铸件
东莞普瑞得五金塑胶制品有限公司	沙田镇	88685118	五金塑胶
东莞盛泓五金塑胶制品有限公司	凤岗镇	87772450	塑胶五金配件
东莞以利沙五金塑胶制品有限公司	塘厦镇	87811756	五金塑胶制品
东莞科进实业有限公司	桥头镇	83458111	五金产品
东莞太阳茂森精密金属有限公司	塘厦镇	87929299	五金冲压产品
东莞番尔康金属制品有限公司	凤岗镇	86803388	五金制品
东莞马士基集装箱工业有限公司	麻涌镇	88826668	集装箱
美兴模具（深圳）有限公司东莞分公司	黄江镇	82300736	模具
东莞才誉五金有限公司	长安镇	81558628	五金配件
东莞捷润五金塑胶有限公司	凤岗镇	87751898	五金制品
东莞横沥田头百汇五金塑胶制品有限公司	横沥镇	83375520	五金配件
东莞浦和冶金有限公司	虎门镇	85150321	轴承
三铃金属制品（东莞）有限公司	麻涌镇	81206829	电镀铜线、电子产品表面处理
首屋尔金属（东莞）有限公司	茶山镇	86414346	五金制品
东莞特鼎五金电子有限公司	清溪镇	86814789	背板
东莞金旺儿童用品有限公司	清溪镇	87867219	婴儿车
东莞市瓦克精密金属科技有限公司	凤岗镇	81286888	五金件
东莞厚街创科五金制品有限公司	厚街镇	82722211	五金制品
东莞财迎电子有限公司	凤岗镇	87770958	五金电子零配件
东莞汉洋五金制品有限公司	长安镇	82762381	五金制品
宜欣塑胶（东莞）有限公司	桥头镇	83454355	其他金属工具
东莞八束易之美五金塑胶制品有限公司	长安镇	85412860	五金配件
东莞兴铜五金有限公司	清溪镇	87091803	五金制品
东莞兆隆五金有限公司	凤岗镇	87751742	铜线和铝线
东莞斯穆碧根柏五金制品有限公司	虎门镇	85191603	模块经营活动
自力钢构(东莞)有限公司	石碣镇	86310711	钢构房屋、钢构桥梁承建
东莞住商益安金属制品有限公司	沙田镇	88863093	剪切钢卷
东莞华震电器有限公司	寮步镇	83218666	喇叭金属零件
东莞亿量五金制品有限公司	大朗镇	81160085	线材
锌辉扬热浸锌(东莞)有限公司	沙田镇	88661928	热浸锌钢铁件

1-5　续表 21

(2012年)

单位名称	所属镇街	联系电话	主要产品(或服务)
东莞万顺昌钢铁制品有限公司	虎门镇	85520198	不锈钢片
新晟五金制品(东莞)有限公司	清溪镇	87733601	五金制品
东莞惠华金属制品有限公司	大朗镇	83188845	铜线
东莞四方技研五金制品有限公司	塘厦镇	87811636	精密冲模
东莞秀特电子有限公司	凤岗镇	87773572	磁石
东莞颖新五金制品有限公司	长安镇	85533709	金属钮扣
东莞建通电子五金有限公司	虎门镇	85565684	端子
东莞原创金属结构有限公司	沙田镇	88688080	金属结构制品
广东紫泉包装有限公司	东城街道	22679188	瓶盖
东莞维信五金塑胶制品有限公司	长安镇	85411861	金属家具加工
东莞华尔泰装饰材料有限公司	万江街道	22716312	铝塑复合板
永金金属材料(东莞)有限公司	长安镇	85330095	锡条
东莞川电电机有限公司	东坑镇	83020001	定子、转子
东莞日联精钢有限公司	塘厦镇	22203677	不锈钢螺丝
东莞信丰五金机械塑胶工业有限公司	长安镇	85411186	相机镜头连接垫
东莞富威钢铁分条有限公司	凤岗镇	87512068	钢铁剪切、分条
东莞精锐电器五金有限公司	高埗镇	88941998	金属制品
东莞升贸锡制品有限公司	虎门镇	85508193	锡制品
东莞益新实业有限公司	塘厦镇	87811000	电子零配件
威廉士制冷设备(东莞)有限公司	清溪镇	87313210	高身雪柜
东莞裕升薄板有限公司	沙田镇	88807688	镀锌薄板
东莞清溪光华制锁厂有限公司	清溪镇	87731333	锁具
东莞万成模具五金制品有限公司	高埗镇	88731998	电脑配件
东莞凤岗雁田财迎五金电子厂	凤岗镇	87770958	摄录机机芯
东莞东运镁业有限公司	常平镇	83500019	镁合金制品
允丰金属(东莞)有限公司	清溪镇	86987599	烤盘
东莞恒旺五金有限公司	横沥镇	83737616	冷板
东莞森永五金塑胶有限公司	寮步镇	83306579	五金制品
东莞伟腾五金塑胶有限公司	厚街镇	85599181	不锈钢餐具、厨具
东莞清溪鸿益五金厂	清溪镇	87732903	五金半成品
东莞翔腾金属制品有限公司	寮步镇	83036688	金属制品
东莞达成金属制品有限公司	虎门镇	85026632	电镀加工文具夹
美达王板和精密金属(东莞)有限公司	松山湖	22893015	各种电子、电器零件金属材料
日立金属(东莞)特殊钢有限公司	茶山镇	81869783	模具钢材
东莞鸿辉五金有限公司	塘厦镇	87933801	铁线
东莞虎门路东昌华五金制造厂	虎门镇	85561811	加工电镀五金文具夹
志联钢线钢缆(东莞)有限公司	长安镇	85312723	钢材加工
东莞泓创五金制品有限公司	塘厦镇	86855688	最脑散热器
东莞智信五金制品有限公司	塘厦镇	87925656	五金制品
东莞茂盈五金科技有限公司	清溪镇	82038300	五金制品及配件
东莞爱福赛保安制品有限公司	黄江镇	83631663	五金
东莞宝金山五金制品有限公司	清溪镇	82068588	五金制品
东莞旭升五金电子有限公司	高埗镇	81309888	五金配件
东莞保来得粉末冶金有限公司	大朗镇	83133077	轴承零配件
东莞宜成制罐有限公司	塘厦镇	87723456	马口铁制品、铁罐

1-5　续表 22

(2012年)

单位名称	所属镇街	联系电话	主要产品（或服务）
东莞智得电子制品有限公司	塘厦镇	87883069	五金厨具
大宝(东莞)模具切削工具有限公司	大朗镇	83182598	切削工具
东莞正荣金属制品有限公司	企石镇	86940999	五金制品
东莞唯可灯饰有限公司	樟木头镇	38819898	灯饰配件
东莞力群金属厂有限公司	麻涌镇	88826058	铁管
东莞宏兴金属制品有限公司	桥头镇	83344310	五金制品
东莞勤德五金制品有限公司	塘厦镇	87724469	计算机五金制品
东莞东盛金属喷涂有限公司	谢岗镇	87760198	喷涂
东莞盛新五金制品有限公司	企石镇	86769005	五金制品
东莞鼎翰铝制品有限公司	谢岗镇	87769786	铝制品
东莞佑能工具有限公司	洪梅镇	88848901	钻头、铣刀、端铣刀
东莞茂森金属冲压有限公司	塘厦镇	87933602	金属冲压件及组件
益龙建材（东莞）有限公司	东坑镇	83885678	轻型建材及配套产品
东莞冠德五金制品有限公司	横沥镇	83723626	冷扎铁、马口铁
东莞东旭金属表面处理有限公司	虎门镇	85565111	音响网、五金电镀制品
东莞济安塑胶五金制品有限公司	高埗镇	88870555	五金饰品
东莞世泉家电五金制品有限公司	东坑镇	83885906	五金制品
东莞建兴塑胶五金制品有限公司	凤岗镇	87753012	五金日用品
米亚精密金属科技(东莞)有限公司	凤岗镇	86802888	高档五金件
东莞顺传五金制品有限公司	清溪镇	87732273	自行车五金零件
东莞坤胜五金制品有限公司	虎门镇	85564158	五金配件
东莞精明五金科技有限公司	凤岗镇	87862898	五金配件
大量（东莞）五金制品有限公司	大朗镇	83110970	金属丝
东莞海金杜门五金制品有限公司	南城街道	22401768	特殊五金冲压件
东莞星志厨具厂有限公司	石碣镇	86634017	厨具
东莞爱可玛金属线有限公司	大朗镇		铜线
东莞金基金属有限公司	虎门镇	85566550	电镀锌铁片
通用设备制造业			
东莞耐力五金配件有限公司	长安镇	85338531	铁螺丝
东莞台一盈拓科技股份有限公司	横沥镇	83798101	金属切削机床
雅美金属制品（东莞）有限公司	大朗镇	83127272	电脑机箱
东莞台端电子有限公司	长安镇	85419090	各种端子
东莞鸿达机械工业有限公司	道滘镇	88313008	机床
东莞百乐仕汽车精密配件有限公司	塘厦镇	87987779	汽车专用配件
堂盛机械（东莞）有限公司	谢岗镇	87130055	机械及五金配套件等
东英精密轴承(东莞)有限公司	沙田镇	88666101	打印机配件
京瓷办公设备科技（东莞）有限公司	石龙镇	86112525	数码复印机、激光打印机及零部件
东莞龙佑五金机械制造有限公司	虎门镇	85518848	精密精铣机床
万宝至精工（东莞）有限公司	虎门镇	85564792	电镀轴芯
东莞鹏驰五金制品有限公司	黄江镇	83668128	螺丝
东莞创机电业制品有限公司	厚街镇	82728888	电动工具
东莞高亿电子五金配件有限公司	塘厦镇	87923840	螺丝
广东欧科空调制冷有限公司	黄江镇	83660888	制冷设备
东莞铨讯电子有限公司	寮步镇	83527668	数码相机及组件
东莞市大将泽精密机械有限公司	横沥镇	83796609	数控机床

1-5　续表 23

(2012年)

单位名称	所属镇街	联系电话	主要产品(或服务)
广东蒙特科瑞莱空气处理设备有限公司	万江街道	22188788	加湿器、除湿机、冷风机、湿膜等
东莞长安东新五金塑胶有限公司	长安镇	85331403	复印机、打印机配件
东莞厚街创机塑胶制品有限公司	厚街镇	82728888	塑胶制品
东莞意达电子有限公司	凤岗镇	87771612	电动油漆喷机
锐德热力设备(东莞)有限公司	长安镇	82380238	回流焊炉
东莞强韧机械铸造有限公司	桥头镇	83455397	铸件
东莞珉强五金塑胶制品有限公司	清溪镇	89137168	铁管
东莞益新五金有限公司	常平镇	83393762	五金制品
东莞今富五金机械有限公司	谢岗镇	87632358	针织机
东莞冠翔电机有限公司	东坑镇	83902873	汽车空压机
东莞玖骏五金有限公司	虎门镇	88622999	电脑、电机及其它精密五金零配
必诺机械(东莞)有限公司	长安镇	85410555	超声波设备
东莞清溪优品电子厂	清溪镇	87311417	计数机
东莞洲亮通讯科技有限公司	道滘镇	88326318	金属餐具和器皿
东莞华懋五金有限公司	常平镇	83399130	螺丝
东泰机械工具(东莞)有限公司	常平镇	83939183	冲床
柯尼卡美能达商用科技(东莞)有限公司	石龙镇	86114300	新型打印装置及其关键部件
东莞利得机电有限公司	道滘镇	88327055	减速机
东莞虎门泰达电子有限公司	虎门镇	85558622	电子计算器
东莞嘉丰机电设备有限公司	寮步镇	83226777	五金机箱等
东莞益鑫电子科技有限公司	大朗镇	86263266	手提打钉机
日立粉末冶金(东莞)有限公司	茶山镇	86170115	气门导管
东莞泰联光学有限公司	长安镇	85535435	照相机、光学零部片、闪光灯等
长成电子(东莞)有限公司	东城街道	22035023	非金属制品模具
东莞日精电子有限公司	塘厦镇	86857999	复印机控制面板
东莞富饶精密五金制品有限公司	虎门镇	85556266	五金制品
东莞明勖机械五金有限公司	大朗镇	83010960	冲床
东莞建越精密轴承有限公司	洪梅镇	88431300	轴承
东莞百利达健康器材有限公司	南城街道	22983092	电子机械衡具
广东尼康照相机有限公司	长安镇	85535435	相机、镜头
金宝电子(中国)有限公司	长安镇	85321555	电子计算机
东莞帝光电子科技实业有限公司	清溪镇	87293808	LED灯具
东莞富鸿齐电子有限公司	樟木头镇	87187028	各类主机轴承
万金机械配件东莞有限公司	凤岗镇	82039188	复印机零配件
东莞泰星五金制品厂有限公司	清溪镇	87386666	螺杆
东莞海益机械配件有限公司	寮步镇	83220188	传感器零件
东莞长谷川金属制品有限公司	横沥镇	83721269	铝梯
日立蓄电池(东莞)有限公司	茶山镇	86400790	汽车铅酸蓄电池
东莞东成空调设备有限公司	黄江镇	83632222	中央冷水机
瑞智制冷机器(东莞)有限公司	虎门镇	85528857	制冷空调设备
东莞瑞智压缩机有限公司	虎门镇	85528857	气体压缩机
东莞大马输送设备有限公司	企石镇	82216389	输送设备、配件
东莞丰裕电机有限公司	塘厦镇	87902888	喷涂环保工业自化设备
东莞奥美佳电子有限公司	凤岗镇	87503835	数码相机
东莞捷讯电子有限公司	樟木头镇	87712009	手提标签机

1-5 续表 24

(2012年)

单位名称	所属镇街	联系电话	主要产品(或服务)
东莞应华精密金属有限公司	寮步镇	82316661	数码相机外壳
东莞宏威数码机械有限公司	南城街道	22901516	旋涂机
东莞明耀金属制品有限公司	塘厦镇	87942266	五金制品
春雨(东莞)五金制品有限公司	大朗镇	83310921	螺丝螺帽
东莞奄美弹簧有限公司	长安镇	85537655	弹簧
东莞艾尔发自动化机械有限公司	大朗镇	83180326	机械手(注塑机)
专用设备制造业			
东莞祥艺机械有限公司	常平镇	82202255	机械
东莞柏兆电子有限公司	长安镇	85540300	电脑主板机
东莞信易电热机械有限公司	大朗镇	83313588	干燥机
忠信制模(东莞)有限公司	横沥镇	83732298	非金属制品模具
万昌五金模具(东莞)有限公司	茶山镇	86480208	模具
东华机械有限公司	东城街道	22806233	注塑机
盘起工业(东莞)有限公司	长安镇	85070387	精冲模
富莱得科技(东莞)有限公司	常平镇	81896936	电动化电渡机械设备
东莞兆旺电子有限公司	塘厦镇	87929567	电子专用设备
永大精密模具(东莞)有限公司	长安镇	85312541	精密模具
东莞高德电动工具有限公司	厚街镇	88639858	木工、电工等电动工具
东莞宇宙电路板设备有限公司	凤岗镇	87569928	电路板水平机组
先锐模具配件(东莞)有限公司	长安镇	85376810	热流管
一胜百模具(东莞)有限公司	松山湖	22897888	精密型模具
东莞明利钢材模具制品有限公司	大朗镇	83316878	精密型腔模
东莞日矿富士电子有限公司	洪梅镇	88431720	液晶背光源用电极
东莞永胜医疗制品有限公司	塘厦镇	87948084	医疗器械
东莞康佳模具塑胶有限公司	凤岗镇	82071360	模具
东莞泛邦电子有限公司	长安镇	85310926	各类电子产品
东莞恒晖彩印机械厂有限公司	凤岗镇	87751438	彩印机器设备
东莞快灵通卡西尼电子科技有限公司	寮步镇	83039222	计算器
台光五金制品(东莞)有限公司	谢岗镇	87685123	精密五金模具、电子五金制品
东莞豪力机械有限公司	茶山镇	88658999	直线封边机
巨力精密设备制造(东莞)有限公司	长安镇	88611555	精冲模
东莞富强鑫塑胶机械制造有限公司	大朗镇	83313753	全自动身拙或型机
东莞科达模具机器有限公司	望牛墩镇	88857718	模坯
东莞运城制版有限公司	常平镇	83395297	凹印版锟
毅昌金型(东莞)五金制品有限公司	谢岗镇	87761209	五金制品、精密模具、小家电等
东莞雷笛克光学有限公司	横沥镇	88975298	光学透镜
峰川模具(东莞)有限公司	凤岗镇	87513998	五金模具
东莞保康电子科技有限公司	樟木头镇	87780831	血糖检测器
东莞皇冠螺丝有限公司	长安镇	85418758	精密螺丝
东莞美博电子有限公司	塘厦镇	82005983	医疗连接器
景旺模具(东莞)有限公司	虎门镇	85504415	模具
东莞亿东机器有限公司	大岭山镇	85785003	全自动注塑机及零配件
东莞毅昌模具制造注塑有限公司	谢岗镇	87761209	五金模具、塑胶注塑件、小家电等
东莞隆富精密模具有限公司	长安镇	85311526	手机按键
东莞极盛电子有限公司	寮步镇	88953118	激光头塑料配件

1-5 续表 25

(2012年)

单位名称	所属镇街	联系电话	主要产品（或服务）
东莞冠皇精密模具塑胶有限公司	樟木头镇	82128128	塑胶制品
东莞佳鸿机械制造有限公司	望牛墩镇	88859861	吹瓶机、模具、全自动焊环机
东莞鸿图金属压铸电器制造有限公司	长安镇	86062888	汽车零部件
东莞东远机械制造有限公司	常平镇	83501527	版制版设备
东莞乙宏精密模具有限公司	塘厦镇	87919391	精密模具
东莞嵩电电子科技有限公司	黄江镇	82302168	模具标准件
捷新精密塑胶钢模(东莞)有限公司	黄江镇	83516669	塑胶产品
东莞永冠铸造厂有限公司	清溪镇	87739480	五金铸件
东莞誉铭新工业有限公司	塘厦镇	86858333	塑胶模具
东莞浩川金属制品有限公司	寮步镇	83281063	五金配件
东莞宝健医疗器械科技有限公司	黄江镇	83625802	电子体温计
东莞朗诚微电子设备有限公司	厚街镇	38855228	其他专用设备
汽车制造业			
东莞奥托泰电器制品有限公司	凤岗镇	87502980	汽车应急灯
东莞山多力汽车配件有限公司	企石镇	86722101	汽车雨刷
广东永强奥林宝国际消防汽车有限公司	寮步镇	83269740	消防汽车
东莞三峰精密技术有限公司	寮步镇	81197733	空调压缩机
东莞井上橡塑加工有限公司	茶山镇	86176862	汽车配件
东莞桥头特比克汽车零件有限公司	桥头镇	83439662	汽车零配件等
东莞吉旺汽车零件有限公司	长安镇	86068932	汽车关键零配件
东莞井上建上汽车部件有限公司	沙田镇	88682171	汽车零部件
格尔翰汽车配件(东莞)有限公司	石排镇	81828988	汽车配件
东莞奈那卡斯精密汽车配件有限公司	大朗镇	82220638	汽车用毛坯件
小仓离合机(东莞)有限公司	石碣镇	86361603	离合器
东莞采升电子有限公司	常平镇	82207988	汽车影音设备
东莞广泽汽车饰件有限公司	厚街镇	85903898	汽车饰件
东莞富国橡塑工业有限公司	大岭山镇	85656968	防振垫
东莞山口实业有限公司	樟木头镇	87128480	汽车塑胶制品
东莞鸿图精密压铸有限公司	长安镇	86062888	铝合金压铸件
东莞恩斯克转向器有限公司	东城街道	22620960	汽车零部件及配件
东莞双叶金属制品有限公司	大岭山镇	85658197	汽车部件
东莞京滨汽车电喷装置有限公司	东城街道	22658290	汽车零部件及配件
东莞大和化成汽车零配件有限公司	桥头镇	83420708	汽车固件
东莞阿尔卑斯电子有限公司	长安镇	85333771	智能汽车钥匙
东莞鸿益雨刷有限公司	茶山镇	86646707	汽车雨刷
东莞联志五金制品有限公司	大朗镇	83195767	汽车刹车盘零件
东莞世技电子有限公司	寮步镇	83224133	防盗器
三樱（东莞）汽车部件有限公司	洪梅镇	82639282	汽车零部件及配件
铁路、船舶、航空航天和其他运输设备制造业			
东莞泰合复合材料有限公司	黄江镇	86913288	自行车零配件
东莞冠捷科技有限公司	塘厦镇	86851177	自行车配件
美尔顿车业(东莞)有限公司	寮步镇	81118000	电动助力车
东莞陇亿自行车配件有限公司	塘厦镇	87723781	铁车架
东莞凯力船舶有限公司	麻涌镇	88280192	船舶配件
广东中远船务工程有限公司	麻涌镇	88286988	金属船

1-5 续表 26

(2012年)

单位名称	所属镇街	联系电话	主要产品(或服务)
爱地雅(东莞)自行车有限公司	寮步镇	88951888	自行车
电气机械和器材制造业			
东莞塘厦力恒电器有限公司	塘厦镇	87724033	多士炉
东莞威德电子科技有限公司	东城街道	23061648	背部按摩椅、座垫
东莞强盛电线电缆有限公司	石碣镇	86633470	电线电缆
东莞新能源科技有限公司	松山湖	88989162	高技术绿色电池
东莞卡妮尔灯饰有限公司	塘厦镇	87723088	台灯
东莞伊斯丹电子有限公司	清溪镇	87338301	变压器、整流器和电感器
东莞乐域光电科技有限公司	石排镇	86550011	光管手提灯
东莞启东电线电缆有限公司	沙田镇	88867234	电线电缆
东莞苏扬灯饰有限公司	桥头镇	83342116	圣诞饰品
东莞威霸清洁器材有限公司	寮步镇	83283988	扫地机、抛光机、洗地毯机等清洁设备
东莞新元电子有限公司	塘厦镇	87815229	锂离子电池
日本电产(东莞)有限公司	高埗镇	88873011	大容量光磁盘驱动器
东莞亿泰电线电缆有限公司	虎门镇	85500951	电线
亚弘(东莞)电器有限公司	塘厦镇	86851766	家用电器
时至灯饰(东莞)有限公司	横沥镇	82301960	灯饰
日本电产三协电子(东莞)有限公司	石龙镇	86111234	新型机电元件
东莞硕宇电子有限公司	虎门镇	85710300	电子灯具
东莞虎门龙眼海克力斯电子有限公司	虎门镇	85554604	电子线
东莞市井南电子有限公司	中堂镇	88410266	新型电子材料、电器及零部件
东莞超霸电池有限公司	塘厦镇	87910215	电池
东莞冠宏电子有限公司	长安镇	88619858	高中频放大器、组合音响、电子钢琴
东莞立诚电子有限公司	石排镇	86532010	电子产品
东莞固邦灯饰电线有限公司	虎门镇	85553167	节日灯饰、红铜线
东莞常禾电子有限公司	虎门镇	85551202	音箱、喇叭、扬声器
东莞基立线缆有限公司	塘厦镇	82061078	电脑连接线
东莞银晖电池制品有限公司	塘厦镇	87723007	锂离子电池
东莞亿得电器制品有限公司	虎门镇	85554635	电热炉
东莞首资宝电器制造有限公司	谢岗镇	87130808	电暖器、浴室柜、灯饰
东莞吉联电线电缆有限公司	虎门镇	85551155	PVC电线
东莞岳丰电子科技有限公司	石碣镇	86634236	电话线连插头
东莞永成电器制品厂有限公司	清溪镇	87738870	吸尘器
东莞清溪华晖五金电器厂	清溪镇	86817099	锅子
东莞新能源电子科技有限公司	南城街道	88989052	电池
东莞升隆电线塑胶有限公司	黄江镇	83608118	电线
东莞立伟电业有限公司	长安镇	86074558	电子接头
东莞联立电器实业有限公司	塘厦镇	87721921	小家电
东莞超冠照明实业有限公司	长安镇	81627688	镇流器
东莞柏杰灯饰有限公司	虎门镇	85551219	塑料五金灯饰
东莞金波罗电业科技有限公司	中堂镇	88886808	电线电缆、光纤电缆、电线连扦头
东莞雅图士电子科技有限公司	塘厦镇	82001800	电子器件
东莞耐迪电子有限公司	茶山镇	86863101	轴承
东莞凯鸿光电科技有限公司	虎门镇	85524576	电器保护管
东莞星地电子有限公司	长安镇	85545651	带插头电线
东莞积信电器有限公司	樟木头镇	87799639	电烤炉

1-5 续表 27

(2012年)

单位名称	所属镇街	联系电话	主要产品（或服务）
东莞嘉盛照明科技有限公司	虎门镇	85700057	灯具
东莞清溪荔横峻凌电子厂	清溪镇	87734725	电子产品
荣文灯饰(东莞)有限公司	长安镇	81667888	灯饰及配件
亚士吉灯饰（东莞）有限公司	石龙镇	88492087	灯饰产品
东莞永德电业制品有限公司	塘厦镇	87901756	电线
东莞大得电线电缆有限公司	企石镇	86787888	电线电缆
东莞启益电器机械有限公司	塘厦镇	87989065	变压器
东莞桥梓周氏电业有限公司	常平镇	83332731	电线电缆PVC胶粒
东莞达晨电业制品有限公司	石碣镇	86631818	电线及电脑周边设备
东莞市雅科精密线材有限公司	东坑镇	83888869	电线、电缆
实盈电子（东莞）有限公司	清溪镇	87318688	连接器
东莞怡盛电业有限公司	大朗镇	83016688	电线电缆
东莞诚信电子塑胶有限公司	虎门镇	85507263	变压器胶架
富士林电子（东莞）有限公司	东坑镇	83882225	连接线
东莞九州电器有限公司	大朗镇	83188854	筒灯
万泰光电（东莞）有限公司	虎门镇	88620666	单模光纤
东莞立贸极细电线有限公司	石碣镇	86302066	电线
东莞邦达五金有限公司	常平镇	83818660	光控开关
乔日电业制品(东莞)有限公司	虎门镇	85562003	开关断路器
东莞艾天电池科技有限公司	横沥镇	88973706	锂离子电池
东莞泰欣照明有限公司	黄江镇	87135999	灯饰
东莞东进照明有限公司	东城街道	22024968	灯饰
东莞千石家电有限公司	横沥镇	83732881	冷气机
东莞美捷电业有限公司	常平镇	83903378	镭射收录机
东莞高力电池有限公司	清溪镇	87739390	干电池
东莞安硕电子有限公司	塘厦镇	87882595	电子式镇流器、微型变压器
松普科技（东莞）有限公司	塘厦镇	87937608	宽带接入网通信系统设备
新宝电机（东莞）有限公司	虎门镇	85504417	线路转换板
东莞丰盛电线电缆有限公司	桥头镇	83343591	铜线
东莞劲捷电子有限公司	厚街镇	85895863	电池充电器
东莞建玮电子制品有限公司	清溪镇	87734800	电脑连接线
永新电线电缆(东莞)有限公司	长安镇	85411045	电线、电脑线、光纤线
东莞新南利电业有限公司	长安镇	85318758	电源线
东莞耀升机电有限公司	清溪镇	87338900	电子零件、压铸产品
呈威电子（东莞）有限公司	横沥镇	83377756	微型变压器
东莞凤岗浸校塘有成电器制品厂	凤岗镇	8600920	电发剪
东莞卡斯特照明有限公司	茶山镇	88655066	照明灯具及其配件
东莞元太电业有限公司	塘厦镇	87881778	电缆
东莞润泰电线电缆有限公司	虎门镇	88620999	电线
东莞佳男五金电镀有限公司	虎门镇	85713636	连续端子、电镀五金制品
东莞迅捷线束有限公司	中堂镇	88412829	电源插头线
谊邦电工材料（东莞）有限公司	东坑镇	22654837	电线
东莞正阳电子有限公司	塘厦镇	87916258	音箱
东莞赫升机电有限公司	塘厦镇	82095588	各类机电设备
东莞世福电器有限公司	塘厦镇	87923483	电源控制盒

1-5 续表 28

(2012年)

单位名称	所属镇街	联系电话	主要产品（或服务）
意拉德电子（东莞）有限公司	横沥镇	82208902	电子控制板
东莞铭励电器制品有限公司	洪梅镇	86227426	电器开关
东莞文邦电线有限公司	清溪镇	87731000	电线电缆
东莞安联电器元件有限公司	虎门镇	85500410	电器开关
东莞丝丽雅电子科技有限公司	东城街道	88772888	塑胶玻璃包装容器
东莞日进电线有限公司	寮步镇	83218997	硅胶电线
飞磁电子材料（东莞）有限公司	清溪镇	87382420	磁芯、磁环
万宝至马达（东莞）有限公司	东城街道	22267409	微电机、其他电机
东莞鸿呈电子有限公司	厚街镇	88636000	电脑连接插头
东莞盛时五金塑胶制品有限公司	塘厦镇	87725890	五金塑胶灯具及配件
东莞巨汉灯饰有限公司	莞城街道	22096948	灯饰
东莞创盟电子有限公司	虎门镇	85505799	电脑周边连接器、连接线
东莞正扬电子机械有限公司	黄江镇	83533290	液位传感器
东莞钜权电器有限公司	万江街道	22183056	厨房电器及其它零配件
东莞恒达电机制造有限公司	谢岗镇	87680606	小型马达
东莞大东电业有限公司	桥头镇	83340838	电线电缆
东莞塘厦伊南电器制品厂	塘厦镇	87880237	连接线
东莞亚岑照明有限公司	凤岗镇	87774926	灯具及照明装置
东莞优电电线电缆有限公司	石碣镇	86632563	电线、电缆
东莞裕新灯饰有限公司	虎门镇	82887578	灯饰
东莞南玻光伏科技有限公司	麻涌镇	88288808	晶体硅太阳能电池
东莞威煌电器制品有限公司	塘厦镇	87727984	电动剪发器
东莞永力电业有限公司	常平镇	83335989	电源线插头
东莞凤岗奥托泰电器制品厂	凤岗镇	87502980	汽车电灯
东莞东骏电器有限公司	南城街道	22401688	电子变压器用铁心片
东莞永大电子有限公司	常平镇	83339366	插头连接线
东莞宏大电器制品有限公司	东城街道	22269073	家用电器
东莞宏桦电器有限公司	塘厦镇	87935001	电风扇
东莞维升电子制品有限公司	黄江镇	83622694	电源线、插头
东莞家利来电器有限公司	常平镇	83390188	风筒
东莞新光电线有限公司	道滘镇	88316705	电线、电缆
东莞宇隆电工材料有限公司	茶山镇	86642861	漆包线
金霸王(中国)有限公司	南城街道	22403615	碱锰电池
东莞艾玛电子有限公司	塘厦镇	87725209	红外线感知灯光控制器
东莞万利信新材料元件有限公司	长安镇	81882000	铝电解、电容器
港芝(东莞)电子制造厂有限公司	塘厦镇	87720639	变压器
东莞华明灯具有限公司	清溪镇	87311200	灯具
东莞宏翔电器有限公司	凤岗镇	87772581	电风扇等
东莞金星电线有限公司	大朗镇	83195297	电线电缆
东莞光距电子有限公司	塘厦镇	87288988	电线、电缆
东莞杰扬五金电器有限公司	东坑镇	83699776	吊灯
东莞荣星电线有限公司	塘厦镇	87913003	电线、电缆
东莞德宏电线电子有限公司	塘厦镇	87724535	电线、电缆
东莞广宇精密电子有限公司	虎门镇	85509706	电线
东莞泰德电机有限公司	东坑镇	83020111	吊扇

1-5 续表 29

(2012年)

单位名称	所属镇街	联系电话	主要产品（或服务）
东莞华兴电器有限公司	清溪镇	82995698	小型变压器
东莞健达照明有限公司	企石镇	21991888	照明灯具
东莞长联电线电缆有限公司	虎门镇	85703585	电线电缆
东莞库柏电子有限公司	长安镇	81605288	变压器
东莞庆泰电线电缆有限公司	常平镇	83330265	电线.电源
东莞华新电线电缆有限公司	大朗镇	83195252	8.0铜杆
东莞毓华电子科技有限公司	企石镇	86668107	开关电源、变压器、
正规电线电缆(东莞)有限公司	黄江镇	83624357	源线、电源插头线组、组装品等
四国电线(东莞)有限公司	清溪镇	87735432	同轴电线
古河汽车配件(东莞)有限公司	清溪镇	87295600	电线及电缆
东莞莹辉灯饰有限公司	虎门镇	85551445	灯饰
东莞瀚宇电子有限公司	大朗镇	83193666	KF线
东莞中钜资讯光电有限公司	厚街镇	85994660	电子原配件
东莞三雄电业制造有限公司	桥头镇	83436611	漆线
东莞统元电源连接有限公司	大朗镇	83101598	电源线、插头、连接器等
东莞港电电器制品有限公司	石排镇	86518228	直发器
东莞堤摩讯传动科技有限公司	横沥镇	87062055	天线控制器
太阳电线东莞有限公司	南城街道	22401739	电线 电缆
东莞汇勋电器制品有限公司	塘厦镇	87880968	家用通风电器具
长青林电子(东莞)有限公司	桥头镇	83340851	电线
东莞华昌导体有限公司	虎门镇	85507296	红铜线
良特电子科技（东莞）有限公司	常平镇	83914041	通讯器材配件
益伸电子（东莞）有限公司	横沥镇	83796198	五金电子
光宝电子(东莞)有限公司	长安镇	86070888	电源供应器
东莞光晋电器有限公司	沙田镇	88800666	五金制品、五金家具及其配件
东莞泽龙线缆有限公司	石龙镇	81388600	特种漆包线、裸铜线、镀锡铜线等
易事特电力系统技术有限公司	松山湖	83681611	UPS不间断电源、EPS应急电源
东莞昭和机电有限公司	东城街道	23068915	电子连接线
东莞光裕照明科技有限公司	塘厦镇	87727255	灯泡
东莞优品电子制造有限公司	清溪镇	87733008	遥控器、计时器、温度计
光宝电源科技（东莞）有限公司	长安镇	86070888	电源供应器
东莞立洋电机有限公司	黄江镇	83364350	连接器
东莞金亿电线科技有限公司	厚街镇	85589098	漆包线
东莞迅城电业有限公司	长安镇	85413308	灯用电器附件及其他照明器具
东莞世谊电子有限公司	塘厦镇	87923483	电源转换器
三发电器制品(东莞)有限公司	塘厦镇	86252838	电烫斗
东莞恒亚电工有限公司	长安镇	85337985	漆包线及漆包绞线
东莞艾科机电设备有限公司	横沥镇	82203118	家用电器
东莞常平金业电器制品有限公司	常平镇	83980008	电源线
达机机电（东莞）有限公司	石龙镇	86184431	微型电磁离合器
东莞巨扬电器有限公司	横沥镇	83728727	感应灯
东莞非太电子有限公司	厚街镇	85599076	USB接口、连接线材及通讯光纤
东莞厚街溪头太空梭电线有限公司	厚街镇	85599076	电脑线
东莞金准电器有限公司	大朗镇	83312620	灯座
东莞合力电器制品有限公司	清溪镇	87731111	搅拌机

1-5 续表 30

(2012年)

单位名称	所属镇街	联系电话	主要产品(或服务)
东莞爱思丽灯饰有限公司	横沥镇	81012302	灯饰
东莞景盛电线材料有限公司	虎门镇	85157538	PVC胶粒
东莞成铭电子有限公司	长安镇	85419999	电子零配件
东莞衡隆电业有限公司	寮步镇	81107395	电线
东莞杰光灯饰有限公司	东城街道	22674459	台灯落地灯
东莞虎门万旭电子有限公司	虎门镇	85552215	电脑连接线
东莞六翊电机有限公司	东坑镇	83382668	风扇马达、定子线圈
东莞忠佑电子有限公司	凤岗镇	86801899	连接线
东莞新能德科技有限公司	寮步镇	88956131	充电池
东莞垣欣电子有限公司	黄江镇	83635311	电感
瑞和肥田电器(东莞)有限公司	厚街镇	85599710	家用电器、塑胶制品
东莞辰达电器有限公司	洪梅镇	86227952	电器开关
立达电线(东莞)有限公司	谢岗镇	86841999	电线
东莞名帝电子产品有限公司	虎门镇	85551447	连接线
东莞中美五金制品有限公司	塘厦镇	87981800	五金制品
东莞黄江永安五金机械有限公司	黄江镇	83600199	厨房设备
东莞艾华电子有限公司	石排镇	86651679	开关
东莞古河东特光电有限公司	塘厦镇	87885167	光扩大器
高桥电机(东莞)有限公司	厚街镇	85591252	电磁离合器
东莞荣铨电器制品有限公司	清溪镇	87739792	变压器
东莞永立电机有限公司	寮步镇	83306898	机电
东莞黑钢电线电缆有限公司	石碣镇	86383061	电线电缆
东莞市万丰科技有限公司	横沥镇	86920001	网络线
东莞昱京电子有限公司	塘厦镇	87849971	变压器
东莞厚街溪头太空梭电线厂	厚街镇	85599076	电线
东莞德龙健伍电器有限公司	清溪镇	87367799	家用电器
世雅电子科技(东莞)有限公司	长安镇	85414388	高效率变频器
东莞荃宝电子制品有限公司	清溪镇	87383811	电子元件
东莞清溪合力电器制造厂	清溪镇	87731111	搅拌机
东莞金山电池有限公司	塘厦镇	87723007	电池
东莞承诠家电有限公司	东坑镇	82809139	风扇
东莞万迪电子有限公司	常平镇	82988519	其他输配电及控制设备
扬宣电子(东莞)有限公司	茶山镇	81833108	电子元器件
东莞诚远家电有限公司	大朗镇	83195040	电风扇
东莞小泉照明有限公司	石龙镇	86189569	照明灯具及配件
东莞展胜电子科技有限公司	常平镇	83397671	多媒体接收器
东莞大焱电器有限公司	东坑镇	83884984	变压器
东莞名星电线电缆有限公司	常平镇	83556398	电线电缆
东莞百实特电子科技有限公司	常平镇	82836825	照明灯、发光标志、应急感流器等
桑野电子(东莞)有限公司	横沥镇	82329818	汽车遮阳板
东莞金泰电线电缆有限公司	厚街镇	86093111	电线电缆
东莞苏泊尔电器有限公司	石碣镇	86365011	电磁炉
永胜(东莞)电子有限公司	塘厦镇	87948084	电脑读书磁头
固邦(东莞)电器有限公司	虎门镇	86096666	节日灯饰、灯饰配件
东莞可比世电子有限公司	黄江镇	83623093	变压器

1-5 续表 31

(2012年)

单位名称	所属镇街	联系电话	主要产品（或服务）
思林菲加热器材(东莞)有限公司	虎门镇	88629188	电子元器件
东莞信浓马达有限公司	凤岗镇	87772818	微电机
计算机、通信和其他电子设备制造业			
东莞伸东电子有限公司	横沥镇	83376470	连接线
东莞麒鸿电子有限公司	常平镇	81033588	喇叭单体
东莞威宇电路板有限公司	虎门镇	85568082	电路板
东莞德宝电子有限公司	莞城街道	38875000	液晶显示器
意创力电子科技（东莞）有限公司	长安镇	81553060	导航仪
东莞联洲电子科技有限公司	凤岗镇	82091688	液晶电视机
东莞和仁昌光电子有限公司	寮步镇	82310298	手机背光源
东莞光宝电脑有限公司	石碣镇	86638923	键盘
东莞中盈电子科技有限公司	黄江镇	86911088	电脑主机
东莞威雅利实业有限公司	长安镇	81588228	电子开关
联胜（中国）科技有限公司	松山湖	22668178	平板显示屏
贝普电子(东莞)有限公司	塘厦镇	86856900	移动硬盘
东莞飞展电子有限公司	塘厦镇	87985212	DVD音响
东莞英可电子有限公司	东城街道	88984021	扩音器
东莞泰升音响科技有限公司	东城街道	38863999	耳机
东莞日经电子有限公司	凤岗镇	87511131	线圈
东莞凤岗嘉辉塑胶五金有限公司	凤岗镇	87777455	打印机及配件
东莞长安富士万微件电子有限公司	长安镇	85312169	电脑零配件
福群科技（东莞）有限公司	塘厦镇	82774488	大容量磁盘驱动器
东莞史特施实业有限公司	东坑镇	81015368	车灯线路板
广东海信光通讯技术要限公司	长安镇	85348008	激光收发器组合
万星光电子（东莞）有限公司	长安镇	81152888	固态电容
东莞锦川电子有限公司	长安镇	85530488	计算机零部件
东莞爱旺电子科技有限公司	黄江镇	83365942	键盘
东莞长安富昌电子有限公司	长安镇	38871661	扬声器
卡士莫实业（东莞）有限公司	高埗镇	38910088	计算机零部件
东莞华晟电子科技有限公司	长安镇	81609588	电子产品
东莞早川电子有限公司	厚街镇	85901115	电子配件
广东百圳君耀电子有限公司	松山湖	28504896	压敏电阻
东莞日翔电子有限公司	茶山镇	86402603	电子产品
东莞泉源电子有限公司	东坑镇	83883111	遥控器
东莞阳天电子科技有限公司	塘厦镇	82062778	电子元件
东莞锦富迪奇电子有限公司	寮步镇	88956666	TFT-LCD平板显示屏材料
广东生益科技股份有限公司	松山湖	22271828	覆铜板
东莞龙杰电子有限公司	清溪镇	87734425	电源线插头
东莞首利科技有限公司	清溪镇	86812888	电元供应器配件
东莞普光液晶显示有限公司	厚街镇	81520001	手机液晶显示屏
健富塑胶五金制品（东莞）有限公司	清溪镇	87338807	电脑机箱
东莞道滘万宝至马达有限公司	道滘镇	88831848	微电机及其他电机
东莞瑞索电子有限公司	塘厦镇	82620705	电子产品
东莞钨珍达盛电子有限公司	谢岗镇	82797299	手机及手机配件
康展电子（东莞）有限公司	塘厦镇	87915950	电子原件

1-5　续表 32

(2012年)

单位名称	所属镇街	联系电话	主要产品（或服务）
辉碧电子（东莞）有限公司	清溪镇	87731085	电源供应器
东莞达伸电子有限公司	横沥镇	88975258	电脑散热风扇
瀚荃电子（东莞）有限公司	常平镇	83397111	连接器
日发电子科技（东莞）有限公司	长安镇	85348787	电脑磁盘读写笔
东莞富士通电装电子有限公司	洪梅镇	88848801	电子元件及组件制
东莞凯世帝电子有限公司	寮步镇	89610271	USB连接线
东莞艾埤特电子有限公司	寮步镇	82815981	电子元器件
东莞凯励电子有限公司	东坑镇	83389798	电子产品
北陆电气（广东）有限公司	东坑镇	83381868	线路板
东莞亨丰电子有限公司	厚街镇	88633868	电脑连接件
台丰印刷电路板（东莞）有限公司	常平镇	83919350	印刷电路板
东莞法母电子有限公司	常平镇	83910283	移动硬盘
东莞冈谷电子有限公司	东坑镇	83384416	电容器
东莞衍通电子资讯有限公司	厚街镇	85988389	电脑机板
东京端一电子（东莞）有限公司	寮步镇	83211170	电子零配件
东莞嘉汇电器有限公司	黄江镇	86912088	电器
东莞大新能率电子有限公司	常平镇	83822970	电子产品
亚南电子（东莞）有限公司	寮步镇	83265079	音响
东莞技研新阳电子有限公司	桥头镇	83434514	电器零配件
韩郁信息技术（东莞）有限公司	桥头镇	89290588	背光源
精成科技电子（东莞）有限公司	黄江镇	83632679	电脑主机板
东莞海正机电有限公司	石碣镇	86366010	激光机芯五金配件
东莞彩显有机发光科技有限公司	清溪镇	87738875	新型平放显示器
天钺电子（东莞）有限公司	横沥镇	83797666	监控设备
东莞耳神电声科技有限公司	万江街道	89027886	音箱
东莞爱铭数码电子有限公司	寮步镇	83038000	DVD激光头
日本电产三协（东莞）工机有限公司	长安镇	87085211	数码相机镜片
诺特电子(东莞)有限公司	塘厦镇	87290991	数字程控调度机
东莞康特尔电子有限公司	高埗镇	88462888	影视录放设备
东莞怡辉五金有限公司	清溪镇	87386488	五金制品、钢材
东莞长安厦岗成铭电子制品厂	长安镇	85419999	电脑机箱
京瓷连接器（东莞）有限公司	石龙镇	88495099	新型电子元器件
东莞尔来德通讯有限公司	黄江镇	87097800	手机按键
东莞奕华电子有限公司	东城街道	88759333	电子产品
东莞栢能电子科技有限公司	厚街镇	85822002	电脑主机
东莞王氏港建电子有限公司	常平镇	83903333	电子产品
东莞顺晟电脑实业有限公司	凤岗镇	86801188	电脑机箱
东莞汉旭五金塑胶科技有限公司	塘厦镇	87880339	散热器
东莞天籁之音电声制品有限公司	厚街镇	85033501	喇叭
伟易达（东莞）通讯设备有限公司	寮步镇	83231806	室内无线电话
东莞联茂电子科技有限公司	虎门镇	88623268	覆铜板
东莞微端电子科技有限公司	常平镇	83975888	新型平板显示器
东莞即辉塑胶电子有限公司	长安镇	85337602	塑胶制品
伟易达（东莞）电讯有限公司	寮步镇	83231806	电子元器件
科广电子（东莞）有限公司	寮步镇	83302929	新型电子元器件

1-5 续表 33

(2012年)

单位名称	所属镇街	联系电话	主要产品(或服务)
大东骏通(东莞)电子有限公司	常平镇	83394379	组合音响
东莞冠坤电子有限公司	清溪镇	87318000	片式电容
东莞新优电子有限公司	横沥镇	82980590	家用电器及其配部件
山进电子科技(东莞)有限公司	桥头镇	86933033	收音机
亚电电子(东莞)有限公司	塘厦镇	87982616	黑胶唱机
东莞庆帮电子有限公司	大朗镇	83319425	喇叭
东莞明瑞电子有限公司	长安镇	86072000	无线网卡
东莞泰克威科技有限公司	桥头镇	81038122	汽车电子产品及配件
东莞中探探针有限公司	虎门镇	85151668	电子测试探针
东莞安美时电子有限公司	常平镇	83394581	网络控制设备
多摩电子(东莞)有限公司	茶山镇	81355688	充电器
东莞泰凯电子有限公司	塘厦镇	82996789	VCD解码板
东莞航天电子有限公司	常平镇	83392291	电话单机
京都电工(东莞)有限公司	长安镇	85428288	电子元件
翰廷电子科技(东莞)有限公司	清溪镇	38850388	电子元件
东莞令特电子有限公司	虎门镇	81518186	压敏电阻、敏感元器件
东莞天铖科技有限公司	厚街镇	85889488	3C产业产品
锦湖光电(东莞)有限公司	高埗镇	81305001	背光源
东莞海声音响科技有限公司	中堂镇	88880328	音箱
东莞卓翰光电科技有限公司	横沥镇	81180610	数码相机零配件
东莞欣德电子有限公司	塘厦镇	87882386	电线
宜来特光电(东莞)有限公司	寮步镇	81122970	TFFLCD平板显示屏
东莞健捷电子有限公司	高埗镇	89911801	半导体分立器件
东莞宏邦光电有限公司	清溪镇	87322250	背光模组加工
东莞领航电子有限公司	塘厦镇	88034706	变压器、整流器
兴科电子(东莞)有限公司	虎门镇	85106058	手机按键
东莞华盛音响制品有限公司	石排镇	86528327	汽车收放音机
东莞中兴电子有限公司	桥头镇	83457860	电子元件
东莞爱美达电子有限公司	横沥镇	83377651	电脑散热器
东莞首富电子有限公司	樟木头镇	87710688	电子产品
东莞凡振工业电子有限公司	谢岗镇	87635181	电子音响、DVD、电子零配件
东莞洲磊电子有限公司	谢岗镇	87631888	磷化镓、磷化锅铟镓
东莞加炜电子有限公司	石碣镇	86310071	电子连接器端子、连接器塑胶壳
东莞科德电子有限公司	常平镇	83391340	铭板
东莞呈越电脑配件有限公司	大朗镇	86913168	液晶显示器支架
东莞泰山电子有限公司	虎门镇	85564813	印刷线路版
东莞达电电子有限公司	石碣镇	86303366	耳机喇叭、耳机麦克风
东莞胜方电子有限公司	东城街道	86216886	导电薄膜
东莞爱美克电子有限公司	凤岗镇	87775085	放大器
奥托仑光电子(东莞)有限公司	茶山镇	86401060	玻璃光学镜片
棠裕电子(东莞)有限公司	清溪镇	87332588	液晶显示器
达创科技(东莞)有限公司	石碣镇	86637008	集线器、路由器
东莞三星视界有限公司	厚街镇	85582000	液晶显示片
东莞长安上角福摩斯托电子厂	长安镇	85541200	组合音响
东莞通华液晶有限公司	东城街道	88774388	液晶显示板

1-5 续表 34

(2012年)

单位名称	所属镇街	联系电话	主要产品（或服务）
东莞国瑞电子有限公司	清溪镇	82063511	电感器
东莞船井电机厂	黄江镇	83665999	液晶电视机
东莞嘉财电业制造厂	大岭山镇	83359040	DVD、电视遥控器、机顶盒等
东莞辰虹实业有限公司	东城街道	22291588	五金制品
东莞宏智电器配件有限公司	谢岗镇	87136136	家用电器配件
东莞欣韵电子有限公司	石碣镇	81399168	电源供应器
东莞铭异精密电子有限公司	石碣镇	86387383	电脑支架
东莞精熙光机有限公司	长安镇	85312190	照相机、复印机主要零部件
东莞南城新科磁电制品有限公司	南城街道	22810033	电脑磁头
千代达电子制造(东莞)有限公司	大岭山镇	88961122	海绵
东莞柏狮精密电子有限公司	麻涌镇	88233068	半导体
东莞东坑先益电子厂	东坑镇	83381857	发光二极管
东莞鹏龙光电有限公司	石碣镇	88787202	平板显示器件、数字照相机等
东莞柏能电子厂	厚街镇	85822002	计算机主板和显卡
东莞时力科技电子厂	长安镇	85415668	电子元件
东莞皓讯电子有限公司	清溪镇	87313056	电脑电子周边线
东莞三协精工科技有限公司	高埗镇	88787202	电子产品
东莞技嘉电子有限公司	黄江镇	83367140	电脑主板
东莞歌乐东方电子有限公司	东坑镇	83387001	音响
东莞华科电子有限公司	大朗镇	83115168	片式电容
东莞富强电子有限公司	东坑镇	83882225	耳机、连接线
东莞久尹电子有限公司	南城街道	22401737	热敏电阻和压敏电阻等
东莞谢岗钨珍电子厂	谢岗镇	82126950	手机外壳
泓凯电子科技(东莞)有限公司	黄江镇	83365942	电脑机箱
飞比达电子元器件（东莞）有限公司	横沥镇	83725088	新型电子元器件
东莞能率科技有限公司	寮步镇	83527668	手机摄像头
东莞迅脉电子有限公司	寮步镇	81196000	新型电子元器件
阿基里斯电子材料(东莞)有限公司	长安镇	85308801	防静电处理
平易电子（东莞）有限公司	常平镇	83820333	印刷电路板
升荣电子(东莞)有限公司	清溪镇	87311036	电脑周边产品
东莞同昌电子有限公司	大朗镇	83318960	PCB（印制电路板）
东莞东英电子工业有限公司	清溪镇	87328201	DVD机蕊
丽清电子科技（东莞）有限公司	黄江镇	86968566	LED车灯
东莞亲荣精密塑胶电子有限公司	凤岗镇	89332701	线圈
东莞加玮华电子有限公司	东城街道	22257469	耳机
东莞超悦电子有限公司	寮步镇	83305007	电脑键盘
东莞鑫联数码科技有限公司	石排镇	86591818	机顶盒
东莞广迎五金塑胶制品有限公司	长安镇	85413055	塑胶机壳
东莞全特电子科技有限公司	虎门镇	85555526	塑胶电子制品
东莞百一电子有限公司	大朗镇	83188045	数字视频编解码设备
富相电子科技(东莞)有限公司	高埗镇	88737888	液晶显示器件
东莞东马电子厂	寮步镇	83308523	微型马达及附件
万事通电子(东莞)有限公司	石碣镇	86633491	耳机麦克
东莞利保迅电子有限公司	茶山镇	86408844	变压器
东莞建冠塑胶电子有限公司	虎门镇	85162899	连接器

1-5 续表 35

(2012年)

单位名称	所属镇街	联系电话	主要产品(或服务)
东莞泰富电子有限公司	高埗镇	88730138	电话
美信音响器材(东莞)有限公司	塘厦镇	86856188	音箱(含喇叭)
东莞嘉茂电子科技有限公司	大朗镇	88606888	喇叭
东莞辉城电子有限公司	望牛墩镇	88520218	电子组件、电解电容器、电源
东莞扩乐格电子器材有限公司	塘厦镇	87923096	影视录放设备
东莞建永数码科技有限公司	塘厦镇	87880818	CD镭射机
易达电源科技(东莞)有限公司	东城街道	22651108	智能化电源设备系统
东莞永保电子有限公司	桥头镇	81176991	锂离子电子
东莞顺牛金属制品有限公司	厚街镇	85931595	金属制品
东莞长安镇时力电子厂	长安镇	85533151	磁臂组合半成品
东莞高盛电子有限公司	常平镇	83813136	电话机
东莞捷盛电子有限公司	东城街道	22026000	零件印制电路板
有声电子(东莞)有限公司	清溪镇	87734351	音频放大器
东莞立德电子有限公司	塘厦镇	87922625	变压器
泰科电子(东莞)有限公司	厚街镇	85817613	通讯终端设备
宝罗电子科技(东莞)有限公司	横沥镇	83712772	新型电子元件
东莞狮龙电子有限公司	寮步镇	83283391	DVD
三洋电子(东莞)有限公司	塘厦镇	87910998	彩电
东莞利源电子有限公司	横沥镇	83723988	灯光控制器
舜全电气器材(东莞)有限公司	虎门镇	85517988	压敏电阻
东莞益衡电子有限公司	凤岗镇	87755689	电源供应器
永泰电子(东莞)有限公司	常平镇	83918040	电脑连接线
东莞三荣通讯科技有限公司	塘厦镇	86851130	手机键
东莞澳利电器制品有限公司	常平镇	83990955	变压器
东莞嘉耀电子有限公司	厚街镇	85930034	电脑功能卡
东莞昱欣电子有限公司	大朗镇	83126168	电子元件
华元电子(东莞)有限公司	清溪镇	86811568	电子产品
恩智浦半导体广东有限公司	黄江镇	83668268	半导体
东莞环宇电子有限公司	凤岗镇	87774838	电子元件
台达电子(东莞)有限公司	石碣镇	86639008	线圈、变压器、直流电源转换器
康舒电子(东莞)有限公司	塘厦镇	87915950	电源供应器
东莞高惠电子有限公司	长安镇	85319188	连接器
东莞沛波电子有限公司	石碣镇	86310316	小型变压器线圈
东莞相川铁龙电子有限公司	常平镇	83395551	电子元件
东莞达宏电子有限公司	清溪镇	87736405	电源供应器
东莞黄江威成科技电子厂	黄江镇	83632679	液晶显示屏
东莞欧珀移动通信有限公司	长安镇	85545555	手机
茂瑞电子(东莞)有限公司	东城街道	87077888	键盘
东莞荣兴五金制品有限公司	大岭山镇	83355911	电脑机壳、五金制品、除草机零配件
东莞林发电子有限公司	厚街镇	83085888	音响插头线
东莞川边电子有限公司	东城街道	22209722	扬声器
东莞鑫佑光电科技有限公司	石排镇	86534198	背光板
东莞昭和电子有限公司	高埗镇	88873451	遥控器
东莞恒扬光电有限公司	横沥镇	83710660	平板显示屏及显示屏材料
东莞松藤电子有限公司	桥头镇	83457291	小型家电制品、塑胶制品等生产

1-5 续表 36

(2012年)

单位名称	所属镇街	联系电话	主要产品（或服务）
智宝电子(东莞)有限公司	塘厦镇	87914676	电解电容器
东莞宇龙通信科技有限公司	松山湖	23075096	新型智能手机
三井高科技(广东)有限公司	长安镇	86070008	新型电子元器件
东莞清溪三清半导体厂	清溪镇	87734139	半导体晶体管
东莞矽德半导体有限公司	清溪镇	87313240	集成电路
东莞电创电子有限公司	道滘镇	88834807	电子元件及组件
东莞台庆精密电子有限公司	黄江镇	83365488	电子零件
东莞广通事务机有限公司	长安镇	85312190	电子元件及组件
捷荣模具工业(东莞)有限公司	长安镇	82387988	精密塑胶、五金模具
东莞大岭山光顺电子厂	大岭山镇	83352904	电子产品
东莞为勤电子有限公司	长安镇	85542016	电子元器件
东莞迅德电器有限公司	清溪镇	87739411	小型变压器
东莞天扬电子有限公司	塘厦镇	82011299	电力电子元器件
东莞德利信电子有限公司	常平镇	83395111	各种机芯产品
广东南方宏明电子科技股份有限公司	南城街道	22407479	电容器
智嘉通讯科技(东莞)有限公司	常平镇	83335430	通讯配件
东莞市捷伟讯电子有限公司	厚街镇	85993708	手机
东莞大迪音响器材有限公司	寮步镇	83326201	音箱
富加宜连接器(东莞)有限公司	沙田镇	88682108	电子连接器
东莞市宝盛五金制品有限公司	清溪镇	87315888	电脑外壳
东莞陆和电子有限公司	中堂镇	88885117	电脑零配件
东莞创慈磁性元件有限公司	石碣镇	86327771	变压器
程品电子科技（东莞）有限公司	石排镇	88935999	高频变压器
特新微电子（东莞）有限公司	茶山镇	86403328	PCB、FPC的机械和镭射钻孔等
永捷电路版(东莞)有限公司	厚街镇	85812542	印制电路板
飞宏(东莞)电子有限公司	清溪镇	87319026	手机充电器
东莞弘电电子有限公司	大朗镇	85550979	新型电子元器件
茂成电子科技（东莞）有限公司	黄江镇	83632688	元器件专用材料
坚力电子（东莞）有限公司	横沥镇	81890360	电子手表
东莞万德电子制品有限公司	东城街道	88775555	硅胶按键
世擎光电（东莞）有限公司	茶山镇	81821666	手机摄像模组
立维腾电子（东莞）有限公司	桥头镇	81038888	电子感应开关
东莞市柏洋电子有限公司	石排镇	81369899	开关电源、充电器
东莞康佳电子有限公司	凤岗镇	87758888	彩色电视
东莞旺宏科技有限公司	长安镇	38851888	鼠标
东莞高美电子有限公司	寮步镇	83300880	电子配件
东莞裕光数码电子有限公司	道滘镇	88382101	电子元件及组件制
东莞红板多层线路板有限公司	长安镇	86060111	电子元器件
东莞芝浦电子有限公司	长安镇	85412371	热敏电阻
东莞新利电子有限公司	塘厦镇	86851599	电子钟表
高效电子(东莞)有限公司	寮步镇	88901888	电脑零配件
东莞全台电子有限公司	东坑镇	83697606	平板显示器
东莞宝顺力电子塑胶制品厂有限公司	大岭山镇	83353827	电子产品音响
东莞美信科技有限公司	企石镇	86761589	电子计算机外部设备
特新电路材料（东莞）有限公司	茶山镇	86403328	多层线路板

1-5　续表 37

(2012年)

单位名称	所属镇街	联系电话	主要产品（或服务）
东莞万士达液晶显示器有限公司	东城街道	22668178	光电子器件及其他电子器件
东莞音音电子绘本有限公司	黄江镇	83668068	电子式音乐卡
东莞万年富电子有限公司	塘厦镇	87724667	线路板
东莞海韵电子有限公司	石碣镇	22610501	电子设备
中名(东莞)电子有限公司	虎门镇	85559636	耳机
东莞天意电子有限公司	石龙镇	86080328	彩票终端机等金融电子产品
东莞太华半导体有限公司	寮步镇	83263688	手机用液晶显示器部件
东莞万德镜片科技有限公司	东城街道	22676816	超薄按键、LML镜片等
东莞华春电子有限公司	中堂镇	88888850	电脑显示卡、数据卡
伟特移动通迅设备（东莞）有限公司	桥头镇	83340841	移动通讯产品
东莞首邦电子有限公司	石碣镇	86632772	变压器电感器电阻
东莞国创电子有限公司	塘厦镇	87720275	片式电阻器
天弘(东莞)科技有限公司	松山湖	22899333	网络游戏机
东莞华龙电子有限公司	横沥镇	83376575	变压器
敦朴光电有限公司	厚街镇	85926660	照相机
国巨电子(东莞)有限公司	塘厦镇	87720275	电阻器
奇烨电子（东莞）有限公司	石排镇	86925028	变压器
东莞奇力新电子有限公司	清溪镇	87730251	线圈
东莞东原电子有限公司	寮步镇	83228000	手机充电器
联一小原光学（东莞）有限公司	长安镇	86240666	光学玻璃毛胚
东莞生益电子有限公司	万江街道	22272074	多层印刷电路板
太阳诱电(广东)有限公司	石碣镇	86636888	电容器、电感器
东莞永腾电子制品有限公司	凤岗镇	87755269	铝制散热片及散热器
东莞盛和电子有限公司	长安镇	86076988	电子产品
东莞永冠电子科技有限公司	万江街道	22033699	DVD播放机
东莞樟木头十和田电子厂	樟木头镇	87713119	收音机、家用音响设备
东莞光阵显示器制品有限公司	清溪镇	87738870	摄像头
极讯电子(东莞)有限公司	寮步镇	88953310	电子元件
东莞普思电子有限公司	长安镇	85538871	高频滤波器
东莞海盛电子科技有限公司	东坑镇	83385859	新型电子元器件
东莞昆盈电脑制品有限公司	厚街镇	85825810	鼠标器
东莞茂林电子有限公司	虎门镇	85562012	空白线路板
东莞福摩斯托电子有限公司	长安镇	85541200	家用电子元件
东莞致力电脑有限公司	清溪镇	87312821	电脑配件
杰群电子科技（东莞）有限公司	黄江镇	83635267	新型电子元器件
东莞康创电子科技有限公司	厚街镇	85889989	收音机
东莞华新半导体有限公司	黄江镇	86968673	集成电路
东莞协盈电脑有限公司	厚街镇	85880090	鼠标
东莞立亚达电子有限公司	石排镇	86511283	电子产品
盛恒达电子(东莞)有限公司	石碣镇	86633718	ADLS路由器变压器电源板
东莞宝山电子有限公司	樟木头镇	87712264	电子产品
东莞进泰电子有限公司	塘厦镇	87725650	音响
东莞市亚通光电有限公司	塘厦镇	82006088	光电子器件
东莞动利电子有限公司	常平镇	83550800	电脑散热风扇
东莞伍联电子科技有限公司	凤岗镇	82097852	鼠标、键盘

1-5 续表 38

(2012年)

单位名称	所属镇街	联系电话	主要产品(或服务)
广东升威电子制品有限公司	塘厦镇	87287777	电位器、编码器
东莞新进电子有限公司	大岭山镇	85613846	电子计算机外部设备
乐依文半导体(东莞)有限公司	长安镇	85647662	集成电路
东莞市旭进光电有限公司	长安镇	85413789	光学镜头
新豪(东莞)电子有限公司	寮步镇	83216200	电脑键盘
东莞高埗微太电子科技有限公司	高埗镇	88876239	数码产品
东莞创群石英晶体有限公司	大朗镇	83119395	石英晶体谐振器
东莞东力电子有限公司	塘厦镇	87723276	DVD机
台达电子零组件(东莞)有限公司	石碣镇	86639008	电脑散热风扇
东莞东聚电子电讯制品有限公司	石碣镇	86631652	鼠标蓝牙耳机
东莞泰硕电子有限公司	大岭山镇	85321851	连接器、散热器
东莞友华通信配件有限公司	寮步镇	22982285	天线
东莞伟时科技有限公司	长安镇	85537565	导光板
东莞裕佳电子有限公司	清溪镇	86814888	光盘驱动器
东莞友华电子有限公司	寮步镇	83326171	端子连接器
东莞泉声电子有限公司	石碣镇	86325251	新型电子元器件
成翔电子(东莞)有限公司	清溪镇	86812888	电源供应器
东莞广濑拓展电子有限公司	石龙镇	86187023	精密机械和电子零部件、电线组件等
东莞友智金属制品有限公司	清溪镇	82130848	五金制品、不断电系统及伺服装置
东莞联桥电子有限公司	茶山镇	86485066	印刷电路板
东莞蒂雅克电子有限公司	长安镇	85548848	音响视听设备
东莞恒忻电子有限公司	塘厦镇	87915567	工率电感、SMD贴片电感、变压器
东莞大朗辉鸿电子厂	大朗镇	83018938	喇叭半成品
东莞旺鸿五金制品有限公司	清溪镇	87302196	电脑机箱
旗利得电子(东莞)有限公司	谢岗镇	87766645	印刷线路板
东莞东坑富港电子制品厂	东坑镇	83882225	电子组件
东莞怡科电子有限公司	长安镇	87086668	汽车移动电话充电器
东莞爱电电子有限公司	桥头镇	83434525	线路板
东莞山本电子科技有限公司	麻涌镇	88227094	印刷线路板
群光电子(东莞)有限公司	清溪镇	87311688	电脑键盘
金笔电子(东莞)有限公司	东城街道	22200489	电子零配件
华玮电子(东莞)有限公司	长安镇	85307001	插座
东莞实英电子有限公司	厚街镇	88630999	电脑接插件
东莞联宝光电科技有限公司	企石镇	86786368	电子产品
东莞创宝达电器制品有限公司	常平镇	83335747	漏电保护器
东莞森泰电子有限公司	凤岗镇	87751663	手机
东莞骅国电子有限公司	厚街镇	85597201	连接器
日本电产精密马达科技(东莞)有限公司	塘厦镇	87720523	微型马达
东莞英格尔电子有限公司	塘厦镇	87934928	电子元件
东莞群翰电子有限公司	常平镇	83824816	连接器
东莞长江电脑制品有限公司	清溪镇	87736209	电脑机箱
华容电子(广东)有限公司	石碣镇	83075098	电容器
东莞近江电子有限公司	桥头镇	81036276	线路主板
东莞康捷电子有限公司	长安镇	85317669	各式电子、电机连接器
东莞福哥电子有限公司	茶山镇	86649438	电位器、编码器、开关及传感器等

1-5 续表 39

(2012年)

单位名称	所属镇街	联系电话	主要产品（或服务）
东莞宇球电子有限公司	寮步镇	83529888	电子插接件
旭丽电子(东莞)有限公司	石碣镇	86638923	键盘
矽谷电子科技（东莞）有限公司	黄江镇	83366696	液晶显示器
东莞艾利博电子有限公司	松山湖	22899100	电子词典和显示器
东莞台霖电子通讯有限公司	大岭山镇	85655858	电脑线连插头
嘉益电子（东莞）有限公司	东城街道	22207821	印制电路板
东莞翊凯电器制品有限公司	清溪镇	86812999	电脑机箱外壳
东莞友俊电子有限公司	清溪镇	87311900	电子五金元器件
东莞广原电子有限公司	石碣镇	86366010	蓝牙耳机
东莞前盛电子有限公司	塘厦镇	87910575	电源供应器
坚田电机(东莞)有限公司	横沥镇	22652988	电子线路钣
东莞东源光电有限公司	东城街道	22633913	光纤跳接线
东莞冠诚塑胶模具有限公司清溪分厂	清溪镇	87315088	遥控器
东莞胜美达(太平)电机有限公司	虎门镇	85111118	电子原件
东莞东煦五金电镀厂有限公司	虎门镇	85564222	LED引线架
东莞宏易电子有限公司	塘厦镇	87881584	音响设备
东莞添威电子制品有限公司	凤岗镇	87779805	电源供应器
振曜电子(东莞)有限公司	大朗镇	83188470	网络交换机
东莞励国照明有限公司	凤岗镇	87759739	LED灯
东莞翔国光电科技有限公司	茶山镇	81833588	印刷电路板
东莞成谦音响科技有限公司	长安镇	89883333	喇叭
东莞友华汽车配件有限公司	寮步镇	83326172	各种天线塑胶配件
东莞宏笙电子有限公司	塘厦镇	87919270	鼠标器
东莞太阳诱电有限公司	石碣镇	86636888	电容器、电阻器
东莞福满生电子有限公司	常平镇	82207777	电脑显示器托架
东莞企达电器制品有限公司	横沥镇	83715169	电子元件
三和盛电子科技(东莞)有限公司	凤岗镇	87862222	数码相机关键件
东莞长安发利达电子厂	长安镇	85531414	电子元件
吉嘉电子东莞有限公司	樟木头镇	87790197	多媒体音箱
东莞盛世科技电子实业有限公司	黄江镇	86914800	电子元器件
富港电子(东莞)有限公司	东坑镇	83882225	变压器
伟创力电源（东莞）有限公司	大岭山镇	85602828	电脑显示器及家用、办公、车用电器
东莞健益五金制品有限公司	茶山镇	86487999	DVD机芯五金件
东莞贯达电子有限公司	高埗镇	88786000	电感、电子元器件、变压器、电感
东莞百吉通信设备有限公司	大朗镇	88603993	通讯设备
东莞高伟光学电子有限公司	寮步镇	83307113	手机摄像头
东莞宏松精密组件有限公司	塘厦镇	28129588	打印机及配件
东莞百音电子有限公司	南城街道	22984320	扬声器
东莞森玛仕格里菲电路有限公司	茶山镇	81822047	多层线路板
华磁电子(东莞)有限公司	石碣镇	86322836	电感器、磁线圈、微型变压器
东莞凯升电子有限公司	塘厦镇	87883521	电脑机箱
东莞昌亿电器有限公司	洪梅镇	88847319	电器开关
东莞合宝电器制品有限公司	横沥镇	83715169	电器开关
快捷达通信设备（东莞）有限公司	常平镇	83936688	数据通
东莞诠盛电器有限公司	厚街镇	85825373	电源插座

1-5 续表 40

(2012年)

单位名称	所属镇街	联系电话	主要产品(或服务)
研鑫电子科技(东莞)有限公司	企石镇	86716856	铁芯
艾利和电子科技(中国)有限公司	松山湖	22899100	MP3和MP4
东莞美隆电声器材有限公司	塘厦镇	86856288	各类型喇叭
东莞万钧电子科技有限公司	洪梅镇	89138000	线路板
东莞汇和电子有限公司	谢岗镇	87768410	印刷线路板
东莞市科隆威自动化设备有限公司	寮步镇	83228201	无铅流焊
联德电子(东莞)有限公司	石碣镇	83072288	电子、电源供应器、电源转换器
东莞美维电路有限公司	东城街道	86228000	印制线路板
广濑电机(东莞)有限公司	常平镇	83817840	连接器
东莞兴鑫电子科技有限公司	虎门镇	85226956	手机按键
东莞鸿爱斯通信科技有限公司	高埗镇	88783009	电子元件
东莞龙升电子有限公司	黄江镇	83536698	变压器
雷兹达电子(东莞)有限公司	长安镇	85327532	电子连接线
锦旭电子(东莞)有限公司	清溪镇	87737118	电脑周边产品
东莞美京电子有限公司	寮步镇	83222371	散热片
圣华电子(东莞)有限公司	塘厦镇	87882707	电子元件及组件
东莞仲屏电子有限公司	石排镇	81868166	扬声器
东莞石龙京瓷有限公司	石龙镇	86119611	照像机、镜头、闪光灯及其零部件
东莞信泰光学有限公司	长安镇	85535435	数码相机
东莞寿广精密电子有限公司	塘厦镇	87909199	塑胶五金配件
东莞长安华南电子厂	长安镇	85307366	磁性产品
东莞珀韵电子有限公司	横沥镇	83720950	音圈
万裕三信电子(东莞)有限公司	长安镇	86069888	电子电容器
东莞保力电子有限公司	石排镇	86511770	充电器
东莞明鑫电子有限公司	企石镇	86944888	电脑主机配件
台达电子电源(东莞)有限公司	石碣镇	86639008	电源供应器、变压器线圈
东莞艾斯光电科技有限公司	东城街道	22667703	新型电子元器件
先锋信泰(东莞)光学有限公司	长安镇	85535435	精密光电电器件
东莞得泰电子有限公司	石碣镇	86316090	耳机发射器、麦克风
东莞东骅电子科技有限公司	清溪镇	33336888	电脑机箱
东莞惠昌电子有限公司	长安镇	85542566	信号线、医疗线、高频线束
东莞东矽电子有限公司	清溪镇	86200050	电源供应器
美锐电路(东莞)有限公司	塘厦镇	87724932	印刷电路板
立信杰(东莞)精密模具制造有限公司	凤岗镇	86800088	连接器插头件
东莞联聿电子有限公司	长安镇	85322996	电脑机箱
雅邦电子(东莞)有限公司	石碣镇	86331999	电子成品组装
东莞力音电子有限公司	石碣镇	86637826	电子线圈、小型变压器
东莞旭福电脑有限公司	清溪镇	87318190	电脑主机板
东莞长安科得电子有限公司	长安镇	85546130	主板机
东莞明崴电子科技有限公司	东城街道	2265628	光电子器件、其他电子器件
最上(东莞)电子有限公司	塘厦镇	87883718	喇叭鼓纸
东莞科泰电子有限公司	南城街道	22408802	合路器
祥发电子(东莞)有限公司	石碣镇	86331999	电源供应器
瑞讯电子(东莞)有限公司	东城街道	88753288	网络卡、路由器
东莞雅士电子有限公司	长安镇	85545115	收放组合机

1-5 续表 41

(2012年)

单位名称	所属镇街	联系电话	主要产品(或服务)
东莞磁威电子科技有限公司	企石镇	86787388	宽带网络话音分离器、脉冲变压器等
东莞群马电子有限公司	东坑镇	83860001	电子零配件
东莞力达电机有限公司	塘厦镇	87727891	微电机及其它电机
广东楚天龙智能卡有限公司	凤岗镇	87509999	IC卡
东莞隆盛达电子有限公司	万江街道	22706295	影碟机
东莞欧陆电子有限公司	长安镇	87088788	电子元件
欧姆龙精密电子(东莞)有限公司	清溪镇	86816688	液晶背光板
东莞泉睿精密五金有限公司	麻涌镇	85315643	五金轨制设备
东莞致通电脑有限公司	清溪镇	87312821	MODEM、MP3等计算机通讯周边产品
东莞明冠电子有限公司	长安镇	85318000	网络卡
广东佳彩数码科技有限公司	企石镇	86727181	机顶盒、液晶电视
希克斯电子(东莞)有限公司	大岭山镇	85601508	充电器
东莞志丰电子有限公司	大朗镇	83183457	蜂鸣器
富声(东莞)电器配件有限公司	虎门镇	85701082	耳机和多媒体喇叭
协发(东莞)电子有限公司	塘厦镇	87720745	电源供应器
东莞大泉传感器有限公司	寮步镇	88953366	传感器
东莞科达五金制品有限公司	石碣镇	86313419	精密驱动器部件
东莞好万年电子制品有限公司	石碣镇	86633278	收音机
东莞艾笛森光电有限公司	横沥镇	81011898	电子产品
东莞明泰电讯设备有限公司	大岭山镇	83356898	各类电话机
东莞易迅电子制品有限公司	高埗镇	88788261	开关电源器、CAC/DC换能器
东莞庆章光机有限公司	清溪镇	87381610	分光镜
东莞亿润电子制品有限公司	高埗镇	88730855	光电子元器件
东莞樟洋电子有限公司	樟木头镇	87197011	数字摄录机、录放机、电源供启器
东莞双盈电子有限公司	清溪镇	87310135	电脑接线和手机连接线
东莞三星电机有限公司	寮步镇	83305000	电源
东莞基杰五金制品有限公司	清溪镇	87735140	电脑机箱
广东惠伦晶体科技股份有限公司	黄江镇	83362809	电子元器材
东莞李洲电子科技有限公司	谢岗镇	87762548	数码管、二极管、线路板
东莞宝星电子有限公司	寮步镇	83288770	微型麦克风
东莞莫仕连接器有限公司	石碣镇	86310328	电脑连接线
锋创电子(东莞)有限公司	长安镇	85398213	音箱
东莞捷仕美电子有限公司	大朗镇	83125678	电子连接器(电脑周边设备)
东莞清溪德丽电子厂	清溪镇	87311036	键盘
东莞冠智电子有限公司	长安镇	85356948	感应触摸胶片玻璃片
东莞诚翰电子有限公司	黄江镇	83536633	线圈
东莞环亚高科电子有限公司	长安镇	85316946	个人数码助理
东莞亚联科技电子有限公司	塘厦镇	87727680	电脑及其周边配件充电器
东莞新劲电子有限公司	塘厦镇	87810780	电脑周边产品
东莞康源电子有限公司	虎门镇	85562002	线路板
东莞精恒电子有限公司	横沥镇	88977068	广播器材
东莞华生精密制品有限公司	樟木头镇	87187900	音响、电子装配等
东莞桥历电子有限公司	桥头镇	86937682	塑胶五金
东莞华鼎电子有限公司	洪梅镇	88847166	液晶显示器
东莞宏致电子有限公司	长安镇	85393066	电子零配件

1-5　续表 42

(2012年)

单位名称	所属镇街	联系电话	主要产品(或服务)
东莞科乐波电子有限公司	寮步镇	83281822	变压器
仪器仪表制造业			
东莞奥得时精密电子有限公司	望牛墩镇	88518719	办公设备零配件
西铁城冠利钟表(中国)有限公司	长安镇	85387288	钟表
先锋高科技(东莞)有限公司	寮步镇	83287704	磁盘驱动器
新和光学(东莞)有限公司	南城街道	22983601	彩管专用特殊胶带
东莞广阳电子有限公司	清溪镇	87899006	电脑电子产品
东莞华仪仪表科技有限公司	清溪镇	81901668	仪器、仪表
镰仓光学(东莞)有限公司	虎门镇	85562870	望远镜及其配件
东莞晓视眼镜制造厂有限公司	凤岗镇	87754133	眼镜
东莞翎乔五金塑胶制品有限公司	道滘镇	88386188	五金制品
高铁检测仪器(东莞)有限公司	南城街道	22400899	试验机
东莞亨域电子有限公司	望牛墩镇	88859838	恒温器、计时器、机械钟
东莞力维时钟有限公司	清溪镇	87732284	时钟
东莞新旭光学有限公司	长安镇	88611999	光学镜片组
陆逊梯卡华宏(东莞)眼镜有限公司	高埗镇	88870241	金属塑胶眼镜
奥泰斯电子(东莞)有限公司	黄江镇	83365026	防盗热感应器
东莞宝元数控科技有限公司	高埗镇	88874202	控制器
东莞侨运表业有限公司	厚街镇	83086066	手表
盈利时表业(东莞)有限公司	大朗镇	83103333	表带
东京光学(东莞)科技有限公司	石龙镇	86185458	大屏幕彩色投影显示器、光学引擎
东莞富鼎兴精密电子科技有限公司	谢岗镇	87686518	电脑周边配件
东莞鸿胜光学眼镜有限公司	常平镇	81897743	眼镜
东莞均益精密五金制品有限公司	石排镇	88937100	五金饰品
东莞嘉泰钟表有限公司	塘厦镇	89899898	钏表及配件
东莞新溢眼镜制造有限公司	长安镇	85540945	眼镜
东莞斯曼塑胶制品有限公司	桥头镇	86551920	纤维胶粒
博世激光仪器(东莞)有限公司	樟木头镇	86907088	激光仪器
东莞蓝创捷特佳电子有限公司	常平镇	83392420	电子测量仪器、智能灯具等
东莞常平土塘大根电子光学制品厂	常平镇	83395446	扫描器镜头
优利德科技(中国)有限公司	松山湖	85729892	电器仪表
来利眼镜制品(东莞)有限公司	樟木头镇	82604067	眼镜配件
峻凌电子(东莞)有限公司	寮步镇	87734726	TFT-LCD平板显示屏材料
脉冲电子(东莞)有限公司	长安镇	85646868	微型马达
丽声实业(东莞)有限公司	虎门镇	86232333	时钟、精密电子零部件
其他制造业			
东莞幸和家庭日用品有限公司	东城街道	22664545	多功能手推车
大蕙日用品(东莞)有限公司	厚街镇	85594741	塑胶晒衣架
东莞新创宠物用品制造有限公司	虎门镇	89966555	宠物用具
东莞大信装饰礼品有限公司	常平镇	86293999	蜡烛灯
东莞立邦礼品灯饰有限公司	塘厦镇	82086818	电光源
东莞市浔兴拉链科技有限公司	大朗镇	82220222	拉链
东莞福泰电子有限公司	长安镇	85318100	碎纸机
欣泰家具(东莞)有限公司	清溪镇	87313008	太阳伞、户外伞
东莞尚馥散热系统有限公司	虎门镇	88623999	铝散热片

1-5　续表 43

(2012年)

单位名称	所属镇街	联系电话	主要产品(或服务)
东莞富美康电器科技有限公司	谢岗镇	87631613	直发器、电吹风
东莞星系手袋厂有限公司	塘厦镇	87939288	其他日用杂品
东莞素艺儿童用品有限公司	道滘镇	88382301	婴儿手推车
东莞晟富电子科技有限公司	寮步镇	81100168	降频器
东莞婴宝幼童用品有限公司	清溪镇	86817000	童车
东莞智富五金制品有限公司	塘厦镇	86853888	电器外壳、散热片、音响面板
广东保点明辉商标标识有限公司	樟木头镇	87797688	织唛、印唛、印刷类商标
东莞肯上精密五金有限公司	长安镇	85335705	五金塑胶件
明门(中国)幼童用品有限公司	清溪镇	87733251	婴儿手推车
东莞宏冠拉链配件有限公司	沙田镇	88866567	拉链
东莞精业拉链有限公司	洪梅镇	88849815	各型拉链、配件
电力、热力生产和供应业			
深南电(东莞)唯美电力有限公司	高埗镇	88463006	天然气发电
东莞众明电力有限公司	寮步镇	83525188	天然气发电
东莞中电新能源热电有限公司	东城街道	22688088	电力
广东省粤电集团有限公司沙角C电厂	虎门镇	85165698	发电
东莞通明电力有限公司	寮步镇	83525188	天然气发电
东莞深能源樟洋电力有限公司	樟木头镇	87198888	发电
东莞虎门电厂	虎门镇	85042288	电力(火力发电)
东莞市科伟环保电力有限公司	横沥镇	83715838	垃圾焚烧发电
东莞市科维环保电力有限公司	横沥镇	83715818	垃圾发电
广东广合电力有限公司沙角发电厂C厂	虎门镇	85135124	火力发电
东莞中科环保电力有限公司	南城街道	22667772	垃圾余热发电
广东电力发展股份有限公司沙角A电厂	虎门镇	85136679	火力发电
燃气生产和供应业			
东莞新奥燃气有限公司	莞城街道	88992299	管道燃气输配等
东莞长安新奥燃气有限公司	长安镇	89992288	管道燃气的建设
建筑安装业			
东莞安泰电业工程有限公司	莞城街道	22465497	高低压输变电、配电、设备安装
批发业			
东莞永泓木业贸易有限公司	大岭山镇	83355145	松木板、中纤板、刨花板
东莞胡连普光贸易有限公司	大朗镇	82973629	汽车零部件连接线
丹标贸易(东莞)有限公司	大朗镇	83111568	辅料
(萨摩亚)伟港国际有限公司东莞代表处	沙田镇		进出口贸易(咨询联络)
华润水泥采购有限公司	沙田镇	81699659	煤炭
莎罗雅(东莞)清洁用品有限公司	长安镇	85358605	清洁用品
锦江麦德龙现购自运有限公司东莞万江商场	万江街道	22178888	商品批发
金光纸业(东莞)有限公司	南城街道	22992511	纸品
大同机械(东莞)销售有限公司	东城街道	22806163	机械设备
东莞市创盛贸易有限公司	长安镇	82289868	钢材制品
东莞金丰物流设备有限公司	道滘镇	88333981	叉车
嘉顿食品贸易(中国)有限公司	南城街道	23024830	蛋糕、饼干、面包等
东莞加德士石油产品有限公司	东城街道	22367236	石油产品储蓄、批发
大船科技(东莞)有限公司	松山湖	22899666	精密轴承
东莞柳道贸易有限公司	长安镇	85394466	热流道条流及配件

1-5　续表 44

(2012年)

单位名称	所属镇街	联系电话	主要产品(或服务)
东莞华港国际贸易有限公司	长安镇	85416451	塑胶原料
东莞联阳金属科技有限公司	麻涌镇	89612188	不锈钢卷板
零售业			
东莞沃尔玛百货有限公司	莞城街道	22323055	超级市场
沃尔玛(东莞)商业零售有限公司	莞城街道	22343111	百货商场
东莞润德商业有限公司	厚街镇	89788109	百货
东莞新奥莞樟燃气有限公司	樟木头镇	87780331	管道天然气
东莞意美汽车服务有限公司	南城街道	85050911	汽车
东莞百安居装饰建材有限公司	南城街道	22719121	其他室内装修材料
东莞美东汽车服务有限公司	寮步镇	82319819	汽车
东莞喜威液化石油气有限公司	南城街道	22497388	液化气
中油碧辟石油有限公司东莞宏伟加油站	南城街道	22404202	汽油
广东吉之岛天贸百货有限公司东莞花园广场分公司	东城街道	22600236	百货
东莞市洛加斯润滑油有限公司	大岭山镇	85617000	润滑油
伟轮叉车(东莞)有限公司	高埗镇	88736868	叉车
东莞永佳中通汽车服务有限公司	厚街镇	81633000	汽车零配件
东莞中升雷克萨斯汽车销售服务有限公司	南城街道	23190999	雷克萨斯汽车
东莞仁孚华星汽车服务有限公司	寮步镇	82222080	奔驰轿车
广东吉之岛天贸百货有限公司东莞第一国际分公司	南城街道	28632988	百货
青岛润泰事业有限公司东莞大朗分公司	大朗镇	83034798	百货
东莞仁孚溢华汽车服务有限公司	南城街道	22902080	汽车
东莞擎达汽车销售服务有限公司	厚街镇	85580180	汽车
道路运输业			
广东省虎门大桥有限公司	虎门镇	85509333	高速公路管理养护
东莞发展控股股份有限公司	东城街道	22083225	高速收费
水上运输业			
东莞深赤湾港务有限公司	虎门港	81297355	公用码头的建设、经营等
东莞虎门龙威客运有限公司	虎门镇	85511759	沿海旅客运输
仓储业			
东莞永得利仓储有限公司	麻涌镇	88236909	物流服务
东莞三江港口储罐有限公司	虎门港	88862888	液体化工仓储服务
住宿业			
东莞御景湾酒店	东城街道	22625029	住宿等
东莞海悦花园大酒店有限公司	长安镇	85318888	餐饮服务
东莞旗峰山酒店有限公司	东城街道	23368888	餐饮服务
东莞丽池海悦酒店有限公司	厚街镇	85885888	住宿等
东莞豪门大饭店	虎门镇	85117888	餐饮
东莞长安酒店	长安镇	85532388	餐饮服务

1-5 续表 45

(2012年)

单位名称	所属镇街	联系电话	主要产品(或服务)
餐饮业			
东莞泛亚饮食有限公司	樟木头镇	87708232	餐饮服务
东莞肯德基有限公司	莞城街道	83588288	快餐
东莞麦长食品有限公司	长安镇	85530791	快餐
东莞麦华食品有限公司	莞城街道	22115051	西式快餐
电信、广播电视和卫星传输服务			
中国联合网络通信有限公司东莞分公司	南城街道	89826239	通信服务
中国移动通信集团广东有限公司东莞分公司	东城街道		移动通信
货币金融服务			
汇丰银行(中国)有限公司东莞分行	南城街道	23093088	金融及理财服务
恒生银行(中国)有限公司东莞分行	东城街道	23138838	金融及理财服务
保险业			
中德安联人寿保险有限公司广东分公司东莞营销服务部	南城街道	22827268	人寿保险
美国友邦保险有限公司东莞支公司	南城街道	22418628	人寿保险
信诚人寿保险有限公司东莞营销服务部	东城街道	22763188	人寿保险
房地产业			
东莞市乐富房地产开发有限公司	樟木头镇	87187088	房地产开发
东莞市阳明渡假山庄开发有限公司	塘厦镇	82275828	房地产开发
东莞市庆丰房地产咨询服务有限公司	东城街道	22619005	房地产开发
麦德龙物业管理(东莞)有限公司	万江街道	22078800	物业管理
东莞水濂山水库商品住宅建造有限公司	南城街道	22403288	房地产开发经营
东莞时富花园开发有限公司	寮步镇	83232328	商品住宅
东莞雁田工业区发展有限公司	凤岗镇	87771905	房地产开发经营
东莞御花苑商品住宅建造有限公司	南城街道	22402268	房地产开发经营
东莞庄士房地产开发有限公司	沙田镇	88660958	房地产开发经营
东莞市金地房地产投资有限公司	南城街道	88991111	房地产开发经营
东莞市富盈房地产开发有限公司	厚街镇	81226161	房地产开发
东莞市庆丰房地产有限公司	东城街道	22619005	房地产中介
东莞东泰花园建造有限公司	东城街道	22482388	房地产
东莞骏豪房地产开发有限公司	塘厦镇	28022593	房地产开发经营
商务服务业			
(丹麦)森海塞尔通信有限公司东莞代表处	东城街道	22360850	业务联络
东莞派诺蒙鞋业服务有限公司	东城街道	22491889	鞋类产品设计
研究和试验发展			
东莞新科技术研究开发有限公司	南城街道	22810033	研究开发磁电制品
体育			
东莞峰景高尔夫有限公司	东城街道	22253459	高尔夫球
东莞长安今宇高尔夫球场俱乐部有限公司	长安镇	85539288	提供高尔夫球娱乐活动
东莞观澜湖高尔夫球会有限公司	塘厦镇	28020888	高尔夫球场及配套设施建设经营管理

1-6 星级酒店名单(2012年)
List of Star-ranking Hotels (2012)

酒店名称	星级	电话	地址
凤岗金凯悦大酒店	五星	87759888	凤岗镇凤深大道158号
豪门大饭店	五星	85117888	虎门镇虎门大道
嘉华大酒店	五星	85928888	厚街镇家具大道1号
富盈酒店	五星	85888888	厚街镇赤岭路段
索菲特御景湾酒店	五星	22698888	东城区迎宾路8号
莲花山庄	五星	85538388	长安镇莲峰北路77号
长安海悦花园大酒店	五星	85318888	长安镇霄边管理区二环路
东莞柏宁酒店	五星	85333333	长安镇德政路222号
石龙金凯悦大酒店	五星	86188888	石龙镇莞龙路西湖路段
喜来登大酒店	五星	85988888	厚街镇S256省道莞太路段
新都会怡景酒店	五星	87883888	塘厦镇环市东路6号
太子酒店	五星	83363333	黄江镇江北路32号
塘厦三正半山酒店	五星	87299333	塘厦镇迎宾大道
汇华国际饭店	五星	83938888	常平镇常平大道2号
帝豪花园酒店	五星	83122222	大朗镇美景中路769号
丰泰花园酒店	五星	85708888	虎门镇S358省道大板地路段
华尔登国际酒店	五星	81028888	桥头镇广场路3号
桥头三正半山酒店	五星	83341868	桥头镇碧莲路
悦莱花园酒店	五星	81118888	寮步镇香市路8号
欧亚国际酒店	五星	82838888	常平镇常东路8号
东莞虎门东方索菲特酒店	五星	82888888	虎门镇虎门大道黄河商业城
寮步金凯悦大酒店	四星	83326328	寮步镇教育路1号
文华大酒店	四星	85911111	厚街镇莞太路新塘路段
东莞宾馆	四星	22222222	莞城区东正路11号
江龙大酒店	四星	85838888	厚街镇S256省道莞太路段
新都会酒店	四星	87713333	樟木头镇维多利商业大道38号
宏远酒店	四星	22418888	南城区宏远路1号
汇美酒店	四星	83918888	常平镇中元路9号
花园酒店	四星	87799888	樟木头镇南城广场
长安酒店	四星	85532388	长安镇中心S358省道旁

1-6　续表 1

(2012年)

酒店名称	星级	电话	地址
司马假日酒店	四星	83391888	常平镇司马管理区
新世纪酒店	四星	83338888	常平镇常平大道8号
梵尔赛酒店	四星	83816888	常平镇下墟工业区
厚街海悦花园大酒店	四星	85885888	厚街镇厚街大道东
汇源美爵酒店	四星	85244888	虎门镇虎门大道
业丰大酒店	四星	83113888	大朗镇莞樟路金朗大道23号
万盈酒店	四星	88828888	麻涌镇麻涌大道
中汇文华大酒店	四星	88788888	高埗镇振兴路
方中假日酒店	四星	86866666	茶山镇茶山大道西28号
半岛酒店	四星	83988888	常平镇北环路
华禧酒店	四星	85383888	长安镇S358省道上沙路段
嘉辉会酒店	四星	87563388	凤岗镇官井头嘉辉路
美怡登酒店	四星	83028888	常平镇中元路
天悦酒店	四星	81812222	石碣镇崇焕路18号
华庭花园酒店	四星	81633333	厚街镇广东现代国际展览中心南侧
新都会璜玛酒店	四星	87633338	谢岗镇花园大道73号
石龙宾馆	三星	86613333	石龙镇绿化中路2号
广彩城酒店	三星	22402088	南城区莞太路
石碣豪华大酒店	三星	86633333	石碣镇新城区
金湖粤海酒店	三星	87869888	塘厦镇塘厦大道南99号
莲城酒店	三星	85536888	长安镇莲峰路接一环路口
黄江假日酒店	三星	83362888	黄江镇黄江大道3号
西湖大酒店	三星	22822888	南城区西平板岭
明苑大酒店	三星	85122918	虎门镇金龙大道南
篁胜酒店	三星	22463888	南城区体育路11号
宝石大酒店	三星	86662188	企石镇振华路1号
恒丰酒店	三星	83343333	桥头镇恒丰新村2号
金岛泰年酒店	三星	82168888	塘厦镇128工业区
绿洲酒店	三星	88832788	道滘镇振兴路160号
沙头酒店	三星	85418888	长安镇沙头管理区

1-6 续表 2

(2012年)

酒店名称	星级	电话	地址
华通城大酒店	三星	86732288	企石镇湖滨南路
丰田酒店	三星	87771199	凤岗镇雁田管理区怡安路
嘉福海港酒店	三星	88682888	沙田镇中心区港口大道17号
中明酒店	三星	88883368	中堂镇新兴路1号
御烽酒店	三星	22186888	万江区107国道拔蛟窝路段
莱莉雅酒店	三星	87507888	凤岗镇永盛商业大街中银大厦
东逸酒店	三星	85396388	长安镇莲峰路103号
鸿茂酒店	三星	83999388	常平镇常黄路
四季酒店	三星	88566666	望牛墩镇新电城A8座
宏信假日酒店	三星	87363888	清溪镇香芒西路
美景湾酒店	三星	83739888	横沥镇沿江路1号
天鹅湖酒店	三星	83338388	常平镇天鹅湖路8号
富豪酒店	三星	83998888	常平镇金美路256号
中青旅山水设计师酒店	三星	21988888	东城区东纵大道189号
亚都酒店	三星	85343888	长安镇长中路115号
金沙亚都酒店	三星	85413888	长安镇靖海中路36号
金澳花园酒店	二星	22496966	东城大道金澳花园A座
耀豪酒店	二星	88865333	沙田镇中心区
银星酒店	二星	83987333	常平镇木抡大道9号
雄狮大酒店	二星	83332198	常平镇振兴路1号
盈丰酒店	二星	83333333	常平镇振兴路中段
新港大酒店	二星	83331000	常平镇新市一街6号
悦华大酒店	二星	83336888	常平镇东兴路275号
海霞酒店	二星	82822888	常平镇板石霞村路段
昇平酒店	二星	83812888	常平镇中元街
冠城酒店	二星	83337788	常平镇中元街常平广场
龙源大酒店	二星	85551028	虎门镇S358省道北栅路段
恒安酒店	二星	88868868	沙田镇横流中心区
海月酒店	二星	85926888	厚街镇涌口海月公园侧
悦凯酒店	一星	83398808	常平镇东元东路28号

1-7 高新技术企业名录（2012年）

List of High-tech Enterprises (2012)

企业名称	所在镇街	行业类别
东莞市鼎立软件有限公司	莞城街道	其他科技推广和应用服务业
广东玉兰装饰材料有限公司	莞城街道	其他纸制品制造
东莞市唯一网络科技有限公司	莞城街道	互联网接入及相关服务
东莞市TR轴承有限公司	莞城街道	轴承制造
广东智通人才连锁股份有限公司	莞城街道	职业中介服务
东莞弘明空调服有限公司	莞城街道	机织服装制造
东莞市政创软件科技有限公司	莞城街道	软件开发
东莞市华南信息科技有限公司	莞城街道	计算机、软件及辅助设备零售
东莞市捷联科技有限公司	莞城街道	互联网信息服务
广东华盈光达科技有限公司	莞城街道	信息系统集成服务
广东宏达工贸集团有限公司	莞城街道	其他建筑安装业
东莞市光华实业有限公司	石龙镇	电力电子元器件制造
东莞泽龙线缆有限公司	石龙镇	电线、电缆制造
泰阳电子（东莞）有限公司	石龙镇	电子元件及组件制造
东莞市广安电气检测中心有限公司	石龙镇	质检技术服务
广东开普互联信息科技有限公司	石龙镇	软件开发
东莞市石龙富华电子有限公司	石龙镇	其他仪器仪表制造业
广东华南药业集团有限公司	石龙镇	化学药品制剂制造
广东众生药业股份有限公司	石龙镇	中成药生产
东莞市龙基电子有限公司	石龙镇	电子元件及组件制造
广东巨龙信息技术有限公司	石龙镇	软件开发
东莞利富高塑料制品有限公司	石龙镇	塑料零件制造
日本电产三协电子（东莞）有限公司	石龙镇	电子元件及组件制造
亚士吉灯饰(东莞)有限公司	石龙镇	照明灯具制造
东莞市龙信数码科技有限公司	石龙镇	软件开发
东莞天意电子有限公司	石龙镇	计算机整机制造
东莞市鸿金顺机械制造有限公司	虎门镇	铸造机械制造
东莞市易辉自动化机械有限公司	虎门镇	其他通用设备制造业
东莞高仪电子科技有限公司	虎门镇	灯用电器附件及其他照明器具制造
东莞市广大制冷有限公司	虎门镇	制冷、空调设备制造
信义汽车玻璃（东莞）有限公司	虎门镇	其他玻璃制品制造
东莞虎彩印刷有限公司	虎门镇	包装装潢及其他印刷
广东威迪科技股份有限公司	虎门镇	污水处理及其再生利用
广东银禧科技股份有限公司	虎门镇	初级形态塑料及合成树脂制造
东莞市科达计算机系统工程有限公司	虎门镇	信息系统集成服务
东莞中探探针有限公司	虎门镇	其他电子设备制造
东莞市联升电线电缆有限公司	虎门镇	电线、电缆制造
东莞康源电子有限公司	虎门镇	印制电路板制造
广东奥其斯科技有限公司	虎门镇	照明灯具制造
信义玻璃工程（东莞）有限公司	虎门镇	其他玻璃制造
东莞常禾电子有限公司	虎门镇	汽车零部件及配件制造
广东力宇新能源科技有限公司	虎门镇	内燃机及配件制造
东莞市适意机械有限公司	虎门镇	其他金属工具制造
东莞联茂电子科技有限公司	虎门镇	电子元件及组件制造

1-7 续表 1

(2012年)

企业名称	所在镇街	行业类别
东莞令特电子有限公司	虎门镇	其他通用零部件制造
兴科电子（东莞）有限公司	虎门镇	电子元件及组件制造
东莞市平波电子有限公司	虎门镇	其他电子设备制造
东莞市妙达电动工具制造有限公司	虎门镇	风动和电动工具制造
东莞市锐升电线电缆有限公司	虎门镇	电线、电缆制造
广东福德电子有限公司	虎门镇	电力电子元器件制造
广东罗尔科技有限公司	东城街道	信息系统集成服务
广东守门神电子科技有限公司	东城街道	交通安全、管制及类似专用设备制造
东莞市博晟电子科技有限公司	东城街道	信息系统集成服务
东莞市港润机械科技有限公司	东城街道	金属成形机床制造
东莞市鸿铭机械有限公司	东城街道	包装专用设备制造
东莞市天唯智能科技有限公司	东城街道	信息技术咨询服务
广东智华计算机科技有限公司	东城街道	信息系统集成服务
岭南园林股份有限公司	东城街道	其他未列明建筑业
东莞博力威电池有限公司	东城街道	锂离子电池制造
东莞大同数控机械有限公司	东城街道	金属成形机床制造
东莞市奕东电子有限公司	东城街道	电子元件及组件制造
东莞市创业电气设备有限公司	东城街道	配电开关控制设备制造
东华机械有限公司	东城街道	塑料加工专用设备制造
东莞科威医疗器械有限公司	东城街道	假肢、人工器官及植（介）入器械制造
东莞生益电子有限公司	东城街道	印制电路板制造
东莞市百分百科技有限公司	东城街道	照明器具生产专用设备制造
东莞市德生通用电器制造有限公司	东城街道	音响设备制造
东莞市高能电气股份有限公司	东城街道	其他输配电及控制设备制造
广东晖速通信技术有限公司	东城街道	通信系统设备制造
东莞美维电路有限公司	东城街道	印制电路板制造
东莞市神州视觉科技有限公司	东城街道	光学仪器制造
东莞市安拓普塑胶聚合物科技有限公司	东城街道	初级形态塑料及合成树脂制造
广东宏远集团药业有限公司	东城街道	化学药品原料药制造
东莞市邦臣光电有限公司	东城街道	照明灯具制造
东莞市凯格精密机械有限公司	东城街道	电子工业专用设备制造
东莞市大忠电子有限公司	东城街道	变压器、整流器和电感器制造
广东建邦计算机软件有限公司	东城街道	软件开发
东莞市慧达环保有限公司	东城街道	环境保护专用设备制造
东莞市嘉腾仪器仪表有限公司	东城街道	光学仪器制造
东莞市事通达机电科技有限公司	东城街道	其他未列明金属制品制造
东莞市新铂铼电子有限公司	东城街道	电子真空器件制造
东莞市源兴光学仪器有限公司	东城街道	光学仪器制造
东莞通华液晶有限公司	东城街道	电子元件及组件制造
东莞拓扑实业有限公司	东城街道	涂料制造
东莞万德电子制品有限公司	东城街道	电子元件及组件制造
东莞市鸿宝锂电科技有限公司	东城街道	电子工业专用设备制造
东莞市立佳精密仪器有限公司	东城街道	其他仪器仪表制造业
东莞市良展有机硅科技有限公司	东城街道	合成橡胶制造

1-7 续表 2

(2012年)

企业名称	所在镇街	行业类别
东莞市伟盈汽车科技有限公司	东城街道	其他电子设备制造
东莞市正新包装制品有限公司	东城街道	塑料薄膜制造
东莞丝丽雅电子科技有限公司	东城街道	运输设备及生产用计数仪表制造
东莞华尔泰装饰材料有限公司	万江街道	建筑装饰业
东莞市吉川机械设备有限公司	万江街道	其他金属加工机械制造
东莞市精诚电能设备有限公司	万江街道	电子工业专用设备制造
东莞市西奥计算机智能科技有限公司	万江街道	计算机外围设备制造
广东大族粤铭激光科技股份有限公司	万江街道	金属切割及焊接设备制造
东莞市金翔电器设备有限公司	万江街道	计算机外围设备制造
广东至诚化学工业有限公司	万江街道	涂料制造
广东五星太阳能股份有限公司	万江街道	燃气、太阳能及类似能源家用器具制造
东莞市银华生物科技有限公司	万江街道	水产饲料制造
东莞市康源节能科技有限公司	万江街道	制冷、空调设备制造
东莞基业电气设备有限公司	万江街道	其他输配电及控制设备制造
东莞市恒生机械制造有限公司	万江街道	其他通用设备制造业
广东广视通科教设备有限公司	万江街道	木质家具制造
东莞市利安达环境科技有限公司	万江街道	环境保护专用设备制造
东莞市铭丰包装品制造有限公司	万江街道	其他未列明制造业
东莞耳神电声科技有限公司	万江街道	音响设备制造
东莞市安默琳节能环保技术有限公司	万江街道	其他金属加工机械制造
东莞市硕源电子材料有限公司	万江街道	锦纶纤维制造
东莞市爱克斯曼机械有限公司	万江街道	纺织专用设备制造
东莞市莱硕光电科技有限公司	万江街道	照明灯具制造
广东宏泰照明科技有限公司	南城街道	其他建筑安装业
广东迪科思信息科技有限公司	南城街道	软件开发
广东凌康科技有限公司	南城街道	信息系统集成服务
广东盛世商潮网络科技有限公司	南城街道	其他互联网服务
东莞市创锐电子技术有限公司	南城街道	电子工业专用设备制造
东莞市思特电子技术有限公司	南城街道	其他未列明信息技术服务业
东莞市艺博达实业有限公司	南城街道	纺织专用设备制造
东莞市朗普工程塑料科技有限公司	南城街道	其他橡胶制品制造
广东华业龙图信息技术股份有限公司	南城街道	测绘服务
东莞宏威数码机械有限公司	南城街道	电工机械专用设备制造
东莞市爱玛数控科技有限公司	南城街道	皮革、毛皮及其制品加工专用设备制造
东莞市福地电子材料有限公司	南城街道	光电子器件及其他电子器件制造
东莞华宝鞋业有限公司	南城街道	皮鞋制造
东莞市高鑫机电科技服务有限公司	南城街道	科技中介服务
广东百思维信息科技有限公司	南城街道	软件开发
东莞市保得生物工程有限公司	南城街道	有机肥料及微生物肥料制造
东莞市杉杉电池材料有限公司	南城街道	锂离子电池制造
广东万维博通信息技术有限公司	南城街道	软件开发
东莞市新雷神仿真控制有限公司	南城街道	其他电子设备制造
东莞市中大科教网络科技有限公司	南城街道	软件开发
东莞市凯诺德软件科技有限公司	南城街道	软件开发

1-7 续表 3

(2012年)

企业名称	所在镇街	行业类别
东莞市领航通通信科技有限公司	南城街道	信息系统集成服务
东莞市佛尔盛机电科技有限公司	南城街道	泵及真空设备制造
广东南方宏明电子科技股份有限公司	南城街道	电子元件及组件制造
东莞新科技术研究开发有限公司	南城街道	工程和技术研究和试验发展
东莞市丰远电器有限公司	南城街道	其他专用设备制造
广东天新软件科技有限公司	南城街道	软件开发
东莞市开创精密机械有限公司	南城街道	弹簧制造
广东数夫家具软件有限公司	南城街道	软件开发
广东新诚智软件科技有限公司	南城街道	软件开发
东莞市创丰科技发展有限公司	南城街道	矿山机械制造
东莞市钜大电子有限公司	南城街道	锂离子电池制造
广东科旺电源设备有限公司	南城街道	变压器、整流器和电感器制造
东莞兆舜有机硅新材料科技有限公司	中堂镇	有机化学原料制造
东莞市铖泰制罐设备有限公司	中堂镇	金属成形机床制造
广东广益科技实业有限公司	中堂镇	食品及饲料添加剂制造
东莞市东兴铝材制造有限公司	中堂镇	其他未列明金属制品制造
东莞理文造纸厂有限公司	中堂镇	机制纸及纸板制造
金元宝弹簧设备（东莞）有限公司	中堂镇	弹簧制造
永磁电子(东莞)有限公司	中堂镇	通信系统设备制造
东莞佳鸿机械制造有限公司	望牛墩镇	其他医疗设备及器械制造
东莞思威特电子有限公司	望牛墩镇	电子元件及组件制造
东莞市亚美精密机械配件有限公司	望牛墩镇	电子工业专用设备制造
东莞山本电子科技有限公司	麻涌镇	印制电路板制造
东莞地龙纸业有限公司	麻涌镇	纸和纸板容器制造
东莞南玻太阳能玻璃有限公司	麻涌镇	平板玻璃制造
东莞市奥莱克电子有限公司	麻涌镇	音响设备制造
东莞市华兰海电子有限公司	麻涌镇	其他未列明制造业
东莞海龙纸业有限公司	麻涌镇	机制纸及纸板制造
东莞玖龙纸业有限公司	麻涌镇	机制纸及纸板制造
东莞市贝特利新材料有限公司	麻涌镇	油墨及类似产品制造
东莞市英芝堂生物工程有限公司	麻涌镇	生物药品制造
广东信力材料科技有限公司	麻涌镇	合成橡胶制造
广东中成化工股份有限公司	麻涌镇	无机盐制造
东莞太平洋博高润滑油有限公司	麻涌镇	原油加工及石油制品制造
广东省东莞电机有限公司	麻涌镇	电动机制造
广东中远船务工程有限公司	麻涌镇	金属船舶制造
东莞市汇美淀粉科技有限公司	麻涌镇	淀粉及淀粉制品制造
广东康达尔农牧科技有限公司	麻涌镇	其他农业
东莞超盈纺织有限公司	麻涌镇	化纤织物染整精加工
东莞南玻工程玻璃有限公司	麻涌镇	平板玻璃制造
东莞市山力高分子材料科研有限公司	麻涌镇	其他合成材料制造
东莞泉声电子有限公司	石碣镇	电子元件及组件制造
品翔电子塑胶制品(东莞)有限公司	石碣镇	塑料零件制造
达创科技（东莞）有限公司	石碣镇	通信终端设备制造

1-7　续表 4

(2012年)

企业名称	所在镇街	行业类别
东莞市前锋电子有限公司	石碣镇	家用厨房电器具制造
台达电子电源（东莞）有限公司	石碣镇	电子元件及组件制造
台达电子(东莞)有限公司	石碣镇	电子元件及组件制造
东莞广发制药有限公司	石碣镇	中成药生产
东莞市智高文具有限公司	石碣镇	文具制造
东莞市盈聚电子有限公司	石碣镇	电子元件及组件制造
东莞达电电子有限公司	石碣镇	其他塑料制品制造
东莞东聚电子电讯制品有限公司	石碣镇	计算机外围设备制造
东莞市金源电池科技有限公司	石碣镇	锂离子电池制造
东莞精锐电器五金有限公司	高埗镇	其他未列明制造业
东莞金富亮塑胶颜料有限公司	高埗镇	塑料零件制造
东莞康特尔云终端系统有限公司	高埗镇	广播电视接收设备及器材制造
东莞宝元数控科技有限公司	高埗镇	工业自动控制系统装置制造
广东福利龙复合肥有限公司	高埗镇	复混肥料制造
东莞市宏达聚氨酯有限公司	高埗镇	初级形态塑料及合成树脂制造
东莞市东田厨具设备有限公司	高埗镇	其他金属制日用品制造
东莞市唯美陶瓷工业园有限公司	高埗镇	卫生陶瓷制品制造
东莞市康德威变压器有限公司	道滘镇	变压器、整流器和电感器制造
银禧工程塑料(东莞)有限公司	道滘镇	初级形态塑料及合成树脂制造
东莞市雄林新材料科技有限公司	道滘镇	初级形态塑料及合成树脂制造
东莞市开泰激光科技有限公司	道滘镇	其他电子设备制造
东莞万泰橡胶有限公司	道滘镇	合成橡胶制造
东莞洲亮通讯科技有限公司	道滘镇	通信终端设备制造
东莞市恒宇仪器有限公司	道滘镇	其他专用仪器制造
东莞市中村绝缘材料科技有限公司	道滘镇	绝缘制品制造
东莞安尚崇光科技有限公司	道滘镇	照明灯具制造
东莞市群跃电子材料科技有限公司	道滘镇	印制电路板制造
台玻华南玻璃有限公司	洪梅镇	平板玻璃制造
广东大众农业科技股份有限公司	洪梅镇	复混肥料制造
东莞市亚洲制药有限公司	洪梅镇	中成药生产
东莞市骏朗自动化科技有限公司	洪梅镇	工业自动控制系统装置制造
广东理文造纸有限公司	洪梅镇	机制纸及纸板制造
东莞市汇星染织有限公司	洪梅镇	化纤织物染整精加工
东莞市绿通高尔夫观光车有限公司	洪梅镇	五金产品批发
广东华坤新能源股份有限公司	沙田镇	电线、电缆制造
东莞市南星电子有限公司	沙田镇	其他电子设备制造
东莞庞思化工机械有限公司	沙田镇	其他专用设备制造
东莞市邦泽电子有限公司	沙田镇	其他专用仪器制造
东莞栢能电子科技有限公司	厚街镇	计算机零部件制造
东莞安达电机有限公司	厚街镇	金属切割及焊接设备制造
东莞市金河田实业有限公司	厚街镇	计算机外围设备制造
东莞市南兴家具装备制造股份有限公司	厚街镇	木材加工机械制造
东莞市东方科技有限公司	厚街镇	计算机外围设备制造
东莞市金银丰机械实业有限公司	厚街镇	皮革、毛皮及其制品加工专用设备制造

1-7 续表 5

(2012年)

企业名称	所在镇街	行业类别
东莞市力凯科技发展有限公司	厚街镇	信息系统集成服务
东莞市意利自动化科技有限公司	厚街镇	皮革、毛皮及其制品加工专用设备制造
东莞市利拿实业有限公司	厚街镇	橡胶加工专用设备制造
东莞朗诚微电子设备有限公司	厚街镇	电子工业专用设备制造
东莞市星士达电子有限公司	厚街镇	音响设备制造
东莞市信诺橡塑工业有限公司	长安镇	初级形态塑料及合成树脂制造
东莞市长江超声波机有限公司	长安镇	其他专用设备制造
万裕三信电子（东莞）有限公司	长安镇	电子元件及组件制造
东莞市维峰五金电子有限公司	长安镇	电子元件及组件制造
东莞市巨冈机械工业有限公司	长安镇	金属切削机床制造
东莞市爱加照明科技有限公司	长安镇	照明灯具制造
东莞市东元新能源科技有限公司	长安镇	污水处理及其再生利用
龙光电子集团有限公司	长安镇	通信系统设备制造
东莞市东阳光电容器有限公司	长安镇	电子元件及组件制造
东莞普思电子有限公司	长安镇	电子元件及组件制造
广东万濠精密仪器股份有限公司	长安镇	光学仪器制造
东莞钜升塑胶电子制品有限公司	长安镇	模具制造
先锐模具配件(东莞)有限公司	长安镇	模具制造
东莞劲胜精密组件股份有限公司	长安镇	电子元件及组件制造
东莞市奥普特自动化科技有限公司	长安镇	电子元件及组件制造
环球石材(东莞)有限公司	长安镇	建筑用石加工
东莞市汇乐清洁设备有限公司	长安镇	其他专用设备制造
东莞福泰电子有限公司	长安镇	其他未列明制造业
东莞广宏电子有限公司	长安镇	电子元件及组件制造
东莞鸿图精密压铸有限公司	长安镇	有色金属铸造
广东冠辉科技有限公司	长安镇	建筑、家具用金属配件制造
东莞市华鹰电子有限公司	长安镇	电子元件及组件制造
东莞市胜蓝电子有限公司	长安镇	电子元件及组件制造
东莞市泰康电子科技有限公司	长安镇	电子元件及组件制造
东莞市扬明精密塑胶五金电子有限公司	长安镇	电子元件及组件制造
东莞信泰光学有限公司	长安镇	光电子器件及其他电子器件制造
东莞市祥鑫汽车模具制品有限公司	长安镇	其他通用零部件制造
东莞市长原科技实业有限公司	长安镇	喷枪及类似器具制造
东莞市星河精密压铸模具有限公司	长安镇	其他未列明金属制品制造
捷荣模具工业（东莞）有限公司	长安镇	其他塑料制品制造
东莞市三姆森光电科技有限公司	长安镇	信息系统集成服务
东莞市奥源电子科技有限公司	长安镇	电子元件及组件制造
东莞市亿辉光电科技有限公司	长安镇	供应用仪表及其他通用仪器制造
广东永强奥林宝国际消防汽车有限公司	寮步镇	社会公共安全设备及器材制造
东莞市科锐机电设备有限公司	寮步镇	其他通用设备制造业
东莞市美之尊电子科技有限公司	寮步镇	音响设备制造
广东西屋电气有限公司	寮步镇	其他未列明电气机械及器材制造
东莞市金业电子科技有限公司	寮步镇	影视录放设备制造
东莞快灵通卡西尼电子科技有限公司	寮步镇	其他文教办公用品制造

1-7 续表 6

(2012年)

企业名称	所在镇街	行业类别
东莞市百味佳食品有限公司	寮步镇	其他调味品、发酵制品制造
东莞市丞冠橡塑制品有限公司	寮步镇	泡沫塑料制造
东莞三联热缩材料有限公司	寮步镇	其他塑料制品制造
广东宏磊达光电科技有限公司	寮步镇	光电子器件及其他电子器件制造
东莞市蓝冠环保节能科技有限公司	寮步镇	燃气、太阳能及类似能源家用器具制造
东莞市永强汽车制造有限公司	寮步镇	汽车整车制造
东莞市友美电源设备有限公司	寮步镇	照明灯具制造
东莞市开关厂有限公司	寮步镇	配电开关控制设备制造
康达新能源设备股份有限公司	寮步镇	发电机及发电机组制造
东莞市科隆威自动化设备有限公司	寮步镇	其他电子设备制造
广东佳景科技有限公司	寮步镇	油墨及类似产品制造
东莞宇球电子有限公司	寮步镇	电子元件及组件制造
东莞市新泽谷机械制造股份有限公司	寮步镇	其他电子设备制造
东莞市飞新达精密机械科技有限公司	寮步镇	其他非金属加工专用设备制造
东莞市骏泰精密机械有限公司	寮步镇	其他电子设备制造
广东新志密封技术有限公司	寮步镇	其他未列明金属制品制造
东莞市嘉龙皮革机械有限公司	寮步镇	缝制机械制造
东莞市蓝威实业有限公司	寮步镇	锅炉及辅助设备制造
东莞日进电线有限公司	寮步镇	电线、电缆制造
东莞唯佳电子有限公司	寮步镇	电力电子元器件制造
东莞长联新材料科技有限公司	寮步镇	其他专用化学产品制造
东莞市中崎机械有限公司	大岭山镇	印刷专用设备制造
东莞市双胞胎饲料有限公司	大岭山镇	饲料加工
东莞光群雷射科技有限公司	大岭山镇	塑料薄膜制造
东莞大宝化工制品有限公司	大岭山镇	涂料制造
东莞市瑞德丰生物科技有限公司	大岭山镇	生物化学农药及微生物农药制造
东莞市新时代新能源科技有限公司	大岭山镇	其他未列明电气机械及器材制造
东莞市奥达铝业有限公司	大岭山镇	铝压延加工
东莞市汇成真空科技有限公司	大岭山镇	其他通用设备制造业
东莞亿东机器有限公司	大岭山镇	塑料加工专用设备制造
东莞市宇佳电子实业有限公司	大岭山镇	其他电子设备制造
东莞金太阳研磨股份有限公司	大岭山镇	其他合成材料制造
东莞市莲盈无纺科技有限公司	大岭山镇	化纤织造加工
东莞锦弘精密机械有限公司	大岭山镇	木材加工机械制造
东莞市台盛环保科技有限公司	大岭山镇	其他金属加工机械制造
东莞市拓斯普达机械科技有限公司	大岭山镇	塑料加工专用设备制造
东莞市优富利电子有限公司	大岭山镇	计算机外围设备制造
环球工业机械(东莞)有限公司	大朗镇	金属成形机床制造
东莞市立旺电子塑胶有限公司	大朗镇	其他电子设备制造
东莞欧德雅装饰材料有限公司	大朗镇	其他塑料制品制造
东莞富强鑫塑胶机械制造有限公司	大朗镇	橡胶加工专用设备制造
东莞华科电子有限公司	大朗镇	电子元件及组件制造
东莞市迈科科技有限公司	大朗镇	镍氢电池制造
东莞信易电热机械有限公司	大朗镇	塑料加工专用设备制造

1-7　续表 7

(2012年)

企业名称	所在镇街	行业类别
东莞市迈科新能源有限公司	大朗镇	锂离子电池制造
东莞市中一合金科技有限公司	大朗镇	有色金属合金制造
东莞市台冠起重机械设备有限公司	大朗镇	起重机制造
大宝(东莞)模具切削工具有限公司	大朗镇	切削工具制造
东莞艾尔发自动化机械有限公司	大朗镇	其他非金属加工专用设备制造
东莞呈越电脑配件有限公司	大朗镇	计算机外围设备制造
东莞市永兴电子科技有限公司	大朗镇	灯用电器附件及其他照明器具制造
广东省东莞市亿达音响制造有限公司	大朗镇	音响设备制造
东莞市毅豪电子科技有限公司	大朗镇	信息系统集成服务
东莞市远峰科技有限公司	大朗镇	导航、气象及海洋专用仪器制造
东莞市科盛实业有限公司	黄江镇	其他未列明电气机械及器材制造
东莞泰德照明科技有限公司	黄江镇	照明灯具制造
东莞正扬电子机械有限公司	黄江镇	电子测量仪器制造
东莞宝迪环保电镀设备有限公司	黄江镇	其他专用设备制造
东莞市星火机电设备工程有限公司	黄江镇	其他通用设备制造业
鹏驰五金制品有限公司	黄江镇	紧固件制造
广东欧科空调制冷有限公司	黄江镇	家用空气调节器制造
广东惠伦晶体科技股份有限公司	黄江镇	电子元件及组件制造
东莞新东方科技有限公司	黄江镇	合成橡胶制造
泓凯电子科技(东莞)有限公司	黄江镇	计算机零部件制造
东莞市宏德电子设备有限公司	黄江镇	其他专用设备制造
广东太阳神集团有限公司	黄江镇	生物药品制造
钰翔精密模具(东莞)有限公司	黄江镇	模具制造
东莞市亚勖电子科技有限公司	黄江镇	信息技术咨询服务
东莞永洪印刷有限公司	樟木头镇	其他出版业
东莞市兄奕塑胶制品有限公司	樟木头镇	塑料板、管、型材制造
东莞市广海大橡塑科技有限公司	樟木头镇	其他橡胶制品制造
东莞积信电器有限公司	樟木头镇	家用厨房电器具制造
东莞市启天自动化设备有限公司	樟木头镇	其他机械设备及电子产品批发
东莞清溪华晖电器有限公司	清溪镇	家用厨房电器具制造
东莞市华源光电科技有限公司	清溪镇	太阳能发电
东莞市万华电子有限公司	清溪镇	其他电子设备制造
东莞市金铮自动冲压设备有限公司	清溪镇	金属切削机床制造
东莞华仪仪表科技有限公司	清溪镇	电工仪器仪表制造
东莞宜安科技股份有限公司	清溪镇	金属结构制造
实盈电子（东莞）有限公司	清溪镇	计算机零部件制造
东莞光阵显示器制品有限公司	清溪镇	光电子器件及其他电子器件制造
东莞华明灯具有限公司	清溪镇	照明灯具制造
广东粤林电气科技股份有限公司	清溪镇	计算机外围设备制造
快意电梯股份有限公司	清溪镇	电梯、自动扶梯及升降机制造
东莞建玮电子制品有限公司	清溪镇	计算机零部件制造
东莞龙杰电子有限公司	清溪镇	其他电子设备制造
模德模具(东莞)有限公司	清溪镇	金属表面处理及热处理加工
东莞市联思电子有限公司	清溪镇	电子元件及组件制造

1-7 续表 8

(2012年)

企业名称	所在镇街	行业类别
东莞泰星五金制品厂有限公司	清溪镇	紧固件制造
东莞格力良源电池科技有限公司	塘厦镇	锂离子电池制造
东莞市中控电子技术有限公司	塘厦镇	其他电子设备制造
东莞市奔迪包装有限公司	塘厦镇	其他塑料制品制造
东莞市凯华电子有限公司	塘厦镇	电子元件及组件制造
东莞市凯昶德电子科技股份有限公司	塘厦镇	电子元件及组件制造
东莞市冠佳电子设备有限公司	塘厦镇	电子工业专用设备制造
东莞市理士奥电源技术有限公司	塘厦镇	其他电池制造
东莞立德电子有限公司	塘厦镇	电子元件及组件制造
广东升威电子制品有限公司	塘厦镇	电子元件及组件制造
东莞市光宇实业有限公司	塘厦镇	电子元件及组件制造
东莞丰裕电机有限公司	塘厦镇	其他金属加工机械制造
东莞正阳电子有限公司	塘厦镇	电子元件及组件制造
广东志成冠军集团有限公司	塘厦镇	变压器、整流器和电感器制造
广东星河生物科技股份有限公司	塘厦镇	食用菌种植
广东坚朗五金制品股份有限公司	塘厦镇	金属门窗制造
东莞市力王电池有限公司	塘厦镇	其他电池制造
东莞市乐科电子有限公司	塘厦镇	电子元件及组件制造
东莞市千岛金属锡品有限公司	塘厦镇	锡冶炼
东莞市亚力通电子科技有限公司	塘厦镇	通信终端设备制造
东莞市三友联众电器有限公司	塘厦镇	电子元件及组件制造
东莞市亚通光电有限公司	塘厦镇	光电子器件及其他电子器件制造
佳辉设备(东莞)有限公司	塘厦镇	电子工业专用设备制造
东莞市楚东电子科技有限公司	塘厦镇	音响设备制造
东莞市欧谛特光电科技有限公司	塘厦镇	电光源制造
东莞建永数码科技有限公司	塘厦镇	音响设备制造
东莞启益电器机械有限公司	塘厦镇	变压器、整流器和电感器制造
东莞市锦润电子有限公司	塘厦镇	光电子器件及其他电子器件制造
东莞领航电子有限公司	塘厦镇	电子元件及组件制造
东莞市升丰电子有限公司	塘厦镇	光电子器件及其他电子器件制造
东莞市倍嘉电池科技有限公司	塘厦镇	其他未列明金属制品制造
东莞勤增实业有限公司	塘厦镇	其他未列明金属制品制造
东莞市澳星视听器材有限公司	塘厦镇	幻灯及投影设备制造
东莞市宙辉电子科技有限公司	塘厦镇	电子元件及组件制造
东莞阳天电子科技有限公司	塘厦镇	通信系统设备制造
东莞永湖复合材料有限公司	塘厦镇	体育器材及配件制造
东莞锐发智能卡科技有限公司	塘厦镇	智能卡设备制造
东莞市林积为实业投资有限公司	凤岗镇	汽车零部件及配件制造
东莞奥托泰电器制品有限公司	凤岗镇	其他原动设备制造
东莞奥美佳电子有限公司	凤岗镇	照相机及器材制造
东莞宇宙电路板设备有限公司	凤岗镇	电子工业专用设备制造
东莞康佳模具塑胶有限公司	凤岗镇	应用电视设备及其他广播电视设备制造
广东楚天龙智能卡有限公司	凤岗镇	通信系统设备制造
东莞康佳电子有限公司	凤岗镇	电视机制造

1-7　续表 9

(2012年)

企业名称	所在镇街	行业类别
嘉力时灯光设备(东莞)有限公司	凤岗镇	照明灯具制造
东莞永腾电子制品有限公司	凤岗镇	电子元件及组件制造
东莞市旭通达模具塑胶有限公司	凤岗镇	塑料零件制造
广东福聚多节能科技有限公司	凤岗镇	灯用电器附件及其他照明器具制造
东莞市大兴化工有限公司	谢岗镇	涂料制造
东莞洲磊电子有限公司	谢岗镇	电子元件及组件制造
东莞市润星机械科技有限公司	谢岗镇	金属切削机床制造
五川音响电子科技(东莞)有限公司	常平镇	音响设备制造
东莞市瀛通电线有限公司	常平镇	电线、电缆制造
良特电子科技（东莞）有限公司	常平镇	通信系统设备制造
东泰机械工具（东莞）有限公司	常平镇	电工机械专用设备制造
广东富林木业科技有限公司	常平镇	胶合板制造
东莞勤上光电股份有限公司	常平镇	照明灯具制造
东莞市环宇文化科技有限公司	常平镇	电子工业专用设备制造
智嘉通讯科技(东莞)有限公司	常平镇	电力电子元器件制造
东莞市华立实业股份有限公司	常平镇	其他家具制造
东莞运城制版有限公司	常平镇	包装装潢及其他印刷
东莞东运机械制造有限公司	常平镇	印刷专用设备制造
东莞市世通国际快件监管中心有限公司	常平镇	其他仓储业
东莞市国研电热材料有限公司	常平镇	电子元件及组件制造
东莞东海龙环保科技有限公司	常平镇	照明灯具制造
东莞龙昌数码科技有限公司	常平镇	玩具制造
东莞欧达电子有限公司	常平镇	电子测量仪器制造
东莞市鼎聚光电有限公司	常平镇	照明灯具制造
东莞市维信电脑科技有限公司	常平镇	信息系统集成服务
永泰电子(东莞)有限公司	常平镇	电子元件及组件制造
快捷达通信设备（东莞）有限公司	常平镇	通信系统设备制造
东莞市宇洁新材料有限公司	常平镇	其他未列明制造业
东莞市汇林包装有限公司	桥头镇	其他纸制品制造
东莞市天益生物工程有限公司	桥头镇	其他调味品、发酵制品制造
东莞市日新传导科技股份有限公司	桥头镇	电线、电缆制造
广东新一信通信发展有限公司	桥头镇	通信系统设备制造
东莞市金培电子有限公司	桥头镇	计算机外围设备制造
东莞兴博精密模具有限公司	桥头镇	其他通用零部件制造
东莞市擎洲光电科技有限公司	横沥镇	光电子器件及其他电子器件制造
东莞巨扬电器有限公司	横沥镇	电光源制造
天钺电子(东莞)有限公司	横沥镇	通信系统设备制造
东莞爱美达电子有限公司	横沥镇	电子元件及组件制造
东莞市安达自动化设备有限公司	横沥镇	电子工业专用设备制造
东莞精恒电子有限公司	横沥镇	其他电子设备制造
广东明家科技股份有限公司	横沥镇	其他输配电及控制设备制造
东莞台一盈拓科技股份有限公司	横沥镇	金属切削机床制造
忠信制模(东莞)有限公司	横沥镇	模具制造
意拉德电子(东莞)有限公司	横沥镇	电子元件及组件制造

1-7 续表 10

(2012年)

企业名称	所在镇街	行业类别
东莞市金鸿盛电器有限公司	横沥镇	其他未列明制造业
东莞雷笛克光学有限公司	横沥镇	灯用电器附件及其他照明器具制造
东莞市中泰模具股份有限公司	横沥镇	汽车零部件及配件制造
广东泰卓光电科技股份有限公司	东坑镇	照明灯具制造
广东迅扬电脑科技股份有限公司	东坑镇	计算机外围设备制造
东莞市艾炜特电子有限公司	东坑镇	电视机制造
广东中德电缆有限公司	东坑镇	电线、电缆制造
东莞市华胜展鸿电子科技有限公司	东坑镇	照明灯具制造
东莞市维美德电子材料有限公司	东坑镇	电子元件及组件制造
东莞市沃德电子科技有限公司	东坑镇	纺织专用设备制造
东莞市新望包装机械有限公司	企石镇	包装专用设备制造
东莞联宝光电科技有限公司	企石镇	电子元件及组件制造
东莞市恒明光电科技有限公司	企石镇	照明灯具制造
东莞市铁生辉制罐有限公司	企石镇	金属包装容器制造
东莞市立敏达电子科技有限公司	石排镇	光伏设备及元器件制造
东莞市旭业光电科技有限公司	石排镇	光电子器件及其他电子器件制造
东莞市智乐堡儿童玩具有限公司	石排镇	玩具制造
东莞市方振塑胶电子制品有限公司	石排镇	塑料零件制造
东莞市富士达电子科技有限公司	石排镇	电光源制造
东莞铭普光磁股份有限公司	石排镇	光电子器件及其他电子器件制造
东莞鑫佑光电科技有限公司	石排镇	电子元件及组件制造
东莞市悠悠美居家居制造有限公司	石排镇	日用塑料制品制造
东莞宇隆电工材料有限公司	茶山镇	铜压延加工
东莞市箭冠汽车配件制造有限公司	茶山镇	汽车零部件及配件制造
东莞荣成塑胶五金制品有限公司	茶山镇	塑料零件制造
东莞市英科水墨有限公司	茶山镇	油墨及类似产品制造
东莞市贻嘉光电科技有限公司	茶山镇	光电子器件及其他电子器件制造
东莞市雄丰配电设备有限公司	茶山镇	配电开关控制设备制造
东莞森玛仕格里菲电路有限公司	茶山镇	印制电路板制造
东莞市金昶电线制造有限公司	茶山镇	金属结构制造
东莞市意普万尼龙科技股份有限公司	松山湖	其他合成材料制造
东莞市星火太阳能科技股份有限公司	松山湖	太阳能发电
广东普赛特电子科技股份有限公司	松山湖	光电子器件及其他电子器件制造
东莞市中之光电科技有限公司	松山湖	照明灯具制造
广东大普通信技术有限公司	松山湖	电子元件及组件制造
东莞市安尔发电子科技有限公司	松山湖	通信系统设备制造
东莞润赢电力科技有限公司	松山湖	信息系统集成服务
东莞市艾斯迪新材料有限公司	松山湖	橡胶零件制造
东莞市纳明新材料科技有限公司	松山湖	其他稀有金属冶炼
广东盈达信息科技股份有限公司	松山湖	信息系统集成服务
东莞市万科建筑技术研究有限公司	松山湖	其他未列明专业技术服务业
广东力优环境系统股份有限公司	松山湖	制冷、空调设备制造
领亚电子科技股份有限公司	松山湖	计算机外围设备制造
广东正业科技股份有限公司	松山湖	其他仪器仪表制造业

1-7 续表 11

(2012年)

企业名称	所在镇街	行业类别
东莞泛亚太生物科技有限公司	松山湖	生物药品制造
广东东阳光药业有限公司	松山湖	化学药品制剂制造
广东生益科技股份有限公司	松山湖	印制电路板制造
广东易事特电源股份有限公司	松山湖	计算机外围设备制造
东莞市科磊得数码光电科技有限公司	松山湖	灯用电器附件及其他照明器具制造
东莞新能源科技有限公司	松山湖	锂离子电池制造
广东雨林木风计算机科技有限公司	松山湖	互联网信息服务
广东电子工业研究院有限公司	松山湖	其他未列明信息技术服务业
广东华南工业设计院	松山湖	专业化设计服务
东莞市劲威智能冲压成套设备有限公司	松山湖	其他金属加工机械制造
东莞易步机器人有限公司	松山湖	电车制造
广东戈兰玛汽车系统有限公司	松山湖	汽车零部件及配件制造
广东三凯新材料股份有限公司	松山湖	其他塑料制品制造
东莞市安美润滑科技有限公司	松山湖	其他专用化学产品制造
广东奥美格传导科技股份有限公司	松山湖	电线、电缆制造
东莞思谷数字技术有限公司	松山湖	其他互联网服务
东莞市天尚太阳能有限公司	松山湖	燃气、太阳能及类似能源家用器具制造
东莞市太平洋计算机科技有限公司	松山湖	信息技术咨询服务
东莞市松庆自动化设备有限公司	松山湖	工业自动控制系统装置制造
东莞市依时利科技有限公司	松山湖	信息技术咨询服务
广东中实金属有限公司	松山湖	其他有色金属压延加工
广东荣文能源科技集团有限公司	松山湖	信息系统集成服务
东莞市华联环保工程有限公司	松山湖	大气污染治理
广东易凌信息科技有限公司	松山湖	其他电信服务
东莞市贝特电子科技股份有限公司	松山湖	电子元件及组件制造
东莞市星擎电子科技有限公司	松山湖	电子元件及组件制造
优利德科技（东莞）有限公司	松山湖	电工仪器仪表制造
艾利和电子科技(中国)有限公司	松山湖	应用电视设备及其他广播电视设备制造
东莞市新东方光电技术有限公司	松山湖	光电子器件及其他电子器件制造
广东洛贝电子科技有限公司	松山湖	家用厨房电器具制造
东莞劲芳生物医药孵化器有限公司	松山湖	生物药品制造
东莞市玮孚电子科技有限公司	松山湖	锂离子电池制造
东莞市百大新能源股份有限公司	松山湖	锅炉及辅助设备制造
东莞市华科制造工程研究院有限公司	松山湖	工程和技术研究和试验发展
东莞市帕马智能停车服务有限公司	松山湖	其他未列明信息技术服务业
东莞市锐源仪器股份有限公司	松山湖	电子测量仪器制造
东莞瑞柯电子科技股份有限公司	松山湖	汽车零部件及配件制造
东莞市苏普尔电子科技有限公司	松山湖	通信系统设备制造
东莞市泰斗微电子科技有限公司	松山湖	其他电子设备制造
东莞市泰通科技实业有限公司	松山湖	农业机械服务
东莞市腾宇龙机械能源科技股份有限公司	松山湖	皮革、毛皮及其制品加工专用设备制造
国云科技股份有限公司	松山湖	其他未列明信息技术服务业
东莞市威特隆仓储设备有限公司	松山湖	其他未列明电气机械及器材制造

中国统计出版社最新图书简目

(仅供参考,以最后出书为准)

统计资料

中国统计年鉴-2013
中国统计摘要-2013
国际统计年鉴-2013
2013中国发展报告
中国第三产业统计年鉴-2013
中国区域经济统计年鉴-2013
中国劳动统计年鉴-2013
中国社会统计年鉴-2013
中国城市统计年鉴-2013
中国建筑业统计年鉴-2013
中国人口和就业统计年鉴-2013
中国工业经济统计年鉴-2013
中国商品交易市场统计年鉴-2013
中国房地产统计年鉴-2013
中国能源统计年鉴-2013
中国民政统计年鉴-2013
中国贸易外经统计年鉴-2013
2013中国地区经济监测报告
中国科技统计年鉴-2013
中国农村统计年鉴-2013
中国农产品价格调查年鉴-2013
中国高技术产业统计年鉴-2013
中国教育经费统计年鉴-2013
中国农村贫困监测报告-2013
全国农产品成本收益资料汇编-2013
中国科学技术协会统计年鉴-2013
工业企业科技活动资料-2013
大中型批发零售和住宿餐饮企业统计年鉴-2013
中国价格统计年鉴-2013
第二次全国R&D资源清查资料汇编－工业企业卷
中国住户调查年鉴-2013
中国县域统计年鉴-2013
中国农村全面建设小康监测报告-2013
第二次全国R&D资源清查资料汇编－综合卷
中国人才资源统计报告-2011
中国民族统计年鉴-2013
中国零售和餐饮连锁企业统计年鉴-2013
2010年中国第六次人口普查公报

2013年省级综合统计年鉴系列

北京 天津 河北 山西 内蒙古 辽宁 吉林 黑龙江 上海 江苏 浙江 安徽 福建 江西 山东
河南 湖北 湖南 广东 广西 海南 重庆 四川 贵州 云南 西藏 陕西 甘肃 青海 宁夏
新疆 新疆生产建设兵团

2013年市(县)级综合统计年鉴系列

天津滨海新区 石家庄 唐山 邯郸 太原 大同 长治 阳泉 晋城 朔州 晋中
运城 忻州 临汾 呼和浩特 包头 通辽 沈阳 大连 长春 吉林市 四平 哈尔滨 黑龙江垦区
上海浦东新区 南京 苏州 无锡 常州 徐州 南通 盐城 镇江 宿迁 泰州 连云港 江阴 丹阳
杭州 宁波 绍兴 台州 温州 金华 嘉兴 衢州 舟山 福州 福州经济技术开发区
厦门经济特区 宁德 南昌 上饶 济南 青岛 潍坊 郑州 洛阳 三门峡 南阳 武汉 宜昌
十堰 荆州 咸宁 长沙 广州 东莞 惠州 深圳 桂林 南宁 柳州 来宾 河池 海口 成都 绵阳
贵阳 昆明 庆阳 西安 兰州 银川 乌鲁木齐

2010年人口普查资料系列

中国2010年人口普查资料 北京 天津 河北 山西 内蒙古 辽宁 吉林 黑龙江 上海 江苏
浙江 安徽 福建 江西 山东 河南 湖北 湖南 广东 广西 海南 重庆 四川 贵州 云南
西藏 陕西 甘肃 青海 宁夏 新疆 新疆生产建设兵团 河南省各市2010年人口普查资料丛书
中国分县2010年人口普查资料 中国分乡镇、街道2010年人口普查资料 中国分民族2010年人口普查资料

“十一五”规划教材

统计学（“十二五”规划，黄良文） 抽样调查理论与实践（“十二五”规划，冯士雍）
统计学（“十二五”规划，单微） 试验设计（“十二五”规划，茆诗松） 贝叶斯统计（“十二五”规划，茆诗松）
统计学：从数据到结论（十二五规划，吴喜之） 医学统计学（陆守曾）
非参数统计（吴喜之） 概率论与数理统计（茆诗松） 现代金融投资统计分析（李腊生）
多元统计分析（任雪松） 应用时间序列分析（王振龙） 统计指数理论及应用（徐国祥）
经济计量学教程（贺铿） 质量管理统计方法 （茆诗松） 统计实验系列教材（许涤龙）
社会统计学（蒋萍） 市场调查与预测（蒋志华） 统计学原理（非统计专业用，朱胜）
国民经济核算教程(杨灿) 概率论与数理统计(经济、管理类专业使用，朱胜）

重点图书

挑大学选专业2013—高考志愿填报指南 挑大学选专业2013—考研择校指南